Regulating and Managing Banks in India

Regulating and Managing Banks in India is a comprehensive coursebook that combines the study of three key aspects of banking: the role of banks in an economy, the need for banking regulations and the significance of regular bank management practices. The book explains the basics of banking functions and emphasises the paramount importance of banks in the overall Indian financial system. It highlights the role of banks in promoting long-term economic prosperity by drawing from theories of economic growth and explains how banks play a key role in managing short-run economic fluctuations. It provides technical details on quantification and management of wide varieties of banking risks and aspects of banking regulations, and draws a roadmap for future banking regulations, management of non-performing assets (NPAs), the impact of developments in information technology (IT) and IT-enabled services (ITES), and digitalisation in the banking business. Simple numerical examples are provided to facilitate easy comprehension and appeal to students as well as professionals. The author combines a balanced academic rigour with his experience of working at the Reserve Bank of India, where he was involved in the conduct of monetary policy and banking supervision.

Amaresh Samantaraya is Professor of Economics at the School of Management, Pondicherry University, and visiting faculty at the Indian Institute of Management (IIM) Kozhikode. He was associated with the Reserve Bank of India (RBI) as an economist in the Monetary Policy Department, as also in the erstwhile Department of Economic Analysis and Policy and the Department of Banking Supervision. He also visited the Bank of England, the Bank of Korea, the Monetary Authority of Singapore and the Swiss National Bank as part of academic collaborations and training and exchange programmes sponsored by the RBI.

Regulating and Managing Banks in India

An Economic Perspective

Amaresh Samantaraya

CAMBRIDGE
UNIVERSITY PRESS

CAMBRIDGE
UNIVERSITY PRESS

Shaftesbury Road, Cambridge CB2 8EA, United Kingdom

One Liberty Plaza, 20th Floor, New York, NY 10006, USA

477 Williamstown Road, Port Melbourne, VIC 3207, Australia

314–321, 3rd Floor, Plot 3, Splendor Forum, Jasola District Centre, New Delhi – 110025, India

103 Penang Road, #05–06/07, Visioncrest Commercial, Singapore 238467

Cambridge University Press is part of Cambridge University Press & Assessment, a department of the University of Cambridge.

We share the University's mission to contribute to society through the pursuit of education, learning and research at the highest international levels of excellence.

www.cambridge.org
Information on this title: www.cambridge.org/9781009556453

First published 2025

A catalogue record for this publication is available from the British Library

ISBN 978-1-009-55645-3 Hardback
ISBN 978-1-009-55644-6 Paperback

Contents

Part II Banks and the Economy

Figures

Tables

Boxes

Acknowledgements

While writing this book, I have received encouragement, active support and assistance from several individuals. Valuable contributions of all of them are acknowledged here with sincere gratitude.

To begin with, I must express my sincere gratitude to C. Rangarajan and Y. V. Reddy, both eminent economists and former governors of the Reserve Bank of India (RBI), and Bandi Kamaiah, my PhD supervisor, for all their valuable teachings, blessings and constant encouragement in my academic pursuits. My learning and understanding of economics and related policy issues evolved with their guidance and handholding.

My exposure to the conduct of monetary policy and banking regulations, while working as a research officer and subsequently as an assistant adviser or assistant general manager in the RBI (1999–2010), has been very useful. I had the good fortune of working in the Monetary Policy Department (2005–08) of the RBI, which helped in exploring the nuances of monetary policymaking. Working in the erstwhile Department of Banking Supervision (2008–10) was critical for gaining crucial insights on the complex aspects of banking regulations and supervision. During this period, interaction with many of my former colleagues in the RBI was quite a good learning experience. I must place on record significant contributions of Michael Debabrata Patra (presently the deputy governor of the RBI), A. Prasad, Ranjit Kumar Pattnaik, Abraham Mathew, Rajnish Kumar, Sitikantha Pattanaik, R. Kesavan, Himanshu Joshi, Siddartha Sanyal, Harendra Behera, Indranil Bhattacharyya, Sarada Prasan Mohanty, Sudarsana Sahoo, J. B. Singh, Rajmal, Rajeev Jain, Satyananda Sahoo and Dipankar Mitra, among others, in this regard.

Interaction with many bankers and former bankers was quite beneficial in gaining valuable insight on the practical aspects of risk management and general banking management practices in the banks. I have benefitted a lot from interactions with Shashi Bhusana Moharana (State Bank of India), S. Suresh Kumar (Canara Bank) and S. Ravindran (Indian Bank). I am grateful to each of them.

From the day I commenced drafting various chapters, I have been in constant touch with professors Rudra Sensarma of the Indian Institute of Management, Kozhikode, and Jitendra Mahakud of the Indian Institute of Technology, Kharagpur, on the topics and issues covered in the book. Their valuable inputs and feedback guided me in improving the overall content of this book. I am immensely thankful to both of them.

I am indebted to my present employer, Pondicherry University, for providing necessary infrastructure and a conducive atmosphere for writing this book. Several friends and colleagues at the university have been quite supportive and a source of constant encouragement. I must acknowledge, M. Ramadass, R. Pravakara Raya, Gurmeet Singh (former vice-chancellor), K. Tharanikkarasu, V. Mariappan, D. Lazar, P. Sridharan, A. Subramanyam Raju, H. Prathap Kumar Shetty, B. B. Mohanty, Pradeep Kumar Parida, Prasant Kumar Panda, A. Sankaran, N. Kubendran, R. Lusome, H. Yasmeen Sultana, Sampad Kumar Swain, M. Vijayakumar, R. Segar, M. P. T. Sagayaraja, S. Murugaiyan, K. Mahesh, S. Kalaivanan and R. Swarnaraj, among others. I must also acknowledge assistance received from my PhD scholars while writing this book. I am especially thankful to Aleena Jose and Abhishek Kumar Chaubey, who have read all the chapters and provided important feedback from a student's perspective.

My family's constant support and encouragement is highly commendable. Particularly, my parents and elder brother, Ashok *bhai*, have always appreciated my work and stood behind me in all my academic endeavours. My wife, Silpi, and younger brother, Ashutosh, shared all household responsibilities and sacrificed their own comfort to help me work on the book without any interruption. I am indebted to each of them. I could not give due care and attention to my daughter, Archisha, and son, Archit, as work pressure during the last couple of years was quite heavy. I am thankful for their understanding and cooperation.

Last but not least, Anwesha Rana of Cambridge University Press has been a great support from the very proposal stage to the final completion of this book. I gratefully acknowledge her guidance and constant encouragement. I am also thankful to Priyanka Das and Anandadeep Roy of the Press for their timely support.

Needless to mention, errors and deficiencies in the book, if any, are my sole responsibility.

27 October 2024 **Amaresh Samantaraya**

Abbreviations

ABF	assessed bank finance
AD–AS	aggregate demand–aggregate supply
AFS	available for sale
ALCO	asset–liability committee
ALM	asset–liability management
AMA	advanced measurement approach
ARC	asset reconstruction company
ASF	available stable funding
ATM	automated teller machine
AUM	assets under management
BBB	Bank Boards Bureau
BCBS	Basel Committee on Banking Supervision
BCP	business continuity plan
BFS	Board for Financial Supervision
BIA	basic indicator approach
BIS	Bank for International Settlements
BOB	Bank of Baroda
BOI	Bank of India
BOP	balance of payments
BPLR	benchmark prime lending rate
BR Act	Banking Regulation Act, 1949
BSE	Bombay Stock Exchange

CALCS	capital adequacy, asset quality, liquidity, compliance and systems
CAMELS	capital adequacy, asset quality, management, earning, liquidity, and system and control
CARE	Credit Analysis & Research Limited
CASA	current account and savings account
CBDC	central bank digital currency
CBI	Central Bureau of Investigation
CBLOs	collateralised borrowing and lending obligations
CBS	core banking solution
CCB	capital conservation buffer
CC	cash credit
CCyB	countercyclical capital buffer
CD	certificate of deposit
CDO	collateralised debt obligation
CEO	chief executive officer
CET1	Common Equity Tier 1
CGFMU	Credit Guarantee Fund for Micro Units
CIBIL	Credit Information Bureau (India) Limited
CIC	credit information company
CMD	chairman and managing director
CP	commercial paper
CPI	consumer price index
CRA	credit rating agency
CRAR	capital to risk-weighted assets ratio
CRISIL	Credit Rating Information Services of India Limited
CRMC	credit risk management committee
CRMD	credit risk management department
CRR	cash reserve ratio
CVC	Central Vigilance Commission
DBT	direct benefit transfer
DCCB	district central cooperative bank

DEA	data envelope analysis
DFI	development finance institution
DICGC	Deposit Insurance and Credit Guarantee Corporation
DPG	deferred payment guarantee
DRTs	Debt Recovery Tribunals
DSIB	domestic systemically important bank
DUPN	derivative usance promissory notes
DvP	delivery versus payment
EAD	exposure at default
EBR	export bill rediscounting
ECB	external commercial borrowing
ECGC	Export Credit Guarantee Corporation of India
ECR	export credit refinance
EI	exposure indicator
EL	expected loss
EMI	equated monthly instalment
EMD	earnest money deposit
EPS	earnings per share
EXIM Bank	Export–Import Bank of India
EYI	equal yearly instalment
FALLCR	facility to avail liquidity for LCR
FBIL	Financial Benchmarks India Private Limited
FCNR	foreign currency non-resident
FDIC	Federal Deposit Insurance Corporation
FEDAI	Foreign Exchange Dealers Association of India
FEMA	Foreign Exchange Management Act, 1999
FERA	Foreign Exchange Regulation Act, 1973
FII	foreign institutional investor
FIMMDA	Fixed Income Money Market and Derivatives Association of India
FIP	financial inclusion plan
FPO	follow-on public offer

forex	foreign exchange
FSB	Financial Stability Board
G10	Group of Ten (countries)
GDP	gross domestic product
GFC	global financial crisis
GNPAs	ratio of gross non-performing assets to total advances
GSDP	gross state domestic product
GST	goods and services tax
GTB	Global Trust Bank
HDFC	Housing Development Finance Corporation
HFT	held for trading
HSBC	Hongkong and Shanghai Banking Corporation
HTM	held to maturity
HQLA	high-quality liquid asset
IBC	Insolvency and Bankruptcy Code, 2016
ICAAP	Internal Capital Adequacy Assessment Process
ICICI	Industrial Credit and Investment Corporation of India
ICRA	Investment Information and Credit Rating Agency of India Limited
IDBI	Industrial Development Bank of India
IDFC	Infrastructure Development Finance Company
IFCI	Industrial Finance Corporation of India
IMF	International Monetary Fund
IMPS	Immediate Payment Service
IMS	information management system
INR	Indian rupee(s)
IOB	Indian Overseas Bank
IPB	Indian private bank
IPO	initial public offering
IRB	internal rating-based
IRDAI	Insurance Regulatory and Development Authority of India
IT	information technology

ITES	information technology-enabled services
JLF	Joint Lenders' Forum
KCC	Kisan Credit Card
KPI	key performance indicator
KYC	Know Your Customer
LAF	liquidity adjustment facility
LCR	liquidity coverage ratio
LCs	letters of credit
LGD	loss given default
LGE	loss given that event
LIC	Life Insurance Corporation of India
LOLR	lender of last resort
LTRO	long-term repo operation
M&As	mergers and acquisitions
MBS	mortgage-backed security
MCLR	marginal cost of funds-based lending rate
MD	managing director
MFI	microfinance institution
MICR	magnetic ink character recognition
MPBF	maximum permissible bank finance
MRMC	market risk management committee
MSF	marginal standing facility
MSME	micro, small and medium enterprise
MTM	monetary transmission mechanism
MUDRA	Micro Units Development and Refinance Agency
NABARD	National Bank for Agriculture and Rural Development
NBFC	non-banking financial company
NCC	National Credit Council
NDA	National Democratic Alliance
NDTL	net demand and time liabilities
NEFT	National Electronic Funds Transfer

NHB	National Housing Bank
NII	net interest income
NIM	net interest margin
NNPAs	ratio of net non-performing assets to net advances
NPA	non-performing asset
NPAT	net profit after tax
NPB	new private bank/new Indian private bank
NRE	non-resident external
NREGA	National Rural Employment Guarantee Authority
NRI	non-resident Indian
NRO	non-resident ordinary
NSDP	net state domestic product
NSE	National Stock Exchange
NSFR	net stable funding ratio
NWC	net working capital
OBS	off-balance sheet
OECD	Organisation for Economic Cooperation and Development
ORMC	operational risk management committee
OSMOS	Off-Site Monitoring and Surveillance
OTC	over the counter
PAC	primary agricultural credit society
PAN	permanent account number
PBT	profit before tax
PCARDB	primary cooperative agriculture and rural development bank
PCFC	pre-shipment credit in foreign currency
PD	probability of default
PE	probability of occurrence of loss event
PF	provident fund
PFAS	pawnbroker for all seasons
PFRDA	Pension Fund Regulatory and Development Authority
PLR	prime lending rate

PMJDY	Pradhan Mantri Jan Dhan Yojana
PNB	Punjab National Bank
POS	point of sale
PSB	public sector bank
PV01	present value of a basis point
RBC	real business cycle
RBI	Reserve Bank of India
RCCI	rural cooperative credit institution
RMC	risk management committee
RMD	risk management department
ROA	return on assets
RPMC	risk policy and monitoring committee
RRB	regional rural bank
RSAs	ratio of stressed assets to advances
RSF	required stable funding
RTGS	real-time gross settlement
S4A	Scheme for Sustainable Structuring of Stressed Assets
SARFAESI	Securitisation and Reconstruction of Financial Assets and Enforcement of Security Interest
SBI	State Bank of India
SCARDB	state cooperative agriculture and rural development bank
SCB	scheduled commercial bank
SD	standard deviation
SDF	standing deposit facility
SDR	Strategic Debt Restructuring
SEBI	Securities and Exchange Board of India
SFA	stochastic frontier analysis
SHG	self-help group
SIDBI	Small Industries Development Bank of India
SIP	systematic investment plan
SLBC	state-level bankers' committee

SLR	statutory liquidity ratio
SOP	standard operating procedure
SWIFT	Society for Worldwide Interbank Financial Telecommunications
TB	treasury bill
TDS	tax deducted at source
TFP	total factor productivity
TLTRO	targeted long-term repo operation
TOD	temporary overdrafts
TSA	the standardised approach
UCB	urban cooperative bank
UCO Bank	United Commercial Bank
UCPDC	Uniform Customs and Practices for Documentary Credit
UEL	unexpected loss
UK	United Kingdom
UPI	Unified Payments Interface
US	United States
USD	United States dollar(s)
UT	union territory
UTI	Unit Trust of India
VAR	vector auto-regression
VaR	value at risk
VAT	value added tax
VRS	Voluntary Retirement Scheme
VSAT	very small aperture terminal
WTO	World Trade Organization

Prologue

An economy is characterised by a variety of macroeconomic indicators such as gross domestic product (GDP), employment, savings and investment, general prices, interest rates, taxes and government borrowing/debt, banking and finance, exports, imports, and so on. Amongst all, GDP, which captures aggregate production or output of a country, stands out as the most important barometer to measure overall economic activity. Production of goods and services in a country generates commensurate income for various stakeholders engaged in the production process and enables them to buy and consume various goods and services. Economic welfare in a country is assessed by the amount of goods and services produced and consumed by its citizens. In a rich country like the United States or Japan, with higher level of production and income generation, the citizens can afford a high level of standard of living. They enjoy access to nutritious food, quality health care, better air conditioning, automobiles and vacation, and so on. On the contrary, a sizeable number of citizens in poor or low- and middle-income countries lack access to even basic needs like food and safe drinking water, reflecting low standard of living.

The growth theories explain, inter alia, how the rich countries in the world could achieve and sustain their economic progress over a long period of time stretching more than a century, and also why many countries in Africa and Asia have not been able to do so. Particularly, proximate causes are identified in terms of accumulation of capital through mobilisation of savings, population growth supplying labour or workers, and improvement of labour productivity through innovations and technological changes. A more fundamental role is assigned to economic and political institutions.

In the aforementioned process of attaining and sustaining economic prosperity in an economy, banks play a special role. In fact, the very functioning and progress of any modern economy is inconceivable without banks and other entities of the financial system. First, banks are financial intermediaries which generate deposits from the public and utilise the mobilised deposits to provide loans and undertake investments. In this process, banks play a crucial role towards augmentation of savings and efficient allocation of resources for productive investments. Consequently, banks assume a vital role towards achieving and sustaining economic growth in a longer-term perspective.

Second, monetary policy is widely used as the most important macroeconomic policy tool for economic stabilisation. It helps in moderating the underlying short-term economic fluctuations around potential output and promotes price stability. For conduct of monetary policy, bank credit acts as a dominant channel of monetary transmission.

Third, banks constitute the backbone of the payments and settlement system in any modern economy.

On the contrary, the underlying features such as problem of information asymmetry and excessive procyclicality in bank lending, mismatch in liquidity of bank loans and deposits, and so on, make banks prone to various types of banking risks. If such risks are not mitigated, they can manifest in insolvency and liquidity problem for the banks and can potentially hurt the economy severely.

Thus, banks have tremendous potential to promote economic welfare and are beneficial to modern society. However, there is an imperative need to ensure prudential functioning of banks with appropriate regulation and supervision to avoid possible injurious impacts on the economy due to any financial mismanagement and excessive risk taking.

In the Indian context, the banking system is the most dominant component of the entire financial system. Since the establishment of Bank of Hindustan in 1770, the first bank in India, the banking system has evolved with many transformations in all dimensions. The bank nationalisation of 1969 and 1980 phenomenally expanded banking services. The expansion was quite visible in terms of geographical spread of bank branches, massive growth in bank deposits and credit. Adoption of international best practices in banking regulations and modernisation of the banking system with comprehensive reforms since the early 1990s facilitated significant improvement in the performance and soundness of Indian banks.

In this backdrop, this book endeavours to cover all the relevant issues related to banks and the banking system in India from an economist's perspective. The issues broadly cover (*a*) the role of banks for an economy, (*b*) the rationale for and details of banking regulations and (*c*) general bank management practices. All of these issues are discussed in the context of the Indian banking system.

The organisation of the book and the chapter-wise coverage of different aspects of banks and banking are outlined here. The book is divided into the following five parts.

Part I: Introduction to Banking in India

Chapter 1 provides an introduction to the banks as financial intermediaries and explains day-to-day banking functions and activities. It highlights that the fundamental function of a bank is to mobilise bank deposits from the general public and to deploy the same as bank loans and investments. Using key items of assets and liabilities appearing in a *bank balance sheet*, the chapter discusses the salient features of various banking activities and operations. The *statement of income and expenditure* of a bank is used to supplement this discussion on the nature banking business. Key banking indicators, mainly derived from the *bank balance sheet* and the *statement of income and expenditure*, are used to assess profitability and financial health of a bank. Other ancillary functions of a bank such as issue of guarantees, letters of credit, bancassurance, and so on, are highlighted to understand a host of financial services which are provided by a modern bank. This chapter also delineates the everyday activities in a bank branch, which form the critical operational unit for the entire bank.

In **Chapter 2**, a broad overview of the overall financial system in India is outlined, and within that the overwhelming position of the banking sector is explained. This chapter provides important information on the structure of the Indian banking sector and progress in banking performance using key banking indicators. The Indian banking system comprises three types of banks: commercial banks, cooperative banks and regional rural banks (RRBs). Commercial banks dominate the Indian banking system. In turn, public sector banks (PSBs), Indian private banks (IPBs) and foreign banks are three major categories of commercial banks, distinguished in terms of ownership of the banks. They are the mainstream commercial banks in India, in addition to recently established small finance banks and payment banks. The salient features of all mainstream commercial banks, their constituents and broad information about their banking performance are presented in this chapter. The chapter also touches upon the role of the apex bank in India—that is, the Reserve Bank of India (RBI). The Indian banking system witnessed significant policy reforms since the early 1990s, which contributed to sweeping transformations in the system. Banks have become sound and more resilient and improved their profitability and efficiency, as well as diversified their portfolio with the introduction of innovative products. Details of these reforms and their implications for the Indian banking and financial sector are provided in this chapter.

Part II: Banks and the Economy

Banks play a critical role in an economy, promoting its economic prosperity. **Chapter 3** highlights how banks facilitate mobilisation of savings, convert the same into productive investments and augment efficient allocation of resources. The chapter explains this by underscoring the role of banks in resolving size and maturity mismatches in the preferences of savers vis-à-vis that of borrowers. The ability of banks in reducing lending risks with expertise in credit appraisal, monitoring the end-use of loans and risk diversification is also discussed. As suggested in the theories of economic growth, mobilisation of savings and accumulation of capital are of paramount importance for achieving and sustaining economic growth. In addition, efficient allocation of resources boosts factor productivity and propels long-term economic prosperity. The chapter also highlights the significance of banks as the backbone of the payments and settlement system in an economy.

Any economy witnesses short-term economic fluctuations within the broad long-term trend of economic prosperity. This is popularly referred to as the *business cycle* phenomenon. Economic slowdown or contraction during the downswing entails job losses and falling income. It causes hardship for the workers and producers. Economic upswings are generally associated with high inflation. The latter undermines the standard of living of the general public. Economic fluctuations can be moderated with appropriate monetary policy action. In **Chapter 4**, we discuss various factors causing economic fluctuations and how monetary policy can be used to achieve greater economic stability. Banks play a central role in transmitting monetary policy impulses. In this perspective, the chapter highlights the role of banks in an economy in short-term output stabilisation and inflation control.

Thus, Chapters 3 and 4 cover the important role of banks and banking both in terms of enhancing economic prosperity in the long run and moderating economic fluctuations in the short run.

There is a third dimension of how the banks can be helpful for an emerging economy like India. This is pertaining to addressing the concerns regarding regional economic disparity. **Chapter 5** highlights how the Indian economy suffers from uneven economic prosperity across different states. Despite stated policy objectives under the central planning to promote economic equality, inter-state economic disparity prevailed and the market-oriented reforms since the early 1990s further aggravated the problem. The rich states became richer while the poorer states lagged behind further. The chapter explores to what extent banking services, particularly bank lending, can mitigate economic disparity across the states. It is observed that the share of economically prosperous regions and states is much higher in overall bank deposits and credit. The ratio of bank credit to net state domestic product (NSDP) was found to be on the higher side for the richer states. The chapter observes that there is a scope for promoting banking services, particularly accelerating lending in the poor states to improve their economic standing. Needless to mention, complementary policies to improve physical infrastructure and governance need to be put in place for creating an industry-friendly ecosystem as a necessary prerequisite. Broadly, this chapter advocates that banking services can be used as a vehicle of development to overcome economic disparity in India.

It is to be noted that Chapter 5 has its relevance in analysing the important link between regional economic disparity in India and similar skewed distribution of banking and in prescribing methods to improve bank lending in the poorer states to correct economic distortion. However, it is not a core chapter in the book. A reader may skip the chapter, if they are not keen to look at the regional distribution aspect of banking services, and may proceed to the next chapter; they will not miss the flow of the discussion.

To sum up, all three chapters in this part underscore the important role of banks in an economy. Books on economics and banking, in general, do not cover the aforementioned issues exclusively, or they fall short of adequate emphasis. In this perspective, the chapters are useful for students of economics to integrate the relevance of banking in economics. Similarly, students of banking and professionals can gain useful insights into how banks are important from an economics perspective.

An analogy can be drawn between banks in an economic system and nuclear plants in a country. The nuclear plants are very useful as a cheaper, environmental-friendly source of energy. The nuclear arsenal acts as a credible deterrent against any foreign aggression. Similarly, the banks are helpful for promoting economic prosperity as discussed. However, accidents in the nuclear plants can potentially have devastating consequences. Banking crises, similarly, can cause serious economic disruptions. This fundamentally justifies the requirement of suitable banking regulations, which would contain banking risks within prudential limits and ensure continuity of beneficial services of the banks to society. In Part III of the book, regulatory issues pertaining to banks are covered.

Part III: Banking Risks, Regulations and Risk Management

Chapter 6 explains the underlying factors causing banking risks. It explains that information asymmetry inherent in bank lending entails the problem of adverse selection and moral hazard, which in turn are the root causes of default risk. Not all borrowers pay back loans as per agreements; in several cases, the banks suffer losses due to loan delinquencies. Excessive procyclicality of bank loans exacerbate the aforementioned problems. Moreover, the alchemy of banking converts liabilities with shorter maturity (bank deposits) into assets with longer maturity (bank loans), which is the root cause of liquidity risk in banks. There are numerous incidents in which such problems led to *bank runs* and in extreme cases resulted in large-scale bank failures due to the contagion. Any business including manufacturing and trade involves a variety of risks. But the nature and manifestation of risks in banking is quite extensive. This justifies adequate and extensive regulation of banks as compared to non-financial business entities.

Moreover, there is a requirement of protecting depositors' interest in banking from ethical and natural justice point of view. Depositors are not involved in business decisions of banks, although they contribute bulk of the funds for banking business. They suffer the most when there are bank failures. Thus, there is a moral responsibility to protect their interest through appropriate bank regulations.

Chapter 6 identifies major types of risks such as credit risk, liquidity risk, interest rate risk, market risk and operational risk in banking business. To assess the magnitude of banking risks, it is necessary to measure each such variety. The chapter provides technical details for measurement of banking risks.

Chapter 7 provides an overview of the evolution of banking regulations. It explains how stringent requirements for commencement of banking business are used as a screening procedure to weed out undesirable entities. Administrative controls on different aspects of the banking business, including lending, fixing interest rate on loans and deposits, governance and management, are used to encourage safe and sound banking. Moreover, central banks are set up to institutionalise a facility like *lender of last resort* (LOLR) to overcome transient liquidity problem in banks, and *deposit insurance* is used to protect depositors from financial losses if there are bank failures. All these are helpful for promoting public confidence in banks and reduce the scope for *bank runs*. Finally, Basel norms on capital adequacy juxtaposed with prudential requirements of asset classification, income recognition and provisioning have emerged as the modern toolkit for banking regulations. The Basel capital adequacy norms have witnessed several rounds of revisions and upgradations influenced by experiences like the global financial crisis (GFC) of 2007–08. The chapter covers all technical details pertaining to Basel capital adequacy requirements, which are used as standards of international best practice for banking regulations.

Even if regulatory norms are well designed, banking soundness and prudence cannot be safeguarded without ensuring effective implementation of these regulations. Well-designed regulatory requirements need to be supplemented by measures which ensure adherence to such prescriptions by the banks. The process of banking supervision is used by banking regulators to monitor actual implementation of the regulatory prescriptions as well as to assess the financial health of banks on a continuous basis. This process involves *on-site inspection* of books of the banks by visiting bank premises, supplemented by *off-site surveillance* of various banking indicators to evaluate their financial health. Based on the inspection report, respective banks are awarded scores and ratings by the regulators. If the scores or ratings are below a certain threshold, the banks concerned are prescribed appropriate corrective action. Chapter 7 briefly explains how banking supervision is performed by the RBI for the banks in India.

Banking risks cannot be avoided completely. But with the adoption of robust risk management procedures and practices, the risks can be mitigated. Banks in India have their own internal mechanism to comply with regulatory requirements on risk management. In addition to that, it is in their own interest to contain banking risks so that they remain solvent and healthy. This is in the long-term interest of the shareholders and bank management. In this perspective, **Chapter 8** outlines risk management framework of the banks in India. It provides necessary details of the organisational structure and procedures followed by banks for containment of different types of banking risks.

Until here the book covers issues related to banks from the macro or systemwide perspective. The role of banks for the economy and regulatory issues pertaining to banks have wider dimensions pertaining to the entire economy or the overall banking system. In Part IV of the book, the focus is on activities of individual banks. It explains general bank management practices.

Part IV: Managing the Banking Business

Managers of banking business peruse the broad objectives of profitability, solvency and liquidity. Being a commercial entity, the primary objective of the banking business is to maximise profit and shareholders' equity value. A bank's profitability can be raised by increasing its interest and non-interest income over interest and operational costs. Given that loans and investments constitute the bulk of a bank's assets, and deposits and borrowings are its main liabilities, the net interest income (NII) broadly determines its overall profit. NII is nothing but a bank's interest income over interest costs. Second, a bank continues to be solvent as long as its assets are in excess of its liabilities or the bank has a positive net worth. If a large chunk of a bank's loans becomes delinquent, then the bank may suffer from insolvency, ultimately leading to its collapse. Moreover, despite having positive net worth, a bank may have transient liquidity problem if its liquid assets fall short of liquid liability. In that case, the bank may fail to meet deposit withdrawal obligations and may encounter *bank runs*. If the liquidity problem persists, that may lead to serious disruptions in its banking business.

General banking management pertains to day-to-day business decisions on the assets and liabilities of a bank, while pursuing the overall objectives of profitability, solvency and liquidity. These decisions are related to the composition of various items of assets and liabilities and their pricing.

Banking managerial decisions pertaining to the assets side of the bank balance sheet, particularly for loans and investments, are covered in **Chapter 9**. Profit of a bank can be maximised by expanding the volume of its loans and investments as well as by charging higher interest rate on them. However, the bank cannot be reckless in this regard. Aggressive lending and investments, particularly the highly risky variety, may raise default risk. It diminishes a bank's solvency conditions. Similarly, a bank needs to maintain a reasonable balance between liquid assets and liabilities. So lending and investment decisions entail very complicated exercise. Proper credit appraisal of borrowers and taking into account various types of risks involved in each variety of lending are very challenging. Also, the loans need to be priced based on the costs of funds, risk profile of the borrower, tenure and type of loans, and so on. A branch manager adheres to the extant guidelines of the RBI and the internal policy of the bank and, juxtaposed with their own managerial acumen, takes business decisions on lending. Necessary details in this regard are provided in Chapter 9. The chapter also highlights strategic investment decisions of the banks.

Similarly, managerial decisions connected to bank deposits and borrowings are covered in **Chapter 10**. Banks mobilise a variety of deposits. Some deposits like current and saving account deposits are payable on demand. On the contrary, time deposits are of longer term and payable on maturity. For a bank, current and saving account deposits are more attractive from the point of view of profitability, while they pose considerable liquidity risks. No interest is paid on current account deposits and interest paid on savings account deposits is relatively low. On the other hand, with a fixed term to maturity, time deposits do not pose much liquidity risks. But interest paid on such deposits at a higher rate undermines banking profitability. Moreover, there has to be reasonable balance between the maturity profile of the assets and liabilities of the banks; otherwise, the banks may face liquidity problem. Depending on the mismatch in assets versus liabilities across different maturity buckets, a bank may need to aggressively expand deposits of certain maturity, while it may require to moderate deposit growth in some other maturity bucket. Accordingly, the pricing of deposits need to be undertaken. Furthermore, the interest rates on deposits and lending have to be synchronised with the monetary policy stance of the RBI. In the context of the management of banking liabilities, the strategies for borrowing from the RBI, other banks and financial institutions or markets are covered. During the post-reform period, banks have resorted to the use of financial derivatives significantly. Chapter 10 also highlights about the management of off-balance sheet (OBS) items.

Part V: Performance of Banks in India and Contemporary Issues

Banking sector reforms adopted in India since the 1990s have phased out government control on them in many aspects. In the new ecosystem, adequate operational autonomy and enhanced competition are expected to improve banking performance in all financial parameters. In **Chapter 11**, an attempt is made to review the performance of banks in India, as reflected in various indicators of profitability, productivity and efficiency. It is observed that most of the parameters of profitability and operational efficiency across the bank groups have improved during the post-reform period. Particularly, it is heartening to note that PSBs have performed better than their private sector counterparts on several aspects. However, as regards allocative efficiency, there has been no noticeable improvement.

Lastly, based on the discussion in the preceding chapters, **Chapter 12** reviews some contemporary issues pertaining to the Indian banking system and provides the future roadmap. This chapter covers issues such as the recent high incidence of non-performing assets (NPAs); bank mergers and consolidation; the debate over public versus private ownership of banks; the use of information technology (IT) and information technology–enabled services (ITES) and the impact of digital innovations in payments and settlement, environmental concerns and green banking; proposals for future banking regulations; and so on.

Overall, this book endeavours to provide an optimal balance between theoretical underpinnings and banking management practices for facilitating a comprehensive understanding of banking and its related issues. The book also covers in detail the regulatory aspects and supervisory practices from the perspectives of both the banking regulator and a banker. The requirements of both academics and professionals are kept in mind to present a holistic approach. The book is expected to be useful for students and researchers interested in banking and finance. It can also be helpful to candidates aspiring to join the banking industry or seeking promotion in their current job in a bank.

The reader is requested to bring to the author's notice any errors—conceptual, technical or otherwise. Despite the author's best efforts to provide correct and updated information, it is possible that the banking management practices in a particular bank deviate in some aspect from the generalised version presented in this book. There could also be revisions and upgradations in any of the risk management aspects or decision-making procedures since the book was written. The author will be thankful to receive valuable feedback from the reader and will hopefully be able to incorporate the same in the next edition of this book after due deliberation.

Part I

Introduction to Banking in India

1

About Banks and Banking

Learning Objectives

- To introduce banks and the business of banking
- To understand banking business using the balance sheet of a bank
- To explain various items of assets and liabilities in a bank balance sheet
- To describe the key items in the income–expenditure statement of a bank and derive indicators of bank profitability and other major parameters
- To briefly highlight the various ancillary services provided by a bank
- To outline the role of bank branches which are the basic functional units for banking operations

1.1 Introduction

In any modern economy, dealing with banks has become an integral part of everyday life. Bank offices or branches are a familiar sight in marketplaces in cities and towns. The setting up of automated teller machines (ATMs) as a form of extension of bank branches has further expanded the presence of banks. Not only urban centres and small towns, but even the rural parts of India today are no longer unfamiliar with banks and banking. It is quite common for the general public to avail ordinary banking services like obtaining a bank loan for business or farming, operating a savings bank deposit account, taking a home or automobile loan, using a credit or debit card or making or receiving small denomination payments using the Unified Payments Interface (UPI). The reader may have some exposure to banks and banking activities in her day-to-day life. However, not everyone may be quite aware about the technical aspects of banking operations and the banking business. Many may not have adequate understanding about various types of assets and liabilities of banks and the technical details related to various banking products and functions. In this chapter, we provide the basic details about a bank and its activities to facilitate a comprehensive understanding of the banking business. The objective is to provide a formal introduction to banks and banking in the Indian context.

Section 1.2 describes ordinary banking services in the form of opening bank deposit accounts, facilitating financial transfers and extending loans. In the process, a typical bank acts as an interface between savers and borrowers. The bank is a legal entity incorporated under the law of the land. The legal provisions in India defining banks and banking functions are also briefly discussed.

Banks are basically commercial entities, with profit maximisation as their key objective. Like any other commercial organisation, two basic financial statements in the form of (*a*) the balance sheet and (*b*) the income and expenditure statement are quite helpful in developing a broad understanding of the functions and business operations of banks. Both summarise wider aspects of their activities. Section 1.3 explains the main functions and commercial activities in banking based on the balance sheet of a bank in India. Similar aspects are described using the income and expenditure statement of a bank in section 1.4. Section 1.5 highlights select ancillary functions or activities undertaken by a modern-day bank beyond the conventional lending and deposit-taking operations.

In India, banks operate under a branch banking system. Under this arrangement, a wide network of bank branches undertake usual banking operations. Important activities like mobilisation of deposits, disbursement of loans and other ordinary banking functions are carried out by such branches. Thus, bank branches form the operational units at the base level. A brief outline on operational aspects such as opening deposit accounts, extending bank loans and managing currency or cash in bank branches in India is provided in section 1.6.

1.2 Conventional Banking and Legal Provisions

Conventional banking involves two fundamental activities—namely, deposit collection and provision of loans. A bank acts as a financial intermediary between savers and borrowers. On the one hand, a bank provides an avenue for savers to deposit their surplus funds. On the other, it deploys the funds mobilised through such deposits in the form of loans to borrowers.

Savers are a set of people or institutions having spending requirements lower than their current earnings and wealth. They are conventionally known as *surplus spenders* (Pierce and Tysome, 1985). Savers are the ultimate lenders. The list of surplus spenders includes households, corporates and small business entities, government bodies, and so on. In India, a very large proportion of bank deposits are held by households, followed by private corporates and the government. For example, as on 31 March 2022, the share of households in the total deposits of scheduled commercial banks (SCBs)[1] was 62.63 per cent, while the shares of corporates and the government were 22.24 and 8.97 per cent, respectively (RBI , n.d.1).

The simple reason behind the need to borrow is spending requirements of firms, households and governments being in excess of their current earnings and accumulated wealth. Such borrowers are conventionally known as *deficit spenders.*

Firms and enterprises require vast amounts of funds for the setting up of factories, the construction of buildings, the purchase of machines or equipment, and so on. Such spending requirements often overwhelmingly exceed their current profits and retained earnings. So they heavily rely on borrowing or external financing. Big corporates can access funds directly by issuing corporate bonds and selling their equity shares in the capital market. Often they also avail project loans and working capital loans from banks. Small enterprises, however, do not enjoy the advantage of accessing funds in the capital market. They are thus primarily dependent on loans from banks to meet their borrowing requirements. Many households too avail bank loans to fund expensive purchases like a home or an automobile. The cost of an apartment or car very often exceeds the amount of accumulated savings and the current income of ordinary households. Similar to small business enterprises, households also do not have access to the equity and bond markets and turn to bank lending to fund such purchases. Households also use bank loans to meet their expenditure needs for consumer durables. The introduction of credit cards has further facilitated the use of bank loans for

[1] SCBs are commercial banks which appear under schedule 2 of the Reserve Bank of India (RBI) Act, 1934. These include all public sector banks (PSBs), Indian private banks (IPBs), foreign banks, regional rural banks, small finance banks and payment banks operating in India.

even routine purchases like groceries, fruits and vegetables, flight and train tickets, and so on. Governments borrow through issue of government bonds and treasury bills to fund their expenditure in excess of their own resources such as tax and non-tax receipts. Needless to mention, all governments across developed and developing countries borrow through issue of government securities. However, in the case of the latter, the reliance on borrowing is quite extensive as the scope for raising tax revenue is limited due to a variety of reasons. These include, inter alia, lower tax base due to weak economic conditions, poor tax governance, and so on.

In his popular book *Modern Banking* (1947), R. S. Sayers defines the conventional banking business as covering three main aspects. These are as follows:

- Changing cash for bank deposits and bank deposits for cash
- Transferring bank deposits from one person or corporation to another
- Giving bank deposits against bills of exchange, government bonds or the secured promises of businessmen to repay

In the following sections, we elaborate on the aforementioned functions of a bank.

1.2.1 Mobilisation of Savings in the Form of Bank Deposits

Readers must be familiar with bank deposits. There are several types of bank deposits. Many of us might have a *savings bank deposit account* in a commercial bank such as State Bank of India (SBI), Bank of Baroda (BOB), Indian Bank, Housing Development Finance Corporation (HDFC) Bank, Industrial Credit and Investment Corporation of India (ICICI) Bank, and so on. Opening a savings bank deposit account in a bank mainly serves two purposes: first, it is a safe and convenient means of keeping our savings; second, such accounts facilitate easy payment and settlement. Banks pay nominal interest on such deposit accounts. Deposits in savings bank accounts can be withdrawn through a withdrawal slip or cheque submitted by the authorised person. As per regulatory requirements, depositors need to submit a set of documents to establish their identity under the Know Your Customer (KYC) norms to avoid money laundering. The KYC documents for individuals generally include their passport, voter identity card, driving licence, Aadhaar card, permanent account number (PAN) card (issued by the income tax authority), and so on. For proprietary concerns, the acceptable KYC documents include their registration certificate, sales and income tax returns, goods and services tax (GST) or value added tax (VAT) certificate, certificate or licence issued by the municipal authorities, and so on. Banks also follow some simple eligibility criteria for different types of customers. Generally, savings bank accounts entail minimum deposit requirements. However, in August 2014, a special variety of savings bank deposits was introduced under the Pradhan Mantri Jan Dhan Yojana (PMJDY) in India which relaxed the requirement of maintaining a minimum balance in deposit accounts for the poor.

Many of us may also be familiar with fixed deposit accounts offered by banks. Such deposits have a fixed period of maturity. The maturity period may vary from a week to several years. Banks pay market-related interest rates on such deposits which are higher than the interest rate(s) paid on savings bank accounts. Details about various types of bank deposits offered by banks in India are provided in Chapter 10 in this book.

Deposits are received by banks in the form of cash or transfer of deposit claims. A customer can add to her balance in a deposit account by depositing cash in the bank branch or at its ATM. Otherwise, one can also transfer funds from another bank account through electronic transfer, cheques or drafts, and so on. Thus, bank deposits are 100 per cent covered by the assets offered by depositors to the concerned bank. Any bank is liable to pay its depositors the amount they have deposited either on demand or on the maturity date. Hence, bank deposits are treated as liabilities of the respective banks.

As indicated earlier, in addition to their utility as a safe mode of savings, bank deposits also facilitate payment and settlement. They constitute a form of money.[2] Amounts in a savings bank deposit account have the inherent characteristic of instantly being converted into cash. The same can also be used for undertaking payments through online transfers, debit cards, UPI, and so on. Banks in India also generally permit withdrawal of amounts deposited in a fixed deposit account before maturity without much difficulty. Necessary guidelines are provided in Chapter 10 in this book.

Depositors will be inclined to place their savings in a bank deposit as long as they have confidence in the ability of the bank to readily meet their deposit withdrawal demands. This capacity of a bank to meet deposit withdrawal demands depends on whether adequate liquid assets or funds are available

---

[2] 'Money' is a form of financial asset which serves three major functions: (*a*) medium of exchange, (*b*) unit of account and (*c*) store of value.

with it. Cash balances are the most liquid form of assets. The liquidity of other assets depends on how quickly they can be converted into cash without any loss of market value. For example, a treasury bill or a government bond is highly liquid as it can be readily sold in the bonds market and can be converted into cash at the prevailing market rate. On the other hand, finding a ready buyer for a piece of land or plot is a time-consuming process. The owner of the land or plot may eventually sell at a price below the market rate if they cannot wait longer to find a suitable buyer. Hence, a piece of a land is not a liquid asset.

A bank has to maintain an adequate amount of liquid assets on a continuous basis. Any difficulty in meeting deposit withdrawal demands due to inadequate liquid assets may lead to impairment of public confidence in the bank. Extreme situations of such damage to depositors' confidence may lead to what are known as *bank runs*.[3] Such episodes have had devastating consequences on several occasions with bank failures and severe disruptions of economic activities. Details of such banking crises are provided in Chapter 6 in this book.

1.2.2 Transfer of Bank Deposits: Enabling Payment and Settlement

The second key aspect of banking entails transferring of funds from one depositor's account to that of another. Households, businesses and government entities undertake numerous transactions as part of their day-to-day activities. Businesses or traders make payments to their employees, raw material suppliers, agencies providing transport, providers of security and legal services, and so on, on a regular basis. They also pay rent, taxes, electricity bills and interest charges. Likewise, they receive numerous payments from the sale of their products and services. Government entities undertake similar transactions. Households make regular payments for their routine purchases using debit cards, online transfers, payments through cheques as also remit funds to other individuals or households.

---

[3] A 'bank run' is a situation in which depositors rush to a bank to withdraw all their deposits for fear of the bank failing to meet future deposit withdrawal demands. Such events take place when depositors and the general public have concerns about the liquidity position and overall financial health of a bank. Often such concerns are based on actual financial difficulties of the concerned bank, but they may also sometimes be caused by misperceptions or rumours. Nevertheless, any general concern leading to 'bank runs' is a self-fulfilling prophecy, details of which are discussed in Chapter 6 in this book.

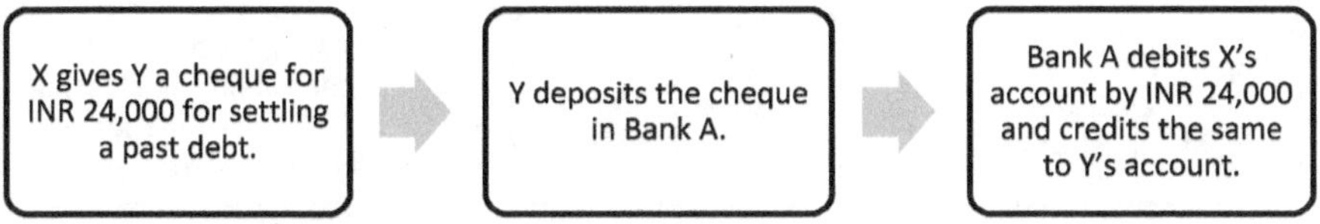

Figure 1.1(a) Transfer of funds when entities have deposit accounts in the same bank

Source: Prepared by the author.

Large transactions undertaken by any of the aforementioned stakeholders often involve the banking channel. Let us explain with simple examples how funds are transferred across different entities using the banking channel.

Suppose an entity X has to make a payment of, say, INR 24,000 to another entity Y. One simple way of making the payment is by using cash. Another popular way is using the banking channel. Assume both X and Y have deposit accounts in Bank A. It may be convenient for X to issue a cheque for INR 24,000 drawn on Bank A in favour of Y. On receipt of the cheque from X, the same can be deposited by Y in Bank A to get the proceeds from X. In this case, the transfer is relatively easy. The deposit account of X in Bank A needs to be debited (deducted) by INR 24,000 and that of Y needs to be credited (added) with INR 24,000. This is depicted in Figure 1.1(a).

The process of transfer becomes a little complicated if they have deposit accounts in different banks. Say, X has a deposit account in Bank A and Y in Bank B. In this case, Y receives the cheque for INR 24,000 from X for its claim. It will deposit the cheque in Bank B. In turn, Bank B will present the cheque to the ‘clearing house’[4] to get the claim from Bank A on behalf of Y. The clearing house is operated by the central bank of the country or its agents. Our central bank is the RBI.

In the clearing house, for facilitating the settlement, the current account[5] of Bank A maintained with the RBI will be debited by INR 24,000 while that of Bank B will be credited with the same amount, effecting the transfer of

---

[4] A clearing house is an institutional mechanism provided by a central bank like the RBI or its agent commercial bank in different cities and towns to facilitate cheque transfers amongst the banks.

[5] Commercial banks maintain a deposit account with their central bank, like the RBI in our country, in the form of current account to facilitate financial transactions between themselves as also with the central bank.

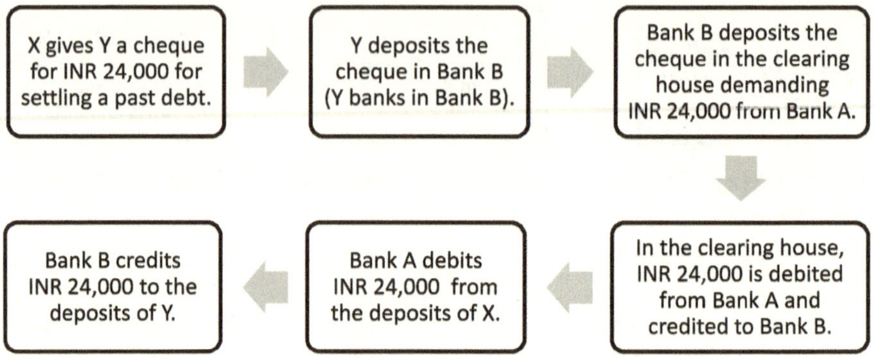

Figure 1.1(b) Transfer of funds when entities have deposit accounts in different banks

Source: Prepared by the author.

funds from Bank A to Bank B. Subsequently, the deposit account of X in Bank A will be debited by INR 24,000 and that of Y in Bank B will be credited with the same amount. Figure 1.1(b) illustrates this transfer of funds from X to Y through their respective banks.

It may be noted that on any given day, Bank A may be receiving several claims from Bank B on behalf of its depositors. Similarly, Bank B may also be receiving numerous claims from Bank A on account of dues from depositors of Bank B payable to depositors of Bank A. The net claims of Bank A from Bank B or vice versa may be calculated by consolidating all the claims and counterclaims amongst the depositors of Bank A and Bank B. Accordingly, the current accounts of Bank A and Bank B in the RBI can be debited or credited. For example, let us assume, taking into account all claims and counterclaims, INR 5 crore is the net claim of Bank A on Bank B; then the account of Bank A held with the RBI needs to be credited and that of Bank B needs to be debited by INR 5 crore. Consequently, at the bank level, the corresponding bank deposits of the entities involved in the claims and counterclaims need to be credited and debited appropriately.

Under the real-time gross settlement (RTGS) procedure used by banks for inter-bank settlements, banks settle dues amongst themselves on a real-time basis. Thus, if several payments are to be made from Bank A to Bank B and vice versa, such transfers are made on a gross basis, item by item in sequence. Assume Bank A needs to pay INR 5 crore to Bank B to settle a payment from one of its customers to a customer of Bank B. This transaction

Box 1.1 Distinction between gross and net settlements

Assume Sridevi and Sanjib are customers of Bank A and Ramakrishnan and Joseph are customers of Bank B. Let us consider a scenario where Sridevi is supposed to pay an amount of INR 10 lakh to Ramakrishnan and Joseph is supposed to pay INR 6 lakh to Sanjib.

Under net settlement, considering the obligations of the customers of Bank A and Bank B, a net amount of INR 4 lakh needs to be transferred from Bank A to Bank B. This is netting the INR 6 lakh payable from Joseph to Sanjib (from Bank B to Bank A) against the INR 10 lakh that is payable by Sridevi to Ramakrishnan (from Bank A to Bank B).

Under gross settlement on a real-time basis, first INR 10 lakh will be transferred from Bank A to Bank B to settle the payment of Sridevi to Ramakrishnan. A separate transfer of INR 6 lakh from Bank B to Bank A will be undertaken to settle the payment from Joseph to Sanjib. Gross settlement ensures that payer bank maintains the required amount of funds to be transferred to the payee bank for each transaction. If there is a default in one transaction in the sequence, remaining transfers cannot be undertaken. Therefore, the gross settlement procedure requires each bank to maintain adequate funds with the central bank to avoid any default.

or payment is carried out independently, irrespective of any other transaction on behalf of other customers. If there is a second payment of, say, INR 3.6 crore to be made on behalf of other customers of both banks, the same is undertaken separately rather than netting the two individual transactions. This is explained in Box 1.1.

As described here, the use of bank deposits facilitates safer and faster transfer of funds across individuals, businesses and government entities. Thus, banks function as the vital institutional infrastructure for the payment and settlement system in any modern economy.

1.2.3 Bank Lending and Investments

The fundamental function of banks is to convert bank deposits into loans and investments. There are many varieties of bank loans. Through bank loans in the form of project loans, a bank provides funding to a business entity to set up a production facility. Households avail home loans to buy an apartment or construct a house. Details on different varieties of bank loans are discussed in the following sections. Borrowers availing bank loans repay the loan along with interest charges over a period of time. On the contrary, investments by banks involve acquiring various types of assets such as bonds, equity, foreign exchange (forex), gold, and so on. Banks earn income on such assets in the form of capital gains, if the selling price of such assets at a later date exceeds the purchase price. Moreover, bonds also give regular income in the form of periodic coupon payments. The bulk of the investment portfolio of banks consists of government securities.

Banks carry out conversion of bank deposits into loans and investments in accordance with the fractional reserve system. The same is elaborated in the paragraphs that follow.

Suppose a bank, namely Bank A, has just started its operations and has received INR 10,000 in cash as deposits. Let us ignore the capital, reserves and other liabilities of Bank A for the moment to simplify our analysis. We will include them in our analysis in the following section. The receipt of INR 10,000 raises the deposits of Bank A by INR 10,000 under its liabilities, as also adds to the cash balances INR 10,000 under the assets side as shown in Table 1.1(a).

Accepting deposits, maintaining the accounts and carrying out transactions related to deposit accounts involve some transaction costs. Moreover, a bank needs to pay interest on its deposits too. By holding INR 10,000 in its vault, the bank does not earn any income. It can earn interest income by deploying the deposited amount in some profitable opportunity like giving a loan. Thus, it does not make any sense for Bank A to hold the entire amount of INR 10,000 in its reserves or as idle cash with itself.

On the contrary, can the bank exhaust the entire amount of INR 10,000 for lending and earn maximum interest income and profit? The answer is no. Utilising the entire deposit of INR 10,000 for lending may lead to liquidity problems in the bank. This is because bank loans are contractual in nature with a prior agreement on the schedule of repayments. A bank cannot demand repayment of its loan from the borrower before the due date in many cases.

Table 1.1(a) Receipt of cash balances as deposits

Liabilities	(in INR)	Assets	(in INR)
Deposits	10,000	Cash	10,000
Total	**10,000**	**Total**	**10,000**

If the bank expends the entire sum of INR 10,000 in lending, it will fail to meet the withdrawal demands of depositors prior to the scheduled repayment of the loan. As a matter of fact, banks usually maintain a portion of their deposits in the form of reserves, partly to meet the statutory requirements of maintaining a minimum balance of cash reserves and partly to meet the cash withdrawal and fund transfer demands of depositors.

The statutory requirement for banks operating in India to maintain cash reserves is popularly expressed in the form of the cash reserve ratio (CRR). Under section 18 of the Banking Regulation (BR) Act, 1949, and section 42 of the RBI Act, 1934, every bank in India needs to maintain a certain minimum proportion of its net demand and time liabilities (NDTL) in the form of cash reserves with itself or in the form of balances held with the RBI. The NDTL for a bank is calculated by removing its paid-up capital,[6] liabilities to the RBI, the National Bank for Agriculture and Rural Development (NABARD), Export–Import (EXIM) Bank of India and National Housing Bank (NHB) and net liabilities in the inter-bank call-money and notice-money market. Necessary details on CRR regulations are provided in section 18 of the BR Act, 1949, and section 42 of the RBI Act, 1934.

As of 31 August 2024, the RBI has stipulated the CRR to be 4.5 per cent. This implies that if, for example, a bank's NDTL as on 19 May 2023 (the last Friday of the second preceding fortnight) is INR 1,00,000, then the bank needs to maintain a daily average balance of INR 4,500 as cash reserves with itself or as balances held with RBI for the period 17–30 June 2023 (reporting fortnight). Finer details of the daily minimum balance requirements, the definition of NDTL, the reference period, computation procedure, and so on, are provided in the guidelines issued by the RBI from time to time.

Even without the statutory minimum requirements, it is imperative for banks to hold some cash reserves to meet deposit withdrawal demands as they arise. Any failure in a bank's ability to meet deposit withdrawal demands will lead to damaging public confidence in the bank which in turn may lead to a *bank run* as indicated earlier. Despite possessing good-quality loans as assets and reasonable comfort in liquidity, a bank cannot meet unusually high demands for deposit withdrawal. This is because the bulk of bank loans cannot be recalled before the schedule of repayments. In extreme circumstances, *bank runs* may cause the eventual collapse of a bank.

---

[6] Paid-up capital is the amount received from the owners or shareholders of a company in exchange of acquiring ownership or share ownership of the company.

It is a fact that the depositors of a bank ordinarily do not withdraw their entire deposits on a daily basis. The sum of deposit withdrawals from a typical bank on any particular day is usually limited to a small fraction of its total deposits. Beyond the regular deposit withdrawals, the bank also needs to maintain some additional balance to fulfil inter-bank transfer requirements. This includes transfer of funds on behalf of bank depositors as explained earlier. So it is prudent for the bank to keep a fraction of its deposits in the form of reserves or cash balances and lend out the remaining portion. This system is popularly known as the *fractional reserve system* in banking. Needless to mention, this fraction or minimum balance of reserves to be maintained by a bank is guided partly by statutory requirements and partly by the past experience of deposit withdrawal patterns of customers. Even then, the total requirement of cash balances or reserves to be maintained by a bank on a day-to-day basis is only a small fraction of its total deposits. For example, as on 31 March 2022, the proportion of the total liabilities[7] of SCBs that was kept as 'cash and balances with RBI' was about 5.4 per cent (RBI, 2022b).

Keeping excess cash reserves in idle form obviously is not a good business option for a bank. Rather, such excess funds should be lent or invested so that the bank can fully exploit the interest earning prospects of these funds. Interest earned from loans and investments by a bank over the interest paid on deposits, after meeting operational expenses, determines its profitability.

Now let us return to Bank A. Say, based on its own past experience, it assumes that maintaining 10 per cent of its deposits as cash reserves is adequate to meet the combined requirements of maintaining the statutory minimum reserves and usual withdrawal demands. In that case, it will be optimal for Bank A to lend out INR 9,000 and keep INR 1,000 as cash reserves out of the total deposits of INR 10,000. Accordingly, the composition of assets in Bank A can be modified as shown in Table 1.1(b).

Table 1.1(b) Use of deposits as bank loans and reserves

Liabilities	**(in INR)**	**Assets**	**(in INR)**
Deposits	10,000	Cash Reserves	1,000
		Bank Loans	9,000
Total	**10,000**	**Total**	**10,000**

[7] The total liabilities include borrowings from the RBI, other banks and non-banking financial institutions, along with the capital and all types of deposits.

Loans generally constitute the bulk of banking assets. As on 31 March 2022, the share of bank loans in the total assets of SCBs in India was 56.3 per cent while that of investments was 26.7 per cent (RBI, 2022b). Details about the management of loans and investments in the banking business are provided in Chapter 9 in this book.

To sum up, mobilisation of deposits from the public, conversion of such deposits into loans and investments, and transfer of deposits across different stakeholders facilitating payment and settlement are the three main functions of a bank. The business of banking primarily entails the management of deposits, loans and investments in such a manner that a bank's interest income on loans and investments over the interest cost on deposits is maximised and sustained. As a commercial entity, the main objective of a bank is to maximise its profit. However, as detailed in Chapter 6 in this book, the banking business involves a wide variety of risks. Mindless pursuit of aggressive lending in search of profit can potentially lead to raising banking risks excessively and may lead to banking crises. In this perspective, we will elaborate in Part III and Part IV of this book how banking management centres around the fundamental principles of profitability, solvency and liquidity. In the process, banks mainly focus on maximising risk-adjusted returns in the banking business.

1.2.4 Legal Aspects of Banks and Banking in India

In India, a popular way of defining banking is derived from the BR Act, 1949. According to section 5(b) of this Act, 'banking' is the acceptance of deposits of money from the public for the purpose of lending or investment. Such deposits are repayable on demand or otherwise and withdrawable by cheque, draft, order or otherwise. The BR Act, 1949, has specified the type of business activities which a bank in India is permitted to undertake and also stipulated a list of prohibited activities for banks.

Section 5(c) of the BR Act, 1949, has defined a 'bank' or 'banking company' as an entity which transacts the business of banking in India as per section 5(b). It excludes from such definition companies engaged in manufacturing or trading activities which accept deposits of money from the public merely for supporting their manufacturing or trading business.

Thus, the BR Act, 1949, clearly demarcates the scope of banking as the business of accepting deposits from the public, repayable on demand as in the case of current account deposits or savings account deposits or on the date of maturity as in the case of fixed deposits, as indicated earlier. The deposits generated by banks are used for the purpose of lending and investment in approved securities. In this way, banking involves the transformation of one set of securities to another set possessing different characteristics. Deposits are small in size, highly liquid and have short maturity periods. On the contrary, loans are large in size, illiquid and have long maturity periods. A large part of bank loans have fixed schedules of repayment. Home loans are often repaid in 20–30 years. The repayment period for car loans is up to 7 years and that for term loans for corporates can be 10–15 years. This is 'alchemy' in banking (M. King, 2016).

Needless to mention, the nature and scope of banking have witnessed significant transformation over time. Banking has become very sophisticated with the emergence of innovative financial instruments and specialised activities. Moving beyond ordinary banking functions as discussed earlier, banks have considerably expanded to take the form of wider financial conglomerates providing a variety of services, including project financing, underwriting and insurance, and so on.

In India, banking and quasi-banking services are provided by a variety of financial institutions. Historically, India had cooperative banks, often with exclusive focus on financing agriculture and rural economic activities. A special type of institutions, namely regional rural banks (RRBs), were created in the 1970s to cater to the needs of specific regions. RRBs were established under the joint ownership of the Government of India, a public sector bank (PSB) and the concerned state government. In 2015, guidelines were issued by the RBI to establish small finance and payment banks to meet small-scale financing requirements. Small finance banks provide specialised banking services such as small loans, deposits, insurance, and so on, to low-income individuals and underserved communities. Payment banks provide basic banking services like deposit taking, fund transfers, net banking and the issue of ATM or debit cards, but are not permitted to extend bank loans. Needless to mention, commercial banks have an overwhelming position in the entire banking system in India. Details about commercial banks and their vital place in the Indian financial system are provided in Chapter 2. Commercial banks in India are mainly classified in terms of ownership as follows:

- *Public sector banks (PSBs)*: The majority shareholder in such banks is the Government of India. After the mega amalgamation of 2019–20, there are 12 PSBs—namely, Bank of Baroda (BOB), Bank of India

(BOI), Bank of Maharashtra, Canara Bank, Central Bank of India, Indian Bank, Indian Overseas Bank (IOB), Punjab & Sind Bank, Punjab National Bank (PNB), State Bank of India (SBI), United Commercial (UCO) Bank and Union Bank of India. SBI is the largest bank in India. As a group, PSBs dominate the overall banking business in India.

- *Indian private banks (IPBs)*: As the name suggests, these are privately owned banks. The new IPBs which were established during the post-reform period have significantly expanded their business since the 1990s. A total of 21 IPBs were operating as of 31 March 2022. The leading IPBs which have grown in size considerably are Axis Bank, HDFC Bank and ICICI Bank.
- *Foreign banks*: Such banks are of foreign origin and established under the law of a country other than India. They also have their head office outside India. The list of leading foreign banks currently operating in India includes Citibank, the Hongkong and Shanghai Banking Corporation (HSBC) and Standard Chartered Bank.

In this book, unless otherwise specifically mentioned, by banks we mainly refer to commercial banks in India. In the following sections, we will explain the main banking activities drawing from the *balance sheet* and the *statement of income and expenditure* of banks. This will provide us further insight into what commercial banks do.

1.3 Major Banking Activities: Drawing from the Balance Sheet of a Bank

The balance sheet of a bank reveals its financial position at a given point of time. It contains two broad types of items, namely (*a*) assets and (*b*) liabilities. Assets include items which are due to the bank from its borrowers and other receivables. A loan is a bank's due from a borrower. Hence, it is an asset. On the contrary, liabilities cover items which the bank owes to its depositors and lenders and other payables. Bank deposits are payable to the depositors by the bank. Therefore, bank deposits are a form of liability of a bank. As explained in the preceding section, conventional banking involves mobilisation of deposits and deployment of these deposits as loans and investments. However, in reality, the banking business deals with a variety of assets and liabilities. The balance sheet of a bank provides a summary statement of its various assets and liabilities as on the last date of a particular period. It may refer to the end of a financial year or calendar year or a particular quarter in a year, such as 31 March 2022, 31 December 2022, and so on.

To understand the nature of activities of a bank in greater detail, we need to be familiar with the items which appear in the balance sheet of a bank.

Banks prepare their balance sheets and get them audited by statutory auditors (as per the BR Act, 1949, and the RBI Act, 1934). Banks in India are required to prepare their balance sheet and financial results in accordance with the statutory format or specification laid down as per the BR Act, 1949; the Companies Act, 1956; and guidelines issued by the RBI from time to time. These statements are submitted to the RBI and other regulatory agencies.

The annual balance sheet (*statement of assets and liabilities*) and financial results for banks operating in India are prepared for every financial year (ending on 31 March). For example, for the financial year 2021–22, the balance sheet is prepared as on 31 March 2022. Similar statements are also prepared for all the four quarters in the financial year. Summary information on audited key balance sheet items and financial results are placed on the official websites of the respective banks with detailed information published in their annual reports.

The statement of assets and liabilities (balance sheet) of SBI as on 31 March 2022 is presented in Table 1.2.

Table 1.2 A summary statement of assets and liabilities of SBI

(As on 31 March 2022)

Capital and liabilities	**(in INR crore)**	**Assets**	**(in INR crore)**
Capital	892	Cash and balances with RBI	2,57,859
Reserves and surplus	2,79,196	Balances with banks and money at call and short notice	1,63,393
Deposits	40,51,534	Investments	14,81,445
Borrowings	4,26,043	Advances	27,33,967
Other liabilities	2,29,932	Fixed assets	37,708
		Other assets	3,39,923
Total	**49,87,597**	**Total**	**49,87,597**

Source: SBI's audited financial results for the year ending 31 March 2022, obtained from its official website, https://sbi.co.in/documents/17826/17948/130522-SBI+RESULTS+MARCH+2022.pdf/cfd901ce-df71-47e7-8c9f-63cbd5b110ab?t=1652433396257 (accessed 27 January 2023).

1.3.1 Broad Items under the Liabilities Side

Various items under the 'liabilities' side of a bank's balance sheet or summary statement of assets and liabilities are given in the left-hand column of Table 1.2. These are ordered as per their duration of maturity as narrated in the sections that follow. Deposits constitute the most dominant item under the liabilities of a bank. As seen in Table 1.2, the share of 'deposits' in the 'total liabilities' of SBI was as high as 81.2 per cent in 2021–22, while that of 'borrowings' was only 8.5 per cent.

1.3.1.1 Capital

The first item—that is, 'capital'—is a long-term source of funds for banks. The amount of capital, particularly common equity, represents the stake of the owners and shareholders. The share of capital in the total assets and liabilities of SBI is quite minuscule. This signifies the extent of leveraging in the banking business. The amount of capital should work as a cushion for depositors in case of any bank failure, but the scope for that is very limited given its miniscule proportion. Under the present prudential banking regulatory norms, banks are mandated to maintain a certain minimum proportion of capital in relation to their risk-weighted assets.[8] For example, if the total risk-weighted assets of a bank are INR 1,00,000 and the minimum capital to risk-weighted assets ratio (CRAR), also known as capital adequacy ratio, is 9 per cent, then the bank is supposed to maintain a minimum of INR 9,000 as capital. In Chapter 7, we have provided details of the items included under the definition of 'capital', assignment of risk weights to various types of assets and technical aspects of CRAR calculations. Therein, we have also discussed other regulatory prescriptions related to capital such as *minimum leverage ratio*, *capital conservation buffer*, and so on.

Capital adequacy requirement is the principal regulatory tool for promoting financial stability in the banking system. As indicated in the preceding paragraph, the share of capital in the overall liabilities of a bank is very small and the owners or managers of banks leverage the overall banking business with public deposits. Banking involves various types of risks such as

[8] Weighted average of assets using presumed riskiness of each asset used as weights. The RBI has provided necessary guidelines to banks for assignment of such weights. Details of the same are discussed in Part III of this book.

credit risk, liquidity risk, interest-rate risk, market risk, operational risk, and so on. Credit risk arises due to the default of the borrower to repay the loan amount or make interest payments as per the repayment schedule. Liquidity risk arises when a bank fails to meet its liability obligations like deposit withdrawal or take advantage of a fresh loan or investment opportunity due to scarcity of liquid fund availability. Interest-rate risk for a bank arises due to adverse impact of interest-rate movements on its income and profitability. Market risk is caused due to any adverse movement in the price of banking assets such as bonds, equity or gold deposits, reducing their value in the bank's balance sheet. Operational risk arises due to deficiencies in the systems or procedures, omissions and commissions by the bank staff or natural calamities which cause losses to the bank. Details of such banking risks are provided in Chapter 6.

Taking into account the quantum of risks embodied in lending, banks charge higher rates of interest on riskier loans. There is a direct link between the risk and the return on a loan or investment. The stake of bank owners in the overall risk is limited to the amount of capital. If their stake in the banking business is not at a reasonable minimum, the owners of the bank will be tempted to undertake excessive risks in search of high returns and lend to or invest in risky projects. Ultimately, the depositors will suffer the adverse consequences of such excessive risk taking. To guard the interest of depositors and promote the safety and soundness of the banking system, banking regulators prescribe minimum capital adequacy requirements for banks. Under this requirement, banks need to maintain a minimum amount of capital linked to the quantum of risks embodied in their asset portfolio. Thus, the minimum capital requirement plays a critical role in banking regulation across countries. Chapter 7 provides further details on this aspect.

1.3.1.2 Reserves and Surplus

'Reserves and surplus' includes various types of items such as capital reserves, statutory reserves, share premiums payable to shareholders, revenue and other reserves, as well as the balance in the 'profit and loss account'. These items are treated as long-term liabilities. The amount of profit can be used flexibly as per the requirement of the bank, while other items can be used only for specific purposes. Therefore, the bulk of the amount under this head cannot be deployed as advances or investments by banks. A part of the 'reserves and surplus' is also included under 'capital' for minimum capital adequacy requirements as per the Basel prudential norms.[9]

1.3.1.3 Deposits

'Deposits' accounted for over four-fifths of the total liabilities in Table 1.2. Deposits are a form of financial savings kept with banks for safe keeping and facilitating payment and settlement as explained earlier. They are mainly of three types as follows:

- *Current account deposits*: Such deposits are payable on demand, with no interest usually paid on them. Generally, businesses and institutions hold current account deposits to facilitate their payments and settlements.
- *Term deposits*: Such deposits have fixed terms such as one year, five years, and so on, and are payable on maturity. They are popularly referred to as *fixed deposits*. Depositors earn interest on such deposits, and generally deposits with longer maturity terms pay higher interest rates though this is not always the case. For example, during 2021–22, the interest rate offered on one-year fixed deposits was the highest across banks in India as against those on three-year or other longer-term fixed deposits. Depending on the liquidity conditions of banks and expectation of future demand for loans, banks offer different rates of interest on such deposits.
- *Savings account deposits*: The general public in India is quite familiar with this variety. It is a hybrid type as such deposits are payable on demand similar to current account deposits but also earn interest like fixed deposits. Interest paid on these deposits is much lower compared to that on fixed deposits. For example, the interest rate on savings account deposits offered by SBI as on 29 August 2022 was around 2.70 per cent while that offered on fixed deposits of one-year and above was in the range of 5.45–5.65 per cent.

Bank regulators and the top management of banks regularly monitor the share of current account and savings account (CASA) deposits in the total

[9] The Basel prudential norms prescribe capital adequacy requirements for banks. The details of these norms are discussed in Chapter 7.

deposits for assessing the liquidity risk as also the cost of deposits. It may be noted that a lower share of CASA deposits involves lower liquidity risk for a bank as they signify the proportion of bank deposits subject to withdrawal on demand. On the other hand, a lower share of CASA deposits also entails a higher cost of deposits for banks as the interest paid on fixed deposits is generally higher than on CASA deposits.

The share of CASA in the total deposits of a bank varies from year to year depending on overall economic and financial conditions. For example, for Allahabad Bank,[10] the share of CASA deposits increased to 49.5 per cent in 2018–19 from 45.8 per cent in 2016–17. The share of CASA deposits also varies across banks at a particular point of time depending on, inter alia, their respective business model and depositor base. For example, the share of CASA deposits across commercial banks in India varied from 29 per cent to 51 per cent in 2018–19 (RBI, n.d.1).

In recent years, with increasing competition amongst banks to attract more customers, several innovative products have been introduced to suit individual requirements. One such innovation is flexible deposit accounts. Under this feature, any amount beyond a certain threshold limit in a savings deposit account is automatically placed as a fixed deposit. Such amount under fixed deposit can be flexibly withdrawn just like any savings account. Based on the period for which the amount is held under fixed deposit, the customer earns higher interest income as applicable for the relevant maturity period.

1.3.1.4 Borrowings

Banks in India borrow money from the RBI, other banks and financial institutions. Recourse to such 'borrowings' depends on the demand for bank loans and opportunities for investment on the one hand and funds generated through deposits on the other. Typically, these borrowings are short-term in nature and subject to higher interest rates. The shortest term of borrowing can be overnight. A bank's overnight borrowing from the RBI under the liquidity adjustment facility (LAF) involves a 'repo' transaction. Under this arrangement, a particular bank can place government securities with the RBI as collateral and borrow funds at the fixed repo rate. Banks also borrow from the RBI at variable repo rates for longer durations.

[10] Allahabad Bank was an erstwhile PSB which was merged with Indian Bank in 2020.

Another popular market for banks for overnight borrowing is the *call money market*. It is an inter-bank market where a bank in need of funds can borrow from another bank at a mutually negotiated interest rate. No security collateral is required for such borrowing. The weighted average of interest rates charged by different banks for lending in the call money market is known as the *call money rate*. Banks also borrow from the inter-bank notice money market, where the duration of borrowing can be up to 15 days.

Banks further borrow from other financial institutions such as mutual funds and insurance companies in collateralised money market segments such as market repo and collateralised borrowing and lending obligations (CBLOs). Details of such borrowings by banks are provided in Chapter 10.

1.3.1.5 Other Liabilities

'Other liabilities' in a bank's balance sheet include a variety of items. However, none of them is of much significance from the perspective of the overall banking business. Such items include bills payable, inter-office adjustments, interest accrued, provision for income tax, tax deducted at source (TDS), interest tax and related provisions. Bills payable may include various liabilities such as drafts, cheques, transfers, payslips, and so on, which are payable by the bank on behalf of its customers. All other items are self-explanatory.

1.3.2 Broad Items under the Assets Side

The various assets in a bank's balance sheet appear in the right-hand column of Table 1.2. Such items are arranged as per their maturity profile but in reverse order as compared to the arrangement of items under the liabilities side. Let us briefly discuss the different types of bank assets in the following sections.

1.3.2.1 Cash and Balances with the RBI

The first item is 'cash and balances with the RBI'. This is the most liquid form of assets for a bank. Cash in hand includes the total amount of domestic currency notes and coins and foreign currency notes at the bank's disposal along with cash balances available in its foreign branches. Balances with the RBI are as good as cash. Cash balances with the bank and balances with the RBI are maintained to meet the statutory CRR requirements as also for facilitating inter-bank settlements. As such balances do not earn interest, banks prefer to maintain minimum amounts under this item just sufficient to meet the statutory requirements and demand for deposit withdrawals. This is reflected in the lower share of 'cash and balances with the RBI' at around 5.2 per cent of the total assets in Table 1.2.

1.3.2.2 Balances with Banks and Money at Call and Short Notice

Assets under 'balances with banks and money at call and short notice' are also very liquid. A bank generally maintains deposits in other banks in both current and fixed deposit accounts. A bank also lends to other banks in the 'call and notice money market'. Lending in the 'call money market' is generally on overnight basis, while that in the 'notice money market' can be for periods up to 15 days. Lending in these markets is largely safe as lending decisions can incorporate the current financial conditions of the borrowing bank, and such conditions do not often change very drastically overnight or within a fortnight.

1.3.2.3 Loans and Advances

Bank loans and advances have an overwhelming share in the total assets of a bank. Bank loans (appearing as 'advances') accounted for nearly 54.8 per cent of the total assets in Table 1.2. The share of loans and advances is partly driven by prevailing economic conditions. It was relatively subdued during the late 2010s due to the economic slowdown in India, high non-performing asset (NPA) overhang and low credit demand. Under good economic conditions, the share of bank loans is generally observed to be higher. For example, the share of bank loans in the total assets of the same bank—that is, SBI—was 59.4 per cent in 2006–07.

Within different categories of bank assets, loans and advances are the most attractive for a bank due to their higher interest earning. These are of several sub-categories as detailed in the following paragraphs.

The first variety is *cash credits, overdrafts and loans repayable on demand.* Notwithstanding the specific maturity duration of such assets, they are repayable on demand. Cash credit is generally provided for the working capital requirements of firms and businesses. Overdraft facilities are usually extended to firms or corporates against securities like fixed deposits or the fixed physical assets of the borrower. The maximum maturity period of such loans is one year. For SBI, the sum of 'cash credits, overdrafts and loans repayable on demand' constituted close to 26.1 per cent of the total advances during 2021–22.

Term loans, the second variety, are the most popular form of bank loans availed by households. Term loans such as typical home loans or automobile loans usually entail a schedule of repayment under the contract in the form of regular monthly instalments. Term loans to corporates for setting up a new project, buying equipment, and so on, have a flexible repayment schedule. In many cases, this involves the ballooning approach or a negotiated loan repayment schedule. Usually term loans are not payable on demand before the maturity date or due date. Related details are provided in Chapter 9. Term loans generally have a longer maturity period as indicated earlier. The share of 'term loans' in the total 'advances' of SBI was 67.8 per cent during 2021–22.

Bill discounting is a major function of commercial banks. Bills discounted or purchased by banks are the third variety of bank loans. These involve tripartite agreements. For example, let us assume a manufacturer M in Delhi supplies goods to a dealer D in Chennai. After shipping the goods, M has to wait for payment until the delivery of the goods to D. This may take a long time. The manufacturer suffers due to the opportunity cost of delay in payment until delivery. To avoid this, the M can approach Bank A in Delhi to discount the bills pending receipt from the D under a tripartite agreement. Under this agreement, Bank A will pay the bill amount to M which is basically a loan to D. Finally, D repays the amount of the bill plus interest as applicable to Bank A as per the agreement. This is explained in Figure 1.2. Bills purchased and discounted are generally of shorter-term maturity and constitute a small fraction of the total bank loans. For SBI, this share was 6.1 per cent during 2021–22.

Further details of different types of bank loans and related management strategies for such loans are provided in Chapter 9.

1.3.2.4 Investments

The portfolio of *investments* is the second largest component of banking assets. Its share in the total assets of SBI was 29.7 per cent during 2021–22 (Table 1.2). It includes securities such as government bonds and treasury bills, other approved securities (such as state development loans), shares, debentures, and so on. In contrast to banks loans, most assets in the

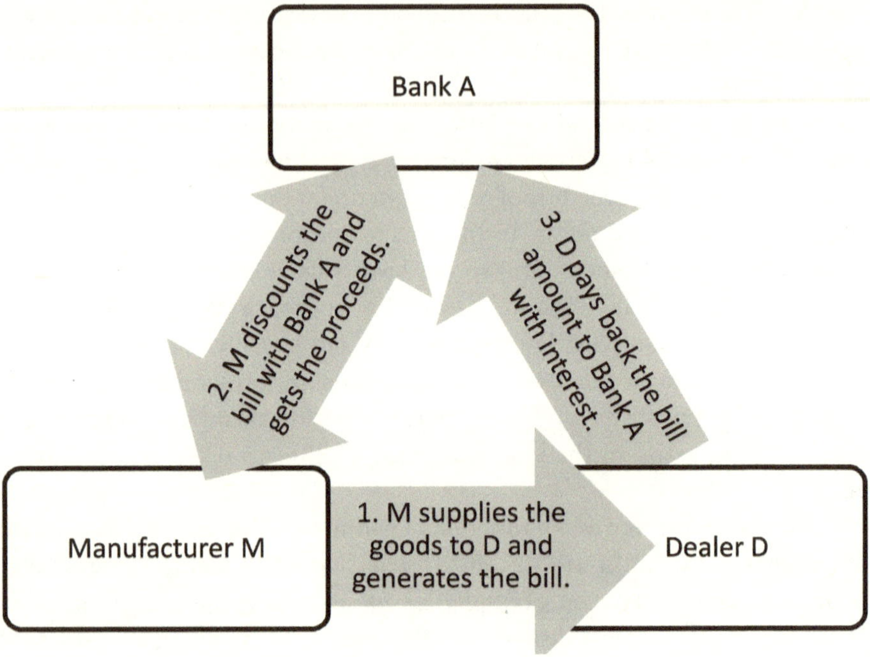

Figure 1.2 Bill discounting

Source: Prepared by the author.

investment portfolio of a bank are traded actively in the secondary market.[11] Thus, they are reasonably liquid.

Government securities constitute the bulk of the investment portfolio of commercial banks in India. During 2021–22, this share was as high as 78.4 per cent for SBI. As government securities are free of default risk, a higher proportion of such securities augments the safety and soundness of a bank. It also enhances the liquidity of the bank's asset portfolio as the secondary market in government securities is very vibrant. Guided by this, the RBI stipulates maintenance of a certain minimum proportion of a bank's NDTL in the form of liquid assets[12] including government securities and other

[11] A secondary market is a market in which investors (banks) buy or sell securities from or to other investors (banks).

[12] Cash balances of a bank over and above the CRR obligation are also included under the SLR.

approved securities under the statutory liquidity ratio (SLR) requirement. As of 31 August 2024, the SLR is stipulated to be 18 per cent by the RBI.

1.3.2.5 Fixed Assets and Other Assets

Fixed assets in a bank's balance sheet include immovable assets such as the buildings and premises, fixtures and furniture, automobiles, ATMs, and so on, owned by the bank. These are basically used for the very functioning of the bank and not directly for any commercial purpose. So fixed assets are non-banking assets. In fact, under section 9 of the BR Act, 1949, banks in India are prohibited from holding immovable property for more than seven years other than for their own use. Similarly, under section 8 of the BR Act, 1949, banks in India are debarred from the buying, selling or bartering of goods other than for the realisation of security interest. Goods include various types of moveable assets, bullion, stocks, shares, and so on.

Finally, under *other assets* in Table 1.2, items such as stationery and stamps, debit balances in inter-office accounts, interest accrued, tax paid in advance, non-banking assets acquired in satisfaction of claims, and so on, are included. Both these forms of assets are of negligible importance in the overall banking business.

* * *

To summarise, the balance sheet of a bank provides a broad understanding of its main activities. The balance sheet of SBI (the biggest bank in India) as presented in Table 1.2 revealed that bank deposits are the dominant source for funding various banking assets. Bank loans and investments overwhelmingly dominate a bank's asset portfolio. Thus, the banking business fundamentally entails the mobilisation of deposits and deployment of such deposits in the form of interest-earning assets such as loans and investments. Keeping in mind that the assets and liabilities of a bank embody various types of risks, successful banking demands judicious lending and designing of a portfolio of deposits so that the composite objectives of profitability, solvency and liquidity can be optimally pursued.

Profit maximisation is the primary objective of banking business as banks are basically commercial entities. In the following section, we will present the 'income and expenditure statement' of a bank to understand how we can obtain its profitability indicators.

Solvency of a bank requires continuously maintaining a positive 'net worth', which is defined as the surplus position of assets over the liabilities of a bank. Given that banking involves various types of risks, the assets of a bank may suddenly shrink if some of the bank's loans become delinquent or if any adverse movements in market prices depreciate the market value of the bank's assets. Similarly, provisioning requirements for bad loans and investments may raise the liabilities of a bank. In view of such circumstances, conducting the banking business strategically calls for continuous monitoring and management of various assets and liabilities so as to keep the bank solvent. This is a necessary prerequisite for nourishing continuous public faith in the bank. More importantly, the emergence of any adverse development affecting a bank's solvency needs to be handled with prompt and swift corrective action.

It may be noted that solvency is more of a long-term requirement. Despite sound solvency conditions, the banking business may be vulnerable to serious disruptions if a bank suffers from adverse liquidity conditions in the short run. The liquidity problem arises when liquid assets fall short of liquid liabilities. A deficient liquidity position may constrain a bank from meeting its deposit withdrawal demands or from taking advantage of an attractive loan proposal. If the liquidity problem is severe, it may lead to a *bank run* risking the collapse of the bank. Therefore, every bank is required to maintain a comfortable liquidity position in the short run in addition to its long-term solvency.

Thus, general bank management entails judicious selection of assets and liabilities so as to pursue the combined objectives of profitability, solvency and liquidity in a balanced and synchronised manner. Practical aspects of bank management, including product design, fixing the interest rates to be charged on loans and deposits, undertaking asset–liability management (ALM), and so on, are discussed in detail in Chapters 9 and 10.

1.4 Income and Expenditure Statement of a Bank and Key Banking Indicators

The balance sheet of a bank, as discussed in the previous section, explains its financial position at a given point of time. However, this is not sufficient to get a comprehensive picture of the bank's business. To gain insight into the performance of a bank during a period of time (interval between two points of time), its *statement of income and expenditure* is very helpful. As a commercial entity, a bank's most important objective is profit maximisation. To gain deeper insight into various factors contributing to the profitability of a bank, we need to examine its statement of income and expenditure.

Summary items from the income and expenditure statement of SBI are provided in Table 1.3. This statement refers to the financial year 2021–22.

Let us now discuss the major items appearing in this statement.

1.4.1 Major Items under Income and Expenditure

The items comprising the *income* of a bank are broadly divided into two categories: (*a*) interest income and (*b*) other income. The former is the primary source contributing to 87.2 per cent of the total income in Table 1.3. Within this, (*a*) interest on advances and discount of bills and (*b*) income on investment are the main items. In this case, they constitute 54.4 and 26.9 per cent of the total income, respectively. Interest income on various types of advances and discount of bills, as discussed in section 1.3, is self-explanatory. Income on investment includes interest income on various fixed income securities like bonds and treasury bills and the dividend

Table 1.3 Summary income and expenditure statement of SBI

(For the financial year ending on 31 March 2022)

Income	**(INR crores)**	**Expenditure**	**(INR crores)**
Interest earned (a)+(b)+(c)+(d)	2,75,457	Interest expended	1,54,754
(a) Interest/discount on advances/bills	1,71,824	Operating expenses (e)+(f)	85,979
		(e) Employees cost	50,144
(b) Income on investment	84,877	(f) Other operating expenses	35,836
(c) Interest on balances with RBI and other inter-bank funds	4,378		
(d) Others	14,378		
Other Income	40,564		
Total	**3,16,021**	**Total** (excluding provisions and contingencies)	**2,40,729**

Source: SBI's audited financial results for the year ending 31 March 2022, obtained from its official website, https://sbi.co.in/documents/17826/17948/130522-SBI+RESULTS+MARCH+2022.pdf (accessed 27 January 2023).

earned on shares and stocks. Profit from the sale of securities held under the investment portfolio is not included here. The amount of interest income under 'others' is very small.

Other income in Table 1.3 consists of several sub-categories. First, banks earn income from commissions or fees pertaining to government agency services, issue of letters of credit and guarantees, charges for remittances and transfers, brokerage on securities, rent on lockers, and so on. Second, from the sale of both financial and physical assets, a bank earns a sizeable income. This includes the sale of bonds and shares held under its investment portfolio. Third, other items include profit from the sale of forex, dividends received from subsidiaries and joint ventures and miscellaneous items.

On the expenditure side, the largest item is 'interest expended' which constituted 64.3 per cent of the total expenditure in Table 1.3. The second largest item, *employees cost* (within *operating expenses*), formed 20.8 per cent of the total expenses.

1.4.2 Key Banking Indicators

To get a comprehensive picture of the financial condition of a bank, regulators, the bank's management and other stakeholders continuously monitor a set of key banking indicators. We can derive information about the various financial indicators of a bank from its balance sheet and statement of income and expenditure. Such indicators help in assessing the financial health of a bank and its business. In Chapter 11, we provide the conceptual details of such indicators and use the same to assess the performance of banks in India. In the sections that follow, we present a brief discussion on a few such indicators for SBI as provided in Table 1.4.

1.4.2.1 Profitability and Efficiency Indicators

In Table 1.4, we have three types of profitability indicators. *Operating profit*, the first one, is calculated as the total income *minus* interest cost and operating expenditure. It is estimated to be INR 75,292 crore for SBI for the year 2021–22 based on the information provided in Table 1.3. Operating profits formed 31.3 per cent of the total expenditure and 87.6 per cent of the operating expenses of SBI in 2021–22.

As discussed earlier, banking involves various types of risks and not all loans are repaid as per schedule. Due to various reasons including changing

Table 1.4 Key financial indicators: SBI

(For the financial year ending 31 March 2022)

Indicators		INR crores
1. Operating profit (before provisions and contingencies)		75,292
2. Provisions (other than taxes) and contingencies		24,452
of which provisions for NPAs		*14,087*
3. Profit before tax (PBT)	[1–2]*	43,422
4. Tax expense (credit)		11,746
5. Net profit (after tax)	[3–4]	31,676
Select Analytical Ratios		(in per cent)
(i) Capital Adequacy Ratio (Basel III)		13.83
(ii) Common Equity Tier 1 Ratio (CET 1)		9.94
(iii) Earnings per Share		35.49
(iv) Percentage of Gross NPAs		3,97
(v) Percentage of Net NPAs		1.02
(vi) Return on Assets (ROA)		0.67

Source: SBI's audited financial results for the year ending 31 March 2022, obtained from its official website, https://sbi.co.in/documents/17826/17948/130522-SBI+RESULTS+MARCH+2022.pdf/cfd901ce-df71-47e7-8c9f-63cbd5b110ab?t=1652433396257 (accessed 27 January 2023).

Note: *After adjustment of the exceptional item of INR 7,418 crores.

business conditions, change in policy and sometimes intentional default, some loans or assets become delinquent or NPAs. There are regulatory prescriptions to provide for such NPAs. By deducting such provisions and contingencies from the operating profit, we can obtain the second measure of banking profitability, popularly referred to as *profit before tax* (PBT). This is a more realistic measure of a bank's profit. Further, excluding the taxes applicable, we get the *net profit after tax* (NPAT) which is available for the shareholders of the bank for appropriation.

In addition to these profitability indicators, regulators, the bank's management and analysts also look at the various analytical ratios listed in Table 1.4 to deduce the financial health of a bank in terms of safety and soundness, efficiency and productivity.

- *Earnings per share (EPS)*: This measure is popularly used to assess the profitability of a company. For a bank, the EPS is obtained by dividing its NPAT by the outstanding shares. In Table 1.4, the EPS at 35.49 per cent for SBI reflects the rate of return to its shareholders.

- *Return on assets (ROA)*: This is the ratio of the NPAT of a bank to its average total assets. For example, in Table 1.4, the ROA for SBI was 0.67 for 2021–22. It is the ratio of its NPAT during 2021–22 to the average of assets held as on 31 March 2021 and 31 March 2022. It reflects how efficiently the bank has constructed its loan and investment portfolio.

1.4.2.2 Capital Adequacy and Asset Quality

The CRAR measures the proportion of capital of a bank as a percentage of its risk-weighted assets. The amount of capital in a bank reflects the real stake of the bank owners or shareholders in the banking business. In a way, the amount of capital in a bank measures the maximum amount of loss that the bank owners can absorb if some assets become delinquent. The same implies the degree of protection that the depositors and lenders of the bank enjoy.

Let us understand this by a simple example without consideration of risk weights. Assume that a bank has extended a loan from which the dues along with interest charges are INR 100 crore. Say, the bank holds equity capital of INR 10 crore. Let us assume that the borrower defaults on the loan after repaying INR 92 crore and the bank is unable to recover the remaining INR 8 crore. In this case, the depositors of the bank will not suffer much as the loss of INR 8 crore can be absorbed by the bank out of its capital of INR 10 crore. However, had the amount of capital been INR 5 crore, then the bank could have absorbed a maximum of INR 5 crore out of the loss of INR 8 crore. The remaining loss of INR 3 crore would have fallen on the depositors. Thus, higher capital of a bank implies a higher loss absorbing power.

In reality a bank's asset portfolio includes a variety of loans and investments. The risk embodied in each asset item varies. To calculate the actual risk exposure in the asset portfolio of a bank, one needs to calculate the risk-weighted assets of the bank. Following similar logic to that in the preceding paragraph, we can infer that a higher level of capital in proportion to the total risk-weighted assets of a bank will reflect a better risk absorption capacity. Thus, a higher CRAR of a bank implies greater safety and soundness of the deposits in the bank.

Technical details on the definition of capital, assignment of risk weights for various categories of assets and calculation of CRAR are provided in Chapter 7.

As of March 2024, the RBI has stipulated the minimum capital adequacy ratio under Basel III for banks operating in India to be 11.5 per cent. This is the sum of a minimum CRAR of 9 per cent and capital conservation buffer of 2.5 per cent. For a systemically important bank like SBI, the minimum capital adequacy ratio is stipulated to be 12.1 per cent. As shown in Table 1.4, the capital adequacy ratio for SBI at 13.83 per cent as on 31 March 2022 is higher than the minimum requirement. Within the overall capital, common equity tier 1 is more durable and its higher proportion reflects better quality of the capital.

The percentage of gross or net NPAs of a bank reflects the proportion of loans or assets which have become delinquent. This indicates the degree of default risk for a bank. Higher NPA ratios are signs of weakness and vulnerability. For SBI, the net NPA ratio at 1.02 per cent during 2021–22 was relatively comfortable.

* * *

To sum up, it is observed that interest income and interest expenditure mainly explain the movement in the operating profit of a bank. Adjusting for the provisioning on problem loans and tax liabilities, the amount of *net profit* of a bank is determined. Strategic business decisions in banking involve pricing of deposits and lending and choosing a judicious mix of deposits and loans and are critical for promoting a bank's profitability. Key indicators as listed in Table 1.4 act as a checklist to assess whether the business activities undertaken by a bank are on prudential lines and to what extent the banking business is profitable, safe and sound.

1.5 Other Functions of a Bank

In the previous sections, we have identified the primary functions of a bank in terms of mobilisation of deposits, deploying such deposits in the form of loans and investments and facilitating transfers of funds. In addition to these, banks also undertake several ancillary or secondary functions which are briefly discussed in the sections that follow. Some of these are linked to the primary functions of deposit mobilisation and lending.

1.5.1 Issuing Guarantees

Usually, participation in the tendering process for the construction of a building or the outsourcing of services by many public and private institutions requires the submission of a bank guarantee. For example, a university hiring an agency to construct academic buildings may insist that all the parties bidding in the tendering process deposit a bank guarantee for a certain amount. This *tender guarantee* ensures the financial commitment and performance obligation of the contracting agency to the university if it wins the contract. Banks issue tender guarantees on behalf of such agencies.

Similarly, there are *guarantees of payment* issued by banks on behalf of buyers to sellers of goods. There are also *contract execution guarantees* which serve as security for providing a service or delivering goods as per the contract. Another variety known as *performance guarantees* are issued on behalf of, say, a construction company to complete the construction of a building. By issuing such guarantees on behalf of their customers, banks facilitate the smooth conduct of business by the concerned parties.

It may be noted that bank guarantees are non-fund-based facilities. The concerned bank need not make any payment against guarantees issued unless a guarantee is invoked. Hence, bank guarantees are considered contingent liabilities or *off-balance sheet* (OBS) items. Banks charge fees for issuing bank guarantees. Details about the technicalities of issuing bank guarantees are provided in Chapter 10.

1.5.2 Opening Letters of Credit

Banks open letters of credit (LCs) which are essential instruments for the conduct of foreign trade. Assume a buyer (importer) in India places an order for 100 computers from a seller (exporter) in the United States (US). The parties may enter into an agreement on the specifications of the computers and prepare the bills incorporating applicable insurance, customs duties, and so on. However, the US exporter may have concerns on the realisation of the payment if it is not assured about the financial credentials and payment commitment of the Indian importer. The US exporter may have difficulties in enforcing the contract in India if the Indian importer defaults on the payment. Therefore, the US exporter may insist that the Indian importer open an LC with a bank, which works like a bank guarantee. The LC declares the commitment of the issuing bank to pay the exporter on behalf of the importer subject to certain terms and conditions. It works as follows:

1. Say, the Indian importer requests its bank, SBI, to open an LC in the prescribed format. This includes the quantity and quality specifications of the goods to be imported along with other information.
2. The LC is sent to the US exporter's bank, Bank of America, which is known as the *advising bank*. The advising bank informs the US exporter about the receipt of the LC.
3. If the US exporter accepts the LC, it ships the goods to the Indian importer and sends the *bill of lading* to the LC opening bank (SBI in this case) for payment.
4. SBI makes the payment to the US exporter through the confirming bank (which can be the same as the advising bank, that is, Bank of America) and recovers the amount from the Indian importer.

This example explains a simple commercial LC. It is illustrated through a chart in Figure 1.3.

Thus, an LC promotes foreign trade by assuring payment on behalf of the importer. Like bank guarantees, an LC is an OBS item or contingent

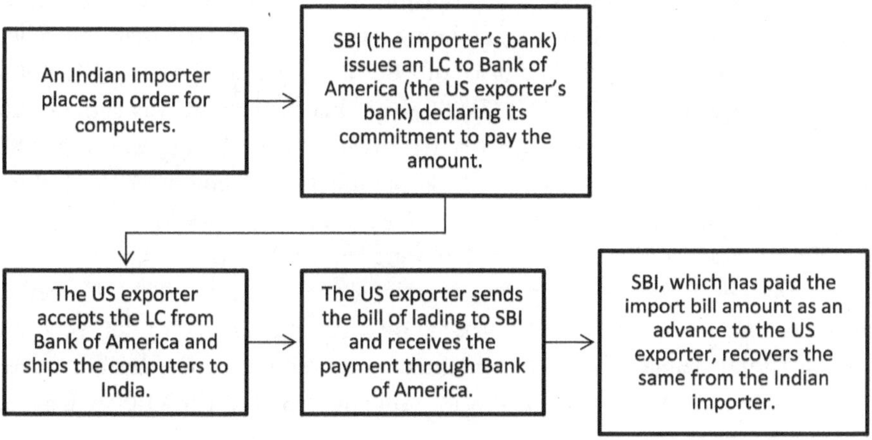

Figure 1.3 Letter of credit facilitating foreign trade

Source: Prepared by the author.

liability. The issuing bank, like SBI in this case, charges a fee from the Indian importer to issue the LC. It may also insist on some security collateral against the facility.

1.5.3 Dealing in Forex: Spot and Forward Transactions

Banks through their specialised branches undertake the purchase and sale of leading foreign currencies like the US dollar (USD), pound sterling, euro, yen, and so on. Banks are key players in both the spot and forward markets trading in foreign currencies.

In the spot market, foreign currencies are purchased or sold instantly like any other commodities such as pens or readymade garments. For buying foreign goods, Indian importers require foreign currencies like USD, euro, pounds sterling, and so on, which are accepted by foreign exporters. Banks supply such foreign currencies to Indian importers. Indian exporters similarly earn foreign currency by selling their goods and services abroad and deposit the proceeds in their respective banks. Many such exporters maintain foreign currency denominated deposit accounts. Thus, by buying and selling foreign currencies, banks play an important role in supporting importers and exporters. These are known as *spot transactions* in foreign currencies.

It may be noted that generally there are time lags involved between entering an agreement to buy goods from a foreigner and making the payment. Between these two points of time, forex rates often fluctuate. Let us assume that an Indian buyer signed an agreement with an American seller to buy 100 IBM computers at a price of USD 1,000 per computer. So the total payment requirement is USD 1,00,000. Say, this agreement was signed and the purchase order placed on 1 February 2023. If the exchange rate is INR 82 per USD on 1 February 2023, the total payment requirement of the Indian buyer is INR 82,00,000.

Let us assume that the computers were received by the Indian importer on 31 March 2023, with the payment to be made on 1 April 2023. However, if the exchange rate is INR 84 per USD on 1 April 2023 due to depreciation of the Indian rupee, the actual payment requirement of the Indian buyer becomes INR 84,00,000. This is the amount equivalent to USD 1,00,000 as on 1 April 2023.

Thus, the Indian buyer suffers a loss of INR 2,00,000 due to exchange rate fluctuation between 1 February and 1 April 2023. To guard against such loss, the Indian buyer can enter into a forward contract with a bank for delivery of USDs at the exchange rate of INR 82 per USD on 1 April 2023 by paying the applicable fees. Similarly, an Indian exporter can buy a forward contract for selling USDs to a bank at a specified rate in future to save it from any adverse consequences due to exchange rate fluctuations. Banks are leading players in the forward market for foreign exchange. Thus, by buying and selling foreign currency at forward rates, banks help customers to avoid losses from fluctuation of exchange rates.

Other than foreign trade, Indians travelling abroad for business or on a pleasure trip as tourists require foreign currencies to pay for various transactions undertaken in the country concerned. Banks sell foreign currencies to such customers and facilitate smooth cross-border movement of people. Banks also sell traveller's cheques, which are like a demand draft on a foreign bank and can be used conveniently to obtain foreign currency when travelling abroad. Use of travellers' cheques protects the traveller from theft of foreign currency. Nowadays, with the growing popularity of international credit or debit cards, the use of traveller's cheques is diminishing.

1.5.4 Merchant or Investment Banking

Merchant banking is concerned with some specialised financial services provided to large corporates and high-net-worth individuals. These services generally pertain to underwriting, loan servicing, managing initial public offering (IPO) and fundraising for corporates or advisory or specialised services for mergers and acquisitions, trading with other companies, and so on. These activities have come to be popularly referred to as *investment banking*. Some internationally reputed investment banks are JP Morgan, Goldman Sachs, Edelweiss, and so on. Major PSBs and IPBs in India also undertake merchant or investment banking activities as part of their usual business.

1.5.5 Bancassurance

Bancassurance is an arrangement between a bank and an insurance company (partner) in which the bank sells the insurance products of its partner. Under this arrangement, bank branches actively market and sell insurance products to their customers. Sometimes, banks attach the sale of insurance products to their own loan products. For example, banks persuade customers to buy insurance for their home when taking home loans. The partner insurance company benefits due to access to a wide market of bank customers. The bank earns commission from selling insurance products without any risk exposure or disposition of funds. During the post-reform period, bancassurance has been widely offered by leading Indian banks.

1.5.6 Other Functions

In addition to the functions discussed in the preceding sections, banks in India also undertake certain other ancillary or secondary functions, including:

- acting as trustees or executors;
- providing locker facilities for the safe keeping of valuables such as gold and jewellery, land and property documents, and so on;
- issuing demand drafts for the transfer of funds;
- periodic payment or collection of utility charges such as electricity bills, telephone bills, and so on; and
- discharging certain agency services on behalf of the government such as collection of taxes, opening and operating of provident fund (PF) accounts, provision of government-funded social welfare schemes and services, and so on.

1.6 Basic Operational Activities at Bank Branches

The preceding discussion about banks and banking has been carried out considering a bank as a single entity or company. However, banks in India, as mentioned, follow the *branch banking system*. In this system, banks operate through a large number of branches spread across the country. Leading banks in fact have branches numbering in the thousands. As on 31 March 2023, the number of bank branches of SBI, PNB and Canara Bank were 25,087, 11,270 and 10,131, respectively (RBI, n.d.1). Smaller PSBs had between 1,600 and 3,500 branches. Among IPBs, the bigger ones like Axis Bank, HDFC Bank and ICICI Bank had over 5,000 branches each, while small ones had a few hundreds.

In the branch banking system, broad policy decisions related to the overall banking business are taken at the head-office level. Such decisions pertain to, inter alia, overall targets for lending and deposit growth, including component-wise targets for lending and deposits, procedures and risk limits for lending, the treasury business, interest rates, ALM, maintenance of capital, reserves and provisioning, tax planning, profit sharing, human resource management, and so on. The bank's branches function as the operational units for the entire bank. The zonal or regional offices of PSBs directly control and monitor the activities of the branches under their jurisdiction within the broad guidelines and targets stipulated by the head office. Branches of IPBs and foreign banks are mostly controlled by their head office directly. Decisions and functions related to lending, mobilisation of deposits, issuance of guarantees, opening of LCs, transfers of funds, currency management, and so on, are actually undertaken at the branch level.

The zonal or regional offices of a bank assign targets on important banking operations to the branches in accordance with the policy guidelines and procedural details delineated by the head office. These targets are set for the entire financial year as also for each month in a year separately. An indicative list of items for which targets are assigned to bank branches in general is as follows:

1. Total deposits
   (*a*) Savings deposits
   (*b*) Current deposits
   (*c*) CASA deposits
   (*d*) Term deposits
2. Total advances
   (*a*) Agricultural loans
   (*b*) Micro, small and medium enterprise (MSME) loans
   (*c*) Retail loans
   (*d*) Priority sector loans
   (*e*) NPAs
   (*f*) NPA upgradation
   (*g*) Cash recovery
3. Aggregate income and expenditure
   (*a*) Interest income
   (*b*) Non-interest income
   (*c*) Interest expenditure
   (*d*) Non-interest expenditure
   (*e*) Operating profit

These items are self-explanatory and have been discussed in the preceding sections. Bank branches play a vital role in undertaking banking activities keeping in mind the targets assigned by the head office or zonal office on the aforementioned items. They execute the actual banking business of deposit taking, lending, OBS activities, and so on, in conformity with the overall policy and operational guidelines set by the top management.

In the following sections, the three main micro-level activities at a representative bank branch, all of them operational practices—namely (*a*) opening of deposit accounts, (*b*) disbursement of loans and (*c*) currency or cash management—are highlighted. This will supplement our previous discussion on the major functions of banks.

1.6.1 Opening Deposit Accounts

Bank branches function as the face of a bank for a variety of banking transactions. Such branches establish the physical and tangible interface between a bank and its customers. Customers approach a bank branch for opening deposit accounts, taking loans and obtaining other banking services.

Opening deposit accounts is a relatively simple job for branch managers. Relevant guidelines are issued by the RBI and the head office of the bank for opening different types of deposit accounts. These guidelines, inter alia, stipulate (*a*) KYC norms to guard against money laundering, terrorist financing and tax avoidance through fraudulent bank accounts; (*b*) agreements or norms on the mode of operation of the account; (*c*) nominee details; and (*d*) the interest payable.

As indicated earlier, KYC norms are used to establish the identity of the customer. Under these norms, banks are required to seek at least one of the prescribed documents like passport, driving licence, voter's identity card issued by the Election Commission of India, job card issued by the National Rural Employment Guarantee Authority (NREGA), Aadhaar card, PAN card issued by the Income Tax Department, and so on, along with the photograph(s) of the applicant(s). For certain types of special services, more than one document is required. For example, for opening fixed deposit accounts, having a PAN card is mandatory as per the extant guidelines prevailing in July 2023. Similarly, for availing direct benefit transfers (DBTs), banks insist on the submission of a copy of the Aadhaar card. For companies, institutions or proprietorship firms, relevant documents including their certificate of incorporation, memorandum of association, articles of association, registration certificate, sales or income tax returns, and so on, are required.

Prospective depositors fill the bank account opening form. After verification and confirmation of eligibility norms, relevant deposit accounts are opened and deposit amounts received from the customers. At the branch level, necessary efforts are made so as to meet the deposit growth targets set by the head or zonal office.

1.6.2 Extending Bank Loans

Unlike opening deposit accounts, extending loans and advances is a very tedious exercise. Bank branches play a critical role in the context of the lending business of a bank, summarised as follows:

- *Identifying prospective borrowers*: In a competitive banking system such as in India, the role of branch managers in identifying and drawing in new borrowers and continuing business with existing borrowers is of paramount importance. They need to continuously look for prospective clients, monitor the financial requirements of existing clients and generate business for the bank by using interpersonal skills. Proactive and dynamic branch managers are always found to be successful in mobilising more loans, irrespective of whether households are looking for retail loans or corporates project loans or working-capital loans. Borrowers would be inclined to continue business with a branch even if the bank charges a marginally higher interest on loans so long as banking services are provided seamlessly in a customer friendly manner.
- *Credit appraisal and risk management*: All forms of loans entail risk of loss due to non-repayment, and excessive loss on loans is a credible threat to the very survival of a bank. The bulk of loans are generated at the branch level. Therefore, due diligence of branch managers while sanctioning loans is absolutely critical for ensuring the safety and soundness of the entire bank. Bank branches must thus undertake meticulous and detailed credit appraisal combining both formal and informal information about loan seekers.
- *Monitoring and recoveries*: Post-sanction monitoring of the use of loans by borrowers is necessary to ensure productive deployment of the funds for the stated purpose. With close proximity to the

> borrowers, branch managers help to effectively monitor the end-use of the funds and related business activities of the borrowers. Branch managers also promptly initiate corrective action as per legal provisions if borrowers deviate from loan-contract stipulations. Bank branches are responsible for taking necessary measures for loan recovery or undertaking loan restructuring depending on the scope of revival of the account. The sincerity, professional competence and accurate judgement of branch-level officials are vital to this process.

In Chapter 9, we will provide detailed information about the management of loans and investments by banks. So we postpone further discussion on strategic management decisions on bank lending until then.

The composition of the loan portfolio of a bank branch depends on its geographical location (rural or urban) and client base. Rural branches have a higher proportion of retail loans, including agricultural loans, while urban branches serve a client base dominated by corporates and high-net-worth individuals and undertake non-fund-based business activities. Many banks have specialised branches to undertake specific businesses like corporate finance or home loan processing exclusively.

The processing of retail loans like home loans and automobile loans is relatively simple. The branch manager just needs to follow a formula-based approach as per the head office guidelines and there is little scope for discretion at the branch level. However, dealing with corporate loans is more complicated and involved. Bank branches enjoy more flexibility and discretion in processing and sanctioning project loans and working capital loans for corporate clients.

1.6.3 Managing Currency or Cash

Maintenance of an optimal amount of currency or cash balances at the branch level is of critical importance and must be undertaken considering the following two factors: on the one hand, the balances should be sufficient to meet the withdrawal demands of depositors; on the other, the same should not be more than a threshold[13] as excess idle balances do not earn interest

[13] Compliance with statutory requirements on minimum cash reserves is a head-office concern.

income. In this context, currency or cash management at the branch level is a major day-to-day activity in a bank.

In conventional practice among banks in India, the head or zonal office sets the branch-wise limits for maintenance of daily cash balances, popularly known as *retention capacity* or *maximum cash-holding limit*. It is believed that the average receipts and payments of a particular branch in the previous year are taken into account to fix its retention capacity. Each branch is required to not keep cash balances in excess of its assigned retention capacity. For example, if the retention capacity of a branch is set at INR 20 lakhs, it should not hold cash balances in excess of INR 20 lakhs.

It may be mentioned that prior to the use of electronic transfers, ATMs, debit cards, and so on, bank branches used to maintain higher levels of cash balances on salary days (the first week of any month). In recent years, with use of information technology (IT)-enabled banking services like electronic transfers and ATMs, no significant seasonal spike is observed as regards cash withdrawal demands at the branch level.

Generally, branches find it possible to comfortably meet deposit withdrawal demands within their assigned retention capacity. How do branches deal with demands for cash withdrawal in excess of the available balances on a particular day?

On such occasions, the bank branch generally approaches the *currency chest* to provide the required cash by transferring funds. *Currency chests* are maintained by the RBI and its designated banks in certain cities and towns. Bank branches generally have arrangements with them to supply the required cash when needed. Say, Branch 1001 of Bank A is facing deficit of cash on a particular day. Bank A may have an arrangement with Bank S which maintains a currency chest in the town in which the said branch is operating. In that case, Branch 1001 of Bank A can approach Bank S for extra cash by transferring the required amount of funds.

However, nowadays the concerned branch often approaches a nearby branch of another bank to get extra cash as needed. Computerisation and faster fund transfers through the electronic mode have facilitated easy access to cash from a nearby bank branch and hence reduced dependence on currency chests.

In the post-Covid-19 period, there has been widespread use of UPI-based digital payment platforms such as Paytm, Google Pay, Rupay, PhonePe and other mobile apps for small transactions. Even small retail shops, tea stalls and roadside vegetable and fruit vendors readily accept payments using UPI. Accordingly, there is less dependence on cash or currency for payments. This has reduced the pressure on bank branches as regards their currency management responsibilities. Towards the end of 2022, the RBI had introduced central bank digital currency (CBDC) on a pilot basis. If the public adopts CBDC widely for regular payments, the reliance on currency or cash for day-to-day transactions will further reduce. This will considerably relieve bank branches of the burden of currency management.

1.7 Tendency towards Greater Centralisation

It may be noted that for certain banking functions, decisions are taken at the head-office level and branch-level officials are not involved in the process. For example, a bank's investments in government securities, corporate bonds and equities, forex management, and so on, are undertaken at head-office level by the treasury department. Similarly, for advances beyond certain threshold limits, approval is accorded by authorities at a higher level like officers in the zonal or head office. With growing business activities on the above accounts in banks, there is greater tendency for centralisation.

Over time, reliance on IT for providing essential banking services has been growing. There is wider access to banking services, particularly deposit of money and withdrawal, through bank ATMs. Even printing of bank account details is possible at select ATMs. Through mobile and internet banking, transfer of money can be carried out from anywhere, including from the comfort of home. Use of credit cards, debit cards and digital payment aggregators for regular transactions is increasingly becoming popular all over India. All these have reduced work pressure on bank branches and reduced the need for customers to visit bank branches for ordinary banking business. Several leading banks in India have started processing and servicing home loans and corporate loans through mobile applications. The mobile banking apps provided by leading banks have facilitated the integration of several financial services on one platform. Beyond traditional banking services like money transfers, opening of fixed deposits and deposit withdrawals, these mobile apps also facilitate seamless transactions related to financial investments, purchase of insurance products, payment of user bills and online shopping solutions. Thus, the use of IT and IT-enabled services (ITES) has radically transformed the channels through which banking services are provided. For these reasons also, there is a move away from availing banking services through bank branches and a tendency towards greater centralisation.

1.8 Conclusion

This chapter provided an introduction to banks and banking business. Banks are conventionally financial intermediaries which mobilise deposits from savers and use such funds for lending and investment. Banks and banking activities have evolved over time with the introduction of several innovative products and services. A bank's balance sheet encapsulates various types of deposits, borrowings, loans and investments. One gains useful insights into banking business by observing the transformation of liabilities like bank deposits into assets like loans and investments. This transformation entails certain challenges as the characteristics of such assets and liabilities are dissimilar in terms of liquidity, size, term to maturity, and so on. Managing such challenges is at the core of banking strategies. Details of these issues are provided in Parts III and IV of this book.

The primary objective of the overall banking business is to maximise profitability. To understand the various factors that determine bank profitability, we used the brief income and expenditure statement of a bank. This was supplemented with key banking indicators to assess the overall performance of a bank. The chapter also highlighted key ancillary services provided by banks such as investment banking, issue of bank guarantees and LCs, forex operations, bancassurance, and so on, which have gained increasing importance in modern banking business.

Bank branches act as the key functional units for delivering banking services in a branch banking system. The chapter underlined their critical role in the overall banking business to gain useful insights into the functioning of banks.

Revision Questions and Problems

1. What are the major functions of a commercial bank under conventional banking?
2. Briefly explain the importance of deposits and loans in a bank's balance sheet to highlight its role as a financial intermediary.

3. Why do banks closely monitor the proportion of CASA deposits within their overall deposit portfolio?
4. Write a short note on 'bill discounting' under a tripartite arrangement.
5. Discuss how banks promote foreign trade by (*a*) issuing LCs and (*b*) undertaking forex transactions.
6. How do bank branches manage demands for deposit withdrawals in excess of cash balances available with them?
7. Is there growing centralisation in banking business within individual banks, relieving pressure on bank branches? Justify your answer with relevant facts.

2

The Indian Banking System

Learning Objectives

- To provide an outline of the Indian financial system and its key constituents
- To describe the role of different types of financial markets and financial institutions in the Indian financial system and highlight their relevance
- To highlight the comparative importance of the banking sector in the Indian financial system
- To trace the evolution of banking in India from a historical perspective
- To describe the banking sector reforms since the early 1990s which shaped various dimensions of the turnaround in the sector
- To outline the composition and relative strength of different banking groups comprising Indian commercial banks
- To summarise the progress of commercial banking in India

2.1 Introduction

The Indian financial system has evolved over time, keeping pace with the country's economic development and changing policy paradigms. Since independence, the overall policy paradigm assigned a critical role to the banking sector in financing the Indian development process. Initially, efforts involved bringing large commercial banks under government control, facilitating a massive expansion in banking since 1969. To supplement commercial banks, cooperative banks were activated and regional rural banks (RRBs) were established with the specific objective of promoting the financing of agriculture and rural economic activities. The post-reform period[1] witnessed the emergence of a broad-based financial sector in India with the development of different segments of the financial markets and other financial institutions.

It is important to note that notwithstanding the development of other constituents of the Indian financial system during the post-reform period, commercial banks continued to be the dominant segment. Chapter 1 provided an introduction to banking in general. In this chapter, we will discuss in some detail the banking system in India.

Section 2.2 provides an overview of the Indian financial system, particularly with the objective of gaining a comparative perspective on commercial banks. This section introduces the key constituents of the Indian financial market such as the equity market, government securities market, corporate bond market, money market and forex market. Information about different financial institutions in India such as cooperative banks, RRBs, non-banking financial companies (NBFCs) and development finance institutions (DFIs) is also provided. Next, section 2.3 traces the evolution of commercial banking from a historical perspective. Comprehensive reforms pertaining to banking introduced since the early 1990s have effected a significant turnaround in various dimensions of the banking sector in India. Salient features of these reform initiatives are highlighted in section 2.4. This is followed by a discussion on the structure of commercial banking in section 2.5. A brief overview of the progress in commercial banking in India is presented in section 2.6. The broad conclusions of the chapter are provided in section 2.7.

2.2 Indian Financial System

The financial system in India consists of various types of entities. These provide financial services to different sets of savers and borrowers in line with their specific requirements. For example, the capital market caters to the

[1] India introduced comprehensive reforms since the early 1990s in various segments of the economy covering the industrial sector, external sector, financial sector and government finances in response to the economic crisis of 1991. This period witnessed gradual market orientation and relaxation of government control over various economic activities. The period since the financial year 1992–93 is popularly referred to as the post-reform period in India.

funding requirements of large industry and business, while cooperative banks and RRBs meet those of small borrowers in rural areas. The structure of the Indian financial system is schematically depicted in Figure 2.1. The overall financial system can be divided into two broad components: (*a*) financial markets and (*b*) financial institutions.

2.2.1 Indian Financial Markets

The major components of the Indian financial market are the equity market, government securities market, corporate bond market, money market and forex market. These markets provide the required platforms for direct transactions between savers and borrowers. Each of the markets serves the requirements of specific types of borrowers and savers as explained in the following sections.

2.2.1.1 Equity Market

The equity market or stock market plays a critical role in serving the long-term funding requirements of big corporate borrowers. A popular way for big businesses to fund long-term projects is to sell a portion of their ownership, known as equity shares, in the stock market. Assume that a manufacturing firm such as Tata Motors or Reliance Industries plans to set up a new factory. The concerned firm can meet only a part of the financing requirements for this project out of its own profits or retained earnings. Given the huge amount of costs involved in setting up a factory, it requires external finance or borrowing to meet the remaining part of the funding requirement.

One popular option for the firm, as mentioned, is to sell a portion of its equity shares and generate the necessary funds. For that the firm needs to register itself in a stock market. In India, the Bombay Stock Exchange (BSE) and the National Stock Exchange (NSE) are popular stock markets. After getting registered in the stock market and obtaining a credit rating from a recognised rating agency,[2] the firm can issue IPOs. In this regard, necessary requirements as stipulated by the equity market regulator, the Securities and

---

[2] In India, ICRA Limited and CRISIL Limited are two major domestic credit rating agencies. At the global level, Standard and Poor's (S&P) Global Ratings, Moody's Ratings (earlier Moody's Investors Service) and Fitch Ratings are popular credit rating companies.

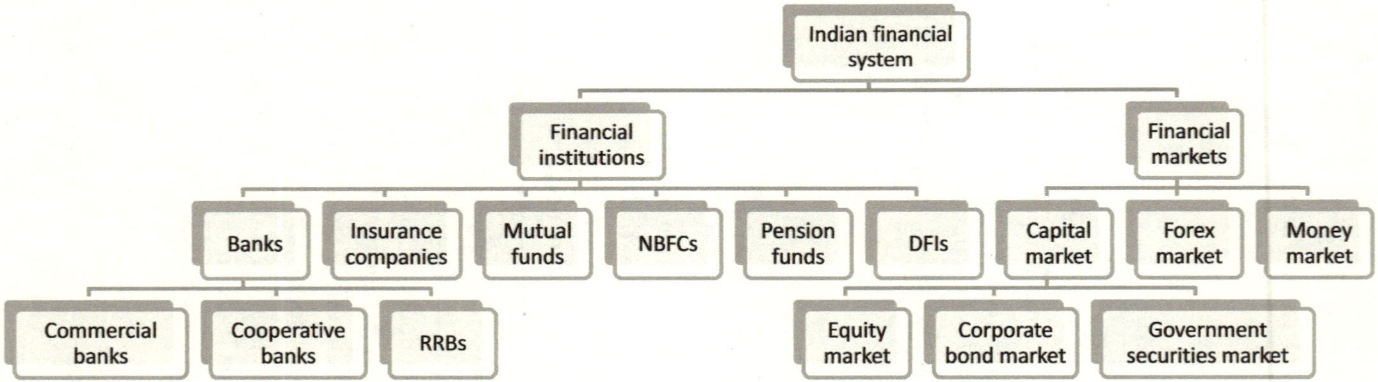

Figure 2.1 Structure of the Indian financial system

Source: Prepared by the author.

Exchange Board of India (SEBI), are to be adhered to. The concerned firm uses the services of investment banks or the corporate banking units of commercial banks to decide on the minimum price of the equity under the IPO, the timing of the issue, and so on.

The actual share price in the IPO depends on the demand for the same in the stock market. The general public, mutual funds and foreign institutional investors (FIIs) are the major buyers in this market.

There are several pros and cons of generating funds through equity sale which are as follows:

- *Advantage for the firm (borrower)*: There is no burden of repayment of funds or capital generated through the equity sale as equity is perpetual.
- *Disadvantage for promoters or major shareholders of the firm (borrower)*: The profits of the firm need to be shared with the minor shareholders.
- *Advantage for buyers of equity shares or IPOs (savers)*: The rate of return on equity shares, referred to as dividends, is generally higher than that on other forms of savings like a fixed deposit in a bank.
- *Disadvantage for buyers of equity shares or IPOs (savers)*: Return on equity is volatile. The dividend paid to shareholders depends on the profitability or loss of the firm which fluctuates in line with evolving business conditions and the performance of the firm. Such conditions are dynamic, based on economic cycles of recession and boom, entry of new players producing the same product, innovations in the product, changes in tastes and preferences of consumers, government regulations, and so on. Moreover, if the firm is in financial turmoil and there is need to wind it up, the share owners are accorded last priority in the order for claims on the firm's assets.

The equity market facilitates direct lending and borrowing. No intermediary is involved between the savers and borrowers in the process. There is a vibrant secondary market for sale and purchase of equities. The shares of listed companies are actively traded on the BSE and the NSE. The market prices of shares are very dynamic and change tick by tick. Depending on the prevailing market prices at the time of the sale as compared to the purchase price, existing shareowners make a profit or loss. For example, if Mr Ashok had purchased equity shares of Reliance Industries at INR 500 per share and sold them at INR 600 per share after a year, the capital gain for him is INR 100 per share. Thus, Mr Ashok made 20 per cent annual profit (calculated as [{INR. 600 – INR 500}/INR 500]*100) on this account.

In India, with a series of reform initiatives, a very active and vibrant equity market has developed during the post-reform period. The major reforms include:

- statutory powers to SEBI as the regulatory body for the equity market with the enactment of the SEBI Act, 1992;
- repeal of the Capital Issues (Control) Act, 1947, in 1992, abolishing statutory control on the floating and pricing of primary issues;
- implementation of disclosure and investor protection guidelines framed by SEBI;
- establishment of the NSE in 1994;
- dematerialisation of securities through the depository system and their transfer through electronic book entry;
- introduction of risk containment measures such as adoption of the mark-to-market margin system, setting intra-day trading and exposure limits, provisions for constituting a trade guarantee fund, and so on; and
- allowing FIIs registered with SEBI to participate in the capital market, significantly expanding the investor base.

These reforms promoted the safety and integrity of the Indian equity market and helped in mobilisation of long-term funds by Indian corporates. The market capitalisation in the BSE increased gradually from INR 1.88 trillion in 1992–93 to INR 5.72 trillion in 2002–03. This substantially increased to INR 63.88 trillion in 2012–13 and subsequently to INR 264.07 trillion in 2021–22 (RBI, n.d.2). Despite a negative market sentiment around the world due to the geopolitical conflict related to the Russia–Ukraine war, spread of Omicron, policy normalisation in advanced economies with the withdrawal of monetary policy accommodation, and so on, the Indian equity market performed quite satisfactorily in 2021–22. The BSE Sensex increased by 18.3 per cent while the Nifty (the NSE index) surged by 18.9 per cent in this period,[3] outperforming major equity market indices around the world. The

[3] This is calculated as the percentage change in 2021–22 indices as compared to the previous year.

total market capitalisation of BSE-listed companies increased by 29.2 per cent in 2021–22.

There has been growing participation of retail investors in the Indian equity market. This is evident from the opening of 3.5 crore new demat accounts during 2021–22 as compared to 1.4 crore during 2020–21. Resource mobilisation through IPOs, follow-on public offers (FPOs) and rights issues surged by 26.1 per cent in 2021–22 to INR 1.4 trillion.

2.2.1.2 Corporate Bond Market

Another option for big corporates for funding their projects is through issue of bonds in the corporate bond market. A bond is a financial instrument with a face value and fixed term to maturity. At the end of the maturity period, the issuer of the bond (here, the firm) pays the holder of the bond (the saver) an amount equal to the face value. For example, say, a firm M has issued a one-year bond with a face value of INR 100. A saver S has purchased this bond in the corporate bond market on 1 January 2020. Then, on 1 January 2021, M needs to pay S, or the holder of the bond, an amount of INR 100 for redemption.

Zero-coupon bonds are purchased at less than face value—say, at INR 90 for a face value of INR 100. The excess of the face value over the purchase price is the return on the bond. Here, the return is INR 10, which is INR 100 over INR 90. The *capital gain* for S in this case is INR 10. This is explained on the right side of Figure 2.2.

Corporate bonds are actively traded in the secondary market. The original purchaser of a bond need not hold it until maturity. Say, in our example, S sells the bond to P at INR 94 on 24 March 2020. Then, the return for S on this bond is INR 4—excess of the selling price of INR 94 over his purchase price of INR 90. If P holds the bond until maturity, she will receive the full face value of INR 100 from the issuer M. Accordingly, the return for P on the bond is INR 6, which is the difference between INR 100 and her purchase price of INR 94. This is explained on the left side of Figure 2.2.

If P does not wish to hold the bond until maturity, she can sell it to someone else in the secondary market, and so on. Ultimately, the person who possesses the bond at the time of maturity gets the amount equal to the face value from the issuer M.

We can similarly calculate the returns on zero-coupon bonds with multi-year maturity.

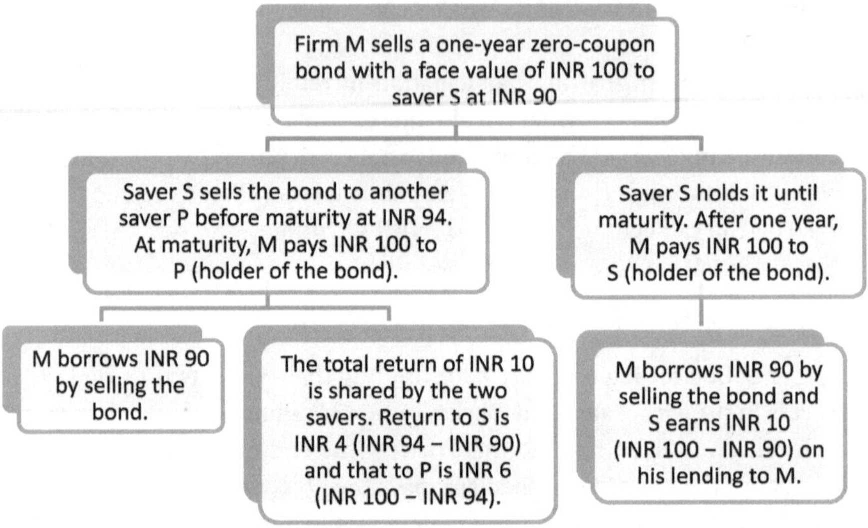

Figure 2.2 Fund mobilisation by issue of bonds

Source: Prepared by the author.

In coupon bonds, periodic coupon payments are made by the issuer of the bond, which are an additional return for the buyer of the bond (saver). For example, if a five-year bond with a face value of INR 100 offers a 6 per cent annual coupon rate, then at the end of each year, the holder of the bond will receive INR 6 from the issuer. If S has bought this bond at INR 90 and held it until maturity, his total return on the bond will be INR 40. This is the sum of INR 10 (as capital gain) and INR 30 (as coupon payments of INR 6 each for five years). If the original buyer of the bond does not hold it until maturity and sells it in the secondary market, we can accordingly calculate the returns to the buyer(s) of the bond as we did in the case of zero-coupon bonds.

There are several advantages for firms or borrowers in generating funds or capital through the sale of bonds. The cost of borrowing through issue of bonds is often cheaper than equities. After redemption of bonds on maturity, the firm or borrower is relived from the burden of parting with its future profits unlike in equity sale. Bonds also provide flexibility for repayment of the borrowed funds, allowing the firm to choose a suitable term to maturity at the time of issue. From the savers' or lenders' point of view, there are certain advantages too. The rate of return on bonds is relatively stable. The savers or lenders receive a fixed value (face value of the bond) from the issuer of the bond on maturity (along with fixed coupon payments, if it is a coupon bond). Fluctuations in market prices of bonds are relatively low compared to those of equities.

During the post-reform period, policy initiatives were introduced to develop an active corporate bond market in India. However, because of several shortcomings, the market could not take off until the early 2020s. As observed by the Committee on Financial Sector Assessment (RBI, 2009), the demand for corporate bonds has been low due to large issuance of risk-free government securities and low-risk subordinated debt issued by banks to meet tier-2 capital requirements under the Basel capital adequacy norms. Poor transparency in reporting and disseminating information on trading, absence of delivery versus payments (DvP) for settlement, lack of pricing of spreads over the benchmark yield curve and TDS were flagged as other key impediments. The said committee recommended several regulatory and legislative reforms for further development of the corporate bond market in India.

Following the recommendations of the High Level Expert Committee on Corporate Bonds and Securitisation (SEBI, 2005), chaired by R. H. Patil, several initiatives were undertaken to overcome the deficiencies in primary issuance and secondary market transaction processes. DvP-based settlements were introduced for over-the-counter (OTC) trades in corporate bonds from December 2009. The RBI permitted repo in corporate bonds since March 2010 for bonds with a rating of AA or above. Now, secondary market transactions in corporate debt instruments are reported on a platform operated by the Fixed Income Money Market and Derivatives Association of India (FIMMDA). Consequently, the corporate bond market has become more active. During 2022–23, primary issuances in the private corporate bond market amounted to INR 7.6 trillion as compared to INR 6 trillion in the preceding year. Outstanding corporate bonds stood at INR 42 trillion as on 31 March 2023. The latter was nearly 15.4 per cent of India's gross domestic product (GDP). But the bulk of fund mobilisation is still undertaken through private placements which accounted for 98.8 per cent of the total resources mobilised through the corporate bond market (RBI, 2023a).

2.2.1.3 Government Securities Market

The government funds spending requirements in excess of its resources through issue of government bonds or securities. In the government securities market, government bonds of various maturities are traded. The major players in this market in India are banks, primary dealers[4] and the RBI. With the introduction of several reforms in the government securities market since the early 1990s, it has become very vibrant. Key reform initiatives in this regard have included:

- introduction of an auction system for the sale of government securities in 1992;
- commencement of secondary market transactions in government securities through subsidiary general ledger (SGL) accounts since 1994;
- introduction of primary dealers in 1995 and satellite dealers[5] in 1996 to make the government securities market more liquid and active;
- allowance of participation of insurance companies, private corporates and financial institutions along with FIIs to broaden the investor base; and
- introduction of a DvP system to reduce settlement risks.

These reforms provided much-needed impetus towards improving the liquidity and pricing of government securities. The gross market borrowing of the government increased from INR 0.18 trillion in 1992–93 to INR 1.82 trillion in 2002–03 and subsequently to INR 22.37 trillion in 2021–22 (RBI, n.d.1). The volume of secondary market transactions increased multi-fold from INR 1.27 trillion during 1995–96 to INR 25.8 trillion during 2005–06 and further to INR 340.92 trillion during 2021–22 (as per RBI, 2023a).

[4] The RBI permitted establishment of a system of primary dealers as special institutions or participants for promoting an active government securities market in India in March 1995. The primary dealers had the obligations for underwriting the sale of government securities and actively trading in the government securities market, making such securities highly liquid. SBI DFHI, PNB Gilts, ICICI Securities Primary Dealership, Nomura Fixed Income Securities, Goldman Sachs (India) Capital Markets, and so on, are popular primary dealers. They helped in the development of an active government securities market in India.

[5] The RBI had issued guidelines for setting up satellite dealers in 1996. These satellite dealers were envisaged to supplement the banks and primary dealers towards development of an active government securities market in India.

The term to maturity of government bonds in India is often long, up to 40 years. As a consequence of the policy-driven elongation of the maturity profile of government securities, the average maturity of such securities increased from 5.7 years in 1995–96 to 14.1 years in 2004–05. The range of maturity of new loans increased from 2–10 years to 5–30 years during the comparable period. The maturity pattern of the Government of India dated securities issued during 2022–23 reveals that 48.9 per cent of the same consisted of securities with over 10 years' maturity. Instruments with less than five years' maturity accounted for 19 per cent of such securities and the remaining 32.1 per cent share was comprised by securities with 5–10 years' maturity.

The equity market, corporate bond market and government securities market together constitute the capital market in India. Within this, the government securities market is a special category as the RBI is the issuer of primary government securities and regulates trading in this market. On the other hand, SEBI regulates issues and trading in the equity and corporate bond markets. However, SEBI itself does not participate in the buying or selling of equities or corporate bonds.

2.2.1.4 Money Market

Financial instruments with less than one-year maturity terms such as treasury bills, certificates of deposit (CDs), commercial papers (CPs), and so on, are traded in the money market. The money market in India has several categories.

First, let us discuss inter-bank money markets such as the call, notice and term money markets. In the overnight call money market, banks borrow and lend amongst themselves to meet day-to-day liquidity requirements. This has been the core of the Indian money market since long. In the notice money market, the duration of inter-bank borrowing is 2 to 14 days. The term money market is the third uncollateralised inter-bank money market. The term to maturity of the lending or borrowing in the term money market varies from 15 days to 1 year. The term money market was dormant for various reasons. As a follow-up to the recommendations of the Working Group on the Money Market, chaired by N. Vaghul (RBI, 1987), the administered interest rate in the term-money market was done away with in 1989. Further, regulatory limits on term money transactions were removed, and from 2001, term money liabilities were exempted from CRR maintenance. With several such initiatives, the average daily turnover in the term money market had increased from nearly INR 1.9 billion in 2001–02 to INR 10.12 billion in 2006–07. The average daily volume in the call money market in 2021–22 was INR 90.6 billion as compared to INR 109.9 billion in 2020–21. The market share of the call money market was 2 per cent during 2021–22 (RBI, n.d.2).

Second, since August 2005, collateralised segments like market repo and CBLOs have grown in prominence. In market repo or CBLOs, securities are traded on a short-term basis with an agreement to reverse the transaction within a stipulated period of time. Say, in a 14-day market repo, Bank A has sold government securities worth INR 1 crore to Bank B. This is akin to Bank A borrowing funds from Bank B by offering government securities as collateral. After 14 days, the transaction is reversed—that is, Bank A repays INR 1 crore to Bank B along with interest charges and gets back its securities. The *repo rate* is the interest rate that Bank B charges to Bank A for providing funds for 14 days. Mutual funds and financial institutions are the prominent lenders in the CBLO market while PSBs are the leading borrowers. In the market repo also, mutual funds are major lenders while foreign banks and IPBs are key borrowers. With the underlying security collateral, this market minimises the default risk. The collateralised repo market also integrates the money market and government securities market. By 2006–07, the collateralised market accounted for nearly 70 per cent of the total volume of transactions in the Indian money market.

Third, there is a special overnight repo market in India operated by the RBI under its LAF. In this market, one party is the RBI and the counterparty is a bank which borrows from the RBI. The repo rate charged by the RBI under the LAF is a fixed rate and is 6.5 per cent as of August 2024. It is popular as the RBI's policy rate for the conduct of the monetary policy. The RBI also conducts variable rate term repo, details of which are discussed in Chapter 10.

Fourth, in addition to the issue of dated government securities[6] for meeting its expenditure needs in excess of its resources as discussed in the previous section, the government also issues *treasury bills* (TBs) for market borrowing. This is the main instrument for short-term government borrowing. There are three varieties of TBs issued by the RBI on behalf of the government differentiated by term to maturity. These are 91-day TBs, 182-day TBs and 364-day TBs. Further details on TBs are provided in Chapter 9.

---

[6] Government dated securities are government bonds with more than one-year original term to maturity.

Finally, CPs and CDs have become popular money market instruments in India during the post-reform period. CPs are unsecured money-market instruments issued by private corporates to raise short-term funds. Corporate borrowers were permitted to issue CPs in 1990. The issuer of CPs needs to meet several eligibility criteria such as having a tangible net worth of above INR 4 crore, bank-sanctioned working capital limits, its accounts with banks not being NPAs and a minimum credit rating equivalent to A3 by a SEBI-registered credit rating agency (CRA). The maturity of CPs varies from seven days to one year, and they can be issued in denominations of INR 5 lakh and multiples thereof. They are purchased at discount. Banks are the main lenders in the CP market.

In the reverse, banks borrow short-term funds from private corporates and high-net-worth individuals by issuing CDs. CDs are negotiable money market instruments. CDs issued by banks have maturity periods of seven days to one year. They are issued in denominations of a minimum of INR 1 lakh and multiples thereof. CDs are also purchased at discount like CPs. Both CPs and CDs are traded in the secondary market, and since July 2010, all such transactions are reported on a platform operated by FIMMDA.

Fresh issuance of CDs in the primary market during 2022–23 stood at INR 6.7 trillion as compared to INR 2.3 trillion in the previous year. New issuance of CPs, however, declined to INR 13.7 trillion in 2022–23 as compared to INR 20.2 trillion in 2021–22. For further details on the money market in India, readers may refer to RBI (2006a, 2023a).

2.2.1.5 Forex Market

The forex market facilitates the purchase and sale of leading foreign currencies such as the USD, pound sterling, euro, yen, and so on. Banks are the major players in the Indian forex market. Unlike other segments of financial markets, there is no lending or borrowing involved in the forex market. It basically facilitates the purchase of a foreign currency in exchange for Indian rupees (INR) or vice versa. Foreign investors are required to convert their respective currencies to INR prior to buying Indian equities or bonds. Similarly, when Indian investors buy equities or bonds in foreign markets, they first need to buy foreign currencies in exchange for INR and then use the proceeds to buy foreign equities or bonds. Thus, the forex market plays a facilitating role in cross-border capital flows. Similar conversion of INR to a foreign currency like USD is required to buy our imports. Our exporters convert their foreign currency earnings to INR. Thus, the forex market promotes foreign trade. Such exchange of currencies is also required for the cross-border movement of people.

During the post-reform period, the Indian economy adopted outward orientation by liberalising imports, initiating a medium-term export promotion strategy and encouraging cross-border investment flows. It thus became increasingly integrated with the rest of the world in terms of trade, investment and the movement of people. Commensurately, it was also required to develop a vibrant forex market. Transition to a market-determined flexible exchange rate regime in 1993 helped the Indian forex market acquire increasing depth. Liberalisation of a series of rules on foreign transactions since the early 1990s played a critical role in this regard. One such change was the replacement of the Foreign Exchange Regulation Act (FERA), 1973, by a more liberal Foreign Exchange Management Act (FEMA), 1999. Freedom to cancel and rebook forward contracts of any tenor, allowing cross-country options on a back-to-back basis, hedging of external commercial borrowings (ECBs), extension of trading hours in the inter-bank forex market, and so on, were other important measures.

With these reforms, the monthly turnover in the forex market in India increased from USD 17.1 billion in July 1996 to USD 546 billion in March 2006. It further increased to USD 2012.7 billion in March 2022. Inter-bank transactions dominated the overall transactions in the forex market. They accounted for 86.5 per cent of the total forex transactions in July 1996. After falling to a low of nearly 75 per cent during the 2000s, this share increased to 80.7 per cent in March 2022 (RBI, n.d.2).

India's exchange rate policy during the post-reform period has been widely hailed to have stood the test of time. Despite several unexpected adverse developments[7] on the external and domestic fronts, India's forex rate movements have remained reasonably stable except for a few episodes of minor turbulence.[8]

---

[7] Some such developments include the Asian financial crisis of 1997, the fallout of the Pokhran nuclear test and border tensions in the late 1990s, the global financial crisis (GFC) of 2007–08, the geopolitical conflict due to the Russia–Ukraine war in 2022, and so on.

[8] Such episodes included the Asian crisis of 1997, the GFC of 2007–08 and the recent geopolitical concerns due to Rusia–Ukraine war since 2022.

The discussion thus far covered key segments of the Indian financial markets. Let us now turn to Indian financial institutions.

2.2.2 Indian Financial Institutions

Financial institutions include different categories of banks and non-banking financial companies (NBFCs). These are financial intermediaries which mobilise funds from savers or lenders and use such funds in turn to lend to ultimate borrowers. Financial institutions facilitate indirect lending unlike financial markets where savers lend directly to borrowers.

Within the set of financial institutions in India, banks have an overwhelming presence. The Indian banking sector has mainly three important constituents. These are (*a*) commercial banks, (*b*) cooperative banks and (*c*) RRBs. Amongst them, commercial banks are of paramount importance in terms of size, spread and operations. The NBFCs in India are composed of a variety of institutions including finance companies, insurance companies, mutual funds, pension funds, and so on. The Indian financial system also includes a set of DFIs with a sector-specific focus.

We have already discussed commercial banking in Chapter 1. The present chapter provides greater details about commercial banks in India in subsequent sections. The remaining part of this section discusses the other segments of the Indian banking system and other financial intermediaries.

2.2.2.1 Cooperative Banks

Cooperative banks and RRBs have been operating along with mainstream commercial banks in India. The cooperative movement in the country has a long history which commenced in 1904. After independence, the cooperative credit system was assigned significant importance under the overall strategy to boost rural credit. The government played an active role in the formation and promotion of cooperatives. The First Five-Year Plan (1951–56) had emphasised on multi-purpose service cooperatives towards agricultural and rural development.

Over time it was observed that while the cooperative credit system was successful in providing much-needed finance to agriculture and ancillary activities, it did not serve the economy to its full potential. Several inadequacies were identified in its functioning and credit delivery. Some such deficiencies were

- involvement of several agencies in the regulatory arrangements for cooperatives with overlapping functions;
- inadequacy in the quantum of credit due to funding constraints and undue delays in the sanctioning of credit;
- excessive bureaucratic control and lack of coordination between administrative departments pertaining to agriculture and cooperatives;
- weak organisational structure and lack of training and skill upgradation of the workforce;
- ineffective audit over cooperative operations; and
- poor loan recoveries.

Several initiatives were undertaken from time to time to address these issues and strengthen the Indian cooperative system. The organisational structure of the cooperative system in India can be broadly distinguished into two segments: (*a*) rural cooperative credit institutions (RCCIs) and (*b*) urban cooperative banks (UCBs). A snapshot of these segments, key policy initiatives and performance indices is provided in the following sections.

2.2.2.1.1 Rural Cooperative Credit Institutions (RCCIs)

RCCIs, or rural cooperative banks, are popular financial cooperatives functioning in India. They were assigned a critical role for financing agriculture and rural economic activities until the 1970s when commercial banks were confined to urban centres. They were the main purveyors of formal credit to farmers.

RCCIs are divided into two categories. The first category caters to short-term funding requirements and has a three-tier structure. State cooperative banks operate at the top in the respective states. At the district level in each state, there are district central cooperative banks (DCCBs); and at the grassroots level, primary agricultural credit societies (PACSs) function as the face of the entire rural cooperative structure.

- *PACSs*: These are popularly referred to as primary societies. They are formed by members residing within a particular locality having an interest in promoting the true spirit of cooperative brotherhood. The membership of primary societies is not restricted to any caste, creed or faith and is also not limited to borrowers or non-borrowers. Primary societies generate funds in the form of share capital, deposits of members and non-members and loans from the DCCB and the government. They provide loans only to their members who are basically farmers. The operations of each primary society are limited to a small locality like a village. The members of a society often have close acquaintance with each other.

- *DCCBs*: These are popularly referred to as central cooperatives. A DCCB is a federation of primary societies in a specific region like a district, or *taluk*. Some of them have more than one office in different towns within a district. Central cooperatives also have individual members from business, finance, other areas of professional expertise and other sections of society. They mobilise deposits from their constituent primary societies, individual members, municipalities, local bodies, universities, quasi-government bodies, and so on. Their share capital, reserve funds and borrowings from their state cooperative bank serve as additional sources of funds. All such resources are used for on-lending to their constituent primary societies.
- *State cooperative bank*: The state cooperative bank is a federation of central cooperatives. It is the apex body in the rural cooperative credit structure of each state. It generates funds from the National Bank for Agriculture and Rural Development (NABARD) and acts as a conduit for lending to central cooperatives. Its share capital and deposits contributed by member central cooperatives are its major sources of funds. It also generates funds from the urban rich in the form of deposits. As the constituent central cooperatives cannot borrow or lend amongst themselves, the state cooperative bank acts as a platform to redistribute the surplus or deficit funds amongst them.

The second category is RCCIs providing long-term finance. For this category, the state cooperative agriculture and rural development banks (SCARDBs) operate as the apex institution at the state level. The primary cooperative agriculture and rural development banks (PCARDBs) function as the base-level operational units. They support agricultural development by providing long-term funding to promote capital formation in rural India.

The agricultural credit-related functions of the RBI were transferred to NABARD after its establishment in 1982. Consequently, NABARD emerged as the apex institution on policy planning and providing refinance facilities to rural financial institutions. To strengthen the financial position of NABARD, since 1996–97, the RBI has been providing INR 400 crore annually.

Guided by the recommendations of several committees, key reform initiatives were undertaken to improve the management, autonomy and financial position of and credit delivery through cooperative institutions since the early 2000s. The Expert Committee on Rural Credit, chaired by V. S. Vyas, and the Task Force to Study the Functioning of the Cooperative Credit System and Suggest Measures for Its Strengthening, chaired by Jagdish Capoor, are two such important committees. Bringing parity with commercial banks, prudential norms on income recognition, asset classification and provisioning for PACSs, or primary societies, were introduced since 2009–10.

2.2.2.1.1.1 Recent Improvement in the Performance of Rural Cooperatives

With active policy initiatives to strengthen rural cooperatives in India, there have been encouraging developments in recent times, particularly as regards their profitability, asset quality and loan recoveries. Although rural cooperatives accounted for nearly 13 per cent of the total credit flow to agriculture in 2021–22, this is a quite dismal performance as compared to their share of 64 per cent in 1992–93 (RBI, 2019b). The amount of profit registered by state cooperative banks was INR 14 billion in 2021–22; the ratio of NPAs to loans outstanding was 6.7 per cent and the recovery to demand ratio was 90.5 per cent. This is an improvement compared to the consolidated profit of INR 2.2 billion and NPAs to loans outstanding ratio of 12.4 in 2007–08.

Amongst the DCCBs, or central cooperatives, 308 posted a consolidated profit of INR 20.9 billion in 2021–22 while the remaining 43 incurred a loss of INR 6.7 billion. The combined NPAs to loans ratio was 11.7 per cent while the loan recoveries to demand ratio was 74.9 per cent. In 2007–08, 261 DCCBs registered a consolidated profit of INR 8.5 billion while the remaining 108 incurred a total loss of INR 9.9 billion. Thus, all the DCCBs put together posted a profit of INR 14.2 billion in 2021–22 as compared to a loss of INR 1.4 billion in 2007–08. The NPAs to loans ratio was also higher at 18.5 per cent (as per various issues of the RBI's *Report on Trend and Progress of Banking in India*).

The story for the primary societies is also similar. Out of a total of 95,633 PACSs operating in 2008–09, only 37,291 (39 per cent) registered a profit while 45,869 (47.9 per cent) incurred losses. In 2020–21, out of 1,02,599 PACSs, 47,297 (46.1 per cent) were profit-making while 37,419 (36.5 per cent) incurred losses. As compared to a total loss of INR 10.7 billion in 2008–09, the PACSs recorded a profit of INR 9.8 billion in 2020–21 (as per various issues of the RBI's *Report on Trend and Progress of Banking in India*).

Notwithstanding the improvements in profitability and asset quality, there are a considerable number of DCCBs and PACSs which are loss-making. The concerns on their financial health and underperformance as regards serving the desired objectives remain. The case of rural cooperatives providing long-term finance in particular is worse. In 2020–21, the ratio of NPAs to loans outstanding was 33.2 per cent for the SCARDBs while that for the PCARDBs was 44.5 per cent. The PCARDBs incurred a loss of INR 4.7 billion in 2020–21 (as per various issues of the RBI's *Report on Trend and Progress of Banking in India*).

2.2.2.1.2 Urban Cooperative Banks (UCBs)

The establishment of UCBs in India dates back to the pre-independence era. Many urban cooperative credit societies were set up in the erstwhile Bombay and Madras provinces during 1919–38. They facilitated the collection of local savings and lending to meet the consumption needs of members. The main drive was to provide financial accommodation to members, relieving them from the clutches of moneylenders. The usefulness of such agencies in financing small traders, factory workers and the urban middle classes was well recognised. The RBI's Working Group on Industrial Financing through Cooperative Banks (1968) had emphasised on the role of urban cooperative institutions in catering to the needs of small-scale industries. Over time, there have been continuous efforts to strengthen UCBs and improve their performance. Guided by the *Vision Document*, 2005, the RBI initiated several reform measures for UCBs, mainly pertaining to their financial restructuring and ALM (RBI, 2005c).

A quick look at the current status of UCBs reveals the following. As on 31 March 2022, 47 out of 1,514 UCBs had extended advances of more than INR 1,000 crore. They accounted for 49.8 per cent of the total advances of the UCBs. There were 216 UCBs with advances of less than INR 10 crore each, and together they accounted for just 0.4 per cent of the total advances of the UCBs. Most such small UCBs had only a single branch. The presence of UCBs is highly concentrated in the states of Andhra Pradesh, Gujarat, Karnataka, Maharashtra and Tamil Nadu. The UCBs with a larger depositor base and wider geographical presence are categorised as tier-2 UCBs. There were 701 tier-2 UCBs in 2021–22 accounting for 92.4 per cent of the total deposits and 92.6 per cent of the total advances (as per various issues of the RBI's *Report on Trend and Progress of Banking in India*). The remaining 813 UCBs were under the tier-1 category with limited geographical spread and a small depositor base.

Operating under RBI supervision, out of 1,514 UCBs in India in 2021–22, 153 were accorded the top rating 'A', 203 were accorded 'B+' and another 740 were given a rating of 'B'. These three categories accounted for 69.8 per cent of the total advances of the UCBs. There were 1,302 UCBs with a CRAR of more than 12 per cent and another 122 with a CRAR in the range of 9–12 per cent. The net NPA ratio of the UCBs stood at 4.4 per cent in 2021–22. The NPAT of the UCBs in 2021–22 was INR 2,881 crore and the ROA was 0.43 per cent (as per various issues of the RBI's *Report on Trend and Progress of Banking in India*). These prudential and profitability indicators suggest strengthening of the UCBs in recent times.

UCBs with multi-state operations are regulated by the Government of India and state-specific ones are regulated by the respective state governments. Drawing from the BR Act, 1949, the RBI has regulatory and supervisory authority over UCBs, particularly with regard to banking-related operations.

The cooperative banks in India put together accounted for nearly one-tenth of the total assets of SCBs in 2017–18 (RBI, 2019b). In a cross-country perspective, this share was close to the share of financial cooperatives in the US but quite low as compared to the share of nearly 51 per cent in France. The comparative share of financial cooperatives in Brazil and China was low at about 3 per cent.

Cooperative banks in India mainly suffer from internal vulnerabilities pertaining to access to funds, lack of competency and professionalism in management, political interventions in loan disbursements, and so on. Increasing competition from commercial banks has added to the problem. However, given the importance of cooperative banks in terms of a massive financial inclusion quotient, their wider outreach covering villages and small towns, there is a need to revitalise the loss-making units and strengthen the overall cooperative structure.

2.2.2.2 Regional Rural Banks (RRBs)

RRBs were established in 1975 to promote rural credit with the active coordination and involvement of the local administration with commercial banks. It was envisaged that RRBs would emerge as specialised institutions with the joint participation of commercial banks, the central government and the respective state governments. The central government was stipulated to subscribe 50 per cent of the required capital to set up the RRBs. The remaining 15 and 35 per cent were subscribed by the state government and a sponsor bank, respectively. It was contemplated that the RRBs would integrate the funding capacity and professional competency of commercial banks with the rural outreach and micro-focus of cooperative banks. This combination was envisaged to make the RRBs prominent regional or rural-oriented financial institutions promoting lending to targeted groups such as farmers, agricultural labourers and artisans along with small traders and entrepreneurs in rural areas. The RBI is the regulatory authority for the RRBs drawing from the provisions of the BR Act, 1949, while NABARD undertakes inspection of their banking activities.

Because of various deficiencies, the actual achievements of the RRBs on credit delivery remained underwhelming. Poor capital structure, rising operational expenses, mismanagement and lack of professionalism led to a large number of RRBs incurring losses, risking their very survival. The number of loss-making RRBs were 40 out of 196 in 2002–03 (as per various issues of the RBI's *Report on Trend and Progress of Banking in India*). The sum of the net losses of such RRBs was INR 2.15 billion. Rise in both interest expenses and operating expenses mainly contributed to the incurring of such losses. Wage bills accounted for a large part of the rise in operating expenses.

In this backdrop, reform initiatives were undertaken towards improving the financial health of RRBs and imparting operational autonomy. On the one hand, restructuring and amalgamation within RRBs weeded out the loss-making entities and recapitalisation of the viable ones strengthened their financial position. On the other, a prudential regulatory framework similar to that applicable to commercial banks was extended to RRBs. Subsequent developments are summarised as follows:

- Since commencement of the consolidation process in 2005, the number of RRBs was reduced from 196 in 2005 to 91 in March 2008. RRBs with a negative net worth were recapitalised. The total amount of required recapitalisation was nearly INR 18 billion in 2007–08.
- Consequently, the financial performance of the RRBs improved. In 2009–10, 79 RRBs out of a total of 82 became profit-making. The consolidated net profit of the RRBs recorded an annual increase of 41.1 per cent to INR 18.8 billion in 2009–10. The aggregate credit increased from nearly INR 485 billion in 2006–07 to INR 836 billion in 2009–10 (as per various issues of the RBI's *Report on Trend and Progress of Banking in India*).

- The financial position of the RRBs was again in the red by the late 2010s with a consolidated net loss of INR 5.5 trillion, mainly triggered by high loan delinquencies. The gross NPA ratio of the RRBs was 9.5 per cent in 2017–18 and further increased to 10.7 per cent in 2018–19 (as per various issues of the RBI's *Report on Trend and Progress of Banking in India*).
- In the backdrop of continuing losses in 2019–20, there was a further requirement of recapitalisation of the RRBs. The Covid-19 pandemic delayed the process. A total of INR 81.7 billion was sanctioned for the recapitalisation of RRBs in 2021–22. By the end of March 2022, NABARD had released the central government share of nearly INR 32 billion after the proportionate infusion of an equivalent amount by the state governments and sponsor banks. This benefitted 22 RRBs. Consequently, there was a turnaround in the performance of the RRBs. The consolidated net profit of the RRBs increased to INR 32.2 billion in 2021–22. The gross NPA ratio improved to 9.1 per cent. The outstanding advances of the RRBs stood at INR 3,628.4 billion as of 31 March 2022. However, the share of RRBs in the total bank credit to agriculture remained low at 11 per cent in 2021–22 (as per various issues of the RBI's *Report on Trend and Progress of Banking in India*).

This underscores the fact that notwithstanding the stated objective of rural cooperatives and RRBs to cater to the financial needs of agriculture and the rural sector, their combined share in agricultural lending has remained low at around 25 per cent in the early 2020s. Commercial banks have an overwhelming share of nearly three-fourths in the overall credit to agriculture from the banking system. This emphasises the standing of commercial banks even in lending to agriculture.

2.2.2.3 Non-Banking Financial Companies (NBFCs)

NBFCs are registered under the Companies Act, 1956 and 2013, and undertake the business of lending, insurance, asset management, hire purchase, leasing, wealth management, and so on. NBFCs have assumed increasing importance in the Indian financial system since the 1980s. They are regulated by both the Ministry of Company Affairs and the RBI. Some leading NBFCs are Shriram Finance, Bajaj Finance, Mahindra & Mahindra Financial Services, Aditya Birla Finance, Muthoot Finance, and so on.

The total number of NBFCs operating in India had significantly increased from 7,063 in 1980 to 25,085 in 1991 and further to 39,454 in 1995. The bulk of the NBFCs are very small in size. NBFCs mainly cater to the needs of borrowers who fail to obtain funding from banks and the capital market. Given the importance of these entities and the need for ensuring their financial prudence, the Narasimham Committee on the Financial System (RBI, 1991) had laid down regulatory requirements for NBFCs. Accordingly, the RBI stipulated necessary norms for their registration and various prudential requirements. As on 31 March 2019, there were 82 deposit-taking NBFCs and 9,461 non-deposit-taking NBFCs (as per various issues of the RBI's *Report on Trend and Progress of Banking in India*). The latter accounted for more than 85 per cent of the total assets of the NBFCs. Amongst the non-deposit-taking NBFCs, there were 274 entities having an asset size of INR 500 crore or more. They are treated as systemically important NBFCs. The third variety of NBFCs consisted of 99 housing finance companies.

The distribution of the credit portfolio of NBFCs suggests that around 55–60 per cent of the total credit is deployed as loans to industry and another 20 per cent as retail loans (as per various issues of the RBI's *Report on Trend and Progress of Banking in India*). Within industry, larger companies received the bulk of the loans while the share received by the MSME sector was miniscule.

2.2.2.3.1 Insurance Companies, Mutual Funds and Pension Funds

There are certain special types of NBFCs with a very large presence in the Indian financial system. These include insurance companies, mutual funds and pension funds. They are not registered with the RBI and their affairs are overseen by sector-specific regulators. These types of NBFCs are largely as follows:

- *Insurance companies*: These include companies which provide life insurance services such as the Life Insurance Corporation of India (LIC), SBI Life, HDFC Life Insurance, Kotak Life Insurance, and so on, and also those which provide general insurance services like motor insurance and health insurance such as the Oriental Insurance Company, National Insurance Company, Bajaj Allianz General Insurance, Tata AIG General Insurance Company, ICICI Lombard General Insurance Company, and so on. The total insurance premiums mobilised by life insurance companies in 2021–22 stood at

INR 6.9 trillion out of which INR 4.3 trillion was due to LIC alone. The gross direct premiums of general and health insurance mobilised in 2021–22 were INR 2.2 trillion out of which the premiums generated by public sector general insurance companies amounted to INR 0.8 trillion (IRDAI, 2023). Insurance companies are regulated by the Insurance Regulatory and Development Authority of India (IRDAI).

- *Mutual funds*: UTI (Unit Trust of India) Asset Management, SBI Mutual Fund, and so on, generate funds from small investors by selling units to them and invest the mobilised funds in the equity and bond markets. The assets under management (AUM) of equity-oriented mutual funds stood at INR 13.7 trillion in 2021–22. Mutual funds mobilised a substantial amount of funds through systematic investment plans (SIPs). Resources mobilised through SIPs amounted to INR 2.5 trillion in 2021–22 (SEBI, 2023). This signifies growing retail participation in the equity market. Mutual funds are regulated by SEBI.
- *Pension funds*: Pension subscribers buy units of pension funds and the funds so generated are lent to support long-term projects in general. The returns generated from these loans are used to pay pensions to beneficiaries or subscribers. The leading pension funds in India include LIC Pension Funds, SBI Pension Funds, UTI Retirement Solutions, HDFC Pension Management Company, Tata Pension Management, and so on. The first three of these accounted for the bulk of the business. The total AUMs for SBI Pension Funds, LIC Pension Funds and UTI Retirement Solutions as on 31 March 2023 were INR 3.4 trillion, INR 2.5 trillion and INR 2.4 trillion, respectively (PFRDA, 2024). The Pension Fund Regulatory and Development Authority (PFRDA) is the regulatory body for pension funds.

2.2.2.4 Development Finance Institutions (DFIs)

Historically, DFIs—namely the Industrial Development Bank of India (IDBI), Industrial Credit and Investment Corporation of India (ICICI), Industrial Finance Corporation of India (IFCI), NABARD, and so on, played a critical role in promoting financial support to specific sectors. ICICI was set up in 1955 to provide medium-term and long-term project financing services to Indian industry and businesses. It was part of a collaboration of the Government of

India with the World Bank and Indian industry. IDBI was set up in 1964 as a DFI. Its services extended beyond conventional project financing. It strived to achieve balanced industrial growth across all parts of India by specifically focusing on the development of backward areas. IFCI was established in 1948 as a statutory corporation under the Ministry of Finance to provide financial support towards promotion of diversified growth of Indian industry. IFCI was privatised in the early 1990s and listed in the stock market to generate funds. NABARD, established in 1981, acts as the central agency to coordinate and promote rural credit. It provides refinance facilities towards encouraging flow of credit to build rural infrastructure. It also acts as the supervisor for cooperative banks and RRBs.

India adopted a market-oriented policy regime in the early 1990s and introduced reforms to develop a broad-based financial sector. One such effort to develop the banking sector was to promote the entry of private and foreign banks. ICICI and IDBI exploited the opportunity to set up ICICI Bank and IDBI Bank, respectively. ICICI Bank was established as part of the ICICI Group in 1994. In 2002, ICICI Personal Financial Services and ICICI Capital Services were merged with ICICI Bank. It has established itself as a leading private bank. IDBI Bank was established in September 2004 and the undertaking of IDBI was transferred to IDBI Limited in October 2004. Subsequently, the present entity, IDBI Bank, came into existence in 2008.

At present, three key DFIs serving different categories of financial needs are Export–Import (EXIM) Bank of India, National Housing Bank (NHB) and Small Industries Development Bank of India (SIDBI).

- *EXIM Bank*: It was established as a specialised institution in 1982 with the objective of promoting, financing and facilitating foreign trade. The bank helps exporters by providing various financial services such as corporate banking, lines of credit, buyer's credit, overseas investment finance, and so on. It also provides advisory services in terms of identifying opportunities and risks related to foreign trade and investment in different countries.
- *NHB*: It was established in 1988 as the apex institution for housing finance. Its major objective is to promote a sound, healthy and cost-effective housing finance system. It has supervisory authority over housing finance companies and also provides financial support for on-lending to the housing sector.

- *SIDBI*: It was established in 1990 to act as the principal financial institution to cater to the requirements of small-scale industries. Its mandate is to promote and finance small-scale industries, along with coordinating with other agencies engaged in similar activities.

Apart from the institutions discussed in the preceding paragraphs, microfinance institutions (MFIs) have emerged as an important vehicle to provide financial support to the poor in the recent decades, particularly to those largely left unbanked by formal institutions like commercial and cooperative banks and RRBs. In this evolution process, MFIs and self-help groups (SHGs) have considerably expanded their presence in several parts of the country.

2.2.3 Dominance of Commercial Banks

It may be noted that until the mid-1990s, the capital market in India was quite narrow-based. The money market, mutual funds and forex market were not very developed. Even the government securities market was in the nascent stage. During the post-reform period, conscious policy efforts helped in the development and strengthening of these segments. As observed by Panagariya (2020), the corporate debt market in India had a late start and is yet to become vibrant. The corporate debt to GDP ratio was around 16.6 per cent in the late 2010s (Panagariya, 2020) . IPOs as a source of funds still remain small despite deepening of the equity market. Panagariya concluded that bank credit will continue to be of paramount importance for borrowers in India until new issues of equity and debt take off on a large scale.

Table 2.1 provides data pertaining to the various constituents of the Indian financial system to highlight their relative importance. The information therein confirms that commercial banks dominate the Indian financial system. As a percentage of GDP, the total bank credit extended by SCBs was nearly 71 per cent and their total investment was close to 26 per cent in 2019–20. Bank credit is largely extended to private households and businesses, while the bulk of the investments of banks are in government securities. Thus, put together, bank lending to the private sector and the government was nearly 100 per cent of the GDP. Both the bank credit and investment of SCBs as a proportion of GDP have gradually and significantly increased from 18.8 per cent and 9.3 per cent, respectively, in 1979–80.

Table 2.1 Key indicators of banking and finance in India (as percentage of GDP)

Items	1979–80	1989–90	1999–2000	2009–10	2019–20
Commercial banks: credit	18.8	22.2	23.5	51.0	71.2
Commercial banks: investment	9.3	14.1	16.6	21.8	25.7
Credit disbursed by RRBs	0.2	0.7	0.7	1.2	2.0
Cooperative banks: credit	3.4	2.1	2.6	1.6	1.4
Funds raised through equity issues*	NA	NA	NA	1.7	2.1
Funds raised through debt issues†	NA	NA	NA	3.5	4.7
Assets under management of mutual funds	NA	NA	5.8	9.6	15.3
Credit disbursed by all financial institutions‡	1.2	2.1	3.7	1.4	0.9
Market borrowings by central and state governments	2.8	2.3	6.1	9.8	10.7

Source: Primary data obtained from RBI's *Handbook of Statistics on Indian Economy*, https://data.rbi.org.in/DBIE/#/dbie/reports/Publication/Time-Series%20Publications/Handbook%20of%20Statistics%20on%20the%20Indian%20Economy (accessed 24 June 2022), and SEBI's *Handbook of Statistics, 2022*, https://www.sebi.gov.in/reports-and-statistics/publications/may-2023/handbook-of-statistics-2022_74606.html (accessed 14 May 2024). Calculation of figures as percentage of GDP by the author.

Note: (*a*) *Equity issues include public issues, rights issues, QIPs (qualified institutional placements) and preferential allotments. †Debt issues include public issues and private placement of corporate bonds. ‡Data pertains to IDBI, IFCI, ICICI, SIDBI, IIBI (Industrial Investment Bank of India), LIC, GIC (General Insurance Corporation of India), SFCs (state financial corporations), SIDCs (state industrial development corporations), and so on. (*b*) NA: Not available.

Lending by other segments of the financial sector in India is quite modest. For example, funds generated through equity and debt issues in 2019–20 were 2.1 per cent and 4.7 per cent of GDP, respectively. Within the non-banking segment, only the AUM of mutual funds is noteworthy. As a share of GDP, it increased from 5.8 per cent in 1999–2000 to 15.3 per cent in 2019–20.

Within the banking system, in 2019–20, the outstanding credit disbursed by RRBs was 2 per cent of GDP while that of cooperative banks was 1.4 per cent. In fact, for cooperative banks, the credit to GDP ratio has broadly witnessed a declining trend from its peak of 3.4 per cent in 1979–80. Even in the area of agricultural finance, in which rural cooperatives and RRBs were envisaged a special role, the share of commercial banks is overwhelming. During the seven-year period of 2015–22, the share of commercial banks in the total credit flow to agriculture was in the range of 70–77 per cent. The share of cooperative banks was in the range of 11–17 per cent and that of RRBs was 11–13 per cent (RBI, 2022b: 97, table V.1).

These facts indicate the significance of commercial banks in India.

2.3 Evolution of Banking in India: A Historical Perspective

In ancient India, some rudimentary forms of money lending by indigenous lenders like *sahukar*s and *marwadi*s were prevalent. Such people usually lent against security collaterals such as jewellery, land titles, utensils and even domestic cattle like cows or goats. The origin of formal banking in India can be traced back to 1770 with the establishment of Bank of Hindustan. The evolution process since then has been a long journey, with many twists and turns.

Mainly, two landmarks in the evolution of commercial banks in India are noteworthy. The first is bank nationalisation and social control on bank credit since the 1970s which facilitated the rapid expansion of banking. The second is the banking sector reforms introduced since the 1990s which strengthened the safety and soundness of banks and provided them operational autonomy in a competitive environment. Let us begin with the run-up to the first landmark event.

After India's independence from British rule in 1947, inter alia, attaining rapid economic development became a top policy priority. The erstwhile Planning Commission of India played the anchoring role in overall central planning, which, among others, involved mobilisation of resources and their optimal allocation. In this endeavour, banking and financial services were assigned a significant part. To promote the use of banking resources in accordance with national priorities, the erstwhile Imperial Bank of India was converted into a public sector bank and SBI came into being in 1955. By the late 1960s, it was realised that the stated socioeconomic objectives of the government, including employment creation in rural areas, poverty eradication and development of agriculture and small-scale industries, remained unfulfilled. Lack of access to bank finance was identified as a key impediment in the realisation of these objectives. It was observed that banking services were limited to urban centres and towns and largely catered to the requirements of big industry and commerce. A need was felt for social control of banks so that banking services could be extended to the hitherto neglected agriculture, small-industry and rural sectors. As part of the objective of ensuring the use of bank credit to serve various sectors and sections of society in the best possible way as per national priorities, major commercial banks were gradually brought under government control.

2.3.1 Bank Nationalisation and Banking Expansion

In this backdrop, 14 large banks[9] were nationalised in 1969 and another 6 in 1980. This led to considerable government control over the commercial banking system. This was the first major event with significant implications for the massive expansion of banking in India.

After bank nationalisation, banks began to open branches across the length and breadth of the country. The number of branches of commercial banks more than doubled from 8,262 in 1969 to 16,936 in 1974, in a span of just five years. Prior to this, a similar doubling of the number of bank branches took nearly two decades. The number of bank branches in 1947 was 4,288. The impact of bank nationalisation was reflected in key banking indicators. The average growth of the deposits of SCBs nearly doubled to 20.3 per cent during the 1970s as compared to 10.4 per cent in the 1960s. In the corresponding period, the average bank credit growth expanded to 18.5 per cent from 13.5 per cent. The 1980s sustained banking expansion and witnessed average growth of deposits and credit at 18.1 and 16.8 per cent, respectively (calculated based on RBI, n.d.2).

The banking sector in India assumed a predominantly public sector character after bank nationalisation. It not only promoted overall savings and investments in the country, but also significantly augmented lending to socially prioritised economic activities like agriculture, rural artisans, small-scale industries, exports, and so on. Banks became instrumental in promoting economic development under the centrally planned regime.

By the early 1990s, it was realised that while the Indian banking system had expanded rapidly as a consequence of bank nationalisation, there were increasing concerns over the commercial viability of several banks. The

[9] These banks had deposits of more than INR 50 crore each.

administered interest rate regime and minimum priority sector lending requirements[10] associated with the process of social control posed serious challenges to bank efficiency and profitability.

With increasing deficit financing of the government, there was a concomitant requirement of raising the SLR from around 30 per cent in the early 1970s to 38.5 per cent by September 1990. This was effectively a process of financial repression, enabling government borrowing from banks at a cheaper rate through statutory pre-emptions. Furthermore, banks were required to set aside a significant portion of their deposits in the form of CRR balances, which were gradually raised from 4 per cent in December 1974 to 15 per cent in July 1989.

This process of financial repression and directed credit at concessional rates compelled banks to pay lower interest rates on bank deposits. A natural corollary was to charge higher interest rates to the private commercial sector so as to cover operational costs. These twin effects resulted in sub-optimal outcomes in terms of both mobilisation of savings and industrial investment. The banking system was constrained to underperform in serving the economy as compared to its true potential. There were serious challenges to the financial health of many banks with perceived political interference in the sanctioning of loans, high operating costs mainly due to wages and salaries paid to the massive workforce and mounting NPAs.

Thus, overarching government control and lack of commercial considerations had serious negative implications in the form of the declining profitability and efficiency of banks. Adoption of new norms of accounting and income recognition in 1992 revealed the true state of their financial health. In 1992–93, it was observed that half of the PSBs had a negative net worth and one-third of them were loss making. NPAs were at an alarming level, at nearly one-quarter of the aggregate loan portfolio of the PSBs. For

[10] Priority sectors cover those sectors which are considered to be of top priority from the national and social interest point of view, but are neglected for lending by banks when driven by commercial considerations alone. Such sectors include agriculture, small-scale industries, MSMEs, retail trade, small business, micro credit, education, advances to SHGs, funds provided to RRBs, and so on. The minimum priority sector lending as a percentage of the total credit of each bank is set at 40 per cent. The norms are liberal for foreign banks given that these banks do not have a rural branch network. Details of priority sector lending are provided in Chapter 9.

some banks, NPAs were as high as 25 to 40 per cent of their respective loan portfolio.

At that point, it became imperative to introduce a series of urgent corrective measures to strengthen the Indian banking system. A weakening and fragile banking system leads to serious crisis and financial instability and severely damages public faith in banking and finance. Lack of public confidence in the soundness and stability of banks is detrimental to the mobilisation of bank deposits and hence harmful for the generation of savings and capital formation, having serious adverse consequences for the overall economy.

2.3.2 Banking Sector Reforms

Banking sector reforms were a vital component of the comprehensive reforms introduced in India in response to the economic crisis of 1991. As indicated earlier, this was the second landmark event in the Indian banking arena. Key reform initiatives included

- phasing out of statutory pre-emption of banking resources;
- provision of operational autonomy to banks in banking decisions related to lending and determination of interest rates;
- adoption of global best practice in terms of banking regulation and supervision;
- liberalisation of entry of private and foreign banks; and
- adoption of prudential regulatory norms on capital adequacy, income recognition and provisioning to strengthen the safety and soundness of banks, aligning with international best practices.

Given the importance of these measures, the necessary details are discussed separately in section 2.4.

These policy initiatives promoted the operational autonomy of banks and contributed to significant improvements in their efficiency and profitability. Increasing competition from new-age private banks was formidable. During the 1990s, new private banks like Axis Bank,[11] ICICI Bank and Global Trust Bank started increasing their prominence by introducing modern banking

[11] Axis Bank was previously UTI Bank.

with customer-friendly products and ambience. PSBs also took charge and adapted to the new competitive environment. Overall, the banking system witnessed significant transformation in several aspects including reorientation of business models, adoption of new products and technology, risk management techniques, manpower adjustment, and so on. In the process, the reforms facilitated the emergence of a very modern, vibrant and sound banking system in India. It played a remarkable role promoting high and sustained growth during the post-reform period.

2.3.3 Metamorphosis of SBI and Other PSBs in India

To gain useful insight into the process of evolution of commercial banking in India, we can refer to the gradual transformation of SBI, the largest bank in the country. Other PSBs also share a similar history and have undergone parallel evolutionary processes. A summary of the evolution of SBI is delineated in the paragraphs that follow, borrowing from the information provided on its official website.[12]

The origin of SBI can be traced back to the Bank of Calcutta, established in the city of Calcutta (present-day Kolkata) in 1804. It was renamed Bank of Bengal in 1809. Subsequently, the Bank of Bombay and the Bank of Madras were established in 1840 and 1843, respectively. The three were popularly referred to as presidency banks and operated in the erstwhile presidencies of Bengal, Bombay and Madras. Contrary to popular belief, the presidency banks were not established to promote economic prosperity in India (under British rule); rather, the objective was to meet the requirements of imperial finance and the needs of local European commercial interest.

In terms of ownership, the presidency banks were joint-stock companies with limited liability. Up to 80 per cent of the total share capital was privately owned and the remaining 20 per cent was owned by the respective provincial governments. The banks were allowed to issue bank notes, used for payment of public revenues within a restricted geographical area. Subsequently, the Paper Currency Act, 1861, assigned the sole power of issuing paper currency to the Government of India, and the authority of the presidency banks to issue bank notes was withdrawn.

---

[12] The official website of SBI is https://www.sbi.co.in.

The banking operations of the presidency banks evolved in sync with the changing economic environment. India witnessed rapid changes facilitating trade and commerce in the period of 1875–1900 through the following developments:

- Laying of railroads commenced in several parts of the country.
- New irrigation networks in the Madras Presidency, Punjab and Sind facilitated the production of cash crops and opened up prospects for exporting farm products.
- The spread of tea and coffee plantations in the hills of Assam and the Nilgiris were associated with this process of commercialisation.

Consequently, India's international trade expanded more than six-fold. The three presidency banks supported this process of commercialisation and international trade.

In 1921, the three presidency banks were merged to set up the Imperial Bank of India. It was assigned a quasi-central banking role, including as a banker to the government and other banks, along with commercial banking functions. With the establishment of the RBI in 1935, the Imperial Bank was relieved from quasi-central banking activities.

India adopted central planning since the early 1950s, after her independence from British rule in 1947. It envisaged the exercise of greater government control on the use of banking resources for the socioeconomic development process. Consequently, the Imperial Bank was nationalised and became SBI in 1955. In 1959, SBI took over former state-associated banks: State Bank of Bikaner and Jaipur, State Bank of Hyderabad, State Bank of Indore, State Bank of Mysore, State Bank of Patiala, State Bank of Saurashtra and State Bank of Travancore.

During the post-reform period, in the process of consolidation and efforts to build big banks, all these subsidiaries were gradually merged with SBI over the period of 2008–17. At present, SBI is the biggest bank in India with nearly one-fifth of the aggregate deposits and advances of all SCBs.

The historical transformation of other PSBs is largely similar to the evolution of SBI. Several commercial banks were set up in various Indian cities in the late nineteenth and early twentieth centuries to facilitate trade and commerce. Allahabad Bank was established in 1865 in Allahabad (now Prayagraj), Punjab National Bank (PNB) in 1894 in Lahore (now in Pakistan), Bank of India (BOI) in 1906 in Bombay (now Mumbai), Canara Bank in

1906 in Mangalore, Indian Bank in 1907 in Madras (now Chennai), Bank of Baroda (BOB) in 1908 in Baroda (now Vadodara), Central Bank of India in 1911 in Bombay (it was also the first Indian commercial bank wholly owned and managed by Indians), Union Bank of India in 1919 in Bombay, and so on. All these banks initially began as privately owned commercial banks and provided facilitating services for trade and commerce in their respective regions. As indicated earlier, 14 such large banks were nationalised in 1969 and 6 others in 1980.

In the following section, we will discuss the banking sector reforms since the early 1990s and subsequent developments.

2.4 Banking Sector Reforms in India

In the backdrop of the economic crisis of 1991, comprehensive reforms were introduced in India. The initiatives covered broadly policies related to the industrial sector, foreign trade and investment, fiscal reforms and the financial sector. In the newly market-oriented environment, banking sector reforms constituted an integral part of the financial sector reforms.

The banking sector reforms were undertaken with two broad objectives. First, it was imperative to improve the financial health of banks and promote banking efficiency and profitability. Second, with greater global integration of the Indian economy since the early 1990s, it was necessary to align the regulatory and supervisory practices pertaining to banks with international best practices.

As discussed in the preceding section, since the bank nationalisation of 1969, there was tremendous success in the expansion of commercial banking in India, with significant penetration in rural and semi-urban areas. However, excessive control over banking activities and statutory pre-emption of banking resources through SLR and CRR stipulations impaired the financial health of banks. By the early 1990s, it was realised that for strengthening banks and making them vibrant, there was an urgent need for course correction. The necessary blueprint to guide the path and direction of the same was provided by the recommendations of two important committees,[13] both chaired by M. Narasimham. The details of these reforms are extensively

[13] These were the Committee on Financial Systems (1991) and the Committee on Banking Sector Reforms (1998).

discussed by Rangarajan (1998), RBI (1999b) and Samantaraya (2015) and summarised in the sections that follow.

2.4.1 Phasing Out of Statutory Pre-Emption

The government played a proactive role in the economic development process adopted by India under central planning. There was an imperative need for massive government expenditure to carry out developmental activities. With limited scope for tax revenue mobilisation, rising government expenditure required higher government borrowing. The gross fiscal deficit of the Government of India, which reflects the quantum of government borrowing, reached an alarming level in the 1980s. As a percentage of GDP, it more than doubled from an average of 3.3 per cent during the first half of the 1970s to 7.7 per cent during the second half of the 1980s (calculated based on RBI, n.d.2).

To facilitate rising government borrowing, the minimum SLR stipulations were raised in that order. SLR determines the proportion of deposits[14] to be maintained in approved securities. Rising SLR requirements create more demand for government securities from banks. By September 1990, the minimum SLR had reached 38.5 per cent. The CRR was also gradually raised to as high as 15 per cent by July 1989. Put together, the SLR and the CRR pre-empted more than half the bank deposits by the late 1980s.

The interest rates on SLR securities were artificially kept low so that the government could avail funds at cheaper rates. Annual redemption yields on the Government of India's long-term securities (15 years and above) were within the range of 9–12 per cent during the late 1980s as compared to the SBI advance rate of around 16.5 per cent and an average call money rate of around 10 per cent during the comparable period. No interest was paid to banks on CRR balances up to 3 per cent[15] of NDTL. Banks earned nominal interest linked to the bank rate on CRR balances above this. Overall, returns on both investments in SLR securities and CRR balances were not remunerative.

[14] SLR is stipulated as a certain proportion of the NDTL of banks to be maintained in government and other approved securities. The RBI is authorised to classify various liabilities to be included under the NDTL as per section 42(1)(c) of the RBI Act, 1934. The latest definition of NDTL is provided in the 'master circular' on CRR and SLR issued by the RBI on 1 July 2014. Bank deposits, with some adjustments, constitute the most important component of NDTL.

[15] This was the statutory minimum CRR prevailing at that time.

Banks were left with limited options for deploying the remaining resources in profitable avenues. This was further constrained by priority sector lending requirements.

As part of the banking sector reforms, the post-reform period witnessed gradual reduction of the SLR and the CRR so that banks were relieved from the statutory pre-emption of a significant part of banking resources. The SLR was gradually reduced since the early 1990s and brought down to the then prevailing statutory minimum of 25 per cent by October 1997. Similarly, the CRR was brought down in a phased manner to 4.5 per cent by August 2003. Thus, reduction in the SLR and the CRR released nearly a quarter of the bank deposits for profitable deployment by banks.

However, the investment of banks in government securities was in excess of minimum SLR requirements in the 1990s. Such excess investment was guided by commercial considerations rather than statutory impositions. This is because, with the introduction of the auction system and other reforms in the government securities market, returns on such securities became attractive. Further, under the Basel capital adequacy norms (discussed in the sections that follow), government securities were assigned 'zero' credit risk. This incentivised investment in such securities over lending to businesses and households.

2.4.2 Deregulation of Interest Rates

Prior to the 1990s, interest rates in banking were heavily regulated. From 1975–76 to 1980–81, banks were prescribed minimum lending rates (13.5 per cent) and ceiling rates (19.5 per cent) by the RBI. Since 1981–82, the prescription of the minimum lending rate was withdrawn, but that of ceiling rates was retained. The ceiling rate was, however, gradually revised downwards to 16.5 per cent by 1987–88. Besides these prescriptions, banks were required to charge concessional interest rates for priority sector lending. The proportion of such lending was stipulated to be a minimum of 40 per cent of the outstanding credit of a bank. This process of financial repression led to lower earnings for banks with adverse implications for their profitability and financial health. Moreover, the administered interest rate regime seriously curtailed the allocative efficiency of bank credit.

As indicated in the preceding section, lower earnings on lending translated to lower interest payments on bank deposits. A regulatory norm required the maximum deposit rate of a bank to be two percentage points lower than the minimum lending rate. Lower interest rates on bank deposits kept overall savings at sub-optimal levels and undermined capital formation in the country.

In this backdrop, deregulation of bank interest rates constituted a key component of the banking sector reforms. The related policy changes were as follows:

- Bank lending rates for credit limits of over INR 2 lakh were freed in October 1994. In 1996–97, banks were asked to announce their maximum spread over prime lending rates (PLRs)[16] for all advances other than consumer credit to impart greater transparency. Banks were permitted to prescribe separate PLRs for the 'loan' and 'cash credit' components and also separate spreads for both in February 1997.
- As regards deposits, in October 1995, banks were allowed to fix their own domestic term deposit rates for deposits with over two years' maturity. In July 1996, this freedom was extended to interest rates on term deposits of above one-year maturity.
- Thus, by 1997, banks acquired considerable autonomy in determination of interest rates on both their loans and deposits, except for a couple of segments like lending of less than INR 2 lakh, export credit and interest paid on savings bank accounts and foreign currency deposits.

However, it was observed that banks merely announced their respective benchmark prime lending rates (BPLRs) to meet statutory requirements. The pricing of the bulk of high-value loans had no strong link with the BPLR for many banks. To improve transparency in the pricing of loans, the RBI introduced the *base rate system*, effective from July 2010. Under this system, a reference rate called the *base rate* was to be fixed by banks taking into account factors such as the cost of deposits, operational cost and risk premium. Banks were advised to link their lending rates to their respective base rates.

The RBI's interest-rate policy prescriptions for banks were further refined in the late 2010s. An internal benchmarking system, namely the marginal

[16] The prime lending rate (PLR) of a bank is the interest rate charged to its most creditworthy borrower at minimum risk. Banks were required to announce their respective PLRs.

cost of funds-based lending rate (MCLR) system, was introduced in April 2016. Further, an external benchmarking system was introduced in October 2019. Many banks are now following the MCLR system for corporate loans and a variety of retail loans. The external benchmarking procedure based on the RBI's fixed repo rate under LAF is used for setting the interest rate on home loans by most banks today.

These interest-rate deregulations provided operational autonomy to banks in India. Bank lending rates became market-determined based on the RBI's monetary policy stance, the bank's cost of funds and the risk profile of its borrowers. Banks acquired flexibility to fix interest rates on deposits, inter alia, based on overall liquidity conditions and their ALM considerations.

2.4.3 Introduction of Prudential Regulatory and Supervisory Norms

In the early 1990s, India adopted prudential norms on banking regulation and supervision aligning with international best practices. The aim was to promote the safety and soundness of banks within an overall liberal set up. These initiatives were mainly guided by the recommendations of the Narasimham Committee on the Financial System (RBI, 1991). Prudential measures on banking regulation covered standards on capital adequacy, income recognition, asset classification and provisioning. Rigorous off-site surveillance supplemented on-site inspection as part of the task of updating banking regulations. The salient features of these measures are discussed in the following sections.

2.4.3.1 Capital Adequacy

Prior to the introduction of prudential regulations in the early 1990s, there was no correspondence between the capital of a bank and the risk embodied in its business. It is imperative to tightly align the capital position of a bank with the quantum of risks it is undertaking. A bank should possess the required amount of capital to absorb any rise in banking risks due to adverse economic conditions, weak financial condition of its borrowers, and so on. A higher capital requirement concomitant to higher risks creates a disincentive for a bank to take undue risks and alleviates excessive leveraging. These issues are comprehensively discussed in Chapter 7.

With the adoption of the Basel prudential norms, the RBI required banks to calculate their risk-weighted assets ratio. Maintaining a minimum capital level linked to their risk-weighted assets was made obligatory. Learning from the experience of the global financial crisis (GFC) of 2007–08, capital adequacy norms were upgraded. The revised norms, popularly referred to as Basel III, enhanced the quantum of minimum capital requirements as well as improved the quality of capital. New norms on stable funding and liquidity requirements were also introduced. Overall, the Basel III revisions improved the macroprudential and counter-cyclical characteristics of the capital adequacy norms. Details of such reforms, including technicalities related to the definition of capital and calculation of risk-weighted assets, are provided in Chapter 7.

2.4.3.2 Income Recognition

The new norms on income recognition revised the existing procedure of accounting income from interest and principal repayments in banking. Earlier, income dues from NPAs were taken into account on accrual basis. The new norms required banks to count income from an asset only if income is actually realised and not to consider overdues from NPAs as income. They made the assessment of income more realistic.

2.4.3.3 Asset Classification and Provisioning for NPAs

The prudential norms on asset classification required the treatment of banking assets on which repayments of principals and interest charges were overdue as NPAs. Within NPAs, the assets were further classified as substandard, doubtful and loss assets mainly based on the duration they were overdue. Classification of assets into various types of NPAs and the related provisioning requirements have witnessed several rounds of revision since the early 1990s. Banks are required to make provisioning in alignment with the quality of the assets: the poorer the quality of the NPAs, the higher the proportion of provisioning required. Details on extant guidelines on asset classification and provisioning norms are given in Chapter 7.

It is important to note that NPAs are doubly taxing for a bank. First, they dry up a bank's resources on account of non-receipt of scheduled loan repayments. Second, provisioning on NPAs compels the bank to set aside a part of its existing resources. Introduction of asset classification and provisioning norms helped in correctly assessing the financial health of banks. It also entailed application of corrective measures to reduce loan delinquencies.

2.4.3.4 Inspection and Supervision of Banks

Framing suitable banking regulatory norms and guidelines is a necessary step to strengthen banking sector stability. But it is not sufficient. There is a complementary need to ensure that regulatory prescriptions are adhered to by banks in letter and spirit. This necessitates the need for constant monitoring of the financial health of banks and confirming that banks are strictly following stipulated guidelines. This task is accomplished by banking supervision. The supervisory framework of the RBI underwent significant improvements during the post-reform period, details of which again are provided in Chapter 7.

2.4.4 Encouraging Entry of Private Banks

The Indian banking sector is dominated by PSBs. Prior to the 1990s, the dominance of the PSBs was even stronger. Lack of competition and weak motive to improve the operational efficiency of the PSBs was considered a factor contributing to the suboptimal performance of the entire banking sector. In this perspective, the Narasimham Committee (RBI, 1991) had recommended liberal entry of new private sector banks to improve competitiveness and foster efficiency in the Indian banking system. Improved efficiency was expected to come from upgrading of technology, introduction of innovative products and adoption of management skills conforming to international best practices.

Guided by these recommendations, guidelines for the entry of new private banks (NPBs) were introduced in January 1993. Three financial institutions, namely UTI, HDFC and ICICI, received in-principle approval to set up new banks. With the addition of more banks, the total number of NPBs went up to 10 by 1995–96. *Report on Trend and Progress of Banking in India, 1995–96*, published by the RBI, observed that in terms of net profit, the performance of the NPBs was far superior to that of other banking groups including foreign banks. The NPBs enjoyed a lower spread between the cost of mobilising deposits and interest earned on their assets. Data on some such indicators are provided in section 2.5. The report also asserted that given their superior financial performance, the NPBs are likely to be the torchbearers of technological upgradation and efficiency in banking. It is no surprise that one of these (HDFC Bank) today has emerged as the second largest bank in India.[17]

As on 31 March 2020, the outstanding deposits of the NPBs stood at INR 35,038 billion and advances at INR 31,158 billion. Their share in the overall deposits and advances of all SCBs was estimated to be 25.1 and 30.2 per cent, respectively.

India also adopted similar liberal policies for foreign banks since the 1990s. The number of foreign banks operating in India doubled from 23 in 1993–94 to 46 in 2019–20.

2.4.5 Computerisation and Mechanisation in Banking

The first industrial revolution took place in the early eighteenth century with scientific invention and widespread adoption of methods of mass production using electro-mechanic techniques. Since the last century, the IT revolution has left its mark, making the production process highly knowledge-intensive. Scientific advances in the areas of electronics, computers and communications technology have led to the widespread use of IT and ITES in production and distribution networks worldwide. Given the role of IT and ITES towards augmenting productivity and efficiency, many describe the phenomenon as the 'second industrial revolution' or the 'third wave'. The banking sector in advanced countries was an early beneficiary of this process, which brought fundamental changes in their data processing and storage, banking operations and customer service.

In India, initiatives towards computerisation and mechanisation of the banking industry were visible starting from the 1980s. This commenced with the computerisation of bank branches, adoption of magnetic ink character recognition (MICR)–based solutions for clearing operations in metropolitan cities and computerisation of settlement operations in all clearing houses managed by the RBI. Advancements in this direction were further strengthened during the post-reform period with the following steps:

- India joined the Society for Worldwide Interbank Financial Telecommunications (SWIFT) network, integrating with the global financial network in 1991.

[17] This is the case in terms of HDFC Bank's share in the outstanding advances of SCBs in 2021–22.

- The establishment of BANKNET, a payment network set up by the RBI, facilitated early realisation of outstation cheques by linking seven cities, namely Mumbai, Delhi, Chennai, Kolkata, Bangalore, Hyderabad and Nagpur.
- Based on the recommendations of several important committees,[18] a wide range of reform initiatives were undertaken towards promoting computerisation in banking, adoption of core banking solutions and improvement of payment and settlement systems.
- The establishment of a very small aperture terminal (VSAT) network provided a reliable communications backbone for exclusive use in banking and finance.
- A system of DvP was introduced in transactions involving government securities.
- Suitable amendments to extant regulations such as the RBI Act, 1934, and the Bankers' Books Evidence Act, 1891, the enactment of the Information Technology Act, 2000, and so on, provided the required legal framework in the changed scenario for strengthening the use of IT and ITES in Indian banking.
- Adoption of RTGS and National Electronic Funds Transfer (NEFT) not only facilitated faster fund transfers but also strengthened the security of banking transactions and played a role in avoidance of fraud.

The post-reform period in India witnessed branch computerisation at various levels in a phased manner, rapid expansion of ATM facilities, adoption of electronic transfer of funds though RTGS and NEFT, significant penetration of credit and debit cards, introduction of internet and mobile banking, and so on. Wide application of IT and ITES in banking promoted efficient data management, faster funds transfer, better analysis and decision-making and improved customer service, among others.

Overall, the reforms discussed in the preceding sections have significantly strengthened the safety and soundness of banking, improved customer

---

[18] These included the Committee on Computerisation in Banks (chaired by C. Rangarajan, 1988), Committee on Technology Issues Relating to Payments System, Cheque Clearing and Securities Settlement in the Banking Industry (chaired by W. S. Saraf, 1994) and Committee for Proposing Legislation on Electronic Funds Transfer and Other Electronic Payments (chaired by K. S. Shere, 1996).

service, upgraded the payment and settlement system and, most importantly, augmented banking efficiency in India.

2.5 Commercial Banks in India

As in other banking systems across the world, the Indian central bank—that is, the RBI—is the backbone of its overall banking system. The RBI was set up in 1935 under the RBI Act, 1934. Like the Federal Reserve System in the US and the Bank of England in the United Kingdom (UK), the RBI is not a regular bank. It is the apex bank in India entrusted with traditional central banking functions such as the issue of currency notes, banker to the government, government debt management, forex management, banker and lender of last resort (LOLR) to banks, regulator and supervisor of banks, and so on. During the post-reform period, with the emergence of monetary policy as the major macroeconomic policy tool, the RBI has become more popular as the monetary authority. Details of the functions of the RBI are provided on its official website[19] and in Reserve Bank Staff College (2017).

The functions and working of the RBI have a strong association with banks in several ways. To begin with, banks need a licence from the RBI for commencing their business. The RBI is the banker for banks. The members of the public keep their deposits with and obtain loans from banks. Commercial banks in turn maintain balances with the RBI and borrow from it in the normal course of business. The RBI also provides an LOLR facility to banks which are under stress. It is the regulator and supervisor of banks. Details of this aspect will be discussed in Chapter 7. The RBI's 'clearing house' constitutes the main platform facilitating transfers of funds amongst banks and hence is the central part of the payment and settlement system. Banks work as the major conduit for transmission of the RBI's monetary policy impulses. The RBI plays a critical role as a regulator or facilitator in several other activities of banks such as transactions in the government securities market, forex market, money market, and so on. Given this role of the RBI as the central bank, many treat it as part of the Indian banking system although it is not a regular bank.

[19] The official website of the RBI is https://www.rbi.org.in.

Besides the RBI, as mentioned, the Indian banking system has three major constituents. These are (*a*) commercial banks, (*b*) cooperative banks and (*c*) RRBs. We have already briefly discussed cooperative banks and RRBs in section 2.2. Among the three constituents, commercial banks are the overwhelmingly dominant segment in terms of volume of business, geographical spread and varieties of banking activities. The structure and composition of commercial banks are discussed in the following sections.

It may be noted that apart from these players in the Indian banking system, there are three specialised banking institutions, namely NABARD, EXIM Bank and NHB, to which we referred earlier. They are not mainstream banks but play an important role in facilitating the flow of bank credit to specific sectors.

In terms of composition based on ownership criteria, mainstream commercial banks can be divided into three types. These are (*a*) PSBs, (*b*) IPBs and (*c*) foreign banks.

2.5.1 Public Sector Banks (PSBs)

PSBs are predominantly owned by the Government of India, with more than 50 per cent share-capital ownership. As discussed earlier, SBI became the first PSB in 1955. Seven state-associated banks were merged with SBI in 1959 and are popularly referred to as associates of SBI. Subsequently, 14 big banks were nationalised in 1969 and another six were added to the list in 1980. So by the time India introduced reforms in the early 1990s, there were a total of 28 PSBs operating in India.

As indicated earlier, following the recommendations of the Narasimham Committee (RBI, 1991), there has been a process of consolidation by merger of several PSBs. The process started with the gradual merger of the associate banks of SBI with SBI itself, one by one over the period 2008–17. Then Dena Bank and Vijaya Bank were merged with BOB in 2019. In 2020, 10 more were merged to form four PSBs. Thus, as of August 2024, a total of 12 PSBs are operating in the country. The list of PSBs prior to and after the merger is given in Table 2.2. Partly, the recent initiatives on bank consolidation were triggered by high loan delinquencies in the PSBs during the 2010s which had a strong negative impact on bank credit growth.

Prior to the merger of various PSBs in 2020, there were 18 PSBs as listed in Table 2.3(a). Data on the deposits and advances of all 18 PSBs as on 31 March 2020 are also provided therein. It may be noted that, put together,

Table 2.2 List of PSBs in India after recent mergers

S. No.	Name of the bank (at present)	Name(s) of the bank(s) (prior to the merger)	Percentage share in total advances of SCBs (2021–22)	Percentage share in total deposits of SCBs (2021–22)
1	Bank of Baroda	(*a*) Bank of Baroda, (*b*) Dena Bank and (*c*) Vijaya Bank (2019)	6.4	6.1
2	Bank of India		3.4	3.7
3	Bank of Maharashtra		1.1	1.2
4	Canara Bank	(*a*) Canara Bank and (*b*) Syndicate Bank (2020)	5.8	6.3
5	Central Bank of India		1.4	2.0
6	Indian Bank	(*a*) Allahabad Bank and (*b*) Indian Bank (2020)	3.2	3.5
7	Indian Overseas Bank		1.2	1.5
8	Punjab and Sindh Bank		0.5	0.6
9	Punjab National Bank	(*a*) Punjab National Bank, (*b*) Oriental Bank of Commerce and (*c*) United Bank of India (2020)	6.0	6.7
10	State Bank of India	(*a*) State Bank of India, (*b*) State Bank of Bikaner and Jaipur, (*c*) State Bank of Hyderabad, (*d*) State Bank of Indore, (*e*) State Bank of Mysore, (*f*) State Bank of Patiala, (*g*) State Bank of Saurashtra and (*h*) State Bank of Travancore (2008–17)	22.4	23.6
11	UCO Bank		1.0	1.3
12	Union Bank of India	(*a*) Andhra Bank, (*b*) Corporation Bank and (*c*) Union Bank of India (2020)	5.4	6.0

Source: *RBI Annual Report, 2020–21*; *Statistical Tables Relating to Banks in India*, 2021–22, downloaded from RBI website, https://data.rbi.org.in/DBIE/#/dbie/reports/Publication/Time-Series%20Publications/Statistical%20Tables%20Relating%20to%20Banks%20in%20India (accessed 4 January 2023).

Note: The years of merger are in parentheses.

Table 2.3(a) Deposits and advances of PSBs as on 31 March 2020

S. No.	Bank	Deposits	Percentage share*	Advances	Percentage share†
1	Allahabad Bank	2,28,609	1.6	1,42,965	1.4
2	Andhra Bank	2,12,609	1.5	1,57,742	1.5
3	Bank of Baroda	9,45,984	6.8	6,90,121	6.7
4	Bank of India	5,55,505	4.0	3,68,883	3.6
5	Bank of Maharashtra	1,50,066	1.1	86,872	0.8
6	Canara Bank	6,25,351	4.5	4,32,175	4.2
7	Central Bank of India	3,13,763	2.2	1,51,101	1.5
8	Corporation Bank	2,05,355	1.5	1,27,399	1.2
9	Indian Bank	2,60,226	1.9	1,97,887	1.9
10	Indian Overseas Bank	2,22,952	1.6	1,21,333	1.2
11	Oriental Bank of Commerce	2,30,108	1.6	1,57,959	1.5
12	Punjab and Sind Bank	89,668	0.6	58,412	0.6
13	Punjab National Bank	7,03,846	5.0	4,71,828	4.6
14	State Bank of India	32,41,621	23.2	23,25,290	22.6
15	Syndicate Bank	2,81,270	2.0	1,84,399	1.8
16	UCO Bank	1,93,203	1.4	1,01,174	1.0
17	Union Bank of India	4,50,668	3.2	3,15,049	3.1
18	United Bank of India	1,37,615	1.0	67,523	0.7
	All PSBs	90,48,420	64.7	61,58,112	59.8

Source: *Statistical Tables Relating to Banks in India*, 2019–20, downloaded from RBI website, www.rbi.org.in.

Note: Deposits and advances are in INR crore. *Share of deposits of bank as a percentage of total deposits of all commercial banks. †Share of advances of bank as a percentage of total advances of all commercial banks.

the PSBs accounted for close to 60 per cent of the advances[20] or loans of all commercial banks. Their share in the deposits was even higher at 64.7 per cent. This reflects the sheer dominance of the PSBs in the Indian banking sector.

During the post-reform period, mainly the entry of NPBs gradually moderated the share of PSBs in both the deposits and advances of SCBs. In the

[20] Bank credit or loans appear as advances in the balance sheet of a bank.

early 1990s, the share of PSBs was close to 90 per cent, which had gradually declined to 75–80 per cent by the early 2000s (Table 2.4).

Among the PSBs, the share of SBI in deposits and advances has been preponderant. As on 31 March 2020, the share of SBI in the deposits of SCBs stood at 23.2 per cent and that in advances was 22.6 per cent. This implies that the share of SBI in the deposits and advances of the PSBs was more than one-third. Its share in the overall deposits and advances of SCBs in 2021–22 was 23.6 and 22.4 per cent, respectively (Table 2.2). Despite consolidation, no other PSB stands anywhere close to that. The shares of the other four large PSBs, namely BOB, Canara Bank, PNB and Union Bank of India were within the range of 5–7 per cent.

2.5.2 Indian Private Banks (IPBs)

As on 31 March 2020, there were 22 IPBs operating in the country. The list of IPBs and data on their deposits and advances are provided in Table 2.3(b). It may be observed that the share of IPBs in the total advances of SCBs was 35.2 per cent as on 31 March 2020. Their share in deposits was 29.8 per cent. During the early 1990s, their share both in deposits and advances of all SCBs was close to 5 per cent (Table 2.4). This reflects the growing importance of IPBs in the overall banking business in India.

It may be noted that the bulk of the increasing share of IPBs is contributed by NPBs. Three such banks, namely Axis Bank, HDFC Bank and ICICI Bank, together accounted for a little over 60 per cent of the total deposits and advances of IPBs as on 31 March 2020. Among them, HDFC Bank stood out as the second largest bank in India, next to SBI, with a share of 9.6 per cent in the advances of SCBs and 8.2 per cent in the deposits (Table 2.3[b]).

As per advances of banks in India, as on 31 March 2020, three NPBs joined the club of the top five commercial banks. Their names and percentage shares (within parenthesis) in the total advances of SCBs were as follows: (*a*) SBI (22.6), (*b*) HDFC Bank (9.6), (*c*) BoB (6.7), (*d*) ICICI Bank (6.3) and (*e*) Axis Bank (5.5). Notwithstanding the merger of 10 PSBs in 2020–21 to form 4 PSBs as listed in Table 2.2, HDFC Bank and ICICI Bank continued to be part of the top-five banks club. As per their shares in advances, the top five banks in 2021–22 were (*a*) SBI (22.4), (*b*) HDFC Bank (11.2), (*c*) ICICI Bank (7), (*d*) BoB (6.4) and (*e*) PNB (6).

Table 2.3 (b) Deposits and advances of IPBs as on 31 March 2020

Sl. No.	Bank	Deposits	Percentage share*	Advances	Percentage share†
1	Axis Bank	6,40,105	4.6	5,71,424	5.5
2	Bandhan Bank	57,082	0.4	66,630	0.6
3	City Union Bank	40,832	0.3	33,927	0.3
4	CSB Bank	15,791	0.1	11,366	0.1
5	DCB Bank	30,370	0.2	25,345	0.2
6	Dhanlaxmi Bank	10,904	0.1	6,496	0.1
7	Federal Bank	1,52,290	1.1	1,22,268	1.2
8	HDFC Bank	11,47,502	8.2	9,93,703	9.6
9	ICICI Bank	7,70,969	5.5	6,45,290	6.3
10	IDBI Bank	2,22,424	1.6	1,29,842	1.3
11	IDFC First Bank	65,108	0.5	85,595	0.8
12	IndusInd Bank	2,02,040	1.4	2,06,783	2.0
13	Jammu & Kashmir Bank	97,788	0.7	64,399	0.6
14	Karnataka Bank	71,785	0.5	56,964	0.6
15	Karur Vysya Bank	59,075	0.4	46,098	0.4
16	Kotak Mahindra Bank	2,62,821	1.9	2,19,748	2.1
17	Lakshmi Vilas Bank	21,443	0.2	13,828	0.1
18	Nainital Bank Limited	7,679	0.1	3,829	0.0
19	RBL Bank	57,812	0.4	58,019	0.6
20	South Indian Bank	83,034	0.6	64,439	0.6
21	Tamilnad Mercantile Bank	36,825	0.3	27,716	0.3
22	Yes Bank	1,05,364	0.8	1,71,443	1.7
	All PSBs	41,59,044	29.8	36,25,154	35.2

Source: *Statistical Tables Relating to Banks in India*, 2019–20, downloaded from RBI website, www.rbi.org.in.

Note: Deposits and advances are in INR crore. *Share of deposits of bank as a percentage of total deposits of all commercial banks. †Share of advances of bank as a percentage of total advances of all commercial banks.

This suggests that the banking sector reforms during the post-reform period have created a level playing field in Indian banking. The new entrants—that is, NPBs—have been able to compete with the incumbent PSBs, and two of them found place among the top five banks in 2021–22. This is, as mentioned, despite the merger of several PSBs.

Overall, it has been observed in the recent years that the share of PSBs is declining and that of IPBs increasing commensurately in the banking business (Table 2.4). However, it is the new entrants that have primarily contributed to the rising share of IPBs. Among the 22 IPBs listed in Table 2.3(b), the number of NPBs is 9. These are Axis Bank, Bandhan Bank, HDFC Bank, ICICI Bank, IDBI Bank, IDFC First Bank, IndusInd Bank, Kotak Mahindra Bank and Yes Bank. Together they accounted for 85.3 per cent of the advances and 83.5 per cent of the deposits of all IPBs as on 31 March 2020.

The NPBs introduced modern banking in several respects, including computerisation and digital banking, flexible and customer-friendly deposit and loan products, modern banking premises, superior business models, and so on. They even provided longer banking hours. ICICI Bank was the first bank to introduce 8.00 a.m.–8.00 p.m. banking in several of its branches in the early 2000s. With lucrative pay packages, they attract managers with better skills and competency. As a result, they have rapidly expanded their business volume as compared to incumbent PSBs and IPBs.

2.5.3 Foreign Banks

As indicated in the previous section, India adopted a liberal policy towards foreign banks during the post-reform period. Correspondingly, there has been a gradual increase in the presence of foreign banks in the country. As on 31 March 2020, 46 foreign banks were operating in India. They together accounted for 4.2 per cent of the advances and 4.9 per cent of the deposits of all SCBs. Table 2.3(c) lists the top 20 foreign banks in descending order of their share in advances.

It may be observed from Table 2.3(c) that the share of individual foreign banks in the overall banking business in India is miniscule. None of them have a share in advances or deposits more than 1 per cent. Moreover, out of 46 foreign banks, the top five accounted for close to 70 per cent of the total banking business of the entire group. This reflects the insignificant share of the rest of the foreign banks. Nevertheless, these foreign banks play an important role in supporting foreign trade and investment with their home countries.

2.5.4 Small Finance Banks and Payments Banks

Apart from the mainstream banks discussed in the previous paragraphs, recently small finance banks and payments banks have been established to

Table 2.3 (c) Deposits and advances of top 20 foreign banks as on 31 March 2020

S. No.	Bank	Deposits	Percentage share*	Advances	Percentage share†
1	HSBC	1,24,903	0.89	76,581	0.74
2	Standard Chartered Bank	1,00,395	0.72	76,214	0.74
3	Citibank	1,57,869	1.13	66,508	0.65
4	Deutsche Bank	59,910	0.43	51,068	0.50
5	Bank of America	39,638	0.28	23,589	0.23
6	DBS Bank	35,652	0.26	19,131	0.19
7	BNP Paribas	21,256	0.15	14,924	0.14
8	JPMorgan Chase	28,386	0.20	14,683	0.14
9	MUFG Bank	19,585	0.14	13,251	0.13
10	Sumitomo Mitsui Banking Corporation	14,480	0.10	10,920	0.11
11	Barclays Bank	14,439	0.10	10,284	0.10
12	Mizuho Bank	14,506	0.10	9,416	0.09
13	Shinhan Bank	7,634	0.05	7,356	0.07
14	Credit Agricole	6,551	0.05	5,041	0.05
15	American Express	2,129	0.02	3,987	0.04
16	Australia and New Zealand Banking Group	4,548	0.03	3,265	0.03
17	Rabobank	4,637	0.03	2,532	0.02
18	Woori Bank	3,511	0.03	2,134	0.02
19	Bank of Nova Scotia	3,381	0.02	1,807	0.02
20	Bank of Bahrain and Kuwait	2,641	0.02	1,580	0.02
	All Foreign Banks	6,84,289	4.90	4,28,072	4.16

Source: Statistical Tables Relating to Banks in India, 2019–20, downloaded from RBI website, www.rbi.org.in.

Note: Deposits and advances are in INR crore. *Share of deposits of bank as a percentage of total deposits of all commercial banks. †Share of advances of bank as a percentage of total advances of all commercial banks.

meet small-scale financing requirements of customers. In 2017, two small finance banks were set up with the basic objective of providing small loans, deposits, insurance, and so on, to low-income individuals and underserved communities. The number of small finance banks had increased to 11 in

2021–22. Their combined share in the advances of all SCBs was nearly 1.1 per cent. Similarly, India Post Payments Bank was established in 2020 as the first payment bank to provide basic banking services like deposit taking, fund transfers, net banking and issue of ATM or debit cards. A total of four payment banks operated in 2021–22. Their combined share in the total deposits of SCBs was quite insignificant at 0.1 per cent. Given the miniscule proportion of the banking business undertaken by small finance banks and payment banks, as also the limited scope of their banking operations, we shall not refer to such entities in the remaining part of this book. We shall confine to mainstream commercial banks, namely PSBs, IPBs and foreign banks.

2.6 Progress of Banking in India

The banking sector in India has made significant progress in various dimensions over time. First, following bank nationalisation (since 1969), there was rapid growth in banking. As indicated earlier, the number of bank branches and volume of advances and deposits witnessed multifold expansion. Second, the post-reform period (since the early 1990s) has seen improvement in safety and soundness along with acceleration in volume of the banking business. Moreover, this period has also seen banks acquiring operational autonomy, introduction of innovative and customer-friendly banking products, digital banking and use of ITES, adoption of international best practices in banking regulation and supervision, and so on. In Chapter 11, a detailed analysis is presented on the performance of banks. It is observed that the post-reform period has helped in improving profitability, productivity and operational efficiency. In many parameters, PSBs have outperformed even the NPBs. However, as regards allocative efficiency, the performance of banks in India has not been encouraging.

In the following paragraphs, an attempt is made to provide a quick review of the progress of banking in India as compared to overall economic activity.

Figure 2.3 presents bank credit and deposits as a percentage of GDP in India since 1950–51. This reflects progress in the volume of the banking business in relation to the economy. The ratio of bank credit to GDP has gradually increased from less than 10 per cent in the early 1950s to more than 50 per cent in recent years (Figure 2.3). The expansion of bank deposits is even faster. The ratio of bank deposits to GDP has progressively risen from around 10 per cent in the early 1950s to nearly 70 per cent in the recent years.

Moreover, Figure 2.3 also suggests that the pace of progress in banking in relation to the economy has not been that smooth; rather, it has involved a couple of significant jumps. For example, the ratio of bank credit to GDP hovered around 10 per cent until the mid-1970s and witnessed a slow and gradual increase. The ratio touched close to the 20 per cent level in the late 1970s and stayed at around the same point for the next two decades. The period of 2000–10 witnessed a quite rapid rise in the ratio. It jumped from 21.7 per cent in 1999–2000 to 50.1 per cent in 2009–10. During the entire 2010s, the ratio remained close to the 50 per cent mark. The ratio of bank deposits to GDP also reflects a similar pattern, but the path of progress has been relatively smooth.

First, it may be emphasised that the Indian economy has experienced faster growth since the 1990s (post-reform period) compared to the first three decades after independence. The rising ratio of bank credit and deposits with respect to GDP suggests even higher growth of bank credit and deposits as compared to that of the economy.

Second, within the broad trend of bank deposits and credit in relation to GDP, the performance of different bank groups is not uniform. There are differences in the business model, operational details, client base and variety of products across bank groups such as PSBs, IPBs and foreign banks. Accordingly, there are changing shares in advances and deposits for PSBs

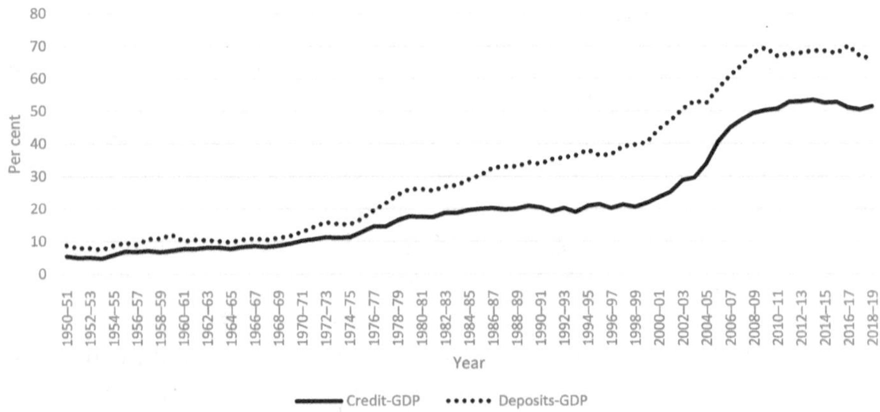

Figure 2.3 Trend of bank credit and deposits as percentage of GDP

Source: Prepared by the author based on data obtained from RBI's *Handbook of Statistics on Indian Economy*, https://data.rbi.org.in/DBIE/#/dbie/reports/Publication/Time-Series%20Publications/Handbook%20of%20Statistics%20on%20the%20Indian%20Economy (accessed 24 June 2022).

versus IPBs as highlighted in the previous section. In Table 2.4, the broad trends in shares of different bank groups in overall deposits and bank credit are provided since 1969.

It may be observed that since 1980, there has been a declining trend in the share of PSBs in both overall deposits and bank credit. Until 1990, the drop in the share of PSBs was relatively slow but became prominent during the post-reform period. For example, the drop in their share in the overall bank credit of SCBs was 3.6 percentage points between 1980 and 1990 as compared to 10.2 percentage points between 1990 and 2000 and 15.8 percentage points between 2010 and 2020 (Table 2.4). A similar pattern was observed for the changing share of PSBs in deposits too.

With the liberal entry of private banks, the share of IPBs in overall deposits and credit witnessed an increasing trend during the post-reform period. Largely, the fall in the share of PSBs was compensated by the rise in the share of IPBs. As noted in the previous section, Table 2.4 also reveals that mainly NPBs contributed to the bulk of the increasing share of IPBs. The share of foreign banks did not change significantly.

Third, we can observe variations in lending patterns across different bank groups. This can be derived from the movement of the credit–deposit ratio which measures the proportion of bank deposits deployed as bank credit.

Table 2.4 Percentage share in total deposits and credit of SCBs

	1969	1975	1980	1985	1990	1995	2000	2005	2010	2015	2020
Bank deposits											
PSBs	83.5	84.1	90.8	90.2	88.5	82.6	79.2	74.6	74.5	73.0	63.0
Foreign banks					5.0	7.5	5.5	4.6	5.2	4.6	4.8
IPBs	16.5	15.9	8.7	8.4	4.1	6.9	11.6	17.4	17.3	19.4	29.0
of which											
NPBs							*5.0*	*11.2*	*12.6*	*14.7*	*25.1*
Bank credit											
PSBs	84.1	85.3	90.4	89.1	86.8	82.6	76.4	71.1	74.4	70.9	58.6
Foreign banks					6.2	7.6	8.1	6.7	5.1	5.1	4.1
IPBs	15.9	14.7	8.7	8.6	3.7	6.9	12.5	19.3	18.0	21.3	34.5
of which											
NPBs							*4.5*	*13.5*	*13.3*	*17.0*	*30.2*

Source: *Statistical Tables Relating to Banks in India*, various issues, downloaded from RBI website, www.rbi.org.in.

Table 2.5 Bank-group-wise credit–deposit ratios

	2000	2005	2010	2015	2020
SBI and associates*	50.35	56.31	77.43	82.07	68.06
Nationalised banks	46.38	61.17	71.33	73.77	
Foreign banks	72.21	87.18	70.34	80.85	62.56
IPBs	49.04	70.34	76.86	86.36	87.16
of which					
NPBs	*50.27*	*77.61*	*80.68*	*88.92*	*99.83*

Source: Statistical Tables Relating to Banks in India, various issues, downloaded from RBI website, www.rbi.org.in.

Note: *For 2020, the figure pertains to PSBs.

The other major alternative for banks is to utilise their deposits in the form of investments, mainly in government securities. Bank credit earns higher interest as compared to government securities. A higher credit–deposit ratio reflects aggressive banking. As regards the movement of the credit–deposit ratio, we observe the following from Table 2.5:

- Both PSBs and IPBs had a similar credit–deposit ratio of around 50 per cent in 1999–2000. This was the period when the Indian economy witnessed moderate growth of around 5 per cent or so. With acceleration of the economy during 2003–08, when India had a dream run registering economic growth of close to 9 per cent, there was a significant rise in the credit–deposit ratio.
- The rise in the credit–deposit ratio was faster for IPBs as compared to PSBs. This reflects aggressive banking mainly by NPBs which to led three of them finding place in the top-five banks of India in 2019–20.
- However, with incidence of high NPAs, there was a relative slowdown in lending by PSBs, and their credit–deposit ratio declined to 68.1 per cent in 2019–20. On the contrary, IPBs continued their aggressive lending, achieving a credit–deposit ratio of 87.2 per cent in 2019–20.

2.7 Conclusion

This chapter has provided a broad introduction to the Indian financial system and its key components such as various forms of financial markets and financial institutions, including different types of banks and NBFCs. It has highlighted that commercial banks enjoy overwhelming dominance in the entire financial system. This was followed by a brief account of the evolution of commercial banking in India from a historical perspective. Two particular events, namely the bank nationalisation of 1969 and wide-ranging reforms since the early 1990s, found special mention. The first helped in the massive expansion of banking in the country. The second strengthened safety and soundness and expanded the scope of banking in several respects along with significant acceleration of the banking business in India. The post-reform period witnessed NPBs emerging as leading players in the industry despite the overall dominance of government-owned banks.

Revision Questions and Problems

1. Write a short note on the key segments of the capital market in India.
2. What is the major distinction between financial markets and financial institutions as regards their role in the mobilisation of savings and capital formation in a financial system?
3. Compare the advantages to a firm or borrower in raising funds for setting up a factory by selling equity shares versus corporate bonds.
4. What are the different constituents of the Indian banking sector? How important are commercial banks amongst them?
5. What are the different categories of commercial banks operating in India distinguished in terms of ownership? Briefly compare the performance of these banking categories or groups during the post-reform period.
6. Using information on the number of bank branches and volume of deposits and advances, narrate how banking services in India witnessed spectacular growth after the bank nationalisation of 1969.
7. Briefly discuss the history of evolution of PSBs in India.
8. Explain the rationale for the following banking sector reforms during the post-reform period towards strengthening Indian banks in a market-oriented environment:
   (*a*) reduction of SLR and CRR to relieve banks from the statutory pre-emption of banking resources;

(*b*) deregulation of interest rates on loans and deposits;
(*c*) liberal entry of IPBs and foreign banks; and
(*d*) promotion of computerisation in the banking sector.

9. How do you see the impact of liberal entry of new private banks on the Indian banking system?

Part II

Banks and the Economy

3

The Role of Banks in an Economy

Learning Objectives

- To highlight the proximate causes of economic growth in the long-run based on theories of growth and particularly to underscore the role of savings
- To explain the role of banks in mobilisation of savings and augmentation of capital formation by resolving size and maturity mismatches in the preferences of savers vis-à-vis those of borrowers
- To explain the role of banks in mobilisation of savings and augmentation of capital formation by moderating risks in lending through gaining expertise in risk management and risk diversification
- To underscore the role of banks in resolving the problem of information asymmetry in the credit market and facilitating its efficient functioning
- To emphasise on the role of banks as the backbone of the payment and settlement system in an economy
- To empirically assess the role of banks towards mobilisation of savings and support of economic growth

3.1 Introduction

The state of the economy of a country is characterised by several indicators such as GDP, consumer price index (CPI), balance of payments (BOP), money stock, government expenditure, savings and investment, interest rate, and so on. Such indicators represent different aspects of an economy. For example, BOP captures international transaction of goods and services as also cross-border capital flows. CPI is a proxy for general prices. Amongst all these,

GDP is the most important indicator and popularly used as a barometer to measure the size of economic activity in a country. It captures the sum of market values of all final[1] goods and services produced in a country during a particular period such as a year or a quarter. Standard macroeconomics textbooks[2] provide details about the concept and measurement of such indicators.

GDP is treated as a proxy for the total amount of income generated in an economy. Owners of capital and land, suppliers of raw materials and other factors of production such as workers, entrepreneurs, and so on, earn their income by participating in the production of goods and services. The total revenue earned from the sale of goods and services produced is distributed amongst these stakeholders. For producing more output, higher number of workers, larger amount of capital and raw material, and so on, are required. Accordingly, more output entails generation of more aggregate income for all the stakeholders who participated in the production process.

Furthermore, one spends one's income on various goods and services so that one can maximise one's utility or satisfaction by consuming goods and services in as much quantity as possible. More consumption leads to more satisfaction. This is under the assumption of positive marginal utility[3] from consumption of goods and services irrespective of the amount consumed. To gain maximum satisfaction, the entire amount of income earned by participating in the production process should get completely exhausted in buying various goods and services.[4] In other words, more income generated

---

[1] Final goods and services are directly consumed while intermediate goods and services are used as inputs to produce final goods and services. The same good can be final or intermediate depending on the context. For example, if wheat flour is used to make *chapati* for domestic consumption, it is a final good. On the contrary, if wheat flour is used as an input by a baker to manufacture bread, it is an intermediate good.

[2] See, for example, Barro (2008); Karlan and Morduch (2021); Mankiw (2010).

[3] Marginal utility is the amount of utility derived from consumption of the last unit of a good or service.

[4] In a dynamic analysis in which an individual lives for more than one year or a specific period, she will not consume her entire income in the current year or relevant period. Rather she will save a part of the income to facilitate future consumption in the consumption smoothening process. Incorporating such dynamic analysis will make our discussion more complicated but the main conclusions of the static analysis can be maintained.

from the production of higher level of output is translated to more expenditure on goods and services.

Thus, GDP which measures the market value of all final goods and services produced in an economy is a proxy for the total income generated as also equal to the aggregate expenditure incurred on various goods and services in a particular period—say, a year. As the amount of consumption of goods and services is a barometer to measure the standard of living, one can use the GDP of a country as an indicator of its national economic welfare.

However, use of GDP for assessing individual economic welfare or standard of living in a country may be misleading. A vastly populated country may have a larger GDP, but its per head consumption will be lower. For example, the GDP of India was much higher at USD 2.66 trillion in 2020 as compared to USD 0.75 trillion for Switzerland. But the per capita GDP of India at USD 1,928 in 2020 was much lower than USD 87,367 for Switzerland. This is because India had a population of 1.38 billion in 2020 while that of Switzerland was 8.67 million. For this reason, while comparing economic welfare or the standard of living across nations, economists use per capita GDP or income as the most popular indicator.

In a way, the fundamental quest in the study of economics is to understand the long-term trend and determinants of the per capita income of a country. First, it helps to gain insight into how the standard of living has progressed over time. Second, and more importantly, we learn how to engineer appropriate public policy initiatives so that a higher standard of living can be achieved.

In Figure 3.1, the historical pattern of per capita income[5] for India since 1950–51 is depicted. It suggests that during the first three decades of independence,[6] the trajectory of per capita income was relatively flat. This was the period when India experienced comparatively slow economic growth at around 3.5 per cent per annum. The average annual growth of per capita income from 1951–52 to 1980–81 was 1.4 per cent. It became relatively steeper during the post-reform period, when per capita income grew at a faster rate of around 4.6 per cent on average.

---

[5] Per capita net national income at constant prices (base year: 2011–12) is used as a measure of per capita income.

[6] India became politically independent from British colonial rule in 1947.

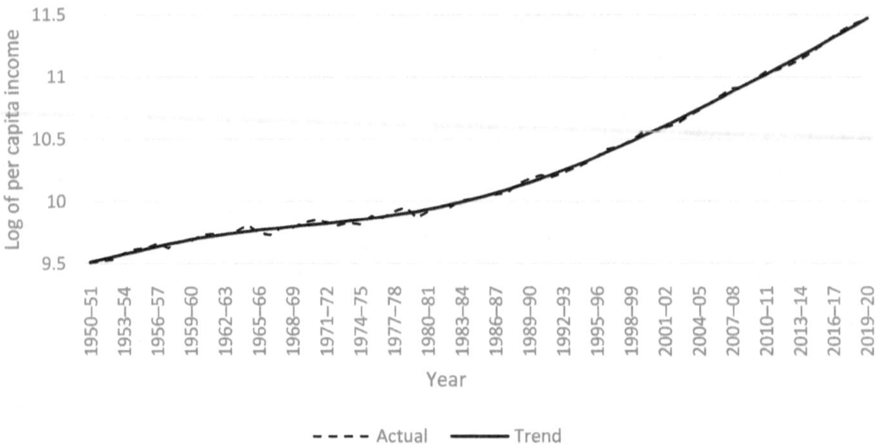

Figure 3.1 Historical trend of per capita income in India

Source: Calculated by the author based on data obtained from RBI's *Handbook of Statistics on Indian Economy*, https://data.rbi.org.in/DBIE/#/dbie/reports/Publication/Time-Series%20 Publications/Handbook%20of%20Statistics%20on%20the%20Indian%20Economy (accessed 24 June 2022).

Note: The data pertain to the log of per capita income (net national income) at constant prices. The trend is obtained by applying the Hodrick–Prescott filter to the log of per capita income.

In this chapter, we explain the role of banks in shaping the long-term path of prosperity in an economy, borrowing ideas from economic growth theories. Such theories emphasise addition to factories and equipment, expansion of the number of workers, and improvement in the technology of production and skill of workers to explain long-term growth. The amount of savings mobilised in an economy is the key determinant for augmenting investment, which is nothing but an increase in factories and equipment. Banks play a critical role in any country in promoting savings mobilisation and converting such savings into productive investment. Therefore, the role of banks in promoting long-term prosperity cannot be overemphasised.

Apart from these aspects, there is another important dimension to the role of banks in modern society. Banks constitute the core of the payment and settlement system. Currency and banking channels backed by deposits are used as the medium of payment for various purchases and settlements of debt. Banks and their branches form the major conduit through which currency issued by the RBI is distributed to the public. Moreover, a vast share of transactions and settlements of debt are carried out using banking channels such as cheques, credit and debit cards, electronic transfers, and so on.

Thus, the paramount role of banks in an economy can be explained in terms of their relevance for facilitating economic growth through promotion of savings and investment and functioning as the mainstay of the payment and settlement system. In this chapter, we highlight these aspects.

The chapter is organised as follows. In section 3.2, we begin by briefly providing essential insights on the determinants of long-term economic growth and highlight the crucial role of banks in augmenting savings and economic prosperity based on theories of growth. In section 3.3, we explain how banks facilitate mobilisation of savings and augment capital formation resolving the size and maturity mismatches in the preferences of savers versus those of borrowers or investors. The role of banks in resolving the problem of information asymmetry and helping efficient functioning of the credit market is discussed in section 3.4. Diversification of asset portfolios and consequent risk mitigation by banks is covered in section 3.5. The pivotal role of banks as the backbone of the payment and settlement system is narrated in section 3.6. Finally, relevant discussion linking bank deposits, savings rates and the growth of per capita income based on Indian data is presented in section 3.7. The broad conclusions of this chapter are set out in section 3.8.

3.2 Theories of Economic Growth and the Role of Banks

In economics, growth theories explain the various factors determining the long-term pattern of economic progress. Neoclassical growth theories suggest that growth in per capita output (income) in an economy is mainly explained by accumulation of per head capital and improvement in technology of production. This can be derived from the standard production function as given below:

$$Y = A\,f(K, L) \tag{3.1}$$

In equation 3.1, Y stands for output, A stands for total factor productivity (TFP), and K and L represent stock of capital and labour, respectively. Finally, f denotes the general functional form, relating output to capital and labour.

Let us assume that the equation satisfies all standard assumptions of the neoclassical production function such as constant returns to scale[7] in K and L, positive but diminishing marginal productivity[8] of K and L and Inada conditions.[9] The property of constant returns to scale suggests that by changing both capital and labour by a given proportion, output will vary by the same proportion. This can be explained as follows:

$$\lambda Y = A\, f(\lambda K, \lambda L) \tag{3.2}$$

In equation 3.2, if we multiply both K and L by λ, then the output Y is also multiplied by λ. For example, if $\lambda = 2$, it implies that doubling of K and L each leads to doubling of Y.

If we assume $\lambda = 1/L$, then equation 3.2 can be modified as $(1/L)Y = A\, f(K/L, L/L)$. The same can be rewritten as

$$y = A\, f(k) \tag{3.3}$$

where y is per capita output and k is per capita capital.

Thus, using the assumption of constant returns to scale, we can transform the production function in aggregate form in equation 3.1 to per capita form as given in equation 3.3. The last equation suggests that per capita output is determined by TFP and per capita capital. In other words, change in per capita output (y) is determined by two factors, namely (*a*) technological change and (*b*) change in per capita capital (k).

While neoclassical growth theories treat technological improvement as exogenous, endogenous growth theories explain the process of technological progress within underlying economic growth dynamics. Readers may refer to standard textbooks on theories of economic growth for further details.[10]

---

[7] Returns to scale captures change in Y due to simultaneous change in both K and L by a constant proportion.

[8] Marginal productivity of K captures changes in Y due to a unit change in K, keeping L constant. Similarly, marginal productivity of L captures changes in Y due to a unit change in L, keeping K constant.

[9] $\lim_{K\to 0} \frac{\partial Y}{\partial K} = \infty$ *and* $\lim_{K\to\infty} \frac{\partial Y}{\partial K} = 0$ and $\lim_{L\to 0} \frac{\partial Y}{\partial L} = \infty$ *and* $\lim_{L\to\infty} \frac{\partial Y}{\partial L} = 0$

[10] See Acemoglu (2009) and Barro and Sala-i-Martin (2004).

Per head capital at any point of time in turn is determined by investment rate, depreciation rate and growth rate of the population. Investment adds to capital stock as by definition investment is change in the capital stock in the current period over that in the previous period. On the contrary, depreciation rate captures the wear and tear of capital stock while in use in the production of goods and services. The growth rate of the population is important as higher population causes lower per head capital.

3.2.1 Role of Savings in Growth Theories

It is important to note that the investment rate in an economy is critically determined by the savings rate. More savings facilitate availability of higher amount of funds to buy more machines and equipment and set up more factories.

The growth theories discussed in the preceding paragraphs also assume that capital is subject to diminishing marginal productivity. This suggests that as increasing amounts of capital are added to the economy, the incremental output for each successive additional unit of capital gradually declines. Lower incremental output leads to lower incremental savings. This is because savings are dependent on income (output). A steady fall in incremental investment caused by falling incremental savings further reduces incremental output. The spiral effects decelerate growth in per capita output as the economy becomes more capital intensive.[11] The economy keeps growing in per capita terms as long as the net addition to per capita capital outweighs the depreciation. This phase is technically termed as the *transitory phase.*

With a gradual decline in the rate of incremental per capita investment, a stage will come when the net addition to capital is exactly equal to the depreciation (the rate of which is assumed to be a constant). At such stage, growth in per capita output ceases as per capita capital stock becomes stationary. This state is known as the *steady state.*

Figure 3.2 shows both the transitory phase and the steady state in the process of economic growth. The *X*-axis depicts k and *Y*-axis represents both investment and depreciation. Investment is equal to savings in a closed economy.[12] Per capita investment and savings are given by $s.\mathrm{f}(k)$. Here, s is the

[11] This happens as per capita capital gradually increases.

[12] In a closed economy, we do not consider existence of cross-border capital flows. Otherwise, if there are net foreign investment inflows into the domestic economy,

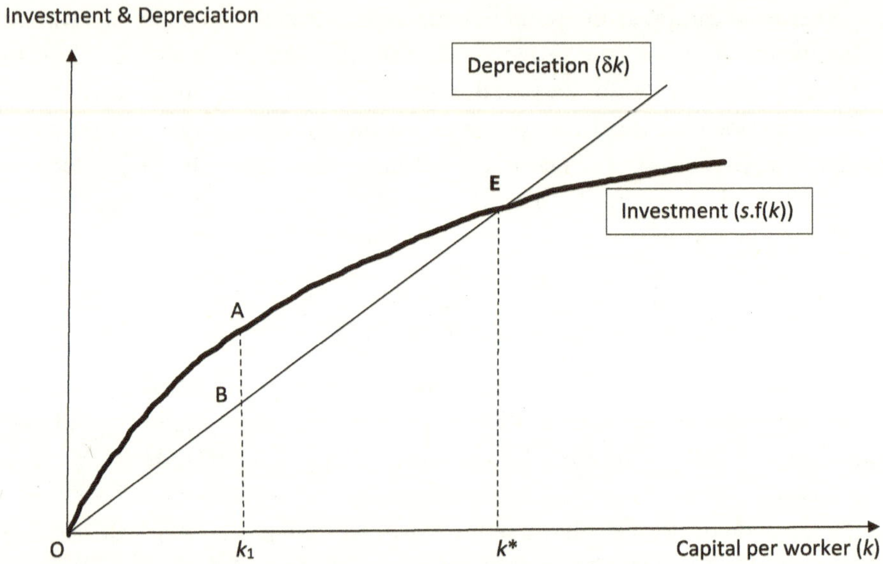

Figure 3.2 Transitory and steady state of economic growth

Source: Prepared by the author.

savings rate and f(k) is the per capita output. The investment is represented by the upward sloping curve. The depreciation is given by δk, where δ is the depreciation rate. The upward sloping line represents the depreciation. All are in per capita terms. The vertical difference between the bold curve and the line measures the net addition to k. This is the difference between the gross investment and depreciation. At per capita capital k_1, the net addition to capital is given by the vertical line segment AB.

It may be observed from Figure 3.2 that for any level of per capita capital less than k^* (to the left of k^*), the investment is higher than the depreciation. So there is net addition to the capital stock. In other words, the growth rate of k is positive. From equation 3.3, we can infer that for such values of k, the growth rate of per capita output or income is also positive. Thus, when the economy's k is within the range of 0 to k^*, the economy is in a transitory phase. In this phase, both k and y experience positive growth.

---

then domestic investment is the sum of domestic savings and net foreign investment inflows. The latter represents net foreign savings used by the host country for domestic investment.

At k^*, the per capita investment and depreciation exactly match. Thus, at k^*, the net addition to k is 'zero'. So y does not change. Hence, at k^*, the economy is said to be at the steady state. Please note that while per capita output does not grow at the steady state, aggregate output can exhibit positive growth as long as there is positive population growth.[13]

However, technological progress (increase in TFP) can help an economy to overcome stagnation in per capita income even at high levels of k and can induce perpetual growth in y.

For our discussion, what is important is to underscore the role of banks in this growth process. Particularly, our focus is on how banks help augment savings and investment in an economy.

From the perspectives of the growth theories discussed in the previous paragraphs, savings play a critical role in promoting economic prosperity. In the transitory phase, increase in the savings rate[14] leads to increase in the per capita stock of capital[15] which in turn augments per capita income. As the economy reaches the steady state, the per capita capital and income cease to grow. But even in the steady state, any reduction in the savings rate will cause a plunge in the per capita capital and hence will lead to a fall in per capita income.

3.2.2 Role of Banks in Promoting Savings and Economic Growth

Banks play a vital role in the mobilisation of domestic savings and conversion of these savings into productive investments in factories and machines. The special role of banks in this regard can be explained in the following ways:

- Banks as financial intermediaries solve the problem of size and maturity mismatches between the preferences of savers and those of borrowers. Without banks, contradictory preferences of savers vis-à-vis those of borrowers would have ceased mobilisation of savings and undermined productive investment.

[13] Per capita output is the ratio of aggregate output and population. In other words, aggregate output is the product of per capita output and population. Hence, the growth rate of aggregate output is the sum of the growth rate of per capita output and that of population.

[14] Savings rate is defined as the ratio between aggregate domestic savings and GDP.

[15] This is for a given depreciation rate and population growth rate.

- Lending entails various types of risks, mainly the risk of default by the borrower. The problem of *information asymmetry* and associated issues of *adverse selection* and *moral hazard* have the potential of causing market failure in the lending business. Banks with their expertise in credit appraisal and monitoring and possessing rich information on a large pool of borrowers overcome the problem of information asymmetry and make lending a viable business activity.
- Banks use their vast pool of deposits for lending to diversified business activities and a wide range of borrowers. The diversified portfolio of loans reduces the overall risk in lending as explained by the financial portfolio theory.[16]

These points are elaborated in the following sections.

3.3 Role of Banks in Resolving Size and Maturity Mismatches

Savings and investment play a critical role in achieving and sustaining economic growth in a long-term perspective as discussed in the preceding section. Higher domestic savings support higher investment, and installation of more machines and factories helps in producing more output. Banks facilitate mobilisation of savings and promote investment by reconciling differences in the preferences of savers vis-a-vis those of borrowers. Such differences in preferences can be in the form of size and maturity mismatches.

The size or amount of savings of each individual saver is often quite small compared to that of loan required by a borrower. For example, for buying an apartment, a borrower may require INR 50 lakh. For setting up a factory, an entrepreneur may need INR 1,000 crore. On the other hand, an individual saver usually saves a couple of thousands or lakhs at any point of time. In the absence of banks, borrowers seeking funds for buying an apartment or setting up a factory would have to approach a large number of savers individually. This process would be tedious and require much time and effort. Moreover, there is high probability that many savers may not have adequate familiarity with the borrowers. Without proper acquaintance and trust, they may not be forthcoming in lending. In that case, neither can savings be mobilised

[16] The portfolio theory suggests that by combining assets of different risk characteristics, the overall risk in the portfolio of assets can be minimised for a given return.

nor potential investments undertaken. Banks as intermediaries collect small savings of numerous savers, and the pooled savings facilitate meeting the large borrowing requirements of home loan seekers or entrepreneurs. Thus, banks bridge the size mismatch inherent in saving versus borrowing.

Similarly, there is a contradiction in maturity period preferences of savers versus those of borrowers. Savers prefer a shorter maturity period for their savings. They want to retain the option to withdraw their savings on demand. On the contrary, borrowers prefer to pay back their loan over a longer maturity duration. For example, a home loan seeker would like to pay back their loan over 20 or 25 years. Paying back the loan in a year or two may not be feasible for them; otherwise they would have waited a couple of years to buy the home out of their own resources rather seeking a loan.

In the absence of banks, savers with shorter maturity preferences on their savings would not have lent out to a home loan seeker requiring a longer period for loan repayment. This would have undermined realisation of savings and investments in the economy. Banks resolve such maturity mismatches by providing the opportunity for savers to deposit their savings with a shorter maturity option while meeting the requirement of longer maturity preferences of borrowers. The theoretical work by the Nobel laureates of 2022 in economics, Douglas Diamond and Philip Dybvig, has provided detailed insights into how banks offer liquid instruments to savers in the form of bank deposits on the one hand, while on the other they also meet the long-term financing requirements of borrowers (Diamond and Dybvig, 1983). Banks turn the liquid assets (bank deposits) of savers into illiquid assets through their lending.

Thus, by resolving the size and maturity mismatches in the preferences of savers versus those of borrowers, banks facilitate augmentation of savings and investments in an economy. As suggested by various growth theories, mobilisation of savings and augmentation of capital stocks are critical for ensuring long-term economic prosperity. This underscores the useful role of banks towards supporting economic progress.

3.4 Role of Banks in Resolving the Problem of Information Asymmetry in the Credit Market

The issue of *information asymmetry* is popularly explained by using the 'problem of lemons' (also known as the 'problem of lemons and peaches') propounded by Nobel laureate economist George A. Akerlof (1970). For the smooth functioning of markets, both buyers and sellers should have full information about the product under consideration. In some cases, like the old car market, the buyer is not fully aware of the quality and condition of a used car while the seller (user) may have the accurate information. Without full information, the buyer may not be willing to pay the appropriate price for a good-quality used car while the existing car owner may not be interested in selling it at an unreasonably low price. This may lead to market failure. The product will remain unsold as the price offered by the buyer does not match the price demanded by the seller.

The credit market or market for loanable funds in an economy plays an important role in augmenting its prosperity. Let us understand this with a simple example. Say, a couple of budding entrepreneurs or a start-up contemplate setting up a factory for manufacturing robots which can assist in day-to-day household work. The funding requirements for the project may run into, say, INR 1,000 crore. But the entrepreneurs in this case may have their own resources of, say, only INR 100 crore. They require a loan from the credit market to meet the remaining funding requirement of INR 900 crore. If the credit market helps them in obtaining the loan, their plan to set up the factory to manufacture robots can materialise. Society benefits from using robots as household help. The entrepreneurs can earn profits from their business. The production of robots can create employment for a large number of engineers and workers. Raw material suppliers and ancillary service providers such as transport operators, security agencies, and so on, can also benefit in the process. Even the government can gain from tax collection from the income and profit earned by all the stakeholders in the process of production and sale of robots.

However, similar to the market for the used car, the credit market also encounters the problem of information asymmetry. The borrowers and lenders are the two sets of principal players in this market. The budding entrepreneurs or potential borrowers would have better familiarity with the profit potential of the robot manufacturing business. They would also know if they intend to default on the loan wilfully. On the contrary, individual lenders (savers) may have limited expertise for appropriately assessing the profit potential of robot making. The majority of them would be ordinary households engaged in farming, teaching, government services, factories, self-employment, and so on. They would also not be experts in reading the mind of the borrowers to assess their sincerity and intention to pay back the loan. Further, individual lenders may not have adequate time and expertise to monitor the end-use of the funds by the borrowers.

Thus, in the credit market, there is information asymmetry between lenders and borrowers. In the absence of adequate information about the profit potential of proposed projects and credit quality of borrowers, risk-averse lenders would insist on imposing high-risk premiums to cover potential mistakes of wrong selection. This would end in higher interest rates being charged to all borrowers. The situation is similar to potential buyers of used cars having reservations over paying the price demanded by the car seller, being unaware of the actual condition of the cars. The owners of good-quality used cars fail to find suitable buyers, and the market fails. Similarly, high creditworthy borrowers find it unreasonable to pay higher interest rates demanded by lenders due to high-risk premiums. In such circumstances, the credit market fails to function. High creditworthy borrowers with potentially profitable projects do not get loans, and society fails to exploit the inherent benefits from production and consumption.

In the aforementioned example, if the budding entrepreneurs fail to obtain loans for INR 900 crore due to the information asymmetry problem in the credit market, their plan to produce robots would not materialise. Consequently, the various benefits to the different stakeholders as discussed would also not be realised. This would be a potential loss for society as a whole.

Fortunately, banks enter here to the rescue of society by resolving the problem of information asymmetry in the credit market. They do so in the following ways:

- First, banks have vast exposure to a variety of borrowers engaged in a host of business activities and occupations. With long experience in the banking business, they possess reasonable expertise in the credit appraisal of loan seekers.
- Second, many loan applicants may have already engaged in some banking business in the past, and banks have the advantage of knowing the banking history of borrowers. Banks have less information asymmetry as compared to individual lenders or savers.
- Third, because of the exposure of banks to a variety of economic activities and borrowers, they possess information about prevailing economic and business conditions. Based on the rich historical data at their disposal, banks are better placed to objectively assess the

future business potential of different industries. This helps them to appropriately select borrowers and economic activities or industries to lend to.

- Fourth, banks continuously monitor the end-use of funds by borrowers. In case of default on loans, banks can gain management control and exercise power in the day-to-day business decisions of the (borrower) firm. This acts as a deterrent against default by borrower firms. Needless to mention, post-default recovery depends on economic and political institutions including the promptness and effectiveness of the regulatory authorities and judiciary. Nevertheless, banks stand in a better position to resolve the information asymmetry problem inherent in the credit market as compared to ordinary savers or lenders.

Thus, banks facilitate optimal functioning of the credit market by overcoming the problem of information asymmetry. In the process, they contribute to promoting production, income generation and overall economic welfare.

3.5 Risk Moderation in Lending through Diversification

As discussed earlier, with a large pool of savings available, banks have adequate scope to lend to a large section of borrowers. A bank's borrowers are spread across different regions. They are engaged in a variety of occupations or industries. Lessons from financial portfolio management suggest that the amount of risk embodied in a portfolio of diversified assets is lower than the sum of risks embodied in the individual assets which are the constituents of that portfolio. This can be explained with an example.

Let us assume that a bank has lent to six borrowers. Say, each borrower needs to pay back their loan over five years. The annual repayments of the loan or instalments (in lakh) for each borrower in this hypothetical example are given in Table 3.1. We can calculate the risk associated with each borrower from the variability or uncertainty of their annual loan repayments. A typical way of assessing uncertainty is by calculating the ratio of standard deviation (SD) to the mean of the stream of repayments.

In Table 3.1, the ratio of the SD to the mean for the respective borrowers is given in the 10th row. The ratio of the SD to the mean for the entire loan

Table 3.1 Calculation of risk in a loan portfolio

(Loan repayments in INR lakh)

Period of repayment	Borrower 1	Borrower 2	Borrower 3	Borrower 4	Borrower 5	Borrower 6	Overall portfolio
Year 1	7.2	21.3	12.3	10.6	8.1	23.4	82.9
Year 2	6.4	24.5	14.2	12.1	12.4	26.9	96.5
Year 3	9.1	18.6	11.6	9.3	6.9	10.4	65.9
Year 4	8.6	14.9	4.5	15.1	3.2	18.5	64.8
Year 5	4.5	20.1	13.9	8.2	14.6	21.2	82.5
Total repayment	*35.8*	*99.4*	*56.5*	*55.3*	*45.2*	*100.4*	*392.6*
Mean repayment	*7.2*	*19.9*	*11.3*	*11.1*	*9.0*	*20.1*	*78.5*
SD of repayments	*1.8*	*3.5*	*4.0*	*2.7*	*4.5*	*6.2*	*13.3*
Ratio of SD to mean	*0.26*	*0.18*	*0.35*	*0.24*	*0.50*	*0.31*	*0.17*

Source: Calculated by the author based on a hypothetical loan portfolio of a bank.

Note: SD stands for 'standard deviation'.

portfolio (all six borrowers) is given in the 10th row of the last column. It is calculated to be 0.17. It may be observed that this number is lower than the corresponding figure for any of the six borrowers. Among all the borrowers, Borrower 2 has the lowest risk with the ratio at 0.18. This shows that due to diversification of risk, the amount of risk embodied in the entire portfolio of six loans is lower than the amount of risk embodied in any of the constituent loans.

With exposure to a cross section of borrowers engaged in diversified economic activities, banks reduce the overall risk in their balance sheet. A potential loss due to adverse developments in a particular industry or region can be compensated by income from other industries or regions which perform well. Moreover, from dealing with a variety of borrowers and acquired expertise in processing loan applications and monitoring, banks enhance their scope for prudent lending. The theoretical work of Nobel laureate Douglas Diamond (1984) suggests that diversification improves the risk tolerance of banks for each loan. Banks mitigate the overall risk in lending due to risk diversification.

Reduced risk augments the safety and security of bank deposits and builds the confidence of savers in banks. Details about banking risks and related management issues are covered in Part III of this book.

3.6 Banks as the Backbone of the Payment and Settlement System

Prior to the invention of money, people exchanged one good or service for another to meet their day-to-day requirements. A farmer in need of milk bought it from the milkman in exchange for his farm produce, say, rice. A carpenter in need of a towel or *dhoti* got the same from a weaver by providing his services in making furniture. This system of exchanging one good or service against another is popularly known as the *barter system*. It prevailed in the past when the requirements of human beings were limited. The barter system was of course fraught with many deficiencies. First, there was the requirement of double coincidence of wants for the barter system to be functional. When the farmer seeks milk from the milkman, the milkman in turn should be ready to accept rice in exchange. This is explained in Figure 3.3(a).

However, in real life, a double coincidence of wants seldom occurs. The milkman in our case may not require rice and may demand cooking oil in exchange for milk from the farmer. Then the farmer has to first look for a trader who is ready to offer oil in exchange for his rice, after which the farmer can provide oil to the milkman to procure milk. This requires two transactions to facilitate exchange in three goods. Barter thus becomes a complicated process involving several goods and services from multiple suppliers. This is explained in Figure 3.3(b).

The second challenge that the barter system encounters is related to establishing exchange rates for each pair of goods and services. If rice is to

Figure 3.3 (a) Double coincidence of wants in the barter system

Source: Prepared by the author.

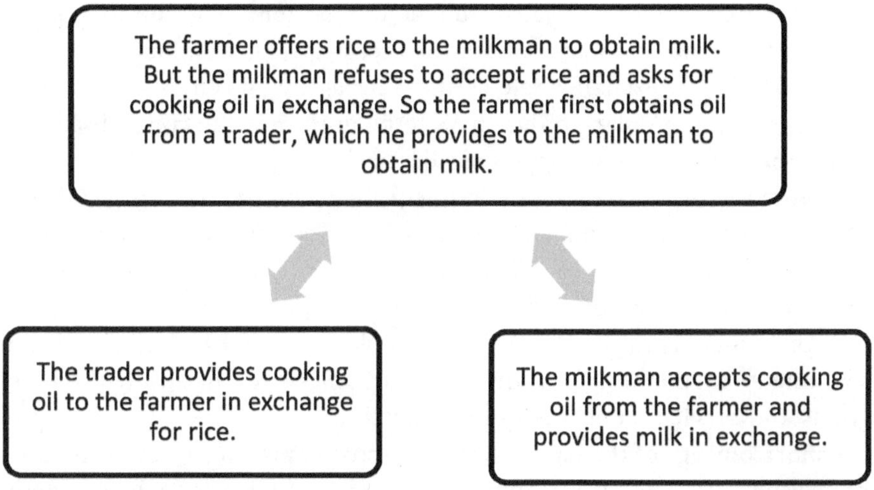

Figure 3.3 (b) Lack of double coincidence of wants in the barter system

Source: Prepared by the author.

be exchanged for milk under barter, both the farmer and the milkman need to determine the exchange rate of rice for milk—that is, the amount of rice to be exchanged for each litre of milk. For exchanging two products, the barter system requires one exchange rate. Exchanging three products—say, rice, milk and cooking oil—under barter requires fixing three exchange rates. These are the exchange rate between rice and milk, between milk and cooking oil and between rice and cooking oil.

If n number of goods and services are consumed in an economy, the first good needs to have n-1 exchange rates with the remaining goods and services; the second good needs n-2 exchange rates, and so on. In this manner, a total of $n(n-1)/2$ exchange rates are required if n goods are used in the economy under barter. Thus, if there are four goods traded in the economy using barter, it requires six exchange rates. It is not that difficult to remember six exchange rates. In the real world, however, people consume hundreds of goods and services. Even for dealing with 50 goods under barter, one has to remember 1,225 exchange rates which is almost impossible. This underscores the enormous challenges in a barter system and at the same time reflects how money is useful to society in facilitating transactions. The use of money requires just one exchange rate for each good purchased and sold. We buy different goods and services where the price of each of them is expressed in terms of rupees.

The third issue is related to standardisation. Not all apples are homogenous, and they vary in terms of size, shape, taste and texture. When we need to fix the exchange rate of one commodity for others, obviously all the units of a particular product have to be uniform and standardised. The fact of the matter is no two apples are identical.

Moreover, several commodities like fruits and vegetables are perishable. They cannot be stored for long periods for future exchange against other goods and services. It is also difficult to carry goods from one place to another to facilitate the process of exchange.

As human beings moved from simple lives in hamlets and tribal settlements to more modern towns and urban centres, naturally the set of goods and services consumed significantly expanded. In the backdrop of the shortcomings of the barter system discussed previously, the need for a new system of exchange was inevitable. Money as a common denominator to facilitate exchange of goods emerged as the obvious operative solution. Initially, commodities like seashells or precious metals were used as money. A common exchange rate for each good or service in terms of units of metals like copper, gold and silver resolved the problems encountered in the barter system. For example, certain ounces of gold were used to define one gold coin (one unit). Each good or service was expressed in terms of units of gold coins. This resolved the problem of double coincidence of wants as a farmer could buy milk using gold coins rather than carrying his rice to make an exchange. Each gold coin was identical and served as the unit of account. Moreover, gold coins emerged as an effective store of purchasing power and could be used for buying goods and services in the distant future. Such forms of money are popularly referred to as *commodity money*.

Thus, money emerged as a convenient medium of exchange, store of value and unit of account in ancient urban centres around the world. This facilitated the smooth progress of trade and commerce too. Bank cheques and currency notes issued by central banks like our RBI are widely used as the modern form of money for carrying out regular transactions and settlements of debt. They are known as *paper money*. Paper money replaced commodity money with its advantages of safety and convenience. Currency notes like an INR 500 note issued by the RBI are known as *fiat money*. They do not have any intrinsic value in themselves. People accept them as a medium of exchange because they are legal tender backed by the implicit mandate of the Government of India.

Small transactions such as buying fruits and vegetables or small household and stationery items, payment of bus fares, and so on, are carried out using currency. The RBI issues currency notes of various denominations such as INR 10, INR 20, INR 50, INR 100, INR 200 and INR 500. These currency notes reach the public mainly through various bank branches and their ATM units. On the other hand, high-value transactions such as the purchase of a car, a home, airline tickets, and so on, are generally carried out by issue of cheques, swiping credit or debit cards or online payment. All such transactions are carried out through the banking channel. Moreover, settlement of payments for transactions involving larger amounts (several thousands, lakhs or crores) across individuals and institutions takes place through the banking channel too. In this process, the bank account of the payer is debited by and that of payee is credited with the said amount. Many times the payer and the payee may hold deposit accounts in different banks. So inter-bank transactions have become very large in terms of both the volume and the quantum of transfers or payments. With the adoption of IT and ITES in the banking industry, there has been greater reliance on various forms of electronic transactions such as the use of debit or credit cards, online transfers, inter-bank electronic transfers and cheque clearings using ITES. The Indian public is very familiar with National Electronic Funds Transfer (NEFT), real-time gross settlement (RTGS), Immediate Payment Service (IMPS), Unified Payments Interface (UPI)-based digital payments, and so on, to facilitate their banking transactions in the online mode.

According to RBI sources, the share of electronic transfers in the total volume of non-cash retail payments was 95.4 per cent in 2018–19 (RBI, 2019a). This increased to 99.6 per cent in 2022–23 (RBI, 2023a).

Thus, the banking system constitutes the backbone of the payment and settlement system in an economy. It is akin to the blood circulatory system in the human body. Any disruption in the normal functioning of banks is severely detrimental to the conduct of trade and transactions and has the potential to cause severe setbacks to the entire economy. The event of withdrawal of INR 500 and INR 1,000 currency notes in November 2016 in India, popularly referred to as 'demonetisation', caused serious disruptions to trade and commerce during late 2016 and early 2017 (see Box 3.1). Its negative impact on the economy and the country's employment situation is widely discussed (PHD Chamber of Commerce and Industry, 2017; Nataraj, 2017). This event underscores the damaging consequences of even a temporary disruption to the payment and settlement system.

Box 3.1 The 2016 demonetisation in India

On 8 November 2016, Prime Minister Narendra Modi surprised the entire nation by announcing discontinuance of currency notes of INR 1,000 and INR 500 denominations. Such notes ceased to be legal tender. This event, popularly referred to as *demonetisation*, resulted in the sudden invalidation of currency notes worth INR 15.4 trillion, constituting 86.9 per cent of the total currency in circulation. The government justified the move for overcoming the triple menaces of the black economy, counterfeiting of high-value Indian currency notes and terrorist financing. Many economists and commentators were apprehensive about this sudden disruption in the payments system and its adverse consequences paralysing transactions in goods and services.

In the aftermath of the demonetisation, the general public suffered from severe hardships for a few months on several accounts. Limited spread of electronic modes of payment made purchase of daily needs like groceries and vegetables extremely difficult. Limited availability of currency notes of other denominations and restrictions on the amount of withdrawals of such notes from banks and ATMs resulted in the formation of very long queues for cash withdrawals at bank counters and ATMs. There were even reported deaths of people standing in long queues under the sun. Until two months after the demonetisation, new currency notes of INR 500 and INR 2,000 denominations were not available adequately. The overall currency in circulation witnessed a negative growth of –19.2 per cent during November 2016–October 2017 as against a growth rate of 14.9 per cent during the comparable period in the preceding year.

Demonetisation-related disruptions of economic activities in the cash-based segments caused loss of livelihood for a large number of people. Even the government acknowledged a transient adverse impact of the demonetisation on the economy. But it pleaded with the general public to bear with the short-term pain in pursuit of the long-term gains of control on black money and tax evasion. It is important to note that despite accelerated growth in bank deposits (due to deposit of currency notes of the invalidated INR 1,000 and INR 500 denominations) immediately after the demonetisation and softening of bank lending rates, there was not much recovery in bank credit. This reflected lack of credit demand with economic slowdown.

More than seven years have passed since the demonetisation, but the debate on its benefits versus losses continues to remain unsettled. The benefits are listed mainly in terms of better tax compliance, decline in the currency–GDP ratio, rapid digitalisation of the payments system and arresting of terrorist financing. The adverse consequences of the demonetisation are highlighted in terms of undue hardship to the general public, disruption of day-to-day transactions, loss of livelihood for many workers in the informal sector and a transient economic slowdown. Reflecting the bipolar views across the political spectrum, several opposition parties observed 8 November 2017 as 'Black Day' while the government celebrated the same date as 'Anti-Black-Money Day'.

3.7 Empirical Evidence

This section presents empirical evidence on interlinkages between banking aggregates and key macroeconomic indicators in light of the discussion presented in the preceding sections. Particularly, we examine the association between savings and economic growth and assess the extent to which the banking sector helps in augmenting savings in an economy.

3.7.1 Savings and Economic Growth

As discussed earlier, growth theories have assigned an important role to savings in propelling economic growth. Particularly, neoclassical growth theories suggest that during the transition phase, increase in the savings rate supports increase in per capita capital which in turn leads to growth in per capita income. In the steady state, when per capita income ceases to grow, the prevailing savings rate helps in maintaining the existing per capita level of capital and income. Any fall in the savings causes a fall in per capita capital, and accordingly the per capita level of income plunges. In the Indian context, Mohan (2008) has provided evidence on the long-term association between savings and economic growth for the period 1950–2008.

The savings rate during the first two decades after India's independence was relatively low at around 10 per cent or so. The average growth of per capita income during this period was around 1.8 per cent. The average savings rate increased to nearly 18 per cent during the 1970s and 1980s. This higher savings rate was also associated with a higher per capita income growth of 2.3 per cent.

The average savings rate during the 1990s further increased to close to 23 per cent. The same period witnessed a higher per capita income growth of 3.7 per cent on average. The savings rate in India since 2004–05 has been above 30 per cent. The average growth of per capita income from 2004–05 to 2019–20 was also higher at nearly 5 per cent.

This discussion suggests a close link between savings and economic growth in the Indian context, confirming lessons drawn from theories of economic growth.

3.7.2 Role of Banks in Augmenting Savings

In the preceding sections, we have explained how banks through financial intermediation help in mobilisation of savings. The following discussion provides supporting evidence of the role of banks in promoting domestic savings in India.

We have already discussed the event of bank nationalisation. The rise of the savings rate in India since the 1970s is widely related to the bank nationalisation of 1969. It led to the opening of bank branches across the country. Citizens in small towns and rural areas used banks to deposit their savings. As a proportion of GDP, bank deposits increased from around 10–11 per cent prior to 1968–69 to above 25 per cent since 1979–80. Correspondingly, domestic savings rates doubled from around 10 per cent prior to the bank nationalisation to close to 20 per cent by the late 1970s. These developments evidence the role of banks in augmenting domestic savings.

Similarly, banking reforms since the early 1990s, as detailed in Chapter 2, helped in reducing government control on banks and provided them operational autonomy. The portfolio of both assets and liabilities of banks witnessed introduction of innovative instruments. Adoption of the Basel prudential norms on capital adequacy, regulations on asset classification, income recognition and provisioning, and so on, contributed to improving the strength and soundness of banks. Competition from new Indian private banks and foreign banks improved operational efficiency and productivity. Necessary details on the performance of banks are provided in Chapter 11.

Overall, the Indian banking sector became stronger and safer. This led to substantial mobilisation of bank deposits. The bank deposits-to-GDP ratio increased to an average of 56.6 per cent during the 2000s and further climbed to a range of 66–70 per cent during the 2010s. Correspondingly, the savings rate in India accentuated to nearly 30 per cent since the early 2000s. Along with financial sector reforms, improvements in corporate profitability and fiscal discipline played a complementary role in raising the savings rate in India, which cannot be ignored. Mohan (2008) has provided a detailed account of these aspects.

Figure 3.4 presents a scatter plot of the growth of bank deposits and savings in India. Consistent with the discussion in the previous paragraphs, the scatter plot reveals a positive association between the growth of bank deposits and savings in India.

Thus, we observe two important facts. First, the rising growth rate in per capita income in India was associated with higher savings rates. Second, higher growth rates of bank deposits facilitated higher growth of domestic savings. Combining these two facts, we can infer that banks play a critical role in supporting economic growth.

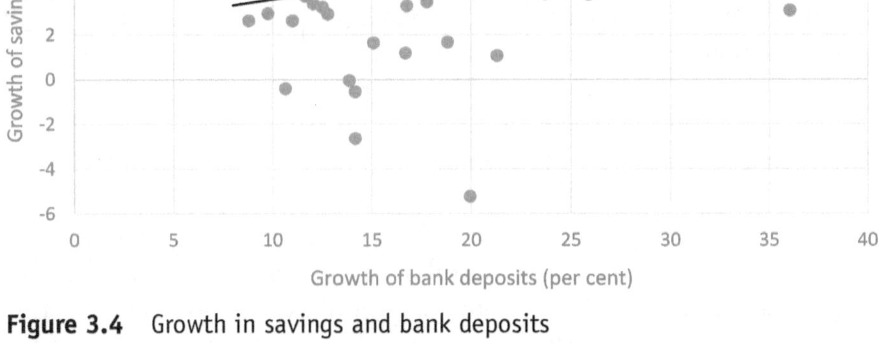

Figure 3.4 Growth in savings and bank deposits

Source: Prepared by the author based on data obtained from RBI's *Handbook of Statistics on Indian Economy*, https://data.rbi.org.in/DBIE/#/dbie/reports/Publication/Time-Series%20Publications/Handbook%20of%20Statistics%20on%20the%20Indian%20Economy (accessed 28 June 2022).

3.8 Conclusion

In this chapter, our endeavour was to understand how banks play a critical role in promoting the long-term economic prosperity of a nation. Growth theories assign an important role to savings in driving economic growth. Savings get converted into investments by banks and other segments of the financial system. Investments add to the existing stock of capital and facilitate production of increasing levels of output. Any setback to the generation of savings ceases investments and hence upsets economic growth.

Banks play a vital role in mobilisation of savings and conversion of such savings into productive investment in factories and machines. They do so by resolving the size and maturity mismatches in the preferences of savers vis-à-vis those of borrowers, enabling effective functioning of the credit market by overcoming the problem of information asymmetry, risk moderation through monitoring and diversification, and so on. It is also important to note that banks are special as they help meet the funding requirements of small borrowers whom the capital market does not serve. Some empirical evidence are cited to suggest that rising savings rates have been associated with acceleration of growth of per capita income in India. We also observed a positive link between mobilisation of bank deposits and overall savings. Broadly, these findings are consistent with the received wisdom on the role of banks towards enhancing economic prosperity.

In addition to helping in mobilisation of savings and augmenting capital formation, banks are useful for society as the backbone of the payment and settlement system. They support transaction of goods and services and facilitate settlement of debt.

Revision Questions and Problems

1. What are the key determinants of economic growth propounded by theories of growth? Highlight the role of savings in this context.
2. Discuss the role of banks in mobilisation of savings and augmentation of capital formation by resolving size and maturity mismatches in the preferences of savers versus those of borrowers.

3. How can the problem of information asymmetry in the credit market jeopardise its very functioning and potentially undermine mobilisation of savings and capital formation? How do banks overcome this problem and help the credit market function optimally?
4. How do banks function as the backbone of the payment and settlement system in any modern economy?

4

Economic Fluctuations, Monetary Policy and the Role of Banks

Learning Objectives

- To explain short-term economic fluctuations and their impact on society
- To explore the reasons behind such fluctuations using relevant economic theories
- To analyse how monetary policy can moderate short-term economic fluctuations
- To emphasise the role of banks in the monetary transmission mechanism
- To present empirical evidence examining the role of banks in the monetary transmission mechanism

4.1 Introduction

In Chapter 3, we discussed the role of banks in augmenting savings and supporting economic growth in the long-term perspective. In macroeconomics, 'long-run' refers to the period in which all prices are flexible. In practice, long-run economic growth and developmental discussion for a country generally cover several decades.

There is another important dimension of economic growth often observed. This is in the form of short-term economic fluctuations. Short run refers to a time period in which the prices of some goods are assumed to be rigid or inflexible. The evolution of Keynesian macroeconomics in the aftermath of the Great Depression of the 1930s highlighted the occurrence of such regular short-term economic fluctuations. It was suggested that there are certain phases in which the economy witnesses rapid growth (boom) followed by periods of economic slowdown (recession). The periodic recurrence of such economic booms and recessions is popularly referred to as the *business cycle* phenomenon.

The question is why we need to be concerned with short-run economic fluctuations.

Our concerns arise as excessive economic fluctuations can have serious adverse effects on society. During economic downswings, sales, production and employment levels plummet. Most households earn their livelihood by participating in the production process in one form or the other. Fall in production and sales adversely affects the profits of industry and unemployment causes loss of income for households. Consequently, the livelihood and standard of living of people at large suffer. Any social-welfare-maximising government cannot afford serious risks to the livelihood and standard of living of its citizens.

Similarly, periods of economic boom, particularly if driven by rising aggregate spending[1] in the economy as compared to the production capacity, cause high inflation. Inflation is nothing but a tendency of continuous surge in the general prices. With rising prices, people can afford to buy fewer goods and services for a given income. Thus, high inflation adversely affects the standard of living of households. Moreover, it is widely believed that high inflation is inimical to economic growth. High inflation hurts the incentive to save and widens foreign trade deficit. It distorts the price-signalling mechanism and leads to suboptimal allocation of resources in an economy. Periods of economic boom are also associated with reckless lending and lead to future financial crises. Therefore, there is an argument to arrest overheating during economic upswings.

For avoiding the costs of excessive economic fluctuations, there are relevant public policy prescriptions. Effective policy making in this regard requires correct analysis of the related causal factors as a necessary prerequisite. In macroeconomics, these inherent fluctuations in economic activity are explained by various theories emphasising different explanatory factors.

---

[1] Aggregate spending is the sum of the aggregate consumption expenditure of households, investment spending, government expenditure and exports over imports.

There is a popular way of separating short-run cyclical fluctuations from the behaviour of the aggregate output in the long run. This is undertaken by removing the secular trend output from the actual output. Mathematically,

$$\text{Cyclical GDP} = \text{Actual GDP} - \text{Trend GDP} \tag{4.1}$$

As per capita income or per capita GDP is a popular indicator used for assessing the standard of living across countries, it is pertinent to focus on per capita income in macroeconomic analysis. In this context, equation 4.1 can be discussed in per capita terms. Neoclassical growth models use the assumption of constant returns to scale to translate growth dynamics from aggregate GDP terms to per capita GDP conveniently as discussed in Chapter 3.

Figure 4.1 depicts the movement in the cyclical per capita income for India covering the period 1950–51 to 2019–20. Cyclical per capita income is obtained by removing trend per capita income from the actual per capita income series. We have constructed trend per capita income by using the Hodrick–Prescott filter on the per capita income (net national product at constant prices) series as applied popularly in the literature (Barro, 2008). It can be observed from Figure 4.1 that the Indian economy has witnessed extensive short-term fluctuations. Particularly, fluctuations were prominent during the 1960s and 1970s. During the post-reform period beginning with the early 1990s, there has been considerable moderation in economic fluctuations. This moderation reflected in terms of both the lower amplitude and the longer duration of economic upswings.

The theoretical underpinnings of short-run economic fluctuations have evolved over time. They include (*a*) the Keynesian *animal spirit*, (*b*) the *real business cycle* (RBC) theory originally due to Kydland and Prescott (1982) and its more general form under *equilibrium business cycle models*, (*c*) the price misperception theory and (*d*) the new Keynesian sticky price model. In the section that follows, these theories are briefly explained.

Standard macroeconomics textbooks[2] use aggregate demand–aggregate supply (AD–AS) analysis to explain the determination of aggregate output and general prices in an economy. They combine ideas derived from growth

[2] See Barro (2008); Romer (2011); Karlan and Morduch (2020).

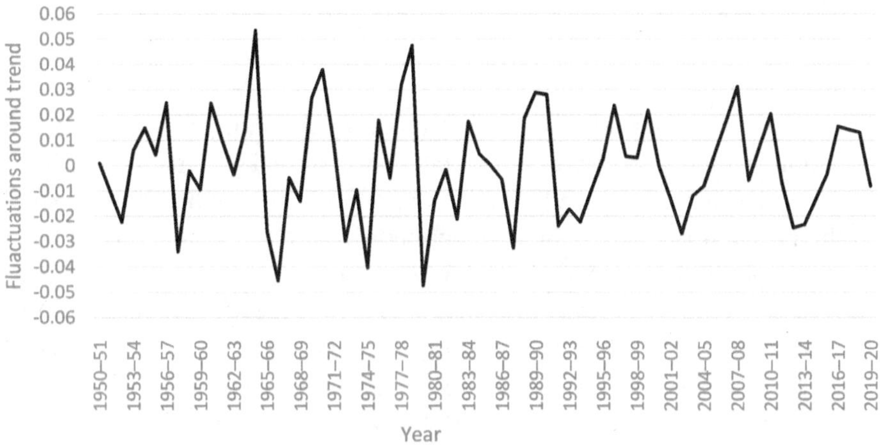

Figure 4.1 Cyclical pattern of per capita income of India

Source: Prepared by the author based on data obtained from RBI's *Handbook of Statistics on Indian Economy*, https://data.rbi.org.in/DBIE/#/dbie/reports/Publication/Time-Series%20Publications/Handbook%20of%20Statistics%20on%20the%20Indian%20Economy (accessed 18 July 2022).

Note: Cyclical per capita income is obtained by detrending per capita income (in logarithmic form) for India. Trend per capita income (in logarithmic form) in turn is constructed using the Hodrick–Prescott filter.

theories to explain the long-run pattern of the economy through an analysis of short-term economic fluctuations. Theories of economic growth delineated in the preceding chapter suggest that factors like accumulation of capital and labour and improvement in factor productivity determine the long-run supply-side conditions or production capacity. On the other hand, short-run economic fluctuations are traced to variation in aggregate expenditure and short-term supply-side shocks.

As indicated earlier, economic fluctuations cause several hardships for different stakeholders. Their occurrence cannot be done away with completely. However, appropriate macroeconomic policy initiatives can moderate such fluctuations. Particularly, fiscal and monetary policy actions have become popular mainstream policy tools to mitigate the swings of economic booms and recessions.

Adoption of fiscal discipline and consolidation across advanced and emerging economies in the last two to three decades has diluted the emphasis on fiscal policy in overall macroeconomic stabilisation other than in crisis situations. Consequently, there has been greater reliance on monetary policy for moderating short-run economic fluctuations. All advanced and emerging economies rely heavily on monetary policy for macroeconomic management.

Monetary policy relates to the decision of the monetary authority on variation in money supply or policy rates so as to make availability of bank credit easier or more difficult, depending on overall spending as compared to the production capacity in an economy. Variation in availability of bank credit causes variation in aggregate consumption and investment spendings funded by bank loans, thus affecting aggregate expenditure. In India, the RBI is entrusted with the responsibility for conducting monetary policy. If there are overheating conditions (rise in aggregate spending exceeding the production capacity) and high inflationary pressure, the RBI tightens the monetary policy. It raises interest rates and makes bank loans costlier. High lending rates reduce demand for bank credit and thus stem the flow of home loans, automobile loans, project loans, working-capital loans, and so on. This, in turn, reduces the purchase of homes or apartments, automobiles, investments and overall spending. Fall in overall spending as compared to the quantity of goods and services produced results in building up of an unplanned inventory. Accumulated inventories lead to a drop in prices and scaling down of production. Thus, dampened aggregate demand finally results in lower inflation and economic growth decelerates.

On the contrary, under recessionary conditions, the RBI reduces interest rates and promotes easy availability of bank credit, thus inducing pick up in investments, purchase of apartments and automobiles and higher levels of economic activity. This may entail quick running down of inventories and producers striving to scale up the level of production to maintain planned inventories. Thus, monetary accommodation–induced rise in aggregate demand facilitates faster growth.

Banks are the key constituents of the monetary system. They play a fundamental role in the transmission of monetary impulses to influence aggregate spendings in an economy. Particularly, monetary policy–driven changes in bank lending rates and availability of bank loans are found to have a strong bearing on aggregate consumption and investment spendings. In view of these aspects, existence of a well-functioning, stable and vibrant banking system is a necessary precondition for the effective conduct of monetary policy. Details of the monetary transmission mechanism (MTM) and the role of banks in the process are presented in the later part of this chapter. Therein, we highlight the significant role of banks in the monetary transmission mechanism, thus emphasising their contribution towards arresting economic fluctuations. We also provide related empirical evidence.

The rest of this chapter is organised as follows. In section 4.2, we provide a summary of theoretical ideas explaining short-run economic fluctuations under the business cycle phenomenon. In section 4.3, an outline of the technical details of monetary policy and how it plays a critical role in controlling economic fluctuations is provided. In section 4.4, the role of banks in the MTM is explained, and section 4.5 presents related empirical evidence. The broad conclusions of the chapter are presented in section 4.6.

4.2 Short-Run Economic Fluctuations: Theoretical Explanations

In macroeconomics, short-run economic fluctuations are explained by various theories. Keynesian macroeconomics explains the business-cycle phenomenon emphasising demand-side factors while the RBC theory focuses on supply side explanations. Price misperception and sticky price models highlight the role of monetary factors causing economic fluctuations. Details of these theories are discussed in the following sections.

4.2.1 Keynesian Demand-Side Explanations

A sudden stock market crash in 1929 led to a severe economic downfall in the US during the 1930s, popularly referred to as the *Great Depression*. It stands out as the worst period of economic slowdown in US history. It caused severe output contraction, job losses and price deflation.[3] During 1929–33, output in the US fell by around 30 per cent and industrial production was down by roughly 47 per cent. The unemployment rate increased to a peak of nearly 25 per cent in 1933 (Barro, 2008; Royal Swedish Academy of Sciences, 2022). During this period, leading economies in Europe also witnessed a similar economic setback. Great Britain suffered from severe economic depression in the early 1930s and the worst impact in France was felt during 1933–36. Japan and countries in Latin America could not escape the economic depression, but the impact was mild and short-lived.

[3] Falling general prices, where the percentage change in a price index like CPI in a period over the same in the previous period is negative.

Standard textbooks on macroeconomics explain how this event brought about a directional change in thinking on the way the economy works. Prior to the Great Depression, mainstream economic thinkers, popularly referred to as *classical economists*, dominated the discourse on economic analysis. They believed that flexibility in the determination of prices, interest rates, wages, and so on, guided by the forces of supply and demand in the product, capital and labour markets, respectively, along with the operation of *Say's Law of Markets* can ensure prevalence of full employment conditions. The latter suggests that any amount of output produced in an economy can be sold out. According to this line of thought, production of goods and services generates factor income in various forms such as wages, salaries, profits, interest payments, and so on. Production of more output requires engagement of larger volumes of various factors of production and hence leads to generation of higher factor incomes. Higher income generated from more production consequently generates higher demand for the goods and services produced. This school of thought ruled out the possibility of a general situation of *glut*.

Any situation of unemployment or overproduction was thought to be transient in nature. Adjustment of prices, wages or interest rates would lead to wiping out any mismatch in demand and supply in the product, labour and capital markets, respectively. For example, for a while the production of goods may be higher than purchases. This imbalance puts downward pressure on prices, as producers who are not able to sell their products at the current prices would try to get rid of their excess inventories by reducing prices. The adjustment process continues until the equilibrium price is reached at which the supply of goods exactly matches the demand. Similarly, flexible adjustment of wages can bring equilibrium in the labour market and any temporary unemployment disappears over time.

The Great Depression witnessed a prolonged period of high unemployment and overproduction. This was a serious challenge to classical economic thinking. It also provided an opportunity to John Maynard Keynes to come up with an alternative explanation on the working of the economy. The Keynesian *general theory* was more appealing and consistent with the empirical facts prevalent during the Great Depression.

Keynesian analysis emphasised the role of *effective demand* in the determination of equilibrium output and employment in an economy. One of the basic premises of Keynesian analysis is that the actual demand for goods and services could be deficient as compared to the amount of goods and services produced at times. This is because the entire amount of factor income received in the form of wages, salaries, profits, interest income, and so on, may not be spent by households and firms in the same period. A part of the income would be saved. Depending on the state of mind of households and firms, aggregate spending on consumption and investment could vary. If households are optimistic about their future income prospects, they may tend to spend more. On the contrary, if they have doubts about their employment and earning prospects in the future, they are likely to save more now so that they can use their current savings for future consumption. Thus, their current consumption spending plumets. Similarly, firms invest more or less depending on their assessment of and expectations about future sales and business prospects. It is believed that fluctuations in investment expenditure in an economy are much more volatile compared to those in consumption expenditure.

Thus, Keynes advocated that upward and downward swings in aggregate spending on consumption and investment are mainly caused by perceptions and expectations of households and firms about current economic conditions and future prospects. These perceptions and expectations are shaped by the psychological swings, popularly referred to as the *animal spirit*, of consumers and producers. Supply-side factors such as stock of capital, labour and technology of production determine the production capacity or *potential output* in an economy as suggested by growth theories. However, in the short run, the actual production and employment are predominantly determined by demand-side factors such as aggregate spending on consumption and investment. Thus, fluctuations in the *animal spirit* of consumers and producers lead to fluctuations in actual aggregate spending, referred to as *effective demand*, which in turn causes fluctuations in actual output in the short run around the potential output. This is the gist of Keynesian analysis explaining the causes of short-term fluctuations in output and employment in an economy.

Based on these understandings, Keynes suggested that the classical idea of an economy operating at full-employment level and without a general situation of *glut* does not hold always. Such a situation can be considered as a special case. Aggregate demand can very much deviate from the potential output of the economy at any point of time. If the aggregate demand is higher than the potential output, it causes an economic boom. On the contrary, if aggregate demand is deficient, it causes economic slowdown.

Thus, Keynesian analysis of short-run economic fluctuations has two critical aspects. First, it suggests that the state of mind of consumers and producers has a strong influence on their expenditure decisions. Variation in optimism or pessimism of consumers and producers causes fluctuations in aggregate expenditure. Second, aggregate expenditure or demand is of paramount importance in the determination of equilibrium output and employment.

There is another way to reject the classical idea of full-employment equilibrium. Under classical thought, the assumption of flexibility of wages is critical for achieving full-employment equilibrium in the labour market. Keynes suggested that workers strongly resist wage cuts as that will undermine their current standard of living. This leads to downward nominal wage rigidity assumptions under Keynesian analysis. With downward nominal wage rigidity, any fall in general prices raises real wages paid to workers. Real wage is the ratio of nominal wage and general prices. If the nominal wage cannot fall (due to nominal wage rigidity), any drop in prices raises the ratio. Higher real wages discourage demand for labour and hence may reduce employment and output. This hinders the economy reaching the full-employment equilibrium level of output. Downward rigidity in nominal wages hampers smooth adjustment of real wages in the labour market to clear the demand–supply gap.

4.2.2 Real Business Cycle (RBC) Model

Keynesian analysis, as discussed in the previous section, heavily emphasised demand-side factors and largely ignored supply-side considerations. Overcoming such deficiencies, *equilibrium business cycle models* were developed which followed a holistic approach. Such models explicitly take into account the underlying microeconomic foundations in the determination of equilibrium employment and wage rates in the labour market, equilibrium amount of savings and investments along with interest rate in the capital market, and so on. Equilibrium business cycle models incorporate the behaviour of firms and households, drawing from microeconomic analysis, to provide a complete picture. Determination of equilibrium levels of employment and wage rates is derived from the behaviour of firms which demand labour vis-à-vis that of households which supply labour. Taking into account interlinkages across various markets for labour, capital and output, equilibrium business cycle models are capable of explaining the behaviour of key macroeconomic variables such as aggregate consumption spending, investment, employment, interest rate, wage rate, and so on, along with short-term fluctuations in output. Under general equilibrium analysis, interaction of demand and supply ensures all the constituent markets are clear.

Let us take a simple equilibrium business cycle model known as the RBC model. It is primarily based on the seminal work of Kydland and Prescott (1982). To explain RBC theory, let us use the standard neoclassical production function as discussed in Chapter 3 and reproduced as follows:

$$Y = A\, f(K, L) \tag{4.2}$$

In equation 4.2, Y stands for output, A stands for TFP, and K and L represent the stock of capital and labour, respectively; f denotes the general functional form, relating output to capital and labour. Let us assume that this production function satisfies all standard assumptions of the neoclassical production function such as constant returns to scale in K and L, positive but diminishing marginal productivity of capital and labour and Inada conditions.[4]

The RBC theory suggests that there are short-run fluctuations in output (Y) caused by fluctuations in TFP. Variations in TFP, in turn, could be due to several factors. There could be improvement in TFP due to technological innovations leading to production of the same output in a more efficient way. This reflects in a higher value of A in equation 4.2. A higher A magnifies the amount of output produced with a given amount of capital and labour. The technological innovations could also be in the form of the invention of a new product or production of the same product in a cost-effective manner with the discovery of a rare raw material, and so on. The invention of electricity, computers and the internet are popular examples of such technological revolutions improving TFP.

Similarly, we can identify several non-technological factors which may reduce TFP. These may include a pandemic like Covid-19, natural calamities like earthquakes, severe floods or droughts, or ecological degradations having adverse impact like harvest failures, and so on. Further, there could be a set of sociopolitical factors which may either improve or damage TFP, depending on the direction of the change. Putting in place conducive and inclusive institutions such as a well-functioning democracy, improvements in property rights and enforcement of contracts, a good legal and governance

[4] $\lim_{K\to 0}\frac{\partial Y}{\partial K} = \infty$ *and* $\lim_{K\to\infty}\frac{\partial Y}{\partial K} = 0$ and $\lim_{L\to 0}\frac{\partial Y}{\partial L} = \infty$ *and* $\lim_{L\to\infty}\frac{\partial Y}{\partial L} = 0$

system, and so on, enhances TFP. On the contrary, large-scale social unrest, political instability, strikes and violence, among others, are setbacks to economic activities, causing a fall in TFP. A given amount of capital and labour translates into a lower amount of output in such situations.

The exponents of the RBC theory trace short-run fluctuations in output to such supply-side factors which mainly cause transient variations in TFP. Barro (2008) has provided a detailed account of the same. It can be inferred from the RBC model that variables like real wage rate, real interest rate, employment, aggregate consumption and investment spendings are procyclical in nature. They rise with economic booms and fall during economic slowdowns.

4.2.3 Price Misperception Model

Contrary to the RBC model which traces the causes of economic fluctuations to real factors, another set of economic models focus on monetary factors. Let us begin with the price misperception model under this set. This model owes its intellectual origin to Friedman (1968) and Phelps (1969). Details of the model can be obtained from the seminal work by Lucas (1981).

The price misperception model has some similarities with general equilibrium models. The microeconomic foundations determining equilibrium levels of employment, wage rate, investment, interest rate, output, prices, and so on, in different constituent markets are retained in the price misperception model. Introduction of misperception of households and consumers about general prices is its main innovation. The price misperception model uses the simple fact that individual consumers often observe price changes of such goods and services as they consume. They fail to notice price changes of goods and services that they do not consume.

The expected price (Pe) of workers is based on the prices of the goods and services which they consume. Increase in money supply raises general prices (P). Workers may not notice the rising prices of goods and services which they do not consume. However, producers (sellers of goods and services) notice increases in P. This results in a difference between the real wage (W/P) that producers pay and expected real wage of workers or households (W/ Pe). In fact,

$$(W/Pe) = (W/P)^*(P/Pe) \tag{4.3}$$

If due to price misperception of workers, P is higher than Pe, then P/Pe is greater than unity. In that case, W/P is lower than W/Pe as can be seen from equation 4.3. Lower *W/P* drives higher demand for labour while higher *W/Pe* due to price misperception of workers causes higher labour supply, too. This pushes overall employment *L* to a higher level. Using the production function provided in equation (4.2), we can infer that higher *L* results in higher output *Y*.

Similarly, monetary contraction leads to lower *P*. But workers failing to see fall in prices of goods and services that they do not consume suffer from price misperception. This keeps *Pe* higher than *P*. In that case, higher *W/P* lowers demand for labour by firms while lower *W/Pe* reduces the labour supply as well. Then overall employment and output in the economy contract.

Thus, price misperception of workers can explain short-run economic fluctuations caused by variation in money supply.

It is important to note that price misperception does not last for long. Ultimately, the workers realise the actual change in the general prices due to variation in money supply and they adjust their price expectations. In the long run, P_e=P and hence W/P_e becomes equal to *W/P*. With tapering of the short-run output gain or loss, the economy returns to the long-run equilibrium.

4.2.4 New Keynesian Model

The New Keynesian model explains short-run economic fluctuations mainly using an imperfect market set up. Under perfect competition, both buyers and producers are large in number and individually none of them can influence the market price of the product. They are price takers. Equilibrium output produced by each producer is set by equality of marginal cost of the product to the market price. In this world, marginal cost = marginal revenue = average revenue = price of the product.

On the contrary, actual market conditions in many industries in the real world conform to imperfect competition. For example, the automobile industry in India has a handful of producers, namely Maruti Suzuki, Tata Motors, Mahindra Automotive, Hyundai Motors, and so on. Key producers in the pharmaceuticals industry include Dr Reddy's Laboratories, Alkem Laboratories, Glenmark Pharmaceuticals, Cadila Healthcare, Cipla and Wockhardt. The major players in the IT industry are TCS, Infosys, Tech Mahindra, Wipro and HCL Technologies, among others. In such a market set-up, each producer makes a slightly differentiated product having its unique market within the industry. Each of them enjoys some market power taking advantage of their product uniqueness and a special segment of consumers preferring their product over that of others. Each of such producers takes advantage of their own market power and charges a price higher than their marginal cost. Excess price charged over the marginal cost depends on the market power of the producer or the seller, which in turn depends on the elasticity of demand for the unique product. If demand is inelastic,[5] the producer has greater market power.

No doubt, if such producers charge a higher price, demand for their product declines. But unlike in perfect competition, this will not drive the producer out of the market. If Maruti Suzuki raises its car price, it may induce several potential buyers to buy cars from other producers like Tata Motors or Hyundai Motors or another car manufacturer. But there will be some committed customers who continue their preference for Maruti Suzuki cars. Details of such market set-ups are provided in standard microeconomics textbooks.[6]

This implies that under imperfect market conditions, producers may adopt a *sticky price* strategy at least in the short run. Some firms may not raise the price of their products despite another raising its product price. By holding their prices unchanged, such producers may gain a larger market share by attracting customers from the producer that raised its price. Adopting a sticky price temporarily is feasible for them because of two reasons. First, such firms may already be charging a price above the marginal cost and earning more than normal profit. If reduction in the supernormal profit is less than the potential extra profit earned by attracting new customers (from the firm that raised its product price), then it may motivate them to follow sticky prices. Second, there is a cost involved in terms of effort, time and money in the process of price revision, popularly referred to as *menu cost* (Box 4.1). An effort to avoid menu costs induces firms not to change their product prices frequently.

A study by Alan Blinder (1994), noted economist and former deputy chairman of the US Federal Reserve, revealed a wide variation in the price-setting behaviour of firms. Nearly half of the firms in the sample did not change the price of their product more than once a year. On the other extreme, about one-tenth of the firms changed their prices in the range of once in a day

---

[5] Demand is said to be inelastic when change in demand for a product is relatively weak responding to variation in its price. Demand for the product falls (rises) by lesser amount when the price rises (falls).

[6] See Pindyck and Rubinfeld (2013); Kreps (1990), and so on.

Box 4.1 Menu costs

Menu cost refers to the cost of printing a price catalogue. It covers the time, money and effort spent for printing the catalogue. For a restaurant owner, when prices of cereals, pulses, vegetables, edible oil, meat, eggs, cooking gas and wages of chefs and workers increase, there is a need to raise the prices of the dishes on the menu. For an automobile firm, similarly, there is a need to revise the prices of its cars if there are changes in the prices of the various inputs for production. Setting new prices entails brainstorming sessions of the management of the firm to analyse the details of changing input prices for the future, price elasticity of the product, response of their competitors, and so on. This requires considerable effort and expending of money and time. Moreover, there is also the direct cost of printing the price catalogues, circulating the same to authorised dealers and advertising.

To avoid incurring menu costs, some firms avoid changing prices frequently. Particularly, when inflation is low and transient, a large section of producers would prefer not to change the prices of their products to save on menu costs. On the contrary, when inflation is high and durable, most firms may ignore menu costs and raise their product prices.

to once in a week. Another 30 per cent changed the prices of their products once in a quarter to once in a year.

Under such conditions, monetary policy is non-neutral and has real effects on the economy. Due to stickiness of prices under imperfect competition, increase in money supply may not lead to corresponding increase in prices by all producers. On the contrary, nominal wages are likely to increase with increase in money supply. In the net, real wages increase with sticky prices. Rise in real wages improves labour supply and correspondingly improves output *Y*. This implies that output increases with increase in money supply. Similar arguments can be made to suggest that output declines with fall in money supply.

However, the variation in real output caused by money supply changes is limited to the short run. In the long run, all producers would like to fully exploit their individual market power and charge normal mark-up prices over the marginal cost. Thus, prices do not remain sticky in the long run. Finally, increase in money supply fully gets reflected in general prices and real wages return to the original 'equilibrium' with upward adjustment of prices.

This can be explained using Figure 4.2, where the labour supply curve is given by the upward sloping line. It shows that as real wage (on the Y-axis) increases, there is greater incentive for households to work more and hence the labour supply rises. The original labour demand curve is given by the downward sloping line. It indicates that as there is increase in real wage, there is a fall in demand for labour by firms. This is because at the equilibrium, the profit-maximising firm equates marginal productivity of labour to the real wage rate. With rise in real wages, the profit-maximising firm is required to operate at a level corresponding to a relatively higher marginal productivity to maintain the equality between the real wage and marginal productivity of labour. From the property of diminishing marginal productivity in a standard neoclassical production function, the firm needs to reduce employment of labour to achieve higher marginal productivity. As the firm employs fewer workers, the marginal productivity increases. Thus, higher real

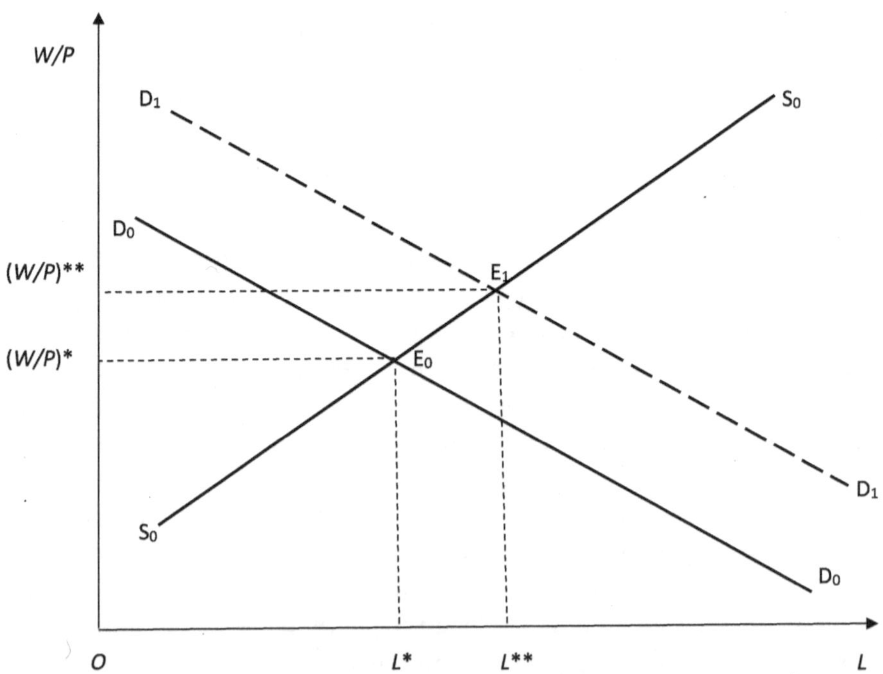

Figure 4.2 Impact of monetary expansion in the labour market: sticky price model

Source: Prepared by the author.

wage corresponds to lesser demand for labour as reflected in the downward sloping demand curve.

Let us assume that the labour market was initially in equilibrium determined by the intersection of the supply curve given by the line S_0S_0 and the original demand curve given by the line D_0D_0. This fixes the equilibrium wage rate at *W/P** and employment at *L**.

With flexible prices, any monetary expansion (contraction) will raise (lower) both the nominal wage *W* and prices *P*, keeping the real wage *W/P* constant. It will not have any impact in the labour market.

However, with sticky prices, monetary expansion leads to higher real money balances *M/P* in the hands of the public. Sticky prices hinder full adjustment of prices *P* when the money stock *M* rises with monetary expansion. The numerator rises more than the denominator, thus leading to rise in the real money balances *M/P*. Higher real money balances induce higher demand for goods and services. As the producers charge a higher price over the marginal cost, they see higher profit opportunity in producing and selling more goods and services in an environment of higher demand for their products.

Higher production of goods and services drives demand for labour. In Figure 4.2, the demand for labour line shifts to the right. The new demand curve is given by the line D_1D_1. Accordingly, the point of intersection between the labour demand and supply lines shifts from E_0 to E_1. Correspondingly, the new equilibrium wage rate and employment are given by *W/P*** and *L***, respectively. It may be noted that the new equilibrium real wage rate and employment are higher than the initial equilibrium. As indicated in equation 4.2, this higher employment leads to higher output.

Therefore, we can conclude that both with sticky prices caused by imperfect competition in production and under the existence of 'menu costs', monetary expansion can lead to higher production of goods and services. Using similar logic, one can argue that monetary tightening can lead to economic slowdown.

In the long run, to hold normal mark-up, firms raise prices so that the long-run price mark-up on and above the marginal cost can be maintained. This leads to prices rising as much as the rise in nominal wages (caused by monetary expansion) while the real wage rate returns to the original level of *W/P** and employment level to *L**.

Thus, under the new Keynesian model, short-run economic fluctuations can be explained due to variation in money supply. It may be noted that while the traditional Keynesian analysis emphasised rigidity of nominal wages to explain economic fluctuations, the new Keynesian model focuses on price rigidities.

In this section, we discussed various factors causing short-run fluctuations in an economy. Our objective was not to examine the relative strength of one theory over another. Rather, we presented a summary of the received wisdom drawing from various schools of thought explaining economic fluctuations. While the RBC model emphasised variation in TFP causing fluctuations over different phases of the business cycle, traditional Keynesian analysis stressed on aggregate expenditure. Later models based on price misperceptions and sticky prices traced the reasons for economic fluctuations to monetary variation. Guided by these ideas, there have been public policy prescriptions to moderate economic fluctuations as discussed in the following sections.

4.3 Role of Monetary Policy in Managing Economic Fluctuations

Following Keynesian prescriptions, economies around the world have been using demand management policies to moderate economic fluctuations. These policies are mainly in the form of (*a*) fiscal policy and (*b*) monetary policy. Fiscal policy takes the form of modulating government expenditure and/or taxation. During periods of economic recession, government expenditure is raised and/or taxes reduced so that aggregate demand increases. Rising government expenditure on various goods and services can revive demand for such goods through standard Keynesian multiplier effects and augment sales and production. On the other hand, reducing taxes raises disposable income in the hands of households inducing higher aggregate consumption spending.

Excessive reliance on fiscal policy and reckless government spending have led to situations of stagflation in several economies including the US during the 1970s. Stagflation entails simultaneous occurrence of economic stagnation and high inflation. Due to persistent deficit financing to engineer high economic growth, several developing countries, particularly in Latin America, have witnessed balance of payments crises. The economic crisis of 1991 in India was also linked to excessive deficit financing during the 1980s.

Consequently, there has been growing adoption of fiscal discipline and consolidation in the last several decades across both industrially advanced and emerging economies. The process of fiscal consolidation, particularly in emerging economies, has been further emphasised and guided by the Washington consensus.[7] Various economies in Latin America and Southeast Asia which suffered economic crises during the 1990s had to adopt structural adjustment and macroeconomic stabilisation programmes under the guidance of the International Monetary Fund (IMF). Fiscal correction and consolidation have been a central element of this programme.

Thus, there has been gradual de-emphasis on deficit financing beyond a limit. Fiscal policy has been used in a constrained manner, particularly under recessionary conditions. However, under extreme situations like the Covid-19 pandemic, governments across countries were compelled to deviate from the fiscal consolidation process. Pressure to arrest severe economic contraction and massive job losses outweighed concerns on high deficit financing. After the pandemic, it has been observed that there is tapering of fiscal stimulus and return to emphasis on fiscal prudence.

With emphasis on fiscal discipline, monetary policy has emerged as the main macroeconomic policy tool to moderate short-run economic fluctuations.

4.3.1 Working of Monetary Policy

Monetary policy is primarily a macroeconomic demand management tool. In India, the RBI is entrusted with the responsibility for conducting monetary policy.

Monetary policy works as follows: It begins with an assessment of the prevailing economic conditions as also the likely out-turn in the near future, maybe over the following year or so. If the projected economic growth or inflationary situation is within a level acceptable to the RBI, perhaps there is no need for fresh policy action. If the economy is under overheating conditions, which implies higher inflationary levels, it requires monetary tightening to moderate aggregate spending and inflation. This is achieved by the RBI raising its *policy rate* (repo rate under the LAF). This is the interest rate charged by the RBI to banks for providing overnight funding. As

[7] Washington consensuses refer to the structural adjustment and macroeconomic stabilisation programmes prescribed by the IMF as part of conditionalities to obtain loans from the IMF by a member country facing BOP crisis.

borrowing for banks from the RBI becomes costly, they in turn pass it on to their borrowers.

Thus, hike in the policy rate as part of the monetary tightening exercise leads to a higher interest rate on bank lending. In turn, higher lending rates charged by banks raise borrowing costs for households and firms. This moderates consumption and investment spending financed by such borrowing and reduces overall spending in an economy. Lower aggregate demand and reduced sales act as a disincentive to more production. This slows down overall production in the economy. Lower demand as compared to the amount of goods and services produced dampens prices as well. Thus, monetary policy can help in moderating growth and inflation during periods of overheating.

Similarly, under situations of economic slowdown and recession, monetary policy can be used for reviving economic growth. Adoption of monetary policy accommodation, which entails lowering of the policy rate, makes borrowing from the RBI cheaper for banks. Banks may pass part of this benefit to their borrowers. With lower costs of borrowing, consumption and investment expenditure may rise, particularly that funded by bank loans. With augmentation of aggregate demand and sales, scope for greater capacity utilisation by industry improves. This may lead to higher economic growth.

A hypothetical example is given in Box 4.2 to illustrate how monetary policy works.

For further details on how monetary policy works to moderate short-term economic fluctuations, the reader may refer to Mishkin (2004) and Barro (2008).

4.4 Banks and Monetary Transmission Mechanism

Monetary transmission mechanism (MTM) explains the process through which monetary policy impulses get transmitted to the economy. Research on MTM emerged as an offshoot of the post-Keynesian versus monetarist debate on the effectiveness of monetary policy.

The post-Keynesians questioned the ability of monetary policy to revive an economy from recessionary conditions. They pointed out that interest rates were quite low during the Great Depression. Despite low interest rates which reflect monetary expansion, recessionary conditions persisted for very long. This led to questioning the effectiveness of monetary policy. The concept of

Box 4.2 A simple illustration of how monetary policy affects the economy

Assume that Anjali plans to purchase an apartment. As her savings are grossly insufficient to buy the apartment, she applies for a home loan of INR 70 lakh from a bank. Assume that considering her credit score, its cost of deposits and other factors, the bank has decided to extend a loan of INR 70 lakh and charge interest at the rate of 10 per cent per annum. Accordingly, say, the bank works out the equated monthly installments (EMI) which Anjali needs to pay the bank to be INR 70,000. This EMI is the sum of a portion of the principal repayment and interest charges. Assuming that Anjali's monthly income is INR 1,20,000 and the minimum amount which she requires to meet other necessary monthly expenses is INR 50,000, she may decide to obtain the home loan and purchase the apartment.

Let us assume that at this point the economy encounters an emerging inflationary situation with signs of overheating. To control inflation, the aggregate spending needs to be reduced. In this perspective, the RBI decides to raise its policy rate from 5 per cent to 6 per cent. The bank, in turn, with its motive of profit maximisation may respond to this hike in the cost of borrowing from the RBI by raising its own lending rates.

The bank's decision on raising its lending rate depends on a variety of factors other than variation in the cost of borrowing from the RBI. These factors include the cost of retail deposits, cost of borrowing from other commercial banks and financial institutions, demand for loans, response of other banks to the hike in the policy rate by the RBI, its own perception about the RBI's commitment to price stability, and so on.

Assume that considering all other factors, the concerned bank raises its home loan rate from 10 to 10.5 per cent. With this revision, let us assume that the EMI for Anjali for the home loan of INR 70 lakh increases from INR 70,000 to INR 74,500.

Now, under the revised EMI, if Anjali proceeds with the home loan, she will be left with only INR 45,500 after meeting the EMI payments. This is less than the INR 50,000 required to cover her other monthly expenses. So she may not avail the home loan right now and instead wait for her income to increase or the EMI to come down, enabling her to meet the requirements for paying the EMI as also her household expenses.

There may be many potential borrowers like Anjali who face a similar situation. With postponement of their decision to avail home loans and purchase apartments, builders would face a fall in the demand for apartments. Hence, builders, in turn, may postpone their earlier plan to build new apartments. This will reflect in a cutting down of demand for cement, iron and steel, other construction materials, electrical appliances and furniture as also of demand for labour and engineers.

Thus, the RBI's decision to raise the policy rate gets translated to reduction in demand for goods and services through changes in the cost and availability of bank credit. This ultimately reflects in some combination of reduction in the production of such goods and services and their prices. Assume a cement manufacturer had earlier planned to produce, say, 1,000 sacks of cement per month, and now it is able to sell only 700 sacks due to deficient demand. It observes piling up of unplanned inventories. It may respond to this by cutting down prices slightly to dispose excess unplanned inventories. If deficient demand conditions persist, the prudent decision would be to downsize production of cement. All other producers may also respond in a similar manner.

This is a simple hypothetical example of how the monetary policy action of the RBI gets transmitted to affect overall production and general prices in an economy.

liquidity trap was used to justify the point. It was suggested that when interest rates are extremely low, monetary policy expansion cannot reduce them any further. In such circumstances, monetary expansion becomes ineffective in raising aggregate spending in an economy.

On the contrary, monetarists under the leadership of Milton Friedman tried to associate the Great Depression with monetary contraction. It was underscored that a large number of bank failures during this period actually signified monetary contraction. The seminal work by Friedman and Schwartz (1963) analysed the historical data for the US for the period 1867–1960 and traced the fluctuations in economic activities to corresponding fluctuations in the growth of money stock. Further, considering the price deflation (negative inflation) that prevailed during the Great Depression, it was argued that real interest rates were actually higher, despite low nominal interest rates.[8] In this

[8] Real interest rate = nominal interest rate – inflation. So if the nominal interest rate = 3 per cent, and inflation = (–)4 per cent, then the real interest rate = 3 – (–4) = 7 per cent.

backdrop, a large body of research works were undertaken to counter the post-Keynesian doubt on the effectiveness of monetary policy.

MTM essentially provides details of the propagation of monetary policy action through various channels. Monetary policy decisions affect medium-term interest rates, foreign exchange rates, asset prices, bank deposits, credit growth, and so on, which in turn impact various components of aggregate expenditure such as consumption and investment spending and net exports, among others. Finally, variation in aggregate expenditure affects economic growth and prices. Clarity in understanding the finer details of channels of monetary transmission is critical for the effective conduct of monetary policy. In a special issue of Fall 1995, *the Journal of Economic Perspective* published select papers on MTM which are widely referred to in the literature. Technical details of various channels of monetary transmission are summarised in Appendix 4A. Our focus here is to highlight the role of banks in MTM.

In traditional Keynesian analysis, it is suggested that monetary tightening (expansion) leads to rise (fall) in interest rates. This is because, there being a given demand for money by the public, monetary tightening (expansion) makes availability of money relatively scarce (plentiful). As interest rate is the price of liquidity or money, scarcity (abundance) of money raises (reduces) interest rates. High (low) interest rates, in turn, discourage (encourage) consumption and investment spending financed through borrowing, thus affecting aggregate expenditure.[9] This policy-driven moderation in the deviation of aggregate expenditure from *potential output* smoothens economic fluctuations. Potential output refers to the long-run production capacity in an economy. It is the output level determined by the long-run equilibrium in the AD–AS model.

Propagation of monetary policy impulses through interest rate variation as explained in the preceding paragraphs is popularly referred to as the *interest rate channel* of monetary policy transmission. Use of traditional Keynesian thinking to explain the MTM in this manner is known as the *money view*.

Needless to mention, for the effective working of the interest rate channel, the role of banks is significant. However, other financial institutions and

[9] In an open economy, the changing domestic interest rate affects cross-border capital flows which in turn influence *net exports* through domestic currency appreciation or depreciation, and consequently impacts aggregate expenditure. This is popularly referred to as the exchange rate channel. Necessary details are provided in Appendix 4A.

markets play a similar role too. This is because all forms of external financing such as borrowing from banks, the capital market, money market, and so on, are affected by changing interest rates.

On the contrary, many economic thinkers, guided by the seminal works of Gurley and Shaw (1955, 1956), believe that banks play a very special role in the MTM. Bernanke (1993), Bernanke and Gertler (1995), Kashyap, Stein and Wilcox (1993), and so on, popularised this view. Under this line of thought, the role of banks is assigned critical importance and seen as different from other segments of the financial system. This is known as the *credit view*. However, the channels under the credit view should not be seen as operating in isolation; rather, they should be treated as complementing and strengthening the traditional Keynesian channel.

MTM under the credit view can be explained in two ways, highlighting the uniqueness of banks and bank assets or liabilities. These are as follows.

4.4.1 Bank Lending Channel

First, let us describe the traditional bank lending channel (Figure 4.3). Monetary accommodation (contraction) leads to higher (lower) growth of bank deposits. This is because monetary variation effected through open market operations or changes in statutory reserves or policy rates causes corresponding changes in bank reserves. As explained in standard textbooks, changes in bank reserves lead to large-scale changes in bank deposits in the deposit multiplication process (Karlan and Morduch, 2020; Mishkin, 2004). It is highlighted that if the banks maintain the reserves to deposit ratio at 10 per cent, a given increase in bank reserves leads to a 10-fold increase in bank deposits in the entire banking system. If the banks maintain the reserves-to-deposit ratio at 5 per cent, the same change in bank reserves leads to a 20-fold increase in bank deposits.

In the second step, higher (lower) growth in bank deposits results in corresponding higher (lower) growth in bank credit. This is because deposits form the main source of funding for bank lending, and it is always profitable for banks to deploy deposits in the form of loans and investments to maximise interest income and profit.

Higher (lower) bank lending facilitates higher (lower) consumption and investment expenditure promoting (reducing) overall aggregate demand. Variation in aggregate demand, in turn, causes corresponding changes in output and prices.

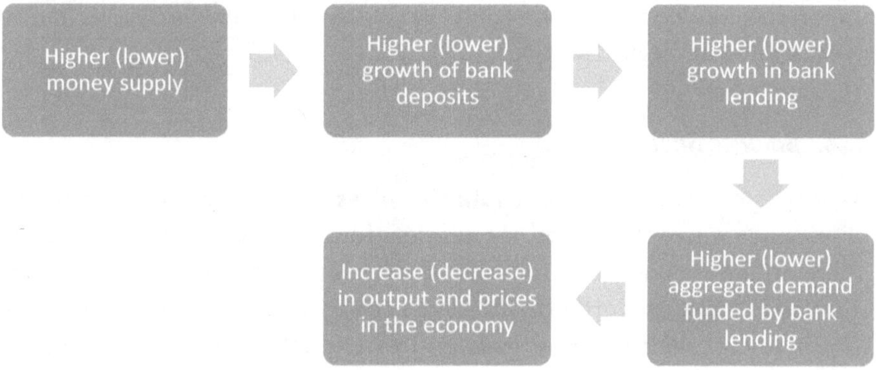

Figure 4.3 Traditional bank lending channel

Source: Prepared by the author.

However, the effective working of this traditional bank lending channel rests on two important conditions. First, in case of monetary tightening, banks should not be able to compensate fall in bank deposit growth by taking recourse to any alternative source of funds. Otherwise, by making up for any fall in deposits, banks can maintain credit flow making monetary policy ineffective. It was observed that in the US, banks generated funds by issuing money market instruments like CDs to partially compensate the fall in bank deposits during monetary tightening. CDs are not subject to statutory reserve requirements unlike retail deposits. This implied weakening of the effectiveness of the traditional bank lending channel.

Second, the impact of bank credit contraction should not be neutralised by borrowers by availing funds from the capital market or other sources of borrowing. Otherwise, trapping other sources of borrowing, the level of investment and consumption spending can be sustained, rendering the bank lending channel ineffective.

However, it is important to note that households and small firms generally do not have access to the equity and bond markets for funding their projects. So the bank lending channel remains relevant as long as there is a set of borrowers like households and small firms which are bank-dependent. Moreover, in the Indian context, the bank lending channel is important as the market size for CDs and CPs (which are used by corporates to raise short-duration funding) is quite small as compared to the banking sector as a whole.

Notwithstanding any weakening of the traditional bank lending channel, banks still remain very relevant in monetary policy transmission. Their importance can be also discussed in the context of the *balance sheet channel* as elaborated in the next section.

4.4.2 Balance Sheet Channel

As discussed in Chapter 3, lending involves the problem of *information asymmetry*, where the lender has deficient information about the borrower. There are also associated problems of *adverse selection* and *moral hazard*. *Adverse selection* occurs due to the tendency and efforts by a high-risk person to camouflage their financial position to look highly creditworthy so as to successfully obtain a loan. On the other hand, *moral hazard* arises due to attempts of the borrower to divert the funds availed through a loan to other high-return high-risk activities deviating from the stated purpose. Details of the same are provided in Chapter 6.

To resolve the information asymmetry problem, banks assess the creditworthiness of loan seekers based on their financial standing derived from their balance sheet position, cash flow projections, debt default history, and so on. If the financial standing and future earning prospects of the borrower are sound, they get a good credit rating. This improves the probability of their obtaining a bank loan. Monetary policy impacts the balance sheet and cash flow position of firms and households in various ways as discussed below and consequently regulates the flow of bank credit.

- Monetary expansion puts excess money in the hands of the general public as compared to their demand. This leads to higher purchase of real goods and services as well as raises their spending on financial or physical assets, including equites. Higher demand for equities raises equity prices and Tobin's Q.[10] This induces firms to raise equity capital for funding investment spendings. Moreover, higher equity prices improve net worth and hence the creditworthiness of firms augmenting bank credit flow and adding to their investments.
- Rising prices of equities and residential buildings due to money supply expansion improve the creditworthiness of households. Households cannot raise funds in the capital market and banks act

[10] Tobin's Q is defined as the ratio between the market value of a firm and the replacement cost of its capital.

as their main source of borrowing. Improvement in creditworthiness promotes bank lending to such households and augments their consumption spending. Higher prices of assets of households due to monetary expansion also raise their consumption expenditure through the *wealth effect*.

- Similarly, monetary contraction leads to falling asset prices. Falling prices of equities, residential buildings and other assets reduce the net worth of potential borrowers and weaken their creditworthiness. This enhances the scope for adverse selection and moral hazard and reduces the flow of bank credit.
- Monetary expansion engenders a low interest–rate environment. This improves the cash flow of existing borrowers. Low-interest payments improve the creditworthiness of firms and households, augmenting bank credit flow. Here again, monetary expansion improves the financial position of borrowers and enhances their eligibility to obtain bank loans. On the contrary, monetary contraction pushes market interest rates up and hence raises the interest payment obligations of firms and households. This adversely affects their cash flows and makes it difficult for them to obtain bank loans.
- Monetary policy expansion raises unanticipated inflation in the economy. This is because unexpected excess money supply as compared to a given money demand by the public is tantamount to more money chasing a given amount of goods and services. Higher demand for goods and services relative to the amount of goods and services available causes unanticipated inflation. The value of financial liabilities or the debt of firms and households declines in real terms due to this unanticipated inflation. On the contrary, the real value of the assets of firms, which are mostly in physical form such as factories, machinery, inventories of finished goods or raw material, does not fall. Overall, the financial position of firms improves with unanticipated inflation and makes them more creditworthy. Similarly, monetary contraction with unanticipated disinflation or deflation reduces the creditworthiness of borrowers by raising the real value of their debt.

Thus, monetary policy action affects the creditworthiness of firms and households in several ways. The changing financial position of loan seekers makes it easier or more difficult for them to avail bank loans. In this manner, the balance sheet channel emphasises the role of banks in monetary policy transmission.

It may be reiterated that both the conventional bank lending channel and the balance sheet channel are more relevant for households and small firms. They do not have the comfort of accessing the equity or bond markets to borrow funds for undertaking investment and consumption spending. Banks are their main source of borrowing. Given this unique aspect, the role of banks in facilitating monetary transmission in an economy cannot be overemphasised.

4.5 Empirical Evidence

A large body of research works empirically analyse the working of various channels of the MTM. In the literature, a debate on the validity of the credit view versus the money view is clearly discernible since the late 1980s. S. King (1986), Kashyap, Stein and Wilcox (1993), Kashyap and Stein (1994), Gertler and Gilchrist (1993, 1994), Kim (1999), Kryshko (2001), Morsink and Bayoumi (2001), and so on, support the dominance of bank lending as a conduit for monetary policy transmission. On the other hand, Romer and Romer (1990), Bernanke and Blinder (1992), and Morris and Sellon (1995) do not support such special role of bank lending.

Let us discuss the empirical evidence of the role of banks in monetary transmission in the Indian context.

Figure 4.4 presents the three-year moving average bank credit growth and economic growth in India during the post-reform period. It uses the three-year moving average growth rate to smoothen the graph. It reveals some association between the growth rate of bank credit and economic growth. Particularly, in the periods 1993–96 and 2001–06, rising growth in GDP was associated with rising growth in bank credit. Similarly, the periods 1996–98 and 2006–13 witnessed deceleration in both GDP and bank credit growth simultaneously.

Table 4.1 presents the average growth rate of bank credit and GDP for different phases during the post-reform period, pointing to close interlinkages between them which are summarised as follows:

- The Indian economy accelerated in the period 1994–97 after economic reforms were introduced from the early 1990s. The average

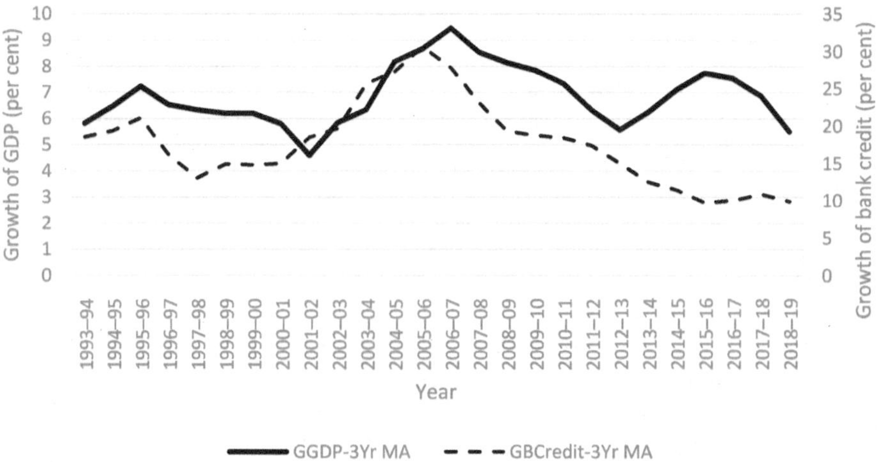

Figure 4.4 Growth of GDP and bank credit: three-year moving average

Source: Prepared by the author based on data obtained from RBI's *Handbook of Statistics on Indian Economy*, https://data.rbi.org.in/DBIE/#/dbie/reports/Publication/Time-Series%20Publications/Handbook%20of%20Statistics%20on%20the%20Indian%20Economy (accessed 18 July 2022).

economic growth accelerated to 7.3 per cent during 1994–97 from 5.1 per cent during 1992–94. This was matched by acceleration of average bank credit growth to 21.1 per cent during 1994–97 as compared to 12.9 per cent during 1992–94.

- The deceleration of economic growth to an average of 5.3 per cent during 1997–2003 was similarly associated with a bank credit slowdown to an average of 16.7 per cent during the same period.
- The Indian economy witnessed its fastest growth of 7.4 per cent during 2003–11. The average bank credit growth commensurately accelerated to 23.7 per cent during this period.
- The deceleration of average economic growth during 2011–16 to 5.7 per cent is also associated with the slowing down of bank credit growth to 15 per cent.
- However, acceleration of economic growth to 6.8 per cent during 2016–20 occurred despite further slowdown of bank credit.

Broadly, this tentative analysis hints at close interlinkages between fluctuations in economic growth in India and similar swings in bank credit growth. Except in the last sub-period in Table 4.1, the evidence support a positive association between bank credit growth and economic growth

Table 4.1 Bank credit growth and economic growth in India

(*Per cent*)

Period	Growth of bank credit	Economic growth	Growth in per capita income
1992–94	12.9	5.1	3.6
1994–97	21.1	7.3	5.3
1997–2003	16.7	5.3	3.4
2003–11	23.7	7.4	5.4
2011–16	15.0	5.7	3.3
2016–20	10.4	6.8	5.4

Source: Calculated by the author based on data obtained from RBI's *Handbook of Statistics on Indian Economy*, https://data.rbi.org.in/DBIE/#/dbie/reports/Publication/Time-Series%20 Publications/Handbook%20of%20Statistics%20on%20the%20Indian%20Economy (accessed 18 July 2022).

during the post-reform period. However, this does not necessarily imply that economic fluctuations are caused by variation in bank credit growth. To establish that, we require application of formal econometric analysis.

A large number of studies have been conducted using appropriate econometric analysis for examining the monetary transmission process in India focusing on banking channels. These studies mainly use time series–based vector auto-regression (VAR) models and panel data techniques. The main findings are summarised as follows:

- Mukhopadhyay (1999) tested the effectiveness of the credit channel by analysing the differential impact of monetary policy across various industries. His empirical analysis suggested that small bank-dependent industries suffered most during periods of quantitative credit controls. As indicated earlier, small firms do not enjoy access to the capital market or money market.
- Pandit et al. (2006) found banks cutting down their lending in response to monetary tightening. PSBs were seen to be more responsive to monetary policy shocks. They also found a strong impact of monetary policy on the credit flow of small banks. Limited ability to fund their lending made their response to monetary tightening more pronounced.
- Nachane, Ghosh and Ray (2006) observed that the impact of monetary policy on bank lending differed across banks depending

on whether banks were constrained by risk-based capital standards, loan delinquencies or liquidity conditions.

- Samantaraya and Kamaiah (2011) observed that the maximum impact of monetary policy on bank investments was realised within six months while that on bank credit was realised after nearly one to two years. They further found that the impact of monetary policy shocks on output became prominent after nearly a year and that on inflation after nearly one and half years. Given the similarity in the longer lag effect of monetary policy on bank credit, output and inflation, they underscored the importance of bank credit as a conduit for transmission of monetary policy impulses.
- Sengupta (2014) established the importance of the bank lending channel during the post-reform period. But she also revealed its weakening strength since the early 2000s. She has attributed such weakening to the greater globalisation of banking operations, liberalisation of the financial markets and the impact of the GFC on international capital flows in India. She found the market-based interest rate and asset price channels becoming stronger during this period.
- Ghosh, Narayan and Garg (2021) have re-examined the differential impact of monetary policy on various banks and bank-loan dependent firms using the latest data (covering up to 2018–19). They confirm the working of the first leg of the bank-based channel of monetary transmission: rise in the RBI's repo rate under the LAF reducing term loans extended by banks with a lag. They observe that an increase in the spread between the call money rate and the LAF repo rate, implying monetary tightening, constrains the liquidity position of banks. However, it is noted that increase in term loans by liquidity-constrained banks does not translate to augmenting the capital expenditure of firms (borrowers). Rather, the loans lead to rise in their current liabilities. On the contrary, rise in the term loans of banks with adequate liquidity results in expanding the capital expenditure of their borrowers.

While there is wider acceptance of the ability of monetary policy to moderate aggregate spending in an economy through monetary tightening, there have been questions on the output augmenting capability of monetary policy accommodations. This is because low interest rates on bank deposits driven by monetary policy accommodation may lead to savers shifting to other forms of saving like buying equities or accumulating non-financial wealth such as gold or land. Eroding of the deposit base may constrain bank credit growth instead of augmenting it. As popularly stated, you can pull a string but cannot push it.

Samantaraya (2015) attempted to examine this asymmetrical impact of monetary policy, focusing on transmission through the bank credit channel. Both demand- and supply-side factors were explicitly considered in the determination of bank credit. It was observed that monetary tightening and the consequent rise in interest rates on bank loans dampened demand for bank lending. On the contrary, a lower interest rate regime driven by monetary accommodation did not promote bank lending because lower interest rates depressed growth of bank deposits which in turn constrained supply of bank credit. Thus, monetary policy accommodation could not help in bank credit expansion while monetary tightening was useful for moderating bank credit growth.

To summarise, the empirical evidence in the Indian context broadly supported the relevance of banks and bank credit in monetary policy transmission.

4.6 Conclusion

Any economy encounters short-run fluctuations, popularly referred to as the business cycle phenomenon. Excessive economic fluctuations cause considerable hardships to different stakeholders. While severe economic recession or slowdown causes painful unemployment, overheating engenders high inflationary conditions. Public policy initiatives are prescribed to moderate such economic fluctuations and reduce hardships to the general public. A good understanding of the causes of fluctuations is a necessary precondition for framing suitable policies for economic stabilisation. This chapter summarised ideas drawing from various schools of thought to explain short-term economic fluctuations.

The chapter also highlighted how monetary policy has emerged as the main policy tool for macroeconomic management aimed at economic stabilisation. Bank credit facilitates transmission of monetary impulses to the economy. The empirical evidence largely support the role of bank-based channels for monetary policy transmission. In this perspective, the chapter underscored the central role of banks towards moderating short-term fluctuations in an economy as banks and bank credit work as important conduits for monetary policy transmission.

Appendix 4A

MTM channels explicitly specify how monetary policy influences the economy. They unravel the black box and provide details of how monetary policy shocks affect aggregate demand through different economic and financial variables. These channels are named depending on the relative importance of a particular economic or financial variable in the transmission process. Mishkin (1996, 2004) has provided a schematic description of the working of key MTM channels.

Money View

The channels which can be placed under the *money view* are (*a*) the interest rate channel, (*b*) the exchange rate channel and (*c*) the asset price channel. The working of these three channels is briefly explained as follows.

Interest Rate Channel

The interest rate channel is basically Keynesian in character. It assumes that variation in money supply for a given demand for money alters interest rates. In the face of fixed marginal efficiency of the investment schedule, higher (lower) interest rates discourage (encourage) investments. This variation in investment expenditure affects aggregate demand and ultimately output and prices. This can be explained based on Mishkin (1996) in terms of the following schematic:

$$M\downarrow \Rightarrow r\uparrow \Rightarrow I\downarrow \Rightarrow Y \,\&\, P\downarrow \qquad (4A.1)$$

This simply depicts that reduction in money supply (M) sequentially causes rise in interest rate (r), discourages investment (I) and finally reduces output (Y) and prices (P).

Exchange Rate Channel

The exchange rate channel is related to the interest rate channel. However, working of this channel requires adoption of a flexible exchange rate regime and considerable global integration of the concerned economy, both in terms of foreign trade and investments. Without restriction on cross-border capital flows, keeping other things constant, foreign investment flows become sensitive to the domestic interest rate. Rise in the domestic interest rate due to monetary tightening makes investing in domestic assets more attractive for foreign investors. This leads to higher foreign investment inflows and consequently greater availability of foreign currencies in the domestic economy. Plentiful availability of foreign currencies as compared to the domestic currency results in appreciation of the latter. With appreciation of the domestic currency, exports become expensive for foreign buyers and imports become cheaper for domestic buyers. Loss of competitiveness of exports thus has adverse consequences for domestic exports while imports rise. Therefore, exports minus imports, referred to as net exports, fall. Finally, aggregate demand which includes net exports as one of its components falls, leading to reduction in output and prices. This is explained schematically as follows:

$$M\downarrow \Rightarrow r\uparrow \Rightarrow \text{Net foreign investment inflows}\uparrow \Rightarrow \text{Exchange rate appreciation} \Rightarrow \text{Net exports}\downarrow \Rightarrow Y \ \& \ P\downarrow \tag{4A.2}$$

It is important to note that the effectiveness of the exchange rate channel heavily depends on central bank intervention in the foreign exchange (forex) market to reduce the volatility of the exchange rate.[11] If the central bank manages the exchange rate and internees in the forex market so that there is no exchange rate variation due to cross-border capital flows, the exchange rate channel does not operate effectively. Moreover, the strength of the elasticity of exports and imports with respect to the forex rate is also an important factor.

---

[11] Central banks like the RBI generally intervene in the forex market to avoid undue and excessive appreciation of domestic currency to protect domestic exporters. They also intervene to avert excessive volatility of exchange rates which has serious adverse implications for foreign trade and hurts foreign investors' sentiments.

Asset Price Channel

The asset price channel is also related to the interest rate channel. There are two ways to explain this channel. The first is related to Tobin's Q and investment decisions while the second is related to the *wealth effect* and consumption expenditure. Existence of a well-developed equity market is critical to the operation of this channel.

With monetary tightening, availability of money becomes inadequate as compared to money demand. The additional requirements of money may be met by liquidating some other assets including equity or other forms of wealth. This can also be explained through portfolio adjustment. Scarcity of money in the entire financial portfolio of the public as compared to other forms of assets, including equity, leads to selling out of other assets in the adjustment process. Selling of equity stocks depresses equity prices (Pe) thus reducing the market value of firms. This, in turn, reduces Tobin's Q (which is the ratio between the market value of the firm and the replacement cost of its capital). Thus, relatively, the replacement cost of capital for firms becomes more expensive as compared to the value of the respective firms in the equity market. This discourages firms from undertaking investment activity by raising equity capital. Fall in investment leads to reduction in output and prices as explained earlier. This is schematically presented as follows:

$$M\downarrow \Rightarrow Pe\downarrow \Rightarrow \text{Tobin's } Q\downarrow \Rightarrow I\downarrow \Rightarrow Y \text{ \& } P\downarrow \quad (4A.3)$$

Similarly, with monetary accommodation, plentiful availability of money as against the demand leads to the public's efforts to reduce the surplus money and adjust the portfolio by buying other assets, including equities. Similar to the earlier explanation, more demand for equities leads to rise in Tobin's Q. Higher market value of firms as compared to the replacement cost of the firms' capital implies that by raising small amounts of equity capital, firms can undertake more investments. High investment consequently leads to rise in output and prices.

As mentioned, operation of the asset price channel can also be explained by taking into account the *wealth effect*. Wealth effect refers to the impact of change in the wealth of households or consumers on their consumption spending. Any decline in wealth makes households or consumers feel poorer and induces reduction in their consumption expenditure. Household consumption expenditure is the most dominant component of aggregate demand in an economy. As indicated earlier, monetary contraction (accommodation) leads to reduction (increase) in asset prices. Through the wealth effect, fall (rise) in asset prices results in reduction (increase) in consumption expenditure and ultimately affects output and prices. This is depicted by the following schematic:

$$M\downarrow \Rightarrow Pe\downarrow \Rightarrow \text{Wealth effect} \Rightarrow \text{Consumption}\downarrow \Rightarrow Y \ \& \ P\downarrow \qquad (4A.4)$$

The impact of monetary policy under the channels hitherto discussed is expected to be uniform across all investors and consumers.

Credit View

Under the *credit view*, bank credit plays a critical role in explaining the MTM. So these channels are known as *credit channels*. The working of these channels can be explained in two ways, namely (*a*) the bank lending channel and (*b*) the balance sheet channel.

Bank Lending Channel

The bank lending channel depicts the traditional explanation of how monetary policy operates. Under this channel, it is assumed that monetary contraction (expansion) leads to fall (rise) in bank deposits. This is obvious as bank deposits form the dominant component of money stock. In the financial intermediation process, bank deposits are the base which determine the scope for lending and investment by banks. Contraction of bank deposits due to monetary tightening thus constrains fund availability to banks for lending and hence reduces bank lending.

Lending to firms involves information asymmetry. Firms have full information about their financial conditions and better understanding about the prospects of the projects in which they are investing.

Prospective lenders generally do not have adequate information on both these aspects. This asymmetry in information inhibits the accessibility of the capital market to small firms and households for raising funds. They are thus heavily dependent on bank lending. Banks with their long association with customers have better information about these firms and do overcome the problem of information asymmetry.

If there is fall in bank credit due to monetary tightening as indicated earlier, these bank-dependent firms are deprived of bank lending, and lack of access to the market for funds compels them to withhold their investment activities. This, in turn, can lead to reduction in output and prices as explained earlier. The working of the bank lending channel can be presented schematically as follows:

$$\text{M}\downarrow \Rightarrow \text{Deposits}\downarrow \Rightarrow \text{Credit}\downarrow \Rightarrow \text{I}\downarrow \Rightarrow \text{Y \& P}\downarrow \qquad (4A.5)$$

However, as mentioned earlier, effective operation of the bank lending channel presupposes two necessary conditions. First, banks do not have access to alternative sources of funding when there is contraction of their deposits. Otherwise, they can take recourse to such sources, compensate for the fall in deposits and maintain the scale of their lending activities. The second condition requires that bank-dependent firms do not have any alternative option to raise funds to finance their projects when bank credit contracts.

Balance Sheet Channel

Introduction of CDs, CPs and other similar financial innovations in the last three to four decades may have diluted the role of the bank lending channel to an extent. This is because CDs help banks to raise resources when monetary tightening reduces bank deposits. Similarly, CPs and access to the capital market open up alternative sources of funds for big firms when bank credit plummets due to monetary tightening. Nevertheless, bank credit is important for monetary transmission operating under balance sheet channels. These channels explain how monetary policy through variation of bank credit can influence investment and household consumption spending, taking into account monetary policy impact on their balance sheet and cash flows. Basically, bank lending entails assessment of the creditworthiness of borrowers in the face of information asymmetry. Monetary policy influences the *net worth* of firms and borrowers.

Now, let us explain how monetary tightening or accommodation affects the net worth of borrowers. First, monetary tightening as discussed under the asset price channel reduces the equity price of firms and thus directly diminishes their net worth. Second, monetary tightening by raising market interest rates blows up interest payments of firms and reduces their cash flow.

Reduction in cash flow, in turn, adversely affects the creditworthiness of firms. Third, monetary tightening leads to unanticipated fall in general prices which increases the value of financial liabilities in real terms, thus reducing the net worth of firms.

Variation in the net worth of firms influences their creditworthiness and accordingly affects the lending decisions of banks. Balance sheet channels explain the impact of monetary tightening on bank credit and investments taking into account the problem of moral hazard and adverse selection. The working of this channel is as follows:

$$\begin{aligned} M\downarrow &\Rightarrow \text{Adverse selection \& moral hazard} \\ &\Rightarrow \text{Credit}\downarrow \Rightarrow I\downarrow \Rightarrow Y \,\&\, P\downarrow \end{aligned} \tag{4A.6}$$

Using households as potential borrowers, one can analyse the impact of monetary policy on the economy through variation in consumption expenditure too.

Revision Questions and Problems

1. What are the major factors causing economic fluctuations popularly referred to as the *business cycle* phenomenon?
2. How does demand for labour respond to rise in real wages?
3. Using sticky price and price misperception assumptions, describe how monetary factors explain economic fluctuations.
4. How does monetary policy work as the key macroeconomic management tool to moderate short-run economic fluctuations?
5. Briefly discuss the MTM and compare the relevance of the credit view versus the money view in this regard.
6. How does bank credit act as a key conduit for monetary policy transmission?
7. How can the importance of balance sheet channels be explained in the context of the information asymmetry problem in lending?

5

Spread of Banking in India

The Regional Dimension

Learning Objectives

- To assess regional aspects of the banking business in India
- To analyse regional disparity in economic prosperity in India
- To link the regional distribution of banking to the regional disparity in economic prosperity
- To draw policy implications for improving inter-state economic disparity in India by overcoming uneven distribution of banking services

5.1 Introduction

India adopted comprehensive economic reforms from the early 1990s in response to the BOP crisis of 1991. The reform initiatives included measures such as liberalisation of industrial policies removing entry barriers and government control on industrial expansion, outward orientation policies promoting foreign trade and investment, overall macroeconomic stabilisation including fiscal reforms and policy initiatives towards developing a broad-based financial sector. As a consequence of these initiatives, India witnessed significant improvements in overall macroeconomic performance during the post-reform period.

For nearly three decades after the introduction of the reforms, the average economic growth was close to 6.5 per cent. This is nearly double the average growth of around 3.5 per cent experienced during the first three decades following India's independence in 1947. Despite an economic slowdown in 2008–09 as a fallout of the GFC, the average growth during 2003–11 was estimated to be 7.4 per cent. This extended period of high and stable economic growth was unprecedented. The percentage of people living below the poverty line gradually declined from 35.97 per cent in 1993–94 to 29.80 per cent during 1999–2000 and further to 21.92 per cent in 2011–12 (as per various issues of the Economic Survey published by the Government of India). Notwithstanding debates on figures relating to the number of the poor,[1] various official committees and working groups—such as the Alagh Committee (1979), the Lakdawala Committee (1993), the Tendulkar Committee (2009) and the Rangarajan Committee (2014), among others—have broadly confirmed the declining trend of the poverty ratio (Planning Commission, 2009, 2014).

The exports-to-GDP ratio substantially improved from less than 6 per cent in the pre-reform period to around 11–17 per cent in the late 2010s and early 2020s. The ratio of current account deficit to GDP has largely been contained within the range of 1–2 per cent during the post-reform period. India stands, as of August 2024, as the fifth largest economy in the world. Its importance as a global economic superpower is getting widely acknowledged. Many Indian companies have taken over leading business firms in different segments around the world. Mittal Steel of Lakshmi Niwas Mittal had acquired the leading European steel manufacturer Arcelor in 2006 and became the largest steel manufacturer in the world. Tata Motors acquired British automobile giant Jaguar Land Rover from Ford Motor Company in 2008. Despite economic contraction in 2020–21 due to the Covid-19 pandemic, India largely bounced back with 9.1 per cent economic growth during 2021–22, followed by 7 per cent growth during 2022–23 (RBI, 2023a). This is noteworthy in the backdrop of the global economic slowdown due to the adverse implications emerging from the Russia–Ukraine conflict. India legitimately aspires to become the third largest economy in the world in the near future.

Notwithstanding these phenomenal economic achievements during the post-reform period, there are some concerns pertaining to the inclusiveness of the growth process. It is observed that despite achieving remarkable economic growth during the post-reform period, performance on employment generation is largely not satisfactory. A related issue is the non-uniform spread of economic prosperity across regions and states. Several states have maintained fast growth rates of above 10 per cent while some others are lagging behind.[2]

---

[1] This is mainly due to differences in methodologies used for poverty estimation.

[2] Richer states such as Gujarat, Maharashtra, Tamil Nadu and Uttarakhand registered average growth rate of 10–13 per cent during India's high growth phase of 2003–11,

Several empirical studies have observed that the degree of dispersion in growth rates across states increased significantly during the 1990s (Ahluwalia, 2000; Bhattacharya and Sakthivel, 2004; Ghosh, 2008). However, some recent studies provided encouraging indications on a few poor states catching up, particularly during the 2000s (Kumar and Subramanian, 2012; Samantaraya et al., 2014).

In this chapter, the main focus is to explore the association between the regional distribution of banking and economic disparity in India, particularly during the post-reform period. The interlinkage between financial development and economic growth has already been discussed in Chapter 3. In this perspective, the association between inter-state disparities in the growth process and banking services in India is explored. Accordingly, useful policy implications are drawn in terms of using bank credit to reduce regional disparity.

The chapter is organised as follows. In section 5.2, we analyse empirically the regional spread of banking in India. This is discussed in terms of the inter-state distribution of bank deposits and credit. Economic disparity across states is considered in section 5.3. In section 5.4, the link between distribution of banking services and inter-state economic disparity is assessed. Important policy implications, particularly to promote balanced distribution of banking services towards moderating inter-state economic disparity, are flagged. The broad conclusions of the chapter are provided in section 5.5.

5.2 Regional Distribution of Banking

India is a country with diversity in many aspects such as geography, climatic conditions, languages, food, clothing, cultural ethos, religious faith and, of course, economic prosperity. The spread of banking and finance across the various regions or states of the country also does not exhibit a uniform pattern. The RBI publishes[3] state-wise annual data on bank credit and deposits. It also provides similar data for various regions in India. The data is available for the following regions: (*a*) central, (*b*) eastern, (*c*) northern, (*d*) north-eastern, (*e*) southern and (*f*) western. The states and union territories (UTs) included

while poorer states such as Assam and Uttar Pradesh posted average growth rate of 5–6.5 per cent.

[3] See the RBI's *Statistical Tables Relating to Banks in India*, various issues (RBI, n.d.1).

under each region are listed in Table 5A.1 (in Appendix 5A). Based on this data, in this section, we assess the regional and state-wise distribution of bank credit and deposits which are the two most important indicators of banking services.

5.2.1 Region-Wise Distribution of Bank Credit and Deposits

Table 5.1 presents region-wise data on bank credit extended by SCBs from 1989 to 2020 (at 10-year intervals). Percentage shares in overall credit are provided in parentheses. A quick look at the table reveals that the 'western' and 'southern' regions accounted for an overwhelming share in the region-wise distribution of bank credit. Their combined share was close to 60 per cent. It is to be noted that 6 of the top 10 major (rich) states were part of these regions. The state-wise ranks based on per capita net state domestic product (NSDP) are provided in Table 5A.2 (in Appendix 5A) for ready reference. The

Table 5.1 Region-wise bank credit in India

(INR billion as on 31 March)

Region	**1989–90**	**1999–2000**	**2009–10**	**2019–20**
Central	83 *(13.1)*	377 *(8.0)*	2,452 *(7.3)*	8,992 *(8.6)*
Eastern	85 *(13.5)*	409 *(8.7)*	2,672 *(8.0)*	7,457 *(7.1)*
Northern	121 *(19.1)*	1,097 *(23.4)*	7,536 *(22.5)*	23,587 *(22.6)*
North-eastern	10 *(1.6)*	37 *(0.8)*	272 *(0.8)*	1,092 *(1.0)*
Southern	170 *(26.8)*	1,237 *(26.4)*	9,074 *(27.1)*	29,418 *(28.2)*
Western	165 *(26.0)*	1,535 *(32.7)*	11,451 *(34.2)*	33,950 *(32.5)*
All India	633 *(100)*	4,690 *(100)*	33,456 *(100)*	1,04,496 *(100)*

Source: *Statistical Tables Relating to Banks in India*, various issues, downloaded from RBI website, www.rbi.org.in.

Note: (*a*) Figures in parentheses are the percentage shares of the respective regions in the overall bank credit outstanding in the relevant year. (*b*) States and UTs placed under different regions are presented in Table 5A.1.

'northern' region accounted for a little above one-fifth of the total bank credit in India. It included 3 of the 10 richest (major) states. Put together these three regions accounted for above 80 per cent of the total bank credit in India.

On the contrary, the other three regions, namely the 'central', 'eastern' and 'north-eastern' regions, accounted for less than one-fifth of the total bank credit. The states from these regions are relatively poor. Not even a single state figured amongst the top 10 rich states (Table 5A.2). It is also important to note that the share of the 'north-eastern' region in overall bank credit distribution was merely around 1 per cent.

This discussion reveals that the distribution of bank credit across regions in India is heavily skewed. It also hints at the association between economic prosperity (per capita NSDP) and share in bank credit.

The regional distribution of bank deposits in India is presented in Table 5.2. It can be observed from the said table that the distribution of bank deposits is somewhat similar to that of bank credit as discussed

Table 5.2 Region-wise bank deposits in India

(INR billion as on 31 March)

Region	1989–90	1999–2000	2009–10	2019–20
Central	164	1,127	5,249	18,682
	(17.1)	*(13.7)*	*(11.4)*	*(13.6)*
Eastern	157	1,110	5,312	17,965
	(16.3)	*(13.5)*	*(11.5)*	*(13.1)*
Northern	229	1,892	10,105	28,441
	(23.9)	*(23.0)*	*(22.0)*	*(20.7)*
North-eastern	20	132	789	2,665
	(2.1)	*(1.6)*	*(1.7)*	*(1.9)*
Southern	195	1,886	9,837	33,721
	(20.3)	*(22.9)*	*(21.4)*	*(24.5)*
Western	194	2,073	14,727	36,029
	(20.3)	*(25.2)*	*(32.0)*	*(26.2)*
All India	960	8,221	46,019	1,37,501
	(100)	*(100)*	*(100)*	*(100)*

Source: *Statistical Tables Relating to Banks in India*, various issues, downloaded from RBI website, www.rbi.org.in.

Note: (*a*) Figures in parentheses are the percentage shares of the respective regions in the overall bank deposits outstanding in the relevant year. (*b*) States and UTs placed under different regions are presented in Table 5A.1.

previously. The economically richer regions, namely the 'western', 'southern' and 'northern' regions, accounted for around 70 per cent of the total bank deposits. The aggregate share of the remaining three regions was less than 30 per cent. Thus, the share of economically poorer regions in aggregate bank deposits was somewhat higher than their share in bank credit. This implies that the credit–deposit ratio of the poorer regions was low compared to that of the richer regions. The same stands confirmed by Table 5.3 which presents region-wise credit–deposit ratios.

Table 5.3 reveals fluctuations in the credit–deposit ratio at the all-India level which generally occur in synchronisation with economic fluctuations. Usually, during an economic boom, the credit–deposit ratio will be high and the same will be low during a downturn. However, it can be observed that irrespective of the swings in the credit–deposit ratio at the all-India level, the ratios for the richer regions were comparatively high. For the poorer regions, the credit–deposit ratios were relatively low. For example, for the 'western' and 'southern' regions, the credit–deposit ratios were in the range of 65–95 per cent. The same for the 'central' and 'eastern' regions were in the range of 33–51 per cent. This implies that part of the resources mobilised as bank deposits from poorer regions were deployed as bank credit in richer regions. There is an element of cross-subsidisation here. Poorer regions financed a part of the economic prosperity of the richer regions.

To gain further clarity on the distribution of bank credit and deposits in India, the next section provides a state-wise analysis.

Table 5.3 Region-wise ratios of bank credit to deposits

(Per cent as on 31 March)

Region	1989–90	1999–2000	2009–10	2019–20
Central	50.3	33.4	46.7	48.1
Eastern	54.4	36.8	50.3	41.5
Northern	52.8	58.0	74.6	82.9
North Eastern	50.1	27.7	34.4	41.0
Southern	87.1	65.6	92.2	87.2
Western	84.7	74.1	77.8	94.2
All India	66.0	57.1	72.7	76.0

Source: Calculated by the author based on bank credit and deposit data presented in Tables 5.1 and 5.2.

Note: States and UTs placed under different regions are presented in Table 5A.1.

5.2.2 State-Wise Distribution of Bank Credit and Deposits

The state-wise distribution of bank credit in India for various years is given in Table 5.4. Data for 19 major states for this purpose were obtained from various issues of *Statistical Tables Relating to Banks in India*, published by the

Table 5.4 State-wise bank credit in India

	1989–90	1999–2000	2009–10	2019–20	1989–90	1999–2000	2009–10	2019–20
Major states	**INR billion**				**Percentage of total bank credit**			
Andhra Pradesh	50	296	2,623	4,061	*7.9*	*6.3*	*7.8*	*3.9*
Assam	7	27	183	707	*1.0*	*0.6*	*0.5*	*0.7*
Bihar	22	83	290	1,355	*3.5*	*1.8*	*0.9*	*1.3*
Chhattisgarh	NA	NA	255	1,001	NA	NA	*0.8*	*1.0*
Gujarat	31	237	1,413	5,453	*5.0*	*5.1*	*4.2*	*5.2*
Haryana	14	71	691	2,715	*2.1*	*1.5*	*2.1*	*2.6*
Himachal Pradesh	4	14	113	313	*0.6*	*0.3*	*0.3*	*0.3*
Jharkhand	NA	NA	223	668	NA	NA	*0.7*	*0.6*
Karnataka	44	279	2,244	6,943	*6.9*	*6.0*	*6.7*	*6.6*
Kerala	22	165	958	3,519	*3.4*	*3.5*	*2.9*	*3.4*
Madhya Pradesh	29	151	714	2,740	*4.6*	*3.2*	*2.1*	*2.6*
Maharashtra	131	1,282	9,953	28,262	*20.7*	*27.3*	*29.8*	*27.0*
Odisha	13	51	444	1,347	*2.1*	*1.1*	*1.3*	*1.3*
Punjab	23	151	950	2,342	*3.7*	*3.2*	*2.8*	*2.2*
Rajasthan	19	111	944	3,345	*3.0*	*2.4*	*2.8*	*3.2*
Tamil Nadu	54	492	3,214	9,659	*8.4*	*10.5*	*9.6*	*9.2*
Uttar Pradesh	54	225	1,340	4,708	*8.4*	*4.8*	*4.0*	*4.5*
Uttarakhand	NA	NA	143	543	NA	NA	*0.4*	*0.5*
West Bengal	50	274	1,697	4,031	*7.8*	*5.8*	*5.1*	*3.9*
All India	633	4,690	33,456	1,04,496	*100*	*100*	*100*	*100*

Source: *Statistical Tables Relating to Banks in India*, various issues, downloaded from RBI website, www.rbi.org.in.

Note: (*a*) Figures in italics are the percentage shares of the respective states in the total bank credit at all-India level in the relevant year. (*b*) NA stands for 'not available'.

RBI. Percentage shares of these states in the total bank credit at the all-India level are provided on the right side of the table in italics.

From Table 5.4, it may be noted that the highest share of around 27–30 per cent in the total bank credit is accounted for by the state of Maharashtra. This was the fifth richest state of India during 2019–20 (Table 5A.2). The second highest share of close to 10 per cent is attributed to Tamil Nadu which stood as the seventh richest state. The share of Karnataka in the total bank credit was around 6–7 per cent. This was the fourth richest state in 2019–20. The second richest state of Gujarat accounted for nearly 5 per cent of the total.

On the contrary, the shares of Assam, Chhattisgarh and Jharkhand in the total bank credit were largely less than 1 per cent each. Similarly, those of Bihar and Odisha were in the range of 1–2 per cent. They were relatively poor states in 2019–20.

A similar pattern was observed in the state-wise distribution of bank deposits in India. As presented in Table 5.5, the richer states of Maharashtra, Karnataka, Tamil Nadu and Gujarat accounted for larger shares in the total bank deposits at the all-India level. The poorer states of Assam, Chhattisgarh, Jharkhand, and so on, contributed to around 1–2 per cent each of the total bank deposits.

We observed earlier that the credit–deposit ratios for the richer 'western' and 'southern' regions were higher as compared to those for the poorer 'eastern' and 'north-eastern' regions. To analyse similar state-wise patterns, related data are presented in Table 5.6. It may be observed from this table that the credit–deposit ratios for Andhra Pradesh, Maharashtra and Tamil Nadu were above 100 per cent for the recent years. The ratios for Gujarat and Karnataka were also on the higher side. On the contrary, the credit–deposit ratios for the poorer states of Assam, Bihar, Jharkhand and Uttar Pradesh were largely in the sub-45 per cent zone. This reiterates the element of cross-subsidisation in banking services as discussed earlier.

5.2.3 Bank Credit–NSDP Ratio

It may be noted that the states of Uttar Pradesh and West Bengal account for a reasonable share in bank credit and deposits similar to some of the richer states (Tables 5.4 and 5.5). But they were relatively poor states in 2019–20. This paradox may be due to the fact that both states are large in terms of the size of their economy. In view of this, there is a need to assess the amount of

Table 5.5 State-wise bank deposits in India

	1989–90	1999–2000	2009–10	2019–20	1989–90	1999–2000	2009–10	2019–20
Major states	**INR billion**				**Percentage of total bank deposits**			
Andhra Pradesh	58	465	2,495	3,279	*6.1*	*5.7*	*5.4*	*2.4*
Assam	13	85	495	1,663	*1.3*	*1.0*	*1.1*	*1.2*
Bihar	56	369	1,015	3,797	*5.8*	*4.5*	*2.2*	*2.8*
Chhattisgarh	NA	NA	484	1,647	NA	NA	*1.1*	*1.2*
Gujarat	51	475	2,165	7,632	*5.3*	*5.8*	*4.7*	*5.6*
Haryana	22	171	1,096	4,758	*2.3*	*2.1*	*2.4*	*3.5*
Himachal Pradesh	9	62	273	1,045	*0.9*	*0.8*	*0.6*	*0.8*
Jharkhand	NA	NA	648	2,377	NA	NA	*1.4*	*1.7*
Karnataka	45	458	2,917	10,754	*4.7*	*5.6*	*6.3*	*7.8*
Kerala	37	389	1,506	5,477	*3.8*	*4.7*	*3.3*	*4.0*
Madhya Pradesh	44	308	1,193	3,988	*4.6*	*3.7*	*2.6*	*2.9*
Maharashtra	138	1,530	12,243	27,550	*14.4*	*18.6*	*26.6*	*20.0*
Odisha	16	127	834	3,388	*1.7*	*1.5*	*1.8*	*2.5*
Punjab	52	386	1,336	4,129	*5.4*	*4.7*	*2.9*	*3.0*
Rajasthan	28	238	1070	4,276	*2.9*	*2.9*	*2.3*	*3.1*
Tamil Nadu	53	559	2,853	9,005	*5.5*	*6.8*	*6.2*	*6.5*
Uttar Pradesh	120	820	3,148	11,550	*12.6*	*10.0*	*6.8*	*8.4*
Uttarakhand	NA	NA	424	1,497	NA	NA	*0.9*	*1.1*
West Bengal	84	606	2,767	8,245	*8.7*	*7.4*	*6.0*	*6.0*
All India	960	8,221	46,019	1,37,501	*100*	*100*	*100*	*100*

Source: *Statistical Tables Relating to Banks in India*, various issues, downloaded from RBI website, www.rbi.org.in; author's calculations of the percentage share of respective states.

Note: (*a*) Figures in italics are the percentage shares of the respective states in the total bank deposits at all-India level in the relevant year. (*b*) NA stands for 'not available'.

state-wise bank credit relative to their respective NSDP. We have presented the bank-credit–NSDP ratio of the major Indian states in Table 5.7.

Table 5.7 shows that there has been financial deepening across states in India during the post-reform period. The ratio of bank credit to NSDP has been largely rising for all the states. Nevertheless, the ratios are found to be higher for

Table 5.6 State-wise ratios of bank credit to deposits

(Per cent)

Major States	1989–90	1999–2000	2009–10	2019–20
Andhra Pradesh	86.1	63.6	105.1	123.8
Assam	51.4	31.5	37.0	42.5
Bihar	39.7	22.5	28.6	35.7
Chhattisgarh	NA	NA	52.8	60.8
Gujarat	61.9	49.8	65.3	71.4
Haryana	61.2	41.4	63.0	57.1
Himachal Pradesh	40.7	22.9	41.4	29.9
Jharkhand	NA	NA	34.4	28.1
Karnataka	95.8	61.0	76.9	64.6
Kerala	59.7	42.3	63.6	64.3
Madhya Pradesh	66.4	49.2	59.8	68.7
Maharashtra	95.1	83.8	81.3	102.6
Odisha	81.4	39.8	53.2	39.7
Punjab	45.0	39.1	71.1	56.7
Rajasthan	66.9	46.7	88.2	78.2
Tamil Nadu	100.7	88.0	112.6	107.3
Uttar Pradesh	44.4	27.5	42.6	40.8
Uttarakhand	NA	NA	33.8	36.3
West Bengal	59.3	45.2	61.3	48.9
All-India	66.0	57.1	72.7	76.0

Source: Calculated by the author based on state-wise bank credit and deposit data presented in Tables 5.4 and 5.5.

Note: NA stands for 'not available'.

richer states in general. The ratio was higher than 100 per cent for Maharashtra in both 2009–10 and 2019–20. The same was higher than 50 per cent for the richer states of Andhra Pradesh, Karnataka, Punjab and Tamil Nadu. For 8 of the 10 richest states, the ratio was above 40 per cent in 2019–20.

On the contrary, the ratio of bank credit to NSDP was relatively lower for poor states. For Assam, Bihar and Jharkhand, the ratio was less than 30 per cent in 2019–20. For other poor states like Chhattisgarh, Madhya Pradesh, Odisha, Rajasthan and Uttar Pradesh, it was in the range of 30–40 per cent.

It is important to note that for West Bengal and Uttar Pradesh, the lower ratios of bank credit to NSDP reflected the lower penetration of banking

Table 5.7 State-wise ratios of bank credit to NSDP

(*Per cent*)

Major states	1989–90	1999–2000	2009–10	2019–20
Andhra Pradesh	18.2	39.8	110.1	52.0
Assam	6.5	8.4	19.8	26.5
Bihar	14.3	17.0	19.5	26.2
Chhattisgarh	NA	NA	28.2	35.4
Gujarat	13.5	23.1	41.5	43.8
Haryana	11.7	14.8	37.4	45.1
Himachal Pradesh	12.8	10.9	26.1	24.2
Jharkhand	NA	NA	23.7	25.5
Karnataka	21.0	28.4	60.6	52.8
Kerala	15.7	24.5	42.9	53.8
Madhya Pradesh	14.9	19.5	35.3	34.1
Maharashtra	25.6	53.0	138.1	131.3
Odisha	11.3	12.2	31.0	32.7
Punjab	14.1	24.5	54.2	54.6
Rajasthan	10.8	13.6	40.0	39.9
Tamil Nadu	18.8	37.6	73.1	66.1
Uttar Pradesh	11.6	13.5	29.2	34.8
Uttarakhand	NA	NA	21.1	26.1
West Bengal	15.3	21.9	49.8	39.6

Source: Calculated by the author based on state-wise bank credit presented in Table 5.4 and NSDP data obtained from RBI's *Handbook of Statistics on Indian Economy*, 2020–21, https://data.rbi.org.in/DBIE/#/dbie/reports/Publication/Time-Series%20Publications/Handbook%20of%20Statistics%20on%20the%20Indian%20Economy (accessed 18 July 2022).

Note: NA stands for 'not available'.

services. The higher share of both the states in bank credit distribution in the cross-state comparison, as discussed earlier, should be interpreted with caution in this perspective.

5.3 Inter-State Economic Disparity

Inter-state economic disparity has been a matter of perennial concern in India. One of the key stated objectives of development planning was to reduce this disparity and achieve balanced growth. However, as demonstrated by Dandekar (1993), achievements in the pre-reform period in this regard were not encouraging. Ranking of states based on per capita NSDP reflected that the poor states in India remained poor while rich states continued to be rich.

The post-reform period did not seem to change the inter-state disparity for the better. The following summarises the findings of several studies which attempted to examine issues related to inter-state economic disparity in India during the post-reform period.

According to Ahluwalia (2000), the post-reform period witnessed removal of many of the controls exercised by the central government and thereby reoriented the role of state governments in many areas that are critical for economic progress. It was expected that with greater manoeuvrability in economic policymaking, poor states would have greater scope to pursue required policies relevant to their own interest. This would facilitate faster growth for them. However, comparing the gross state domestic product (GSDP) growth rates of 14 major states between 1980–91 and 1991–99, he observed that the degree of dispersion in growth rates across states increased during the 1990s. The coefficient of variation in their growth rates increased to 0.27 from 0.15 in the previous decade. It was also observed that per capita GSDP growth rates accelerated in the 1990s among states at the upper end of the spectrum (Gujarat and Maharashtra) while they decelerated in weaker states (Bihar, Uttar Pradesh and Odisha). The Gini coefficient increased from around 0.15–0.16 during the 1980s to 0.20–0.24 during the 1990s, suggesting deterioration of economic parity across states in India.

Bhattacharya and Sakthivel (2004) also observed that regional disparity amongst major Indian states had widened significantly during the 1990s. The poorer states did not perform well and their failure to control population growth made matters worse. The coefficient of variation in terms of per capita income worsened from 0.22 in the 1980s to 0.43 in the 1990s.

Ghosh (2008) reiterated that improved growth performance of the Indian economy during the post-reform period has been associated with increasing regional disparity. His empirical analysis was based on data for 15 major states for the period 1960–2002. He observed that disparity in income across states increased significantly after the implementation of comprehensive reforms from the 1990s. He traced the divergence to inter-state variations in human capital, production structures and physical, social and economic infrastructure.

Kumar and Subramanian (2012) observed that the pace of growth was higher across all major states in the 2000s as against the 1990s. The average growth in per capita income across 21 major states more than doubled from 2.8 per cent during 1993–2001 to 5.8 per cent during 2001–09. Particularly, they highlighted the strong performance of weaker states such as Bihar, Chhattisgarh, Odisha and Uttarakhand during the 2000s. Nevertheless, there was no evidence of convergence as the richer states grew faster and the inequality across states actually increased.

Table 5.8 presents per capita NSDP (at constant prices) for 19 major states. The purpose is to assess relative economic prosperity or inter-state income disparity across such states in different years. It begins with 1989–90, which is a representative year from the pre-reform period. After that three representative years—with 10-year intervals—were chosen from the post-reform period. The latest year, 2019–20, was just prior to the period when India and the rest of the world suffered severely from the Covid-19 pandemic.[4]

One way of assessing inter-state disparity is comparing per capita NSDP of the richest state to that of the poorest. In 1989–90, the ratio of per capita NSDP of Punjab to that of Bihar was 3.3. The ratio increased over time to 5.8 in 2019–20. This is the ratio of per capita NSDP of Haryana to that of Bihar (Table 5.8).

However, deterioration in inter-state disparity looks less severe if we compare the average per capita NSDP of the top five richer states to that of the bottom five poorer states. This ratio increased from 2.5 in 1989–90 to 3.8 in 2019–20. Nevertheless, this does not hide the widening of the income gap across states.

Table 5.9 ranks states over the years according to per capita NSDP. The ranks are in descending order. The state with the highest per capita NSDP among those in the list is assigned the 1st rank. It is the richest state. The state with the second highest per capita NSDP is assigned the 2nd rank, and so on. For example, in 2019–20, the richest state, Haryana, is assigned the 1st rank and the poorest state, Bihar, is assigned the 19th rank (Table 5.9). It may be noted that we have confined ourselves to 19 major states for the ranking.

---

[4] India imposed a nationwide lockdown in two separate spells to cease human contact and minimise casualties or loss of life due to Covid-19, beginning from mid-March 2020. Due to this, the economy witnessed severe contraction registering negative growth of (–)5.8 per cent in 2020–21 (RBI, 2023a).

Table 5.8 State-wise data on per capita NSDP

(*INR*)

Major states	1989–90	1999–2000	2009–10	2019–20
Andhra Pradesh	2,013	15,427	35,677	1,13,927
Assam	1,517	12,282	20,406	60,660
Bihar	1,116	5,786	10,635	30,621
Chhattisgarh	NA	11,629	24,189	75,278
Gujarat	2,644	18,864	49,168	1,64,310
Haryana	3,254	23,222	55,044	1,76,199
Himachal Pradesh	2,250	20,806	43,492	1,42,155
Jharkhand	NA	11,549	21,534	57,246
Karnataka	2,055	17,502	37,294	1,54,861
Kerala	1,705	19,461	47,360	1,49,563
Madhya Pradesh	1,523	12,384	20,959	62,236
Maharashtra	3,414	23,011	54,246	1,52,566
Odisha	1,699	10,622	22,846	82,257
Punjab	3,730	25,631	42,831	1,19,162
Rajasthan	1,716	13,619	24,304	78,390
Tamil Nadu	2,094	19,432	47,394	1,49,329
Uttar Pradesh	1,593	9,749	16,390	44,618
Uttarakhand	NA	13,516	44,557	1,58,919
West Bengal	2,086	15,888	29,799	71,719
Ratio of per capita NSDP of the richest to that of the poorest state	*3.3*	*4.4*	*5.2*	*5.8*

Source: RBI's *Handbook of Statistics on Indian Economy*, various issues, https://data.rbi.org.in/DBIE/#/dbie/reports/Publication/Time-Series%20Publications/Handbook%20of%20Statistics%20on%20the%20Indian%20Economy (accessed 18 July 2022).

Note: (*a*) Data for 2019–20, 2009–10, 1999–2000 and 1989–90 correspond to NSDP data published with the respective base years: 2011–12, 2004–05, 1999–2000 and 1980–81. (*b*) NA stands for 'not available'.

A closer look at Table 5.9 reveals an interesting mix of continuity and change. On the one hand, a large number of states maintained their relative economic status. Richer states like Haryana, Gujarat and Maharashtra continued to remain rich in all the years in our sample. Assam, Bihar, Jharkhand and Uttar Pradesh remained at the bottom of the list throughout. Similarly, Andhra Pradesh and Tamil Nadu maintained their middle-income status across the period under consideration. On the

Table 5.9 State-wise ranks based on per capita NSDP

(Per cent)

Major states	1989–90	1999–2000	2009–10	2019–20
Andhra Pradesh	9	10	10	10
Assam	15	14	17	16
Bihar	16	19	19	19
Chhattisgarh	NA	15	13	13
Gujarat	4	7	3	2
Haryana	3	2	1	1
Himachal Pradesh	5	4	7	8
Jharkhand	NA	16	15	17
Karnataka	8	8	9	4
Kerala	11	5	5	6
Madhya Pradesh	14	13	16	15
Maharashtra	2	3	2	5
Odisha	12	17	14	11
Punjab	1	1	8	9
Rajasthan	10	11	12	12
Tamil Nadu	6	6	4	7
Uttar Pradesh	13	18	18	18
Uttarakhand	NA	12	6	3
West Bengal	7	9	11	14

Source: Ranks assigned to states by the author based on per capita NSDP of the respective states as given in Table 5.8.

Note: (*a*) Rank is based on per capita NSDP (at constant prices). The state with 1st rank is that with the highest per capita NSDP in the corresponding year; the state with the 2nd rank is the second richest, and so on. (*b*) NA stands for 'not available'.

contrary, there have also been some transitions in terms of the poor–rich divide. For example, Odisha gradually moved up in economic prosperity from the 17th rank in 1999–2000 to the 11th rank in 2019–20 while Karnataka moved up from the 8th to the 4th rank. West Bengal fell from the 9th to the 14th rank and Punjab from the 1st to the 9th rank in the comparable period.

To analyse the association between the relative economic prosperity of the major states and banking services, a comparative perspective is presented in the following section.

5.4 Distribution of Banking Services and Inter-State Economic Disparity

In Chapter 3, we have discussed the long-term pattern of progress in an economy as explained by mainstream growth theories. The neoclassical growth model as originally developed by Nobel laureate Robert Solow (1956) suggests that in the transitory phase, as per capita capital stock in an economy increases, it fuels growth of per capita income. However, as the level of per capita capital increases beyond a point, growth in per capita income tappers off. This is due the fact that capital is subject to diminishing returns. This process leads to the 'steady state' equilibrium when at a particular level of per capita capital k^*, per capita income ceases to grow, as shown in Figure 3.2.

One important implication of this analysis is that poor countries can keep adding to their stock of capital and approach the per capita capital levels of rich countries. However, rich countries cannot raise their per capita stock of capital beyond k^* which is the maximum equilibrium level for all countries.[5] In other words, the implication of the neoclassical growth model is that while every economy approaches the steady state level of per capita capital, rich countries will grow slowly while poor countries grow at higher rates. Thus, ultimately all countries would converge to the same level of per capita income. However, empirical analysis based on cross-country data largely suggests otherwise (Barro, 2008; Barro and Sala-i-Martin, 2004). Subsequently, it was suggested that initial economic conditions such as volume of savings, innovation and technological improvements determine economic convergence, popularly known as conditional convergence. The empirical evidence suggested that homogeneous countries have a tendency for convergence while countries with wide disparity in economic conditions do not exhibit such tendency (Barro, 1991; Barro and Sala-i-Martin, 1992; Mankiw, Romer and Weil, 1992).

It is important to note that financial development and scope for saving can be considered as among the important factors determining conditional convergence. We can replicate the same analysis to highlight the issue of conditional convergence for states in India. Banking services can be considered to have significant influence in attaining conditional convergence

---

[5] k^* is the maximum equilibrium level of per capita capital stock which any country can achieve, without technological change. Advanced technological innovation can help a country shift to a higher level of equilibrium per capita capital stock.

across states in India. In this perspective, let us discuss how variation in banking services enjoyed by different states in India can be used to compare inter-state economic disparity.

Table 5.10 presents state-wise ranks according to their ratio of bank credit to NSDP. It again demonstrates that most of the poor states like Assam, Bihar, Jharkhand and Uttar Pradesh have lower ranks in terms of their ratio of bank credit to NSDP. On the other hand, richer states like Karnataka, Maharashtra, Tamil Nadu, Punjab, and so on, appear higher in the order. This is similar to the ranking in terms of economic prosperity (Table 5.9).

Table 5.10 State-wise ranks based on bank credit–NSDP ratios

Major states	1989–90	1999–2000	2009–10	2019–20
Andhra Pradesh	4	2	2	6
Assam	16	16	18	15
Bihar	8	10	19	16
Chhattisgarh	NA	NA	14	11
Gujarat	10	7	8	8
Haryana	12	11	10	7
Himachal Pradesh	11	15	15	19
Jharkhand	NA	NA	16	18
Karnataka	2	4	4	5
Kerala	5	6	7	4
Madhya Pradesh	7	9	11	13
Maharashtra	1	1	1	1
Odisha	14	14	12	14
Punjab	9	5	5	3
Rajasthan	15	12	9	9
Tamil Nadu	3	3	3	2
Uttar Pradesh	13	13	13	12
Uttarakhand	NA	NA	17	17
West Bengal	6	8	6	10

Source: Ranks assigned to states by the author based on the bank credit–NSDP ratio of the respective states presented in Table 5.7.

Note: (*a*) Rank is based on the bank credit–NSDP ratio. The state with the 1st rank is that with the highest bank credit–NSDP Ratio in the corresponding year; that with the 2nd rank has the second highest bank credit–NSDP ratio, and so on. (*b*) NA stands for 'not available'.

The rank correlation coefficient between per capita NSDP and ratios of bank credit to NSDP of states was estimated to be 0.5 in 1999–2000 and 2019–20. The coefficient was 0.6 in 2009–10. However, it was lower at 0.3 in 1989–90.

From this discussion, it appears that with the market-oriented economic policy regime adopted in India during the post-reform period, there are evidence of greater interlinkages between economic growth and banking services. In this perspective, there should be adequate policy focus on improving banking services in the economically weaker states so that inter-state disparity in India could be reduced in a tangible way.

We need to understand that banks lend to creditworthy borrowers and promising industrial projects. Industrial projects and start-ups can flourish with a conducive business environment and supporting physical infrastructure. With the adoption of the nationwide GST, the earlier differences in tax benefits for industry have vanished. Now better governance, faster processing of proposals and approvals, and reduction of corruption are key to attracting investments. The critical issue is removing bottlenecks and providing necessary physical infrastructure like power, roads, railways, ports, communications and IT to facilitate trade and industry. The responsibility for this lies with the respective state governments with the active funding support of the Government of India.

The top management of banks and the RBI need to take into cognisance the lopsided inter-regional distribution of bank credit and deposits. Without compromising on prudential banking norms, they should formulate a strategy on how to spread banking services uniformly across the country and help reduce economic disparity between states. This is easier said than done. Nevertheless, any concrete strategy in this regard needs to emerge from banks rather than be imposed by the government and regulators.

5.5 Conclusion

Economic disparity across states in India has been a perennial concern. Despite the stated policy emphasis under the central planning regime in India, inter-state economic disparity could not be resolved during the pre-reform period. During the post-reform period, concerns on the deteriorating rich–poor divide across states were further aggravated. Mobilisation of savings and channelising such savings into productive capital formation is a major instrument for achieving economic prosperity. Banks play a critical role in a bank-dominated financial system like that of India to support economic prosperity. In this perspective, this chapter attempted to explore the regional distribution of bank credit and deposits in India and its interlinkages with inter-state economic disparity.

It was observed that the spread of banking services in India is highly skewed. This is in terms of regional and inter-state distribution of bank credit and deposits. The chapter traced an association between the state-wise distribution of bank credit and economic growth. Economically poorer states were found to be poorly served by banks. Their share in bank credit and deposits was abysmally low.

There is an imperative need to improve the flow of bank credit in relatively poorer states so that it becomes a vehicle for promoting investment and capital formation in such states. Banks and regulators need to consider this requirement seriously. Supporting policy initiatives in poor states towards improving physical infrastructure such as roads and railways, power and communications, as well as overall governance are critically needed so that banks find creditworthy projects to fund.

Appendix 5A

Table 5A.1 List of states and UTs under various regions

Region	States	UTs
Central	Uttar Pradesh	
	Uttarakhand	
	Madhya Pradesh	
	Chhattisgarh	
Eastern	Bihar	Andaman and Nicobar Islands
	Jharkhand	
	Odisha	
	Sikkim	
	West Bengal	
Northern	Punjab	Chandigarh
	Haryana	Delhi
	Himachal Pradesh	Jammu and Kashmir
	Rajasthan	Ladakh

(Contd)

Table 5A.1 (*Contd*)

Region	States	UTs
North-eastern	Assam	
	Arunachal Pradesh	
	Manipur	
	Meghalaya	
	Mizoram	
	Nagaland	
	Tripura	
Southern	Andhra Pradesh	Lakshadweep
	Karnataka	Puducherry
	Kerala	
	Tamil Nadu	
Western	Goa	Dadra and Nagar Haveli
	Gujarat	Daman and Diu
	Maharashtra	

Source: *Statistical Tables Relating to Banks in India*, 2020–21, downloaded from RBI website, www.rbi.org.in.

Table 5A.2 Ordering of major states in India based on per capita NSDP in 2019–20 (base: 2011–12)

Serial number	State	Amount (INR)
1	Haryana	1,76,199
2	Gujarat	1,64,310
3	Uttarakhand	1,58,919
4	Karnataka	1,54,861
5	Maharashtra	1,52,566
6	Kerala	1,49,563
7	Tamil Nadu	1,49,329
8	Himachal Pradesh	1,42,155
9	Punjab	1,19,162
10	Andhra Pradesh	1,13,927
11	Odisha	82,257
12	Rajasthan	78,390
13	Chhattisgarh	75,278

(*Contd*)

Table 5A.2 (*Contd*)

Serial number	State	Amount (INR)
14	West Bengal	71,719
15	Madhya Pradesh	62,236
16	Assam	60,660
17	Jharkhand	57,246
18	Uttar Pradesh	44,618
19	Bihar	30,621
	All India (per capita net national income)	94,566

Source: RBI's *Handbook of Statistics on Indian Economy*, 2020–21, https://data.rbi.org.in/DBIE/#/dbie/reports/Publication/Time-Series%20Publications/Handbook%20of%20Statistics%20on%20the%20Indian%20Economy (accessed 18 July 2022).

Revision Questions and Problems

1. Comment on the regional or state-wise distribution of bank credit and deposits in India.
2. Do you find any link between inter-state economic disparity in India and distribution of banking services? Justify your answer with relevant facts.
3. Offer your suggestions to improve the balance in distribution of bank loans in India so as to use them as a vehicle for reducing economic disparity across states.

Part III

Banking Risks, Regulations and Risk Management

6

Banking Risks and Rationale for Banking Regulations

Learning Objectives

- To explain how the underlying problems of information asymmetry, excessive procyclicality in bank lending and liquidity mismatch in assets and liabilities make the banking business highly risky
- To discuss episodes of bank runs and contagion leading to banking crises
- To underline the rationale for banking regulation: containing potential disruptions of economic activities due to bank failures and protecting depositors' interest
- To identify various types of risks embodied in the banking business such as credit risk, liquidity risk, interest rate risk, market risk, operational risk, and so on
- To describe a variety of methodologies used for measurement of banking risks

6.1 Introduction

The facilitating role of banks towards promoting and sustaining prosperity in an economy has already been discussed in the preceding chapters. An analogy can be drawn between the banking sector and nuclear plants. Nuclear power has emerged as a formidable alternative to fossil fuels for meeting energy requirements. It has many advantages in terms of proficiency, reliability, ecofriendly aspects and low cost. However, any accident or mishandling in a nuclear plant can potentially cause severe devastation and loss of life. Similarly, the banking sector promotes economic growth in several ways and acts as a critical channel of the MTM to control inflation and mitigate economic fluctuations. At the same time, the banking business entails inherent risks. If the risks embodied in banking are not contained within reasonable prudential limits, they can severely harm the economy.

Any ordinary business involves risks due to fluctuations in sales, production costs, shortage in availability of raw materials, disruptions in the supply chain, employee unrest, deteriorating physical infrastructure, and so on. But the dimensions, configurations and magnitude of risks in the banking business are much wider than those in any non-financial business. Higher risk in banking is mainly explained using underlying bank-specific features such as information asymmetry in and excessive procyclicality of bank lending, scope for *bank runs* and contagion, and so on. Details of these aspects are discussed in section 6.2.

Ben S. Bernanke, Nobel laureate for economics in 2022, has highlighted how failure of banks can aggravate a conventional economic crisis (Bernanke, 1981, 1983). The Keynesian explanation for causes of the Great Depression emphasises the role of deficient aggregate demand. It is suggested that inadequate investment and consumption expenditure driven by the animal spirit of pessimism led to the Great Depression of the early 1930s. During this period, the unemployment rate in the US increased to nearly 25 per cent and industrial production plummeted by close to 46 per cent (Barro, 2008; Royal Swedish Academy of Sciences, 2022). Bernanke's works suggest that bank failures during this period sustained and aggravated the depression in the US for a longer duration covering 1929–33. In this backdrop, there is an imperative need to regulate banks so that overall risks in banking can be contained within manageable limits.

Further, in banking, depositors fund an overwhelming part of the business while bank managers take all the business decisions. Profit from banking is appropriated by bank promoters and shareholders, but bank depositors suffer heavily if there are bank failures. Need for protecting the interest of depositors adds to the aforementioned rationale for banking regulation.

Regulatory prescriptions across countries aim to maintain stability in the banking system on a continuous basis. Hence, it is important to constantly monitor banking activities to detect and decipher risk parameters. If any symptom of vulnerability or instability surfaces, suitable corrective action must promptly be initiated. Continuous monitoring of prudential parameters of banks and banking activity is undertaken through the process of banking supervision.

Banking regulation and supervision are central to ensuring a well-functioning, vibrant banking sector. In this perspective, their role in promoting and sustaining prosperity in an economy can never be overemphasised.

The rest of the chapter is organised as follows. Section 6.2 provides the relevance and rationale for regulation and supervision of banks which is mainly to contain the overall risks in banking and to protect the economy from the adverse consequences of banking crises. As indicated earlier, the banking business is exposed to a variety of risks. The nature and dimensions of various types of risks embodied in banking activities such as credit risk, liquidity risk, interest rate risk, market risk, operational risk, and so on, are delineated in section 6.3. We also discuss concentration of different categories of banking risks in different banking activities. Identifying the entire gamut of banking risks is important. More important is correct quantification of such risks. This is a necessary prerequisite in order to contain the same. In this perspective, section 6.4 explains measurement of core varieties of banking risks. Our main conclusions in this chapter are set out in section 6.5.

6.2 Rationale for Regulation and Supervision of Banks

As detailed in Chapter 1, banks mobilise deposits and use such deposits for lending and undertaking investments. They pay lower interest rates on their deposits and charge higher interest rates from their loans and investments. The net interest income (NII) for banks is the difference between interest earned on loans and investments over interest paid on deposits. Banks also earn non-interest income from the sale of bonds and bullion as well as fees and charges for money transfers, issuance of drafts, bank guarantees and letters of credit (LCs), underwriting services, forex operations, and so on. Similarly, they incur operational costs such as payment of salaries and pensions, rent for office premises, spending on stationery, electricity charges, and so on. The surplus of total income (sum of interest and non-interest income) over total costs (sum of interest and operational costs) constitutes a bank's profit. As commercial entities, the primary objective pursued by banks is profit maximisation.

Like any other business, a bank's profit depends on the movement of different items of income and expenditure. For example, if banks can expand loans and investments rapidly and charge higher interest rates on them, their income increases. This is true provided the loans and interest charges thereon are repaid as per schedule and there is no default in investments. Similarly, banks can reduce their costs if they can manage to mobilise deposits at cheaper cost and rationalise manpower, establishment costs, and so on. Similar is the case for a manufacturing firm. For instance, an automobile firm can earn more profit if it can produce and sell more cars at a higher price and lower its costs of production, including on workers, raw material, establishment, and so on. However, as compared to manufacturing firms, the nature, dimension and extent of variation in the items of a bank's balance sheet and statement of income and expenditure are very wide. Consequently, the degree of fluctuation and uncertainty in flow of profits in banking is much higher. In the following sections, we highlight underlying features in the banking business which make it highly risky.

6.2.1 Rationale for Regulation of Banks

The banking business is associated with illiquid assets and liquid liabilities. This liquidity mismatch in assets and liabilities of banks gives rise to high liquidity risk in banking. Any impairment of public confidence in a bank due to liquidity concerns can lead to *bank runs* which pose severe challenges to the entire banking system with contagion effects. Bank lending entails *information asymmetry* and excessive procyclicality which raise default risks. Several assets in the balance sheet of a bank like bonds, equities and forex reserves are regularly traded and prices of such assets even change tick by tick. Downward movement in prices of such assets adversely affects the bank's balance sheet and this leads to market risk.

If banking risks are not contained within reasonable limits, there could be bank failures which can seriously disrupt economic activities. The rationale for banking regulation derived from these underlying features in the banking business is detailed in the sections that follow.

6.2.1.1 Bank Lending and Information Asymmetry

The problem of *information asymmetry* in economics is widely referred to as the problem of the 'lemons and peaches'. In 2001, noted economists George

Akerlof, Michael Spence and Joseph Stiglitz were jointly awarded the Nobel Prize in Economics for their contributions related to the analysis of markets with asymmetric information. This issue is already highlighted in Chapter 3. Further details are provided in this section.

In standard transactions or exchanges in the marketplace, both buyers and sellers are assumed to have full information about the product. For example, buyers and sellers of apples in the fruit market know well if the apples are of good quality or not. Accordingly, they bargain and determine the price of the apples through mutual negotiation. For a transaction to take place, a necessary precondition is both parties being possessed of full information about the product.

However, there are cases of information asymmetry where one party to the transaction possesses full information while the other does not. Such cases make undertaking business transactions difficult.

Let us consider the case of used or second-hand cars. The car owner or seller knows fully about the actual condition of the used car while the prospective buyer does not possess full information. In such a situation, the seller may demand a higher price knowing that the used car is in good condition (like a peach). But the prospective buyer may wish to buy only at a lower price, having doubts about its condition (like a lemon). Eventually, the transaction may fail due to disagreement on the price. This leads to a situation of market failure.

The literature suggests several ways to enable functioning of the market under information asymmetry. For example, if the seller sets up an impressive showroom for selling used cars, the buyer may feel secure about their credibility. The buyer gets assured about the quality of the used car. This resolves the information asymmetry problem. A real-life example is Maruti Suzuki India Limited setting up True Value outlets to sell used cars.

In banking, the problem of information asymmetry is quite prevalent in lending. The loan seeker is fully aware about their financial position, future income prospects and even their true intention to repay the loan as per the agreement. The bank does not have complete information about the same. Moreover, a borrower always has an incentive to camouflage their financial position and overstate their future income prospects to make themself appear highly creditworthy. It is said that the borrower has to prove to the bank that they do not require a loan in order to improve the probability of obtaining the loan. This entails the problem of *adverse selection*—persons who are not creditworthy make themself look successful to obtain a loan.

Furthermore, bank lending also involves the problem of *moral hazard*. This is related to diverting the borrowed funds to other risky activities, possibly swayed by the temptation of earning high returns in the short run rather than using the loan proceeds for the stated purpose. For example, a borrower who received a bank loan to set up a production plant may use the proceeds to buy equity in the stock market if current returns are high. They may be tempted to earn some extra returns quickly and then use the proceeds to buy equipment or machines for the plant later. However, stock prices are volatile and may move southward suddenly contrary to their expectations. Consequently, they may incur losses and may fall short of funds to set up the plant. In such a case, they would default on the loan, being unable to generate revenue from the proposed production plant.

Thus, problems associated with information asymmetry in lending, namely adverse selection and moral hazard, make the banking business a very risky proposition. Some bank loans and investments become delinquent partly due to these problems. Information asymmetry inherent in bank lending is one of the reasons causing loan defaults, mainly due to misjudgement on the creditworthiness of the borrower. Default on bank loans dries up a bank's fund availability due to non-receipt of projected loan repayments on the due date. Ultimately, the bank incurs loss if it is not able to recover the loan dues.

6.2.1.2 High Procyclicality of Bank Loans

Bank lending across countries is often found to fluctuate with changing macroeconomic conditions. Any economy experiences recurrences of booms and recessions as part of the usual business cycle phenomenon as detailed in Chapter 4.

It is observed that during economic booms, growth of bank credit accelerates rapidly while economic slowdowns are usually associated with low credit growth. This phenomenon is popularly referred to as the *procyclicality* of bank lending. In periods of economic boom, rising asset prices and higher incomes raise the creditworthiness of loan seekers. With irrational exuberance all around, banks tend to dilute credit appraisal standards. This leads to accelerated credit flow during economic upswings. On the contrary, during recessions, sales and income plummet. Asset prices become stagnant or fall. This downgrades the credit rating of prospective borrowers and credit flow from banks slows down. Moreover, economic recessions are also associated with loan delinquencies. This constrains resource availability with banks due to non-receipt of loan repayments and higher provisioning requirements[1] on bad loans. The overall dismal environment and drying up of resources compel banks to adopt an overcautious lending approach. Thus, bank credit slows down during recession.

Like bank lending, non-financial enterprises witness fluctuations in business across different phases of economic boom and slowdown too. However, fluctuations in bank loans are often more pronounced. For example, the Indian economy accelerated from an average growth of 5.8 per cent during 1992–2003 to 7.4 per cent during 2003–11—a jump of roughly 1.6 percentage points. During the corresponding period, real bank credit growth[2] increased from an average of 10.7 per cent to 17.5 per cent—a jump of around 7 percentage points. The Indian economy witnessed deceleration during 2011–20 with average GDP growth of 6.4 per cent. During this period, average growth in real bank credit was nearly 8.3 per cent (as per calculations based on data from the RBI's *Handbook of Statistics on Indian Economy*). This suggests not only that bank loans are procyclical but also that the amplitude of fluctuations in bank lending is much bigger than of those in the real economy.

Interest income from loans and investments constitutes the bulk of the overall income of banks. Interest income is dependent on the volume of loans and investments as also returns on such assets. High procyclicality in lending makes interest income of banks prone to wider variations and exposes banks to volatility in profit.

Higher variation in interest income is not only due to procyclical fluctuations in bank lending, it is also due to procyclical variation in interest rates.

Interest rates vary with swings in economic activity and the consequent response of the monetary authority. Under a standard, textbook approach, monetary authorities like the RBI adopt a low interest–rate policy to revive the economy during periods of economic slowdown and interest rates are raised during periods of overheating and heightened inflationary pressure. Along

[1] As per regulatory norms, banks need to make provisions for different types of assets. For standard assets, the provisioning requirements are low; for NPAs (problem loans), the provisioning requirements are very high. Details on provisioning for such assets are discussed in Chapter 7.

[2] Real bank credit growth in a year is calculated as the difference between nominal growth in non-food credit and inflation in that year.

with the changing monetary policy stance, all interest rates in the economy, including bank lending rates and returns on bonds, change. Changing lending rates and interest rates on bank investments exacerbate fluctuations in the interest income of banks. This explains how bank profitability is exposed to considerable volatility due to fluctuations in both the volume of business or assets and the returns thereupon.

It is observed that high growth of bank loans during economic booms also sows the seeds for loan delinquencies in the future (Misra, Rajmal and Verma, 2016; Samantaraya, 2016). This is because of laxity in credit appraisal during economic upswings as indicated earlier. Thus, high procyclicality of bank lending not only causes fluctuations in bank profitability, it is also a factor responsible for large loan defaults during economic recession.

6.2.1.3 Banking Involves a Variety of Risks

It may be noted that banking intrinsically entails a variety of risks, discussed as follows:

- First, as indicated earlier, bad lending decisions may cause default in repayment of loans. Other factors such as adverse economic conditions, changing preferences of consumers away from the goods produced using the bank loan, competition from imports or even wilful default by borrowers can cause default in loan repayments. This type of risk is known as *credit risk*.
- Second, at times, liquid assets of a bank may fall short of liquid liabilities and a bank may not be able to meet demand for deposit withdrawal or disbursement of fresh loans temporarily. This happens due to mismatch in the liquidity profile of the assets and liabilities in the bank's balance sheet in the short run. A bank may continue to be solvent but there could be shortage of liquid assets. This is known as *liquidity risk*.
- Third, a bank's interest income on its loans and interest costs on deposits and borrowings are sensitive to changes in interest rate. If with increase in the market interest rate due to monetary tightening, interest costs rise more proportionately than interest income, then the bank's NII and profitability are adversely affected. This may happen if interest rates on deposits are highly flexible while the same on loans are relatively rigid or change slowly. Similarly, if a floating

rate loan is funded through a term deposit with a fixed interest rate, any reduction in the market interest rate will reduce the NII of the bank. Such adverse impact of interest rate variation on a bank's profitability is popularly referred to as *interest rate risk.*

- Fourth, banks are exposed to *market risk* which occurs due to fall in the value of assets like bonds, bullion, forex, and so on, due to adverse movement in market prices. Such assets are actively traded in the market and their prices change regularly. Fluctuation in the market price of such assets changes their mark-to-market value in the bank's balance sheet. If prices change unfavourably, it may shrink the value of assets in the bank's balance sheet and reduce its net worth.
- Fifth, banks suffer losses due to inadequate or deficient systems, procedures or people or due to external factors like accidents or natural calamities on several occasions. Such losses are part of *operational risk.*

Details of various types of risks in banking are covered in section 6.3.

6.2.1.4 Bank Runs, Contagion and Systemic Crisis

Public confidence in a bank is of paramount importance for sustaining its business. Any damage to the confidence of depositors can lead to bank runs which have the potential to seriously harm the entire banking system in extreme situations. This will become clear from the following discussion.

Assume a bank suddenly suffers loan delinquencies due to bad lending decisions or because of a recession. Loan delinquencies not only dry up receipts in the form of loan repayments, related provisioning for such troubled assets puts additional pressure on the resources of the concerned bank (Samantaraya, 2016). This curtails its ability to take up fresh lending and earn additional interest income. If the depositors perceive that their bank does not have adequate funds to cover loan defaults, their confidence in the bank gets impaired. They begin to doubt the bank's ability to meet their deposit withdrawal demands. In that situation, luckier is the one who can run to the bank and be the first to withdraw all their deposits. All the depositors may be affected by the herd instinct. The bitter competition amongst them to be the luckiest may drive all of them to run to the bank to be the first in the queue and collect their deposits. This is popularly referred to as a *bank run.*

Even a healthy bank will certainly collapse if all its depositors want their deposits withdrawn at once. Term loans are illiquid with a fixed schedule of repayment. Hence, the bank will find it impossible to meet deposit withdrawals as it will be unable to encash such loans instantly. Needless to mention, when a bank is in bad shape, matters are worse.

This suggests that mismatch in the maturity profile of loans and deposits in banking makes loss of confidence in a bank a self-fulfilling prophecy. Bank runs are caused due to doubts as to the financial standing of a bank. Underlying asset–liability maturity mismatches convert such doubts into reality.

Moreover, at times, trouble in one bank quickly spreads to the entire banking system. This is because banks are interconnected through the payment and settlement infrastructure. Failure of one bank may affect the business of other connected banks who were supposed to receive funds from the failed bank either for themselves or on behalf of customers. Further, the depositors of other banks may start doubting the ability of their own banks to meet deposit withdrawal demands seeing the fate of depositors of the failed bank. This causes a cascading effect and the contagion spreads to the entire banking system.

This is not an imaginary or hypothetical situation. There were several instances of bank runs in the US and Europe in the late 1920s and early 1930s. The resolution costs of such contagion and banking crises are estimated to be huge. Fortunately, in India while there have been sporadic instances of bank runs, such episodes were limited to a handful of cooperative banks and largely remained localised. Global Trust Bank (GTB), a promising private commercial bank, witnessed a bank run in the early 2000s. But the impact was contained by the swift takeover of GTB by Oriental Bank of Commerce. Active and prompt intervention of banking regulators is necessary to arrest the contagion effect. Such interventions[3] generally take the form of announcing a temporary moratorium on deposit withdrawals in the troubled bank, superseding its management, arrangement for merger or takeover, and so on.

Thus, bank runs, mainly triggered by concerns over solvency of a bank, may lead to severe contraction of its deposits. Not only does it encounter massive deposit withdrawals, even fresh deposits are not received. If this leads

[3] Details of the standard operating procedure for such interventions are provided in Chapter 12.

to a contagion, the entire banking system becomes unstable. There may be serious disruption to the normal functioning of an economy. Furthermore, resolution costs of the crisis add to the burden.

The preceding paragraphs have explained how the underlying features of the banking business make it extremely risky. The risks in banking cannot be eliminated completely. However, banking regulations can keep the quantum of risks contained within prudential limits.

There is another compelling reason for regulation of banks on account of ethics and principles of natural justice. Let us discuss the same.

6.2.1.5 Different Stakeholders Managing Banking Business versus Those Bearing Losses

Owners and shareholders contribute to equity capital in ordinary non-financial business activities such as manufacturing and trading, and this constitutes the bulk of their overall funding. They take critical business decisions and themselves bear the loss or appropriate the profits of the business. On the contrary, bulk of the funds used for the banking business is contributed by depositors. The share of equity capital which represents exposure of owners and shareholders in the banking business is very limited. For example, prior to the GFC of 2007–08, the proportion of capital to total assets for many leading banks in the US and Europe was less than 5 per cent. In 2021–22, the *leverage ratio*[4] of several leading banks in India was in the range of 4 to 6 per cent. The owners and management of banks take all business decisions relating to the use of depositors' money in lending and investments. If a bank earns high profits due to prudent and good business decisions, bulk of the profit goes to equity holders. The depositors do not gain much from this. However, if due to reckless decisions of the bank management, the bank incurs losses and becomes insolvent, bulk of the burden falls on the depositors.

Moreover, the problems in one bank generally do not remain isolated. The entire banking system may collapse due to contagion, with an overwhelmingly injurious impact on the economy. To avoid the larger trouble caused by such

[4] Leverage ratio is defined as the ratio of tier-1 capital to total exposure (both on- and off-balance sheet exposure) of a bank. The RBI has prescribed a minimum leverage ratio of 3.5 per cent for India. For systemically important banks (domestic), the minimum leverage ratio is 4 per cent.

contagious effect, it has been seen in the past that the government bails out troubled banks. The burden of such resolution costs is borne by taxpayers.

Thus, while depositors and taxpayers do not have any say in lending and other business decisions of a bank, they suffer most, quite unjustifiably, when it fails due to bad decisions of the bank management. Both from the point of view of protecting interests of depositors and taxpayers and saving the economy from severe adverse consequences, it is imperative that banks are adequately regulated.

Non-financial firms and ordinary business organisations are regulated in each country by various provisions including those on registration and establishment, company laws, labour laws, environmental legislation, tax regulations, and so on. In addition to these, banking companies need further regulation concerned with protecting depositors' interest, lending norms, capital adequacy requirements, asset classification, income recognition, reporting and transparency requirements, and so on.

This discussion explains the imperative need for banking regulation to ensure that the banking business is conducted following prudential principles. Banks should avoid excessive risk taking. Moreover, the regulations should compel banks to have sufficient capital and provisioning to cover risks. The depositors' confidence in the bank also needs to be continuously maintained. Details of such banking regulations are discussed in Chapter 7.

6.2.2 Rationale for Banking Supervision

It is important to note that framing guidelines for banking regulation as indicated earlier is only part of the requirement towards promoting banking safety and soundness. What is more important is effective implementation of the regulatory prescriptions. Well-designed regulatory policies without effective implementation will not be helpful. There is high probability that banks intentionally or otherwise may deviate from the regulatory guidelines, driven by the desire for excessive profit or due to lack of adequate competency. In view of these aspects, it is necessary to continuously monitor banking activities to ensure the adherence of banks to regulatory prescriptions. This is undertaken through banking supervision.

Banking supervision involves both periodic on-site inspection of banks by banking regulators as well as off-site surveillance through analysis of regular reports submitted by banks. Details of the same are discussed in Chapter 7.

To sum up, this section highlighted typical underlying features in banking which expose a bank to a variety of risks. Containment of risks in banking is necessary to stem disruptions in economic activities due to bank failures. This underscores the rationale for banking regulation and supervision. For this purpose, there is a prior requirement of adequate understanding of the nature and dimensions of various types of risks entailed in the banking business. This task is undertaken in the following section.

6.3 Major Types of Risks in Banking

The banking business entails various types of risks. These can be analysed from several perspectives. Some varieties of risks are embodied in the assets side of a bank's balance sheet, while some in the liabilities side. Some others configure based on the developments in the entire balance sheet as also in off-balance-sheet (OBS) items. Each item of assets and liabilities again carries different proportions of various types of risks. For example, the nature, composition and extent of risks embodied in a mortgage loan are different from the same for a corporate working-capital loan. For investment in government securities, these are again completely different.

For long-term solvency and maximising inter-temporal profitability in the banking business, there is need to have a comprehensive understanding about the nature and degree of various types of banking risks.

6.3.1 What Is Risk?

Risk is simply an adverse outcome compared to that which is expected or projected. Let us explain with an example. Assume an automobile manufacturer projected in 2019 that the number of cars they can sell in the year 2020 will be 10,00,000. They may have used a very scientific method of projection based on income forecasts of prospective car buyers, the total demand for cars, number of cars likely to be sold by other car manufacturers, number of cars expected to be imported or exported, and so on. Guided by these projections, say, they adjusted the production capacity in their plant, hired engineers and workers, procured raw materials and produced 10,00,000 cars in 2020. Assume some unexpected developments in 2020 like the unanticipated economic contraction due to the Covid-19 pandemic or an aggressive price cut by a competitor adversely affected their sale of cars. Say, they could sell only 7,60,000 cars as against the projection of 10,00,000. The loss of income or profit due to this adverse deviation reflects the amount of risk for the car manufacturer.

Similarly, each balance-sheet item of a bank can undergo adverse deviation as compared to the projection or plan. A term loan instalment may not be received from a borrower if their business suffers due to economic slowdown or some accident in the plant disrupts production and sale or if they decide to default wilfully, and so on. Likewise, the proceeds from sale of bonds in the secondary market depend on market conditions. On the liabilities side, renewal of deposits depends on the depositors' spending requirements when the deposit matures or the relative interest rate offered in other financial market segments or that offered by other banks, and so on. A bank may also suffer losses if there is any deficiency in the documentation for loans and investments, omission or commission by bank employees, malfunctioning of the software or IT infrastructure employed for record keeping or data storage, or disruption in the enabling payment and settlement system due to some external cause, and so on. Thus, banks are exposed to a variety of events because of which there could be adverse deviation in the actual income flow or profit as compared to what they had planned or conceived a priori.

Risk is associated with the uncertainty of a future event or outcome. Technically, uncertainty cannot be measured, but the amount of risk can be quantified. There is a probability associated with risk. This can be explained with an example.

Let us say a bank has given an INR 20 lakh loan at 10 per cent interest to a borrower for one year. Borrowers are categorised by banks into different classes or groups as per their *credit rating*, which reflects their loan repayment ability or creditworthiness. Say, the present borrower has a credit score which suggests that they are likely to repay the entire amount (principal plus interest charge)—that is, INR 22 lakh with a probability of 0.8. They are likely to pay back a total amount of INR 20 lakh with a probability of 0.1 and INR 21 lakh with a probability of 0.1. The weighted average of their likely repayment amount (using corresponding probability as weights) = (INR 22 lakh × 0.8) + (INR 21 lakh × 0.1) + (INR 20 lakh × 0.1) = INR 21.7 lakh.

In this case, as compared to the desired repayment of INR 22 lakh, the borrower is likely to make a repayment of INR 21.7 lakh. So the amount of adverse deviation in the receipt as compared to what is desired would be INR 22 lakh – INR 21.7 lakh = INR 0.3 lakh. Thus, here the amount of risk involved is INR 30,000. The actual methods applied in banking for measuring various types of risks are discussed in section 6.4.

6.3.2 Types of Risks

The banking business embodies different types of risks. Some important categories of banking risks are discussed as follows.

6.3.2.1 Credit Risk

Credit risk in banking manifests mainly in the form of *default risk* which arises due to non-payment of at least a part of the principal and interest on a loan. For example, say, a bank has given a loan from which the principal and interest due over the years is INR 50 lakh. In case the borrower pays back INR 40 lakh through periodic instalments but defaults on the remaining amount of INR 10 lakh, the adverse deviation in the bank's receipt from loan repayment is INR 10 lakh which is the amount of default risk on the loan.

It may be noted that the security collateral available to the bank needs to be adjusted for calculating the actual credit risk. If the value of the security collateral available to the bank in the aforementioned case is INR 7.5 lakh, then the actual credit risk on the loan is INR 2.5 lakh (calculated as INR 10 lakh – INR 7.5 lakh).

Default risk is applicable to other items of banking assets and liabilities too. For example, there is default risk if payments in an investment—that is, dues from a counterparty or issuer of a security—are not realised. In case of bank guarantees or LCs and financial derivatives, default risk arises if payments are not received from the constituents or counterparties on crystallisation of the committed liability.

In addition to default risk, other major drivers of credit risk in the banking business are as follows:

- *Recovery risk*: Banks generally insist on security collateral from borrowers. In case of default, they use the security collateral to recover the pending dues. However, if there is diminution in value of the security itself, a bank faces uncertainty in recovering pending dues. This is referred to as recovery risk.

- *Concentration risk*: This refers to excessive exposure to a single borrower, counterparty, group of industries, particular type of industry, and so on.
- *Spread risk*: The credit rating of a borrower is dynamic. If due to downgrading of a borrower of a particular type, the market value of the loan diminishes, it is referred to as spread risk.
- *Correlation risk*: The business prospects of a variety of borrowers or industries may be highly correlated. For example, the business of the tyre manufacturing industry is highly correlated with that of the automobile industry. Correlation risk refers to simultaneous default on loans given to different industries which have common risk factors.
- *Currency-induced credit risk*: This refers to the credit risk which arises due to unhedged foreign currency exposures of clients.

Given the predominance of default risk in the banking business, the terms 'credit risk' and 'default risk' are used interchangeably in this book.

6.3.2.2 Liquidity Risk

Liquidity risk arises when a bank is unable to meet withdrawal demand for deposits or request for a loan due to lack of fund availability. It may be noted that on any given day, a bank typically receives funds in various forms such as (*a*) bank deposits from numerous depositors, (*b*) loan repayments from borrowers, (*c*) sale proceeds from investments, (*d*) borrowings from the RBI and other banks, and so on. Similarly, on the same day, the bank disburses funds for (*a*) meeting deposit withdrawal demands, (*b*) extending fresh loans, (*c*) undertaking investments in the form of buying government securities, corporate bonds, forex and gold, among others, (d) lending to other banks and financial institutions, and so on. Obviously, a prudent bank will not prefer to hold idle liquid funds which do not generate interest income. If the bank can meet disbursal requirements from the receipts of funds comfortably, then the banking business is conducted smoothly. The bank can exploit profitable business opportunities optimally. On the contrary, if the proceeds from receipts of funds fall short of disbursal requirements, the bank encounters a liquidity problem. Inability of the bank to meet such immediate deposit withdrawal and loan disbursal or investment requirements out of its own liquid resources is popularly known as *liquidity risk*.

The liquidity problem mainly arises due to non-receipt of funds in any one account as indicated in the previous paragraph. Accordingly, liquidity risk manifests in the following forms:

- *Funding risk*: if the liquidity problem is due to non-renewal of deposits or unanticipated withdrawal of existing deposits
- *Time risk*: when a liquidity problem arises due to non-repayment of loans as per schedule or non-receipt of other income flows of the bank
- *Call risk*: where the liquidity problem arises due to crystallisation of a contingent liability such as a bank guarantee, LC, a derivative product like an 'option' or futures contract, and so on.

6.3.2.3 Interest Rate Risk

Interest rate changes affect a bank's interest earnings, cost of funds, profitability and balance sheet position. Adverse impact of interest rate changes on a bank's profitability and market value of equity or net worth is popularly referred to as *interest rate risk*. It can be viewed from the *earning perspective* when interest rate variation reduces interest earning, raises interest costs and consequently reduces profitability of a bank. Similarly, interest rate risk can be viewed from the *economic value perspective* when we analyse the adverse impact of interest rate variation on a bank's balance sheet, diminishing its equity value. Interest rate risks take various forms. Let us briefly discuss key varieties.

As discussed in Chapter 4, monetary policy is popularly used as a key macroeconomic management tool across countries. It responds to business cycle–related economic fluctuations by changing the interest rate and aggregate spending in an economy with a view to delivering economic and price stability. The changing interest rate affects the NII and profitability of banks. This is because interest rates on loans and deposits behave differently when there are changes in the market interest rate. Lending rates for several types of loans[5] are now linked to the RBI's fixed repo rate under the LAF. As and when there is a change in the RBI's monetary policy rate—that is,

[5] Many banks in India are now using the RBI's fixed repo rate under the LAF as the external benchmark for the interest rate they charge for home loans and some other types of retail loans.

fixed repo rate under the LAF—the lending rates linked to it automatically change. So if there is monetary policy expansion and reductio of the policy rate, it leads to a drop in bank lending rates. On the other hand, if such loans are funded by, say, a three-year term deposit, then the interest rate on such deposit remains unchanged. Thus, interest rate reduction engineered by the RBI's monetary policy reduces a bank's interest income on loans linked to the RBI's policy rate while interest costs on deposits remain fixed—causing a drop in NII. This type of adverse impact of changing interest rates on bank profitability is termed as *repricing risk.*

Even if interest rates on deposits are flexible, but reduction in lending rates due to change in market interest rate is stronger as compared to reduction in interest rate on bank deposits, it can adversely affect the bank's profitability. This type of interest rate risk which arises due to difference in sensitivity of interest earning on assets and that of interest cost on liabilities to variation in market interest rate is referred to as *basis risk.*

Similarly, when there are changes in the interest rate, the *yield curve* does not shift parallelly. The yield curve depicts interest rates on securities of different terms to maturity at a point of time. When interest rates witness downward movement, interest rates on securities with different terms to maturity do not fall by exactly the same amount. It may be possible that the interest rate on a one-year bond drops by 20 basis points while that on a two-year bond falls by 50 basis points. On a five-year bond, the drop could be, say, 35 basis points. In such circumstances, if interest rates paid by a bank on some bank liabilities are linked to the interest rate on one-year bonds and interest charged on several assets is benchmarked to five-year bonds, the bank will witness a drop in its NII. Such type of interest rate risk is known as *yield curve risk.*

Thus, the previous paragraphs summarise some varieties of interest rate risk from the earning perspective referring to fall in NII and profitability caused by adverse change in interest income or cost in non-traded items like bank loans and deposits.

Variation in interest rates may also cause deterioration in a bank's balance sheet due to drop in the market price of tradeable securities in the secondary market. It may be noted that a sizeable portion of a bank's balance sheet takes the form of investments in government securities which are traded regularly in the secondary market. Rise in the market interest rate reduces the mark-to-market price of such securities and hence adversely affects the bank's balance sheet. Details of these aspects are discussed under *market risk* in the section that follows. In fact, variation in the interest rate affects the market value of various interest rate–sensitive assets and liabilities in a bank's balance sheet differently. By summing up the impact on all such assets and liabilities, we can decipher the overall impact of interest rate changes on the market value of a bank's equity. Hence, another dimension of interest rate risk is in terms of assessing the adverse impact of interest rate variation on a bank's equity or net worth.

6.3.2.4 Market Risk

Market risk arises due to adverse movement in the market price of a bank's assets. Let us consider the amount of gold in a bank's balance sheet. If the price of gold moves southward, then the value of gold assets in a bank's balance sheet also witnesses downward revision. Similarly, if the INR–USD exchange rate appreciates from, say, INR 80 per USD to INR 75 per USD, then the rupee value of USD assets in a bank's balance sheet correspondingly falls. Assume a bank holds foreign currency assets worth USD 1 million. At INR 80 per USD, its rupee value is INR 80 million. When the exchange rate becomes INR 75 per USD, the value of the same USD 1 million in the bank's balance sheet declines to INR 75 million. Thus, the value of the bank's forex reserves deteriorates by INR 5 million due to change in the market exchange rate. This quantifies the amount of market risk in holding USD 1 million.

Banks hold a substantial amount of government securities. They are exposed to significant market risk on the portion of government securities which are held for trading. As we know, the price of a bond in the secondary market is inversely related to the market interest rate on the bond. To explain this, let us take the following example.

Say, a one-year zero-coupon bond with a face value of INR 100 is traded in the market on 1 January 2020. As it is a zero-coupon bond, the only return on this bond is the difference between its face value (amount received on maturity) and market price. If it is purchased at INR 90 on 1 January 2020, the investor will get INR 100 (face value) on redemption on 1 January 2021. So the return on the bond is INR 100 – INR 90 = INR 10. The rate of return = (10/90) × 100 per cent = 11.1 per cent. If the bond is purchased at INR 80 on 1 January 2020, the return on the bond = INR 100 – INR 80 = INR 20, and the rate of return = (20/80) × 100 per cent = 25 per cent.

Thus, if the market price of the bond falls from INR 90 to INR 80, the rate of return increases from 11.1 to 25 per cent. This explains the inverse relation between the market price of a bond and the rate of return.

Let us assume that a bank has a portfolio with government bonds worth INR 1,000 crore. If the market interest rate rises, the market value of this portfolio will fall below INR 1,000 crore correspondingly, as the market price of each bond falls. This fall in the market value is the market risk on government bonds.

It may be noted that a portion of the government bonds is earmarked to be held until maturity. On this portion of bond holding, there is no market risk. In the aforementioned example, if the bank wishes to hold the bond until 1 January 2021, it receives the face value of INR 100 on maturity. Then there is no loss of value on this bond and the associated market risk is nil. Only the remaining portion of the bond portfolio which is held for trading in the secondary market is exposed to market risk.

Thus, market risk is concerned with adverse movement in the marked-to-market value of tradeable assets in a bank's balance sheet like bonds, equities, forex, commodities, and so on, due to change in their prices. As and when market prices change on a real time basis, market risk on such assets or securities is calculated. This is the potential loss due to adverse movement in the asset price with certain probability over a particular time horizon. It need not involve actual sale of such assets.

6.3.2.5 Operational Risk

Operational risk in banking is an adverse outcome which arises due to man-made errors or faults of omission or commission, deficiencies in documentation or record keeping, disruptions in IT infrastructure, external events such as damage from accidents or natural calamities, and so on. It is difficult to decipher the amount of operational risk in a bank but roughly the amount should be proportional to the volume of its business.

6.3.2.6 Overall Banking Risks in Different Items of Assets and Liabilities

It may be noted that different items of assets and liabilities in a bank's balance sheet may carry different proportions of the types of risks discussed in the previous paragraphs. For example, a mortgage loan may embody a significant proportion of default risk and some amount of operational risk, but no market risk. Investment in government securities has zero default risk, but if held for trading, it may entail significant market risk.

Identifying the different types of risks embodied in the balance sheet and OBS items of a bank and configuring the sum of risks in the entire banking business are critical for conducting the banking business prudently. It is imperative for the bank's management and regulators not only to correctly decipher various types of risks embodied in the banking business and to measure them precisely, but also to put in place an appropriate risk management and mitigation framework. This can enable banks to serve the economy in the best possible way.

6.4 Measurement of Banking Risks

Identifying various types of risks entailed in banking is one thing while measuring the amount of risk is another. The latter is very challenging. Conventionally, various types of approaches and techniques are employed to measure the quantum of banking risks. Different methods are suitable for assessing different types of risks. We shall cover the measurement of (*a*) credit risk, (*b*) liquidity risk, (*c*) interest rate risk, (*d*) market risk and (*e*) operational risk in this regard. Popular methods used for measuring such risks are outlined in the sections that follow.

6.4.1 Measurement of Credit Risk

Credit risk accounts for the bulk of overall banking risks as loans and investments overwhelm banking assets. Such assets involve potential for default or credit risk. In addition, non-fund activities like issuing bank guarantees, LCs, and so on, also entail credit risk if the counterparty defaults.

Mainly, credit risk in banks is assessed and measured through *credit rating models*. Credit rating models are used to undertake rating or grading of loan seekers and dynamically assess creditworthiness of incumbent borrowers. First, banks assess credit risk on loans based on the credit score or rating of loan seekers to take lending decisions. Second, after lending, the credit risk of borrowers is periodically reviewed using *rating migration* or *rating transition*, which is nothing but an assessment on a borrower moving from one rating category to another over a period of time.

Broadly, measurement of credit risk involves two steps. First, using credit rating or scoring, the probability of default (PD) for borrowers is assessed. Second, PD is used as a critical input along with the quantum of exposure at default and estimation of loss to quantify credit risk. Let us understand the procedure with some more details.

6.4.1.1 Assignment of Credit Rating or Score Using a Credit Rating Model

When a bank receives a loan application, the screening procedure involves rating the loan repayment ability of the borrower using a credit rating model. Credit rating is a quantified assessment of the creditworthiness of a borrower. Based on several factors such as current financial position including debt obligations, present income or cash flows, future sales and profit projections of businesses or corporates along with turnover for several years, and a company's (borrower) market outlook and regulatory issues, credit rating models assess the loan repayment ability of loan seekers. For individual borrowers, past payment history (default or delayed payment on past loans), income from their current occupation or employment, future income projections, demographic profile, availability of guarantee or security collateral, and so on, are taken into consideration.

A typical credit rating for a business or corporate borrower takes into account relevant financial variables such as its projected sales, profits, working capital, retained earnings, composition of liabilities, debt–equity ratio, personal assets–liabilities of the directors or promoters, and so on. Appropriate weights are assigned to these factors and the weighted average is used to obtain a credit score for the borrower. Assignment of a score also depends on the historical data of various firms (borrowers) and the events of their default or non-default in the past.

The credit rating of a borrower is expressed using symbols such as AAA, BBB, and so on, as given in Table 6.1. The same table also provides indicative interpretation of a borrower's loan repayment ability for different rating categories.

Based on different parameters pertaining to the industry risk, business risk, management risk and financial risk of a borrower, they are assigned a rating in the order of AAA, AA, A, BBB, BB, B, CCC and D. For illustrative purposes, on a scale of 0 to 10, borrowers having a score of above 7.5 may be rated as AAA, those having a score of 6.5 to 7.5 may be rated as AA, and so on. Borrowers having a score of less than 2 may be placed under the D category.

Table 6.1 Different rating categories and the creditworthiness of a borrower

Rating category	Interpretation on creditworthiness	Broad category
AAA	Highest degree of safety on timely repayment of debt obligations; represents the lowest credit risk	Investment grade
AA	Very low or marginal credit risk	
A	Low or modest credit risk	
BBB	Moderate degree of safety and credit risk	
BB	Moderate risk of default	Non-investment or speculative grade
B	High risk of default	
C	Very high risk of default	
D	Already in default or expected to default soon	

Source: Collated by the author based on information obtained from official websites of different banks in India.

The highest rated AAA borrower may have minimum risk of default, an AA borrower may have marginal risk and an A type borrower may have modest risk, and so on. Finally, a D-type borrower may be considered as the default category.

Thus, default risk is assumed to increase as we move down in the credit rating grade from AAA to D. Again, for illustrative purposes, borrowers rated AAA may have a default probability of 1 per cent within a one-year time horizon since availing the loan. In other words, it is expected that 1 out of 100 AAA-rated borrowers is likely to default within one year of availing the loan. Similarly, the default probability within a one-year time horizon for BBB-type borrowers could be 5 per cent, that for CCC-type borrowers may be 25 per cent, and so on. Broadly, borrowers with credit rating AAA to BBB are classified as investment grade borrowers. The remaining are non-investment or speculative grade.

Further, for assessing creditworthiness, stability of profit or income flow is considered to be more critical. As loan repayment is scheduled over a period of several years, a borrower with greater stability in their future profit or income flow enjoys better ability to repay the loan.

It is also important to note that credit rating models used for corporate borrowers or government entities are more formal and detailed. Needless to mention, rating models used by individual banks are proprietary and confidential in nature. Obviously, details of the weights allocated to various factors while assigning ratings and PD for different credit ratings are not available in the public domain. In practice, CreditRisk+ developed by Credit Suisse, CreditMetrics by JPMorgan Chase and Altman's Z-Score are popular credit rating models used by several banks. Such models vary from each other in terms of factors considered and the respective weights assigned to them for rating a borrower; otherwise, the essence of the exercise, as discussed, remains the same.

On the other hand, for individual or retail borrowers, banks use simpler rating models. For example, consider mortgage loans. Depending on the type of borrower, such as a government employee (with stable income flow), a self-employed, households with more than one earning member, and so on, banks may have different assessment on PD. These models are also proprietary in nature and details thereof are not available in the public domain. Credit scores assigned by credit information companies (CICs) are popularly used by banks in India for assessing creditworthiness of retail borrowers and pricing of such loans. Such credit scores take into account the past loan repayment habit of a borrower, credit utilisation pattern, pending dues, number of credit facilities availed, and so on. Credit Information Bureau (India) Limited (CIBIL), High Mark Credit Information Services, Equifax and Experian are popular CICs. Under credit scoring, borrowers are assigned a score in the range of 300 to 900. A high credit score for an individual reflects their low default risk. A credit score of above 750 is widely treated as excellent. It is learnt that for calculating the credit score of an individual, CIBIL assigns 30 per cent weightage to payment history, 25 per cent to credit exposure, 25 per cent for credit type and the remaining 20 per cent to other factors.

6.4.1.2 Rating Migration or Transition

The second step to measure PD entails assessment of *rating migration* or *rating transition* of borrowers. This is undertaken as follows.

Say, as on 1 January 2018, there are 100 borrowers rated as AAA-type by a bank using its own proprietary rating model. As on 1 January 2019, based on the latest information available for these 100 borrowers, the credit score may change under the same rating model. Say, on a review, out of these 100 borrowers, 90 are retained as AAA borrowers as on 1 January 2019. Say, the review downgraded 6 out of the above 100 borrowers to AA-type and the remaining 4 to A-type. In this example, not a single AAA-type borrower was downgraded to the default D category. This explains rating migration of AAA-graded borrowers within a year as depicted in Figure 6.1.

Similarly, say, out of 100 BBB borrowers as on 1 January 2018, the rating migration as on 1 January 2019 could be such that three of them are upgraded to A type; 85 retain BBB rating; 10 and 1 could be downgraded to B and CCC types, respectively; and 1 borrower downgraded to the D category.

Lastly, let us assume that out of 24 B borrowers as on 1 January 2018, the rating migration as on 1 January 2019 is such that 16 retain B rating; 2 are upgraded to BB; and 6 slip into the default category, D.

This rating migration suggests that the percentage of AAA-rated borrowers migrating to the default category, D, is 0, as not a single AAA borrower as on 1 January 2018 was downgraded to the D category on 1 January 2019. Amongst BBB-type borrowers, out of 100, only 1 migrated to the D category while 6 amongst the 24 B-type borrowers migrated to the D category. Thus, the rating migration or transition suggests 1 and 25 per cent of BBB- and B-type borrowers, respectively, are likely to default after one year. A similar procedure may be adopted for assessing rating migration for all borrowers under different credit ratings over the years.

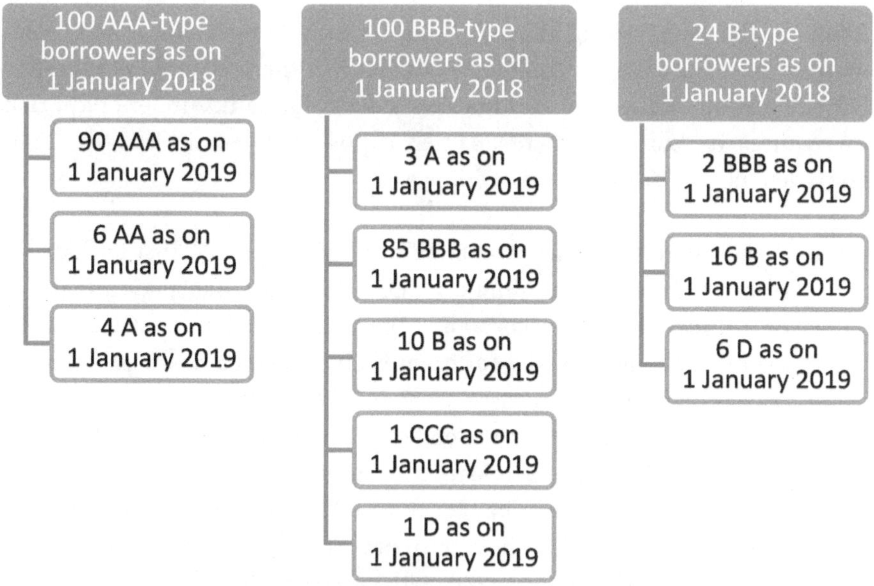

Figure 6.1 An illustration of rating migration

Source: Prepared by the author.

Using such information on rating migration, banks prepare a migration or transition matrix for borrowers in different rating categories. It basically summarises the transition in creditworthiness of different borrowers in the loan portfolio over the years. This helps in calculating PD for a particular borrower which is the first critical element in calculation of losses due to credit risk on a loan.

PD for a particular borrower is calculated as the long-run average of the probability of their migrating to the D type under rating migration in each year. For simplicity, let us assume Borrower X was rated AAA, AA and AA in the years 2020, 2021 and 2022, respectively. Assume, based on historical data, the probability of an AAA-rated borrower migrating to the D type is 0 and that for an AA-rated borrower is 0.015. Then, PD for Borrower X is equal to (0 + 0.015 + 0.015)/3 =0.03/3=0.01, or 1 per cent.

Thus, PD is the average of probability of rating migration to the default category for a borrower over the years. PD over the years need not remain the same due to rating migration as the credit rating itself may vary for a borrower over the years. Similarly, PD for other borrowers can be calculated.

6.4.1.3 Expected and Unexpected Loss Due to Credit Risk

Based on the credit rating or scores and the rating migration of borrowers, we described calculation of PD for a borrower in the preceding paragraphs. For calculation of expected and unexpected loss for banks under credit risk, we require two more ingredients, namely exposure at default (EAD) and loss given default (LGD), discussed as follows:

- EAD is nothing but an estimation of credit exposure—that is, dues from a borrower on a future date. On a term loan like a home loan or a project loan to a corporate, the outstanding amount on the loan is the same as EAD. For example, if the total amount of EMIs outstanding from Borrower X's loan is INR 1,50,000 over two years, then EAD on this loan at the end of two years is INR 1,50,000. On a partially disbursed term loan, loan limit or outstanding amount, whichever is higher, can be treated as EAD. On overdraft and cash credit, EAD will include both current outstanding amounts and the unutilised portion of the facility with necessary adjustments.
- LGD measures the percentage of EAD which cannot be recovered if there is a default on a future date. LGD can be calculated after

adjusting for loan repayments along with interest, security collateral, drawing down of committed facilities, and so on, from EAD. Assume, in the same example of EAD of INR 1,50,000 after two years, recoveries from EMI payments and security collateral from Borrower X are expected to be INR 80,000. Hence, the recovery rate = INR 80,000/INR 1,50,000 × 100 = 53.3 per cent of EAD. LGD is calculated as 1 minus the recovery rate. In the example, LGD = 1 – 0.533 = 0.467, or 46.7 per cent of EAD.

We can calculate expected loss (EL) due to credit risk on a loan as a product of PD, LGD and EAD. For Borrower X, EAD is INR 1,50,000, LGD is 46.7 per cent and PD is 1 per cent; therefore, the EL for this loan is calculated as:

$$\text{EL} = \text{PD} \times \text{LGD} \times \text{EAD} = 0.01 \times 0.467 \times \text{INR } 1{,}50{,}000 = \text{INR } 700.50 \quad (6.1)$$

The EL measures the amount of loss which a bank expects to incur from a loan. The bank covers EL through pricing of the loan and provisioning. Banks charge a higher interest rate if the EL is higher for a loan.

It is important to note that the EL as estimated above is a measure of average loss at a future date with certain probability. The future is unknown and actual outcomes can be different from expected. One can measure the unexpected loss (UEL) which accounts for the variation of actual loss from the expected loss. While UEL is likely, its timing and severity are difficult to assess in advance.

For calculating unexpected loss, we may use a volatility measure like standard deviation (SD) of the rating migration or transition for a borrower over the years. In our example, SD of the rating migration to the D category for Borrower X during 2020, 2021 and 2022 can be calculated as follows:

$$\text{SD} = \text{Standard deviation of } (0, 0.015, 0.015) = 0.00866 \quad (6.2)$$

Then UEL = SD × LGD × EAD = 0.00866 × 0.467 × INR 1,50,000 = INR 606.63.

Banks need to be prepared to cover UEL due to credit risk. Otherwise, realisation of such loss will make a bank insolvent and may lead to its collapse. Through the minimum capital adequacy requirement, banking regulators ensure that a bank is capable of compensating for UELs and such loss does not cause bank instability. If a bank suffers a low capital position, its profit and capital put together may not be able to cover UEL as and when it occurs.

Finally, let us return to the measurement of 'credit risk'. In the previous example, the quantum of credit risk for Borrower X = EL + UEL = INR 700.50 + INR 606.63 = INR 1,307.13. By summing up quantum of credit risk for all the borrowers calculated in the same way, the total amount of expected and unexpected loss in the overall balance sheet and OBS items of a bank can be arrived at. This measures the amount of credit risk in a bank.

Some analysts perceive that the amount of credit risk on a loan is restricted to UEL. Measuring credit risk in that way is an understatement. The actual amount of credit risk should be the sum of EL and UEL as indicated in the previous paragraph. The comfort is the EL is covered by a bank through pricing of loans and provisioning. The UEL needs to be covered by minimum capital requirements.

6.4.1.4 Stress Tests and Scenario Analysis

In the post-GFC scenario, banking regulators in many countries are insisting that banks undertake *stress tests* and *scenario analyses* for assessing evolution of credit risk under different hypothetical situations. For example, if there is a recession, it has adverse consequences for sales and profit generation for business as well as for individual income. This may affect rating migration, PD and EAD estimates. Similarly, with economic recession, the value of security collaterals may depreciate and recoveries in general suffer. This may raise LGD. Overall, under different economic conditions and industry-specific developments, EL and UEL due to credit risk in a bank may vary.

Stress tests facilitate assessing the amount of credit risk in the banking business under different hypothetical and extreme situations. This helps to prepare banks for worst-case scenarios which may be hypothetical but probable. Accordingly, the preparedness of the bank in terms of adequacy of its capital position to face such extreme situations is analysed.

6.4.2 Measurement of Liquidity Risks

Liquidity risk in the banking business is measured using several methods. Most popular amongst them are the gap method and the use of balance sheet indicators.

The *gap method* basically estimates the mismatch between cash inflows and outflows of a bank over different time horizons in the future. Such mismatches are assessed based on expected residual maturities of various items of assets and liabilities. The first step in the gap method is construction of the *maturity ladder.* Second, maturity mismatches in cash inflows and outflows out of various banking transactions are assessed over different time buckets. The quantum of gap, particularly excess of cash outflows over inflows, is then used to quantify liquidity risk in a particular time bucket. This is explained using a hypothetical example as follows.

6.4.2.1 Construction of Maturity Ladder and Estimation of Gap

The day-to-day banking business entails numerous cash inflows and outflows in a variety of ways. Cash inflows for banks arise mainly from mobilisation of fresh deposits and renewal of old deposits, repayment of loans, receipt of interest and fees, sale of securities and other assets, availing credit lines and borrowing from the RBI and other financial institutions. Similarly, cash outflows occur due to withdrawal or non-renewal of deposits, disbursement of new loans, purchase of securities, renewal and upgradation of old loans, use of credit lines provided by the bank, and so on. The assessment of cash flows also covers OBS items.

As indicated, the first step involved in the application of gap analysis is making projections about future cash inflows and outflows and then distributing such inflows and outflows across different time horizons.

As a hypothetical example, let us consider construction of time buckets extending from '1–14 days' to 'above 5 years' as given in Table 6.2. The *maturity ladder* in this example is composed of eight time buckets. The lowest time bucket of '1–14 days' includes all the projected inflows and outflows at the shortest maturity. The longest time bucket of 'above 5 years' includes all the projected inflows and outflows scheduled to be maturing beyond five years.

Liquidity risk is measured by assessing the quantum of mismatch between inflows and outflows over different time buckets. The deficit in liquidity position—that is, the excess of cash outflows over inflows in a time bucket—reflects the quantum of liquidity risk in that bucket. Particularly, gaps in lower time buckets (shorter maturity) are a matter of greater concern.

For example, in Table 6.2, under normal business conditions, the gap for '1–14 days' is estimated to be INR 135 – INR 120 = INR 15 crore. This stands for surplus liquidity position as cash inflows are larger than outflows. In case

Table 6.2 Maturity ladder for assessing liquidity risk under gap analysis

(*INR crore*)

	Normal business conditions			**Bank-specific crisis**			**General market crisis**		
Time horizon	*Inflows*	*Outflows*	*Gap*	*Inflows*	*Outflows*	*Gap*	*Inflows*	*Outflows*	*Gap*
1–14 days	135	120	15	125	125	0	105	120	–15
15–28 days	160	155	5	155	157	–2	141	157	–16
29 days–3 months	200	210	–10	200	214	–14	200	246	–46
3–6 months	450	425	25	428	430	–2	428	530	–102
6–12 months	930	900	30	910	910	0	810	1,202	–392
1–3 years	1,880	1,850	30	1,880	1,850	30	1,650	1,700	–50
3–5 years	3,380	3,300	80	3,380	3,300	80	3,350	3,360	–10
Above 5 years	6,524	6,500	24	6,521	6,500	–21	6,411	6,500	–89

Source: Hypothetical example by the author.

inflows would have been less than outflows, then there would be a liquidity risk—that is, the bank would suffer from shortage of cash to meet outflows from the projected inflows. In Table 6.2, the time bucket '29 days–3 months' under normal business conditions is such a case. In this time bucket, the gap is negative at INR 10 crore which reflects the amount of liquidity risk at this time horizon.

6.4.2.2 Scenario Analysis

Calculation of *gap*, which is the difference between cash inflows and outflows for different time buckets, appears to be a simple exercise. But in reality, it is a very complex and challenging task. It involves projection of cash inflows and outflows for the future under alternative scenarios. In the previous section, we discussed calculation of gap under *normal business conditions*.

It is important to note that the projection of each of the constituent items of cash inflows and outflows over different time buckets is based on both the past experience of a bank as well as assessment of likely economic and financial conditions in the future. As regards future economic and financial conditions, it is prudent to consider alternative scenarios and assess liquidity risk not only under normal business conditions but also under adverse situations.

In Table 6.2, we have considered broadly three likely situations. A baseline scenario assumes *normal business conditions*. In addition to this, we have also included two worst-case scenarios. In one such possible adverse situation, it is assumed that there could be a bank-specific adverse development like some of its loans becoming delinquent. This is a bank-specific unfavourable development and its negative consequences are assumed to be restricted only to the bank. In Table 6.2, its projected impact on cash inflows and outflows is presented under the column 'bank-specific crisis'.

The second adverse situation is more severe. It may be assumed that a large-scale banking fraud has affected several big banks and has shaken public confidence in the entire banking system. This led to a *bank run* initially in these banks and other banks have also suffered due to the contagion. The incident has a systemic dimension affecting all banks harshly. It upsets cash inflows and outflows for all banks and conditions are more challenging for each bank. In Table 6.2, its projected impact on cash inflows and outflows is presented under the column 'general market crisis'.

In Table 6.2, all the negative figures under the 'gap' column in the three different scenarios reflect liquidity deficiency. Such negative numbers measure the quantum of liquidity risk under a particular time bucket. It can be observed from the table that under *general market crisis* conditions, liquidity risk is the maximum across various time buckets. For example, for the '29 days–3 months' time bucket, liquidity risk is calculated to be INR 10 crore under *normal business conditions*. Under *bank-specific crisis*, the liquidity risk rises to INR 14 crore. It is the maximum at INR 46 crore under *general market crisis*.

The gap method is popularly referred to as the flow approach to liquidity risk measurement as it is based on cash inflows and outflows of banks. Details of the gap method that banks in India follow using the statement of structural liquidity prescribed by the RBI for asset–liability management (ALM) are provided in Chapter 8.

6.4.2.3 Balance Sheet Indicators

It is important to note that along with the gap method, banks and bank regulators also use a host of other indicators drawn from a bank's balance sheet to assess liquidity risk. These indicators compare various items of assets and liabilities of a bank to decipher if the bank has a comfortable or distressed liquidity position. The list of such indicators, inter alia, includes:

- *Ratio of liquid assets to near short-term liabilities*: Higher proportion of liquid assets as compared to near short-term liabilities reflects lower liquidity risk. This is because a higher proportion of liquid assets enables meeting demand for funds comfortably.
  - For this purpose, liquid assets include cash and current account balances with other banks (including the RBI) adjusted for excess CRR balances, CDs, money market lending, liquid mutual fund investments, excess unencumbered SLR securities, liquidity support under marginal standing facility (MSF) and 50 per cent of unencumbered non-SLR securities.
  - Volatile portions of CASA and term deposits, a portion of CDs which are scheduled to mature within 30 days, money market borrowings, and so on, are included as part of near short-term liabilities.

- *Ratio of core deposits to total assets*: This indicates the proportion of assets that is funded through a bank's stable deposit base. Higher the ratio, lower is the liquidity risk. For calculating core deposits, bank deposits beyond one-year maturity are included. The core deposits are primary retail deposits mobilised mainly from households which are a stable source of funds for banks. They are differentiated from bulk deposits which are mobilised mainly from high net-worth individuals. The bulk deposits are single rupee term deposits of INR 2 crore and above.
- *Ratio of volatile liabilities to total assets*: Higher proportion of volatile liabilities as compared to total assets reflects higher liquidity risk.
- *Ratio of prime assets to total assets*: Higher proportion of prime assets in the total assets reflects lower liquidity risk. Prime assets are those with undoubted quality or nearly zero default risk. Such assets include government securities, currency and balances with the RBI, and so on.
- *Ratio of liquid assets to total deposits*: Higher proportion of liquid assets as compared to total deposits reflects lower liquidity risk.
- *Ratio of net overnight borrowing to total assets*: This reflects the dependency on overnight borrowing and hence higher liquidity risk.
- *Ratio of illiquid assets to core deposits*: The illiquid assets include loans, mandatory CRR and SLR requirements and fixed assets. Higher proportion of such assets as compared to core deposits reflects high liquidity risk.

These indicators, in various ways, reflect the relative ability of a bank to meet the liquidity demand out of its own resources. Accordingly, they provide a fair idea about liquidity risk in a bank. Moreover, such indicators can be directly derived from the bank's balance sheet and do not require any sophisticated method to measure liquidity risk.

6.4.2.4 Implicit Assessment of Liquidity Risk under LCR and NSFR

Liquidity coverage ratio (LCR) and net stable funding ratio (NSFR) have emerged as the two most important indicators under Basel III to assess the liquidity position of a bank. Both the indicators are explained in the sections that follow. Details about Basel III regulatory norms are provided in Chapter 7.

6.4.2.4.1 Liquidity Coverage Ratio (LCR)

LCR is defined as the ratio of stock of high-quality liquid assets (HQLAs) to total net cash outflow over the following 30 calendar days (TNCO30) expressed in percentage terms. Thus,

$$LCR = HQLAs/TNCO30 \times 100 \quad (6.3)$$

where HQLAs are such assets which can be converted into cash easily and immediately at little or no loss of value. They are mainly composed of cash in hand, excess CRR, government securities in excess of minimum SLR, marketable securities issued or guaranteed by a foreign sovereign (having '0' risk weight), liquidity support available under MSF of the RBI and facility to avail liquidity for LCR (FALLCR). As of August 2024, MSF is up to 2 per cent of the NDTL of a bank and FALLCR is up to 16 per cent of NDTL. The assets mentioned are categorised as level 1 assets. These assets are most liquid. HQLAs also include level 2 assets such as corporate bonds and equities which meet certain conditions. It is stipulated that level 2 assets should not be more than 40 per cent of the total HQLAs. TNCO30 is nothing but total expected cash outflows over total expected cash inflows for a bank for the ensuing 30 calendar days.

The short-term resilience of the liquidity profile of a bank can be assumed to be good if its LCR is above 100. The extent to which the LCR is lower than 100 can be used to assess liquidity risk of a bank implicitly.

6.4.2.4.2 Net Stable Funding Ratio (NSFR)

On the other hand, NSFR can be used to assess the long-term funding risk of a bank. It is defined as the ratio of available stable funding (ASF) to required stable funding (RSF) in percentage terms over a one-year time horizon. Thus,

$$NSFR = ASF/RSF \times 100 \quad (6.4)$$

ASF is calculated as the weighted average of regulatory capital and deposits from retail customers, small business customers, non-financial corporate customers, and so on. The weights (or ASF factor) vary from 0 to 100 per cent reflecting the stickiness of the liability. A higher ASF factor indicates lower liquidity risk or higher stickiness of the liability over a one-year time horizon. In other words, ASF is the reliable portion of liabilities in a bank which are not expected to be replaced or repaid within one year.

RSF reflects liquidity characteristics and residual maturities of various assets and OBS items of a bank. They are mainly unencumbered standard loans with residual maturity of one year or more. RSF factors in the range of 0 to 100 per cent for different assets and OBS items are used for calculation of RSF. An asset with an RSF factor of 100 is illiquid and hence needs to be fully funded by highly stable sources. At the other end, an asset with an RSF factor of 0 is highly liquid.

If NSFR is above 100 for a bank, it reflects that the bank has adequate stable funds to support its business and is not likely to face funding stress. If it is below 100, it implies that the bank needs to raise its stable sources of funding and reduce those assets requiring additional funding.

6.4.3 Methods to Measure Interest Rate Risk

Interest rate risk can be measured in several ways. *Gap analysis* and *duration analysis* are the most popular methods of quantifying interest rate risk. The former is supported by simulation approaches. *Gap analysis* compares the impact of interest rate variation on interest-sensitive assets versus interest-sensitive liabilities at different time horizons and accordingly suggests the net impact on the bank's profitability and asset–liability position. This follows a similar approach using a maturity ladder as discussed earlier for the measurement of liquidity risk. *Duration analysis* helps in measuring the sensitiveness of market price of an asset like a bond or a car loan to variation in interest rate. With aggregation, it helps in assessing the impact of interest rate changes on the asset portfolio of a bank. *Duration gap* derived from the estimation of duration of assets and liabilities measures the mismatch between the two, which in turn can be used to examine the impact of interest rate variation on a bank's equity.

6.4.3.1 Gap Analysis

Under *gap analysis*, let us begin with *simple gap analysis* which requires identification of interest rate–sensitive assets and liabilities in a bank's balance sheet and OBS items. Within liabilities of a bank, capital, reserves and surplus and current account deposits are non-sensitive to interest rate variation. All remaining liabilities are sensitive to interest rate changes on maturity or the repricing date. Among assets, cash, current account balances with the RBI and other banks, shares and units of mutual funds, fixed assets and inter-office adjustment are non-sensitive to interest rate changes. All other assets are sensitive to interest rate on maturity or on the repricing date. Accordingly, *gap* can be computed as follows:

$$\text{Gap} = \text{RSA} - \text{RSL} \tag{6.5}$$

where RSA: interest rate–sensitive assets; RSL: interest rate–sensitive liabilities

If the *gap* is positive, or RSA > RSL, then increase in the interest rate raises a bank's income by a higher amount as compared to rise in the cost of funds. This is under the assumption that the interest rate sensitivity of assets and liabilities is of similar magnitude. The bank encounters interest rate risk under rising interest rate, if the *gap* is negative. In that case, rise in interest cost is higher than rise in interest income and the NII shrinks. On the contrary, if the gap is positive, fall in interest rate causes interest rate risk. Drop in the interest income becomes higher than reduction in the interest cost of the bank.

A popular way of measuring interest rate risk in banks is by applying such gap analysis across different time horizons. In this method, interest rate–sensitive assets and liabilities need to be segregated into different time buckets similar to those used for measuring liquidity risk earlier. Bank regulators provide guidelines on classification of assets and liabilities into different time horizons and construction of a maturity ladder. This is explained with a hypothetical example for Bank X in Table 6.3.

Under each time bucket, we can assess the mismatch between interest rate–sensitive assets and liabilities (placed under the column 'gap' in Table 6.3). This is basically the difference between interest rate–sensitive assets and interest rate–sensitive liabilities and hence reflects the *incremental gap* for the respective time bucket. We have also reported *cumulative gap* in the last column of Table 6.3. The cumulative gap is calculated as the cumulative subtotal of incremental gaps up to a specific time horizon. For example, the incremental gaps for the first three time buckets, '1–28 days', '29 days–3 months' and '3–6 months', in Table 6.3 are –5, –26 and –56 billion, respectively. The cumulative gap up to six months is the subtotal of all three which is equal to –87 billion.

Application of gap analysis over different time buckets helps in measuring the differential impact of changes in interest rates on NII. For example, in Table 6.3, the gap is negative for shorter time horizons while it is positive for the time buckets of '1–5 years' and 'over 5 years'. Bank X can assess that any

Table 6.3 Maturity ladder for assessing interest rate risk under gap analysis

(INR billion)

Residual maturity/Repricing date	Assets	Liabilities	Gap	Cumulative gap
1–28 days	196	201	–5	–5
29 days–3 months	250	276	–26	–31
More than 3–6 months	276	332	–56	–87
More than 6 months–1 year	324	446	–122	–209
More than 1–5 years	528	345	183	–26
Over 5 years	450	248	202	176
Total	2,024	1,848	176	

Source: Hypothetical example by the author.

interest rate hike adversely affects its NII within a time horizon of up to one year. For longer time horizons, NII rises with interest rate hike. It is because, for shorter time horizons with negative gap, rise in interest rate raises interest expenses more than interest income of the bank. On the contrary, for time buckets of '1–5 years' and 'over 5 years' with positive gap, rise in interest rate raises interest income more than interest expenses of the bank.

Such application of gap analysis can measure interest rate risk from an earning perspective. In the following section, under *duration gap*, we shall discuss a method which uses some features of gap analysis to assess the economic value perspective of interest rate risk.

Gap analysis is widely used by banks under their ALM analysis to measure interest rate risk. Nevertheless, it suffers from several limitations which are as follows:

- It ignores yield curve risk.
- It does not take into account economic value impact of variation in interest rate, implications of pre-payment of loans or foreclosure of time deposits, and suffers from over-aggregation.

6.4.3.2 Duration Analysis

Duration is a very popular tool used to assess price volatility of a fixed-income security like a bond. The basic idea is if the residual maturity or duration of a bond is short, its market price does not vary much from its face value. For example, if a bond is about to mature within a week, the bank can always receive the face value of the bond holding it until maturity. Therefore, the bank may not be willing to accept any price which is significantly lower than the face value within a week before maturity. On the contrary, consider the case of a bond having residual maturity of 10 years. In the intermittent period before maturity, the market price of the bond can vary considerably depending on the fluctuation in market interest rates. This suggests that a shorter residual period of maturity for a bond implies lesser adverse deviation in the bond price and hence lower market risk.

Macaulay duration and *modified duration* are widely used to measure interest rate risk (also, market risk) in bonds and any other interest sensitive assets. Macaulay duration is given by the following formula:

$$\text{Macaulay duration} = \Sigma_i\ [C_i/(1+\text{YTM})^i]/V \qquad (6.6)$$

where i runs from 1 to N; N: number of years to maturity; C_i: cash flows including annual coupon payment in year i; YTM: yield to maturity on the bond; V: current market price of the bond

For example, let us calculate the Macaulay duration of an INR 100 (annual) coupon bond with a market value of INR 1,000 and residual maturity of three years. Assume the YTM on the bond is 7 per cent. Accordingly, Macaulay duration on the bond can be calculated as follows:

$$\begin{aligned}\text{Macaulay duration (D)} &= [(100/(1+0.07)^1]/1{,}000 + [100/(1+0.07)^2]/1{,}000\\ &+ [1{,}000/(1+0.07)^3]/1{,}000 = [(100/1.07)\\ &+ (100/1.1449) + (1{,}000/1.2250]/1{,}000\\ &= [93.46 + 87.34 + 897.96]/1{,}000\\ &= 1{,}078.76/1{,}000 = 1.08 \text{ years} \qquad (6.7)\end{aligned}$$

This implies that for this bond, the investor has to wait for 1.08 years on average to receive the present value of future cash flows. This is a single number characterising the bond's price sensitivity or risk to change in interest rate. Longer the Macaulay duration, higher is the price sensitivity and the market risk of the bond. This can be used to compare market risk across different bonds, and the bank or investor can choose bonds with a specific Macaulay duration as per their preference.

Modified duration is based on Macaulay duration and directly measures price sensitivity of a bond, and it is easy to interpret. The formula is as follows:

$$\text{Modified duration} = [D]/[1+(YTM/n)] \quad (6.8)$$

where n: number of coupon payments in a year (in this case, it is 1 – for annual coupon payments)

Using values from our above example for the bond under consideration,

$$\text{Modified duration} = (1.08)/(1+(0.07/1) = 1.08/1.07 = 1.01 \quad (6.9)$$

It can be interpreted that if the market interest rate increases by 1 percentage point, the price of the bond will fall by 1.01 per cent. Thus, modified duration measures interest rate risk on the price of a bond or the marked-to-market value of a bond. By calculating modified duration for all the bonds held for trading, we can derive the amount of interest rate risk in the entire portfolio.

For zero-coupon bonds, Macaulay duration is the same as their residual maturity.

To assess the impact of variation in interest rate on the entire balance sheet of a bank, first we can compute the duration of all assets and liabilities. Based on this, we can compute duration gap which reflects the mismatch between the duration of assets and liabilities of a bank. Accordingly, duration gap measures interest rate risk in the entire balance sheet.

$$\text{Duration Gap (DG)} = [DA - (L/A)(DL)] \quad (6.10)$$

where DA: Macaulay duration of assets in the bank's balance sheet; DL: Macaulay duration of liabilities in the bank's balance sheet; L: market value of liabilities; A: market value of assets

Say, for Bank X, the market value of assets is INR 1,200 billion and that of liabilities (deposits and borrowings) is INR 1,150 billion. The value of equity capital is INR 50 billion. If the Macaulay duration of assets and liabilities for Bank X is calculated as 3.6 and 3.1 years, respectively, then its duration gap can be calculated as follows:

$$\text{Duration Gap (DG)} = [3.6 - (1150/1200)(3.1)] = 3.6 - 2.97 = 0.63 \quad (6.11)$$

It is important to note that duration gap analysis can capture interest rate risk in terms of repricing risk where the sensitivity of both assets and liabilities to interest rate changes is similar. It, however, fails to take into account basis risk.

With a small mathematical manipulation, the estimated duration gap helps in assessing the interest rate sensitivity of a bank's equity as follows:

$$\text{Change in value of bank equity } (\Delta E) = -\text{ DG } [(\Delta r)/(1+r)]A \quad (6.12)$$

where Δ: difference operator; r: interest rate

Assuming rise in interest rate from 6 to 6.25 per cent, the reduction in equity of Bank X in the preceding example can be calculated as follows:

$$\begin{aligned} \Delta E &= -(0.63) \times [(0.0625 - 0.0600)/(1+0.0600)] \times (1200) \\ &= -(0.63) \times (0.0025/1.0600) \times (1200) \\ &= -1.783 \text{ billion} \end{aligned} \quad (6.13)$$

This implies that as the interest rate rises from 6 to 6.25 per cent, the equity of Bank X declines by nearly INR 1.8 billion, reflecting the adverse impact of interest rate risk.

6.4.3.3 Simulation Approaches

Modern-day banking is very complicated, involving a variety of assets and liabilities with sophisticated features. Moreover, the economic environment is highly dynamic. To measure interest rate risk in a more meaningful way in this context, there are advancements using simulation methods. Under these approaches, various assets and liabilities can be segregated and the impact of interest rate on each of them under different interest rate scenarios can be simulated using a comprehensive approach. A bank can distinguish how there is differential impact of increase in interest rate on various types of assets and liabilities.

Using simulations, a bank can examine how the upward swing in interest rate with monetary tightening impacts conditions over the long-term versus short-term horizon. If the impact on short-term liquidity conditions is more severe, it may be required to raise the interest rate on short-term deposits more aggressively (by a higher amount) as compared to that on deposits with long-term maturity. Thus, a simulation exercise can be undertaken to analyse the rise in interest cost on deposits, taking into account the differences in interest cost on short-term versus long-term deposits. Similarly, interest rate risk emanating from each item of the balance sheet and OBS items can be simulated realistically. Sophisticated statistical tools are used for this simulation exercise. This explains the use of *static simulation* exercises.

This can be supplemented by *dynamic simulation* where the future movement in interest rate itself can be simulated using suitable econometric exercises taking into account economic fluctuations, external sector developments and monetary policy response. Accordingly, under a diverse interest rate scenario, differential impact of each interest rate change on the earning prospects and economic value of a bank is simulated. This makes measurement of interest rate risk more involved and realistic. However, the usefulness of the simulation approach is heavily dependent on the nature and appropriateness of the assumptions used in the simulation exercise.

6.4.4 Methods to Measure Market Risk

There are several methods used to assess the quantum of market risk in banking as enumerated in the following sections.

6.4.4.1 Standard Deviation

A simple way of assessing market risk is using the measure of 'standard deviation'. It captures the variation or dispersion of observations in a distribution around their mean value. The market price of a bond varies based on the forces of demand for and supply of the bond in the market.

Let us assume the probability distribution of possible market prices of a bond is given by X_i with probability p_i. It implies that the market price of the bond is X_i in the ith case. Assume, there are a total of N such possible market prices and μ is the arithmetic mean of all N possible values of X_i. Then the standard deviation is given by the following formula:

$$\sigma = \sqrt{(1/N\ \Sigma[(X_i - \mu)^2])} \tag{6.14}$$

A higher value of σ suggests that the possible market values of the bond are widely spread around the expected or mean value. Such wider deviation of market values from the mean implies higher market risk on the bond. On the contrary, a lower value of σ implies lesser deviation of actual outcome from the expected and hence lesser market risk. Similar measures of standard deviation can be applied to other assets such as equities, forex, and so on, which are actively traded in the market.

6.4.4.2 Sensitivity Analysis

In this method, variation in asset value is measured due to change in its price. Let us discuss application of sensitivity analysis for assessment of market risk of a bond. Let Y denote market price (outcome) of the bond and market interest rate (argument variable) be denoted by X. The popular way of undertaking sensitivity analysis is estimating the elasticity of Y due to change in X which can be denoted by ε. This measures the proportionate change in Y due to proportionate change in X. It can be estimated from available historical data on X and Y using the formula:

$$\varepsilon = (\Delta Y/\Delta X) \times (X/Y) \tag{6.15}$$

where Δ: the difference operator

If we multiply ε by 100, it gives the percentage change in the price of the bond due to 1 percentage point change in the market interest rate. For example, if $\varepsilon = -0.02$ for a bond, it implies that 1 percentage point increase in the market interest rate leads to fall in the market price of the bond by INR 2 if the price of the bond was INR 100 before the change in interest rate.

Higher absolute value of ε implies greater fall in the bond price for 1 percentage point increase in the market interest rate and hence higher market risk for the bond. Similarly, the measure of elasticity can be applied to assess the market risk for other price-sensitive assets.

6.4.4.2.1 Present Value of a Basis Point (PV01)

A popular sensitive indicator used by banks to measure market risk is present value of a basis point, or PV01. It directly measures change in the market value of an asset like a bond due to one basis point (one-hundredth of a percentage point) change in the interest rate. For example, if the market price of a bond falls by INR 3.60 due to one basis point increase in the market interest rate, then PV01 of this bond is INR 3.60.

6.4.4.3 Duration Analysis

We have already described the use of *duration analysis* for assessing the impact of interest variation on asset or bond prices under measurement of interest rate risk. As discussed therein, *modified duration* derived from the estimation of *Macaulay duration* of a bond or a portfolio of securities can be used to quantify market risk (adverse variation in market price) due to change in the market interest rate.

6.4.4.4 Downside Potential and Value at Risk (VaR)

It may be noted that conceptually risk is an adverse deviation from the expected value. The measures previously discussed such as standard deviation, sensitivity analysis and duration analysis assess the volatility or variation—both on the upper and the lower sides—in an expected value. Thus, these measures capture both potential profit and loss and do not strictly conform to the concept of risk.

For example, *modified duration* measures market risk of the bond—that is, drop in the market price of the bond when market interest rate increases. It also reflects the profit opportunity when the market interest rate falls. If the numerical value of modified duration for a bond is estimated to be 3.36, it also suggests that the price of the bond goes up by 3.36 per cent when the market interest rate declines by 1 percentage point. So modified duration measures percentage of capital gain and profit potential too.

Overcoming this drawback, *downside potential* solely captures the adverse deviation of an outcome from the expected or planned outcome. It measures potential losses exclusively. It combines the volatility or sensitivity measures discussed earlier with information on statistical distribution of market prices at different probability and is widely rated as the most comprehensive measure of market risk.

Value at risk (VaR) is a popular method of measuring market risk conforming to the concept of downside potential. It measures maximum loss in a portfolio of tradeable assets with a certain probability over a specific period of time under normal trading conditions. For example, let us assume one-day VaR for a portfolio of securities is calculated to be INR 10 crore with 95 per cent probability. This implies that maximum daily loss in this security or portfolio is INR 10 crore in 95 out of 100 cases under normal trading conditions. However, this also suggests that there is a 5 per cent chance that the loss on the security or portfolio can be more than INR 10 crore. Thus, VaR measures maximum loss at a future date due to adverse movement in the price of a bond with a specified probability.

We can explain computation of VaR using a simple numerical example. For that we require three ingredients, namely (*a*) current market value of the portfolio (V), (*b*) standard deviation (SD) of daily historical return of the portfolio and (c) Z-score from the Z-table which measures the spread from mean value of the distribution in terms of standard deviation.

For example, assume that the current market value of a portfolio is INR 2,400 crore, the SD of daily price return estimated from historical data is 0.06 and the Z-score for one-tailed 99 per cent confidence interval is 2.33. Based on this data, we can compute VaR = 2,400 × 0.06 × 2.33 = INR 335.52 crore. This implies that the maximum overnight loss in this portfolio due to changing price of the asset is INR 335.52 crore at 99 per cent probability. It also implies that there is 1 per cent probability that the loss in the portfolio could be more than INR 335.52 crore.

Banks in practice use the historical simulation and Monte Carlo methods to compute VaR in their portfolio of securities. Box 6.1 briefly outlines both these procedures.

6.4.4.4.1 VaR and Backtesting

Backtesting is often conducted to assess the validity of VaR computed values. It compares the actual closing position of the portfolio, ex post, with the estimated VaR value. Accordingly, one can monitor the precision of the estimated market risk derived from VaR calculations.

It is important to note that VaR estimates do not capture the tail risk. As discussed, if overnight VaR for a portfolio is computed as INR 335.52 crore, it suggests that maximum loss on the portfolio is INR 335.52 crore with 99 per cent confidence. Thus, there is 1 per cent probability that the loss can be more than INR 335.52 crore. But the quantum of such potential loss, popularly referred to as tail risk, cannot be derived from VaR computation.

For assessing the market risk of a portfolio of securities, *stress testing* is conducted using the hypothetical movement of market parameters under extreme assumptions. From this exercise, expected shortfall can be calculated applying the extreme value theory. This can supplement the VaR method to reach an informed judgement about potential market risk.

6.4.5 Measurement of Operational Risks

Measurement of operational risk in banks was initially carried out in an ad hoc manner. This is because events or factors causing operational risk are infrequent and do not follow any standard probability distribution. We can discuss three methods mainly used to quantify operational risk in a bank.

Box 6.1 A brief outline of historical simulation and Monte Carlo methods of computing VaR

The *historical simulation* procedure is a simple method for computation of VaR based on historical data on returns. It is widely used for calculation of VaR globally. It requires multiplication of current exposure or market value of the portfolio with daily returns; and from the ordering of the product values, one can derive the VaR at a particular level of confidence. The basic logic behind this method is explained with a numerical example as follows.

Say, data on daily returns on the portfolio for the past 1,000 days is available with us. Assume the rate of return was 0.010 yesterday, 0.012 day before yesterday, and so on. Say, current market value of the portfolio is INR 2,400 crore. Then,computation of VaR can be undertaken as follows:

- Multiply the market value of INR 2,400 crore with each of the daily rates of return for the last 1,000 days. This gives us 1,000 product values such as INR 2,400 × 0.010 crore (using the rate of return for yesterday), INR 2,400 × 0.012 crore (using the rate of return for day before yesterday), and so on.
- Arrange these 1,000 product values (market value multiplied by daily returns) in ascending order.
- The 11th value from the top (11th lowest) in the ordering gives VaR at 1 per cent level of confidence. In this case, the top 10 values in the ordering are excluded as they come within 1 per cent of 1,000 values.

Thus, under this ordering, if the 11th lowest value is INR 112 crore, then VaR is INR 112 crore at 99 per cent confidence. Similarly, if the 51st lowest value is INR 33 crore, then VaR at 95 per cent confidence is INR 33 crore. It is because 10 is 1 per cent of 1,000, and 50 is 5 per cent of 1,000.

VaR is similarly computed using the *Monte Carlo method*. This method starts with calculating mean and standard deviation of the historical daily return data. Both the parameters are used to generate random rates of return using the Monte Carlo random number generation method. Then, as in the historical simulation method, each randomly generated daily rate of return is multiplied by the market value and ordered from the lowest to the highest value. From the ordered ranking, a value at a particular cutoff gives VaR at a specific confidence interval as in the historical simulation method.

These methods are prescribed by the Basel capital adequacy norms, details of which are provided in Chapter 7. The methods are as follows:

6.4.5.1 Basic Indicators Approach

This is the simplest of the three methods. Operational risk for a bank under this method is estimated as a proportion of the *gross income* of the bank which is used as an indicator for overall operational risk exposure. Gross income is computed as the sum of NII and net non-interest income. As per the basic indicator approach,

$$\text{Operational risk} = [\tfrac{1}{3} \textstyle\sum_{1}^{3} (\text{gross income}_i)] \times 0.15 \qquad (6.16)$$

Thus, the quantum of operational risk is calculated as equal to 15 per cent of average of last three years' gross income of a bank. If the gross income for any of the three previous years is negative or nil, then that year needs to be excluded. Moreover, any extraordinary income items and compensation received (namely, insurance) need to be adjusted from the gross income.

6.4.5.2 Standardised Approach

Under this approach, banking activities are divided into eight standard business lines or segments. Different weights or *beta* factors are assigned to these business segments for assessing operational risk. These weights reflect the banking industry's operational risk experience for the respective segments. This is an improvement over the uniform weightage of 15 per cent assigned for all business lines under the basic indicator approach. The weightage or beta factors for different banking segments under the *standardised approach* are as follows:

- 18 per cent: (*a*) corporate finance, (*b*) trading and sales, and (*c*) payment and settlement
- 15 per cent: (*d*) commercial banking, and (*e*) agency services
- 12 per cent: (*f*) retail banking, (*g*) asset management, and (*h*) retail brokerages

Gross income for each of these eight business segments is calculated separately. A weighted average of the segment-wise 'gross income' for last three years is calculated to quantify the operational risk of the bank. Segment-wise *beta* factors as given previously are used as weights. Thus, the formula for calculating operational risk under the standardised approach is as follows:

$$\text{Operational risk} = \tfrac{1}{3} \Sigma_1^3 (\beta_i \times \text{gross income}_i) \qquad (6.17)$$

where β_i is the *beta* factor for the ith segment; gross income_i indicates the amount of gross income for the ith segment

6.4.5.3 Advanced Measurement Approach

As the name suggests, the *advanced measurement approach* is an advanced and scientific method to measure operational risk in banks. This is an approach which takes into account all information, encompassing ingredients like internal and external loss data, scenario analysis and internal control or mitigating factors pertaining to operational risk. Similar to the credit rating model discussed in the context of measurement of credit risk, the advanced measurement approach uses (*a*) estimation of probability of occurrence of loss event (PE), (*b*) parameter for potential financial loss given that event (LGE) and (*c*) exposure indicator (EI) for assessing the impact of operational risks.

Here, EI is the size of operational risk exposure. Historical information on occurrences of risk events and estimated probability for the future are combined to get PE. Necessary adjustment is made for insurance mitigation, if any, to arrive at LGE. Accordingly, expected loss (EL) due to operational risk is calculated as follows:

$$\text{EL} = \text{PE} \times \text{LGE} \times \text{EI} \qquad (6.18)$$

To sum up, in the preceding sections, we have covered different methods of quantifying important varieties of banking risks. Such methods are constantly getting upgraded. Our endeavour here is to provide a foundation to understand different methods of measuring banking risks. Measurement of banking risks is a necessary prerequisite to get an insight about the magnitude of the problem and accordingly to employ risk management procedures as detailed in the following chapters.

Readers may refer to the official websites of the Bank for International Settlements (www.bis.org) and leading banking regulators like the RBI (www.rbi.org.in) to obtain further details about measurement of banking risks.

6.5 Conclusion

This chapter underscored, first, the typical features of bank lending in terms of information asymmetry–related problems of adverse selection and moral hazard and excessive procyclicality which cause credit risks in banking. Second, deposits which constitute the bulk of banking liabilities are highly liquid with a significant portion being withdrawable on demand. On the contrary, a sizeable portion of bank loans have a fixed repayment schedule. Due to this mismatch, any impairment in depositors' confidence snowballs into a bank run and works as a self-fulfilling prophecy exposing a bank's inability to meet deposit withdrawal demands when there is unusually high demand. This is popularly referred to as liquidity risk in banking. Third, if change in the market interest rate affects the interest income on the bank's assets differently as compared to the interest cost on its liabilities so that overall profitability of the bank is adversely affected, the bank suffers from interest rate risk. Interest rate risk also arises due to adverse interest rate movements leading to diminution of the equity value of banks. Fourth, banks are exposed to market risks due to adverse variation in price-sensitive assets in the bank's balance sheet. Fifth, they also encounter operational risks resulting in financial losses due to a variety of reasons such as omissions and commissions of bank employees, faulty documentation, deficiencies in the system, malfunctioning of the communications and IT infrastructure, and external events including natural calamities.

All these risks inherent in the banking business have the potential to cause bank failures and can seriously disrupt economic activities. There have been many instances of bank failures in history, and the resolution costs of such occurrences have been heavy. This underscores the rationale for bank regulation so that the probability of bank failures can be minimised and the contribution of the banking sector to the economy is optimised. Moreover, bank owners and the top management control the banking business with their own miniscule stake. Bank loans and investments, on the other hand, are largely funded by bank depositors. There is thus an imperative need to protect the depositors' interests as it is they who suffer the most when there is a bank failure. This is an additional consideration for regulation of the banking business.

Identification and quantification of different varieties of banking risks is a necessary prerequisite for deciphering the magnitude of overall risks and accordingly framing appropriate banking regulations and adopting risk management practices. In this perspective, the measurement of banking risks is important. The chapter described with relevant technical details a variety of methodologies used for the measurement of credit risk, liquidity risk, interest rate risk, market risk and operational risk in banking.

Revision Questions and Problems

1. What are the different varieties of banking risks?
2. How do you justify the role of banking regulatory provisions in view of the underlying risks in the banking business?
3. Why does the interest of bank depositors need to be protected as a matter of public policy concern?
4. How is liquidity risk unique to the banking business? Why can excessive liquidity risk in banking lead to a bank run?
5. Compare basis risk and yield curve risk.
6. Explain interest rate risk in the banking business both in terms of its impact on a bank's profitability and its net worth.
7. How do credit rating and analysis of rating migration help in measuring credit risk?
8. How do we calculate expected loss (EL) and unexpected loss (UEL) for assessing credit risk on a bank loan?
9. How can a bank measure interest rate risk by using a maturity ladder of interest rate–sensitive assets and liabilities?
10. How can the sensitivity and duration methods be used to measure market risk?
11. Write a short note about value at risk (VaR).
12. What is operational risk in banking? How can we measure operational risk using the standardised approach?

7

Banking Regulations and Supervision

A Broad Overview of Different Forms and Manifestations

Learning Objectives

- To undertake a broad overview of banking regulatory policies towards managing banking risks and reducing the scope of bank failures
- To outline the contours of banking regulatory policies in India in a historical perspective
- To provide details on the adoption in India of the Basel prudential norms on capital adequacy which emerged as the mainstay of banking regulatory policies linking risk embodied in the banking business to minimum capital adequacy requirements
- To provide an outline of the banking supervision procedures of the RBI

7.1 Introduction

In Chapter 6, we identified various types of risks involved in the banking business and their underlying causes. Based on this we underscored the rationale for banking regulation and supervision to contain banking risks. Healthy and vibrant banks facilitate economic progress as explained in the previous chapters. Insolvency of banks and liquidity problems, on the other hand, can severely disrupt real economic activities. Guided by these reasons, banking regulation and supervision are widely treated as the central pillars of public policy across countries towards promoting the safety and soundness of banks. Banking regulations fundamentally strive to follow the twin objectives of (*a*) maintaining the stability of the banking system and (*b*) protecting the interest of bank depositors and borrowers.

The emergence of different kinds of banking risks historically and measures to address them have an analogy with human ailments causing fever and their treatment in medical science. When people suffered from low-grade fever caused by the common flu or cold, paracetamol was invented to treat the same. Subsequently, a new variety of fever known as malaria caused by mosquito bites became a major health concern. Medical research invented chloroquine to treat malaria. Typhoid, traced to infection that spreads through contaminated water and food, emerged as the next form of fever, and fluoroquinolones were developed to treat it. Covid-19 is the newest variant of deadly fever which caused a severe pandemic in 2020. The medical fraternity subsequently devised the required vaccine and treatment for Covid-19 too. Similarly, regulators and analysts try to identify the dimensions and root causes of different types of banking risks. Accordingly, they come up with appropriate regulatory policies to mitigate recurrence of banking crises. With the passage of time, new forms of banking risks emerge or existing forms are found to be aggravated by a different set of factors. Again, banking regulators and analysts seek new solutions to safeguard the banking business. The process is a continuous one.

It is also important to note that banking regulations are not without costs. Banking regulations, by curtailing and controlling the commercial autonomy of banks, to a certain extent impede the achievement of fuller business efficiency. They may compel banks to operate at suboptimal levels. As noted by Goodhart (1998, p. 215), 'regulation is only desirable up to the point where the marginal benefits exceed the marginal costs'. There is a larger consensus that benefits of banking regulations overwhelm the costs. This is appropriately reflected in the worldwide adoption of a variety of banking regulatory policies.

Banking regulatory policies prescribe the norms and procedures for undertaking the banking business, outline methodologies for measurement of banking risks and set prudential parameters for risk mitigation in banks. The banking supervision function undertakes monitoring of the banking business and ensures the adherence of banks to regulatory prescriptions. There is quite a bit of complementarity between these two functions. The 2016 edition of *Federal Reserve System Purposes and Functions*, published by the Federal Reserve System of the US, noted:

> Regulation entails establishing the rules within which financial institutions must operate—in other words, issuing specific regulations and guidelines governing the formation, operations, activities, and acquisitions of financial institutions. Once the rules and regulations are established, supervision—which involves monitoring, inspecting, and examining financial institutions—seeks to ensure that an institution complies with those rules and regulations, and that it operates in a safe and sound manner.

The responsibility for banking regulation and supervision is entrusted to the central bank in most countries. In India, the RBI is the regulator for commercial banks. It is also the regulator for urban cooperative banks while the NABARD is delegated with a similar responsibility for rural cooperative banks and RRBs.

The remaining part of this chapter is organised as follows. A brief account of the evolution of public policy related to banking regulation is presented in section 7.2. It provides a summary of various forms and dimensions of banking regulatory policies. With adoption of the Basel prudential norms, regulatory prescriptions on capital adequacy have become popular as the mainstay of banking regulatory policy since the 1990s. Important features of the first version of the Basel prudential norms adopted in the early 1990s are summarised in section 7.3. With comprehensive strengthening, the second (revised) version of the Basel capital adequacy norms, popularly referred to as Basel II, was adopted in the 2000s. This expanded the scope of banking risk assessment by prescribing several alternative and realistic methods of risk measurement and included operational risk in overall banking risk assessment. It also added norms on a supervisory review process and disclosure norms on risk assessment and capital provision. Details of Basel II are covered in section 7.4. The GFC of 2007–08 exposed the vulnerabilities of the microprudential approach of the Basel II norms. Based on the lessons drawn and introducing several corrective measures, capital adequacy norms were upgraded both on qualitative and quantitative aspects under the Basel III avatar. Norms on liquidity requirements and minimum leverage ratio were also added. Core revisions under Basel III are summarised in section 7.5. Salient features of the banking supervision procedures in India are presented in section 7.6. Finally, the broad conclusions of this chapter are presented in section 7.7.

7.2 Public Policy to Contain Banking Risks: Banking Regulation and Supervision

As detailed in Chapter 6, the banking business inherently entails a variety of risks. Such underlying risks have led to bank runs and bank failures with devastating impact. Many banks collapsed during the early nineteenth century in Great Britain leading to the formation of joint stock companies in 1826 to facilitate wider distribution of risk amongst a large number of proprietors. The collapse of Overend, Gurney & Company in 1866 and the City of Glasgow Bank in 1878 and the crisis in a leading merchant banking house, Baring Brothers, in 1890 were significantly detrimental to the British financial system. The Bank of England had to intervene to effect a 'rescue' in the last episode by arranging a guarantee fund. Another spell of bank failures since 1973 led to the enactment of the Banking Act, 1976, which strengthened the formal role of the Bank of England in banking regulation and supervision in the UK. A large number of banking crises in the US between 1836 and 1914 were considered to be the main reason leading to the establishment of the Federal Reserve System.

The legal framework pertaining to banking companies in India prior to independence was largely in alignment with British law. The Companies Act, 1913, in particular was believed to be a comprehensive law and was applicable to banking companies in India. In the backdrop of several episodes of banking crisis, the Indian Central Banking Enquiry Committee (1929–31) recommended the enactment of a special bank Act. The Act would encompass guidelines on organisation, management, audit and liquidation of banks. The establishment of the RBI in 1935 was helpful in providing an LOLR facility for banks in trouble. Notwithstanding the prevailing public policy concerns and initiatives, as many as 588 banks failed in India during 1939–49 (RBI, 2005a). The RBI submitted a report in 1939 highlighting its concerns on the financial position and functioning of banks in India (particularly referring to non-scheduled banks) and recommending a strong bank Act. The efforts in this regard were again revived in 1943, and finally the Banking Regulation (BR) Act, 1949, saw the light of the day.

The BR Act, 1949, is the mainstay, covering the whole gamut of issues related to the regulation and supervision of banks in India. It provides guidelines on the very inception of banks, conduct of their regular operations and even amalgamations and takeovers. The RBI assumes its regulatory and supervisory role derived from the provisions of the BR Act, 1949. With changing requirements and responding to evolving issues, the BR Act, 1949, has witnessed more than 33 amendments until 2024. Various dimensions of banking risks in recent days have become very complicated with adoption of a high degree of financial engineering and sophistication in banking activities as also greater global integration. Accordingly, the regulatory and supervisory apparatus for the banking sector is continuously being upgraded.

The responsibilities pertaining to the regulation and supervision of banks are often entrusted to central banks. This is because central banks across countries are delegated with the monopoly power of issuing currency notes; they are the banker to banks and provide a platform for inter-bank settlements and clearing facilities. Moreover, monetary policy effectiveness of the central bank is heavily dependent on the response of other banks. The latter act as the major conduit for monetary policy transmission. There is a web of interlinkages and interdependence between the functions of the central bank and those of other banks in the financial system. Therefore, it is widely accepted that the central bank is best placed to effectively discharge the responsibilities relating to banking regulation and supervision. As indicated earlier, in India, our central bank—that is, the RBI—is the regulator and supervisor of commercial banks.

In general, banking regulations have two broad dimensions. Prior to adoption of the Basel prudential norms, banking regulations were largely characterised by administrative control, crisis management through emergency liquidity support and safeguarding the confidence of depositors by provision of deposit insurance. With adoption of the Basel capital adequacy norms since the early 1990s, banks have been given more freedom to undertake risks linked to their capital position. The monitoring of asset quality and provisioning requirements have a similar characteristic of incentivising banks not to take excessive risks.

In this backdrop, the broad elements and manifestations of banking regulation are summarised as follows.

7.2.1 Administrative Control

We have already discussed the imperative need for regulation of banks. Given the inherent risks involved in the banking business and the overarching requirements of protecting the interest of depositors, it is vital to screen the promoters and top management of banks using appropriate criteria.

In this perspective, the establishment of banks and conduct of their business have been subjected to stringent regulatory requirements. First, commencement of the banking business itself involves prior approval of the regulatory authority. In India, section 22 of the BR Act, 1949, stipulates detailed requirements for issuance of banking licences. Under this provision, the RBI is authorised to issue licenses to companies proposing to commence the banking business subject to their satisfying prescribed conditions. Such conditions, inter alia, include the following:

- The company should have the ability to meet deposit withdrawal demands of present and future depositors.
- Conduct of business by the banking company should not be detrimental to the interest of depositors.
- The general character of the bank's management should not be prejudicial to the public interest in India or to the interest of depositors.
- The company should have adequate capital and earning prospects.
- Granting of banking licence to the company should not be detrimental to the operation and consolidation of the banking system.

Entities satisfying the required eligibility criteria and committing to follow stipulated regulatory requirements are permitted to undertake the banking business. The RBI has complete autonomy to set necessary eligibility conditions. It issues banking licences after satisfying itself as to the eligibility of the applicant company. Issuance of a banking licence serves as the first stage of screening to prevent undesirable entities from entering into the banking business.

Related stipulations pertaining to administrative control of the banking business include

- requirements on minimum paid-up capital and reserves;
- eligibility, powers and responsibility of the chairman and members of the board of directors; and
- stipulations on control over the management and supersession of the board of directors under certain extreme circumstances considered as detrimental to a bank and its depositors.

Second, there are a set of regulations related to the conduct of the banking business. These include

- nature and forms of business activity which can be undertaken and those which are prohibited;
- procedures to be followed for lending, deposit mobilisation and operation of accounts; and
- guidelines for determination of interest rates on loans and deposits, and so on.

With liberal policies adopted on lending and pricing of loans and deposits, some such restrictions have been diluted by the RBI in the post-reform period. Banks in India have assumed considerable operational autonomy in this regard since the 1990s.

The third set of requirements are related to accounting provisions, audit and submission of regular reports. To facilitate proper monitoring of banks, there is need for standardisation as regards accounting and reporting of banking activities. The RBI prescribes the accounting principles and format for preparation of the balance sheet, income and expenditure statement and report on other key financial indicators. There are provisions for the scrutiny and verification of the information given in such statements through both internal and external professional auditors. Banks are also required to submit reports on their business to the RBI at regular intervals. The RBI consistently monitors the business activities of banks and their financial position through on-site inspection and off-site surveillance.

Finally, notwithstanding banking regulations and supervision, banking crises cannot be eliminated completely. As and when banking crises occur under certain extreme circumstances, the problem banks need to be shut down and taken over. Banking regulators like the RBI follow certain standard operating procedures (SOPs) in such cases. These include announcement of a temporary moratorium on deposit withdrawal from the troubled bank, superseding its management and, in many instances, arranging for a merger or acquisition by another sound and big banking entity.

7.2.2 Lender of Last Resort (LOLR) Facility

Various regulations and remedial measures related to banking across countries evolved historically in response to banking crises and the growing sophistication of the banking business. As discussed earlier, inherent problems of information asymmetry, adverse selection and moral hazard make loan delinquencies unavoidable. Notwithstanding the best efforts by the bank management and regulators to mitigate risks, banking crises do occur. The alchemy of converting liquid liabilities into illiquid assets in banking results in bank runs and crises when a bank faces large-scale loan delinquencies or any other financial trouble.

A series of banking crises and related severe adverse consequences in several countries witnessed the emergence of central banks as institutional mechanisms providing LOLR facility. Following the Bagehot rule, the Bank of England was the first to provide an LOLR facility since the 1860s. The rule is credited to the eminent British writer on economics Walter Bagehot. He recommended that the Bank of England lend freely against sound collateral to problem banks so that collapse of such banks can be arrested. It may be noted that with the inception of the LOLR facility, Britain did not suffer any serious banking crisis since 1866 until the return of banking problems in 2007 during the GFC. In the US, the financial crisis of 1907 led to the creation of the Federal Reserve Banks in 1913, with one key objective being provision of an LOLR facility.

The LOLR facility provides a cushion to banks in distress in the form of liquidity support from the central bank. The central bank is the monopoly supplier of currency notes in a country and enjoys immense capacity to supply liquidity. Any overwhelming liquidity problem in a bank can be addressed by availing funds from the central bank under LOLR. It enables banks to meet deposit withdrawal demands when facing a severe liquidity crunch and, consequently, to restore confidence of depositors in the bank. This was conceived to arrest *bank runs*, particularly in banks which are solvent but are facing a temporary liquidity problem.

The LOLR facility is provided against eligible collateral at a penalty rate—an interest rate higher than the ordinary discount rate charged by the central bank on its general refinance facility.

In India, section 18 of the RBI Act, 1934, empowers the RBI to provide the LOLR facility to banks.

7.2.3 Safety Net under Deposit Insurance

The sustenance of and success in the banking business heavily hinge on the confidence of depositors. The volume of deposits mobilised by a bank determines its volume of lending and the investment it can undertake. The amount of profit which a bank can earn, in turn, depends on the volume of prudent lending and investment. As long as depositors continue to have faith in the ability of banks to pay back their deposits on demand, deposit mobilisation continues and the banking business prospers.

The LOLR facility, as discussed in the previous section, can be effective in avoiding a banking crisis when a bank is solvent and faces a temporary liquidity problem. But when the problem is more enduring, as witnessed around the Great Depression in the US, the LOLR facility has not been found to be adequate to contain the banking crisis. The next innovation was *deposit insurance*. This was designed in the backdrop of large-scale bank failures in the US in the 1920s and 1930s. Around 600 banks failed in the US on average in each year during 1921–29. The number of bank failures had substantially risen to about 9,000 during 1930–33. Out of these, around 4,000 banks failed in 1933 alone. In response, the Federal Deposit Insurance Corporation (FDIC) was created in 1933 to insure deposits of member banks. As of August 2024, for each depositor of an insured bank, the standard insurance amount is USD 2,50,000. It is reported that since 1934, no customer of member banks has lost money deposited in insured funds due to any bank failure.

In India, while the issue of insuring bank deposits was envisaged in 1948 in the backdrop of banking crises in Bengal, it was given serious thought only after the collapse of Palai Central Bank and Laxmi Bank in 1960. Subsequently, the Deposit Insurance Act was enacted in 1961. With several transformations, the Deposit Insurance and Credit Guarantee Corporation (DICGC) was established in 1978 and the functions of deposit insurance and credit guarantee were integrated. The DICGC is a fully owned subsidiary of the RBI. As of August 2024, the DICGC insures up to INR 5 lakh towards both principal and interest for each depositor in member banks in India. As of 31 March 2023, nearly 98.1 per cent of the deposit accounts of 2,206 registered banks were insured by the DICGC. These included 139 commercial banks and 1,887 cooperative banks. The total amount of insured deposits stood at INR 83.9 trillion which constituted nearly 46.3 per cent of the total assessable deposits of banks (RBI, 2023a).

Deposit insurance assures the safety of the savings of bank depositors (up to a certain amount) and helps in maintaining their confidence in the bank. Thus, deposit insurance implicitly reduces the scope for bank runs.

7.2.4 Statutory Reserves

To address the problem of liquidity risk, banks in many countries have been subjected to minimum statutory reserve requirements. These requirements are generally stipulated in the form of minimum cash reserves and minimum liquid assets in proportion to the liabilities of a bank.

In India, under the CRR requirement, each scheduled bank[1] is stipulated to maintain minimum cash reserves in proportion to its NDTL. Such cash reserves can be maintained by a bank either as cash balances with itself or as deposits in its current account with the RBI. NDTL for a bank is calculated by removing its paid-up capital, liabilities to the RBI, NABARD, EXIM Bank and NHB, and net liabilities in the inter-bank call money and notice money market. Necessary details on CRR are provided in section 18 of the BR Act, 1949, and section 42 of the RBI Act, 1934.

The CRR to be maintained by banks as of August 2024 is 4.5 per cent. Let us understand with an example the calculation of CRR balances to be maintained by banks. A reference is made to reporting Fridays[2] in a calendar for maintenance of CRR. For example, 27 January 2023 was a reporting Friday as per the RBI calendar. Assume that the NDTL of Bank X as on 27 January was INR 1,000 crore. As per the regulation, based on the bank's NDTL as on the last Friday of the second preceding fortnight (a reporting Friday), the bank needed to maintain its minimum CRR balances for the ensuing fortnight. This implies that the bank needed to maintain INR 45 crore (4.5 per cent of INR 1,000 crore) as its minimum CRR requirement for the fortnight 24 February–10 March 2023 on average. Here, 27 January 2023 was the last Friday of the second preceding fortnight for the current fortnight 24 February–10 March 2023. CRR stipulations ensure maintenance of a minimum part of each bank's liabilities in the form of the most liquid assets. This is helpful for avoiding liquidity risks under normal circumstances.

Further, banks in India are also required to maintain a minimum portion of their NDTL in the form of liquid assets such as government bonds and other approved securities under the SLR. Previously, banks were

[1] A scheduled bank is a bank which is listed in schedule 2 of the RBI Act, 1934.

[2] Every alternative Friday subsequent to 29 March 1985 is stipulated by the RBI as the reporting Friday.

subject to a statutory minimum[3] of 25 per cent SLR. The actual minimum SLR stipulation was as high as 38.5 per cent during the late 1980s. Presently, there is no statutory minimum SLR. As of August 2024, the prevailing minimum SLR as stipulated by the RBI stands at 18 per cent. This implies that a bank having an NDTL of INR 1,000 crore as on the last Friday of the second preceding fortnight needs to maintain SLR securities of INR 180 crore for the ensuing fortnight on average. Compelling banks to hold a certain minimum portion of their liabilities in the form of government securities and other specified liquid assets promotes both solvency and liquidity. Solvency conditions improve as government securities are devoid of credit or default risks. The liquidity comfort is due to prevalence of a very active secondary market for government securities.

7.2.5 Rationale for Capital Adequacy Requirements

As discussed earlier, bank lending is not entirely safe. Despite best possible credit appraisals, defaults on loans occur because of certain factors which are beyond the control of borrowers. Such factors may include emergence of economic recession, changes in consumer preferences away from the goods produced by the borrower, disruptions in income generation in households, changes in legal provisions, global factors, and so on. These adversely affect the income flow of the borrower constraining their ability to repay the loan as per the agreement. Sometimes there could be wilful default if the judiciary and law enforcement mechanism are not reasonably effective. There could also be other varieties of banking risks as discussed in Chapter 6.

There is no certainty that the entire amount of loans disbursed by a bank would be repaid and there could be partial default. Both depositors and policy authorities are aware of this. Nevertheless, depositors continue to have confidence in a bank as long as its capital, particularly equity capital,[4] is more than the amount of loan loss. After compensating for loan losses, there should be enough surplus to meet the withdrawal demand of depositors. This can be explained with an example.

Say, the balance sheet of Bank X on a given day has INR 200 crore as equity capital and INR 800 crore as deposits. On the assets side, on the same day,

---

[3] The statutory minimum stipulated the minimum SLR to be prescribed by the RBI. The RBI was allowed to fix the SLR below that level (25 per cent of NDTL).

[4] Equity capital refers to the stake of owners or shareholders in the bank.

assume that Bank X holds INR 700 crore as loans, INR 250 crore as investments and INR 50 crore as cash. Assume the economy suffers from a recession after six months due to unforeseen reasons. This may cause several borrowers of the bank to default on their loans. With consequent loss of assets, assume that the amount of standard loans in the bank's balance sheet six months from now is reduced to INR 550 crore. With availability of equity capital of INR 200 crore, the bank can absorb the loan loss of INR 150 crore (from INR 700 crore to INR 550 crore) and will be left with enough assets in excess of bank deposits. After the loan losses, the total assets of Bank X will stand at INR 850 crore as compared to its deposits of INR 800 crore. This may help depositors to continue to have confidence in the bank despite loan delinquencies.

Had the equity amount been INR 100 crore, the bank would have failed to absorb the loan loss of INR 150 crore fully in our example. The total assets of the bank would have fallen short of its deposits. The consequent panic of depositors would have caused a *bank run*, ultimately perhaps leading to the collapse of Bank X.

Therefore, a higher capital level boosts the confidence of depositors in a bank as it reduces the probability of the bank defaulting on its deposits. Maintaining confidence of depositors is conducive to sustaining and expanding the banking business. Higher equity capital diminishes the probability of a bank becoming insolvent and reduces the amount of liquidity risk and the possibility of a bank run.

According to Admati and Hellwig (2013), in the nineteenth century, banks used to maintain equity to the extent of 40 or 50 per cent of their total assets. During this period, the owners of banks were fully liable for their debts. Subsequently, around 1900, banks in many countries maintained an equity–total assets ratio of close to 20–30 per cent. Maintenance of such high levels of equity was not mandated by any regulation; rather, it emerged voluntarily in the process of interaction amongst different stakeholders like the owners, managers and depositors of banks.

After embracing the Basel prudential norms since the early 1990s, details of which are discussed in the following sections, banks are required to maintain minimum capital adequacy ratios where the minimum amount of capital has a proportional relation to the amount of risk embodied in the banking business. Notwithstanding this requirement, the ratio of equity capital to total assets had declined to less than 5 per cent for many banks in the US and Europe before the onset of the GFC in 2007 (King, 2016). This reveals the vulnerability of banks at the time.

Thus, we can see that a higher level of equity capital mitigates the problem of bank insolvency as well as helps reduce the liquidity problem, augmenting public confidence in banks.

It is important to note that in extreme cases of bad lending decisions or economic recessions, if the loan delinquencies are massive, even higher equity capital would not be able to save the bank from a crisis. In our previous example, Bank X would become insolvent even with higher equity capital of INR 200 crore if loan delinquencies reduce the amount of (standard) loans in its balance sheet to INR 400 crore instead of INR 550 crore. Equity capital of INR 200 crore obviously would be insufficient to cover loan losses of INR 300 crore fully. Thus, higher equity capital can be helpful to avoid a banking crisis only to an extent. Ultimately, prudent banking practices in terms of correct credit appraisal and continuous monitoring of borrowers, obtaining adequate security collateral, prompt corrective action on early signs of weakness, appropriate pricing of loans and provisioning are fundamental for keeping the banking system safe and resilient. This underscores the importance of competency, financial prudence and integrity of the bank management and staff.

Capital adequacy norms aligned the minimum capital required to be maintained by banks with the quantum of risks embodied in their business. This became popular since the 1990s with adoption of the Basel prudential norms across advanced and emerging economies. Details of the same are provided in the following sections of this chapter.

7.2.6 Public Ownership Strengthening Depositors' Confidence

There is another dimension in the Indian context which has helped avert major bank run–like situations in the last half century or so. This pertains to the government ownership of major banks. SBI, India's biggest bank, became a PSB in 1955, as discussed in Chapter 2. In 1969, 14 major banks with outstanding deposits of more than INR 50 crore each were nationalised, followed by another 6 in 1980. They accounted for bulk of the banking business in India. Public confidence in PSBs is quite robust and enduring. It is based on the immense capacity of the government to infuse additional capital and bail out a troubled PSB if there is need. This can be considered a major reason for PSBs in India not suffering from any tendency for a bank run. This is despite the unfolding of serious weaknesses in their financial position in the early 1990s. Incidence of high loan delinquencies in several PSBs during the mid-2010s was a matter of concern. Nevertheless, it did not cause serious impairment to the confidence of depositors in these banks.

The previous sections summarised various forms and dimensions of banking regulatory policies in general and in the Indian context in particular, as they evolved historically. In the following sections, we will concentrate on capital adequacy and other prudential norms which are incentive-based regulatory prescriptions for containment of banking risks. These constitute a major plank of banking regulatory policies around the world today.

7.3 Capital Adequacy and Other Prudential Norms

In the current banking regulatory framework, capital adequacy requirements play a predominant role. Capital adequacy norms under the Basel Accords have evolved with several rounds of revision and upgradation. Along with this, norms on accounting related to asset classification, income recognition and provisioning requirements have become very popular. These prudential norms have evolved as standardised and global best practice banking regulations. We provide a brief account of the same in the sections that follow.

7.3.1 Run-Up to the 1988 Basel Accord

It may be noted that with large-scale bank failures during the Great Depression, banking regulations in advanced economies were strengthened. These regulations usually took the form of controls on borrowing and lending activities, interest rate ceilings, stipulations on composition of asset portfolios and participation in the securities markets, capital structure, firewall between financial and commercial institutions, and so on. Needless to mention, the shape and stringency of such regulations varied across countries. As a consequence of these safety nets and regulations, no major banking crisis occurred in advanced countries from the late 1930s to the mid-1970s.

The situation changed from the late 1970s due to a turnaround in the public policy approach pertaining to the financial sector, partly as a response to the event of *stagflation*. During the 1970s, the US and several other leading economies witnessed simultaneous occurrence of economic slowdown and high inflation. This is popularly referred to as *stagflation*. To tame inflationary pressure, the US undertook monetary tightening under the Federal Reserve chairman Paul Volker. This in turn undermined interest rate ceilings. Several banking regulations were relaxed in the 1980s for promoting a more efficient financial system. Under high competitive pressure, financial innovations in banking led to the sidestepping of regulatory ceilings and restrictions. As observed by many commentators such as King (2016), these events led to the reappearance of large-scale financial disturbances in the US and Europe. Some such notable events included failure of Franklin National Bank of the US and Herstatt Bank of Germany in 1974, Continental Illinois National Bank and Trust Company in 1984, over 1,000 savings and loan associations in the US between 1986 and 1995, and so on. The collapse of Continental Illinois is considered the largest bank failure in the history of the US until the GFC.

Academic research and banking regulatory practices since the early 1980s focused on analysing and improving key aspects of banking regulations pertaining to administrative control, deposit insurance, the LOLR facility, regulatory reserves, and so on. Several deficiencies of the existing LOLR facility and deposit insurance schemes were identified. It was pointed out that such facilities actually accentuated banking risks due to moral hazard problems. Bailouts through deposit insurance made depositors risk-insensitive while choosing amongst banks. The complacency of depositors and LOLR cushion emboldened banks to undertake high-risk lending and investments in search of high returns. Excessive risk-taking made banks prone to loan delinquencies and consequent insolvency risks. In this backdrop, greater banking supervision and monitoring, setting minimum equity capital requirements and the right to wind up troubled banks emerged as credible policy alternatives to moderate moral hazard problems. It was observed that in the US, banks with a strong capital position retained high depositor confidence while safety-net provisions in the form of deposit insurance weakened the banking system (Dowd, 1993).

The late 1980s and early 1990s witnessed greater consensus and convergence across banking regulators of advanced economies on introduction of a standardised regulatory and supervisory framework. As noted by Alworth and Bhattacharya (1998), this new order emerged mainly due to three key developments. First, as indicated in the previous paragraphs, there were far more incidences of banking failures as compared to the preceding decades. Many banks in the US, Norway, Sweden, Japan, the UK, France and Spain witnessed sharp deterioration in asset quality and widespread financial distress during the late 1980s and early 1990s. The resolution cost of such banking problems was estimated to be around 3 to 4 per cent of GDP. So there was an imperative need to make the banking system stronger and more resilient with adoption of a more reliable and credible regulatory framework.

Second, banking activities had witnessed greater financial engineering with a new wave of financial innovation since the 1980s. Banks began to deal with a host of financial derivative products and entered new areas of business, including in fixed securities. This exposed them to new varieties of risks. Accordingly, there was a need to review existing banking regulations and risk management practices.

Third, the world was witnessing greater globalisation both in terms of foreign trade and financial flows. The run-up to the establishment of the World Trade Organization (WTO) in 1995 was filled with fever and excitement for an integrated world. Multilateral agencies like the IMF were pressing for greater global integration of financial markets. The new interconnected environment led to the emergence of global banks having operations across countries. As a corollary, the domestic banking system in a country could not be insulated from any adverse development in a global bank operating at home. Protecting the domestic banking system from any financial weakness in a foreign bank required assurance from concerned foreign bank regulators on the soundness and resilience of foreign banks operating in a host country. This made indispensable the need for uniformity and standardisation in banking regulations across nations.

In this backdrop, under the aegis of the Bank for International Settlements (BIS), Basel, the Basel Capital Accord of 1988 emerged as the new regulatory framework prescribing risk-linked capital adequacy norms. This Accord was set out by the Basel Committee on Banking Supervision (BCBS), consisting of central bank governors of the Group of Ten (G10) countries. The countries included Belgium, Canada, France, Germany, Italy, Japan, the Netherlands, Sweden, Switzerland, the UK and the US. It is believed that the insolvency and consequent collapse of Herstatt Bank in June 1974 seriously disrupted international payments and settlements in the US and other leading economies. Due to its sudden closure, it failed to settle its foreign currency transactions with banks in the US and other countries in different time zones. To avoid such adverse spillover effects, it was felt that not only domestic banks but even foreign banks operating in host countries should be adequately regulated to ensure safety and soundness. This led to the constitution of the BCBS to promote international coordination on banking regulation. With the passage of time, the BCBS has emerged as the global platform to deliberate and frame banking-related regulatory prescriptions.

7.3.2 Basel Accord of 1988

The Basel Accord of 1988, now popularly referred to as Basel I, is a set of guidelines prescribing minimum capital adequacy requirements for the banks of G10 countries. Under this Accord, a bank needs to maintain a minimum level of capital depending upon the quantum of risk-weighted assets it holds. The larger the proportion of risky assets, commensurately higher is the requirement of capital. As equity capital is contributed by the owners and shareholders of a bank, a higher equity capital requirement raises their own risk exposure. This acts as a deterrent to excessive risk-taking by banks. Moreover, as indicated in the previous section, higher capital enhances the loss absorption capacity of a bank and provides greater protection to its depositors. This in turn augments the confidence of depositors in the bank and curbs bank run–like situations.

The Basel Accord, 1988, defined the composition of capital for the purpose of capital adequacy and assigned risk weights for different categories of loans. For assignment of risk weights, credit risk alone was taken into account. All assets were put under four categories of risk weights as follows:

- *No risk ('0' risk weight)*: Cash and its equivalent, government securities (in G10 countries: securities issued by governments of Organisation for Economic Cooperation and Development (OECD) members; in India: securities issued by the Government of India)
- *Low risk (20 per cent risk weight)*: Short-term claims maturing in a year or less, bonds issued by agencies of OECD governments
- *Moderate risk (50 per cent risk weight)*: Mortgages
- *Standard risk (100 per cent risk weight)*: Commercial loans, exposure to non-OECD banks and governments

Necessary guidelines were also provided on the definition and composition of capital to be taken into account for capital adequacy requirements, summarised as follows:

- *Tier 1*: Composed of ordinary paid-up share capital or common shareholders' equity stock, disclosed reserves and any surplus and unallocated reserves, less specified deductions. The RBI prescribed that tier-1 capital be at least half of the minimum (overall) capital adequacy requirements (minimum 4 per cent out of the 8 per cent CRAR).

- *Tier 2*: Includes undisclosed reserves, subordinated debt of more than five years' maturity, general provisions or loan loss reserves, asset revaluation reserves, investment fluctuation reserves and limited life preference shares. It was required that long-term subordinated debt should not exceed half the tier-2 capital.
- *Tier 3*: Mainly consists of short-term subordinated debt with the sole purpose of providing the flexibility to meet a part of the capital requirements for market risk. This was introduced after incorporating capital charge for market risk in 1996.

7.3.2.1 Risk Mitigation under Basel Capital Adequacy Norms

The 1988 Basel Accord linked maintenance of minimum capital to the quantum of risks embodied in a bank's assets, devising a risk-linked capital requirement norm. It was not a legal mandate but more a global best practice norm. The Accord became effective for banks operating in G10 counties other than Japan in 1992. Banks in Japan were given an additional year for its implementation. The related calculations for capital adequacy are explained with a numerical example in Box 7.1.

Let us discuss how capital adequacy requirements control risk-taking by banks. The Basel norms stipulate that the minimum amount of capital to be maintained by a bank is 8 per cent of its total risk-weighted assets. So if Bank Y has total risk-weighted assets of INR 1,000 crore, it is supposed to maintain capital at a minimum level of INR 80 crore. If the actual amount of capital falls short of INR 80 crore, it is a violation of the regulatory norm and Bank Y will invite the relevant penalty.[5] In other words, as long as Bank Y has a capital level of INR 80 crore, it can afford risk-weighted assets worth INR 1,000 crore.

Now, consider a hypothetical scenario where Bank Y receives fresh deposits worth INR 10 crore. As long as Bank Y's capital remains fixed at INR 80 crore, it will be constrained in its options to deploy the additional deposits profitably. It cannot use the additional deposits of INR 10 crore for lending to private corporates or other banks. If Bank Y extends additional loans of INR 10 crore to private corporates, its risk-weighted assets will rise

---

[5] The penalty can take the form of a fine or restrictions on certain business activities of the bank under prompt corrective action. It has not gone to the extent of suspension of licence as of now in India.

Box 7.1 Calculation of minimum capital requirements as per the 1988 Basel Accord: a numerical example

Assume the total assets in the balance sheet of Bank X are INR 1,00,000 crore. The composition of these assets is (*a*) INR 5,000 crore in cash, (*b*) INR 60,000 crore in term loans to private corporates, (*c*) INR 25,000 crore investment in government securities and (*d*) the remaining INR 10,000 crore in loans to other banks in the overnight and term-money markets.

Applying risk weights as per the 1988 Basel Accord, the total risk-weighted assets of the bank can be calculated as follows:

Table 7.1 A numerical example for calculation of minimum capital requirement under the 1988 Basel Accord

Asset category	Amount (INR crore)	Risk weights	Risk-weighted assets (INR crore)
Cash	5,000	0.0	Nil
Loans to private corporates	60,000	1.0	60,000
Loans to government	25,000	0.0	Nil
Loans to other banks (short-term)	10,000	0.2	2,000
Total	1,00,000		62,000

Source: Hypothetical example by the author.

In this calculation, cash is assigned '0' risk weight. The 1988 Basel Accord prescribed that a bank maintain minimum capital equivalent to 8 per cent of its risk-weighted assets. For the total risk-weighted assets of INR 62,000 crore in the example, the minimum capital requirement can be calculated as follows:

$$\begin{aligned}\text{Minimum capital requirement} &= 0.08 \times \text{INR } 62{,}000 \text{ crore} \\ &= \text{INR } 4{,}960 \text{ crore} \qquad (7.1)\end{aligned}$$

Thus, if Bank X wants to continue with its asset portfolio of INR 1,00,000 crore as in our example, it is required to maintain minimum capital of INR 4,960 crore.

to INR 1,010 crore (why?). This will be a violation of the capital adequacy regulation as Bank Y cannot exceed risk-weighted assets of INR 1,000 crore as along as its capital level is fixed at INR 80 crore. On the other hand, the additional deposits of INR 10 crore can be deployed as lending to the government, as this will not raise the risk-weighted assets. The risk-weight assigned for lending to the government is 'nil'. Thus, the Basel capital adequacy regulation mitigates risky lending such as lending to private corporates in this case. It implicitly enforces safe lending options like lending to the government.

At the same time, it is an incentive-based regulation. In our hypothetical example, Bank Y can use the additional deposits of INR 10 crore entirely as fresh loans to private corporates as long as it can infuse the required additional capital. Corresponding to the risk-weighted assets of INR 1,010 crore, the minimum amount of capital required to be maintained by Bank Y is INR 80.8 crore (8 per cent of INR 1,010 crore). So if Bank Y wants to exploit the opportunity of lending to private corporates rather than lending to the government, it needs to infuse additional capital of INR 0.8 crore. This will raise its capital holding to INR 80.8 crore and support risk-weighted assets of INR 1,010 crore.

Thus, the Basel 1988 norms do not necessarily force a bank to use its resources for less risky lending such as to the government. A bank is free to lend to more risky activities and earn higher interest income. For that, the shareholders of the bank need to raise their stake in the banking business (equity capital) or the bank needs to raise funds from the corporate bonds market; it has to raise its capital. Lending to risky activities is not directly controlled, but the requirement of higher capital infusion linked to the risk profile of loans discourages highly risky lending.

7.3.2.2 Limitations of the Basel Accord, 1988

The Basel Accord of 1988 was a welcome initiative for promoting uniformity and global coordination in setting capital adequacy requirements for banks. However, as time passed, some of its limitations became evident. Three such issues are as follows:

- First, the Accord took into account only credit risk for overall banking risk assessment. Other aspects such as market risk, liquidity risk and operational risk were ignored.
- Second, assignment of risk weights was arbitrary and erroneous. For example, loans to a good corporate house like the Tata Group in India are less risky as compared to short-term exposures to a bank on the verge of trouble. Assigning 100 per cent risk weight for loans

to the Tata Group and 20 per cent for loans to a weak bank cannot be justified. The one-size-fits-all approach of treating all corporates or banks as homogeneous for risk treatment was a major point of criticism.

- Third, necessary adjustment in credit risk assessment for risk mitigants like security collaterals, guarantees, credit derivatives, and so on, was not considered. Actual credit risk on loans which have such credit mitigants is lower.

A bank's investment portfolio comprises a significant share of its balance sheet. For SCBs in India, such share was nearly 37 per cent during the late 1990s and early 2000s. Moreover, with the introduction of financial sector reforms, an active secondary market for government securities was developed. Accordingly, the relevance of 'market risk' in overall banking risks became significant. Banks in advanced economies were exposed to considerable market risks even earlier. In view of these aspects, the 1988 Basel Accord was amended in 1996 to include 'market risk' explicitly for calculation of minimum capital requirements.

7.3.3 Adoption of the Basel Capital Adequacy Norms in India

The need to extend the global best practice on banking regulation to emerging economies was seriously felt after the Asian crisis of 1997. The phenomenal economic performance of Southeast Asian nations, popularly referred to as Asian Tigers (Hong Kong, Singapore, South Korea and Taiwan), commenced in the 1960s and stretched over several decades. Quite surprisingly, they suffered a serious setback in 1997 with an economic and financial crisis witnessed in South Korea, Indonesia, Malaysia, Thailand and the Philippines. A 'post-mortem' of the crisis, inter alia, exposed several weaknesses in the banking sector in these countries. The reasons behind the Asian crisis of 1997 were as follows:

- Sustained high growth in the Asian Tigers attracted a huge amount of foreign investment. Over time, in search of high returns, these funds were channelled to speculative investment in real estate and the stock market.
- With a massive speculative attack on the Thai baht in 1997 and its contagion effect in the region, there was a sudden reversal of capital

flows. This led to collapse in real estate and equity prices. Banks suffered heavily due to their sizeable exposure to these sectors.

- In Indonesia, bank lending to the property sector was nearly one-fifth of aggregate lending. Banks in Thailand had similar high exposure to real estate.
- Spiral effect of the banking crisis and economic crisis exacerbated the problem.
- Regulatory and supervisory authorities of the banking sector in these countries did not foresee the adverse consequences of financial globalisation, particularly those of uncontrolled cross-border capital inflows.

Learning from this experience, the policy authorities in emerging economies realised that in order to promote foreign investment, there was a pressing need to strengthen their respective banking sectors. In this backdrop, adoption of the Basel norms for banking regulation became popular to upgrade their regulatory and supervisory frameworks in line with the international standard.

In India, the Narasimham Committee I (RBI, 1991) recommended adoption of capital adequacy norms with a view to strengthening the safety and soundness of the banking sector. Consequently, India adopted the 1988 Basel Accord in April 1992. Its implementation was spread over several years. The RBI had prescribed that banks meet the requirement of maintaining a minimum CRAR of 8 per cent by 31 March 1996. It also defined specific components of capital for this purpose. This minimum capital is usually referred to as regulatory capital. As per the 1988 Basel Accord, regulatory capital was divided into core capital (tier 1) and supplementary capital (tier 2). Subsequently, after amendments in January 1996 and September 1997, tier-3 capital was also included. The composition of each variety has been discussed previously. The minimum CRAR requirement was raised by the RBI to 9 per cent from 2000 (RBI, 2005).

7.3.4 Norms on Asset Classification and Provisioning

Along with capital adequacy norms, banking regulations related to asset classification, income recognition and provisioning have also emerged as global prudential standards. Regulations on asset classification mandate segregating bank assets into performing and non-performing types depending on timely repayment of loans. A loan is classified as an NPA if the principal repayments and/or interest charges become overdue. Depending on the duration of the assets being overdue, NPAs are classified as *substandard*, *doubtful* or *loss* assets. Moreover, there is a requirement for higher provisioning by banks for NPAs.

In India, regulatory guidelines stipulate that assets of banks can be treated as NPAs if interest and/or an instalment of the principal remains overdue for a period of more than 90 days for a term loan. A similar norm of 90 days overdue is suitably applied for bills purchased and discounted, securitisation and derivative transactions undertaken. Agricultural loans are treated as NPAs if loan instalments remain overdue for two or one crop season(s) for short- or long-duration crops, respectively. NPAs up to 12 months are termed as *substandard* assets. NPAs which remain substandard for more than a year are categorised as *doubtful*. The worst quality NPAs are *loss* assets which are identified as a loss by the bank itself or by the auditors or the RBI, provided the amount is not written off wholly by the bank.

The stipulated income recognition norms compel banks not to recognise income on accrual basis from NPAs unless income is actually received. However, if adequate margin is available against term deposits, securities and interest income from those securities, the same can be booked. The entire income accrued and credited to the income account in the past has to be reversed if any such income was booked but not realised due to the asset becoming an NPA.

When a bank's assets become NPAs, not only does it suffer due to income loss but there is an additional burden arising from related provisioning requirements. Every bank is required to make separate provisions for NPAs by setting aside a part of its income from other assets. The amount of provisioning corresponds to the severity of the loan delinquency. For example, loss assets have extremely low recovery potential and banks are required to make 100 per cent provisioning for such assets. Extant guidelines of the RBI also require 100 per cent provisioning for unsecured doubtful assets. For secured doubtful assets, the provisioning requirements are set at 25, 40 and 100 per cent of the secured portion based on the duration for which such assets are kept under the doubtful category. For substandard assets, there is a requirement of general provisioning of 15 per cent on the total outstanding[6] and additional provisioning of 10 per cent for unsecured exposures.

Within these broad norms, there are certain concessions for some desirable activities having strong positive externalities for society such as lending to infrastructure projects. For details, one may refer to the RBI's 'Master Circular on Prudential Norms on Income Recognition, Asset Classification and Provisioning Pertaining to Advances' available on the RBI's official website www.rbi.org.in.

7.4 First Major Revision in the Basel Norms: Basel II

The 1988 Basel Accord marked a good beginning for providing a global standard on capital adequacy requirements for banks. It was the first attempt of its kind to link minimum capital requirements for banks to the risks embodied in their business. However, it suffered from several inadequacies as highlighted in the previous section. There were continuous efforts to overcome these deficiencies. As part of the process, the BCBS came up with substantial revisions to the capital adequacy assessment for banks and released its report *International Convergence of Capital Measurement and Capital Standards: A Revised Framework* in June 2004. The revised norms are popularly referred to as the Basel II Accord. Since then the 1988 Accord is referred to as Basel I.

The Basel II framework consisted of three key pillars, namely (*a*) Pillar 1: minimum capital requirements, (*b*) Pillar 2: supervisory review process and (*c*) Pillar 3: market discipline. A brief description of these pillars is provided in the following sections.

7.4.1 Pillar I: Minimum Capital Requirements

The Basel II Accord substantially improved assessment of the minimum capital requirement for banks in several ways. First, Basel II expanded the scope of overall banking risk assessment by incorporating operational risk along with existing credit risk and market risk considerations under Basel I. Second, overcoming the straitjacket approach for assessing credit

---

[6] This is after making allowance for Export Credit Guarantee Corporation of India (ECGC) guarantee cover and securities available.

risk under Basel I, it adopted a realistic approach. Particularly, it prescribed use of credit ratings for individual borrowers to determine their true creditworthiness. Ratings given by external CRAs and those obtained by applying internal rating models were allowed for this purpose. This facilitated differentiation of borrowers within a particular category, such as private corporates or banks, based on their realistic risk profile. On the contrary, Basel I had assigned uniform risk weights for all borrowers in a particular category, irrespective of their creditworthiness or credit rating. Third, Basel II recommended a variety of methods for measuring different types of banking risks. Banks were allowed to use simpler approaches to assess credit risk, market risk and operational risk to begin with. With gradual improvement in technical expertise and data availability, it was envisaged that more sophisticated and advanced procedures could be adopted over time. The broad objective was making risk assessment in banks more realistic and comprehensive.

7.4.1.1 Assessment of Credit Risk under Basel II: Standardised Approach

Basel II prescribed three procedures for assessing capital adequacy on account of credit risk. These were (*a*) standardised approach, (*b*) internal rating-based (IRB) foundation approach and (*c*) IRB advanced approach. Measurement of credit risk becomes more realistic and comprehensive gradually moving from the first to the third approach in order.

Under the standardised approach, risk weights for assessment of credit risks for individual corporate borrowers were assigned based on their credit ratings by approved CRAs. For example, exposure to corporates with AAA rating was assigned a risk weight of 20 per cent, that for AA-rated borrowers was 30 per cent, and so on (Table 7.2). For banks operating in India, risk weights of 20–125 per cent were assigned for credit risk based on their credit rating. For retail loans, risk weights varied depending on the type of loans. Different risk weights for OBS items were also specifically indicated. For example, risk weights to be assigned for LCs, performance guarantees and financial guarantees were 20, 50 and 100 per cent, respectively. Necessary details are summarised in Table 7.2.

It may be reiterated that assignment of risk weights for credit risk under Basel II became more realistic. As indicated in the preceding paragraph, exposures to the best quality corporate borrowers with the highest credit rating (AAA) were assigned 20 per cent risk weight while that for a weak

Table 7.2 Risk weights specified by the RBI under the Basel II standardised approach for credit risk

Asset portfolio	Risk weight (per cent)
Sovereign exposures	Domestic sovereign (Government of India) exposures: 0 State government exposures: 20 Foreign government exposures: as per sovereign rating
Exposure to banks	Domestic banks and foreign banks operating in India: 20–125 (as per external rating) Foreign banks: 20–150 (as per external rating)
Corporate exposures	AAA-rated: 20 AA-rated: 30 A-rated: 50 BBB-rated: 100 Below BBB-rated: 150 Unrated: 100
Retail loans	75
Retail (individual) residential mortgage loans	Loans up to INR 30 lakh with loan to value (LTV) ≤ 80: 35 Loans up to INR 30 lakh with LTV 80 ≤ 90: 50 Loans above INR 30 lakh and up to INR 75 lakh with LTV ≤ 80: 35 Loans above INR 75 lakh with LTV ≤ 75: 50
Other loans (other than against gold)	125
OBS items	LC: 20 Performance guarantee: 50 Financial guarantee: 100 (credit conversion factor is used as applicable)
Credit risk mitigation	Recognition of available security collateral, guarantees, credit derivatives, regulatory haircut for adjustment, as applicable

Source: Collated by the author based on information obtained from various sources on the official websites of RBI (www.rbi.org.in) and SBI (www.sbi.co.in).

borrower (BBB-rated) was 100 per cent. The risk weight was uniformly 100 per cent for all corporate borrowers under Basel I.

Given the importance of credit ratings for determination of risk weights for corporate borrowers, the credibility and competency of CRAs became critical. Basel II therefore stipulated certain parameters for selecting or shortlisting CRAs.[7]

7.4.1.2 Assessment of Credit Risk under Basel II: IRB Approach

Banks directly deal with individual borrowers. In the process of their long association, they have risk information about their customers. Therefore, it is perceived that a bank's own assessment about the credit risk of its borrowers can be very helpful. In this context, IRB approaches based on a bank's internal credit-rating model improve realistic risk assessment.

We have already explained in Chapter 6 calculation of credit risk under IRB models through credit ratings or scores and rating migration. The foundation and advanced approaches under IRB models mainly differ on determination of key parameters for calculation of credit risk. Under the Foundation IRB approach, PD is calculated by the respective banks while LGD, EAD and maturity (M) are given by the banking regulator or supervisor. Under the IRB advanced approach, all four parameters—namely PD, LGD, EAD and M—are determined by the lending bank.

In December 2011, the RBI had issued draft guidelines relating to the IRB approach for calculation of capital charge for credit risk. As observed by the RBI (2011), there were specific challenges for Indian banks in adoption of the IRB approach. First and importantly, lack of availability of historical data on the rating scores of borrowers and rating migrations for different categories of borrowers was a major handicap. This is a necessary prerequisite for calculation of PD and LGD. Second, traditional classification of assets followed by banks in India as per available data differed from the requirement under the IRB approach. Third, a large number of corporate borrowers in India were not listed, undermining the utility of credit risk models which are heavily reliant on market data.

Most Indian banks follow the standardised approach for assessing the capital requirement for credit risk. They have been preparing seriously to migrate to the IRB approach since the early 2010s and stand at different levels of progress. The RBI has approved adoption of the Foundation IRB approach by several banks on parallel-run basis. For example, as per its Basel

---

[7] Key criteria for selection of CRAs include norms on independence, international access/transparency, disclosure, resources, credibility, no abuse of unsolicited ratings and cooperation with supervisor.

III disclosures (as on 31 December 2022), PNB was permitted by the RBI to conduct parallel run of Foundation IRB with effect from 31 July 2013 while it has expressed its intention to the RBI for implementing the Advanced IRB approach.

7.4.1.3 Assessment of Market Risk under Basel II

As regards calculation of regulatory capital to cover market risk, Basel II prescribed three approaches. These were (*a*) standardised approach following maturity method, (*b*) standardised approach following duration method and (*c*) internal models method.

The first one is the simplest in which risk weights are assigned based on mismatches in the investment portfolio or long and short positions across different time buckets or zones. For example, for a maturity mismatch under the time bucket of less than one month, the risk weight to be assigned is nil; for a mismatch under one to three months, the risk weight is 0.2 per cent; and so on. Mismatches in assets–liabilities under various time buckets are obtained from the maturity ladder constructed under ALM. Details of the same are discussed in Chapter 8. The modified duration method for measuring market risk has already been described in Chapter 6. The technique of VaR used under the internal model method was also discussed therein.

Basel II stipulated accounting for market risk under equity, forex and gold portfolios separately. The RBI determined a general market risk charge of 9 per cent for these assets.

7.4.1.4 Assessment of Operational Risk under Basel II

As regards operational risk, Basel II prescribed three approaches as well. These were (*a*) the basic indicator approach (BIA), (*b*) the standardised approach (TSA) and (*c*) the advanced measurement approach (AMA). Measurement issues for different approaches for assessing operational risk have already been presented in Chapter 6. Lack of external loss data and unavailability of reliable internal loss data are major constraints in adoption of AMA. Moreover, elements of subjective judgement, assessment of internal controls and use of scenario analysis add further challenges. The RBI had issued guidelines for measuring capital charge for operational risk using the TSA approach in March 2010 and the AMA approach in April 2011.

For further details on assessment of risk weights for credit, market and operational risks under various approaches, readers may refer to BIS (2004) and the official website of the RBI (www.rbi.org.in).

7.4.1.5 Minimum Regulatory Capital Requirement

The minimum regulatory capital requirement for banks under Basel II is calculated as the sum of the capital requirements for credit, market and operational risks. Depending on data availability, competency and progress in modelling or computing aspects, banks were permitted to gradually move from simpler to more advanced approaches for risk measurement under each category. The amount of minimum regulatory capital to be maintained by banks was recommended to be 8 per cent of the total risk-weighted assets.[8]

Thus, Pillar I itself was a significant improvement, overcoming major deficiencies of the Basel I Accord. Pillars II and III under Basel II further strengthened and supplemented the minimum capital adequacy requirements.

7.4.2 Pillar II: Supervisory Review Process

Banks were delegated greater responsibilities and assumed more flexibility under Basel II capital adequacy assessment. Particularly, advanced approaches for assessing credit, market and operational risks heavily relied on the internal data and analytical models of banks. The efficacy of capital adequacy norms under Pillar I critically rested on the robustness of the internal risk assessment processes of individual banks. Hence, it was necessary to review the soundness and integrity of the internal risk evaluation procedures and processes of banks. Any scope for laxity or underestimation of risks by banks either due to misusing the permitted flexibility or due to lack of competence needed to be mitigated. Hence, under Pillar II, banking regulators were required to continuously evaluate and monitor such internal procedures and technical analysis within banks as well as keep a close watch on their risk profile. This was part of the supervisory review process under Pillar II.

Also, there was a need to monitor if banks were maintaining the required capital as per the risk-linked assessment under Pillar I. If a bank fell short of maintaining its minimum capital requirement, the banking regulator was to

---

[8] The RBI stipulated a minimum CRAR of 9 per cent since 2000 (RBI, 2005).

initiate prompt corrective action so that the bank makes necessary adjustment on its lending and/or capital position. Furthermore, if any deficiency in the internal risk assessment processes in a particular bank was detected, Basel II empowered the banking regulator to insist on a differential capital obligation for the relevant bank. This amount was incremental over the requirements under Pillar I.

This commensurately entailed additional tasks for bank supervisors.

7.4.3 Pillar III: Market Discipline

As indicated earlier, banks enjoyed a reasonable degree of flexibility in risk assessment under Basel II. To balance this flexibility with market-based discipline, Basel II required banks to reveal and report important information to the public through greater transparency and disclosures. Under Pillar III, banks had to disclose certain qualitative and quantitative information in the public domain at periodic intervals. The qualitative information pertained to conceptual definitions, accounting principles, policies and the system followed by the bank for calculating and reporting various banking indicators. The quantitative indicators included various items in the bank's balance sheet, income and expenditure statement, and information on capital adequacy, asset quality and performance indicators.

7.4.4 Adoption of the Basel II Norms in India

Implementation of Basel II commenced in advanced economies in 2006, and the due date for application in emerging economies was spread over a couple of years after that date. In India there was a parallel run of minimum capital requirements as per the Basel I Accord along with the revised Basel II until 2007. Banks in India had adopted simpler approaches to minimum capital adequacy norms under Basel II by 31 March 2009. The schedule for implementation of advanced approaches was laid down by the RBI in July 2009.

As indicated earlier, adoption of advanced approaches to measure credit, market and operational risks under the Basel II capital adequacy norms concomitantly required rigorous technical analysis, detailed documentation, review and authentication of various banking risk parameters by banks internally. In this perspective, banks were required to put in place their board-approved Internal Capital Adequacy Assessment Process (ICAAP) as part of the regulatory requirements. The ICAAP was envisaged as a bank's internal mechanism to configure its overall risk profile, assess the alignment of its capital requirements with risks embodied in its business and spell out its strategy for maintaining capital adequacy under alternative scenarios of normal and stressed conditions. Each bank had to review its ICAAP at least once a year, with the same being validated by internal and external audit. Each bank was to also submit its ICAAP to the RBI by 30 June every year.

7.4.5 Deficiencies of the Basel II Capital Adequacy Norms

Despite the improvements over Basel I, there were certain criticisms of the regulatory capital prescriptions of Basel II. Such criticisms mainly pertained to (*a*) exclusive focus on microprudential aspects and ignoring of macroprudential dimensions; (*b*) amplification of the procyclical character of bank credit due to inherent variation in risk assessment during different phases of the business cycle; and (*c*) recourse by banks to securitisation and shadow banking activities for risk mitigation under the 'origin and distribute'[9] approach to bank lending. The GFC of 2007–08 exposed various limitations of the Basel II norms, delineated as follows:

- First, it was observed that regulations aiming at individual institutions which are microprudential in character cannot ensure the safety and soundness of the banking system as a whole. According to Aristotle, 'the whole is greater than the sum of its parts'. Perhaps banking regulators across the world had forgotten these sagacious words of the great philosopher. The Basel II norms failed to identify the building-up of systemic vulnerabilities.
- Second, the Basel II norms exacerbated procyclicality in bank lending. During an economic downturn, many firms and individuals

[9] In conventional banking, a bank originates bank loans, and such loans are retained in its balance sheet until paid back along with interest charges. With securitisation, bank loans are bundled together and sold as securities or bonds such as mortgage-backed securities. After securitisation, such loans are removed from the balance sheet of the lending bank and transferred to the investors who have purchased such securities. This is popularly referred to as the 'origin and distribute' model in bank lending through securitisation.

face economic hardship and become vulnerable to default on their loans. Risk exposures to such borrowers rise, reducing the CRAR of a bank. With a lower CRAR, a given level of capital constrains a bank to hold a lower amount of assets or loans. Therefore, the growth of bank loans decelerates during an economic downturn. On the contrary, during an economic upswing, better financial profiles of firms and households reduce risk weights on loans to such entities. Accordingly, the CRARs of banks improve. With a higher CRAR, a bank can extend a higher amount of loans for a given amount of capital. Thus, bank loans expand rapidly during economic booms. The procyclical characteristic of CRAR amplifies swings in bank loans concomitant with business cycle-related economic swings under the Basel II capital norms. Excessive credit growth during economic booms sows the seeds of loan delinquencies that become pronounced during economic recessions.

- Third, securitisation and the use of derivatives for mitigating risks in banking led to sophisticated financial engineering. The regulatory arbitrage also led to mushrooming of shadow banking institutions. Using financial engineering, banking risks were transferred to investment banks and their investors, and consequently the bank's balance sheet appeared to be safe and resilient. The onset of the sub-prime crisis exposed the vulnerability and superficiality of financial engineering, including securitisation. On the role of financial engineering and regulatory deficiencies in causing the GFC, Rangarajan (2009) rightly observed that

> derivative products are a natural corollary of financial development. They meet a felt need. However, if the derivative products become too complex to discern where the risk lies, they become a major source of concern ... Quite clearly, there was a mismatch between financial innovation and the ability of the regulators to monitor them.

In the backdrop of the experience of the GFC of 2007–08, banking regulators and experts deliberated vigorously to improve the Basel capital adequacy regulations. Consequently, capital adequacy regulations were considerably revised, and new liquidity standards were introduced, popularly referred to as the Basel III norms. This became the new global capital adequacy framework for banking regulations.

7.5 Second Major Revision in the Basel Norms: Basel III

The GFC of 2007–08 severely impacted the banking sector in the US and many other advanced economies in Europe, exposing the weaknesses and deficiencies of the Basel II capital adequacy norms. Many analysts and international organisations undertook serious efforts to re-examine the prevailing banking regulatory framework and overcome underlying deficiencies. Early global efforts in this regard were confined to the Financial Stability Forum, a smaller forum of advanced economies under the aegis of BIS. As exposure of emerging economies to the spillover effects of the GFC became evident, the forum became wider, using the platform of G20. A bigger body, the Financial Stability Board (FSB), was set up in 2009 to work on the required improvements in the global regulatory framework for banks.

Deliberations on the GFC traced its genesis to the sub-prime crisis in the US. Insufficient liquidity buffers acted as a trigger for the ensuing crisis. At a fundamental level, the severity of the crisis was attributed to excessive leveraging both on balance sheet and OBS items of banks along with gradual erosion of the level and quality of their capital base (BIS, 2010). Lack of focus on systemic trading and credit losses, a procyclical deleveraging process and interconnectedness of systemic institutions through a web of complex and opaque transactions added to these problems, raising solvency concerns.

Learning from the experience of the GFC and seeking to strengthen the resilience of banks and banking systems, the BCBS framed revised guidelines improving upon the Basel II norms. These guidelines were placed in the public domain for feedback in January 2009, and subsequently, a revised global regulatory framework for banks was introduced in 2010. These norms are popularly referred to as the Basel III norms. Readers may refer to BIS (2010) for further details.

The Basel III norms improved upon the Basel II framework broadly on four accounts. First, it modified the prevailing risk assessment and capital adequacy stipulations of Basel II in several ways. Not only did it raise the quantum of capital requirements under all three pillars of Basel II, it also emphasised improving the quality and composition of regulatory capital, thereby enhancing the resilience of banks to banking risks. Second, it introduced new measures of capital regulation in the form of minimum leverage ratio requirements which stipulated maintenance of good-quality capital by banks in alignment with their overall business, irrespective of risk considerations for different types of banking assets. This is to safeguard against potential manipulation by banks in assigning risk weights for their assets and counter excess leveraging. Third, regulations in the form of maintaining LCR and NSFR were introduced, setting a new global liquidity standard. Fourth, to strengthen capital adequacy and deal with liquidity concerns over different phases of the business cycle, suitable measures were incorporated to address macroprudential, countercyclical and systemic aspects. The salient features of these upgradations are delineated as follows.

7.5.1 Modification of Basel II Norms and Strengthening of Related Capital Charges

Basel III modified all three pillars of the Basel II norms. As regards Pillar I, the Basel III norms strengthened capital adequacy requirements both by raising the quantum of capital charges and by improving the quality of capital. New norms on a capital conservation buffer (CCB), countercyclical capital buffer (CCyB) and additional capital requirement for systemically important banks raised the overall minimum capital requirement. Details of such new measures are discussed in the following sections. As regards improving the quality of regulatory capital, the minimum tier-1 capital requirement was raised from 4 to 6 per cent. Moreover, at least 75 per cent of tier-1 capital was required to be in the form of common shares and retained earnings—the best quality of bank capital. Basel III stipulated phasing out innovative hybrid capital instruments and elimination of tier-3 capital instruments. These instruments were used to cover market risks under Basel I. Basel III also proposed enhancement of transparency by requiring disclosure of all components of capital along with a detailed reconciliation of accounts. Necessary amendments were suggested to raise capital requirements for re-securitisation in the banking and trading books. Moreover, capital requirements were revised to take into account risks from derivatives, repo and securities transactions. To prepare against stressed situations, a new stressed VaR capital requirement was envisaged. Banks were encouraged to use their own internal assessments for securitisation exposures rated by an external CRA.

On Pillar II, there was emphasis on rigorous supervision of OBS exposures, particularly pertaining to securitisation, valuation of complex instruments and other derivative products. There were also suggestions on improving supervisory focus on the management of liquidity risks and stress-testing practices followed by banks.

On Pillar III, there were prescriptions, inter alia, to enhance disclosure of securitisation and OBS vehicles.

7.5.2 Countercyclical and Non-Risk-Based Capital Requirements

The capital adequacy norms under Basel II had two major drawbacks. First, business cycle–related economic fluctuations entailed changing risk weights during phases of economic boom and recession. As indicated earlier, this amplified the procyclicality of bank lending. Second, possible manipulation in assignment of risk weights by banks could lead to excessive leveraging and undermine relevance of minimum capital adequacy norms. In this perspective, Basel III introduced several measures to counter excessive leveraging and reduce procyclicality in bank lending.

First, a minimum leverage ratio of 3 per cent was introduced. This ensures maintenance of a minimum level of capital by banks in proportion to their total assets. This is a non-risk-based capital charge. Under this requirement, only tier-1 capital was included. The main objective of this simple measure was to limit excessive leveraging in the banking business and protect the economy from the painful consequences of the deleveraging process during a crisis. This is independent of changing risk perceptions over different phases of the business cycle.

Second, Basel III introduced a capital conservation requirement which facilitates building up of additional capital buffers during good times. This is above the regulatory minimum as determined by Pillar I requirements. This excess capital can be drawn on in times of stress so as to facilitate credit smoothening when banks incur losses due to loan delinquencies. Basel III prescribed a CCB of 2.5 per cent above the regulatory minimum capital under Pillar I. This buffer is to be comprised of only tier-2 capital.

In addition to the these, Basel III prescribed a CCyB to moderate excessive procyclicality in bank lending. Under this norm, banking regulators can impose a CCyB up to 2.5 per cent of risk-weighted assets to counter building up of system-wide risks during periods of economic boom and very high growth of bank credit. During economic downswings and credit growth deceleration, the CCyB can be reduced to nil. This buffer also needs to be maintained in the form of Common Equity Tier-1 (CET1) capital.

Thus, Basel III not only strengthened capital adequacy norms under Pillar I by enhancing risk coverage, quality and transparency of the capital base, it also supplemented these by incorporating macroprudential and systematic aspects in banking risk assessment in the form of newly introduced measures such as minimum coverage ratio, CCB and CCyB requirements.

7.5.3 Liquidity Standards

The GFC exposed another weakness of the prevailing banking regulatory framework in terms of lacking a harmonised global liquidity standard. In fact, the GFC itself was perceived as a liquidity problem at the beginning. Before the onset of the crisis, asset prices in the US were buoyant and banks were flooded with liquidity. Funds were available readily. The crisis dramatically changed liquidity conditions in a flash. Not only did the market witness sudden evaporation of liquidity, illiquid conditions also persisted for long.

To establish a harmonised global liquidity standard, Basel III adopted a two-pronged approach. First, under LCR, it required banks to maintain sufficient liquidity to compensate for net cash outflow under short-term liquidity stress. This was envisaged to address potential liquidity disruptions within a 30-day horizon. Second, an NSFR requirement was introduced to ensure a minimum threshold of stable sources of funding and protect banks against liquidity problems on a durable basis. NSFR also incorporated contingent liquidity requirements from OBS exposures. The time horizon for consideration under NSFR is one year. In Chapter 6, we have already discussed LCR and NSFR.

7.5.4 Timeline for Implementation of Basel III and 2017 Amendments

Implementation of the Basel III regulations was scheduled to be stretched over a long transition period and varied from one regulatory item to another. Originally, the BCBS had laid out a broad roadmap for smooth transition to Basel III standards from January 2013 to January 2019. Implementation of the minimum leverage ratio was scheduled to commence from January 2015. After a parallel run, it was supposed to migrate to Pillar I treatment from January 2018. Minimum CET1 and total Tier I requirements were scheduled to be executed from January 2013 to January 2015. CCB and CCyB were to become fully effective from January 2019. Moreover, the implementation schedule of Basel III norms varied across countries for different measures.

Subsequently, the BCBS came up with some important revisions to the Basel III norms in 2017 (BIS, 2017). The 2017 reforms were critically confined to use of the IRB approach for credit risk, improving the level and quality of capital and assessment of operational risk.

There were concerns of manipulations in assignment of risk weights by banks to their advantage under the IRB approach. The 2017 reforms debarred use of the IRB approach for equity exposures. Application of the Advanced IRB approach for exposure to banks and other financial institutions and big corporates was done away with. The standardised approach to measure credit risk was refined by introducing a more detailed risk-weight approach instead of application of flat risk weights. For example, a more granular treatment was adopted for corporate and retail exposures, while residential and commercial real-estate exposures were subjected to a more risk-sensitive approach. It was also stipulated that the amount of risk-weighted assets under the IRB approach for any bank cannot fall below 72.5 per cent of risk-weighted assets arrived at using the standardised approach. Say, if the risk-weighted assets of a bank under the standardised approach are calculated as INR 1,00,000, then risk-weighted assets for the same bank under the IRB approach cannot be less than INR 72,500.

The 2017 reforms in Basel III raised the minimum leverage ratio for global systemically important banks. In addition to the minimum leverage ratio of 3 per cent, these banks are required to maintain an additional leverage ratio buffer amounting to 50 per cent of their capital buffer. For example, if for a global systemically important bank, the capital buffer is 4 per cent, then the additional leverage buffer for the bank will be 2 per cent. Thus, this bank needs to maintain a minimum 5 per cent (that is, 3 + 2) leverage ratio.

Measurement of capital requirements for operational risk has been widely viewed as being ad hoc. The 2017 reforms in Basel III envisage simplifying and improving the calculations using a single standardised approach rather than the prevailing multiple approaches discussed in Chapter 6. The proposed framework combines the existing gross income–based measure along with a new dimension incorporating a bank's own internal loss history due to deficient or failed internal systems, processes and people or external events over the past 10 years.

The Covid-19 pandemic during 2020 had devastating economic consequences across countries. Central banks and banking regulators around the world responded by adopting many conventional and unconventional measures to support their economies. This included relaxation of different banking regulatory measures for sustaining bank lending. Postponement of implementation dates of certain provisions of Basel III in many countries was part of these efforts. In several countries, banks were permitted to drawdown their capital and liquidity buffers. The CCyB was reduced in France, Germany, Sweden, Switzerland and the UK. India temporarily eased the LCR requirement and deferred the due date for implementation of the final tranche of CCB.

7.5.5 Adoption of the Basel III Norms in India

The RBI had issued draft guidelines on implementation of the Basel III norms for Indian banks in December 2011. Incorporating the feedback received from different stakeholders on the draft, it issued its final guidelines on 2 May 2012. The roadmap for implementation was spread across January 2013 to March 2018. Full implementation of Basel III for Indian banks was envisaged by the end of the financial year 2017–18, seven months prior to the due date of implementation set by the BCBS—that is, January 2019.

The main components of the Basel III capital and liquidity regulatory norms implemented by the RBI are summarised as follows:

- *Minimum regulatory capital requirements*: Under Basel II, the RBI had already stipulated the minimum CRAR at 9 per cent. This was 1 percentage point above the BCBS recommendation under Basel II. Under Basel III, the RBI retained this ratio at 9 per cent. However, the quality of capital under this requirement was enhanced. The RBI stipulated the minimum CET1 capital to be 5.5 per cent of risk-weighted assets. Accordingly, the minimum ratio of tier-1 capital to risk-weighted assets was fixed at 7 per cent. A transition path was delineated to raise the ratio of CET1 to risk-weighted assets gradually from 4.5 per cent in January 2013 to 5.5 per cent by 31 March 2015.
- *CCB*: The CCB was envisaged to be independent of banking risk measurement as also over and above the minimum regulatory capital of 9 per cent. It was supposed to be accumulated in good times so that it could be used as a buffer by banks during bad times. This is to help banks avoid the violence of the minimum regulatory capital requirement during periods of stress. The CCB was supposed to be maintained in the form of common equity. The RBI had drawn a roadmap to gradually raise the CCB as a proportion of risk-weighted assets from 0.625 per cent as of end-March 2015 to 2.5 per cent by end-March 2018.

- *Leverage ratio*: The RBI had prescribed a parallel run to maintain a minimum tier-1 leverage ratio of 4.5 per cent between January 2013 and January 2017. It stipulated a minimum leverage ratio of 4 per cent for domestic systemically important banks (DSIBs) and 3.5 per cent for other banks with effect from October 2019.
- *Additional requirements for DSIBs*: Cascading effects of failures of big banks can be disproportionately high. To guard against this, the RBI postulated an additional tier-1 capital requirement for big banks over and above the minimum regulatory requirement of 7 per cent. The additional requirement was stipulated to be 0.6 per cent of risk-weighted assets for SBI and 0.2 per cent for HDFC Bank and ICICI Bank.
- *LCR*: LCR is expressed as the ratio of stock of HQLAs to total net cash outflows over the ensuing 30 calendar days. The RBI had provided a roadmap to gradually raise the minimum LCR for banks from 60 per cent in January 2015 to 100 per cent in January 2019. To guard against the adverse impact of Covid-19, LCR norms were temporarily relaxed. The minimum LCR was again raised to 100 per cent with effect from 1 April 2021.
- *NSFR*: Implementation of NSFR was initially deferred from April 2020 to October 2020 in view of the Covid-19 pandemic. Subsequently, the RBI set out a minimum NSFR of 100 per cent with effect from October 2021.
- *CCyB*: CCyB was envisaged to arrest excessive credit growth during economic booms and counter build-up of system-wide risks. The RBI had issued guidelines on CCyB in February 2015 providing details on its composition and use of parameters or indicators for its activation and calibration. However, based on a review, the RBI decided to postpone implementation of CCyB requirements for the time being (RBI, 2022b); as of August 2024 also, it is yet to be implemented.

A summary of minimum regulatory capital, capital buffer, liquidity requirements, and so on, as stipulated by the RBI is given in Table 7.3.

According to the RBI's *Financial Stability Report* published in June 2023, CRAR of SCBs in India had reached a new high of 17.1 per cent in March 2023 and the median CRAR was even higher at 17.9 per cent. Alongside, the CET1 ratio of SCBs had reached a high level of 13.9 per cent with the median CET1 ratio at 15.8 per cent. The leverage ratio of SCBs stood at 7.3 per cent at

Table 7.3 Basel III regulatory capital and other requirements in India

(*Per cent*)

Item	CET1	Total tier 1	Tier 2	Total capital
Minimum capital under Pillar I	5.5	7.0	2.0	9.0
Conservation buffer	2.5			2.5
Minimum capital plus conservation buffer	8.0	9.5	2.0	11.5
Additional requirement for domestic systemically important banks (DSIBs)*		0.2 to 0.6		11.7 to 12.1
Countercyclical buffer				
(not implemented as of August 2024)	0.0–2.5			
Leverage ratio	4 per cent of tier-1 capital to total exposure on balance sheet and OBS items for DSIBs and 3.5 per cent for other banks			
Liquidity coverage ratio (LCR)	Minimum LCR of 100 per cent over 30 calendar days			
Net stable funding ratio (NSFR)	Minimum NSFR (available stable funding to required stable funding ratio) is 100 per cent over a time horizon of one year			

Source: Collated by the author based on information obtained from various sources on the official websites of RBI (www.rbi.org.in) and SBI (www.sbi.co.in).

Note: *Additional tier-1 capital requirement of 0.6 per cent for SBI and 0.2 per cent each for HDFC Bank and ICICI Bank.

the same time. Macro-stress tests conducted by the RBI for assessing credit risk, also reported in the aforementioned report of June 2023, suggested that banks in India are adequately capitalised. This implied that banks in India can withstand adverse stress scenarios without violating minimum capital adequacy standards.

7.6 Banking Supervision in India

It may be reiterated here that framing banking regulatory policies alone cannot guarantee safety and soundness of the banking system. It is equally important to ensure adherence of banks to the regulatory norms in letter and spirit on a continuous basis. Banking supervision undertaken by the concerned authorities serves this purpose. Banking supervision also facilitates regular monitoring of the financial health of banks and urges them to conduct the banking business on prudential lines. The RBI is entrusted with the responsibility for banking supervision in India, deriving such authority from the BR Act, 1949, and the RBI Act, 1934.

Prior to the 1990s, banking supervision was mainly undertaken through on-site inspection of banks. As discussed earlier, the post-reform period witnessed a significant turnaround in conduct of the banking business in India in several dimensions. Moving away from the administered regime of bank credit and interest rates, banks acquired considerable operational autonomy since the early 1990s. The scope of banking expanded from the traditional deposit mobilisation and lending to the introduction of a variety of innovative products on both the assets and liabilities sides of a bank's balance sheet. Banks were also exposed to a large number of OBS items. Adoption of incentive-based regulatory tools like risk-based capital charge, asset classification and provisioning requirements transformed the role of banks in the process of pursuing the objective of risk-adjusted returns in the regular banking business. Concomitantly, there was a significant transformation in banking supervision too.

Given the need for greater focus and upgradation as regards banking supervision in the changing environment during the post-reform period, the RBI created a new department, namely the Department of Supervision,[10] in 1993. It also established a special high-level body in the form of the Board for Financial Supervision (BFS) in November 1994, entrusted with the overall responsibility for supervision of various financial entities in India, including banks. The RBI governor is the chairman of the BFS, and a deputy governor of the RBI assumes the role of vice-chairman. The BFS also includes four directors of the RBI central board as members.

Moreover, the RBI's broad framework for banking supervision was revised to conform to the Core Principles for Effective Banking Supervision,[11] originally prescribed by the BCBS in September 1997 and subsequently revised in September 2012. The RBI adopted the CAMELS approach for banking supervision from the 1990s. This is an acronym for capital adequacy

[10] The name of the department was changed to Department of Banking Supervision (DBS) in the intermittent period (during 1997 to 2019) before reverting to the original name, Department of Supervision, in 2019.

[11] With significant changes in the banking business and risk profile of banks, there was a need to upgrade the core principles. This was carried out in September 2012.

(C), asset quality (A), management (M), earning (E), liquidity (L) and system and control (S).

Under these parameters, the RBI periodically examines banking activities using a two-pronged approach, namely (*a*) on-site inspection and (*b*) off-site surveillance. Through such scrutiny, the RBI keeps a close watch on the status of compliance as regards regulatory prescriptions as well as continuously monitors the financial position of banks to assess their financial prudence, solvency and liquidity. Accordingly, banks are assigned different ratings or grades. Parameters related to (*a*) financial condition and performance, (*b*) management and operating conditions, (*c*) compliance and (*d*) summary assessment based on CAMELS determine a bank's rating.[12] Typically, the ratings assigned are 'strong', 'satisfactory', 'less than satisfactory', 'deficient' and 'critically deficient'. Any bank falling below the prescribed threshold as per the rating is asked to take corrective action accordingly.

The RBI generally conducts an on-site inspection once a year for each bank. For this purpose, the RBI inspection team visits the head office of the bank and select bank branches covering a certain minimum proportion of the bank's business. Usually, the inspecting team consists of officials with expertise in accounting, loan processing, risk assessment, the treasury business, and so on. The team physically inspects and examines the banking books, ledgers, internal guidelines of the bank for undertaking the banking business and risk assessment, documentation for executing various transactions, deployment and rotation of banking personnel for sensitive activities, and so on. Based on the findings of the inspecting team, banks are given scores using the CAMELS parameters. The team submits the annual inspection report to the concerned central authorities in the RBI. The concerned authorities re-examine and scrutinise the report of the inspecting team and prepare the final score and rating of the bank so as to assess whether the bank is strong or deficient. Accordingly, the RBI advises the concerned banks about their status and recommends undertaking necessary corrective action as applicable. For deficiencies in adhering to regulatory guidelines, if any, appropriate penalties are imposed on concerned banks.

However, on-site inspection of banks is not necessarily conducted only annually. Depending on the requirement and preliminary information about

[12] The RBI uses CAMELS for the rating of domestic banks. For foreign banks operating in India, it uses CALCS, an acronym for capital adequacy, asset quality, liquidity, compliance and systems.

the conduct and financial health of a bank, special on-site inspections may additionally be carried out by the RBI.

Moreover, the RBI also undertakes 'off-site surveillance' of banks at more frequent intervals. It established an Off-Site Monitoring and Surveillance (OSMOS) system in 1995 for this purpose. Banks are required to regularly submit data or reports online to the RBI on a host of business and financial indicators such as deposits, loans, liquidity position, profitability indicators, NPAs, capital position, provisions, and so on. Depending on the relevance, some information is obtained on a weekly basis and other information on a fortnightly, monthly or quarterly basis. The concerned RBI officials in the Department of Supervision analyse such data and information. This facilitates assessing the position of the bank on a continuous basis. Particularly, safety and soundness concerns are reported to higher authorities with necessary details and the concerned bank is also informed about the assessment. Off-site surveillance helps in quicker assessment and detection of regulatory concerns for relevant banks and facilitates timely action.

Both on-site inspection and off-site surveillance complement each other in strengthening banking supervision. While on-site inspection is more detailed and extensive, off-site surveillance helps in quick and timely assessment of concerns.

7.7 Conclusion

This chapter presented an overview of banking regulatory and supervisory practices broadly in an Indian perspective. To start with, various forms and dimensions of banking regulations were outlined. We covered administrative control on banks, LOLR facilities, deposit insurance, capital adequacy requirements, and so on, in the evolution of banking regulations. The relevance and utility of each of these were highlighted. The Basel capital adequacy and other prudential norms on asset quality, income recognition and provisioning were embraced as the popular market-oriented and incentive-based banking regulatory tools in India since the 1990s. Necessary details on the origin and upgradation of these norms in the form of the Basel II and Basel III capital adequacy and liquidity regulations were provided. Towards the end, the chapter outlined salient features of banking supervision in India.

Broadly, the chapter covered regulatory and supervisory aspects of risk mitigation in banks which are aimed at promoting the safety and soundness of the overall banking system. Even without regulatory guidelines, it is in the interest of banks to undertake the banking business prudently to maximise their inter-temporal profits as well as for their very survival. In this perspective, it is important to understand how banks manage banking risks. Necessary details are provided in the following chapter.

Revision Questions and Problems

1. How do the LOLR facility and bank deposit insurance provisions reduce the possibility of a bank run if a bank encounters a severe but temporary liquidity problem?
2. How do minimum capital adequacy requirements act as a disincentive for excessive risk taking?
3. Briefly explain the role of supervisory review and disclosure norms under Basel II.
4. What important lessons can be drawn for banking regulations from the GFC of 2007–08?
5. Explain how Basel II capital adequacy norms exacerbate procyclicality in bank lending,
6. What are the major improvements introduced by Pillar I capital adequacy norms under Basel III as compared to the provisions of Basel II?
7. What new norms has Basel III introduced to address macroprudential and countercyclical regulatory requirements?
8. Provide an outline of the banking supervision framework of the RBI.

8

Risk Management by Banks

Learning Objectives

- To provide details of the internal risk management system of banks in India
- To describe how banks in India use a multipronged approach for credit risk management
- To explain the asset–liability management (ALM) system of banks and highlight how the ALM system is used to manage liquidity and interest rate risk
- To discuss how banks in India manage market and operational risk

8.1 Introduction

As we have discussed in the previous chapters, banks as financial intermediaries mobilise deposits from savers and lend out the funds generated to borrowers. The interest income earned on loans and investments over interest cost on deposits is the main source of a bank's profits. We also discussed how the banking business entails a variety of risks. The central aspect of the banking business is maximising risk-adjusted profits. In Chapter 7, we discussed how the policy authorities regulate banking activities to contain risks within reasonable limits and ensure that banks take necessary precautions to mitigate risks.

In this perspective, banks undertake risk management as part of their regular banking operations. Risk management practices adopted by banks serve mainly two purposes. First, they ensure a bank's compliance with regulatory prescriptions in letter and spirit. Second, in the interest of sustaining the banking business and maximising risk-adjusted returns in the long run, the bank undertakes related banking operations to maintain safety and soundness. Risk management within banks is not just a matter of obligation to comply with regulatory requirements, but it is also a necessity for their very survival and sustenance.

As part of the banking sector reforms commenced in India since the early 1990s, the banking regulatory apparatus witnessed a radical transformation. Implementation of international best practices related to capital adequacy norms, asset classification, provisioning and income recognition were the key components of such regulatory reforms. A related reform was the adoption of a risk management system for identifying, measuring and mitigating different types of banking risks. Details of these aspects are provided in Chapters 6 and 7 of this book.

It is pertinent to note that the risk management criteria or parameters within a bank cannot be below the standards prescribed by the RBI. Nevertheless, there are subtle differences as regards the regulatory prescriptions on a particular aspect vis-à-vis internal risk management practices across banks on several counts. For example, the RBI prescribes following the *standardised approach* for calculation of capital charge on credit risk for the capital adequacy requirement. It does not mandate use of advanced internal rating models at the moment. But actual assessment of credit risk within a bank involves use of internal credit rating or score models. Hence, discussion on actual risk management practices within a bank is of considerable interest. These are over and above the regulatory prescriptions discussed in Chapter 7.

It is also important to note that risk management by banks cannot eliminate banking risks completely. Rather, practical risk management is about understanding the different dimensions of inherent risks in the banking business and applying this awareness skilfully to optimise risk-adjusted returns. In this perspective, the risk management framework of banks in India broadly comprises of the following key aspects:

- Putting in place the required organisational structure entrusted with the responsibility of overall risk management. Given its paramount importance, risk management is undertaken under the direct supervision of the top management of a bank. The top management outlines and approves the policies and procedures of a bank pertaining to risk management.

- Undertaking required technical analysis and using suitable models to identify and quantity various types of banking risks. Proper identification and measurement of such risks is a necessary prerequisite for risk management.
- Adherence by bank officials to risk management policies and procedures at the transaction level for all types of banking transactions
- Regular reporting to the top management about risk exposures and continuous monitoring through a well-designed feedback system

Thus, risk management in banks broadly covers identification, measurement, monitoring and mitigation of overall banking risks. It entails appropriate internal controls and mitigation procedures to contain overall risks within prudential limits. We have already discussed the various types of risks involved in the banking business and various methods to measure such risks in Chapter 6. So the identification and quantification facets have already been covered. In this chapter, we focus mainly on the internal monitoring and mitigation aspects of risk management as practised by banks in India.

The discussion in this chapter is based on information on risk management practices obtained from the official websites[1] of the RBI and select Indian banks, namely SBI, BOB, Canara Bank, HDFC Bank, Indian Bank, PNB, and so on.

The chapter is organised as follows. Section 8.2 outlines the broad organisational structure for risk management followed by banks in India. Credit risk stands as the most dominant component of overall banking risks. Necessary information about the multipronged approach that banks follow to mitigate credit risk is provided in section 8.3. Liquidity risk is a major day-to-day concern for banks. Likewise is interest rate risk which arises due to the adverse impact of interest rate fluctuations on a bank's profitability and balance sheet position. Following RBI guidelines, banks in India have put in place their respective ALM systems since the late 1990s to manage liquidity and interest rate risks. Details of the ALM system are provided in section 8.4. Risk mitigation procedures followed by banks in India to mitigate various types of market risks and operational risks are presented in section 8.5. Finally, section 8.6 presents the broad conclusions of this chapter.

[1] These websites were accessed during April–June 2023.

8.2 Organisational Structure for Risk Management: An Integrated Framework

8.2.1 Need for an Integrated Approach

In Chapter 6, we discussed various types of banking risks. In fact, each item of assets and liabilities in a bank's balance sheet is directly or indirectly exposed to a variety of risks. This makes risk management in banks very complicated and challenging. The following example highlights such complexities.

Let us take the example of a simple car loan of INR 10 lakh with a repayment period of five years. Say, the interest rate charged on the car loan is linked to an external benchmark such as the RBI's fixed repo rate under the LAF. Assume this car loan is funded by a term deposit of INR 10 lakh with three years maturity. Now, let us discuss the various types of risks which are linked to this car loan:

- First, the car loan bears default or credit risk if there is default on interest and/or principal repayment(s) by the borrower.
- Second, if the RBI reduces its repo rate, there is a drop in interest income on the car loan as compared to the projection. On the other hand, the interest rate paid by the bank on the term deposit is fixed in nature until renewal (if renewed) after maturity. Drop in interest income from the car loan due to repo rate reduction by the RBI as compared to the fixed interest cost on the term deposit reduces the NII for the bank. Thus, it entails interest rate risk.
- Third, the term deposit which funded the car loan is scheduled to mature on completion of three years. The loan repayment proceeds from the car loan may not cover the entire amount to honour the repayment of the term deposit. This is because the bank is yet to receive the loan repayments for the last two years (out of five years). Thus, the bank needs to arrange for the remaining funding requirement on maturity of the term deposit. This is a form of liquidity risk.
- Fourth, if the bank is able to renew the term deposit on maturity but has to offer a higher interest rate on its renewal, the NII of the bank falls.
- Fifth, if the bank has attempted to protect itself from credit risk on the car loan by using a credit derivative, then the bank is also exposed

to counterparty risk if the protection provider fails to honour the commitment when it is crystalised.

This example highlights how an asset like a simple car loan is associated with a variety of banking risks. Such types of risks are contracted at the transaction or branch level. But given the fact that various types of risks involved in any asset or liability are interlinked, it is imperative that a central authority in the bank undertakes the responsibility for risk management. An integrated approach to risk management is required. Needless to mention, for effective risk management, there has to be two-way communication between the top bank management and the branch-level officials. Our discussion in the following sections will reinforce this point.

There is another reason why the top management should have direct control over banking risk management. The central objective of the banking business is to maximise risk-adjusted returns. Therefore, risk management is integral to the core banking strategy. It cannot be separated from regular business decisions at the highest management level.

8.2.2 Organisational Structure

Based on the reasons discussed earlier and adhering to the RBI's guidelines, banks in India have put in place their respective organisational structures for risk management. Depending on the size of the bank, complexity of its assets and liabilities portfolio, its business model, its geographical spread, and so on, there are minor variations in the structure. The typical organisational structure for risk management in Indian banks is outlined in Figure 8.1.

At the top, risk management is under the direct control of the board of directors. The board has the responsibility to identify various dimensions of banking risks in the balance sheet and OBS items. In conformity with the RBI guidelines and considering the bank's own requirements, the board approves the guidelines for assessing risks in all forms of the banking business, prescribing methods of risk measurement, setting the procedure for risk mitigation, and so on. Such guidelines form part of a policy document of the bank duly approved by the highest authority. Across banks, these policy documents take the form of an integrated risk management policy; an ALM policy; a policy on credit, market and operational risk management; and Internal Capital Adequacy Assessment Process (ICAAP), among others. Every bank undertakes its regular business within the risk appetite

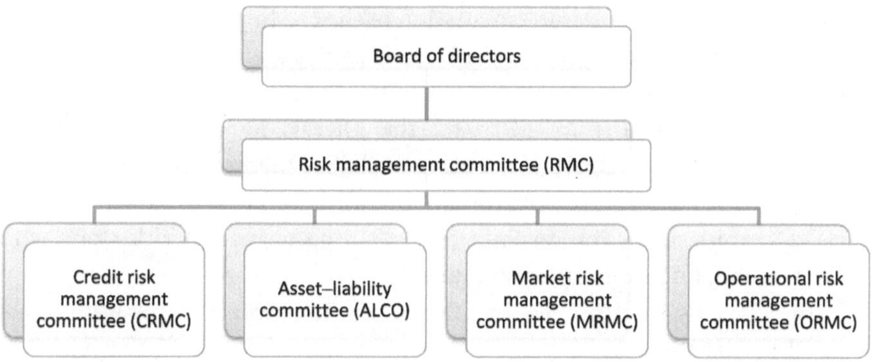

Figure 8.1 Organisational structure for risk management in Indian banks

Source: Prepared by the author.

parameters or limits under the broad guidelines stipulated in such policy document. The board reviews the policy guidelines at least once a year.

In PSBs, a board-level subcommittee designated as the risk management committee (RMC) generally takes up the responsibility of overseeing risk management in the bank. This body formulates and approves policy guidelines for various risks that the bank is exposed to. It receives periodic feedback from branch-level and mid-level bodies within the bank on actual risk crystallisation. It internally monitors compliance with board-approved guidelines in all business decisions having implications for banking risks as well as ensures non-violation of the RBI guidelines on risk management. Depending on the feedback on actual risk configuration and audit, the RMC revises its policy guidelines. In private banks, similar bodies with different nomenclatures take up this responsibility. For example, in HDFC Bank, the risk policy and monitoring committee (RPMC) plays a role akin to the RMC in PSBs.

The RMC is assisted by different internal committees or bodies in managing specific types of risks. As discussed in Chapter 6, mainly banking risks take the form of credit risk, liquidity risk, interest rate risk, market risk and operational risk. Accordingly, banks have formed specific committees to look after different types of risks. These are (*a*) credit risk management committee (CRMC), (*b*) asset–liability committee (ALCO), (*c*) market risk management committee (MRMC) and (*d*) operational risk management committee (ORMC). The names of the respective committees suggest the type of banking risk which each of them addresses. For example, the CRMC has responsibilities related to implementation of the credit policy and procedures set by the RMC. It undertakes credit risk analysis and actual control and management of credit risk in a bank. The ALCO manages liquidity and interest rate risks. The MRMC and the ORMC look after market and operational risks, respectively. In this regard also, there are minor variations across banks. For example, in Indian Bank, there is no separate MRMC. Its ALCO undertakes responsibilities pertaining to market risk along with management of liquidity risk and interest rate risk.

The various committees mentioned in the previous paragraph are headed by the top executives of a bank. For example, in SBI, the ALCO is headed by the chairman while the managing director (risk, compliance and stressed resolution group) plays an important role in overseeing internal risk management in the bank. The deputy managing director, who functions as the chief risk officer, coordinates and acts as the immediate supervisory authority for the risk management department (RMD) and the chief information security officer.

The RMD in banks is entrusted with the actual implementation of risk management policies. It monitors evolving risks at the transaction level and proposes necessary revisions to the policy guidelines, if any, to the RMC. The RMD is headed by top-level officials like a chief general manager (CGM) in the PSBs. Departments responsible for information security and internal audit form a critical part of the overall organisational structure in a bank for risk management. Within the RMD, in big banks like SBI, officers at the level of general manager (GM) or deputy general manager (DGM) are entrusted with the responsibility of management of specific types of banking risks such as credit risk, market risk, operational risk, enterprise and group risk, Basel implementation, portfolio management, and so on. In the following sections we provide details of internal risk management practices in banks.

8.3 Credit Risk Management: A Multipronged Approach

Credit risk manifests in the banking business in various forms. There could be defaults or delays in repayment of loans and advances. In the investment portfolio, the major constituent—that is, government securities—has zero default risk. However, in other treasury operations, defaults by counterparties under various contracts may cause credit risk. In OBS items like issue of guarantees, LCs, letters of comfort and financial derivatives, credit risk may arise if the counterparty fails to deliver as per the contract when the liability crystallises. Needless to mention, credit risk is mainly confined to loans and advances which overwhelmingly dominate a bank's asset portfolio.

As indicated earlier, the credit risk management department (CRMD) of banks under the overall supervision of the CRMC is entrusted with the responsibility for identification, assessment, measurement, monitoring, reporting and control of credit risks. The board-approved credit risk management policy is used as the main template for management of credit risk. Such policy outlines related standards and establishment of systems, procedures and controls. A bank's loan policy is closely associated with its credit risk management. The loan policy generally covers issues pertaining to organisation of the business, assessment of credit facilities and pricing of loans, due diligence in loan sanction, post-sanction follow-up and monitoring of advances, and delegation of financial power, among others. The credit risk management policy in a bank is complimented by its policy and practices on the conduct of stress tests, risk-rating policy for asset categorisation, risk modelling, and so on.

Banks in India follow a multipronged approach to manage credit risk. Let us discuss each component of this framework.

8.3.1 Assessing Creditworthiness, Pricing of Loans and Monitoring

The foundation of credit risk management in a bank is laid by the screening and assessment of creditworthiness of loan seekers. Banks use a variety of credit rating models or credit scores for this purpose. We have already discussed such models in Chapter 6. In fact, all loan proposals received by a bank are processed using credit ratings or scores for taking lending decisions. Depending on the risk factors derived from the credit ratings or scores which are juxtaposed with subjective risk parameters, borrowers are segregated into the low-, medium- or high-risk category. The *credit review mechanism* of a bank lays down the broad guidelines for such assessment. Accordingly, loans to borrowers are priced based on their credit ratings or scores with appropriate imposition of risk premium. Chapter 9 has explained in detail the determination of interest rate charges for borrowers based on their credit rating or score.

It may be noted that internal credit rating models used by banks are verified and validated by external agencies as per the RBI guidelines. This strengthens the robustness of the rating model used by banks.

For corporate borrowers, following the RBI guidelines, banks presently use credit ratings assigned by external rating agencies to obtain an independent and objective opinion about their creditworthiness. Domestic CRAs include Credit Analysis & Research Limited (CARE), Credit Rating Information Services of India Limited (CRISIL), India Ratings and Research, Investment Information and Credit Rating Agency of India Limited (ICRA), Brickwork Ratings India, SME Rating Agency of India and Infomerics. Popular international rating agencies include Fitch, Moody's, and Standard & Poor (S&P Global).

All banks in India have also established a structured *loan review mechanism* and internal *credit audit system* for assessing rating migration and facilitating regular review or audit of large-value loan accounts. The standard assets monitoring committees of banks periodically review accounts which have shown any signs of distress and require close monitoring. These are known as *special mention accounts*. Accordingly, prompt corrective action is envisaged to stem slippage of standard assets to NPAs.

8.3.2 Mitigation of Credit Risk: Conventional Ways

It may be reiterated here that it is impossible to wipe out credit risk completely in bank lending. However, with the adoption of prudent banking management tools, credit risk can be mitigated.

There are several conventional ways of mitigating credit risk. First, after loan disbursals, banks continuously monitor the business activities of borrowers, particularly the end-use of funds. As long as the funds availed through bank loans are judiciously used for the stated purposes, the probability of default is reduced. If there are deviations and consequently any default occurs on loan repayments, the lending bank can exercise its rights on the assets of the borrower and take over its business activities. This acts as a deterrent for diversion of funds by borrowers and reduces the moral hazard problem. Effective monitoring helps in timely action by the lending bank in this regard.

Second, banks often obtain security collaterals from borrowers. Such security collaterals take the form of first priority claim on the assets of the borrower against default on the loan, personal guarantee of the borrower, third-party guarantees, and so on. Mortgage against a home loan, hypothecation of a vehicle against an automobile loan, or use of raw materials and inventories as security collateral for working capital loans helps the lending bank reduce financial losses in case of loan default. Similarly, insisting on a margin requirement also reduces the bank's exposure and implicitly moderates credit risk.

RBI-imposed exposure limits on borrowers or groups of borrowers have been the third conventional tool used for moderating credit risk. Such limits reduce concentration risk and improve diversification of the loan portfolio of banks. Banks in India have put in place loan exposure limits on several counts. There are exposure limits on overall loans and advances to a single borrower or group. Based on different categories of borrowers, there are industry-wise, country-wise and inter-bank exposure limits, among others. Many banks even prescribe exposure limits in terms of credit rating or score category. Within the overall loan portfolio, certain segments like commercial real estate, credit card, exposure to equity, unsecured loans, and so on, are more vulnerable to credit risk. Banks set exposure limits for loans to sensitive sectors and unsecured loans.

While these conventional ways of managing credit risk continue to be the main plank of risk management practised by banks in India, since the 1990s there has been increasing emphasis on the Basel capital adequacy norms and use of financial innovations, summarised in the section that follows.

8.3.3 Mitigation of Credit Risk: Recent Innovations

With widespread adoption of financial innovations in the last two to three decades, banks have taken recourse to financial derivatives to mitigate or manage credit risk. Adoption of the Basel prudential norms requires capital charge on bank loans based on the risk embodied in such assets, as elaborated in the preceding chapters. Securitisation and credit derivatives are used by banks as innovative instruments to reduce credit risk as explained in following sections. Such instruments became popular as they helped banks avoid capital charge on securitised loans. Some financial derivatives also reduced the uncertainties pertaining to future cash flows from existing loan products.

8.3.3.1 Securitisation

In securitisation, the lending bank—that is, the originator of the loans—constructs a portfolio by pooling together a set of its loan accounts and sells it in the form of a financial security or derivative. For example, a set of mortgage loans can be combined to construct mortgage-backed securities (MBSs) which can be sold to investors such as investment banks, pension funds, venture capital funds, and so on. Investors or buyers of such securities become entitled to the cash flows generated from the repayment process of the constituent loans in the portfolio which are securitised.

Once such loans are sold through securitisation or are securitised, they do not appear in the concerned bank's balance sheet. The bank is relieved from capital charge on such loans. Credit risk on such loans for the loan originator or the lending bank is thus concealed. On the other hand, excess amount earned from the sale proceeds of the loan or asset securitisation over the principal adds to the bank's profitability. In other words, excess income earned out of this securitisation process over the principal amount of the loans provides positive net income to banks. Surplus cash flows out of the original loans under securitisation over the cost of investment is the income or profit for the investors or buyers of such financial securities or derivatives. Thus, actual cash flows consisting of principal repayments and interest charges out of the portfolio of securitised loans are partly shared by the lending banks or loan originators with the remaining part going to the investors.

For example, say, a portfolio of loans of Bank X is securitised and sold in the market for INR 1,000 crore. For convenience, let us assume all such loans were securitised on the same day they were originated. Assume, the principal amount of the constituent loans extended by Bank X is INR 910 crore and the future cash flow of loan repayments along with interest charges on such loans is INR 1,100 crore. Ignoring the inflation factor, net income for Bank X is INR 1,000 crore – INR 910 crore = INR 90 crore. On the other hand, net income for the investors is INR 1,100 crore – INR 1,000 crore = INR 100 crore. Thus, total income out of the lending for this portfolio of loans at INR 190 crore is distributed between Bank X and the investors as illustrated in the example.

Further, as observed in the run up to the GFC of 2007–08, investors who bought securities like MBSs, in turn, created a second layer of financial derivatives by pooling the MBSs in their portfolio. This second layer of derivatives took the form of collateralised debt obligations (CDOs). Thus, several layers of financial derivatives were created out of the original bank loans.

Thus, securitisation wipes out credit risk in a bank's balance sheet through a process of financial engineering. It was used as a popular tool in advanced economies prior to the GFC of 2007–08. The GFC exposed the adverse consequences of the mindless use of securitisation to reduce capital charge on credit risk as also in search of high returns.

In India, securitisation of bank loans for managing credit risk has been very limited. The RBI had issued a set of guidelines on securitisation of standard assets in February 2006 involving simple structures and stable ratings. In the post-GFC period, asset quality concerns undermined investor appetite for securitisation the world over. In this backdrop, the RBI refined the regulatory prescriptions on securitisation and issued revised guidelines in May 2012. The extant guidelines, inter alia, include norms on minimum holding period, minimum retention requirement, prohibition of securitisation of single loans, loan origination standards and standards of due diligence (RBI, 2012). Broadly, such regulations envisage mitigation of the moral hazard problem associated with the 'origin and distribute' model in bank lending through securitisation. Banks or originators of the loans are compelled to hold such assets in their balance sheet for a certain minimum period before securitisation is permitted. Moreover, it is ensured that they continue to have some stake in their loans even after securitisation.

8.3.3.2 Credit Derivatives

Credit derivatives became popular tools of credit risk mitigation since the 1990s. They are similar to securitisation as an innovation in the financial engineering process. The mechanism through which credit derivatives are used to mitigate credit risk is explained as follows.

The lending bank which wants to buy a credit derivative to protect itself against credit risk is the *protection buyer*. The loan or asset against which credit risk is covered is known as the *reference obligation*. The agency or counterparty which sells a credit derivative is the *protection seller*. By purchasing a credit derivative, the lending bank or protection buyer transfers credit risk in the reference obligation to the counterparty (protection seller) against a notional value. This involves payment of a fee or premium to the protection seller. In case of a credit event like default on the reference obligation (loan), the lending bank is compensated for the loss by the protection seller. Thus, credit derivatives protect the lending bank from loss due to credit risk. Credit default swaps, interest rate swaps and options are popular credit derivatives used in advanced economies.

It may be noted that unlike in securitisation, the ownership of or entitlement to the assets or loans is not transferred from the lending bank or loan originator to the investors. Credit derivatives are pooled out of a variety of assets such as loans, bonds, account receivables, and so on. Credit risk in such bundles of assets is isolated and traded in the market in the form of credit derivatives. Moreover, in several credit derivatives, uncertainties in future cash flows due to interest rate or exchange rate fluctuations are mitigated. These are OBS items.

Use of credit derivatives for risk management by Indian banks has been very limited, particularly in the domestic market. However, for a variety of external exposures, banks in India have been using several forms of financial derivatives such as interest rate swaps, forward rate agreements and other plain vanilla financial derivatives to mitigate credit risk. Details about such derivatives are provided under OBS items in Chapter 10.

8.3.4 Capital Adequacy Requirements

As detailed in Chapter 7, since the 1990s capital adequacy requirements form the mainstay of banking regulatory prescriptions for credit risk management. As per the RBI's Basel III prescriptions, banks in India are using the *standardised approach* for credit risk measurement. Technical details of the same have been provided in Chapters 6 and 7. Accordingly, banks ensure maintenance of a minimum capital position to comply with the RBI's CRAR stipulations. Besides overall CRAR requirements, banks also adhere to related stipulations as regards the CET1 capital ratio and tier-1 capital ratio, separately. They further comply with the CCB of 2.5 per cent and additional CET 1 requirements of 0.2–0.6 per cent for DSIBs.

Needless to mention, these CRAR stipulations imposed by the RBI cover the capital charge for market and operational risk as well as credit risk. Capital adequacy requirements are envisaged to meet a variety of objectives, including protecting the interest of depositors and creditors against any unforeseen losses as well as discouraging excessive risk taking by banks.

Using alternative macroeconomic scenarios, business projections, and so on, banks undertake stress tests and scenario analyses and make projections on their capital position for nearly five years ahead. Such stress tests are conducted on a quarterly basis. RBI-prescribed scenarios are juxtaposed with bank-specific alternative circumstances for this purpose. Banks also undertake macroeconomic and micro-segment-centric scenario analyses. Business verticals like retail, corporate, agriculture, MSMEs, and so on, are considered as micro-segments for the latter.

This summarises how banks in India undertake management of credit risk.

8.4 ALM System and ALCO

Greater operational autonomy acquired by banks during the post-reform period concomitantly raised their strategic responsibilities in banking management. Consequently, judicious management of assets and liabilities is considered to be the most important to meet the broad objectives of profitability, solvency and liquidity. Business decisions on composition of assets and liabilities, balancing the diverse characteristics of liquidity, interest income, and cost and risk parameters, form the core of overall business strategy. Following RBI guidelines, banks in India have put in place their respective ALM systems. Initially, the ALM system was conceived to address liquidity risk and interest rate risk management. It envisaged balancing assets and liabilities of banks within different time buckets so that excess of liabilities over assets at different time horizons are contained within tolerable limits. For example, if the quantum of liabilities of a bank maturing overnight is less than its assets with corresponding maturity, it does not face liquidity risk. On the contrary, if the amount of liabilities with overnight maturity is higher than assets maturing overnight, the bank encounters liquidity risk. To meet such liability mismatch, the concerned bank needs to borrow from the RBI or approach the money markets. As discussed earlier, persistence of liquidity deficiency or liquidity risk of higher order may lead to erosion of the confidence of depositors and bank run–like situations. The ALM system of a bank assumes paramount importance in this context.

Banks in India established their respective ALM systems from April 1999 adhering to the RBI's guidelines. The ALM guidelines were finetuned in 2007, extending the scope of the ALM system from liquidity and interest rate risk management to covering responsibilities pertaining to asset–liability composition, pricing of assets and liabilities, along with reviewing interest rate outlook, projection of business growth and associated capital and profit planning, review of investment and forex portfolios, and so on. Preparation of structural liquidity statements, maintenance of LCR and NSFR, submission of reports to the regulatory authorities, and conduct of various stress tests to assess the configuration of interest rate risk and liquidity risk under different adverse scenarios, among others, were also added to its responsibilities. Thus,

ALM has gained strategic importance for guiding and undertaking regular banking operations.

In this chapter, we are confined to the relevance of the ALM system for liquidity and interest rate risk management in banks. Its role in broader strategic banking operations is covered in Chapter 10.

8.4.1 ALCO

ALM-related responsibilities in banks in India are entrusted to their respective ALCOs. The ALCO is a decision-making body with responsibility for balance sheet planning based on risk–return considerations. The major responsibilities of ALCOs are as follows:

- Strategic decisions related to management of liquidity and interest rate risks
- Operational issues related to ALM such as formulating the bank's business and management strategy, setting the limits for various risk parameters and monitoring such limits, and initiating prompt corrective action as required
- Ensuring adherence to the prudential limits set by the board
- Articulating key business decisions pertaining to the tenures of deposits, source and mix of other liabilities, sale of assets, tenures of loans and investments, and so on, conforming to overall requirements as regards the desired maturity profile and composition of incremental liabilities and assets
- Guiding the central strategy of the bank on pricing of loans and deposits
- Ensuring availability of adequate liquidity and managing repricing risk
- Conduct of stress tests, undertaking scenario analyses and putting in place a contingent funding plan in this context
- As regards liquidity management, the ALCO monitors the structural liquidity profile of the bank and its LCR and NSFR positions
- Policy documents related to ALM, ICAAP and stress tests are prepared under the guidance of the ALCO

All these functions and responsibilities of the ALCO balance the overall long-term objective of the bank to promote shareholders' wealth with short-run business decisions to maximise the NII and net interest margin (NIM) of the bank. In this perspective, it periodically monitors and reviews the risk–return profile for all business decisions, various sources of funds and deployment of such funds. As part of regular operational decisions, the ALCO sets benchmark lending rates such as the base rate, MCLR, external benchmarking and card rates on deposits. It directs investment activities in consonance with the bank's overall policies on investment, market risk management, trading policy related to forex and derivatives, and so on.

Given its importance, the ALCO is generally headed by the bank's top executive. It also includes heads of all important departments of the bank as its members. Such departments are economic research, credit, investment, treasury or funds management, international banking, and so on. In SBI, the ALCO is headed by the chairman. Its managing directors (MDs) and deputy managing directors (DMDs) are members. The ALM department or support group provides the ALCO with relevant information, technical analysis and all necessary assistance including secretarial support. The ALCO meets at least once a month or more frequently depending on the requirement.

The RMC, a board-level subcommittee, approves various decisions taken by the ALCO and oversees implementation of ALM in banks.

8.4.2 ALM and Management of Liquidity Risk

Liquidity risk arises when a bank fails to honour a liability on maturity due to lack of funds. This can vary across different time buckets depending on asset–liability mismatches within each specified time window. Accordingly, funding requirements can be assessed.

The RBI had prescribed construction of a maturity ladder to assess asset–liability mismatches and consequent funding requirements in its 1999 ALM guidelines (RBI, 1999a). The maturity ladder consisted of eight time buckets, namely (*a*) 1–14 days, (*b*) 15–28 days, (*c*) 29 days–3 months, (*d*) 3–6 months, (*e*) 6–12 months, (*f*) 1–2 years, (*g*) 2–5 years and (*h*) over 5 years. The RBI's 2007 ALM guidelines further divided the *first* time bucket into three, namely (*a*) next day (overnight), (*b*) 2–7 days and (*c*) 8–14 days.

Banks are required to calculate residual maturity for all items under their assets and liabilities portfolio over different time buckets. Accordingly, asset–liability mismatches and consequent liquidity risk are assessed. The RBI's guidelines provide necessary details on how to place different items of a bank's balance sheet across specific time buckets. The RBI's 2007 ALM guidelines on construction of a maturity profile for assessing liquidity risk are reproduced in Table 8A.1. This helps in comparing inflow of funds out of maturing assets and outflow of funds to honour maturing liabilities across different time horizons. This, in turn, enables calculation of cumulative surplus or deficit fund position at different maturity dates.

We have already discussed construction of a maturity ladder of cash inflows and outflows under different time buckets and assessment of liquidity gap in Chapter 6. The chapter highlighted how liquidity risk is assessed under normal business conditions as well as under alternative scenarios with bank-specific and systemic adverse developments.

As prescribed by the RBI's 2007 ALM guidelines, banks are required to prepare their respective *statements of structural liquidity*. A prototype of this is provided in Table 8A.2. Based on the maturity profile of assets and liabilities of a bank, the timing of cash inflows and outflows is assessed over different time horizons. Rupee inflows or outflows arising due to various forex operations are also taken into account. The RBI has prescribed tolerance limits for asset–liability gaps across different buckets. Particularly, asset–liability mismatch up to a one-year time horizon under different time buckets is relevant for assessing liquidity risks. A severe gap, especially excessive liabilities over assets up to one year, provides an early warning signal for evolving liquidity concerns. Banks follow internal prudential limits for asset–liability mismatches. Such limits have to be approved by the board of the bank and monitored by the ALCO as indicated earlier.

Needless to mention, asset–liability mismatches at shorter time horizons are of great concern from the liquidity risk management point of view. As per the RBI's 2007 ALM guidelines, the net cumulative negative mismatch (liabilities over assets) should not exceed 20 per cent of the cumulative cash outflows (liabilities) for the '15–28 days' residual maturity segments. The limit for the gap is tapered down for shorter time buckets. For example, net cumulative mismatches for the time buckets of '8–14 days', '2–7 days' and 'next day' are stipulated not to exceed 15 per cent, 10 per cent and 5 per cent of the cumulative cash outflow in the respective buckets. Thus, the tolerance limit for short-term maturity mismatches is more stringent.

It may be noted that over and above the regulatory guidelines of the RBI on tolerance limits for liquidity mismatches, some banks have their own internal limits for other time buckets too. For example, SBI has stipulated its own tolerance cumulative gap limits of 20 per cent for all time buckets from over 1 month up to 15 years.

Banks in India prepare their statement of structural liquidity on a daily basis and submit the same to the RBI on a fortnightly basis. Banks are also required to monitor their short-term liquidity position for 90-day periods as per the *statement of short-term dynamic liquidity* prescribed by the RBI. A prototype of the same is given in Table 8A.3. It incorporates projections under various hypothetical situations and a variety of outflow commitments.

The Indian economy became highly globalised during the post-reform period. Rationalisation of import tariffs, phasing out of the import quota system and adoption of a market-determined exchange rate system facilitated rapid increase in India's exports and imports. Moreover, liberalisation of cross-border capital flows enhanced financial integration of the Indian economy with leading financial hubs around the world. Banks are major players in the forex market. Rapid increase in international trade and investment has correspondingly raised the currency risk exposures of Indian banks. Currency risk arises if a bank has serious mismatches in its assets versus liabilities denominated in a foreign currency. For example, if a bank has excess USD-denominated liabilities over USD-denominated assets in a particular time bucket, it may face difficulties in meeting the outflow requirements from its USD inflows within that time horizon. This leads to currency risk. Moreover, variation in the INR–USD exchange rate may have implications for the bank's INR liquidity position if there is any mismatch in its asset–liability position denominated in USDs. The ALM is finetuned to also monitor and manage currency risk in the banking business.

8.4.3 ALM and Management of Interest Rate Risk

As discussed in Chapter 6, interest rate risk is a dominant form of banking risk. This arises due to movement of market interest rates having adverse consequences for a bank's profitability and balance sheet position. If interest rates on deposits rise faster than those on loans, then costs of deposits increase by a higher amount as compared to interest earnings on loans. This adversely affects bank profitability. On the contrary, if interest rates on bank deposits are sticky while those on bank loans witness downward movement, a bank's profitability is again adversely affected. Similarly, adverse movements in interest rates can reduce the mark-to-market value of tradeable assets in a bank's balance sheet. This diminishes the market value of a bank's equity.

In India, the reforms since the early 1990s created a market-oriented regime for determination of interest rates in various segments of the financial market as detailed earlier. Banks acquired greater operational autonomy in fixing interest rates on their deposits and loans. The government securities and money markets became active. Such reforms exposed banks to interest rate risks. In this perspective, the RBI's ALM guidelines envisaged adoption of traditional gap analysis for management of interest rate risk.

Traditional gap analysis measures the mismatches between assets and liabilities which are interest-rate sensitive. Such mismatches are monitored over different time intervals, such as (*a*) less than 1 month, (*b*) 1–3 months, (*c*) 3–6 months, (*d*) 6 months–1 year, (*e*) 1–3 years, (*f*) 3–5 years and (*g*) more than 5 years. Assets and liabilities which are not sensitive to variation in interest rates are placed separately. Broadly, interest-rate sensitive assets and liabilities are placed under any one such time bucket based on their residual maturity or repricing date. Table 8A.4 provides necessary details on classification of various items of banking assets and liabilities as per their interest-rate sensitivity and specific time-bucket category.

Using such classification criteria, the mismatch between interest-sensitive assets and liabilities for a particular time bucket can be calculated. The quantum of mismatch is known as the *gap*. As per the RBI's ALM guidelines, if interest-sensitive assets exceed interest-sensitive liabilities under a particular time bucket, the gap is treated as positive. Similarly, if interest-sensitive liabilities are higher than such assets, it is termed a negative gap. This implies that the financial position of a bank deteriorates on rise of market interest rates if the bank has a negative gap in any time bucket. Similarly, downward movement of market interest rates will be harmful for the financial health of the bank if it has a positive gap. Thus, *gap analysis* is used to assess the interest rate risk of banks.

Banks in India have put in place prudential limits for the maximum gap under various time buckets with the due approval of their board and monitored by the ALCO.

8.4.4 LCR and NSFR

Learning from the experience of the GFC of 2007–08 and with the adoption of the Basel III prudential norms, the RBI has further strengthened the liquidity risk management framework of banks in India. Guidelines on LCR under

Basel III were issued in June 2014 (RBI, 2014). The main objective of LCR is to ensure that each bank maintains adequate HQLAs over shorter time horizons to cover liquidity requirements under a liquidity stress scenario. It stipulates that the stock of HQLAs in a bank within a 30-day window should be above the net cash outflows of the bank. Banks in India commenced implementation of LCR norms since 2015 and by 2019 successfully achieved the target of 'above 100 per cent' for LCR.

As per the Basel III guidelines, concerns over long-term funding risks of banks are addressed through implementation of NSFR requirements. The guidelines on NSFR liquidity standards were issued by the RBI in May 2018 (RBI, 2018). With the objective of mitigating future funding stress on banks, NFSR guidelines require conducting the banking business with sufficiently stable sources of funding. They entail assessment of the required stable funding (RSF) of a bank over a one-year horizon based on the liquidity characteristics and residual maturity of various assets in the bank's balance sheet as well as OBS exposures. The amount of available stable funding (ASF) is calculated as the portion of reliable capital and other liabilities over a one-year period. The NFSR, which is the ratio of ASF to RSF, is to be maintained at above 100 per cent. The RBI made NFSR stipulations effective since October 2021 and now banks in India are NSFR compliant.

8.4.5 ALM Information System

ALM is heavily based on granular data on loans, investments, deposits, and so on, across all maturities as well as interest rates applicable to all such items. This requires putting in place a very elaborate information management system (IMS) encapsulating detailed data on different items of a bank's balance sheet. PSBs in particular have widely dispersed branches spread across the country. Prior to the IT and ITES in the Indian banking system, consolidation of data on various banking indicators used to be an extremely cumbersome task. With establishment of advanced IT and networking infrastructures during the post-reform period, banks in India have adopted core banking solution (CBS) systems. This has facilitated real-time data transfer and updates, thus integrating data from far-flung bank branches with the central or head office comprehensively.

The ALCO monitors the residual maturity of various items in a bank's balance sheet based on data on loans, capital market investments and money market exposures including forex operations. Using this historical data, the

ALCO analyses evolving situations related to liquidity and market risk under various hypothetical developments. For example, if the market interest rates increase by 1 per cent, it can have related implications for interest income and costs across different assets and liabilities of banks over different terms to maturity. Accordingly, its impact on the NII, NIM, market risk, liquidity risk, and so on, can be analysed under alternative hypothetical scenarios. A robust and comprehensive ALM database is thus an essential prerequisite for effective functioning of ALM systems in banks.

8.5 Market and Operational Risk Management

8.5.1 Market Risk Management

Market risk in the banking business refers to the adverse impact of movements in market interest rates, forex rates, equity prices, and so on, on a bank's balance sheet position. As per the RBI's Basel III guidelines, banks in India at present follow the *standardised duration approach* for the measurement of market risk and comply with related capital adequacy requirements. The RMC is the concerned authority in Indian banks which puts in place appropriate institutional infrastructure for identification, measurement, monitoring and control of market risk. A bank's MRMC or ALCO undertakes the actual implementation of market risk management.

Banks in India use a host of statistical and non-statistical measures to obtain a comprehensive view of actual market risk exposure. Standard market risk measurement tools, as discussed in Chapter 6—namely VaR, earnings at risk, modified duration, and so on—are used in this regard. Net overnight open position limits, individual gap limits and aggregate gap limits are used to contain market risks of different kinds.

Banks also undertake regular stress tests and scenario analyses to visualise their vulnerability to market risk under some hypothetical but plausible extreme unfavourable shocks. The same are reported to the MRMC or ALCO on a quarterly basis.

The mid-office in a bank monitors treasury operations having implications for market risks on a day-to-day basis and reports the same to the designated authority like the chief risk officer in many banks. A comprehensive report on market risk assessment is submitted to the MRMC or ALCO on a monthly basis.

8.5.2 Operational Risk Management

Managing operational risk in a bank is problematic as its concrete location and measurement is quite challenging. The challenge emanates from the fact that operational risk in banks is hidden but is embedded in the entire banking business. It may manifest in a variety of ways and has the potential to cause massive financial and reputational loss to a bank. Banking frauds and cybercrime-related incidents cause huge financial losses both to bank customers and the bank itself.

The nature of operational risk management in a bank is determined by the volume of its business, diversity, sophistication and complexity embedded in its balance sheet and OBS items, and so on. Banks in India have put in place internal control systems to manage and overcome any deficiency and inadequacy in internal processes and systems, human errors of omission and commission, and losses due to external events. Operation risk management is undertaken under oversight of the bank's board. The policies and manuals pertaining to operational risk management are well laid out and placed on the intranet of banks for easy access by their officials and managers. This includes setting up of a web-based operational risk management system which captures, measures and monitors risk parameters.

Banks undertake risk-control self-assessment to establish the validity of internal controls and undertake necessary upgradations as required. As a backup to reduce potential damage caused by operational risk, banks in India have established business continuity plans (BCPs). The BCP ensures provision of banking services as and when banking operations suffer due to disruptive events. Its main objective is to facilitate business continuity while managing any disruption. The endeavour is to enable the BCP to cover all possible events across the branches of a bank. Banks also undertake periodic checks to verify their preparedness in the face of hypothetical events or disruptions as well as scenario analyses using expert services to examine exposure and potential losses in case of high-severity events.

8.6 Conclusion

The bottom line in the banking business is to maximise risk-adjusted returns. How banks optimise interest and non-interest earnings through undertaking general banking management operations is taken up in Part IV of this book. This chapter covered how banks carry out banking risk management responsibilities. It started by providing an introduction to the organisational structure for banking risk management in Indian banks. It then elaborately discussed credit risk and liquidity risk management in banks. Credit and liquidity risks overwhelm all risks in banking. The chapter also covered briefly the practical aspects of market and operational risk management in Indian banks.

Appendix 8A

Table 8A.1 Time buckets for future cash flows of banks

Heads of accounts	Classification into time buckets
A. Outflows	
1. Capital, reserves and surplus	Over 5 years bucket
2. Demand deposits (current and savings bank deposits)	Savings bank and current deposits may be classified into volatile and core portions. Savings bank (10%) and current (15%) Deposits are generally withdrawable on demand. This portion may be treated as volatile. While the volatile portion can be placed in day 1, 2–7 days and 8–14 days time buckets, depending upon the experience and estimates of banks, the core portion may be placed in over 1–3 years bucket. The above classification of savings bank and current deposits is only *a benchmark*. Banks which are better equipped to estimate the behavioural pattern, roll-in and roll-out, embedded options, etc., on the basis of past data/ empirical studies could classify them in the appropriate buckets, i.e., **behavioural** maturity instead of **contractual** maturity, subject to the approval of the Board/ALCO.
3. Term deposits	Respective maturity buckets. Banks which are better equipped to estimate the behavioural pattern, roll-in and roll-out, embedded options, etc., on the basis of past data/ empirical studies could classify the **retail deposits** in the appropriate buckets on the basis of **behavioural** maturity rather than **residual maturity**. However, the **wholesale deposits** should be shown under respective maturity buckets. (Wholesale deposits for the purpose of this statement may be Rs 15 lakh or any such higher threshold approved by the bank's board.)

(Contd)

Table 8A.1 (*Contd*)

Heads of accounts	Classification into time buckets
4. Certificates of deposit, borrowings and bonds (including subordinated debt)	Respective maturity buckets. Where call/put options are built into the issue structure of any instrument/s, the call/put date/s should be reckoned as the maturity date/s and the amount should be shown in the respective time buckets.
5. **Other liabilities and provisions**	
(i) Bills payable	(i) The core component which could reasonably be estimated on the basis of past data and behavioural pattern may be shown under 'over 1–3 years' time bucket. The balance amount may be placed in day 1, 2–7 days and 8–14 days buckets, as per behavioural pattern.
(ii) Provisions other than for loan loss and depreciation in investments	(ii) Respective buckets depending on the purpose
(iii) Other liabilities	(iii) Respective maturity buckets. Items not representing cash payables (i.e., income received in advance, etc.) may be placed in over 5 years bucket.
6. Export refinance – availed	Respective maturity buckets of underlying assets
B. Inflows	
1. Cash	Day 1 bucket
2. Balances with RBI	While the excess balance over the required CRR/SLR may be shown under day 1 bucket, the statutory balances may be distributed amongst various time buckets corresponding to the maturity profile of DTL with a time-lag of 14 days.
3. **Balances with other banks**	
(i) Current account	(i) Non-withdrawable portion on account of stipulations of minimum balances may be shown under 'over 1–3 years' bucket and the remaining balances may be shown under day 1 bucket.
(ii) Money at call and short notice, term deposits and other placements	(ii) Respective maturity buckets

(*Contd*)

Table 8A.1 *(Contd)*

Heads of accounts	Classification into time buckets
4. **Investments (net of provisions)**	
(i) Approved securities	(i) Respective maturity buckets, excluding the amount required to be reinvested to maintain SLR corresponding to the DTL profile in various time buckets
(ii) Corporate debentures and bonds, PSU bonds, CDs and CPs, redeemable preference shares, units of mutual funds (close ended), etc.	(ii) Respective maturity buckets. Investments classified as NPIs should be shown under over 3–5 years bucket (substandard) or over 5 years bucket (doubtful)
(iii) Shares	(iii) Listed shares (except strategic investments) in '2–7 days' bucket, with a haircut of 50%. Other shares in 'over 5 years' bucket.
(iv) Units of mutual funds (open ended)	(iv) Day 1 bucket
(v) Investments in subsidiaries/joint ventures	(v) Over 5 years bucket
(vi) Securities in the trading book	(vi) Day 1, 2–7 days, 8–14 days, 15–28 days and 29–90 days according to defeasance periods
5. **Advances (performing)**	
(i) Bills purchased and discounted (including bills under derivative usance promissory notes [DUPN])	(i) Respective maturity buckets
(ii) Cash credit/ Overdraft (including temporary overdrafts [TOD]) and demand loan component of working capital	(ii) Banks should undertake a study of behavioural and seasonal pattern of availments based on outstandings and the core and volatile portion should be identified. While the volatile portion could be shown in the near-term maturity buckets, the core portion may be shown under 'over 1–3 years' bucket.

(Contd)

Table 8A.1 *(Contd)*

Heads of accounts	Classification into time buckets
(iii) Term loans	(iii) Interim cash flows may be shown under respective maturity buckets.
6. NPAs (net of provisions, interest suspense and claims received from ECGC/ DICGC)	
(i) Sub-standard	(i) 'Over 3–5 years' bucket
(ii) Doubtful and loss	(ii) 'Over 5 years' bucket
7. Fixed assets/assets on lease	'Over 5 years' bucket/Interim cash flows may be shown under respective maturity buckets
8. Other assets	
Intangible assets	Intangible assets and assets not representing cash receivables may be shown in 'over 5 years' bucket.
C. Off-balance sheet items	
1. Lines of credit committed/available	
(i) Lines of credit committed to/ from institutions	(i) Day 1 bucket
(ii) Unavailed portion of cash credit/ overdraft/ demand loan component of working capital limits (outflow)	(ii) Banks should undertake a study of the behavioural and seasonal pattern of potential availments in the accounts and the amounts so arrived at may be shown under relevant maturity buckets up to 12 months
(iii) Export refinance – unavailed (inflow)	(iii) Day 1 bucket
2. Contingent liabilities Letters of credit/ Guarantees (outflow)	Devolvement of letters of credit/guarantees initially entails cash outflows. Thus, historical trend analysis ought to be conducted on the devolvements and the amounts so arrived at in respect of outstanding letters of credit/guarantees (net of margins) should be distributed amongst various time buckets. The assets created out of devolvements may be shown under respective maturity buckets on the basis of probable recovery dates.

(Contd)

Table 8A.1 *(Contd)*

Heads of accounts	Classification into time buckets
Other inflows/Outflows	
(i) Repos/Bills rediscounted (DUPN)/CBLO/ Swaps INR/USD, maturing forex forward contracts, etc. (outflow/inflow)	(i) Respective maturity buckets
(ii) Interest payable/ receivable (outflow/ inflow) – accrued interests which are appearing in the books on the reporting day	(ii) Respective maturity buckets

Source: 'Appendix – I', Asset–Liability Management (ALM) System, Notifications, RBI, https://rbidocs.rbi.org.in/rdocs/notification/PDFs/80878.pdf (accessed 12 July 2022).

Note: (*a*) Liability on account of event cash flows i.e. short fall in CRR balance on reporting Fridays, wage settlement, capital expenditure, etc. which are known to the banks and any other contingency may be shown under respective maturity buckets. The event cash outflows, including incremental SLR requirement, should be reported against 'outflows – others'. (*b*) All overdue liabilities may be placed in the day 1, 2–7 days and 8–14 days buckets, based on behavioural estimates. (*c*) Interest and instalments from advances and investments, which are overdue for less than one month, may be placed in day 1, 2–7 days and 8–14 days buckets, based on behavioural estimates. Further, interest and instalments due (before classification as NPAs) may be placed in the 29 days–3 months bucket if the earlier receivables remain uncollected.

Table 8A.2 Statement of structural liquidity

Name of the bank ____________________

Statement of structural liquidity as on ____________________

(INR crore)

	Residual maturity										
Outflows	**Day 1**	**2–7 days**	**8–14 days**	**15–28 Days**	**29 days and up to 3 months**	**Over 3 months and up to 6 months**	**Over 6 months and up to 1 year**	**Over 1 year and up to 3 years**	**Over 3 years and up to 5 years**	**Over 5 years**	**Total**
1. Capital											
2. Reserves and surplus											
3. Deposits	XXX	XXX	XXX	XXX	XXX	XXX	XXX	XXX	XXX	XXX	XXX
(i) Current deposits											
(ii) Savings bank deposits											
(iii) Term deposits											
(iv) Certificates of deposit											
4. Borrowings	XXX	XXX	XXX	XXX	XXX	XXX	XXX	XXX	XXX	XXX	XXX
(i) Call and short notice											
(ii) Inter-bank (term)											
(iii) Refinances											
(iv) Others (specify)											

(Contd)

Table 8A.2 *(Contd)*

Outflows	Residual maturity										
	Day 1	2–7 days	8–14 days	15–28 Days	29 days and up to 3 months	Over 3 months and up to 6 months	Over 6 months and up to 1 year	Over 1 year and up to 3 years	Over 3 years and up to 5 years	Over 5 years	Total
5. Other liabilities and provisions	XXX	XXX	XXX	XXX	XXX	XXX	XXX	XXX	XXX	XXX	XXX
(i) Bills payable											
(ii) Provisions											
(iii) Others											
6. Lines of credit committed to	XXX	XXX	XXX	XXX	XXX	XXX	XXX	XXX	XXX	XXX	XXX
(i) Institutions											
(ii) Customers											
7. Unavailed portion of cash Credit/Overdraft/Demand loan component of working capital											
8. Letters of credit/Guarantees											
9. Repos											

(Contd)

Table 8A.2 *(Contd)*

	Residual maturity										
Outflows	**Day 1**	**2–7 days**	**8–14 days**	**15–28 Days**	**29 days and up to 3 months**	**Over 3 months and up to 6 months**	**Over 6 months and up to 1 year**	**Over 1 year and up to 3 years**	**Over 3 years and up to 5 years**	**Over 5 years**	**Total**
10. Bills rediscounted (DUPN)											
11. Swaps (buy/sell)/ Maturing forwards											
12. Interest payable											
13. Others (specify)											
A. Total outflows											
B. Cumulative outflows											

	Residual maturity										
Inflows	Day 1	2–7 days	8–14 days	15–28 days	29 days and up to 3 months	Over 3 months and up to 6 months	Over 6 months and up to 1 year	Over 1 year and up to 3 years	Over 3 years and up to 5 years	Over 5 years	Total
1. Cash											
2. Balances with RBI											
3. Balances with other banks	XXX	XXX	XXX	XXX	XXX	XXX	XXX	XXX	XXX	XXX	XXX
(i) Current account											

(Contd)

Table 8A.2 *(Contd)*

Inflows	Residual maturity										
	Day 1	2–7 days	8–14 days	15–28 days	29 days and up to 3 months	Over 3 months and up to 6 months	Over 6 months and up to 1 year	Over 1 year and up to 3 years	Over 3 years and up to 5 years	Over 5 years	Total
(ii) Money at call and short notice, term deposits and other placements											
4. Investments (including those under repos but excluding reverse repos)											
5. Advances (performing)	XXX	XXX	XXX	XXX	XXX	XXX	XXX	XXX	XXX	XXX	XXX
(i) Bills purchased and discounted (including bills under DUPN)											
(ii) Cash credits, overdrafts and loans repayable on demand											
(iii) Term loans											
6. NPAs (advances and investments)*											

(Contd)

Table 8A.2 *(Contd)*

	Residual maturity										
Inflows	**Day 1**	**2–7 days**	**8–14 days**	**15–28 days**	**29 days and up to 3 months**	**Over 3 months and up to 6 months**	**Over 6 months and up to 1 year**	**Over 1 year and up to 3 years**	**Over 3 years and up to 5 years**	**Over 5 years**	**Total**
7. Fixed assets											
8. Other assets	XXX	XXX	XXX	XXX	XXX	XXX	XXX	XXX	XXX	XXX	XXX
(i) Leased assets											
(ii) Others											
9. Reverse repos											
10. Swaps (sell/buy)/ Maturing forwards											
11. Bills rediscounted (DUPN)											
12. Interest receivable											
13. Committed lines of credit											
14. Export refinance from RBI											
15. Others (specify)											
C. Total inflows											
D. Mismatch (C-A)											

(Contd)

Table 8A.2 *(Contd)*

	Residual maturity										
Inflows	**Day 1**	**2–7 days**	**8–14 days**	**15–28 days**	**29 days and up to 3 months**	**Over 3 months and up to 6 months**	**Over 6 months and up to 1 year**	**Over 1 year and up to 3 years**	**Over 3 years and up to 5 years**	**Over 5 years**	**Total**
E. Mismatch as % to outflows (D as % to A)											
F. Cumulative mismatch											
G. Cumulative mismatch as a % to cumulative outflows (F as a % to B)											

Source: 'Guidelines on Asset-Liability Management (ALM) System: Amendments', https://rbidocs.rbi.org.in/rdocs/notification/PDFs/80878.pdf (accessed 12 July 2022).

Note: *Net of provisions, interest suspense and claims received from ECGC/DICGC.

Table 8A.3 Statement of short-term dynamic liquidity

Name of the bank ____________________

Statement of short-term dynamic liquidity as on ____________________

(INR crore)

Items	1–14 days	15–28 days	29–90 days
A. Outflows			
1. Net increase in loans and advances			
2. Net increase in investments			
(i) Approved securities			
(ii) Money market instruments (other than treasury bills)			
(iii) Bonds/Debentures/Shares			
(iv) Others			
3. Inter-bank obligations			
4. Off-balance sheet items (repos, swaps, bills discounted, etc.)			
5. Others			
Total outflows			
B. Inflows			
1. Net cash position			
2. Net increase in deposits (less CRR obligations)			
3. Interest on investments			
4. Inter-bank claims			
5. Refinance eligibility (export credit)			
6. Off-balance sheet items (reverse repos, swaps, bills discounted, etc.)			
7. Others			
Total inflows			
C. Mismatch (B – A)			
D. Cumulative mismatch			
E. C as a % to total outflows			

Source: 'Asset - Liability Management (ALM) System', https://www.rbi.org.in/scripts/NotificationUser.aspx?Id=16&Mode=0 (accessed 12 July 2022).

Table 8A.4 Interest rate sensitivity

Heads of accounts	Rate sensitivity and time bucket
Liabilities	
1. Capital, reserves and surplus	Non-sensitive
2. Current Deposits	Non-sensitive
3. Savings bank deposits	Sensitive to the extent of interest paying (core) portion. This may be included in the 3–6 months bucket. The non-interest paying portion may be shown in non-sensitive bucket.
4. Term deposits and certificates of deposit	Sensitive and reprices on maturity. The amounts should be distributed to different buckets on the basis of remaining maturity. However, in case of floating term deposits, the amounts may be shown under the time bucket when deposits contractually become due for repricing.
5. Borrowings: fixed	Sensitive and reprices on maturity. The amounts should be distributed to different buckets on the basis of remaining maturity.
6. Borrowings: floating	Sensitive and reprices when interest rate is reset. The amounts should be distributed to the appropriate bucket which refers to the repricing date.
7. Borrowings: zero coupon	Sensitive and reprices on maturity. The amounts should be distributed to the respective maturity buckets.
8. Borrowings from RBI	Up to 1 month bucket
9. Refinances from other agencies	(a) Fixed rate: as per respective maturity (b) Floating rate: reprices when interest rate is reset
10. Other liabilities and provisions	
(i) Bills Payable	(i) Non-sensitive
(ii) Inter-office Adjustment	(ii) Non-sensitive
(iii) Provisions	(iii) Non-sensitive
(iv) Others	(iv) Non-sensitive
11. Repos/Bills re-discounted (DUPN), swaps (buy/sell), etc.	Reprices only on maturity and should be distributed to the respective maturity buckets
Assets	
1. Cash	Non-sensitive
2. Balances with RBI	Interest earning portion may be shown in 3–6 months bucket. The balance amount is non- sensitive.

(*Contd*)

Table 8A.4 (*Contd*)

Heads of accounts	Rate sensitivity and time bucket
3. Balances with other banks	
(i) Current account	(i) Non-sensitive
(ii) Money at call and short notice, term deposits and other placements	(ii) Sensitive on maturity. The amounts should be distributed to the respective maturity buckets
4. Investments (performing)	
(i) Fixed rate/Zero coupon	(i) Sensitive on maturity
(ii) Floating rate	(ii) Sensitive at the next repricing date
5. Shares/Units of mutual funds	Non-sensitive
6. Advances (performing)	
(i) Bills purchased and discounted (including bills under DUPN)	(i) Sensitive on maturity
(ii) Cash credits/Overdrafts (including TODs)/Loans repayable on demand and term loans	(ii) Sensitive only when PLR/risk premium is changed. Of late, frequent changes in PLR have been noticed. Thus, each bank should foresee the direction of interest rate movements and capture the amounts in the respective maturity buckets by which time PLR would be revised.
7. NPAs (advances and investments)*	
(i) Sub-standard	(i) 2–5 years bucket
(ii) Doubtful and loss	(ii) Over 5 years bucket
8. Fixed assets	Non-sensitive
9. Other assets	
(i) Inter-office adjustment	(i) Non-sensitive
(ii) Others	(ii) Non-sensitive
10. Reverse repos, swaps (sell/buy) and Sensitive on maturity bills rediscounted (DUPN)	
11. Other products (interest rate)	
(i) Swaps	(i) Sensitive and should be distributed under different buckets with reference to maturity
(ii) Other derivatives	(ii) Should be suitably classified as and when introduced

Source: 'Asset - Liability Management (ALM) System', https://www.rbi.org.in/scripts/NotificationUser.aspx?Id=16&Mode=0 (accessed 12 July 2022).

Note: *Amount to be shown net of provisions.

Revision Questions and Problems

1. Briefly outline the organisational structure for risk management in Indian banks.
2. What is the rationale for active involvement of the top management of banks in banking risk management?
3. What are the major responsibilities of ALCOs in Indian banks?
4. Briefly explain the conventional ways of credit risk management practised by banks in India.
5. Compare use of securitisation versus credit derivatives for credit risk management.
6. Explain how ALM is used by Indian banks for liquidity and interest rate risk management.

Part IV

Managing the Banking Business

9

Banking Management

Assets Side

Loans and Investments

Learning Objectives

- To explain regular banking management processes pertaining to items on the assets side of a bank's balance sheet
- To provide details about different types of bank loans extended by banks in India and explain the management of such loans
- To describe the procedures followed for the assessment of creditworthiness of loan applicants for different types of loans and consequent lending decisions
- To delineate the procedures followed by banks in India for the determination of interest rates on different types of loans
- To explain the management of the investment portfolio and treasury operations of banks

9.1 Introduction

In the backdrop of our discussion in the previous chapters, it is important to reiterate two key aspects pertaining to the banking business. First, as a financial intermediary, a commercial bank undertakes deposit mobilisation and uses such deposits for lending and investments. Surplus interest income earned on loans and investments over the cost of deposits is the main source of a bank's profit. Needless to mention, to calculate a bank's overall profitability, non-interest income is to be counted and operational costs and taxes need to be adjusted. As a commercial entity, profit maximisation is the prime objective of a bank. Second, we also discussed that lending and investments entail various types of risks. Aggressive lending in search of higher returns inherently involves higher levels of risks. The quantum of risks in the banking business needs to be kept within reasonable limits to ensure banking stability.

Considering these facts, the guiding principle for prudent banking is to strive for optimising risk-adjusted profit. In that direction, the banking business is conducted keeping in mind not only the primary objective of profitability but also considerations of solvency and liquidity.

As regards promoting profitability, banks aim to maximise their NII and non-interest income. The NII is nothing but interest income over interest cost of a bank and accounts for the bulk of banking profitability. Higher NII can be generated by expanding interest income from loans and investments while reducing costs on deposits. Thus, maximising NII requires judicious decision-making in choosing the portfolio of bank deposits, loans and investments and the pricing of products.

Solvency considerations focus on maintaining a positive net worth of a bank on a continuous basis. A positive net worth can be maintained by ensuring a higher amount of assets over a bank's liabilities. A bank's *capital* is the accounting residual which is obtained by subtracting a bank's deposits and other liabilities from its total assets. Capital is the amount that a bank owes to its owners or shareholders. In a sense, the net worth and capital of a bank are the same.

Loan delinquencies reduce the value of assets. If a bank's total assets fall short of its total liabilities due to writing off NPAs, the bank may face insolvency consequences. This may lead to the collapse of the bank. This underscores the need to contain risks in the banking business within reasonable limits so that the assets of a bank continue to be higher than its liabilities.

It is important to note that while solvency of a bank refers to long-term banking stability, there could be impairment of public faith in a bank if there are short-term liquidity problems. This may arise in a situation where a bank suffers from shortage of liquid assets as compared to short-term liabilities. Under such circumstances, the bank may fail to meet deposit withdrawal demands without taking recourse to external funding. The bank facing any difficulty in obtaining external funding and thus failing to meet deposit withdrawal demands can create panic amongst depositors and a consequent *bank run* which may lead to a banking crisis. So prudent banking management requires ensuring a comfortable liquidity position on an ongoing basis. This underscores the need for appropriate balance of assets vis-à-vis liabilities of a bank within different time windows.

Such considerations of profitability, solvency and liquidity form the cornerstones of banking management in a broad sense. Banking management entails strategic decision-making mainly on lending, investments, mobilisation of deposits, fixing of interest rates on loans and deposits, ALM, and so on. The finer details of the practical aspects of banking strategy and policies pertaining to the loan and investment portfolios of banks are discussed in this chapter. This includes business decisions to lend or not to a particular loan seeker, determination of interest charges on bank loans, composition of the loan portfolio, investment and treasury operations, procedures and parameters to assess the creditworthiness of borrowers, and so on. Similar banking management issues pertaining to bank deposits and borrowings are discussed in Chapter 10.

In Table 9.1, we have provided information on asset composition derived from the consolidated balance sheet of SCBs in India for the recent period. It reveals that 'loans and advances' account for nearly 40–60 per cent of the total assets of SCBs. Another 25–40 per cent is accounted for by 'investments'. Given their overwhelming share, strategic decisions on bank loans and investments are critical for conduct of the banking business.

The loan portfolio of banks consists of a variety of loans. Bank loans availed by households are categorised as *retail loans*. Home loans, automobile loans, personal loans, study loans, and so on, fall under this category. Large businesses avail *corporate loans*. Term loans for corporates are generally very large in size and entail longer repayment periods. Such loans are required to commence new industrial projects, expand existing production facilities, upgrade machines and tools, and so on. Businesses also avail working capital loans which are short-term in nature for the purpose of meeting the working capital gap. Such loans are generally availed for buying raw material and payment of wages to workers, among others.

In India, banks extend a special type of retail loan under priority sector lending requirements. Such loans are provided to farmers, small-scale enterprises, exporters, and so on, to meet the developmental objectives of society. Banks charge concessional rates on such loans and commercial considerations are not accorded due significance. We will discuss priority sector loans separately.

As regards investments, the investment portfolio of SCBs is mostly dominated by SLR securities, which are mainly bonds issued by the Government of India and different state governments. As can be observed from Table 9.1, the proportion of 'investments' in the total assets of SCBs has

Table 9.1 Asset composition from the consolidated balance sheet of SCBs in India

(*INR billion*)

Items	1999–00	2004–05	2009–10	2014–15	2019–20	1999–00	2004–05	2009–10	2014–15	2019–20
	Value in INR billion					*Percentage share in total assets*				
1. Cash and balances with RBI	854	1,181	3,658	5,285	7,657	7.7	5.0	6.1	4.4	4.3
2. Balances with banks and money at call and short notice	810	962	1,736	4,583	7,876	7.3	4.1	2.9	3.8	4.4
3. Investments	4,139	8,681	17,290	29,776	46,898	37.3	36.8	28.7	24.7	26.0
Out of which										
3.1 Investments in government securities	2,882	6,989	13,671	24,661	38,810	26.0	29.7	22.7	20.5	21.5
3.2 In other approved securities	252	163	53	4.3	1.0	2.3	0.7	0.1	0.0	0.0
3.3 In non-approved securities	1,005	1,529	3,566	5,111	8,087	9.0	6.5	5.9	4.2	4.5

4. Loans and Advances	4,435	11,511	34,967	73,882	1,03,019	39.9	48.9	58.0	61.4	57.2
Out of which										
4.1 Bills purchased and discounted	431	895	1,895	4,410	3,454	3.9	3.8	3.1	3.7	1.9
4.2 Cash credit and overdrafts	2,416	4,371	13,326	28,772	36,013	21.8	18.6	22.1	23.9	20.0
4.3 Term loans	1,588	6,245	19,746	40,699	63,552	14.3	26.5	32.8	33.8	35.3
5. Fixed assets	155	231	496	805	1,508	1.4	1.0	0.8	0.7	0.8
6. Other assets	712	994	2,122	6,040	13,186	6.4	4.2	3.5	5.0	7.3
Total assets	11,104	23,560	60,269	1,20,370	1,80,144	100	100	100	100	100

Source: *Statistical Tables Relating to Banks in India*, various issues, downloaded from RBI website, www.rbi.org.in.

Note: Figures pertain to end-March of the respective financial year.

significantly declined from around 37 per cent during the late 1990s and early 2000s to about 25 per cent in the 2010s. This is partly due to gradual reduction of SLR requirements by the RBI from 25 per cent during October 1997–November 2008 to 18 per cent since April 2020. Moreover, due to absence of default risks in government securities, banks preferred to invest in such securities to minimise the capital charge requirement on credit risks during the 1990s and early 2000s.

Further details on these aspects are provided in this chapter, which is organised as follows. In section 9.2, we provide details about different types of retail loans and strategic lending decisions pertaining to such loans. Similar details related to management of corporate loans are provided in section 9.3. As indicated earlier, lending to select sectors like agriculture, small-scale enterprises, weaker sections of society, and so on, is considered to be socially desirable from the developmental perspective. Details of this unique form of *priority sector lending* are discussed in section 9.4. In section 9.5, we cover the business strategy of banks in India as regards investments and treasury operations. Finally, broad conclusions are drawn in section 9.6.

9.2 Management of Retail Loans

Retail loans are relatively small in size. They serve the needs of the masses such as households and small firms. These loans in the form of home loans, automobile loans, general-purpose personal loans, credit card loans, and so on, have been very useful for households in improving their standard of living. Using a home loan, one can acquire an apartment and enjoy the comfort of living in one's own house. An automobile loan helps in possessing a car or motorbike and enjoying the convenience of one's own mode of transport. General-purpose personal loans can help a household in meeting various financial needs such as undertaking repairs in one's home, buying consumer durables, meeting health-related exigencies, and so on. Use of credit cards facilitates purchase of daily requirements without making immediate cash payments by availing a very short-term loan.

The retail loan portfolio has significantly grown in importance for Indian banks in the post-reform period, particularly since the early 2000s. Prior to that, households belonging to middle-income categories in India could only afford either a home or a car using their life savings. Lack of availability of bank loans meant the vast majority of middle-income households could not enjoy the comfort of having both home and car simultaneously. Since the 1990s, easy access to retail loans has enabled the middle class to enjoy both facilities. The outstanding amount of retail loans disbursed by SCBs at the aggregate level is presented in Table 9.2. It is to be noted that prior to the GFC of 2007–08, retail loans constituted nearly a quarter of total bank loans. After the GFC, banks in India became more cautious on retail loans and their share in overall bank credit gradually declined. The share dropped to less than one-fifth during the first half of the 2010s. In the recent years, there has been significant pick-up in the share, rising to 26.4 per cent in 2019–20 and further to nearly 30 per cent as of 31 March 2023. Different categories of households such as professionals, the salaried class and the self-employed have benefitted from availing retail loans and acquiring their own homes and automobiles even at the beginning of their work life. Banks have also benefitted from the tremendous business opportunities of lending to such households. Retail loans have emerged as the largest business vertical for leading banks in India.

9.2.1 Types of Retail Loans

Banks in India provide various types of retail loans to households. Popular varieties of such loans are discussed as follows.

Table 9.2 Outstanding retail loans of SCBs in India

(INR billion)

Items	2004–05	2009–10	2014–15	2019–20
Home loans	1,347	3,009	6,285	13,619
Auto loans		638	1,246	3,395
Consumer durables	38	83	153	161
Credit card receivables	84	201	305	1,199
Education loans		369	633	779
Other personal loans	1,201	1,041	2,362	6,941
Total retail loans	2,670	5,856	11,663	27,269
Total loans and advances*	11,057	31,963	64,420	1,03,191
Share of home loans in total retail loans	*50.4*	*51.4*	*53.9*	*49.9*
Share of retail loans in total loans and advances	*24.1*	*18.3*	*18.1*	*26.4*

Source: *Statistical Tables Relating to Banks in India*, various issues, downloaded from RBI website, www.rbi.org.in.

Note: (*a*) Figures pertain to end-March of the respective financial year. (*b*) *Non-food credit.

9.2.1.1 Home Loans

Home loans form the most dominant component of retail loans. For SCBs, the share of home loans has been nearly half the total retail loans since 2004–05 (Table 9.2). Such loans are mainly of three types, summarised as follows:

- Loans availed to construct a new house or buy a newly constructed apartment
- Loans to repair or refurbish an existing house or apartment
- Obtaining a personal loan with a house or apartment as mortgage or security collateral

Home loans are relatively safe as compared to other loans as the mortgage or security collateral provided against such loans is a credible deterrent against default. In case of any default, the bank can always take recourse to repossession—that is, take over the mortgaged property. As the price of housing property generally has a tendency to increase, it may not be difficult for the bank to sell the property and recover its dues.

Home loans are generally long-term in nature. The term to maturity of new home loans is usually 20 to 30 years. The maximum amount of home loan that can be availed from a bank is up to 90 per cent of the house or apartment value if it is less than INR 20 lakh. The loan amount can be up to 80 per cent of the property price if it is above INR 20 lakh. The remaining 10 or 20 per cent of the value of the home or apartment needs to be financed by the borrowers themself. This is popularly referred to as *margin requirement.*

9.2.1.2 Auto Loans

With rapid economic progress witnessed in India during the post-reform period, there has been constant upgradation of standard of living for a vast majority of households. In addition to the high appetite of the rich for luxury cars, burgeoning middle-class households have created considerable demand for cars and motorcycles. Growing non-agricultural income in rural India has added to this demand. Banks have fully exploited this opportunity by providing auto loans at competitive rates. The share of auto loans has been nearly one-tenth of the total retail loan portfolio of SCBs during the 2010s.

Normally, the duration of car loans is up to seven years, with a down payment or margin requirement of 10 per cent. The duration of two-wheeler loans in many banks is up to three to four years. The loan margin requirement for such loans is 15 per cent.

9.2.1.3 General-Purpose Personal Loans

The general public in India seem to have become aspirational. They are continuously upgrading their lifestyle by purchasing modern consumer durables. There is also requirement of financial support to meet the needs of education, health and marriage of children. Banks have come forward to provide general-purpose *personal loans* to households to meet a variety of such needs. In such loans, the utilisation of the amount is not for a specific purpose unlike home loans or auto loans. Personal loans can be used as an add-on loan to construct or repair a house, support children's education, buy a consumer durable, avail a vacation with one's family, and so on. There is complete flexibility on the end-use of personal loans as per the borrowers' requirement. This segment has grown in importance within the overall retail loan portfolio. In recent years, it accounts for nearly a quarter of total retail loans (Table 9.2).

It may be noted that while there is reasonable flexibility in extending personal loans, it is observed that the availability of such loans is generally limited to certain classes like the salaried, pensioners or the self-employed who have an established record of a stable source of income. The interest rates charged for such loans are generally higher than for other loans. The term to maturity is, on the other hand, usually short unlike long-term home loans.

9.2.1.4 Education Loans

Education loans have important implications for the long-term economic prosperity of a society. Growth theories in economics emphasise the role of technological progress and human capital in promoting long-term growth. Acquiring knowledge and skills through education and training is essential for technological progress and development of human capital. In this perspective, banks contribute to the process of improving human capital by providing loans for higher and professional education to meritorious students. While the share of education loans in the total retail loans of SCBs declined from 6.3 per cent in 2009–10 to 2.9 per cent in 2019–20, outstanding education loans of SCBs nearly doubled from INR 369 billion to INR 779 billion during the comparable period (Table 9.2).

9.2.1.5 Consumer Durable Loans

All leading banks in India provide consumer durable loans for users of e-commerce. Such loans are provided in several ways. A popular form is online EMI loans for purchase of consumer durables through online aggregators or shopping portals like Amazon, Flipkart, and so on. Such loans are also provided as point-of-sale (POS) EMI loans while purchasing consumer durables from authorised dealers or retail shops. Many banks aggressively push such loans for pre-selected customers with a good financial standing.

9.2.1.6 Gold Loans

Banks in India provide general-purpose personal loans under a popular variety known as 'gold loans'. As the name suggests, these loans are provided against a pledge of gold coins or gold jewellery. This portfolio is quite secured with gold as collateral. The size of this portfolio, however, is relatively small. For example, for SBI, the size of its gold loan portfolio was less than one-tenth of its overall personal loans as of 31 March 2021.

9.2.1.7 Miscellaneous Items

In addition to the specific varieties of retail loans discussed in the preceding paragraphs, leading banks in India also provide some tailored loans for privileged customers. There are a variety of pre-approved personal loan products offered using aggressive marketing and customer hunt strategies. Banks offer special top-up loans for specific categories of customers like public sector employees, pensioners, and so on. With increasing competition amongst banks to exploit lending opportunities, there is constant innovation in designing tailor-made retail loan products to suit the specific needs of potential borrowers.

As can be seen from the previous discussion, the share of retail loans has been witnessing increasing importance in the credit portfolio of Indian banks. Accordingly, management of such loans has become critical for fostering a successful banking business. In the remaining part of this section, let us focus on management of retail loans.

9.2.2 Credit Appraisal and Designing of Retail Loan Products

It may be reiterated here that profitability, solvency and liquidity considerations have an overarching effect on business decisions pertaining to retail loans like any other vertical in the banking business. Profitability can be enhanced by raising a bank's share in aggregate retail lending. This calls for proper assessment of the requirements of the public for home loans, auto loans, general-purpose personal loans, and so on, and designing suitable products accordingly so as to maximise the bank's share in the retail loan market. Equally important are proper credit appraisal and borrower screening standards so as to minimise loan defaults.

Banks adopt a multipronged strategy to minimise default risk on retail loans. First, an objective assessment of the creditworthiness or loan repayment ability of the borrower is undertaken. This is mainly based on quantitative analysis using information on the loan seeker's past loan repayment history, transactions in their deposit account, CIBIL score, primary income source, and so on. Verifiable records like salary statements and income tax returns are used as supporting documents. This helps in assessing the loan repayment which the borrower can afford. Banks further undertake technical analysis of evolving economic conditions and their impact on the loan repayment ability of prospective borrowers. They also create a right on other assets of the borrower or insist on a guarantee by family members as an additional cushion in case the borrower defaults on the loan.

Second, to enhance the borrower's commitment to loan repayment and minimise losses due to loan default, banks insist on first right charges on the assets obtained (security collateral) out of the bank loan. In case of a home loan, the mortgaged property serves as the security collateral, and the bank reserves the right to repossess the home or apartment acquired by the borrower in case of default. In auto loans, the car or motorbike is hypothecated to the lending bank.

Third, to further strengthen the borrower's loan repayment commitment, banks also impose margin requirements. This compels the borrower to make a minimum downpayment for acquiring an asset using the loan.

It is important to note that the board-approved credit policy prescribes the credit scoring models for the screening of loan applications for different types of retail loans. The template for credit appraisal and determination of appropriate loan amounts for individual borrowers is made available to branch managers. Parameters may include historical data on the applicant's income, assets and liabilities, loan repayment history, composition of family and income of family members, remaining years of service in case of salaried persons, and so on. As branch managers enter information on a host of such financial and personal parameters obtained through the loan application, the credit score for the borrower is automatically calculated. This leads to a straightforward approval or rejection of the loan application as also fixation of the eligible loan amount, if sanctioned.

Needless to mention, different approval limits for loans are fixed for different levels of bank officers. Branch managers at various scales approve loans within their assigned sanction power. For loans above the threshold limit, the loan application is sent to the zonal or regional office or head or central office for approval by a high-level officer or committee as stipulated. For example, according to information obtained from the official website of Canara Bank (a leading PSB) as on 11 May 2023, the maximum credit sanctioning power of a branch manager of a small branch is INR 25 lakh while that of a branch manager of a large branch is INR 75 lakh (Canara Bank, n.d.). The maximum credit sanctioning power of an assistant general manager is INR 5 crore and that of a deputy general manager (DGM) at a regional office is INR 25 crore. Thus, sanctioning power is higher for senior executives of the bank. At the highest level, the managing committee of the board needs to sanction any loan above INR 800 crore.

Prescribed quantitative models have reduced the complexities of loan assessment for retail loans at the branch level. However, banks use a variety of scoring models for rating the creditworthiness of loan applicants in addition to the quantitative approach discussed in the preceding paragraphs. Hybrid scoring models provide scope for augmenting purely quantitative models with the subjective judgement of the bank manager about the loan applicant. Such subjective assessment can be based on the past experience of the bank manager in dealing with the loan applicant, loan delinquency pattern of a particular loan product, and so on. Models which use the past behaviour of a loan applicant as a bank customer are known as behavioural scoring models.

9.2.2.1 Role of Credit Information Bureau (India) Limited (CIBIL)

CIBIL is the leading credit information agency in India. It is the largest repository of borrower information. CIBIL collects, updates and maintains consumer credit information from banks, non-banking financial institutions and other lenders which are its members. Such credit information covers data on the loan history, repayment history and loan defaults of borrowers from member institutions. Member banks can access the required information for loan applicants available with CIBIL and obtain their credit score. This supplements the credit appraisal exercise for those loan applicants who are not existing customers of the concerned bank.

9.2.3 Loan Repayment Methods

Broadly, two different methods are used by banks in India for repayment of retail loans. For the bulk of retail loans such as home loans, auto loans, education loans, and so on, banks follow the *straight loans* method. Under this method, the loan amount is disbursed to the borrower in a lump sum. Over the repayment period, the borrower pays back the loan along with interest in EMIs. In the initial period of loan repayment, EMIs cover a smaller proportion of the principal and a higher proportion of interest charges. Over time, the proportion of interest charges in the EMIs tapers off and that of the principal increases. A hypothetical example is used in Box 9.1 to explain the composition of equal yearly instalments (EYIs) for a home loan. We have used EYIs instead of EMIs for reasons of simplicity.

On the contrary, credit card loans are a variety of *revolving loans* or *evergreen loans*. For credit card loans, a maximum limit for purchases using the card or cash withdrawal is fixed, mainly based on the income of the credit card holder. Within the given limit, the card holder is allowed to make purchases or withdraw cash. They are supposed to pay back the credit availed by the due date which is a fixed date in a calendar month. On repayment of the amount due or used, the original limit is restored.

Let us explain with an example. Assume the maximum purchase limit is INR 1 lakh and that for cash withdrawal is INR 10,000 for a credit card holder, Ms Divya. She can make purchases or undertake cash withdrawals within the respective limits. Until repayment of the credit card bill, the eligible amount for further purchases or cash withdrawals will be restricted to the remaining amount from the overall limit adjusting for the purchases or cash withdrawals

Box 9.1 Composition of EYIs for repayment of a home loan: a hypothetical example

Say, Mr Siddhartha has obtained a home loan of INR 60 lakh from Bank A on 1 January 2021. Assume the bank charges a fixed interest rate of 12 per cent on this home loan. Let us assume that the loan along with interest charges needs to be repaid over 20 years through EYIs.

Let us explain how the proportion of interest charges and principal repayments varies within EYIs paid by Mr Siddhartha over the 20-year period. If the EYIs need to be paid by Mr Siddhartha on 1 January every year, then the first instalment is due on 1 January 2022. The amount outstanding along with interest charges as on 1 January 2022 will be INR 67,20,000. This is the sum of the principal amount of INR 60,00,000 and interest dues of INR 7,20,000.

Assume Bank A has fixed EYIs of INR 8,03,300 for the home loan to Mr Siddhartha. Then in the first instalment of INR 8,03,300 paid on 1 January 2022, the component of interest charges is INR 7,20,000. The remaining INR 83,300 covers repayment of the principal.

On 1 January 2022, the remaining principal amount of the loan is INR 59,16,700. This is the original loan amount of INR 60,00,000 minus the principal of INR 83,300 repaid on 1 January 2022. Adding interest of INR 7,10,004 on the remaining principal amount (12 per cent of INR 59,16,700), the outstanding amount of the loan as on 1 January 2023 is INR 66,26,704. The second EYI that is INR 8,03,300 is paid on 1 January 2023. Out of this, INR 7,10,004 is the interest charge and the remaining amount, INR 93,296, goes towards repayment of the principal. After repayment of the second instalment, the remaining principal amount as on 1 January 2023 is INR 58,23,404.

In this manner, interest charges, principal repayments and outstanding principal over the years can be calculated as given in Table 9.3.

It can be observed from Table 9.3 that for the initial years, the bulk of the EYI goes towards interest payment and a smaller portion is left for principal repayment. Over time, the share of interest charges in the EYI gradually declines with falling outstanding principal dues. Consequently, the share of principal repayment increases within the periodic instalments.

Currently, most Indian banks charge floating interest rates on home loans linked to the external benchmark of the RBI's fixed repo rate under the LAF. Accordingly, interest rates on home loans vary with the changing repo rate. Depending on fluctuations in the home loan lending rates, the interest

Table 9.3 Composition of regular instalments in the straight loan repayment method

As on 1 January of the respective years	Outstanding principal amount (INR)	EYI (INR)	Interest component in EYI (INR)	Principal component in EYI (INR)
2021	60,00,000			
2022	59,16,700	8,03,300	7,20,000	83,300
2023	58,23,404	8,03,300	7,10,004	93,296
2024	57,18,912	8,03,300	6,98,808	1,04,492
2025	56,01,882	8,03,300	6,86,269	1,17,031
2026	54,70,808	8,03,300	6,72,226	1,31,074
2027	53,24,005	8,03,300	6,56,497	1,46,803
2028	51,59,585	8,03,300	6,38,881	1,64,419
2029	49,75,436	8,03,300	6,19,150	1,84,150
2030	47,69,188	8,03,300	5,97,052	2,06,248
2031	45,38,190	8,03,300	5,72,303	2,30,997
2032	42,79,473	8,03,300	5,44,583	2,58,717
2033	39,89,710	8,03,300	5,13,537	2,89,763
2034	36,65,175	8,03,300	4,78,765	3,24,535
2035	33,01,696	8,03,300	4,39,821	3,63,479
2036	28,94,600	8,03,300	3,96,204	4,07,096
2037	24,38,652	8,03,300	3,47,352	4,55,948
2038	19,27,990	8,03,300	2,92,638	5,10,662
2039	13,56,049	8,03,300	2,31,359	5,71,941
2040	7,15,475	8,03,300	1,62,726	6,40,574
2041	Nil	8,03,300	85,857	7,15,475

Source: Hypothetical example by the author.

amount will vary, unlike in our example where the interest rate was assumed to be fixed at 12 per cent. Nevertheless, the broad trend of a lower share of the principal repayment component within the EYI for initial years and higher share of the same in later years remains unchanged.

The calculation of the interest and principal repayment components for EMIs is similar to that discussed for EYIs in the preceding paragraphs. Mainly, 20 annual instalments under EYIs become 240 monthly instalments under EMIs.

already made. Say, if Ms Divya has made purchases worth INR 60,000 using her credit card as on the date, her eligible amount for further purchases is reduced to INR 40,000, which is INR 1,00,000 – INR 60,000. After Ms Divya pays back the amount due along with interest as applicable, her purchase limit is again restored to INR 1 lakh. Thus, credit cards provide a revolving loan facility.

It may be noted that banks allow for partial repayment of the total amount due. In such cases, they charge interest on the availed credit amount which is a major source of earning from the credit card business. Non-payment of the minimum dues on credit card purchases by the due date attracts penalty charges.

9.2.4 Pricing of Retail Loans

Each bank has its comprehensive policy on lending rates, adhering to relevant RBI guidelines. Such policy is duly approved by the board of directors or any high-level committee of the bank so authorised by the board. The ALCO plays a critical role in decision-making related to lending rates as discussed in Chapter 8. As per the RBI guidelines, banks can apply either floating or fixed interest rates on their loans. Floating rate loans are required to be linked to internal or external benchmarks, a brief history of which is provided in Box 9.2. Details of these procedures are provided in the RBI's 'Master Direction: Reserve Bank of India (Interest Rate on Advances) Directions, 2016', as updated on 10 June 2021 (last updated on 12 September 2023). This can be obtained from the official website of the RBI (www.rbi.org.in).

The reference benchmark needs to be explicitly mentioned as part of the terms of the loan contract. The policy for fixing the spread over the benchmark rate for specific borrowers need to be approved by the bank's board of directors. It is the central or head office of the bank which fixes the margin above the repo rate according to a formula based on the CIBIL rating and other financial parameters of borrowers. These parameters include the monthly or annual income of the borrower, their outstanding assets and liabilities, availability of unencumbered security collateral, their demographic profile and type of occupation such as government or private corporate employee, self-employed, daily-wage worker, and so on. The retail loan policy, credit score models, loan sanction procedures and limits, and related guidelines are placed on the intranet for ready reference of the bank

Box 9.2 A brief history of benchmarking of lending rates in India

During the post-reform period in India, there has been continuous effort to improve monetary policy transmission by improving alignment of bank lending rates with the monetary policy rate or stance of the RBI. Particularly in the 2010s, there were several rounds of revision that the RBI prescribed on benchmarking bank lending rates. In each successive round of revision, the process became more transparent and the link with the RBI's policy rate became stronger.

It was observed by the late 2000s that despite development of a broad-based financial system in India as a consequence of the financial sector reforms introduced since the early 1990s, interest rates in the banking sector were not integrated with interest rates in the money and bond markets. Banks merely revised the benchmark prime lending rate (BPLR) in line with the changing monetary policy stance to meet statutory requirements. But the effectiveness of the BPLR was quite limited as the pricing of the bulk of high-value loans had no strong link with it. Therefore, actual lending rates of banks did not move in sync with the interest rates in the money and bond markets. There was an imperative need to make lending rates in the banking sector market determined. In this perspective, the RBI introduced an internal benchmarking system for bank lending rates in the form of the *base rate* system from 1 July 2010.

The base rate system required each bank to have only one base rate to be used for internal benchmarking of its lending rates. Banks were supposed to announce the base rate in a transparent manner, taking into account the cost of funds for different tenures. The board of directors or ALCO was supposed to review the base rate every quarter. It was also stipulated that banks cannot change the methodology for setting their base rate prior to three years from the date of its finalisation. The base rate system was applied for all floating rate rupee loans during the period July 2010–March 2016 until the introduction of a revised internal benchmarking procedure under the *marginal cost of funds-based lending rate* (MCLR) system.

Internal benchmarking for setting floating lending rates was made more detailed and granular with introduction of the MCLR system from April 2016. The MCLR consists of four components, namely (*a*) marginal cost of funds, (*b*) negative carry-on account of CRR, (*c*) operating costs and (*d*) tenure premium. Details on calculation of each of these components are provided in the RBI's 'Master Direction' updated on 10 June 2021 (RBI, 2021a). The MCLR system further refined the transparency in setting internal benchmarks for bank lending and strengthened the benchmark's alignment with the cost of deposits and operating costs of banks. Banks are required to publish MCLR for a range of tenures from overnight to one year. Publishing MCLR for higher-order tenures is optional. Banks review and publish such MCLRs for different maturities once a month on a preannounced date.

It may be noted that under the MCLR system, the floating lending rates charged to borrowers not only reflect the cost of funds and operational costs of a bank, but also incorporate credit risk premium and considerations of business strategy, market competition, market liquidity of the loan, and so on. Since 2016, many banks have used MCLR for benchmarking of floating rate rupee loans for corporate lending. For certain types of retail loans, some banks are using internal benchmarking linked to the MCLR too.

External benchmarking for floating lending rates on retail and personal loans was introduced in October 2019 and the same for MSME loans was introduced in April 2020. Banks are allowed to use an external benchmarking system for other types of borrowers too. The RBI has stipulated various interest rates which can be used for external benchmarking. These include (*a*) the RBI's fixed repo rate under the LAF, (*b*) three-month or six-month treasury bills (TBs) rate published by Financial Benchmarks India Private Limited (FBIL) and (*c*) any other benchmark market interest rate published by FBIL. It is understood that all SCBs in India, except one, are using the RBI's fixed repo rate under the LAF for external benchmarking during 2023. For several types of retail loans, including lending to MSMEs, banks are following the external benchmarking system.

There are a few categories of loans exempted from application of benchmarking of lending rates. The RBI's 'Master Direction' provides a list of such categories (RBI, 2021a).

staff. The branch managers collect required information while processing the loan application and enter the same for analysis into the prescribed template. On entering this information, the interest rate to be charged to the borrower is calculated using the automated system.

Banks during 2023–24 follow external or internal benchmarking for pricing retail loans as per the RBI's guidelines. Since October 2019, a vast majority of banks in India are using the RBI's repo rate under the LAF as the external benchmark for a variety of their retail loans. With the introduction of the MCLR system in 2016, banks are using their respective MCLRs as the internal benchmark for their corporate and some retail loans. For example, as per information obtained from SBI's official website (www.sbi.co.in) in June 2023, it benchmarks its home loans to the RBI's fixed repo rate while its lending rates for car loans and loans for consumer durables under e-commerce are linked to its MCLR. Its MCLR was 8.5 per cent since 19 April 2023. On the other hand, for its car loans, BOB uses the RBI's fixed repo rate as its external benchmark unlike SBI.

Banks charge differential interest rates to borrowers depending on their credit scores. As per information obtained from SBI's official website, for borrowers with CIBIL scores above 750, the interest rate charged on regular home loans is 9.15 per cent while that for borrowers with CIBIL scores between 700 and 749 is 9.35 per cent. Necessary details are provided in Table 9.4. It shows how higher interest rates are charged to borrowers with lower CIBIL scores. Table 9.5 provides information on the interest rate charged by SBI on new car loans. This table explains how the spread over its MCLR changes with the credit score for different borrowers.

As per RBI stipulations, for fixed interest rate loans for tenures less than three years, the applicable interest rate should not be below the benchmark rate for similar tenures.

Based on this discussion, Table 9.6 summarises relevant information on eligible loan amounts, margins and security collateral requirements, and types of interest charges for popular kinds of retail loans in India.

Table 9.4 SBI's home loan rates across different CIBIL scores

CIBIL score	Interest rate on regular home loan (per cent)	Interest rate on top-up home loan (per cent)
750 or more	9.15	9.55
700–749	9.35	9.75
650–699	9.45	9.85
550–649	9.65	10.15
No CBIL score	9.35	9.75

Source: SBI's official website, www.sbi.co.in (accessed 5 June 2023).

Table 9.5 SBI's car loan rates across different Credit Information Corporation scores

CIC score	Interest rate on new car loans of 3–5 years duration (per cent)	Interest rate on new car loans of above 5 years duration (per cent)
775 or more	MCLR + 0.15 = 8.65	MCLR + 0.25 = 8.75
757–774	MCLR + 0.25 = 8.75	MCLR + 0.35 = 8.85
721–756	MCLR + 0.50 = 9.00	MCLR + 0.60 = 9.10
700–720	MCLR + 0.75 = 9.25	MCLR + 0.85 = 9.35
650–699	MCLR + 1.05 = 9.55	MCLR + 1.15 = 9.65
−1 (101–200)	8.75–9.10	

Source: SBI's official website, www.sbi.co.in (accessed 5 June 2023).

Note: (*a*) CIC score refers to credit score obtained from the Credit Information Corporation. (*b*) One-year MCLR for SBI was 8.50 per cent from 19 April 2023.

9.3 Management of Corporate Loans

Despite development of different segments of the financial system during the post-reform period, as discussed in Chapter 2, trade and business in India are heavily dependent on banks for funding their long-term projects as well as for meeting working capital requirements. While the post-reform period opened up the possibility for large corporates to fund their long-term projects by accessing the equity and corporate bond markets, small enterprises can meet such requirements from the banking sector alone.

Needless to mention, strategic business policies and day-to-day operations of banks pertaining to corporate loans need to be in compliance with extant regulatory guidelines. The RBI has laid down detailed stipulations on the types of business activities to lend (or not lend) to, exposure limits for individual firms or groups to avoid concentration of bank lending, setting lending rates, and so on. During the post-reform period, banks have acquired greater operational autonomy for lending to corporates and determining applicable interest rates. Banks have their own board-approved loan policy for corporate lending which generally covers key aspects of their lending strategy, including details of credit appraisal procedures, risk assessment and the pricing of loans. The loan sanctioning authority at different levels of managerial positions is clearly defined. Bank managers need to be well versed with the loan policy and follow the same in letter and spirit while sanctioning loans. Banks also undertake active monitoring and follow-up after sanction

Table 9.6 Summary characteristics of different types of retail loans

Characteristics	Home loans	Auto loans	Education loans	Personal loans	Credit card loans
Type of loan	Secured and straight	Secured and straight	Unsecured or secured and straight	Unsecured and straight	Unsecured and revolving
Eligible loan amount	Multiple of take-home salary or income subject to a ceiling Up to 80–90 per cent of the home value	Multiple of take-home salary or income subject to a ceiling Up to 80–90 per cent of the on-road price of the vehicle	Up to INR 10 lakh for studies in India and up to INR 20 lakh for studies abroad	Multiple of take-home salary or income subject to a ceiling	Multiple of take-home salary or income subject to a ceiling
Security collateral	Mortgage of the property	Hypothecation of the car or motorbike	Up to INR 4 lakh: No security INR 4–7.5 lakh: third-party guarantee Above INR 7.5 lakh: tangible security collateral	Not required	Not required
Margin requirement	10–20 per cent	10 per cent	Up to INR 4 lakh: nil Above INR 4 lakh for studies in India: 5 per cent Above INR 4 lakh for studies abroad: 15 per cent	Not required	Not required
Interest rate	Fixed rate or flexible rate (repo rate + 2.8 per cent)	Fixed rate	Concessional fixed rate	Fixed rate	Fixed rate of around 2–2.5 per cent per month

Source: Collated by the author based on information obtained from official websites of SBI, BOB, Canara Bank, Indian Bank, PNB, and so on.

and disbursement of loans to ensure that the loans are utilised for the purpose for which they were obtained. The ALCO outlines the policy on lending rates applicable to corporate loans based on the internal or external benchmark, tenure of the loan and risk parameters. In general, the corporate loan policy provides adequate flexibility to branch managers on lending and loan pricing decisions.

Senior-level executives provide focused attention to promote corporate loans. By setting up specialised branches for corporate lending, banks have been able to address the specific needs of big borrowers from trade and industry. The officers and staff of such branches are well trained and have expertise in meeting the business requirements of corporate borrowers. Each corporate borrower is unique in terms of loan requirements and there is tough competition amongst bankers to capture corporate business. Without flexibility and autonomy to corporate branch managers, no bank can optimise business opportunities in this segment.

The specialised corporate bank branches have evolved as single-window service centres providing a whole gamut of services to corporate clients under one roof. These include project finance, working capital finance, trade finance, issuing of LCs for foreign trade, advisory and consultancy services on commercial and financial matters, issue of bank guarantees and insurance services, assistance in forex operations, cash management and collection for clients, and so on. A large part of the ancillary services such as issuing of LCs, bank guarantees, forex derivatives and underwriting services, among others, are non-fund-based services and fall under OBS activities, details of which are covered in Chapter 10.

Corporate loans can be distinguished from retail loans on the following accounts:

- Corporate loans are provided to meet the financial needs of trade and industrial units registered under the Companies Act, 1956 and 2013. On the contrary, retail loans are generally provided to individuals and smaller firms to meet their consumption needs, personal finance and small business-loan requirements.
- The amount of corporate loans is often very large in size, contrary to the small loan requirements in the retail segment.
- Unlike in retail loans, the lending bank needs to continuously monitor the activities and related financial consequences for corporate loans

during the post-sanction period. This often involves additional lending to meet a variety of financial requirements.

- Lending to corporates involves a very tedious process of credit appraisal as summarised in the sections that follow while that for retail loans is relatively simple.
- Interest rate decisions for retail loans at the branch level are simple and straightforward and only require conforming to the guidelines stipulated by the head office. In the case of corporate loans, branch managers enjoy some flexibility and scope for negotiation and bargaining.

Broadly, corporate loans are of two types, namely (*a*) term loans or project finance loans and (*b*) working capital loans. General bank management issues pertaining to lending and pricing decisions for such loans are discussed in the following sections.

9.3.1 Term Loans

9.3.1.1 Purpose of the Loan

Industrial units undertake regular investment for setting up factories and buying machines and equipment. Banks provide *term loans* to such units which basically involves lending for purchasing assets like land, heavy machines and equipment, construction of buildings, and so on. Broadly, term loans for new projects cover three components, namely land, buildings and machinery.

9.3.1.2 Credit Appraisal

The process of credit appraisal for corporate loans is very rigorous and exhaustive as compared to that for retail loans. It begins with submission of a loan proposal or project report by the prospective borrower. This contains detailed information on the type of industrial or commercial project for which the loan is sought. It can be a fresh project or capacity expansion of an existing production facility. Projected cash flows with minute details under various heads of income and expenditure constitute a critical part of the project report. Banks undertake extensive analysis mainly as regards economic considerations, technical feasibility and financial viability of the proposed project.

It is pertinent to note that profitability of any project critically depends on revenue earned from sale of the products manufactured. The prevailing demand conditions in the economy, in turn, determine the volume of sales. Hence, the need for assessing the prevailing and evolving economic conditions for profitability of a project cannot be overemphasised. This assessment necessarily involves comprehensive macroeconomic analysis such as the prospects for economic growth, overall demand conditions, competition from producers of the same product both domestically and abroad (through imports), prospects for export, movement in general prices, government borrowing programmes and monetary policy stance, and so on. Further microeconomic aspects such as cost of production, market structure in the specific industry and margin requirement, among others, are also important.

The second important aspect is the technical feasibility of the proposed project. This covers issues related to the very manufacturing of the product such as physical infrastructure, availability of raw materials required for production, use of updated or the latest technology, availability of engineers and workers, and so on. Physical infrastructure includes access to the production facility through roads, shipping facilities, type of land and building used to set up the factory, communications, electricity supply, water supply, and so on. The feasibility of procuring the required machines and plants, either from domestic producers or through imports, needs to be taken into account. Finally, government regulations related to environment and labour, any restriction on producing the proposed goods, the government's policy on tax or subsidy for the product, and so on, also constitute key inputs. Broadly, the issues related to technical feasibility of the proposed products cover enabling factors as also bottlenecks concerned with their production.

Third, the financial viability of the project is of the ultimate importance. Financial viability focuses on the reliability of projected cash flows which are the key component for assessment of the loan repayment ability of the borrower. Turnover in the last three years for the company and projected cash flows are rigorously scrutinised. Needless to mention, for projected cash flows, account must be taken of both revenue and cost aspects. Financial indicators and statements such as current and projected debt–equity ratios, profitability measures, fund flow statements, current ratio, interest coverage ratio, ratio of net fixed assets to liability, debt service coverage ratio, and so on, are critical considerations for assessment of the future financial position of the borrower. Technical tools like sensitivity analysis are employed to assess the impact of various hypothetical changes in financial and economic variables on projected cash flows. For example, if market interest rates move upwards, the interest coverage ratio is impacted. Similarly, if domestic currency depreciates, import costs of machines and equipment rise.

Besides such objective assessment of creditworthiness, banks also examine the character and credibility of borrowers. Information available in the public domain as also that obtained from past banking relations with the borrower helps in this regard.

It is important to note that banks conduct internal or in-house proprietary credit rating analysis based on the information and analysis discussed in the previous paragraphs. Their internal or in-house rating models are not available in the public domain. This impedes detailed examination of credit appraisal for corporate loans. Along with their internal rating, banks also use ratings assigned by popular external CRAs for broader assessment of the creditworthiness of borrowers. Such rating agencies include Moody's, Standard & Poor (S&P Global), Fitch, ICRA and CRISIL.

Readers may refer to Bhattacharya (2011) and Singh and Dutta (2013) for finer details on assessment of project financing by banks.

9.3.1.3 Duration of Project Loans and Repayment Method

The term to maturity for project loans varies according to the purpose. The repayment period for loans availed to purchase machines and equipment is not extended beyond 7–10 years as most machinery items are covered by guarantees for such period. The repayment period for land and building components is longer, often up to 15 years.

The tenure of a term loan for projects consists of three distinct components. They are as follows:

- *Implementation period*: The time period from when the loan is availed to set up the factory and install machines and equipment up to commencement of production
- *Moratorium period*: The time period from commencement of production to breakeven, when loan repayment begins. Some treat the entire duration from availing a term loan until commencement

of loan repayment as the moratorium period—it usually varies from 6 to 24 months.

- *Repayment period*: Period of loan repayment after the moratorium period. Bank managers directly dealing with the client have flexibility in determining the loan repayment period, depending on the cash accrual of the project.

The schedule and pattern of loan repayment for corporate term loans is different from the EMI approach for retail loans discussed earlier.

On corporate term loans, interest dues are debited on a monthly basis after the moratorium period. The principal amount is paid back in equal instalments as per the agreement. In many project loans, banks follow a *ballooning approach* or *negotiated repayment schedule*. Under this approach, principal repayment instalments progressively rise with higher capacity utilisation and cash accrual by borrowers over time. With the passage of time, there is greater scope for higher sales and revenue generation from the project. Accordingly, banks allow lower principal repayments at the beginning of the repayment period. Progressively, regular principal repayments are raised like the gradual filling of air in a balloon and its expansion to full capacity.

9.3.1.4 Security and Margin Requirements

Machines and equipment purchased for a project using a term loan are hypothecated to the bank. A margin of 15–25 per cent is generally insisted upon on loans for such components. The margin amount required is deposited by the borrower in their current account maintained with the lending bank.

Land purchased or leased and buildings constructed using project loans are often mortgaged with the bank. The margin requirements on the proportion of the project loans used for construction of buildings generally vary from 25 per cent to 40 per cent while that for purchase of land goes up to 100 per cent.

In addition to these requirements, banks also insist upon guarantees from the borrowing company and sometimes even personal guarantees of the director(s) of the company on term loans. Depending on availability and requirements, some banks also obtain guarantees from the sister concerns of the borrowing company.

9.3.1.5 Pricing of Project or Term Loans

Under the RBI's extant guidelines, banks enjoy considerable flexibility in fixing lending rates for project loans. As discussed in the previous section, banks follow internal or external benchmarking to fix lending rates for corporate borrowers as per their board-approved interest rate policy.

For floating interest rates on corporate term loans, banks in India since 2016 use either their internal MCLR benchmark or an external benchmark like a TB rate for a particular maturity (say, the market interest rate on 91-day or 270-day TBs). Actual spread over the benchmark for a particular borrower is determined by their credit rating. If the rating of a borrower is good, the spread of the lending rate over the benchmark charged to the borrower is lower.

Since October 2019, the fixed repo rate under LAF had emerged as a popular external benchmark. With the RBI's accommodative monetary policy during the Covid-19 pandemic, the repo rate under the LAF was reduced to 4 per cent in May 2020. This favoured corporate borrowers. But high inflationary conditions since February 2022 forced the RBI to raise the repo rate to 4.4 per cent in May 2022. Subsequently through a series of hikes, it had reached 6.5 per cent by February 2023. This automatically raised lending rates charged to corporate borrowers using the repo rate as the benchmark. Consequently, it is learnt that many banks have now switched to MCLR-based internal benchmarking under pressure from their corporate clients. Details about MCLR and external benchmarking have been provided in Box 9.2.

9.3.2 Working Capital Loans

9.3.2.1 Purpose

Term loans facilitate setting up the production facility including procurement of machines and equipment. They meet the medium-term or long-term funding requirements of corporates. However, business enterprises also require funds for their day-to-day operations, including procurement of raw materials, employment of workers and engineers, payment of electricity bills and other user charges, and so on. After the goods are manufactured, some time is required to sell the same and receive the proceeds. So there is a time lag between procuring raw materials, hiring manpower and incurring other operational expenses to manufacture goods and receipt of the sale proceeds.

This duration is known as the *operating cycle*. Firms or borrowers require funding support from banks to meet expenses within the operating cycle which is facilitated through working capital loans.

9.3.2.2 Credit Appraisal and Setting the Limits for Working Capital Loans

The working capital requirement is assessed by banks following standard credit appraisal methods similar to those used for term loans. Independent evaluation of the creditworthiness or bankability of the credit proposal is undertaken using the standard procedure as discussed earlier. Approval is obtained from the appropriate sanctioning authority in accordance with a bank's scheme of delegation of credit sanctioning power. For loan limits above INR 20 lakh or a turnover value of above INR 100 crore (per annum), banks insist upon submission of the loan seeker's audited balance sheet for the last three years. As is the case for term loans, a credit information report is obtained from rating agencies like CIBIL, Equifax, Experian, and so on, as an additional input to the internal credit rating models to assess the creditworthiness of borrowers.

For calculating the working capital limit, banks in India broadly follow three methods explained briefly as follows.

9.3.2.2.1 Turnover Method

Assessment of the working capital limit under the turnover method begins with the bank scrutinising projections on gross annual sales turnover submitted by the borrower and arriving at accepted or realistic projections. Under this method, the working capital gap is fixed as 25 per cent of the accepted turnover. Discounting the margin of 20 per cent of the working capital gap (eligible amount), the remaining portion is calculated as the working capital limit for the borrower.

Table 9.7(a) presents a hypothetical example of calculation of the permissible bank finance or working capital limit using the turnover method. As compared to the projected sales of INR 56 crore submitted by the borrower, the bank's own assessment reduces it to INR 52 crore. Accordingly, the working capital gap is calculated as 25 per cent of INR 52 crore, which is INR 13 crore.

From a working capital gap of INR 13 crore, permissible bank finance can be calculated as 80 per cent of INR 13 crore (after adjusting for the margin requirements or deducting actual net working capital [NWC], whichever is

Table 9.7(a) Calculation of working capital limits: turnover method

S. No.	Particulars	Amount (INR crore)
1	Projected sales (submitted by the borrower)	56.0
2	Accepted projection of sales by the bank	52.0
3	Working capital gap (25 per cent of 2)	13.0
4	Minimum margin required (5 per cent of 2)	2.6
5	Actual net working capital	2.0
6	Maximum permissible bank finance (3-4 or 3-5, whichever is lower)	10.4

Source: Hypothetical example by the author

lower). Actual NWC is nothing but excess of current assets of the borrower over current liabilities. In our example, 80 per cent of the working capital gap is INR 10.4 crore. The actual NWC is INR 2 crore. Accordingly, permissible bank finance for working capital requirements is calculated as INR 10.4 crore.

9.3.2.2.2 Assessed Bank Finance (ABF) or Maximum Permissible Bank Finance (MPBF) Method

Under ABF or MPBF, the bank assesses the working capital requirements of corporate borrowers by calculating their total current assets and total current liabilities (excluding bank borrowings). A detailed study of the borrower's business operations and production or processing cycle of the industry is undertaken to evaluate reasonable build-up of current assets of the borrower by using bank finance. Banks emphasise proper classification of current assets and liabilities based on approved guidelines. Projections of inventories and receivables are made based on key factors such as past trend, operational needs, industry trend and inter-firm comparisons, and relevant market developments. Accordingly, the working capital gap is calculated as the difference between the current assets and current liabilities of the borrower, adjusting for bank borrowings.

A hypothetical example is given in Table 9.7(b) to explain calculation of maximum permissible working capital limit. In this example, the total current assets of the borrower stand at INR 250 crore while their total current liabilities are placed at INR 188 crore. The amount of bank borrowings is INR 76 crore. Thus, the amount of current liabilities excluding bank borrowings is INR 112 crore. Accordingly, the working capital gap is calculated as INR 250 crore – INR 112 crore = INR 138 crore.

Table 9.7(b) Calculation of working capital limits: MPBF method

S. No.	Particulars	Amount (INR Crore)
1	Total current assets	250.0
2	Less: current liabilities excluding bank borrowings	112.0
2A	*Bank borrowings*	*76.0*
3	Working capital gap (1-2)	138.0
4	Minimum stipulated margin (25 per cent of 1)	62.5
5	Actual net working capital	52.0
6	Maximum permissible bank finance (3-4 or 3-5, whichever is lower)	75.5
Memo	Current ratio (current assets/current liabilities)	1.33

Source: Hypothetical example by the author.

The margin requirement is minimum 25 per cent of the current assets which works out to be INR 62.5 crore. Excluding that, the permissible bank finance works out to be INR 138 crore – INR 62.5 crore = INR 75.5 crore. This is compared with an alternative measure of permissible bank finance obtained from the difference between the working capital gap and the actual NWC of the borrower. In this example, the actual NWC is INR 52 crore. So the alternative permissible bank finance is calculated as INR 138 crore – INR 52 crore = INR 86 crore. Between the two measures of permissible bank finance, the lower one is chosen as the working capital limit. Thus, in this example, the amount of MPBF is calculated as INR 75.5 crore.

It may be noted that non-fund-based limits are also included within MPBF calculations. Moreover, while assessing MPBF, banks ensure that the borrower has a current ratio of 1.33, interest coverage ratio of 2.1, asset coverage ratio of 1.5:1, debt–equity ratio of 3:1, and so on. Banks use different criteria for certain types of borrowers such as construction companies, MSMEs, and so on.

9.3.2.2.3 Cash Budget Method

Banks set working capital limits under the *cash budget method* on the basis of projected cash flows and estimates of cash credit. This method is more suitable for those borrowers who witness seasonal fluctuations in their cash flows. Borrowers engaged in industries like construction, sugar, tea or software development or traders or merchants who do not have a predetermined production or trading cycle belong to this category. Under this method, cash inflows over the months are assessed taking into account cash sales, debtors' realisations, advances from customers and miscellaneous receipts, among others. Similarly, cash outflows on account of operational expenses, payments to creditors, repayments of term loans, and so on, are considered. The difference between cash inflows and outflows gives the surplus or deficit position for borrowers over the months. Working capital limits are set so as to meet peak deficit (over the months) financing requirements.

9.3.2.3 Duration of Working Capital Loans and Repayment Method

Working capital loans are revolving in nature. A working capital limit is sanctioned for the borrower based on the methods delineated in the preceding discussion. Depending on the borrower's cash flow under the operating cycle, banks design a suitable loan repayment schedule. Interest is charged on outstanding dues within the limit.

Working capital limits are reviewed and renewed annually. For renewal of the facility, standard procedures similar to the credit appraisal methods followed while sanctioning fresh working capital loans are applied.

9.3.2.4 Security and Margin Requirements

Inventories of finished goods and raw materials procured using the working capital loans, properties such as land and buildings, securities, gold, and so on, are used as security collaterals. In several cases, banks offer unsecured working capital loans based on the financial statements, credit scores, tax returns, and so on, of borrowers.

The margin requirement is up to 25 per cent of the turnover or current assets depending on the method used to compute the working capital limit.

9.3.2.5 Pricing of Working Capital Loans

Banks follow a standard benchmarking system linking the interest rate charged on working capital loans to their MCLR or an external benchmark as discussed in the case of project loans to corporates. The spread on the benchmark is mainly determined by the bank's cost of funds and the credit rating or score of borrowers.

9.3.3 Consortium Lending

At times, loan requirements for projects are very large, exceeding the funding capacity of a particular bank. Not being able to exploit an attractive business opportunity due to insufficient fund availability leads to a potential loss. Further, regulatory exposure limits are imposed to avoid loan concentration. As per the RBI circular 'Large Exposures Framework' issued on 3 June 2019, credit exposure to a single counterparty (borrower) is limited to a maximum of 20 per cent of a bank's tier-1 capital (RBI, 2019c). Similar exposure limit for a group of connected counterparties is fixed at 25 per cent. A lending bank already having exposure to a particular borrower will be constrained in providing more loans to the same borrower if the loans exceed the exposure limit. In such circumstances, the bank can resort to consortium lending or syndicated loans where a group of banks come together to finance the project. Moreover, the RBI has also stipulated that consortium lending needs to be followed for lending proposals of more than INR 500 crore (RBI, 2019c).

Infrastructure projects like construction of roads and highways, power, seaports and airports, and so on, generally require massive funding, and banks resort to consortium lending for such projects. Recently, it was reported that an SBI-led consortium is expected to fund Adani Group's INR 340-billion polyvinyl chloride (PVC) project in Mundra, Gujarat (Krishnan, 2023).

The operational details of consortium loans are briefly discussed as follows:

- The borrower approaches several banks with its project loan proposal and obtains their individual sanction.
- The group of lenders (banks) meet and appoint one of them as the *lead bank*.
- The lead bank approaches a *lender legal counsel* to draft the loan document and shares the same with the members of the consortium.
- The consortium loan uses common discipline in valuation of the primary security like land, buildings, machines and equipment; uniform rules and regulations including margin requirements and drawing power calculation; and so on.
- There are joint inspection and quarterly review of the consortium loan by members.
- However, the quantum of loans provided by each bank and their pricing differ across consortium members depending on their respective fund availability and risk appetite.

Consortium lending reduces banking risks due to individual misjudgement or malfeasance. Joint involvement of several banks in risk assessment, processing and follow-up procedures reduces errors likely to be committed by a single bank, intentionally or otherwise. It is afterall said that two heads are better than one.

Sometimes, consortium lending follows a different procedure compared to that described earlier. It may be that instead of approaching many banks simultaneously, the borrower may request a single bank to finance its project. The concerned bank processes the request and approaches other interested banks to co-fund the project. After other banks agree to the proposal, the remaining procedures as discussed are followed. This form of consortium lending is popularly referred to as *down-selling.*

In many Western countries, consortium loans are referred to as syndicated loans. Down-selling is informally known as roadshow.

9.4 Priority Sector Lending: Agricultural and MSME Loans

Availability of finance is a major instrument for achieving economic prosperity, details of which have already been discussed in Chapter 3. But there is a paradox in the role of finance in augmenting an individual's economic welfare. Formal finance like bank loans can be availed only by the creditworthy who are perceived to have the ability to pay back loans. The poor who are not considered creditworthy do not benefit from bank loans and cannot often take up new ventures to emerge from impoverished conditions. In a nutshell, one can say formal finance helps the rich become richer but does not enable the poor to overcome poverty. This underscores the imperative need for financial inclusion.

After nearly two decades of central planning adopted since the early 1950s, it was realised that banks in India were largely confined to urban areas and catered to the needs of large trade and business enterprises. The vast majority of rural masses did not benefit from banking services. This gave rise to the philosophy of *social control* of banking in the late 1960s as an imperative need to expand banking services to hitherto neglected sectors and areas. As discussed earlier, the nationalisation of 14 major commercial banks in 1969[1] was a significant move in this direction.

---

[1] Subsequently, six more banks were nationalised in 1980.

Another very significant initiative in this direction was the imposition of mandatory *priority sector lending* requirements. This obliged banks to extend a certain minimum proportion of their overall lending to specified activities and individuals. The initiative commenced in 1968 and saw several rounds of revision over time. Since 1985, Indian banks have been required to ensure extending a minimum 40 per cent of their overall lending to priority sectors. Recognising that foreign banks are confined to urban centres, they are given some concession in this regard. Foreign banks with less than 20 branches operating in India are required to meet a minimum target of 32 per cent for export credit within the overall 40 per cent priority sector lending. They need not meet sub-targets as regards loans to agriculture and rural credit. Details about priority sector lending are provided in Box 9.3.

9.4.1 Role of Branches in Priority Sector Lending

It may be noted that the branch managers and staff play a critical role in assessment of borrowers and management of loans under priority sector lending. Unlike retail and corporate loans, formula-based credit score models are not very useful in assessing creditworthiness and determining the loan amount in priority sector lending. This is because many potential borrowers often do not possess financial statements like balance sheets, income–expenditure statements, salary slips, income tax returns, and so on, for assessing their creditworthiness. In this regard, the professional judgement of branch managers is of paramount importance.

All the branches of a bank are not treated equally for fixing priority sector lending targets, notwithstanding the overall target for any particular bank. For example, the agriculture sector target of 18 per cent of total loans is a bank-level target. However, the branches of any bank are differently placed to meet the target uniformly. Urban branches may not have adequate scope for lending to agriculture but rural branches located in areas with fertile land and better irrigation facilities are more aptly placed to generate agricultural loans. Rural branches of leading PSBs contribute to nearly four-fifths of their total agricultural loans. The zonal or regional offices of a bank take into consideration the relative strength of branches under their control to fix targets for such loans.

The priority sector lending targets for bank branches are often set in quantum terms and towards ensuring a certain percentage growth over the actual amount of sectoral credit in the preceding year. Say, the agricultural

Box 9.3 Priority sector lending in India

The first move towards priority sector lending can be traced to the decision of the erstwhile National Credit Council (NCC) in July 1968 desiring bank lending to agriculture and small-scale industries on a priority basis. The NCC was an important policymaking body on bank credit with the finance minister as its chairman and the RBI governor as vice-chairman. Subsequently, in February 1972, the RBI issued guidelines specifying areas and sectors defined as the priority sector. In November 1974, banks were instructed to meet a minimum target of one-third of their respective total advances for the priority sector, to be achieved by March 1979.

As a follow up to the recommendations of the working group chaired by K. S. Krishnaswamy, the RBI issued modified guidelines on priority sector lending on 29 October 1980. The new guidelines raised the overall target to a minimum 40 per cent of total advances, to be achieved by March 1985. It also outlined sub-targets for various sectors or activities which are detailed as follows.

The *agriculture* sector employed a little over 60 per cent of the workforce in India in the early 1980s. Despite its declining share in overall GDP since independence, the sectoral share of agriculture was close to 30 per cent in the 1980s. To eradicate poverty and reduce income inequality, improving per capita income in the agriculture sector has been considered pivotal. In this backdrop, the importance of bank lending to agriculture cannot be overemphasised. The sub-target for priority sector lending to agriculture in the overall advances of a bank has been set at 18 per cent. Out of the overall target for agriculture, a three-fourth share is allotted to direct agricultural advances such as loans to farmers in the form of crop loans and tractor loans, loans to persons engaged in allied activities like dairy, goat rearing, poultry farming and pisciculture, and so on. Indirect agricultural priority sector loans consist of loans to agricultural cooperative societies; farmers' service societies; refinances to RRBs; loans for distribution of fertilizers, seeds and other agricultural implements; and so on.

Small-scale industries are important in India in terms of both employment generation and share in overall manufacturing output. MSMEs provided employment to close to 60 million in 2015 and were the second largest employment generating sector (next only to agriculture). There were nearly 26 million MSME units in 2015, accounting for close to 45 per cent of value added in Indian manufacturing. The classification of a particular enterprise under MSMEs is undertaken based on the investment threshold in plant and machinery at original cost and annual turnover. Such thresholds have been revised from time to time. Since July 2020, enterprises are classified into different categories as per the following criteria.

Table 9.8 Manufacturing enterprises and enterprises rendering services

Micro enterprise	Investment in plant and machinery not more than INR 1 crore and annual turnover not more than INR 5 crore
Small enterprise	Investment in plant and machinery not more than INR 10 crore and annual turnover not more than INR 50 crore
Medium enterprise	Investment in plant and machinery not more than INR 50 crore and annual turnover not more than INR 250 crore

At the time of formulating priority sector lending guidelines in the 1970s, this sector was even more critical for the Indian economy as regards employment, share in industrial output and exports.

Both direct loans to MSMEs as well as indirect finance to various agencies which support them are included under priority sector lending. Loans to agencies cover loans for setting up industrial estates, loans to state industrial corporations for financing MSMEs, and loans to those supplying inputs to and marketing products of artisans and village and cottage industries. Indirect finance to MSMEs also covers subscription to bonds issued by the NABARD with the objective of financing the non-farm sector exclusively as well as funds provided to the Small Industries Development Bank of India (SIDBI), state finance corporations, and so on. There is a sub-target of 12 per cent for loans to micro-enterprises.

The *services* sector today accounts for more than half of India's GDP. During the 1970s itself, policymakers were aware of its huge potential. Accordingly, loans to small road and water transport operators, professionals and self-employed persons, retail trade, small businesses, education and housing were also covered under priority sector lending requirements.

Weaker sections of society do not possess the required security collateral to obtain loans from banks while they need the funding support the most to break the vicious cycle of poverty. Under priority sector lending provisions, the sub-target for weaker sections has been gradually raised from 10 per cent of the overall advances of a bank in 2020–21 to 12 per cent, to be achieved by

2023–24. The weaker sections for this purpose comprised small and marginal farmers, landless labourers, tenant cultivators, sharecroppers, artisans, persons belonging to the Scheduled Castes (SCs) and Scheduled Tribes (STs), and so on.

In due course of time, it was observed that there was substantial under-recovery in priority sector loans. This posed challenges to the profitability and financial health of the banking sector. The Committee on the Financial System (RBI, 1991) made serious observations in this regard and recommended reduction of the minimum priority sector lending target from 40 to 10 per cent in a phased manner. Given its political sensitivity, this recommendation was not implemented. However, during the post-reform period, several initiatives were undertaken to rationalise priority sector lending which are already highlighted in Chapter 2.

credit disbursed by a branch was INR 100 crore in 2020–21. The zonal office may expect the same branch to raise agricultural credit by 10 per cent in 2021–22. Then the target for 2021–22 becomes INR 110 crore. This target may raise or reduce the ratio of agricultural loans to the total loans of the concerned branch depending on the overall growth in lending. Branch managers are expected to be proactive in regularly monitoring such loan accounts.

The following sections provide further details of management by branches of different types of priority sector loans.

9.4.1.1 Agricultural Loans

Under broad guidelines laid out by the top management of a bank, bank managers take lending decisions within their sanction limits. For amounts higher than the sanction limit of branch managers, higher authorities in the zonal office or the head office accord required approvals. Branch managers assess the creditworthiness of farmers by taking into account their land holdings, quality of land, water source for cultivation, marketability of the crop, net worth, and so on. Information obtained from fellow farmers and rural development officers in the local administration is also used along with that provided by the loan applicant themself. No formal credit score model is used for this purpose. Branch managers often determine the loan amount based on their personal judgement. Loans up to INR 3 lakh can be extended without requiring any security collateral like land.

It may be noted that the maximum limit for agricultural loans to be treated as priority sector lending as of July 2023 is fixed at INR 50 lakh. Moreover, state-level bankers' committees[2] (SLBCs) in different states provide overall guidance for determination of loan limits for different crops like sugarcane, bananas, paddy, and so on.

There is widespread belief that farmers in rural areas face unnecessary procedural hassles in obtaining bank loans. In an innovative initiative to promote hassle-free credit availability to farmers, the Government of India introduced the Kisan Credit Card (KCC) Scheme in 1998. This facilitated purchase of agricultural inputs and availing of related services by farmers on credit at any time. By 31 December 2022, 3.89 crore farmers had benefitted with a consolidated KCC limit of INR 4,51,672 crore. In 2018–19, the KCC facility was extended to fisheries and animal husbandry. By the end of 2022, nearly one lakh KCCs had been issued for the fisheries sector and five lakh for animal husbandry (RBI, 2023a).

Interest rates charged for agricultural loans are generally low. Large loans (above INR 3 lakh) are linked to the repo rate under the LAF. In early 2022, interest rates on such loans were within the range of 8.5 to 9 per cent (RBI, 2023a). Short-term agricultural loans up to INR 3 lakh are available at 7 per cent interest under the Modified Interest Subvention Scheme. To encourage timely repayment of loans, an additional subvention of 3 per cent is given for prompt and timely repayment of loans.

9.4.1.2 MSME Loans

Small loans (up to INR 5 lakh) to MSMEs under priority sector lending are assessed informally, without credit score models. Experience of the borrower in manufacturing the product, their future business plans, ability and scope for marketing, type of technology used for production, and so on, are considered by branch managers to assess creditworthiness as also fix the loan amount. For loans above INR 20 lakh, branch managers often obtain documentary information from loan applicants. The list includes invoices and bills to assess turnover, information on procurement of various inputs

---

[2] An SLBC is a consultative and coordinating body of all financial institutions in a state.

and raw materials for production, number of workers employed, and so on. Banks generally insist on a security collateral for large loans. Working capital loans and term loans for big MSMEs are very similar to loans to large corporates as regards security and margin requirements, credit appraisal and repayment methods, as discussed earlier. However, on each account, liberal and concessional norms are followed for MSME lending. For example, for working capital loans, the margin requirements insisted on by many banks are lower at 10–15 per cent of the eligible amount for MSMEs as compared to 25 per cent for corporate loans. Similarly, working capital limits are renewed once in two years for MSMEs while renewal is undertaken annually for corporate loans.

Interest rates charged on MSME loans were linked to the RBI's fixed repo rate under the LAF since 2019. In early 2022, interest rates charged by a PSB on such loans were within the range of 8.5 to 9 per cent. After monetary tightening commenced from May 2022, there were concerns on the rising costs of borrowing (linked to the rising fixed repo rate) by MSMEs. Many banks since then have linked the interest rates charged for MSME lending to their MCLR.

9.4.1.3 Loans to Services

Loans for trading and other services are more formal and document-based. Registration of the borrower is mandatory, and banks insist on submission of audited balance sheets and income–expenditure statements for the previous three years along with related projections for the next three years. Security collateral, although not mandatory, is generally insisted on by banks. Out of the total expenditure needs, generally the borrower is asked to cover a minimum margin of 20 per cent.

9.4.1.4 MUDRA Loans

The National Democratic Alliance (NDA) government under the leadership of Prime Minister Narendra Modi assumed office in May 2014 and introduced several policy initiatives to promote the overall economic prosperity of India. Some key policy initiatives of this government to foster financial inclusion were the introduction of the Pradhan Mantri Jan Dhan Yojana (PMJDY) and Micro Units Development and Refinance Agency (MUDRA) loans. The PMJDY requires banks to open no-frills accounts for the poor, named basic savings bank deposit accounts, merely based on the submission of a photograph of the depositor along with their signature or thumb impression given before a bank official. The maximum amount of deposits permitted in such accounts is INR 50,000. By August 2022, 46.11 crore beneficiaries had opened PMJDY accounts and the total deposit balances held in such accounts were INR 1,71,616 crore (RBI, 2023a).

MUDRA loans are envisaged to provide loans up to INR 10 lakh to small business enterprises in the manufacturing, trading and services sectors as well as allied agricultural activities. These are provided in the form of both term loans and working capital requirements. The margin requirement for MUDRA loans up to INR 50,000 is nil and that for amounts above INR 50,000 is 10 per cent. No processing fees are charged for loans up to INR 5 lakh. A guarantee for five years is provided under the Credit Guarantee Fund for Micro Units (CGFMU) to incentivise lending under this scheme.

9.5 Management of Investment Portfolio and Treasury Operations

As discussed earlier, the second largest component of the assets side of a bank's balance sheet is its 'investment portfolio'. The share of the investment portfolio has been nearly a quarter of the overall assets of SCBs in the early 2020s (RBI, 2022b). The share was in fact higher at nearly 35–40 per cent during the late 1990s and early 2000s. The reduction in the share of the investment portfolio is partly policy-driven as minimum SLR requirements were reduced from 25 per cent in 1997 to 18 per cent by April 2020. Other factors such as fluctuations in demand for bank credit, incidence of bank NPAs and related risk management requirements, and so on, are also relevant.

The investment portfolio has special significance for banks. First, bulk of the investment portfolio is in the form of SLR securities, a large part of which are government bonds issued by the central and state governments. These are devoid of default or credit risk and provide considerable stability to the overall assets of a bank. On the flip side, the assets under this portfolio earn lower returns as compared to loans and advances. Second, assets under the investment portfolio have wider terms to maturity ranging from shorter maturities of a week to longer maturities of 40 years at the time of issue. This helps in managing maturity mismatches in the assets and liabilities of banks, details of which have already been provided in Chapters 7 and 8. Further, such securities are actively traded in the secondary market and hence are highly liquid. Considering these facts, judicious decision-making on the size and composition of the investment portfolio in the banking business is critical.

9.5.1 *Composition of Investment Portfolio*

Table 9.9 provides information on the composition of the investment portfolio of SCBs in India. It is evident that SLR securities account for bulk of the investment portfolio. SLR securities are composed of bonds and TBs issued by the Government of India, bonds issued by state governments and other approved securities. Other securities include, for instance, bonds issued by petroleum marketing companies. In recent years, the share of SLR securities has been around 80 per cent of the overall investment portfolio of banks (Table 9.9).

Table 9.9 Composition of investment portfolio of SCBs in India

Item	2019	2020	2021	2019	2020	2021
	Value in INR billion			Percentage share in total investment		
1. SLR securities	33,811	37,473	44,625	79.5	81.0	82.6
2. Commercial papers	904	1,045	826	2.1	2.3	1.5
3. Shares issued by						
3.1. PSUs	115	141	98	0.3	0.3	0.2
3.2. Private corporate sector	696	754	640	1.6	1.6	1.2
3.3. Others	64	57	52	0.2	0.1	0.1
4. Bonds/Debentures issued by						
4.1. PSUs	1,348	1,257	1,210	3.2	2.7	2.2
4.2. Private corporate sector	2,688	2,266	3,089	6.3	4.9	5.7
4.3. Others	1,700	1,917	1,493	4.0	4.1	2.8
5. Instruments issued by						
5.1. Mutual funds	210	356	311	0.5	0.8	0.6
5.2. Financial institutions	984	977	1,671	2.3	2.1	3.1
Total investments	42,519	46,244	54,017	100.0	100.0	100.0

Source: *RBI Bulletin*, various issues, 2019–22, https://www.rbi.org.in/Scripts/BS_ViewBulletin.aspx (accessed in 2022).

Note: Figures pertain to end-March of the respective financial years.

Securities issued by the Government of India are of varied maturities. Long-term dated government securities or bonds have original terms to maturity from 5 to 40 years. TBs are money market instruments having terms to maturity of less than one year. Popular TBs with high demand in the Indian financial market are those of 91-day, 182-day and 364-day maturity. Both dated government securities and TBs of different maturities are actively traded in the secondary government securities market. TBs are basically zero-coupon instruments and are purchased at a discount. For example, assume the face value of a 91-day TB is INR 100 and is purchased at INR 98 in the auction. As the purchase price is less than the face value, it is said that the TB is purchased at a discount. The rate of return is calculated as the percentage change between the face value and the purchase price of the bond in annualised terms. For example, for a 91-day TB, annualised return in this case is $[(100 - 98)/98] \times 100 \times 4 = 2.04 \times 4\% = 8.16\%$. The percentage return on this TB is multiplied by 4 to convert it into annualised return.

On the contrary, the bulk of dated securities bear coupons which are paid once in six months. Let us consider the example of a one-year government bond with, say, a 4.8 per cent coupon rate. This bond may be purchased at a discount, at par or at a premium depending on demand and supply conditions. A bond is said to be sold at a premium when its market price is above its face value. The scope for buying this bond at par or at a premium arises as it provides six monthly returns of INR 4.80 (for a face value of INR 100). This coupon earning is added to the difference between the face value and the market price of the bond to determine total returns. For example, if the purchase price of the bond is INR 95 (at a discount), the total return on the bond will be the sum of the capital gain of INR 5 (= INR 100 – INR 95) and the coupon value of INR 9.60 (= INR 4.80 × 2) which is INR 14.60. On the contrary, if the bond is purchased at a premium, say, at INR 102, there is a capital loss of INR 2 (= INR 100 – INR 102). However, the total return on the bond is still positive at INR 7.60. This is the sum of the capital loss and coupon earnings on the bond.

Other than such bonds and TBs issued by the Government of India, SLR securities also include state development loans which are basically securities issued by various state governments in India. The share of state government securities in overall SLR securities is relatively small.

Apart from investments in SLR securities, banks also invest in shares, bonds, mutual funds, and so on. It may be observed from Table 9.9 that the share of investments in bonds or debentures is in the range of 11–13 per cent of the overall investment portfolio of SCBs. Investments in bonds or debentures issued by the private corporate sector account for close to half this number. Investments in instruments issued by financial institutions comprise around 2–3 per cent of the overall investment portfolio. Investments in shares contribute to roughly another 1.5–2.1 per cent.

9.5.2 Management of Investment Portfolio

Management of the investment portfolio of banks is critical for the overall banking business due to several aspects. As discussed earlier, bulk of such investments are devoid of default risk and highly liquid. The maturity spectrum of such investments is also quite extensive. Therefore, the investment portfolio not only reduces overall credit and liquidity risk in a bank's balance sheet, it also aids in balancing asset–liability mismatches.

Business decisions on various assets in the investment portfolio of a bank are taken at the head-office level. The treasury department under the strategic policy guidance of the ALCO of a bank generally manages the investment portfolio. These matters are, however, regulated by the RBI guidelines in this regard. Bank executives and managers responsible for investment decisions need to be familiar with such guidelines and ensure strict adherence to them. The latest guidelines in this matter are provided in 'Master Direction: Classification, Valuation and Operation of Investment Portfolio of Commercial Banks (Directions), 2021', issued by the RBI (2022a). This provides details of classification of investments, conditions for migration across different categories, valuation, prudential system, role of the board, and so on. In the following paragraphs, we have summarised some important aspects from the RBI's 'Master Direction'.

As per the RBI guidelines, banks need to classify their entire investment portfolio under three heads, namely (*a*) held to maturity (HTM), (*b*) available for sale (AFS) and (*c*) held for trading (HFT). Classification of securities in any of these categories is determined by the bank at the time of acquiring the security. The same is documented in the records appropriately.

Those securities which the bank intends to hold until maturity are categorised as HTM. Such securities cannot be sold prior to maturity. On the other hand, those securities which the bank intends to hold for trading in the secondary market and not until maturity are classified under the HFT category. Banks undertake sale or purchase of government securities in the secondary market to take advantage of short-term variation in market price. HFT securities need to be offloaded within 90 days. The remaining securities in the bank's investment portfolio which are neither categorised as HTM nor HFT are placed under AFS.

According to RBI stipulations, the share of HTM in the overall investment portfolio of a bank shall not exceed 25 per cent. Securities which are to be included in the HTM portfolio are mainly SLR securities. Non-SLR securities which were included under HTM prior to September 2004 can be part of this portfolio too. After September 2004, only a few special types of non-SLR securities can be added under HTM. These include (*a*) recapitalisation bonds issued by the Government of India towards infusing capital in the same bank and held in the investment portfolio, (*b*) equity of subsidiaries and joint ventures, (*c*) long-term bonds issued by companies engaged in infrastructure activities, and so on. However, such non-SLR securities will not be counted for the purpose of the 25 per cent ceiling for the HTM category. 'Master Direction' also provides the conditions under which the ceiling can be exceeded.

As per the RBI guidelines, the composition of HFT and AFS within the remaining 75 per cent of the investment portfolio can be determined by a bank based on its capital position, trading strategies, risk management capabilities, tax planning, expertise and skills of its managers, and so on.

'Master Direction' also provides guidelines for shifting securities from one category to another. For example, securities held under HTM can be shifted only at the beginning of the accounting year with the approval of the board of directors. Such transfers are subject to certain conditions laid down by the RBI. There are also detailed guidelines on valuation of securities, income recognition and risk management of the investment portfolio.

The RBI guidelines require all banks to frame and adopt a comprehensive investment policy. This policy should be duly approved by the bank's board of directors. The policy document, inter alia, stipulates appropriate prudential limits for investments and delineates the proper risk management apparatus. Investment proposals entail similar credit risk analysis as undertaken for bank loans. Banks are expected to put in place a robust internal credit rating system for investments as well. The board of directors is required to constitute an investment committee which is supposed to take decisions on investments. This committee is accountable for all business decisions of the bank related to its 'investment portfolio'.

9.5.3 Treasury Operations

The treasury department of a bank undertakes business transactions related to the investment portfolio under the overall guidance of the ALCO and the investment committee. Treasury operations mainly involve transactions in SLR and non-SLR securities, forex, and so on. Such operations are undertaken to profitably deploy the surplus funds of a bank so as to optimise risk-adjusted returns.

Treasury operations heavily depend on the evolving economic situation and existing liquidity conditions. For example, during the Covid-19 pandemic of 2020–21, many banks in India witnessed muted credit demand while their deposit growth was robust. Banks managed this surplus liquidity situation by aggressive investment in government securities and corporate bonds. They also had to deal with lower returns on investments due to rising market prices under high demand pressure. So officials manning treasury operations need to be alert to the evolving economic and liquidity situations and promptly respond in managing the overall investment portfolio.

The treasury department of banks also assists in compliance with the RBI's SLR regulations. Banks need to maintain currency and balances with the RBI suitably to meet minimum CRR and SLR norms. In most banks, the banking operations and accounts department monitors the CRR and SLR position on a continuous basis. Based on its advice, the treasury department must adjust holding of SLR securities to meet the minimum requirements.

The post-reform period in India has witnessed growing integration of the Indian economy with the rest of the world. There have been quantum jumps in cross-border trade in goods and services as also manifold increases in international capital flows. India adopted a market-determined exchange rate regime and facilitated development of a very active forex market. In this backdrop, first, banks in India have also become highly active in the forex market. The treasury department looks after business transactions in the forex market such as buying and selling of foreign currencies. This is supported by information on inward and outward remittances in foreign currency obtained from branches dealing with foreign currency transactions. Second, banks provide active support to customers in managing their foreign currency flows. Such customers basically include exporters, importers and those involved in cross-border investments. Third, they offer a host of financial derivatives such as options, swaps and forwards in foreign currency trade to hedge against risks from adverse movement of exchange rates against popular foreign currencies. Forex operations include both exchange-traded derivatives and OTC transactions.

9.6 Conclusion

As a commercial entity, the primary objective of a bank is to maximise risk-adjusted returns from the banking business. Expansion of loans and advances and promotion of investments are directly helpful in raising the interest income of banks. Associated pricing of such loans and returns on investments are equally important. Given that loans and investments embody a variety of risks, banks need to be cautious in assessing the riskiness of such assets and incorporating potential risks in the pricing of their products. Thus, decisions on loans and investments based on assessment of associated risks and their suitable pricing are fundamental to the conduct of the banking business. In this chapter, we have provided necessary banking management details for different types of loans and investments. The chapter has highlighted practical aspects of banking management pertaining to the assets side of a bank's balance sheet.

Particularly, we observed that the management of the investment portfolio of banks is more centralised, under the direct supervision of the ALCO and the investment committee and executed by the treasury department. A comprehensive loan policy envisaged and approved by the board broadly guides the lending decisions of branch managers. Branch managers largely follow the guidelines and credit scoring models prescribed by the central authority in case of retail loans while their personal judgement is critical for assessing the creditworthiness of loan applicants in priority sector loans of small size. For corporate loans, although the central authority prescribes broad guidelines, branch managers enjoy considerable scope for negotiations and bargaining. The pricing of a large part of the loan portfolio of banks is as per the internal or external benchmarking prescribed by the RBI. Under this broad guideline, banks have considerable autonomy and loans are priced taking into account a variety of factors including the RBI's monetary policy stance, cost of funds for the bank and the risk profile of the borrower.

Revision Questions and Problems

1. How important are bank loans and investments in the overall balance sheet of SCBs in India?
2. Compare retail and corporate loan products in terms of (*a*) size of the loans, (*b*) type of borrowers and (*c*) end-use of the funds.
3. Briefly discuss the major varieties or types of retail loans extended by banks in India in the post-reform period.
4. Explain the credit appraisal practices and other procedures followed for processing corporate loans in India, both for project or term loans and for working capital loans.
5. How are working capital loans obtained by corporates or businesses different from project loans?
6. Explain how external or internal benchmarking is used by banks in India for determination of interest rates for loans and advances.
7. How do banks determine the spread over an internal benchmark like MCLR for fixing interest rates for different borrowers? Explain with an example.
8. What is the importance of the investment portfolio for management of credit and liquidity risk in a bank's balance sheet?
9. Priority sector lending has special significance for financial inclusion in India. Discuss in detail priority sector lending by banks in India.
10. Briefly explain management of the investment portfolio and treasury operations of banks in India.

10

Banking Management

Liabilities Side

Deposits and Borrowings

Learning Objectives

- To describe regular banking management processes pertaining to items on the liabilities side of a bank's balance sheet
- To explain various types of deposits offered by banks
- To outline broad banking strategies on management of the deposits portfolio and pricing of deposits
- To explain borrowings undertaken by banks from different sources and related strategies
- To delineate various types of OBS items of banks

10.1 Introduction

In Chapter 9, we discussed management of banking assets such as bank loans and investments. Broad considerations on profitability, solvency and liquidity guide overall strategic decisions on the volume and type of bank lending and pricing of loans. Operational decisions related to items on the liabilities side of a bank's balance sheet are equally important and are covered in this chapter.

During the post-reform period, banks assumed adequate operational autonomy as regards deposit mobilisation and fixing of interest rates on deposits as well as exploration of several sources of borrowings. This has created a highly competitive environment for mobilising deposits by attracting customers through aggressive marketing and pricing strategies. Banks are heavily reliant on borrowings not only for day-to-day liquidity management but also to raise capital from the market for meeting tier-2 capital requirements under the Basel norms.

OBS items such as bank guarantees, LCs, acceptances and endorsements have been offered by banks in India to facilitate trade and business. Contingent upon failure of the counterparty to honour the underlying transaction, any OBS item can become an effective liability. Hence, such items are popularly referred to as *contingent liabilities*. These items are not real bank liabilities as long as they are not crystalised. During the post-reform period, not only has the volume of transactions in traditional OBS items like bank guarantees and LCs significantly multiplied, new financial derivatives mainly pertaining to foreign exchange (forex) contracts have also become very popular. Given the importance of OBS items in the banking business in recent times, this chapter also briefly discusses management of these items.

As discussed in Chapter 8, the ALM system adopted by banks in India since the late 1990s has emerged as a comprehensive tool to analyse, monitor and take corrective action for managing a bank's balance sheet. Its mandate goes beyond containing the asset–liability gap of banks across different time buckets within tolerable limits to manage liquidity and interest rate risk. The ALM system has many critical macro-level functions such as overall profit planning and business growth for banks. Strategic decisions pertaining to the composition of bank liabilities such as deposits and borrowings and the pricing of deposits are part of the ALM exercise. The ALCO under the overall guidance of a bank's board discharges the responsibilities related to ALM. The treasury department takes care of the operational aspects.

The rest of this chapter is organised as follows. Section 10.2 provides detailed information about the composition of bank liabilities, particularly its main components of deposits and borrowings. The strategies followed by banks in India for determining the composition of deposits and their pricing are covered in section 10.3. Similar strategies for borrowings by banks are presented in section 10.4. Related information pertaining to management of OBS items by banks in India is provided in section 10.5. The broad conclusions of the chapter are presented in section 10.6.

10.2 Major Liabilities-Side Items in a Bank's Balance Sheet

This book has already introduced the reader to a bank's balance sheet in Chapter 1. It was observed that on the liabilities side of the balance sheet of a typical commercial bank, 'deposits' constitute the most dominant item.

Their share was nearly 79.3 per cent in the total liabilities of SCBs in 2021–22. The share for PSBs was even higher at 84.3 per cent (calculated based on data from RBI, 2022b). Deposits are of various types differing in terms of maturity, payment of interest, and so on. Retail deposits are the most popular form of bank deposits and account for the bulk of bank liabilities in India. Retail deposits are available for the general public. Households have accounted for 50–60 per cent of term deposits and 80–90 per cent of savings account deposits during the post-reform period (calculated based on data from RBI, n.d.1). Retail deposits differ from special types of high-value deposits such as bulk deposits and certificates of deposit (CDs) which are available to select high-net-worth individuals or companies. CDs are money market instruments and can be traded in the secondary market. Banks in India offer the following types of retail deposits.

10.2.1 Types of Retail Deposits Offered by Banks in India

Details of various types of deposits that can be offered by banks in India and rate(s) of interest payable on the same are provided in 'Master Direction: Reserve Bank of India (Interest Rate on Deposits) Directions, 2016', issued by the RBI on 3 March 2016 and updated on 2 July 2021. A large part of our discussion in this section is borrowed from this document. Let us confine to the most popular varieties of retail deposits offered to the general public.

10.2.1.1 Current Account Deposits

Current account deposits are payable on demand. Such accounts do not have any restriction on the number of cash deposits and withdrawals, and they are also are not subject to any limit on the amount of daily transactions. On the flip side, the minimum balances required to be maintained in current account deposits are generally higher. Also, no interest is paid on balances in current account deposits. While having several customised options for instant and seamless payments is the advantage for a customer holding a current account deposit, the main disadvantage is loss of interest income. Current account deposits are mainly held by businesses, merchants and enterprises that are required to undertake high-value and frequent banking transactions. Many societies, associations and institutions like universities also hold current account deposits.

10.2.1.2 Savings Account Deposits

Savings account deposits are the most popular bank deposits held by the general public. They have accounted for nearly one-third of the total bank deposits of SCBs in the late 2010s and early 2020s (calculated based on data from RBI, 2019b, and RBI, 2022b). Banks pay interest on savings account deposits. The balances held in such accounts are withdrawable on demand using withdrawal slip, cheque, ATM, online transfer, and so on. Interest paid on savings bank accounts is low as compared to that on fixed term deposits. Also, as per the norm, banks can impose restrictions on the number and amount of withdrawals. There are daily limits on the maximum amount that can be withdrawn through an ATM. If the deposit balances in savings bank accounts fall below the minimum balance requirement, banks impose a small financial penalty on the customer. Many banks offer 'zero balance' savings bank account facilities on salary accounts. Salary accounts are nothing but ordinary savings bank accounts to which the salary of the depositor is regularly credited by their employer.

10.2.1.3 Term Deposits

The general public may be familiar with *term deposits* which are also popularly referred to as *fixed deposits*. As the name suggests, such deposits have fixed terms to maturity ranging from 7 days to 10 years. The customer does not have the right to demand withdrawal of such deposits before their date of maturity. However, in actual practice, banks allow such withdrawal to meet exigencies like large medical expenses, costs of children's education, and so on. As per the RBI guidelines, premature withdrawal facility is available for all term deposits up to INR 15 lakh accepted from individuals. Term deposits account for bulk of the bank deposits in India. Such deposits accounted for nearly 60 per cent of the total deposits of SCBs in the late 2010s and early 2020s (calculated based on data from RBI, 2019b, and RBI, 2022b).

There are some varieties of term deposits offered by banks in India with special features. For example, *notice deposits* are fixed deposits which can be withdrawn by giving one-day notice. *Recurring deposits* are a special variety where periodic (monthly, quarterly, and so on) deposits are made in the account for a certain period. On fixed deposits with reinvestment option, the maturity amount is auto-renewed on the date of maturity if there is no explicit request by the depositor to redeem the amount. Say, a one-year fixed deposit (under reinvestment option) is scheduled to mature on 29 August 2022. If the customer does not explicitly opt for its redemption, it will be auto-renewed for one more year on 29 August 2022. Its revised date of maturity becomes 29 August 2023. The interest rate applicable to auto-renewed deposits is that prevailing on the date of renewal.

These varieties fall under the broad category of 'domestic rupee deposits'. Banks in India also offer deposit accounts for non-resident Indians (NRIs).[1] Such accounts are opened and operated as per the provisions of the Foreign Exchange Management (Deposit) Regulations, 2000, which are amended from time to time. NRIs can open both foreign currency–denominated and rupee-denominated deposit accounts as detailed in the following sections.

10.2.1.4 Non-Resident Ordinary (NRO) and Non-Resident External (NRE) Deposit Accounts

Banks in India allow NRIs to open rupee-denominated deposit accounts. There are two such types, namely, (*a*) non-resident ordinary (NRO) accounts and (*b*) non-resident external (NRE) accounts.

NRO deposits can be opened to keep any income earned by NRIs in India. Such income may include rent, dividends, interest income, pension, and so on. Interest earned by NRIs on NRO deposits is taxable at the rate of 30 per cent. Interest earned on NRO accounts after tax is repatriable. The principal amount is also repatriable subject to a maximum of USD 1 million in a financial year. Such accounts can be opened jointly with other NRIs or Indian citizens.

NRE deposits are opened to keep foreign earnings of NRIs. Both the balances and interest income on NRE deposits are tax-free. Also, both the principal and interest earnings are repatriable and can be transferred to a foreign currency non-resident (bank) account, popularly referred to as an FCNR(B) or FCNR deposit account. NRE accounts can be jointly opened with other NRIs, too.

---

[1] An NRI is an Indian citizen who resides in a foreign country for employment or business for more than 180 days in a financial year.

10.2.1.5 FCNR Deposit Accounts

NRIs can open FCNR accounts with banks in India. These are foreign currency–denominated accounts. Most banks in India offer FCNR deposits in any of six foreign currencies, namely, US dollar, euro, pound sterling, yen, Australian dollar and Canadian dollar. FCNR accounts can be opened to deposit money earned overseas in a foreign currency. Interest paid on FCNR balances is free from income tax in India. These accounts are fixed deposits with maturity varying from one year to five years. Both the principal amount and interest earnings on such accounts are fully repatriable. Overdraft facility is provided in FCNR accounts.

As FCNR deposits are denominated in foreign currencies, they do not suffer from exchange rate fluctuations vis-à-vis the Indian rupee. This is a major attraction which leads NRIs to prefer FNCR deposits as compared to NRE or NRO deposits.

10.2.2 Borrowings of Banks

The second largest item on the liabilities side of a bank's balance sheet is *borrowings*. The share of borrowings in the total liabilities of SCBs in 2021–22 was 7.7 per cent. This is not that significant compared to the share of deposits at nearly 80 per cent. The share of borrowings was even lower earlier. It was a mere 3.2 per cent in 1997–98 and increased to 4.8 per cent in 2003–04 (calculated based on data from RBI, 2022b). Further, reliance on borrowings is not uniform across bank groups. In 1997–98, the share of borrowings in the total liabilities of PSBs was 2.2 per cent while that for foreign banks was much higher at 15.1 per cent. The share for IPBs was closer to that of PSBs at 2.4 per cent. In 1997–98, foreign banks accounted for nearly two-fifths of the total borrowings of SCBs. High reliance of foreign banks on borrowings was due to their low deposit base. However, since then PSBs and IPBs have taken increasing recourse to borrowings, particularly from non-banking institutions and agencies, for reasons explained in the subsequent paragraphs. This reduced the share of foreign banks in the total borrowings of SCBs to 7.7 per cent in 2021–22. The share of PSBs and IPBs commensurately increased to around 45 per cent each (calculated based on data from RBI, 2022b).

It is widely perceived that with development of different segments of the financial market like the equities, bond and money markets, and so on, and non-banking financial companies (NBFCs), savers gain access to non-banking savings instruments. Generally, interest rates on bank deposits are low as compared to returns on capital and money market instruments of similar maturities.

With development of financial markets and growth of non-banking financial institutions, savers look for increasingly more non-bank avenues for savings in search of high returns. Non-bank entities such as insurance companies, mutual funds, pension funds, and so on, lend part of the resources generated from savers to different segments of the financial system. Banks borrow such resources available in the capital and money markets to support their funding requirements. In terms of volume, there has been multi-fold increase in the borrowings of SCBs. They increased from INR 257.8 billion in 1991–92 to INR 16,632.8 billion in 2021–22.

Bulk of the borrowings of banks in India are from domestic sources. In 2021–22, domestic borrowings constituted 73.7 per cent of the overall borrowings of SCBs (RBI, 2022b). Banks borrow mainly from three domestic sources, namely (*a*) the RBI, (*b*) other banks and (*c*) other institutions and agencies. In 2021–22, nearly 90 per cent of the domestic borrowing of SCBs was from other institutions and agencies. The share of borrowing from the RBI was 7.8 per cent and the remaining 2.9 per cent of domestic borrowing was from other banks.

It is important to note that banks take recourse to borrowings for a variety of reasons. They borrow from the RBI to tide over short-term liquidity requirements. They borrow from other banks also mainly to meet day-to-day liquidity deficiencies. On the other hand, borrowings from other financial institutions and agencies are undertaken to raise tier-2 capital and tap funds from these sources.

Borrowings certainly add to a bank's resources. Moreover, there are significant advantages in raising funds through long-term borrowing. It reduces liquidity risks of a bank and also improves its asset–liability management by supporting funding of long-term projects.

On the contrary, borrowings also have several disadvantages from the point of view of banks. First, the cost of borrowings is often higher than that of retail bank deposits. Notwithstanding lower interest earnings, savers prefer to hold bank deposits as such deposits facilitate seamless payments, have easy withdrawal options and enjoy insurance protection. As in many countries, bank deposits in India up to INR 5 lakh are insured by the Deposit Insurance and Credit Guarantee Corporation (DICGC). Second, the borrowings portfolio entails market risks as many instruments thereunder are traded actively. External borrowings may carry exchange rate risks too. Banks need to appropriately configure the risks embodied in their borrowings portfolio and accordingly undertake suitable risk management measures. Different types of borrowings availed by banks in India are summarised as follows.

10.2.2.1 Borrowings from the RBI

Notwithstanding that they constitute less than one-tenth share of the domestic borrowings of SCBs, borrowings from the RBI are very popular. Banks avail funds from the RBI under different windows and under a variety of considerations. One of the initial responsibilities of central banks like the RBI was to provide an LOLR facility to banks under severe liquidity stress. In the past, the RBI also provided reserves to the banking system for funding seasonal requirements. Moreover, it had been providing various sector-specific refinances to banks, including export credit refinance (ECR). Under ECR, banks used to avail funding from the RBI linked to their incremental outstanding export credit as against a cut-off date. The interest rate on ECR was linked to the bank rate[2] and the duration could be up to 180 days. In 1997, the RBI had established a *general refinance* facility under which refinance was provided up to 1 per cent of the average outstanding aggregate deposits of a bank in 1996–97. The general refinance facility was available for a duration of eight weeks. For the first four weeks, the interest rate applicable was the bank rate; and for the second spell of four weeks, it was the bank rate plus 1 per cent.

The period since the early 2000s witnessed the RBI switching over to market-oriented facilities for funding banks. Operationalisation of the LAF from June 2000 was one such significant initiative. The LAF envisaged the RBI lending to banks on overnight basis at the fixed repo rate. For longer duration

---

[2] Bank rate is the standard interest rate at which the RBI buys or rediscounts bills of exchange or other commercial papers to provide general refinance facility to the commercial banks. Since early 2000s, bank rate is linked to the RBI's fixed repo rate under the LAF. As of 29 August 2024, bank rate is 6.75 per cent, which is 25 basis points above the RBI's repo rate. During the late 1990s, when there was no LAF, the bank rate was the RBI's main discount rate to provide refinance facilities to the banks. Repo rate is a fixed interest rate charged by the RBI for overnight funding to a bank under the LAF. It is the official policy rate used by the RBI to convey its monetary policy stance, since adoption of inflation targeting in 2016. It is also known as policy repo rate. As of 29 August 2024, the RBI's repo rate stands at 6.50 per cent.

borrowing from the RBI, ECR remained the only standing facility. Interest payable on ECR was aligned with the fixed repo rate under the LAF. However, there was growing concern on interference of sector-specific standing facilities like ECR in smooth monetary policy transmission. Consequently, the ECR facility was phased out in 2014–15. It was replaced by a new market-oriented system to provide system-level liquidity based on the SLR holding of banks.

As of August 2024, borrowing options for banks from the RBI include a range of liquidity management facilities. These cover overnight facilities at the very short end as also longer-term options extending to a couple of years.

Availing funds from the RBI under repo operations is the most popular means for banks to manage short-term liquidity deficiencies. The RBI provides overnight funding to banks at the fixed repo rate under the LAF. This is the single policy rate used by the RBI for its monetary policy operations. As of 31 August 2024, the fixed repo rate is 6.5 per cent. There is no restriction on the amount of borrowing under the fixed repo facility as long as a bank can offer eligible SLR securities as collateral. LAF operations are conducted by the RBI on a daily basis.

Banks can also borrow from the RBI under variable term repo. A bank can avail a 14-day repo facility on reporting Fridays.[3] The amount of lending and applicable variable repo rate are determined by the RBI based on market liquidity conditions. Banks can borrow from the RBI under variable term repo within a range of overnight to 13 days. However, this facility is not available on a regular basis. Depending on its assessment of market liquidity conditions, the RBI exercises its discretion to conduct such repo operations.

Banks which are in need of emergency liquidity support under difficult situations can borrow from the RBI under the marginal standing facility (MSF). This provides short-term liquidity at a penal interest rate. The interest rate charged for MSF is higher than the fixed repo rate. As on 31 August 2024, the MSF interest rate is 6.75 per cent (25 basis points above the fixed repo rate under the LAF). A bank can avail funds under MSF up to its excess SLR holdings plus an amount equivalent to 2 per cent of its NDTL. For example, say, the NDTL of Bank X is INR 1,000 crore. As on 31 August 2024, the minimum SLR requirement for banks is 18 per cent of NDTL. Therefore, the

[3] Reporting Fridays are indicated by the RBI in a calendar and are basically alternate Fridays on which banks submit various returns to the RBI. The duration between two reporting Fridays is one fortnight.

minimum amount of SLR securities to be maintained by Bank X is INR 180 crore. Let us assume the actual position of SLR securities held by Bank X at present is INR 250 crore. Then excess amount of SLR securities = INR 250 crore – INR 180 crore = INR 70 crore. Moreover, the amount equivalent to 2 per cent of NDTL = 0.02 × INR 1,000 crore = INR 20 crore. Thus, under MSF, Bank X can borrow up to INR 90 crore. This is sum of INR 70 crore of excess SLR securities and INR 20 crore which is 2 per cent of the bank's NDTL.

Since February 2020, banks can avail long-term borrowing from the RBI under long-term repo operations (LTROs). The duration of LTROs can vary from one to three years. Since March 2020, banks can also borrow under targeted long-term repo operations (TLTROs) for on-lending to specific sectors or instruments such as investment-grade corporate bonds, commercial papers, non-convertible debentures, and so on. Both LTROs and TLTROs are variable rate repo facilities. The amount of lending and interest rate applicable are determined by the RBI based on its assessment of market liquidity conditions. The RBI has not fixed any regular calendar for conduct of LTROs and TLTROs and provides such facilities at its discretion.

10.2.2.2 Borrowings from Other Banks

Banks borrow from each other mainly in the *call money market* which is the overnight inter-bank market in India. It may happen that on a particular day Bank A is in need of funds to finance a large borrower, say, X. Bank A is likely to receive a huge amount of loan repayment on the next day from another customer, say, Y. In such a case, if it does not wish to forego the profit opportunity of lending today to X, it can take recourse to the call money market. It can avail funds from other banks which have surplus funds. Using the borrowed funds from the call money market, Bank A can exploit the lending opportunity today and pay back its lenders the next day out of the loan repayment receipts from Y.

Borrowing in the call money market does not require any security collateral. Obviously, the interest rate charged by banks in this market will not be less that the standing deposit facility (SDF) rate of the RBI. As on 31 August 2024, the SDF rate is 6.25 per cent (25 basis points below the RBI's fixed repo rate under the LAF). Any bank with surplus funds has the option of depositing the same with the RBI SDF and earning interest income at the SDF rate. Such banks will be interested in lending to a bank in the call money market only if they are offered an interest rate higher than the SDF rate. With the latest LAF corridor designed by the RBI, the call money rate is observed to be revolving around the fixed repo rate (Samantaraya, 2023).

Banks in India also borrow from other banks in the *notice money market*, in which the tenure of borrowing is up to 14 days. However, the notice money market is not very active.

10.2.2.3 Borrowings from Other Institutions and Agencies

Banks also avail borrowings from other financial institutions and agencies. As indicated earlier, this contributes to nearly nine-tenths of the domestic borrowings of SCBs. Such an overwhelming share is due to several reasons. First, with the adoption of the Basel prudential norms on capital adequacy, banks were required to augment their capital position in relation to risk-weighted assets to comply with minimum CRAR requirements. This compelled them to raise tier-2 capital in the domestic capital market by issuing subordinated debt.

Second, non-bank participants have been debarred from the call money market since 2005. They are allowed to lend in the market repo and collateralised borrowing and lending obligations (CBLO) market which have emerged as the dominant collateralised money markets in India. Mutual funds are found to be major lenders in both the market repo and the CBLO market. Other financial institutions are significant lenders in the market repo. PSBs are major borrowers in the CBLO market and foreign banks and IPBs have been borrowing heavily in the market repo.

External borrowings became important for banks in India during the post-reform period. Banks gained flexibility on different accounts to tap foreign sources of funding. The RBI (2005b) observed that granting pre-shipment credit in foreign currency (PCFC) and export bill rediscounting (EBR) to exporters significantly contributed to raising the external borrowings of banks. Banks were allowed utilisation of funds raised through buy–sell swaps for granting such loans. In the late 2010s and early 2020s, external borrowings have contributed to nearly a quarter of the overall borrowings of SCBs.

10.3 Business Strategies for Mobilisation of Bank Deposits

In this section let us focus on general bank management decisions pertaining to bank deposits and their pricing. Coordinated efforts with the active involvement of the board of directors and the ALCO for strategic decisions at the top level and different levels of managers and staff at the branch level are of paramount importance in mobilisation of bank deposits. Overall macroeconomic conditions which determine demand for bank credit and the relative liquidity position of a bank provide broad guidance for its approach to deposit mobilisation. Higher credit demand in the face of a bank's deficient fund position obviously drives an aggressive approach for deposit mobilisation. Similarly, deficit demand for bank credit and investment opportunities within the risk–return requirements of a bank may force it to limit deposit growth. Within the broad approach on deposit growth, ALM requirements of a bank determine its endeavour to promote deposit growth under different maturities. In the following sections, we provide further details on these aspects.

10.3.1 Composition of the Bank Deposits Portfolio

As regards the composition of domestic rupee deposits, banks in India follow a judicious approach to balance long-term and short-term maturity. Long-term deposits are in the form of term deposits or fixed deposits. Short-term deposits are popularly referred to as CASA deposits, an acronym for current account and savings account deposits.

Within CASA, banks do not pay any interest on current account deposits. But such deposits pose liquidity risks to banks as they are payable on demand. Banks pay a lower interest rate on savings account deposits. Similar to current account deposits, savings bank accounts also pose liquidity risks to banks. Such deposits are practically payable on demand notwithstanding daily limits on the number of transactions and amount of withdrawals.

Fixed deposits are more durable and do not pose much liquidity risk to banks as they have a pre-scheduled maturity date. But they are costly as interest rates paid on fixed deposits are much higher than those on savings account deposits. Table 10.1 provides information on interest rates paid by two leading banks in India, namely SBI and HDFC Bank, on their deposits (as on 29 August 2022). It may be observed from this table that interest rates offered by both these banks on their fixed deposits of more than one-year maturity are nearly double those offered on savings account deposits.

Banks try to maintain their CASA deposits in a proportion close to the industry average. For example, say, in the entire banking system, the ratio of CASA deposits to total deposits is 40 per cent. Every bank tries to

Table 10.1 Interest rates on deposits of SBI and HDFC Bank

(As on 29 August 2022; per cent)

Type of deposit	Term to maturity	SBI	HDFC Bank
Fixed deposits	7–45 days	2.90	2.75–3.25
	46–179 days	3.90	3.25–3.75
	180–210 days	4.55	
	211 days–less than 1 year	4.60	
	6 months–less than 1 year		4.65
	1 year–less than 2 years	5.45	5.50
	2 years–less than 3 years	5.50*	5.50
	3 years–less than 5 years	5.60	6.10
	5 years–up to 10 years	5.65	5.75
Savings bank accounts		2.70	3.00†

Source: Official websites of SBI (www.sbi.co.in) and HDFC Bank (www.hdfcbank.com) (accessed on 29 August 2022).

Note: (*a*) Interest rates offered on term deposits provided in this table are for deposits of less than INR 2 crore and applicable to ordinary citizens. Higher interest rates are offered to senior citizens and on deposits of more than INR 2 crore. (*b*) *Except for domestic term deposits for 1,000 days for which the rate of interest was 6.10 per cent. (*c*) †Interest rate on savings bank deposits of less than INR 50 lakh.

maintain a similar ratio (40 per cent in this instance). This is to avoid any cost disadvantage as compared to its peers. Given that CASA deposits are cheaper, a higher proportion of CASA deposits for a particular bank facilitates overall lower costs for its deposits.

In the recent years, IPBs have been very successful in raising their share in overall CASA deposits in the banking system. Their share in current account deposits increased from 40.7 per cent as of end-March 2021 to 45.5 per cent as of end-June 2022. During the same period, their share in savings account deposits increased from 27 to 33 per cent (RBI, 2022b, 2023a, 2023b). This was possible with increasing emphasis on end-to-end banking service delivery through digital channels like opening CASA accounts using smart phones, aggressive marketing for personal and credit card loans, and so on. Higher share of CASA contributes significantly to raising NII or profitability. To recover the fall in their share, PSBs have been trying to come up with innovative strategies too. In March 2022, in a letter to bank staff,[4] the SBI

[4] *Hindu Business Line*, 20 September 2022.

chairman had stressed on mobilising high-value current account deposits and popularising innovative cash management products amongst clients. Emphasis was placed on strengthening business from corporate customers and the rich by providing a host of banking services under one roof as also by appointing dedicated relationship managers.

Based on a bank's ALM requirements at any point of time, the ALCO undertakes analysis of its comparative asset–liability position across different maturities. Accordingly, the strategy for mobilisation of deposits under different maturities is designed so as to ensure that the mismatches between assets and liabilities in different time buckets remain within prudential norms. This process provides overall guidance on the composition of the portfolio of deposits of different tenures.

At the branch level, managers play a pivotal role in mobilisation of deposits based on their active involvement and strengthening of relationship banking. Branch managers are not involved in the determination of interest rates on deposits. But by updating customers about any upward revision of interest rates, they can aggressively pursue deposit mobilisation in such segments. Downward revision of interest rates on deposits obviously upsets customers. In such situations, branch managers need to inform customers about the reasons for lowering of interest rates. This may be part of the changing monetary policy stance or for other reasons. In fact, customers need to be made aware that the lowering of interest rates, if any, is not specific to their bank; rather, it is uniform across banks. Personal bond of branch managers with their customers can help in accelerating deposit mobilisation or moderating slowdown in deposit growth, as required.

The use of internet banking and mobile banking has no doubt reduced the scope for personal interface with customers to some extent. Nevertheless, friendly customer service such as enabling seamless opening and redeeming of deposits, facilitating smooth banking transactions, and so on, always helps in sustaining banking ties with customers. In this context, the role of branch managers in promoting deposit mobilisation cannot be overemphasised.

10.3.2 Decisions on Interest Rates on Deposits

Decisions on interest rates offered on bank deposits are of strategic importance for banks. They affect the overall funding cost of banks as deposits are the main source of funds for the banking business. Therefore, interest rate decisions on deposits are of paramount significance for determination of the overall profitability of banks. Determination of interest rates on deposits is also important on several other accounts. Changing interest rates on deposits of different maturities can accelerate or moderate mobilisation of deposits of different tenures by a bank. Hence, interest rate decisions on deposits are closely intertwined with the bank's approach on both overall mobilisation of deposits and their maturity profile. Similarly, pricing decisions also need to take into account the competitive environment within which banks are operating. Particularly during the post-reform period, banks in India have enjoyed greater operational autonomy to determine interest rates on their deposits, and there is significant increase in competition amongst banks. Therefore, pricing of deposits has become more challenging for banks.

According to the RBI's regulatory requirements, banks are to put in place a comprehensive policy on interest rates on deposits duly approved by their board or by any other committee as per the direction of the board. The RBI's 'Master Direction: Reserve Bank of India (Interest Rate on Deposits) Directions, 2016' stipulates that each bank pay a uniform interest rate to all its depositors on deposits of the same type and tenure. There should not be any negotiation between customers and a bank in the matter of interest rate determination. As per the RBI guidelines, interest rates on deposits offered by banks need to be transparent, reasonable and consistent. The schedule of interest rates paid on bank deposits should be disclosed in advance.

On term deposits, interest rates vary mainly on the basis of term to maturity. Table 10.1 provides information on interest rates offered by two leading banks in India for different tenures of fixed deposits. It is evident from the said table that in general higher interest rates are offered on deposits with longer maturities. However, this is not always true. For example, the highest interest rate of 6.10 per cent was offered by HDFC Bank on its fixed deposits of 3–5 years' maturity while the interest rate on the longest maturity of 5–10 years was only 5.75 per cent. The highest interest rate of 6.10 per cent was offered by SBI on its '1,000-day' fixed deposits. During the same period, SBI offered 5.65 per cent on fixed deposits of 5–10 years maturity.

Banks take decisions on interest rates offered on their deposits based on several factors. Key factors include demand for loans and liquidity conditions in a bank, asset–liability gap or balance across various time buckets, and overall monetary policy stance of the RBI as briefly explained in the sections that follow.

10.3.2.1 Asset–Liability Gap Considerations across Different Time Buckets

As indicated earlier, the ALM system in banks assesses and monitors gaps between their assets and liabilities across different time buckets. Accordingly, deposit mobilisation under different time buckets can be aggressively pursued or discouraged to maintain the balance. For example, if there are excess liabilities as compared to assets within the 'three–five years' time bucket, the bank may try to discourage mobilisation of deposits with three–five years maturity. It can afford to pay a low interest rate on such deposits.

On the contrary, if there are excess assets over liabilities within the 'one–two years' time bucket, the bank can fill the gap by mobilising more deposits with one–two years' maturity rather than cutting down advances under this time bucket to bridge the gap. Accordingly, the bank can pursue aggressive pricing of fixed deposits with one–two years' tenure to facilitate rapid growth of such deposits. Thus, based on asset–liability mismatches across various time buckets, banks strategize mobilisation of deposits under different tenures and also pricing of such deposits.

10.3.2.2 Macroeconomic Conditions and Flow of Bank Credit

Evolving macroeconomic conditions impact the demand for bank loans and also have implications for loan delinquencies. For example, during 2019–20 and 2020–21, the demand for bank loans in India was muted. The growth rate of bank credit was 6.1 per cent in 2019–20 and 5.5 per cent during 2020–21 (RBI, n.d.2). This was in the backdrop of signs of economic slowdown commencing since 2016–17 and severe economic contraction witnessed in 2020–21 due to the Covid-19 pandemic. Under these conditions, banks were very cautious about future demand for bank credit and many adopted a wait and watch policy. As a precaution, many banks emphasised on mobilising deposits with shorter time horizons so as to avoid pricing risks with longer-duration deposits. This was reflected, for instance, in SBI offering its highest interest rate of 7 per cent on deposits with one–two years tenure between 8 May and 1 August 2019 while interest rates on deposits with other tenures were less than this. Interest rates on deposits with more than two years' maturity were within the range of 6–6.75 per cent. A similar pricing strategy was continued by SBI until 10 November 2019.

With signs of economic revival after the pandemic, there was pick-up in bank credit growth in India. It accelerated to nearly 10 per cent in 2021–22.

With high demand for bank credit, SBI and other banks shifted their focus to longer-term deposits which was reflected in aggressive pricing of such deposits. In its 15 August 2022 revision, SBI offered its highest interest rate of 6.10 per cent on fixed deposits of 1,000 days. In its 15 October 2022 revision, it offered its highest interest rate of 6.25 per cent on deposits of two–three years' maturity.

Thus, banks in India change their pricing strategy for deposits depending on the changing conditions for credit demand.

10.3.2.3 Monetary Policy Stance

Most importantly, the RBI's monetary policy stance significantly impacts interest rates. The RBI has been relying on market-oriented liquidity management under its monetary policy operating procedure since the early 2000s. Consequently, banks have been fixing interest rates on their deposits guided by the RBI's monetary policy stance. Since the mid-2010s, the RBI has been using the fixed repo rate under its LAF as the single most important policy rate. It hikes the repo rate to signal tightening of monetary policy while reduction of the same reflects monetary policy accommodation. Banks pick up the RBI's signal on its interest rate stance and accordingly respond by altering their interest rates suitably.

Needless to mention, the entire banking system responds to changes in the RBI's policy rate. But the response in terms of the quantum and timing of changing bank-specific interest rates on deposits is not uniform. In other words, the overall direction of variation of interest rates on deposits across banks is found to be similar. Raising (reduction) of RBI policy rates is followed by increase (decrease) of bank deposit interest rates by all banks. But the quantum of change in such interest rates varies across banks. The response also differs in terms of different time lags. Some banks respond immediately while others adopt a wait and watch policy for a couple of months. These bank-wise differences in response to the RBI's monetary policy signal are determined, inter alia, by prevailing liquidity conditions and asset–liability mismatches of individual banks, as discussed earlier.

In Box 10.1, we have compared interest rates offered by SBI on its deposits with the RBI's fixed repo rate under the LAF to provide some empirical evidence on how banks determine interest rates on their deposits in response to the changing monetary policy stance of the RBI. Given that the banking system in India is akin to an oligopoly market, there is a close alignment in interest rates. The response of other major banks is similar to SBI's decision on interest rates following a signal from the RBI on its monetary policy stance.

Box 10.1 RBI's monetary policy stance and changing interest rates on SBI's deposits

Since the early 2000s, the RBI has been emphasising liquidity management as its principal monetary policy operating procedure. Under this approach, various liquidity management operations of the RBI aim at setting the trajectory of the call money rate, which is the key operating target. Policy-driven changes in the call money rate set the path of other interest rates in the financial system, including interest rates on deposits and loans of banks. Over time, the RBI's fixed repo rate under the LAF has emerged as the single policy rate signalling its monetary policy stance and setting the trajectory for the 'call money rate'.

In this perspective, let us compare the movement of the RBI's repo rate and SBI's interest rates on deposits to assess the extent to which monetary policy transmission is effective. The comparison also provides an insight into the behaviour of banks as regards setting their interest rates.

Figure 10.1(a) depicts the movement of the fixed repo rate under the LAF and SBI's interest rate on its deposits of one–two years' maturity.

It is evident from Figure 10.1(a) that largely movement of SBI's interest rate on deposits of one–two years' maturity followed that of the RBI's fixed repo rate. Since April 2012, the RBI has been following monetary policy accommodation except on a handful of occasions. The interest rate offered by

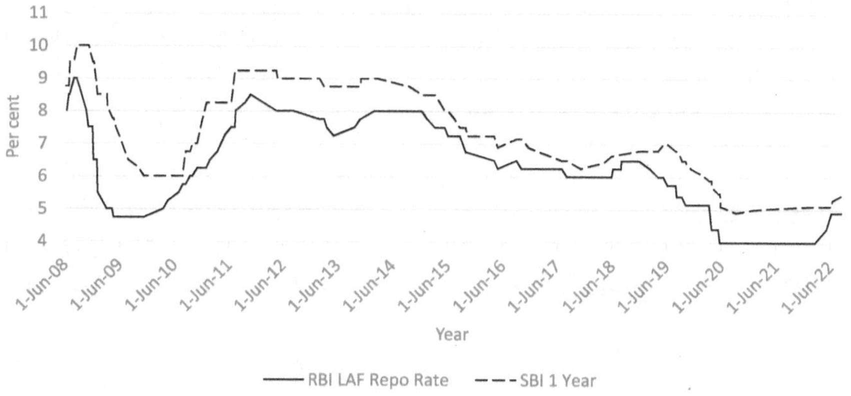

Figure 10.1(a) RBI's fixed repo rate and SBI's interest rate on deposits of one–two years' maturity

Source: Prepared by the author based on relevant data obtained from the official websites of RBI (www.rbi.org.in) and SBI (www.sbi.co.in).

Figure 10.1(b) SBI's interest rates on deposits of 1–2 and 5–10 years' maturity

Source: Prepared by the author based on relevant data obtained from the official websites of RBI (www.rbi.org.in) and SBI (www.sbi.co.in).

SBI on its deposits of one–two years' maturity very much followed the RBI's monetary policy signal. Detailed date-wise data on the RBI's fixed repo rate and SBI's interest rates on deposits are provided in Table 10A.1.

Do interest rates on deposits of banks across all tenures move similarly? To verify this, Figure 10.1(b) plots movements of SBI's interest rates on deposits of 1–2 and 5–10 years maturity together.

It can be observed from the graph that interest rates on deposits of both tenures as offered by SBI have moved together from 2008 to 2022. The direction of adjustment was reasonably similar.

As indicated in the preceding discussion, decisions on determining the composition of deposits and related pricing issues are the prerogative of the ALCO of a bank. Managers at the branch level have a limited role in these matters.

10.4 Strategic Decisions on Borrowings

As discussed earlier, borrowings account for less than one-tenth of the total liabilities of SCBs in India. This share is quite small compared to the nearly 80 per cent share of bank deposits. Nevertheless, the business strategy of banks on borrowings is quite important for a variety of reasons.

Day-to-day borrowings from the RBI and other banks are mainly driven by the transient liquidity management considerations of a bank. Every day, banking resources drain out due to deposit withdrawals, money transfers, disbursement of loans, investments in government securities and corporate bonds, and so on. Similarly, repayment of existing loans, fresh deposits, receipt of fees and interest income, proceeds from sale of securities, and so on, result in inflow of funds. It is impossible to make precise projections of such fund inflows and outflows. The ALM strategy of banks aims at containing liquidity concerns within prudential limits. Yet often banks get exposed to transient liquidity deficiencies. To meet the shortage of funds on an overnight basis, banks heavily depend on the RBI's LAF window and inter-bank call money market. Banks need to keep a close watch on liquidity requirements on an ongoing basis and accordingly approach the RBI or other banks to procure overnight funds. The treasury department of a bank takes care of operational aspects in this regard.

As regards borrowing on an overnight basis, banks broadly have two options. Banks with surplus eligible securities above minimum SLR requirements can fully exploit the RBI's LAF window. Otherwise, they can borrow in the inter-bank call money market. If a bank borrows from the RBI under the LAF, it cannot seek any flexibility as regards the interest rate charged by the RBI. The bank can borrow at the fixed repo rate which is determined by the RBI based on its monetary policy stance. However, borrowing banks enjoy some bargaining power in the call money market. This is an OTC facility. Depending on the systemic liquidity position and a bank's liquidity requirements, it can negotiate to get funds at a cheaper rate.

As regards other facilities of the RBI like variable term repo, MSF, LTRO and TLTRO, and so on, the RBI has complete discretion to determine the quantum and pricing of the borrowing based on market liquidity conditions. A bank does not have any choice in this regard.

Borrowings from other institutions and agencies were not that important prior to the 2000s. RBI's *Report on Trend and Progress of Banking* used to contain a table on important banking indicators for SCBs. During the late 1990s, the report used to include information on 'borrowings from the RBI' and 'liabilities to banks' along with bank deposits in the liabilities side of the consolidated balance sheet of SCBs. Borrowings from other institutions and agencies did not appear in that table. However, as indicated in the preceding discussion, during the later part of the post-reform period, borrowings from sources other than the RBI and other banks have gained momentum. The need for generating subordinated debt to augment tier-2 capital and tapping other sources of funds are the prime factors behind this. Initiatives to generate more non-deposit resources in the market repo and the CBLO market to maximise fund availability for gainful deployment (fully exploiting opportunities for lending and investment) have become more popular. In the market repo and the CBLO market, interest rates are determined through the auction process.

Thus, as regards borrowings from the RBI under its LAF window, banks do not have any influence on the cost of borrowing though there is flexibility on the amount. Banks can borrow any amount depending on availability of surplus SLR securities which are accepted as collaterals in the LAF window. In all other forms of borrowing, borrowing banks participate in the auction process or OTC negotiations to determine the amount of borrowing and its cost. While borrowing banks do not completely control the final outcome, their participation in the auction process has some influence on quantity and pricing decisions in such borrowings.

As regards managerial and operational aspects, the head office or central office of banks discharges the responsibilities pertaining to their borrowings in all forms. The treasury departments of banks undertake necessary transactions while their ALCOs oversee and provide policy guidelines for related business decisions. Branch-level officials are not involved in such operations.

10.5 Off-Balance Sheet (OBS) Items

The banking sector in India has witnessed introduction of many innovative products during the post-reform period. Banks strove to find new ways of improving income and profit by venturing into areas not hitherto explored. One such area is raising fee-based income from OBS items. As the name suggests, such items do not appear in a bank's balance sheet until occurrence of some specific events related to them. These items are also popularly referred to as *contingent liabilities* as they effectively become liabilities on occurrence of certain conditions, as detailed in the following paragraphs.

OBS items are largely non-fund-based banking activities—that is, they do not require allocation or exposure of funds or credit. For example, issuing of bank guarantees or popular financial derivatives like forwards or options does not involve lending or funds upfront. On the other hand, banks benefit from earning fees and income from issuance of such products. This helps in raising the return on assets (ROA) of banks as such items raise the numerator without affecting the denominator.

However, on occurrence of contingent events, OBS items affect a bank's financial position. For example, if the customer for whom a bank has issued a bank guarantee fails to meet the commitment or requirements as per the contract, then the bank needs to make up for the losses of the beneficiary. This transforms a contingent liability into an effective or tangible liability in the bank's balance sheet. Similarly, if the movement in the forex rate is adverse to a bank as per a forward contract for delivery of US dollars, then the resultant loss will reflect in reduction of the bank's profit.

The RBI publishes data on three broad OBS items for different bank groups. These are (*a*) forward exchange contracts, (*b*) guarantees given, and (*c*) acceptances, endorsements, and so on. It can be observed from Table 10.2 that OBS exposures of SCBs in India have significantly increased since the early 2000s. In 1999–2000, the total OBS exposure of SCBs was around half the total liabilities. By 2009–10, OBS exposures had become nearly 1.75 times the total liabilities of SCBs. The share of OBS items in the total liabilities of foreign banks and IPBs is found to be much higher than that of PSBs.

10.5.1 Conventional OBS Items

Several items under contingent liabilities in the Indian banking system were widely used even prior to the reforms. Some such popular items were various types of bank guarantees, LCs and the unavailed portion under a line of credit or overdraft. During the post-reform period, with greater globalisation of the Indian economy, the scope and volume of items like LCs have increased manifold. In the process of financial development, the post-reform period in India has also witnessed emergence of several new forms of financial derivatives. Details of such items are discussed in the sections that follow.

10.5.1.1 Bank Guarantees

Bank guarantees are very popular OBS items which have been dealt with by Indian banks since long. Such instruments are relatively simple as explained in the following paragraphs. Bank guarantees are broadly of two types: financial guarantees and performance guarantees.

Table 10.2 OBS exposures of SCBs in India

Item	1999–2000	2009–10	2019–20	1999–2000	2009–10	2019–20
	As percentage of total liabilities			Percentage change over previous year		
PSBs						
Forward exchange contracts	15.2	21.6	19.6	32.3	-7.3	-16.4
Guarantees given	4.8	7.4	4.6	2.0	29.2	-5.7
Acceptances, endorsements, and so on	5.5	10.6	6.6	23.1	-23.0	11.9
Total contingent liabilities	26.3	39.7	30.9	23.7	-7.4	-10.0
IPBs						
Forward exchange contracts	58.3	98.8	103.7	49.4	-5.4	13
Guarantees given	9.7	13.7	7.9	39.5	29.4	2.4
Acceptances, endorsements, and so on	11.2	82.4	4.3	14.5	19.1	-19.2
Total contingent liabilities	79.3	194.9	115.9	43.5	5.8	10.6
Foreign banks						
Forward exchange contracts	281.3	1,206.5	858.7	28.5	-17.0	17.1
Guarantees given	19.2	13.8	12.8	12.1	4.7	0.9
Acceptances, endorsements, and so on	41.7	378.2	115.0	43.3	41.7	29.5
Total contingent liabilities	342.2	1,598.5	986.5	28.4	-7.8	18.2
SCBs						
Forward exchange contracts	38.4	118.8	105.6	31.4	-14.3	10.9
Guarantees given	6.1	8.7	6.2	7.2	25.6	-1.6
Acceptances, endorsements, and so on	8.4	47.3	13.4	27.4	19.3	16.8
Total contingent liabilities	52.9	174.8	125.3	27.6	-5.6	10.8

Source: RBI's *Report on Trend and Progress of Banking in India*, various issues.

Let us discuss with some examples. Say, a buyer A wishes to purchase goods from a manufacturer X to be delivered at a future date. Assume manufacturer X promises to deliver the goods to buyer A after six months but insists on an advance payment of INR 1 crore now. A may be ready to pay the advance amount but may not have adequate familiarity with X. It may ask X to provide a bank guarantee to compensate it for the advance amount in case the latter fails to supply the goods. In that case, X may approach its bank to issue a bank guarantee on its behalf. With the bank guarantee of INR 1 crore as backup, A may not hesitate to pay the advance and the deal can be fructified.

In this example, the bank guarantee involves three stakeholders. These are the principal debtor, manufacturer X, on whose behalf the bank has issued the guarantee; the beneficiary, buyer A (the creditor); and the bank which acts as surety. This is a *financial guarantee.* It involves the commitment of the bank to pay the buyer an amount of INR 1 crore if the supplier or manufacturer fails to deliver the goods. It is not an ordinary liability as the bank does not have a payment obligation to buyer A as long as manufacturer X meets its commitment in delivering the goods. This bank guarantee is a contingent liability as the payment obligation of the bank under the guarantee actually crystalises contingent upon the failure of manufacturer X to meet its commitment. Thus, the primary obligation is that of manufacturer X while for the bank it is a secondary obligation. The bank charges applicable fees to its customer—that is, manufacturer X—to issue such guarantee. This is a non-fund-based activity for the bank as no funds or loans need to be provided by it when it issues the guarantee.

Similarly, when a buyer purchases goods on credit from a wholesaler or manufacturer, the latter may ask for a bank guarantee to protect it from any losses arising due to failure of the buyer to make payments in the future. In this instance, the roles of the buyer and the manufacturer reverse as compared to the previous example. The buyer becomes the principal debtor, and the wholesaler or manufacturer is the creditor.

Bank guarantees have been widely used in the tendering process. Generally, participants or contractors in all tendering processes need to furnish *earnest money deposits* (EMDs) or *tender deposits* while submitting their bid. EMDs involve blocking of funds for participants and loss of potential income from productive use of such funds. To avoid this, participants in tendering alternatively submit bank guarantees, popularly known as *bid bond guarantees.* This is a win-win situation for both contractors and banks.

Contractors save themselves from loss of interest income and banks benefit from earning fees on issue of guarantees.

All these instances are examples of financial guarantees. Banks have been helping trade and business by issue of such instruments. Nevertheless, banks have to carefully scrutinise requests to issue such guarantees so that the contingent liability does not crystalise as an effective liability. Banks need to thoroughly satisfy themselves of the ability and capacity of the principal debtor to honour the commitment or obligation to the beneficiary. Banks follow detailed guidelines for proper assessment of such requests such as verifying the credentials of the customer or principal debtor, including their past record, legality of and RBI restrictions on the purpose and amount of the guarantee, adequacy of margin and security collaterals offered by the principal debtor, and so on. Banks also generally obtain a counter-guarantee from the principal debtor to avoid potential losses if the guarantee crystalises.

Deferred payment guarantees (DPGs) are a variety of financial guarantees issued for purchase of capital goods by firms. Purchase of a machine by a manufacturer may involve payment of a huge sum—say, thousands of crores. Generally, a downpayment of, say, 15 per cent is made to procure the machine. The remaining amount is paid in instalments over a period of time as mutually agreed by the buyer and the seller. As the repayment in instalments may cover a long period, the seller of the machine may insist on a DPG. Issue of a DPG by a bank thus facilitates the procurement of the machine.

It is important to note that banks are generally encouraged to issue financial guarantees but exercise reasonable caution in dealing with performance guarantees. *Performance guarantees* are issued by banks as assurance that the customer will perform their commitment as per the contract. The commitment here is not in terms of financial transactions like payment for good; it is to deliver goods on time (say, within six months). Similarly, in the tendering for, say, construction of an airport terminal or stadium, the financial guarantee is limited to covering the EMD or tender deposit. In this case, a performance guarantee may also be insisted upon for completion of the construction within the specified time. Obviously, the quantum of risk is higher in performance guarantees as compared to that in financial guarantees. Hence, banks are advised to exercise greater caution while issuing performance guarantees.

It is important to note that as per the legal provisions, banks need to promptly honour bank guarantees when they are invoked by the beneficiary, contingent upon failure of the principal debtor to meet their obligation. Banks need to regularly monitor their OBS position due to issue of guarantees and follow due diligence in cancelling the guarantees issued on expiry or surrender.

If the firm seeking a bank guarantee is already a customer of the bank availing the cash credit (CC) facility, the guarantee is issued within the sanctioned limit as per the arrangement. Under this arrangement, generally 75 per cent of the guarantee amount is covered under the CC facility with appropriate security and the customer has to give a new security collateral for the additional 25 per cent. If the guarantee-seeking customer does not have a CC facility, generally the bank insists on security collateral from the customer covering the entire guarantee amount.

One of the most popular OBS items issued by banks are LCs. We have already discussed the details of LC issue in Chapter 1. With significant rise in the volume of foreign trade during the post-reform period in India, issue of LCs by banks to facilitate foreign trade has increased manifold. Banks need to conform to various stipulations of the Uniform Customs and Practices for Documentary Credit (UCPDC), Foreign Exchange Management Act (FEMA), guidelines issued by the RBI and Foreign Exchange Dealers Association of India (FEDAI), and so on, for dealing with issuance of LCs.

10.5.2 OBS Items in the Form of Financial Derivatives

The Indian economy witnessed greater global integration during the post-reform period, in terms of both foreign trade and capital flows. Concomitantly, there was tremendous escalation in the volume of transactions involving leading foreign currencies including US dollars, euros, yen, and so on. India adopted a market-determined exchange rate regime from the early 1990s. This led to fluctuation in the market exchange rate of the Indian rupee vis-à-vis US dollars, euros, and so on, depending on the demand for and supply of the respective foreign currencies in the forex market. To protect against adverse impact of exchange rate fluctuations on their income and profit, exporters and importers avail financial derivatives.

We have discussed in Chapter 1 with a simple example how a *forward contract* in forex saves an Indian importer from potential loss due to depreciation of INR against USD. It was discussed how an Indian importer who had bought IBM computers from the US needs to pay INR 84,00,000 instead of INR 82,00,000 for the same USD 1,00,000 worth of computers due to depreciation of INR against USD. This can happen if the INR–USD exchange rate changes from INR 82 per USD to INR 84 per USD between the time when the import order is placed and the time when payments are made after receiving the consignment. To protect against the loss of INR 2,00,000 due to the INR depreciation, the Indian importer can buy a forward contract from a bank so that it can buy USDs at the rate of INR 82 per USD in the future (at the time it needs to make the payment for the imports).

Banks sell such forward contracts to importers and help them *hedge* against the risk of rupee depreciation. A forward contract is a simple form of *financial derivative.* A financial derivative is an instrument which derives its value from an underlying transaction in a financial asset. It entails a right or obligation to undertake a transaction in a financial asset in the future. For example, a three-month forward contract is an arrangement between a protection buyer (say, an importer) and protection seller (say, a bank) to buy USD 1,00,000 at, say, INR 82 per USD, three months ahead. Thus, the contract specifies today the rate at which the underlying financial asset like USDs can be transacted at a future date.

Popular financial derivatives are futures, forwards, options and swaps. The reader may refer to Hull and Basu (2018) for a comprehensive understanding of financial derivatives.

Futures are standardised contracts undertaken in an *exchange market* to deliver and pay for an asset on a future date at a predetermined price. India's NSE is one of the world's largest exchange markets which facilitates transactions in futures, mainly in equities and bonds. The protection buyers of futures do not enjoy flexibility, unlike forward contracts, as the futures are standardised in terms of size, tenure and currency. However, the advantage with futures contracts is that they eliminate counterparty risk. Exchanges such as the NSE guarantee honouring the transaction. Futures contracts are very popular in equities and government securities too.

Options are another popular form of derivatives and hedge against adverse fluctuations in the price of the underlying asset without foregoing the potential of benefitting from favourable price changes. For example, in the situation previously discussed, the importer has purchased today a three-month forward contract to buy USDs at INR 82 per USD. In case INR appreciates three months from today to INR 79 per USD, it is a disadvantage for the importer. They have to buy USDs at INR 82 under the forward contract, whereas in the spot market USDs are available at INR 79 per USD. In an *option*, the protection buyer does not suffer this disadvantage. If they have a *call option*, they enjoy the right to buy USDs at INR 82 per USD on the specified date but does not have an obligation to do so. Similarly, a *put option* gives the right to the protection buyer (say, an exporter) to sell the underlying asset (say, USD) at the pre-specified price, but they not have an obligation to do so if it is not advantageous for them.

Swaps are financial derivatives which facilitate exchange of income flows from two different sets of securities. Say, the protection buyer may enter an agreement to exchange income flows from a security earning a flexible interest rate against another earning a fixed interest rate from the protection seller.

From the mid-1990s, banks in India have been permitted to use a variety of financial derivatives to help their customers hedge against exchange rate risk. In April 1997, cross-currency derivatives with the INR as one leg were introduced. From July 2003, INR–forex options were permitted. Banks are using financial derivatives to hedge against various types of risk, including exchange rate risk in their own portfolio. Mainly forwards, options and swaps are popularly used in the Indian financial market. As can be observed from Table 10.2, *forward exchange contacts* account for an overwhelming share in the OBS items of banks in India. As a percentage of the total liabilities of SCBs, the share of forward exchange contracts significantly increased from 38.4 per cent in 1999–2000 to 118.8 per cent in 2009–10, before moderating slightly to 105.6 per cent in 2019–20.

Amongst bank groups, for PSBs, the share of *forward exchange contacts* in their total liabilities has been fairly moderate. It increased from 15.2 per cent in 1999–2000 to 19.6 per cent in 2019–20. However, forward exchange contacts constituted nearly half their overall OBS items. On the contrary, the share of forward exchange contacts in total liabilities as also in overall OBS items is disproportionately high for foreign banks and IPBs. Particularly, for foreign banks, the share of forward exchange contacts was nearly 8.5 times their total liabilities in 2019–20. Their share in the overall OBS items of the banks was nearly 90 per cent.

Within SCBs, foreign banks have accounted for around half the overall volume of OBS items in recent times. The share of PSBs is about one-fifth. In the total exposure of forward exchange contracts of SCBs, the share of foreign banks was 51.8 per cent in 2021–22 while that of PSBs was 15.4 per cent. The remaining was accounted for by IPBs.

As per the RBI guidelines, banks in India follow detailed risk management and corporate governance procedures for managing their exposures in OBS items. The top management of banks monitors the exposures in the derivative markets. Risk management processes are integrated in terms of setting prudent risk limits for OBS exposures, sound risk measurement procedures, continuous monitoring and reporting. Banks have put in place comprehensive internal controls and audit procedures given the rapid rise in exposures related to OBS items.

10.6 Conclusion

In the perspective of maximising risk-adjusted returns and promoting solvency and liquidity considerations, general bank management issues pertaining to bank liabilities are critically important. In this chapter, we have discussed various types of deposits that banks in India offer and various types of borrowings they undertake. Bank deposits comprise nearly 80 per cent of the liabilities of SCBs and borrowings account for a little less than 10 per cent.

As regards deposits, we discussed the strategic decisions of banks on the volume and composition of different types of deposits and the pricing of such deposits. We discussed that along with broad macroeconomic factors, the monetary policy stance and fluctuations in bank credit growth, strategic decisions of banks in India on mobilisation of deposits and their pricing were mainly influenced by the asset–liability balance under different time horizons. Banks in India resort to borrowings from the RBI and other banks to address temporary liquidity deficiencies on a day-to-day basis. On top of that, in the recent years they are found to be borrowing from non-banking institutions in the capital market and money market. Related issues are highlighted in this chapter.

OBS items are growing in the banking business in India partly due to the drive of banks to raise non-interest income from fees and commissions charged on contingent liabilities in a more competitive environment. Growing business requirements at home as also the process of greater global integration of the Indian economy have raised the demand for such products. This chapter highlighted rapid expansion in the volume of OBS items in the banking business in India and related risk concerns. Accordingly, it also outlined banking management practices for OBS items.

Appendix 10A

Table 10A.1 RBI's fixed repo rate under the LAF and SBI's interest rates on deposits

(Per cent)

Date	Repo rate	SBI 1–2	SBI 5–10	Date	Repo rate	SBI 1–2	SBI 5–10
1 Jun 2008		8.75	9.00	15 Jan 2015	7.75		
12 Jun 2008	8.00			4 Mar 2015	7.50		
25 Jun 2008	8.50			10 Apr 2015		8.25	8.25
30 Jun 2008		9.50	9.00	11 May 2015		8.00	8.00
30 Jul 2008	9.00			2 Jun 2015	7.25		
16 Aug 2008		10.00	9.25	17 Jul 2015		7.75	7.75
20 Oct 2008	8.00			19 Aug 2015		7.50	7.25
3 Nov 2008	7.50			29 Sep 2015	6.75		
1 Dec 2008		9.50	9.00	5 Oct 2015		7.25	7.00
8 Dec 2008	6.50			5 Apr 2016	6.50		
1 Jan 2009		8.50	8.50	1 Sep 2016		7.15	7.00
5 Jan 2009	5.50			4 Oct 2016	6.25		
5 Mar 2009	5.00			24 Oct 2016		7.05	6.50
9 Mar 2009		8.10	8.50	17 Nov 2016		6.90	6.50
13 Apr 2009		7.75	8.25	29 Apr 2016		6.90	6.25
21 Apr 2009	4.75			1 Jul 2017		6.50	6.25
4 May 2009		7.50	8.00	2 Aug 2017	6.00		
15 Jun 2009		7.00	7.75	1 Nov 2017		6.25	6.00
27 Jul 2009		6.50	7.50	28 Feb 2018		6.40	6.50
5 Oct 2009		6.25	7.25	28 Mar 2018		6.40	6.75
9 Nov 2009		6.00	7.25	28 May 2018		6.65	6.75
19 Mar 2010	5.00			6 Jun 2018	6.25		
20 Apr 2010	5.25			30 Jul 2018		6.70	6.85
2 Jul 2010	5.50			1 Aug 2018	6.50		
27 Jul 2010	5.75			28 Nov 2018		6.80	6.85
17 Aug 2010		6.75	7.50	7 Feb 2019	6.25		
16 Sep 2010	6.00			4 Apr 2019	6.00		
1 Oct 2010		7.00	7.50	9 May 2019		7.00	6.60
2 Nov 2010	6.25			6 Jun 2019	5.75		

(Contd)

Table 10A.1 *(Contd)*

(Per cent)

Date	Repo rate	SBI 1–2	SBI 5–10	Date	Repo rate	SBI 1–2	SBI 5–10
7 Dec 2010		7.75	8.50	1 Aug 2019		6.80	6.50
3 Jan 2011		8.25	8.50	7 Aug 2019	5.40		
25 Jan 2011	6.50			26 Aug 2019		6.70	6.25
17 Mar 2011	6.75			10 Sep 2019		6.50	6.25
3 May 2011	7.25			4 Oct 2019	5.15		
16 Jun 2011	7.50			10 Oct 2019		6.40	6.25
11 Jul 2011		9.25	9.25	10 Nov 2019		6.25	6.25
16 Jul 2011	8.00			10 Jan 2020		6.10	6.10
16 Sep 2011	8.25			10 Feb 2020		6.00	6.00
25 Oct 2011	8.50			10 Mar 2020		5.90	5.90
17 Apr 2012	8.00			27 Mar 2020	4.40		
24 Apr 2012		9.00	8.75	28 Mar 2020		5.70	5.70
7 Aug 2012		9.00	8.50	12 May 2020		5.50	5.70
29 Jan 2013	7.75			22 May 2020	4.00		
1 Mar 2013		8.75	8.75	27 May 2020		5.10	5.40
19 Mar 2013	7.50			10 Sep 2020		4.90	5.40
3 May 2013	7.25			8 Jan 2021		5.00	5.40
20 Sep 2013	7.50			15 Jan 2022		5.10	5.40
29 Oct 2013	7.75			15 Feb 2022		5.10	5.50
1 Nov 2013		9.00	9.00	4 May 2022	4.4		
28 Jan 2014	8.00			8 Jun 2022	4.9		
18 Feb 2014		9.00	8.50	14 Jun 2022		5.30	5.50
18 Sep 2014		8.75	8.50	13 Aug 2022		5.45	5.65
8 Dec 2014		8.50	8.25				

Source: RBI's *Handbook of Statistics on Indian Economy*, 2021–22, https://data.rbi.org.in/DBIE/#/dbie/reports/Publication/Time-Series%20Publications/Handbook%20of%20Statistics%20on%20the%20Indian%20Economy (accessed 18 July 2022); table on historical retail term deposit rates obtained from SBI, https://sbi.co.in/web/interest-rates/interest-rates/deposit-rates (accessed 13 August 2022).

Note: (*a*) Repo rate is the RBI's fixed repo rate under the LAF. (*b*) SBI 1–2 is the interest rate offered by SBI on deposits of 1–2 years' maturity. For some periods like 2010–11, this referred to the interest rate offered on deposits of 1 year to 554 days' maturity. (*c*) SBI 5–10 is the interest rate offered by SBI on deposits of 5–10 years' maturity. For some periods like 2008–11, this referred to the interest rate offered on deposits of 5–8 years' maturity.

Revision Questions and Problems

1. What are the advantages and disadvantages of a bank having a higher proportion of CASA deposits?
2. Briefly describe how asset–liability mismatches in different time buckets influence a bank's strategy on composition of its deposit portfolio.
3. How are interest rate decisions on bank deposits relevant for mobilisation of deposits by a bank in general? How do such decisions influence composition of deposits of different terms to maturity?
4. Explain the relevance of the RBI's monetary policy stance for interest rate decisions of banks in India.
5. Compare the advantages and disadvantages of overnight borrowing options of banks from the RBI's LAF window versus the call money market.
6. What are the main factors contributing to the multi-fold increase in the borrowings of banks in India from 'other institutions and agencies' during the post-reform period?
7. Briefly compare the advantages and disadvantages of forwards, futures and options as hedging instruments against exchange rate risk in the forex market.
8. How would you assess the growing importance of both traditional OBS items and modern financial derivatives in the overall banking business in India during the post-reform period?

Part V

Performance of Banks in India and Contemporary Issues

11

Profitability, Productivity and Efficiency of Banks

Learning Objectives

- To explain the concepts of profitability, productivity and efficiency in the banking business
- To analyse the trend of profitability, productivity and operational efficiency of banks in India during the post-reform period
- To compare the performance of different bank groups and leading banks in terms of profitability, productivity and operational efficiency
- To explore the performance of banks as regards allocative efficiency
- To draw important policy implications for improving banking performance in India

11.1 Introduction

Banks are basically commercial entities and maximising profit is the main objective in the banking business. Profit for banks arises from broadly two sources. The major source is interest income from loans and investments over interest cost on deposits and borrowings, popularly referred to as net interest income (NII). We have observed earlier in this book that deposits constitute the bulk of the liabilities of a bank and loans and investments overwhelmingly dominate a bank's assets. Therefore, NII constitutes the main source of a bank's profit. A bank has to choose a judicious mix of deposits and loans as also appropriately price such products to maximise its NII. The second source of profit for banks is earnings in the form of fees, commissions and charges, and so on.

However, banks cannot ignore the risks involved in various banking products. Generally, higher risk is associated with higher returns. Prudent banking entails containment of overall risks within reasonable limits; otherwise excessive risks may wipe out the entire profit. In exceptional situations, excessive risk may even cause complete collapse of a bank. In view of these aspects, optimising risk-adjusted returns without compromising solvency and liquidity aspects is the ultimate goal in the banking business.

It is important to note that profitability can be maximised through improving banking efficiency and productivity. In banking, productivity is popularly measured in terms of per employee business and profit. This closely resembles the concept of labour productivity used in microeconomics. Higher business per employee reflects higher productivity.

Bank profitability in the long run depends on how efficiently and effectively banking resources are put to use. Efficiency in banking can be discussed in two different contexts. First, *operational efficiency* refers to minimising the cost of banking operations including wages and salaries of employees. Lower gap between interest cost and interest earning for a given level of assets represents higher banking efficiency. Second, *allocational efficiency* assesses distribution of banking services across different regions, economic activities, borrower groups, and so on. Better allocational efficiency is associated with more effective use of banking resources through judicious and balanced lending across sectors and individuals. Allocative efficiency is closely linked to the developmental goals of an economy.

It may be noted that many researchers and commentators use the terms *productivity* and *efficiency* interchangeably. However, as indicated earlier, there is a subtle difference between the two. Productivity measures output per unit of factor input. Labour productivity is total output divided by total units of labour. In banking, it can be measured as *business per employee* or *profit per employee*. On the other hand, efficiency is a broader concept. It is a comprehensive indicator assessing how all factors of production are effectively used in the banking business. Thus, efficiency is a summary measure of the combined productivity of funds, employees, technology, management, and so on. The concept of *total factor productivity* (TFP), already discussed in Chapter 3, is used to measure efficiency through econometric analysis. The word 'productivity' in TFP creates the confusion. Further details on these concepts are provided in the following sections of this chapter.

During the pre-reform period, particularly after the bank nationalisation of 1969, banks in India were heavily regulated. Banking resources were statutorily pre-empted by raising CRR and SLR requirements. Priority sector lending commitments compelled banks to lend to agriculture, small-scale industries and socially backward communities, ignoring profitability and banking soundness requirements. Regulation of bank credit and pricing of loans and deposits were directed to ensure flow of bank credit to the desired sectors as per the developmental objectives under central planning. Obviously, commercial considerations were not given due importance. Introduction of comprehensive reforms since the early 1990s accorded reasonable operational autonomy to banks in India. Promoting the financial health of banks through market-oriented prudential norms became a policy priority. This induced a turnaround in the profitability, productivity and operational efficiency of banks. Particularly, PSBs became more vibrant and stepped up their efforts to match IPBs and foreign banks on profitability, productivity and efficiency parameters.

It is pertinent to note that efficient and profitable banks are necessary for the proper functioning of a sound banking system. Weak banks cannot help society to benefit from mobilisation of savings and capital formation. Sustained economic prosperity requires efficient and profitable banks. In this background, this chapter presents various issues related to banking profitability, productivity and efficiency in India, particularly during the post-reform period.

The chapter is organised as follows. In section 11.2, conceptual and measurement issues related to profitability of banks are delineated. This section also reviews the performance of various bank groups and leading banks in India as regards profitability during the post-reform period. Likewise, conceptual and measurement issues related to banking productivity as also performance of banks in India on these aspects are covered in section 11.3. Similar discussion on operational efficiency is carried out in section 11.4 using conventional banking indicators and supplemented by findings of popular empirical studies. This analysis of profitability, productivity and efficiency of banks in India also provides a comparative perspective on the performance of PSBs vis-à-vis IPBs and foreign banks. Section 11.5 undertakes a comprehensive analysis on allocative efficiency of banks in India. Finally, section 11.6 concludes the chapter identifying important policy implications.

11.2 Profitability of Banks in India

The broad parameters of profitability, productivity and efficiency are popularly used to assess financial performance in banking. All three are interrelated but distinguished in conceptual terms. As indicated in the introduction to this chapter, with the adoption of banking sector reforms in India since the 1990s, banks acquired adequate operational autonomy during the post-reform period. Various types of government control and statutory pre-emption of banking resources were phased out. Entry of new Indian private banks (NPBs) and foreign banks promoted competition and there was tremendous pressure on PSBs to improve their performance. In this perspective, the present section provides information on the profitability of banks in India during the post-reform period.

11.2.1 Concept and Measurement of Bank Profitability

In economics and finance, the concept of *profitability* has a simple connotation. Profit basically measures excess income or revenue earned out of a business over the cost incurred. For a manufacturing firm, profit is total revenue earned out of the sale of its products over total costs incurred in the production process. While calculating total costs, operational costs such as electricity bills, transportation, maintenance of accounts, advertising, and so on, are covered along with production costs including wages and salaries of workers, expenditure on purchase of raw material, interest payments on loans and advances, and so on. In retail trading, profit reflects the difference between total earning received from the sale of goods in a retail store or shop over all forms of costs involved in procuring, storing, preparing bills and facilitating the sale of such goods.

Based on the types of cost components which are deducted from the total income or revenue, profit is expressed as 'gross' or 'net'. *Gross profit* is nothing but total revenue or income from a business over production cost. *Net profit* is arrived at after deduction of some items such as operational costs and taxes from gross profit.

In banking, profit can be measured in various ways. *Gross profit* of a bank broadly consists of two elements, namely (*a*) NII and (*b*) non-interest income. NII is nothing but interest earning out of lending and investment of a bank over interest cost on bank deposits and borrowings. As discussed earlier, loans and investments constitute the bulk of a bank's assets. Hence, interest income from loans and investments constitutes the major component of a bank's income or revenue. Similarly, bank deposits and borrowings account for the bulk of a bank's liabilities. Accordingly, interest cost on deposits and borrowings is of paramount importance for a bank. Therefore, NII accounts for the bulk of the gross income or profit of a bank. The second component, *non-interest income*, arises from earnings such as fees or commissions for issuing bank guarantees, LCs, bank drafts, cheque books, and so on, and providing locker facilities and profit from sale of forex, bonds, and other assets. Non-interest income also includes earnings from dealing in various financial derivatives.

The *operating profit* of a bank can be calculated as gross profit minus operational costs including wage bills, rent for buildings, electricity bills, stationery, advertising, and so on. In other words, operating profit is defined as total earnings minus total expenses of a bank excluding provisions and contingencies.[1]

Return on Assets (ROA) is a very comprehensive measure of the profitability of banks. It is defined as the ratio of *net profit* to *average assets* of a bank. The numerator is obtained by deducting the provisions and contingencies of a bank from its operating profit and adjusting for taxes. The denominator is the arithmetic average of assets at the beginning and the end of the period for which ROA is calculated. Say, in the financial year 2019–20, net profit of Bank A is INR 2,000 crore. If the total assets of Bank A as of end-March 2019 and end-March 2020 are INR 80,000 crore and INR 1,00,000 crore, respectively, its ROA for 2019–20 = (INR 2,000)/[(INR 80,000 + INR 1,00,000)/2] = INR 2,000/INR 90,000 = 0.0222 = 2.22 per cent.

ROA broadly reflects how effectively the resources of a bank are put into use. So it implicitly measures efficiency in resource use. Details about popular indicators of operational efficiency of banks are discussed in section 11.4.

It is obvious that profit maximisation on a sustained basis is the fundamental objective of a bank as a commercial entity. This is the single most important objective of banks in their day-to-day operations. Interest income can be enhanced either by expanding the quantum of loans and investments or by charging higher interest rates on lending or through both these avenues. Sustaining bank profitability is equally important. Lending involves a variety of risks and repayment of loans has an element of uncertainty. Delinquency

[1] This is noted in the explanatory notes to RBI's *Statistical Tables Relating to Banks in India*, 2019–20.

of bank loans and related provisioning requirements may lead to incurring of losses in the future if excessive aggressive lending is pursued by a bank to maximise current profit.

On the other hand, management of bank deposits balancing cost and liquidity criteria is critical for minimising the cost of funds. Having a higher share of CASA deposits reduces the overall cost of funds but exposes banks to higher liquidity risks. On the contrary, raising the proportion of fixed or long-term deposits reduces liquidity risks but entails higher interest costs.

So raising the profitability of a bank by augmenting NII requires adoption of a comprehensive strategy managing both deposit mobilisation and lending. Details of the same have been discussed in Chapters 9 and 10.

11.2.2 Performance of Banks in India as per Profitability

Banks in India acquired adequate operational autonomy both in framing their policies on lending and deposit mobilisation and in pricing their products by the late 1990s. Therefore, it can only be expected that the profitability of banks would have improved during the post-reform period.

11.2.2.1 Profitability of Different Bank Groups

Table 11.1 presents broad profitability indicators for various bank groups in India. Let us begin with interest income which is overwhelmingly dominant for determining overall banking profitability. It can be observed from Table 11.1 that the post-reform period in India witnessed gradual moderation in the ratio of interest income to assets. For SCBs as a whole, the ratio gradually declined from 10.27 per cent in 1991–92 to 7.20 per cent in 2004–05. Since the mid-2000s, there was a reversal in the trend with the ratio gradually rising up to 8.18 per cent in 2014–15. There was a second turning point in in 2019–20 with the ratio declining to 7.22 per cent. This broadly reflected the changing monetary policy stance of the RBI. During 1997–2003, the Indian economy witnessed a marginal deceleration in GDP growth to 5.3 per cent on average as compared to 6.4 per cent during 1992–97. In an effort to support rapid economic expansion, the RBI pursued an accommodative monetary policy from 1997 to 2004. This reflected in CRR reduction from 11 per cent in January 1998 to 6 per cent by April 2003. The monetary policy-driven reduction in lending rates partly explains the reduction in the ratio of interest income to assets of SCBs until 2004–05. Moreover, rapid

Table 11.1 Bank-group-wise profitability trends in India

(Per cent)

Bank groups	1991–92	1994–95	1999–2000	2004–05	2009–10	2014–15	2019–20
			Ratio of interest income to total assets				
PSBs	10.18	8.61	8.92	7.42	7.46	8.12	6.84
IPBs	9.72	7.67	7.60	6.61	7.60	8.81	8.07
Foreign banks	11.61	9.88	9.93	6.33	5.99	6.71	5.74
SCBs	10.27	8.63	8.97	7.20	7.37	8.18	7.22
			Ratio of non-interest income to total assets				
PSBs	NA	NA	1.29	1.49	1.19	0.91	1.13
IPBs	NA	NA	1.58	1.60	1.87	1.72	1.75
Foreign banks	NA	NA	2.54	2.67	2.26	1.99	1.43
SCBs	NA	NA	1.42	1.59	1.41	1.15	1.35
			Ratio of operating profit to total assets				
PSBs	1.84	1.26	1.46	2.39	1.87	1.70	1.66
IPBs	2.08	1.99	2.11	1.93	2.68	2.86	2.90
Foreign banks	5.06	3.93	3.24	3.16	3.70	3.36	2.83
SCBs	2.08	1.49	1.66	2.36	2.17	2.00	2.15
			Return on assets (ROA)				
PSBs	0.28	0.25	0.57	0.95	0.97	0.46	−0.23
IPBs	0.57	1.16	0.90	1.06	1.28	1.68	0.51
Foreign banks	1.56	1.87	1.24	1.61	1.26	1.84	1.55
SCBs	0.39	0.43	0.66	1.01	1.05	0.81	0.15

Source: RBI's *Report on Trend and Progress of Banking in India*, various issues; RBI's *Statistical Tables Relating to Banks in India*, various issues, downloaded from RBI website, www.rbi.org.in.

Note: NA stands for 'not readily available'.

expansion of bank credit to nearly 30 per cent during 2004–07 led to faster increase in the denominator (total assets). This contributed to the decline of the ratio too. Greater autonomy to banks to determine their lending rates in a highly competitive environment could also be a significant factor.

The pattern in the movement of the ratio of interest income to assets across different bank groups was not uniform. It is true that the ratio was lower for all bank groups during the later part of the post-reform period as compared to the initial part. But the ratio for IPBs at 9.72 per cent was the lowest across all bank groups in 1991–92 and became the highest at 8.07 per cent in 2019–20. On the contrary, for foreign banks, the ratio was highest at 11.62 per cent in 1991–92 and became the lowest across all bank groups at 5.74 per cent in 2019–20.

Table 11.1 also presents information on the ratio of non-interest income to assets for different bank groups for the purpose of comparison. The ratio did not witness much variation across bank groups.

It is pertinent to note that similar to how variation in interest rates on loans and investments was in tune with the changing monetary policy stance, changes could be observed in the pattern of interest rates on bank deposits too. Moreover, greater operational autonomy and a competitive environment would have also impacted different items under operating costs. Therefore, information on operating profits will give a broader perspective on bank profitability. It can be observed from Table 11.1 that the ratio of operating profit to assets for SCBs had gradually increased from 1.49 per cent in 1994–95 to 2.36 per cent in 2004–05. Afterwards, there was broadly a declining trend.

PSBs were found to be improving their ratio of operating profit to assets since the mid-1990s until the mid-2000s. It appears they were successful in controlling interest costs and operating costs aggressively to more than compensate the drop in their ratio of interest income to assets during this period. However, the ratio of operating profit to assets of PSBs witnessed continuous moderation after the mid-2000s. This is despite a rising ratio of interest income to assets during the mid-2000s to mid-2010s.

IPBs and foreign banks exhibited very different patterns as regards their ratio of operating profit to assets. Foreign banks witnessed broadly a moderation in the ratio from 5.06 per cent in 1991–92 to 2.83 per cent in 2019–20. On the contrary, for IPBs, the ratio improved from 2.08 per cent to 2.90 per cent during the comparable period.

Finally, let us talk about the ROA of banks which is the most comprehensive measure to assess bank profitability. As provisions and contingencies are covered in calculating ROA, this measure partly takes into account risks entailed in the lendings and investments of banks.

The ROA of SCBs was found to be gradually improving during the earlier part of the post-reform period. It registered an increasing trend from 0.39 per cent in 1991–92 to 1.05 per cent in 2009–10. Reversing the trend, it marginally came down to 0.81 per cent in 2014–15 and drastically dropped to 0.15 per cent in 2019–20. The broad pattern in the movement of ROA for PSBs exactly mirrored that for SCBs. For PSBs, ROA became negative at (–)0.23 per cent in 2019–20, largely reflecting their burden of high loan delinquencies during the 2010s. The ratio of gross NPAs to total assets of PSBs, which was 1.3 per cent in 2009–10, gradually increased to 8.9 per cent in 2017–18. The ratio remained stubbornly high at 7.3 and 6.3 per cent, respectively, in the following two years. High NPAs required more provisioning for loan delinquencies and adversely affected the ROA of PSBs.

It is interesting to note that foreign banks largely maintained their ROA throughout the post-reform period with only some minor fluctuations. IPBs exhibited continuous upward movement in ROA until the mid-2010s. In fact, they raised it by more than 1 percentage point within a quarter century of banking reforms, which is the highest gain across all bank groups. While both IPBs and foreign banks suffered declining profitability in 2019–20, their ROA figure remained close to their respective levels in 1991–92.

Thus, different indicators broadly reflected comfortable profitability for different bank groups before some concerns on negative net profit experienced by PSBs in the recent years. Both interest income and operating profit as a proportion of assets have been reasonably good.

11.2.2.2 Profitability of Leading Banks in India

It is obvious that the pattern of profitability of a group of banks indicates the average performance of the members of the group. All members need not conform to the group average. In this perspective, to understand how individual banks have fared on the profitability front during the post-reform period, let us discuss bank-wise performance.

To simplify our analysis, we have selected a sample of big banks from each group using the volume of advances in 2009–10 as the criterion. Considering the *differences* in the nature and scope of the banking business, particularly between Indian and foreign banks, we have fixed different cut-off levels. For Indian banks (PSBs and IPBs), we have shortlisted those with advances above INR 1,00,000 crore in 2009–10. For foreign banks, the threshold level is fixed as INR 20,000 crore. We have selected seven PSBs and three each amongst IPBs and foreign banks as the sample. The ratios of interest income to assets of these sample banks are provided in Table 11.2.

It can be observed from Table 11.2 that all the PSBs in our list except BOB broadly reflected the same pattern in the movement of their ratio of interest

Table 11.2 Ratio of interest income to total assets of leading banks in India

(Per cent)

Bank	1991–92	1994–95	1999–2000	2004–05	2009–10	2014–15	2019–20
PSBs							
Bank of Baroda	10.08	9.43	8.91	6.79	6.61	6.25	6.78
Bank of India	10.18	7.76	8.45	6.35	7.14	7.29	6.61
Canara Bank	11.13	9.17	8.92	6.86	7.74	8.41	6.90
Central Bank of India	9.98	8.07	9.04	7.59	7.30	8.78	6.86
Punjab National Bank	10.06	8.94	9.52	6.70	7.88	8.03	6.70
State Bank of India	10.03	8.73	8.49	7.05	7.04	7.94	6.74
Union Bank of India	10.26	9.15	9.48	6.86	7.47	8.73	7.13
IPBs							
Axis Bank	NA	5.17	7.25	5.10	7.09	8.40	7.30
HDFC Bank	NA	0.37	5.83	6.02	7.97	8.96	8.27
ICICI Bank	NA	4.34	7.06	5.61	6.92	7.91	7.25
Foreign banks							
Citibank	9.72	10.14	10.51	6.52	6.05	7.20	6.39
HSBC	10.17	9.21	7.84	5.83	5.58	6.21	6.01
Standard Chartered	13.11	9.10	10.62	6.69	6.09	7.72	6.41

Sources: RBI's *Report on Trend and Progress of Banking in India*, various issues; RBI's *Statistical Tables Relating to Banks in India*, various issues, downloaded from RBI website, www.rbi.org.in.

Note: (*a*) The 2019–20 figure for Bank of Baroda is not strictly comparable with corresponding figures of the previous years, as Dena Bank and Vijaya Bank were merged with Bank of Baroda in 2019. The figure for 2019–20 is that of the combined entity after amalgamation, while for other years the figures pertain to Bank of Baroda prior to the merger. (*b*) NA stands for 'not readily available'.

income to assets as that observed for PSBs as a group. The ratio gradually declined from 1991–92 until the mid-2000s. Afterwards, the ratio increased until the mid-2010s before falling again in 2019–20. As discussed earlier, this movement largely reflected the shifts in the monetary policy stance of the RBI. Only for BOB, the ratio of interest income to assets kept falling till the mid-2010s and the trend reversed with a marginal rise in 2019–20.

The IPBs in our sample witnessed continuous improvement in the ratio of interest income to assets during the post-reform period. In fact, for HDFC Bank, the ratio phenomenally increased by nearly 8 percentage points. This distinctive feature of rising interest income as compared to assets could not be discerned when we discussed IPBs as a group earlier. The ratio for the foreign banks in our sample, however, reflected a similar pattern to what was observed for that group as whole.

Information on the ratio of net profit to assets and ROA for the banks in our sample is provided in Table 11.3. The numerator both for the ratio of net profit to assets and ROA is the same—that is, net profit. There is a minor difference in the denominator. In the ratio of net profit to total assets, the denominator is the total assets for the corresponding year, while in ROA the denominator is the average of total assets in the corresponding year and the preceding year. Table 11.3 presents data on the ratio of net profit to total assets for the sample banks for the period 1992–93 to 2004–05 while the same for ROA covers the period 2004–05 to 2019–20. As readily available continuous

Table 11.3 Ratio of net profit to total assets and ROA of leading banks in India

(Per cent)

	1991–92	1994–95	1999–2000	2004–05	2004–05	2009–10	2014–15	2019–20
Bank	**Net profit to total assets**				**ROA**			
				PSBs				
Bank of Baroda	0.44	0.56	0.86	0.71	0.75	1.21	0.49	0.06
Bank of India	0.24	0.17	0.31	0.36	0.38	0.70	0.27	-0.43
Canara Bank	0.95	0.77	0.43	1.01	1.01	1.30	0.55	-0.32
Central Bank of India	0.21	-0.41	0.36	0.52	0.53	0.66	0.21	-0.35
Punjab National Bank	0.58	0.30	0.75	1.12	1.17	1.44	0.53	0.04
State Bank of India	0.18	0.59	0.78	0.94	0.99	0.88	0.68	0.38
Union Bank of India	0.34	0.62	0.29	0.99	1.10	1.25	0.49	-0.53
				IPBs				
Axis Bank	NA	0.41	0.76	0.89	1.21	1.67	1.83	0.2
HDFC Bank	NA	0.09	1.03	1.29	1.47	1.53	2.02	2.01
ICICI Bank	NA	0.43	0.87	1.20	1.59	1.13	1.86	0.81
				Foreign banks				
Citibank	2.11	2.09	1.43	1.77	2.84	0.96	2.43	2.55
HSBC	1.64	1.11	0.96	1.28	1.27	0.88	1.33	1.61
Standard Chartered	-5.92	0.34	1.83	1.61	1.97	3.03	2.42	1.78

Source: RBI's *Report on Trend and Progress of Banking in India*, various issues; RBI's *Statistical Tables Relating to Banks in India*, various issues, downloaded from RBI website, www.rbi.org.in.

Note: NA stands for 'not readily available'.

data could not be accessed for the entire period for either ratio of net profit to total assets or ROA, we have followed this approach of presenting data for two sub-periods with a common year (2004–05) for suitable comparability.

It can be observed that broadly the ratio of net profit to total assets and ROA improved for all the PSBs in our sample until 2009–10, except two. For SBI and Union Bank of India, the increasing profitability trend was observed only up to the mid-2000s. Moreover, Central Bank of India had posted negative profit for a couple of years in the 1990s. All the PSBs in our list experienced decline in ROA during the 2010s. In fact, in 2019–20, half the PSBs incurred losses. ROA for Bank of India, Canara Bank, Central Bank of India and Union Bank of India was negative in the range of (–)0.32 per cent to (–)0.53 per cent. This is mainly due to the high level of loan delinquencies experienced during the 2010s.

Loan delinquencies of IPBs and foreign banks were much lower as compared to those for PSBs. Hence, as can be seen from Table 11.3, they could raise their ratio of net profit to assets and ROA until the mid-2010s. By 2019–20, some of them witnessed a drop in their profitability, although none in our list incurred losses. Interestingly, HDFC Bank, Citibank and HSBC could improve their profitability in 2019–20 as compared to 2014–15.

11.3 Productivity of Banks in India

11.3.1 Concept and Measurement of Bank Productivity

To explain the concept of productivity, let us return to the *production function* introduced in Chapter 3. It specifies the technical relation between the output of a producer and the factor inputs used in the production process. Mathematically, a production function can be represented as:

$$Y = A\,f(K, L) \qquad (11.1)$$

In equation 11.1, Y stands for output, A stands for TFP, and K and L represent stock of capital and labour, respectively. Finally, 'f' denotes the general functional form, relating output to capital and labour. This suggests K amount of capital and L amount of labour are used to produce Y amount of output. The properties of this production function are the same as those of equation 3.1 presented in Chapter 3.

We can define the productivity of a factor of production such as labour or capital in marginal or average terms. Increase in output by increasing one unit of a factor of production while keeping the remaining factor input(s) constant is referred to as marginal productivity of that factor of production. Let us assume, using a particular technology of production, one machine and two workers produce 100 units of output. Let us also assume that by employing an additional worker—that is, employing a total of three workers with the same one machine—total output increases to 120 units. Here, the marginal productivity of the third (new) worker is 20 units. This is 120 *minus* 100.

Similarly, average output of a factor of production is obtained by dividing the total amount of output by the total units of the factor of production used in the production process. In our example, when two workers were used (along with one machine) to produce 100 units of output, the average productivity of a worker was 50—that is, 100 divided by 2. As an additional worker is employed, the average productivity of the workers drops to 40, which is 120 divided by 3. This measure of average productivity of labour is popularly referred to as *labour productivity*. In other words, labour productivity refers to the total output divided by the number of workers used in the production process. Higher labour productivity in a production activity implies higher amount of output produced by an average unit of labour. For further details on factor productivity, the reader may refer to popular textbooks on microeconomics.[2]

In banking, *business per worker* and *profit per worker* are popularly used to measure productivity. Both terms are derived from the concept of labour productivity. If the managers and staff of a bank are well motivated, trained with the required skill set and work hard, it helps in expanding the volume of loans and deposits. Proper credit appraisal while sanctioning loans and monitoring of their end-use by competent bank staff can reduce loan delinquencies. The interest rate policy adopted by banks with correct macroeconomic analysis, including precise assessment of the competitive environment and evolving economic conditions, is crucial for raising bank profitability. This also requires appropriate use of econometric and statistical models by the bank's economists and analysts. To sum up, overall labour productivity encapsulating competency, sincerity and commitment of a bank's officers and staff is critical for promoting business volume and profitability.

---

[2] See, for instance, Pindyck and Rubinfeld (2013) and Mankiw (2016).

11.3.2 Performance of Banks in India as per Productivity

11.3.2.1 Productivity of Different Bank Groups

Table 11.4 presents two broad indicators of productivity, namely (*a*) *business per employee* and (*b*) *business per branch* for different bank groups, borrowing from RBI (2008). The *business per employee* of SCBs had increased manifold from around INR 47 lakh in 1991–92 to INR 118 lakh in 1998–99 and subsequently to INR 522 lakh in 2006–07. Within 15 years, the number had increased more than tenfold. Similarly, the *business per branch* of SCBs had also increased significantly from around INR 9 crore to INR 79 crore during the comparable period.

Improvement in productivity was registered across bank groups, notwithstanding the variation in degree. PSBs had improved their *business per employee* more than tenfold from INR 45 lakh in 1991–92 to INR 471 lakh in 2006–07. IPBs did even better by raising employee productivity more than twentyfold during the comparable period. Foreign banks raised their employee productivity nearly fivefold.

It is important to note that despite faster growth of employee productivity in PSBs and IPBs, the level could not match that of foreign banks. For example, the *business per employee* of PSBs in 2019–20 was INR 471 lakh as compared to INR 995 lakh for foreign banks. Bank group-wise *business per branch* figures convey a similar story (Table 11.4).

Table 11.4 Bank-group-wise productivity indicators

(*INR lakh*)

Bank groups	**1991–92**	**1998–99**	**2006–07**
	Business per employee		
PSBs	45.15	105.78	470.99
IPBs	33.48	193.95	694.07
Foreign banks	199.47	504.81	995.09
SCBs	46.66	117.72	521.94
	Business per branch		
PSBs	8.93	20.90	66.83
IPBs	4.87	25.24	133.16
Foreign banks	149.96	349.04	1,004.10
SCBs	9.12	22.75	79.39

Source: RBI's *Report on Currency and Finance, 2006–08*, vol. 2.

11.3.2.2 Productivity of Leading Banks in India

Bank-wise data on *business per employee* are provided in Table 11.5. All the PSBs in our sample witnessed significant improvement in labour productivity, using business per employee as proxy. Of course, there are minor differences in the pace of improvement. For example, SBI witnessed a nearly twentyfold increase in labour productivity within two decades from the late 1990s to the late 2010s while that for BOB and Canara Bank was less than fifteenfold.

The IPBs in our sample did not witness any significant jump in labour productivity between 1999–2000 and 2019–20. Their business per employee hardly doubled during this period. The improvement amongst the foreign banks was better than that of the IPBs but was dwarfed by the achievements of the PSBs.

It is important to note that the labour productivity of the PSBs in our sample surpassed that of leading IPBs. Business per employee of the PSBs in our sample, except one, was higher than any of the IPBs in 2019–20. This

Table 11.5 Business per employee of leading banks in India

(INR lakh)

Bank	1999–2000	2004–05	2009–10	2014–15	2019–20
		PSBs			
Bank of Baroda	143	310	981	1,889	1,877
Bank of India	136	320	1,333	2,069	1,940
Canara Bank	135	351	983	1,435	1,763
Central Bank of India	93	207	712	1,138	1,406
Punjab National Bank	106	277	808	1,319	1,814
State Bank of India	111	243	636	1,234	2,105
Union Bank of India	135	347	853	1,446	2,006
		IPBs			
Axis Bank	1,249	895	1,111	1,371	1,727
HDFC Bank	942	806	590	1,010	1,749
ICICI Bank	595	880	765	832	1,275
		Foreign banks			
Citibank	1,161	1,360	1,980	2,463	4,363
HSBC	467	779	1,136	2,678	5,061
Standard Chartered	572	786	1,083	1,900	2,713

Source: RBI's *Report on Trend and Progress of Banking in India*, various issues; RBI's *Statistical Tables Relating to Banks in India*, various issues, downloaded from RBI website, www.rbi.org.in.

is a heartening development of the 2010s, reflecting a turnaround in labour productivity in PSBs. However, the PSBs lagged behind foreign banks substantially. For the foreign banks in our sample, business per employee stood in the range of INR 4,363–6,352 lakh in 2019–20, while for the PSBs the range was INR 1,406–2,462 lakh.

The total output in a financial company like a bank can be represented by either business volume or profit generated. Using business volume as proxy, we discussed previously labour productivity in a bank in terms of *business per employee.* Using volume of profit as proxy for output, we can alternatively measure labour productivity in terms of *profit per employee.* In Table 11.6, we have presented bank-wise data on *profit per employee.* As per this criterion, all the foreign banks in our sample have improved their labour productivity consistently during the post-reform period. The PSBs seem to have improved their labour productivity until the late 2000s. After that there was a decline in profit per employee during the 2010s due to decline in their profitability.

Table 11.6 Profit per employee of leading banks in India

(*INR lakh*)

Bank	1999–2000	2004–05	2009–10	2014–15	2019–20
		PSBs			
Bank of Baroda	1.07	1.71	8.00	7.00	1.00
Bank of India	0.33	0.80	4.39	3.70	−5.90
Canara Bank	0.45	2.48	7.35	5.00	−4.00
Central Bank of India	0.31	0.93	3.30	1.53	−3.27
Punjab National Bank	0.63	2.42	7.31	5.00	1.00
State Bank of India	0.33	2.07	4.46	6.02	5.79
Union Bank of India	0.87	2.81	7.47	5.00	−8.00
		IPBs			
Axis Bank	6.91	7.03	12.00	17.00	2.40
HDFC Bank	9.60	8.80	5.98	10.00	24.00
ICICI Bank	7.83	11.00	9.00	16.00	8.25
		Foreign banks			
Citibank	19.22	21.75	18.32	59.00	104.05
HSBC	4.36	8.90	11.73	34.25	71.58
Standard Chartered	10.27	11.50	26.31	41.79	44.23

Source: RBI's *Report on Trend and Progress of Banking in India*, various issues; RBI's *Statistical Tables Relating to Banks in India*, various issues, downloaded from RBI website, www.rbi.org.in.

Amongst the IPBs in our sample, *profit per employee* improved for Axis Bank and ICICI Bank until the mid-2010s after which it deteriorated. HDFC Bank maintained rising profit per employee figures until 2019–20.

As discussed earlier, the net profit of a bank is affected by provisions and contingencies. Higher provisions due to loan delinquencies affected the net profit of leading PSBs during the 2010s. Loan delinquencies occur due to various reasons such as the changing economic environment, government policy or wilful default, negligence or incompetency of the bank staff in credit appraisal and/or monitoring end-use of the funds. In the last account, we can associate productivity or competency of the bank staff with bank profitability, and hence *profit per employee* as a measure of labour productivity cannot be ignored. Nevertheless, we consider *business per employee* as a better proxy for the labour productivity of banks as in our view the total business of a bank is a better indicator of output in the banking business. Accordingly, we acknowledge significant improvement in the labour productivity of PSBs during the post-reform period, even overtaking the performance of NPBs.

11.4 Operational Efficiency of Banks in India

11.4.1 Concept and Measurement of Bank Efficiency

The concept of *labour productivity* as discussed in the previous section has a narrow scope in assessing banking performance. A broader way of assessing a bank's performance is to examine how overall banking resources including manpower, funds, and physical and technological infrastructure are effectively combined and exploited to maximise long-term bank profitability.

In microeconomics, TFP, a popular concept, reflects the efficiency of combining various factors of production to produce a particular amount of output. In equation 11.1, A represents TFP. It implicitly measures the efficiency or productivity of all the factors of production in combination. A higher value of TFP suggests that given amounts of capital and labour are combined more efficiently to produce a higher amount of output. On the contrary, a lower value of TFP suggests production of lesser quantity of output by the same amounts of capital and labour due to technical inefficiency. Technical details on measurement of productivity in industry and related complications are provided in standard economics textbooks.[3]

[3] See, for example, Mankiw (2010).

Such efficiency is referred to as *operational efficiency.* In banking, a host of indicators are used to assess operational efficiency, discussed as follows. These indicators are published by the RBI in various issues of *Statistical Tables Relating to Banks in India* and *Report on Trend and Progress of Banking in India.*

- *Net interest margin (NIM)*: NIM is NII divided by the average earning assets of a bank. Average earning assets are calculated as the arithmetic average of earning assets held by the bank at the beginning and the end of the concerned period. The logic for using NIM as an indicator of efficiency is very simple. NIM can be low if either interest expenses are high or interest earnings are low or both. High-interest expenses reflect higher returns on savings for depositors. On the other hand, low-interest earnings for a given asset base implies borrowers availing funds from the bank at a low cost. Both reflect efficient financial services provided by the bank in terms of converting deposits into loans and investments. Hence, low NIM is used as proxy for higher efficiency in banking services.
- *Intermediation cost*: This is another balance sheet indicator widely used to assess efficiency in the banking business. It is the operational expenses of a bank. It measures how cost-effectively banking resources are converted into banking assets.
- *Wage bills*: Salaries and compensation to employees constitute a significant component of operational costs. A bank is more efficient if its wage bills as a proportion of total expenses are low.

11.4.2 Performance of Banks in India as per Operational Efficiency

11.4.2.1 Operational Efficiency of Different Bank Groups

Information on various efficiency indicators for different bank groups in India is provided in Table 11.7. A summary of the same is as follows:

- There was no perceptible change in the NIM of SCBs during the post-reform period. It varied within a broad range of 2.54–3.31 per cent without exhibiting any systematic pattern. Nevertheless, it is observed that NIM was lower in the recent period as compared to the

Table 11.7 Bank-group-wise efficiency indicators in India

(Per cent)

Bank groups	1991–92	1994–95	1999–2000	2004–05	2009–10	2014–15	2019–20
				NIM			
PSBs	3.22	2.92	2.70	3.18	2.29	2.35	2.37
IPBs	4.02	2.69	2.13	2.51	2.90	3.37	3.43
Foreign banks	3.92	4.24	3.85	3.54	3.96	3.54	3.26
SCBs	3.31	3.00	2.72	3.08	2.54	2.64	2.81
			Ratio of intermediation cost to total assets				
PSBs	2.61	2.83	2.52	2.28	1.61	1.60	1.84
IPBs	2.98	2.01	1.85	2.18	2.10	2.23	2.28
Foreign banks	2.26	2.73	3.21	3.05	2.52	2.17	1.86
SCBs	2.60	2.76	2.49	2.32	1.78	1.80	2.01
			Ratio of wage bills to total expenses				
PSBs	NA	NA	21.01	23.79	14.79	13.19	17.53
IPBs	NA	NA	10.82	11.80	12.73	11.99	12.31
Foreign banks	NA	NA	11.38	16.13	23.48	17.32	15.63
SCBs	NA	NA	19.28	21.18	14.85	13.10	15.76

Source: RBI's *Report on Trend and Progress of Banking in India*, various issues; RBI's *Statistical Tables Relating to Banks in India*, various issues, downloaded from RBI website, www.rbi.org.in.

Note: NA stands for 'not readily available'.

corresponding figures in the early 1990s, implying improvement in the operational efficiency of SCBs.

- During a large part of the post-reform period, NIM for PSBs was lower than that for IPBs and foreign banks. This implies that PSBs were more successful in improving their efficiency.
- The ratio of intermediation cost to total assets of SCBs witnessed a gradual decline from the mid-1990s until the late 2000s. During the 2010s, the same moved upwards marginally. As per this indicator, efficiency gain by different bank groups was not uniform. The ratio witnessed a gradual reduction for foreign banks during the 2000s and 2010s. For PSBs, the decline commenced since the mid-1990s

earlier than for foreign banks. On the contrary, for IPBs, the ratio marginally increased during the 2010s. As per intermediation cost, PSBs performed better than IPBs and foreign banks in improving operational efficiency during the post-reform period.

- PSBs substantially reduced the ratio of wage bills to total expenses from 23.79 per cent in 2004–05 to 14.79 per cent in 2009–10. The implementation of the Voluntary Retirement Scheme (VRS) by PSBs in the early 2000s to rationalise manpower requirements and control wage bills certainly played a role in this reduction. In 2019–20, this ratio had increased to 17.53 per cent for PSBs, but it was still lower than the figure of 21.01 per cent for 1999–2000. On the contrary, for IPBs and foreign banks, the ratio of wage bills to total expenses was higher in 2019–20 as compared to that in 1999–2000.

11.4.2.2 Operational Efficiency of Leading Banks in India

Table 11.8 presents bank-wise data on NIM which suggests that there was a reduction in the NIMs of the PSBs in our sample. For Canara Bank and Union Bank of India, this reduction was more consistent for the entire post-reform period. For BOB, Central Bank of India and PNB, there was a temporary increase in the respective NIMs in 2004–05, breaking the declining trend. However, for all the PSBs in our sample, NIMs were lower in 2019–20 as compared to the early 1990s. This implies an improvement in the operational efficiency of these banks during the post-reform period.

For all the IPBs in our sample, NIMs during the 2000s and 2010s were higher as compared to their respective NIMs during the 1990s. The foreign banks had a mixed pattern. Similar to the IPBs, the NIMs of Citibank and Standard Chartered were higher during the recent years as compared to the 1990s. However, for HSBC, the NIM was lower in the recent years.

It is important to note that the NIMs of all the PSBs in our sample were lower than those of the IPBs and foreign banks during 2014–15 and 2019–20. This implies higher operational efficiency of the PSBs.

Let us now examine how leading banks in India managed their intermediation costs. The PSBs in our list witnessed gradual reduction in the ratio of intermediation cost to total assets from 1991–92 to 2019–20 (Table 11.9). Of course, within this broad trend, there were minor and transient aberrations for some. Nevertheless, for each bank, the ratio was lower in the 2000s and 2010s as compared to the 1990s.

Table 11.8 NIM of leading banks in India

(Per cent)

Bank	1991–92	1994–95	1999–2000	2004–05	2009–10	2014–15	2019–20
PSBs							
Bank of Baroda	2.92	3.59	2.92	3.15	2.35	1.92	2.45
Bank of India	2.25	2.59	2.31	2.36	2.30	1.91	2.38
Canara Bank	4.42	3.60	2.64	2.86	2.35	1.86	1.85
Central Bank of India	2.80	2.46	2.96	3.46	1.54	2.41	2.22
Punjab National Bank	3.42	2.85	2.99	3.17	3.12	2.87	2.17
State Bank of India	3.63	3.25	2.65	3.03	2.35	2.86	2.57
Union Bank of India	3.81	3.32	2.74	2.85	2.35	2.30	2.19
IPBs							
Axis Bank	NA	2.67	1.36	1.94	3.05	3.37	2.94
HDFC Bank	NA	0.23	2.62	3.46	4.13	4.14	4.05
ICICI Bank	NA	1.44	1.54	1.69	2.19	3.07	3.23
Foreign banks							
Citibank	3.25	4.72	4.54	4.29	4.04	4.13	4.22
HSBC	4.02	4.20	2.75	3.52	3.51	2.97	3.63
Standard Chartered	3.43	2.45	4.29	3.72	4.18	4.25	3.58

Source: RBI's *Report on Trend and Progress of Banking in India*, various issues; RBI's *Statistical Tables Relating to Banks in India*, various issues, downloaded from RBI website, www.rbi.org.in.

Note: The 2019–20 figure for Bank of Baroda is not strictly comparable with corresponding figures of the previous years, as Dena Bank and Vijaya Bank were merged with Bank of Baroda in 2019. The figure for 2019–20 is that of the combined entity after amalgamation, while for other years the figures pertain to Bank of Baroda prior to the merger.

On the contrary, all the three IPBs in our sample witnessed a rise in their ratio of intermediation cost to total assets during the 2000s and 2010s. For the foreign banks again, there was a mixed trend.

Similar to what we observed in the case of NIMs, the ratios of intermediation cost to total assets for the individual PSBs in our sample were relatively lower than those for IPBs in the recent years.

11.4.2.3 Evidence from Econometric Analysis

It is important to note that several empirical studies have been carried out to assess banking efficiency in India during the post-reform period using

Table 11.9 Ratio of intermediation cost to total assets of leading banks in India

(*Per cent*)

Bank	1991–92	1994–95	1999–2000	2004–05	2009–10	2014–15	2019–20
			PSBs				
Bank of Baroda	2.17	2.50	2.22	2.09	1.51	1.12	1.69
Bank of India	2.11	2.57	2.49	2.03	1.47	1.36	1.63
Canara Bank	2.85	2.78	2.48	1.91	1.44	1.4	1.63
Central Bank of India	2.95	3.09	3.00	2.46	1.35	1.86	2.02
Punjab National Bank	2.48	2.93	2.82	2.36	1.75	1.82	1.49
State Bank of India	2.37	2.96	2.41	2.19	2.01	2.00	1.97
Union Bank of India	3.10	2.57	2.47	1.74	1.41	1.67	1.44
			IPBs				
Axis Bank	NA	1.25	0.98	1.54	2.26	2.18	2.02
HDFC Bank	NA	0.18	1.47	2.11	2.93	2.59	2.21
ICICI Bank	NA	2.68	1.27	1.97	1.58	1.85	2.10
			Foreign banks				
Citibank	1.85	3.27	3.87	3.62	2.35	2.22	2.08
HSBC	2.56	2.97	2.35	2.43	2.11	2.33	1.82
Standard Chartered	2.31	4.24	3.32	2.26	2.60	2.27	1.97

Source: RBI's *Report on Trend and Progress of Banking in India*, various issues; RBI's *Statistical Tables Relating to Banks in India*, various issues, downloaded from RBI website, www.rbi.org.in.

Note: (*a*) The 2019–20 figure for Bank of Baroda is not strictly comparable with corresponding figures of the previous years, as Dena Bank and Vijaya Bank were merged with Bank of Baroda in 2019. The figure for 2019–20 is that of the combined entity after amalgamation, while for other years the figures pertain to Bank of Baroda prior to the merger. (*b*) NA stands for 'not readily available'.

a variety of econometric tools such as multiple regression analysis, data envelope analysis (DEA), stochastic frontier analysis (SFA), and so on. Widely cited studies in this area include Kumbhakar and Sarkar (2003); Das, Nag and Ray (2005); Sensarma (2005); RBI (2008), and so on. One recent study is Baral and Patnaik (2023). The main findings of these studies are summarised in Appendix 11A. Broadly, these studies provide evidence in favour of enhanced banking efficiency in India during the post-reform period, particularly since the late 1990s.

To sum up, the preceding sections highlighted improvements in the profitability, productivity and operational efficiency of banks in India during the post-reform period. Particularly, PSBs were successful in taking advantage of the operational autonomy and greater competitive environment under the deregulated regime. They performed better than Indian private and foreign banks on many indictors of banking productivity and operational efficiency. This is consistent with the observations of noted experts (Mohan, 2005; Chakrabarty, 2013).

11.5 Allocative Efficiency of Banks in India

As observed previously, broadly the performance of banks in India has improved after the banking reforms adopted since the early 1990s. However, the drive for improving profitability, productivity and operational efficiency might have led to neglect of certain groups, regions and economic activities. If weaker sections of society, backward regions and activities like agriculture and small enterprises are neglected in the process of improving banking profitability and operational efficiency, it leads to concerns of financial inclusion. This dilutes the *allocative efficiency* of banking from the developmental perspective. It is thus important to explore how banks in India have performed on this account.

In a public speech delivered in 2013, K. C. Chakrabarty, the former deputy governor of the RBI, highlighted that while banks in India had been successful in improving operational efficiency during the first two decades after banking deregulation, there were rising concerns on account of allocational efficiency. In fact, he blamed the improved operational efficiency attained by banks for causing deterioration in allocative efficiency (Chakrabarty, 2013).

Chakrabarty highlighted the deterioration in banking allocational efficiency in 2013 as compared to 1994 using a host of indicators. These included the falling share of rural branches in the total branches of SCBs; low growth of credit and deposit accounts in rural areas as compared to overall growth; drop in the share of agriculture, small-scale industries and small-sized loans in credit deployment; and so on. Based on these factors, he concluded that improving productivity and operational efficiency in banking did not help all sections of society during the post-reform period. He attributed this to lack of banking penetration; failure to leverage new technology to create products, business models and delivery channels to spread banking services to all; and undue focus on wholesale business. He also listed a few initiatives undertaken by the RBI in the early 2010s to improve the allocational efficiency of banking in India. Key initiatives included (*a*) revision of priority sector norms in 2012, (*b*) regulatory mandate to open a minimum one-fourth new branches annually in unbanked rural areas, (*c*) liberal norms for domestic SCBs to open new branches in centres with populations less than one lakh and (*d*) implementation of a financial inclusion plan (FIP) during 2010–13 and 2013–16 (Chakrabarty, 2013).

In the following sections, let us assess and review the allocational efficiency of banks in India by including information for the latest period.

11.5.1 Regional Distribution of Banking

In Chapter 5, we have reviewed distribution of banking services in India across states. We observed that poorer states have weaker access to banking services. Here, we attempt to compare availability of banking services across different regions in India distinguished in terms of the rural–urban divide. Table 11.10 provides data on population group–wise distribution of banking services in India for different centres or areas. Broadly, the centres are distinguished in terms of the following categories: (*a*) rural, (*b*) semi-urban, (*c*) urban and (*d*) metropolitan. According to the RBI's *Statistical Tables Relating to Banks in India*, the population of 'rural' centres is less than 10,000 and that of 'metropolitan' centres is 10 lakh and above. The population of 'semi-urban' and 'urban' centres is in the range of 10,000–1,00,000 and 1,00,000–10,00,000, respectively. The following figures indicate the falling share of rural branches in the overall banking business:

- Rural areas accounted for 58.2 per cent of the bank branches of SCBs in 1991–92. The opening of bank branches across the country was mainly facilitated by the bank nationalisations of 1969 and 1980.
- A gradual decline in the share of rural centres saw rural branches accounting for only 34.9 per cent in 2019–20.

It is pertinent to note that the declining importance of rural centres was not only confined to distribution of bank branches. A similar trend was also observed in the distribution of bank credit and deposits:

- As regards the distribution of bank credit of SCBs, rural centres accounted for nearly 20 per cent share in 1991–92 (Table 11.10). This gradually declined to less than 10 per cent by 2019–20. The share of

Table 11.10 Distribution of banking services of SCBs in India

Regions/Centres	1991–92	1994–95	1999–2000	2004–05	2009–10	2014–15	2019–20
	Distribution of bank branches						
Rural	35,269	33,004	32,734	32,082	30,075	45,136	52,387
Semi-urban	11,356	13,341	14,407	15,403	21,409	34,874	42,240
Urban	8,279	8,868	10,052	11,500	15,964	22,489	27,314
Metropolitan	5,666	7,154	8,219	9,370	17,639	24,014	28,102
Total	60,570	62,367	65,412	68,355	85,087	1,26,513	1,50,043
Memo:							
Rural Branches as percentage of total branches	58.2	52.9	50.0	46.9	35.3	35.7	34.9
	Percentage distribution of bank credit						
Rural	20.1	15.9	12.9	13.9	11.5	9.5	9.1
Semi-urban	16.7	15.1	14.1	12.4	11.0	11.6	13.0
Urban	22.0	17.7	17.3	18.4	17.7	17.1	18.6
Metropolitan	41.1	51.4	55.7	55.3	59.7	61.7	59.3
Total	100	100	100	100	100	100	100
	Percentage distribution of bank deposits						
Rural	15.1	13.7	14.7	12.2	9.2	10.3	10.9
Semi-urban	19.6	18.8	19.7	16.9	13.5	14.8	16.5
Urban	23.3	22.2	23.0	21.5	20.7	22.0	21.6
Metropolitan	42.0	45.3	42.6	49.4	56.6	53.0	50.9
Total	100	100	100	100	100	100	100

Source: Calculated by the author based on data obtained from RBI's *Handbook of Statistics on Indian Economy*, various issues.

'semi-urban' and 'urban' centres also witnessed a similar declining trend. On the contrary, the 'metropolitan' centres, which accounted about 40 per cent of the bank credit in 1991–92, raised their share to nearly 60 per cent in 2019–20.

- Centre-wise shares in bank deposits exhibited a similar pattern to that of bank credit. The share of 'metropolitan' centres increased from 42 per cent in 1991–92 to 50.9 per cent in 2019–20. The remaining three categories witnessed a decline in shares. But compared to bank credit, the fall in the share of bank deposits in rural areas was less severe.

It is also important to note that over the last 30 years, there would have been transitions of centres from 'rural' to 'semi-urban', from 'urban' to 'metropolitan', and so on, with gradual increase in population. Consequently, the falling share of rural centres may be partially due to such transitions of several centres from a low-population category to a high-population category.

11.5.2 Distribution of Bank Credit

Information on sectoral deployment of credit is provided in Table 11.11. We get a mixed picture on allocative efficiency from this table. On the one hand, it is clear that the share of agriculture, micro and small-scale industries in the outstanding non-food credit of SCBs has dropped by half during the post-reform period. It gradually declined from nearly 30 per cent in 1991–92 to 15.6 per cent in 2019–20. The share of medium- and large-scale industries, which varied in the range of 35–40 per cent until 2014–15, also plummeted to about 25 per cent in 2019–20.

On the contrary, the share of personal loans has increased during the post-reform period from 9.2 per cent in 1991–92 to 26.4 per cent in 2019–20. 'Housing loans' constituted nearly half the personal loans. Thus, the redistribution of the sectoral loans of SCBs suggests that an almost 15 per cent drop in the share of agriculture, micro and small-scale industries was compensated by a proportional increase in the share of personal loans.

Another way of assessing the allocational efficiency of bank credit is by examining the distribution of loans as per loan size. Table 11.12 provides information on distribution of the outstanding bank credit of SCBs according to the credit limit. Information could be obtained only up to 2011–12 beyond which the RBI stopped publishing the same in its annual publication *Statistical Tables Relating to Banks in India*.

It can be observed from Table 11.12 that during the post-reform period, the share of small-sized loans has gradually declined. The share of loans up to INR 2 lakh in the outstanding total bank credit had dropped from 35.5 per cent in 1991–92 to 9.5 per cent in 2011–12. On the contrary, the share of large loans of above INR 10 crore increased from 37 per cent to 67.1 per cent during the comparable period.

Thus, broadly, the changing distribution of bank loans based on sectoral share and population size of the centre points to deterioration in allocational efficiency during the post-reform period in India. However, the significant rise in the proportion of personal loans provides some comfort in this regard.

Table 11.11 Sectoral deployment of bank credit of SCBs in India

(*INR crore*)

Sectors	1991–92	1994–95	1999–2000	2004–05	2009–10	2014–15	2019–20
Agriculture	18,157	23,983	44,381	1,25,250	4,15,741	7,65,880	12,03,176
Micro and small-scale Industries	18,150	27,638	52,814	74,588	2,06,401	3,80,028	4,03,051
Medium and large-scale industries	47,090	74,672	1,47,319	3,52,304	11,05,051	22,77,599	25,43,800
Personal loans	11,187	18,884	51,639	2,55,981	5,85,633	11,66,348	27,26,864
of which							
Housing loans (including under priority sector)	NA	NA	18,525	1,26,797	3,00,929	6,28,535	13,61,880
Total	**1,21,335**	**1,84,710**	**3,75,127**	**9,99,788**	**30,39,615**	**60,02,952**	**1,03,19,097**
Memo: share in total credit (per cent)							
Share of agriculture, micro and small-scale industries	29.9	27.9	25.9	20.0	20.5	19.1	15.6
Share of medium and large-scale industries	38.8	40.4	39.3	35.2	36.4	37.9	24.7
Personal loans	9.2	10.2	13.8	25.6	19.3	19.4	26.4
Housing loans	NA	NA	4.9	12.7	9.9	10.5	13.2

Source: Calculated by the author based on data obtained from RBI's *Handbook of Statistics on Indian Economy*, various issues.

Note: NA stands for 'not readily available'.

Table 11.12 Distribution of bank credit as per loan size

(*Per cent*)

Credit limit range	1991–92	1994–95	1999–2000	2004–05	2009–10	2011–12
Percentage share in outstanding bank credit as per size of credit limit						
Up to INR 25,000	22.0	16.2	7.9	3.7	1.3	1.6
INR 25,000–INR 1 lakh	7.7	5.8	NA	NA	NA	NA
INR 1 lakh–INR 2 lakh*	5.8	5.6	14.4	13.6	9.5	7.9
INR 2 lakh–INR 5 lakh	5.5	5.2	6.2	9.6	7.7	7.5
INR 5 lakh–INR 10 lakh	4.0	3.3	3.2	6.1	4.9	4.3
INR 10 lakh–INR 25 lakh	5.8	4.9	4.2	5.4	5.8	5.7
INR 25 lakh–INR 50 lakh	5.9	5.0	3.9	3.2	3.4	3.3
INR 50 lakh–INR 1 crore	6.6	6.3	4.7	3.1	2.8	2.6
INR 1 crore–INR 10 crore	25.7	27	23.1	15.9	12.8	11.3
Above INR 10 crore	11.3	20.9	32.3	39.3	52.0	55.8
Memo items						
Less than INR 2 lakh	35.5	27.6	22.3	17.3	10.8	9.5
More than INR 1 crore	37.0	47.9	55.4	55.2	64.8	67.1

Source: RBI's *Report on Trend and Progress of Banking in India*, various issues; RBI's *Statistical Tables Relating to Banks in India*, various issues, downloaded from RBI website, www.rbi.org.in.

Note: (*a*) *For 2009–10 and 2011–12, the credit limit was INR 25,000–INR 2 lakh. (*b*) NA stands for 'not readily available'.

11.5.3 Distribution of Bank Deposits

As regards the distribution of deposits of SCBs in India, the household sector accounts for the dominant share. During the post-reform period, its share in total deposits witnessed a decline from 67.6 per cent in 1999–2000 to 58 per cent in 2009–10. Afterwards it witnessed an increasing pattern and reached 63.5 per cent in 2019–20 (Table 11.13). A similar pattern was observed for term deposits too. This reflected the approach of banks towards mobilisation of retail deposits versus bulk deposits (from financial and non-financial corporates). Year-wise trends suggest that the actual turning point was the year 2006–07. The share of households in term deposits was the lowest at 47.9 per cent and that in total deposits was 57.4 per cent in 2006–07. Perhaps prior to the GFC of 2007–08, banks had emphasised mobilisation of bulk deposits from corporates. Understanding the vulnerability of bulk deposits on account of liquidity risks and realising the importance of retail deposits

Table 11.13 Distribution of bank deposits of SCBs in India

(Per cent)

Sectors	1994–95	1999–2000	2004–05	2009–10	2014–15	2019–20
Savings account deposits						
Household sector	87.5	87.3	86.1	85.2	83.1	82.4
Out of which						
Individuals	NA	79.2	77.3	74.2	74.3	78.1
Corporate sector (non-financial)	0.2	0.1	0.5	0.6	0.7	3.8
Corporate sector (financial)	0.6	0.8	0.7	0.4	0.4	0.4
Government sector	6.1	6.7	7.2	8.6	11.3	8.2
Term deposits						
Household sector	67.9	64.3	52.2	50.2	53.0	57.8
Out of which						
Individuals	NA	55.6	41.1	38.5	43.3	50.5
Corporate sector (non-financial)	3.5	3.4	9.5	17.0	11.7	17.4
Corporate sector (financial)	5.6	8.3	10.1	14.2	10.8	7.3
Government sector	8.0	9.5	17.6	15.1	15.5	8.3
Total deposits						
Household sector	69.2	67.6	60.7	58.0	60.1	63.5
Out of which						
Individuals	NA	57.0	48.4	45.2	49.3	55.6
Corporate sector (non-financial)	4.2	3.8	8.7	14.8	10.1	15.3
Corporate sector (financial)	6.7	7.7	7.8	10.0	8.2	5.5
Government sector	9.2	10.1	14.6	13.5	14.4	8.4

Source: RBI's *Report on Currency and Finance, 2006–08*, vol. 2; RBI's *Statistical Tables Relating to Banks in India*, various issues, downloaded from RBI's official website, www.rbi.org.in.

Note: NA stands for 'not readily available'.

from households in terms of reliability and durability, there was a shift in focus after the GFC. This resulted in the rising share of households in term deposits.

The share of households in savings account deposits witnessed a gradual decline from 87.3 per cent in 1999–2000 to 82.4 per cent in 2019–20. Nevertheless, households maintained more than four-fifths share in overall savings account deposits. Thus, as regards allocational efficiency, the distribution of deposits does not raise any significant concern.

To sum up, our analysis suggests that the allocational efficiency of banks in India has deteriorated on several counts during the post-reform period. Banking services in terms of spread in bank branches and distribution of deposits and bank credit are not favourable for rural centres. Instead, metropolitan centres have found rapid expansion of banking services in this regard. There is evidence of falling shares of agriculture and small-scale industries in distribution of bank credit. Also, the share of large borrowers has expanded at the expense of small-sized loans. The only silver lining is improvement in the share of personal loans, implying that a large number of middle-class borrowers have benefitted from bank lending during the post-reform period.

11.6 Conclusion

In the preceding sections, we reviewed the profitability, productivity and efficiency of banks in India during the post-reform period. It was perceived that the banking sector reforms introduced since the early 1990s helped banks to perform better on these parameters. As regards profitability, except some concerns regarding loan delinquencies in the 2010s, largely banks in India fared well. There were signs of improvement in terms of productivity and operational efficiency across different bank groups. On account of both labour productivity and operational efficiency, the improvement in performance of PSBs was noteworthy. However, there were concerns about the deteriorating allocative efficiency of banks.

It was observed that incidence of high loan delinquencies for banks, particularly for PSBs, led to deterioration of profitability and efficiency parameters during the 2010s. For promoting banking soundness and financial performance of the Indian banking sector, this experience provides valuable lessons. The RBI and individual banks need to learn from the mistakes, misjudgements, malfeasances and external factors which led to bank NPAs during this period. Necessary corrective action can be helpful in avoidance of recurrences. Suggestions on strengthening the regulatory and supervisory aspects as discussed in Chapter 12 will definitely be helpful in this regard.

The improvement in the productivity and operational efficiency of banks in India during the post-reform period bodes well for their role in promoting economic prosperity. We have already underscored the role of banking services in promoting the economic prosperity of society as a whole by augmenting savings mobilisation and capital formation as well as forming the backbone of the payment and settlement system. However, it is also pertinent to distinguish between private profit and social benefit as regards banking services. Profitability considerations in the banking business are confined to the owners or shareholders and managers of the bank alone. But we cannot ignore the fact that banking services entail positive externality as associated with a public good. Practically, banking services involve non-rivalry and non-excludability. Opening of a deposit account by someone does not exclude another person from opening their own deposit account. Similarly, as long as two individuals are creditworthy, the bank generally lends to both to maximise its profitability. Thus, we need to keep in mind that social welfare aspects associated with banking services are higher than the sum of the private profits earned by the shareholders of the bank. In this context, the need for improving the allocational efficiency of banks in India cannot be overemphasised. At the same time, the drive for better allocational efficiency cannot be at the cost of financial prudence. It has to be pursued with deft balancing of associated risks and returns. The task is easier said than done.

Appendix 11A

Several studies were undertaken using a variety of economic tools to empirically examine banking efficiency in India, particularly to assess the improvement in the post-reform period. These studies used a variety of methods of econometric analysis such as the multiple regression model, DEA and SFA. In a nutshell, multiple regression analysis examines how the dependent variable such as output or profit is determined by a set of factor inputs (explanatory variables) like workers, fixed assets, funds, and so on. In DEA and SFA, the benchmark or best practice frontier is constructed assuming optimal use of resources. If a particular bank lies on this frontier, it is the most efficient bank. As a bank moves away from the best practice frontier, it is treated as less efficient. In general, loans and advances, investments and suitable indicators for OBS businesses are used as banking sector outputs while bank deposits, borrowings, employees and fixed assets of a bank are used as inputs for constructing the best practice frontier. Providing details of such econometric analysis is beyond the scope of this book. The reader may refer to the respective studies for the same. The broad findings of a set of widely cited studies which examined banking sector efficiency in India during the post-reform period are summarised in the paragraphs that follow.

Kumbhakar and Sarkar (2003) observed that during their study period of 1985–96, the TFP growth of PSBs was moderate. There was no significant improvement in TFP growth during the 1990s for PSBs. The TFP growth of IPBs was found to be somewhat higher than that of PSBs. Moreover, IPBs experienced higher TFP growth in the 1990s as compared to the 1980s. They concluded that reduction in regulatory distortions was yet to deliver the anticipated improvement in banking efficiency.

The following studies which covered the period beyond the late 1990s broadly observed improved banking efficiency, mostly using DEA- and SFA-based analysis. Das, Nag and Ray (2005) estimated the cost, technical and profit efficiency of banks for the period 1997–2003. They observed that since 1999–2000, there was noticeable improvement in the profitability of banks. Their empirical analysis suggested that the profit efficiency of banks was closely linked to their size. In a deregulated regime, banks had greater freedom to choose a proper combination of credit and investment portfolios and also enjoyed adequate flexibility as regards resource management in day-to-day operations. Bigger banks had advantages in terms of greater manoeuvrability and could improve their profit efficiency by higher amounts. Within different bank groups, PSBs were successful in improving their profit efficiency considerably while the profit efficiency of IPBs moved erratically. The profit efficiency of foreign banks was relatively higher although there was no improvement in the level during the period of the study.

Sensarma (2005) observed improvement in the cost efficiency of banks during his period of study (1986–2003). He asserted that with the banking sector reforms and infusion of greater competition, it was natural that banks reduced cost of financial intermediation, and hence cost efficiency improved. Amongst different bank groups, domestic banks were found to be more efficient than foreign banks. In most of the years in the study, PSBs performed better followed by NPBs and foreign banks. There was no appreciable intertemporal change in the cost efficiency of Indian banks. The bigger banks were found to be relatively less cost-efficient. Profit efficiency takes into account both revenue and cost aspects of banking operations. Sensarma (2005) found that while PSBs and IPBs had similar profit efficiency, after deregulation, IPBs performed better than PSBs. He attributed the better profit efficiency of private banks to improvement in service quality. Better service quality of private banks was facilitated through flexible banking hours, upgradation of technology, elegant and modern-looking banking premises, promptness of the banking staff, and so on. However, PSBs outperformed foreign banks with higher profit efficiency consistently.

RBI (2008) observed that banks in India performed better during 1998–2007 as compared to 1992–98 in terms of cost efficiency. Based on DEA estimates, the cost efficiency of banks in India was calculated to be 0.42 in 1991–92. This implied that banks could have reduced costs by 58 per cent given the feasible technology and input–output bundles observed for them. The cost efficiency of banks improved to 0.51 in 1997–98 and further to 0.71 in 2006–07. The growth rate of cost efficiency was estimated to be 20.8 per cent during 1992–98, while the same accelerated to 39.7 per cent during 1998–2007. The ownership of banks did not impact cost efficiency performance. Bank size and scope for diversification were found to be helpful in improving banking efficiency. Within different bank groups, the State Bank group was found to be enjoying the highest cost efficiency in 2006–07 at 0.85, followed by NPBs at 0.83.

Moreover, RBI (2008) also deconstructed cost efficiency into technical and allocative efficiency. It was observed that bulk of the improvement in cost efficiency is due to progress in technical efficiency which measures a bank's ability to maximise output for a given set of inputs. It improved from 0.57 in 1991–92 to 0.63 in 1997–98 and further to 0.84 in 2006–07. In this regard, the growth in efficiency was nearly 33.4 per cent during 1998–2007 as compared to 9.5 per cent during 1992–98. On the contrary, the progress as regards allocative efficiency was weaker during 1998–2007 with a growth rate of 3.22 per cent as compared to 12.03 per cent during 1992–98. Allocative efficiency assesses the ability of a bank to optimise input-use proportionately given the prices. However, bank group–wise assessment suggests that PSBs performed better in terms of allocative efficiency during 1998–2007 as compared to 1992–98. Thus, for PSBs, gain in allocative efficiency was also reasonable like that in technical efficiency.

In a recent study, Baral and Patnaik (2023) have estimated the TFP of banks in India using data for the period 2000–19 and derived efficiency change and technical change in banking performance therefrom. To elaborate, change in TFP can have two sources. First, there can be an upward movement in the best practice index itself. Assume that Bank A was the best performer in a particular period with the highest index. In the following period, Bank A may be seen to improve its own index value. This reflects a positive technical change. Second, say, Bank B had an index lower than the best practice index of Bank A in the previous period. In the following period, Bank B may have improved its own index value coming closer to that of Bank A. This is a positive technical efficiency change by Bank B which is basically a catching-up phenomenon. Econometric analysis undertaken by Baral and Patnaik (2023) revealed improvement in TFP[4] during 2000–19 for banks in India. Particularly, 30 out of 36 Indian banks in the sample showed improvement in TFP. The best performers included a mix of PSBs and IPBs, including the largest bank, SBI. A large part of the rise in TFP was due to augmentation of technical change. The top three in the list with the highest technical change included two PSBs, among which there was SBI. On the other hand, private banks led the enhancement in catching-up–relative efficiency change.

Revision Questions and Problems

1. What are the popular indicators of banking profitability?
2. How did different bank groups perform in terms of profitability indicators during the post-reform period in India?
3. How do you compare *productivity* and *efficiency* in the banking business conceptually?
4. Briefly explain the difference between *operational efficiency* and *allocative efficiency* in banking services.
5. How would you analyse banking sector performance in India in terms of operational efficiency during the post-reform period?
6. How would you analyse banking sector performance in India in terms of allocative efficiency during the post-reform period?
7. How would you compare the performance of public sector banks during the post-reform period in terms of profitability and efficiency as against that of other bank groups in India?

[4] This was by using the Malmquist TFP index.

12

Contemporary Issues and Future Agenda

Learning Objectives

- To revisit the recent problem of high bank loan delinquencies in India and its implications
- To review policy responses for arresting bank loan delinquencies and their effectiveness
- To examine the banking consolidation process in India through mergers and acquisitions (M&As) and its relevance
- To discuss the debate on public versus private ownership of banks in India
- To outline recent developments in digital banking and fintech
- To highlight recent developments in green banking in the light of environmental concerns and global warming
- To draw a broad roadmap for future banking regulations with capital requirements in a simplified but effective form and an innovative central bank liquidity facility

12.1 Introduction

In the preceding chapters, we broadly covered all critical aspects of banking in an Indian perspective. We began with an introduction to the banking business and Indian banking system in Part I of the book. We discussed that deposit mobilisation and use of such deposits for lending and investment form the core of the banking business. We also highlighted how modern banking has become more sophisticated with the adoption of financial engineering and several ancillary functions. In the Indian financial system,

SCBs continue to be of paramount importance despite development of other segments including the capital market during the post-reform period. Necessary details in a comparative perspective were provided.

This was followed by a discussion on the role of banks in an economy in Part II. Drawing from growth theories, we discussed how through mobilisation of domestic savings and facilitation of capital formation along with efficient resource allocation, banks support long-term economic prosperity. The critical role of banks in the MTM towards moderating economic fluctuations in the short run was also highlighted. It was underscored that banks can be helpful in addressing the economic disparity across states in India by promoting banking services in backward regions or states.

The banking business inherently entails a variety of risks. In this context, various types of banking risks, their quantification, regulatory prescriptions and the risk management framework of banks were covered in Part III. Awareness about banking risks and containing such risks within reasonable limits is an integral part of the banking business; otherwise, like a nuclear disaster, banking failures can be severely damaging. Banking crises can impede economic prosperity as was evident during the Great Depression of the 1930s and GFC of 2007–08. Such situations undermine monetary policy effectiveness.

Thus, Part II highlighted how banks serve society by promoting long-term prosperity and moderating short-term economic fluctuations. On the contrary, Part III flagged the harmful consequences of unrestrained banking risks for an economy. This underscored the imperative need for appropriate banking regulation and adoption of prudent banking practices. Details of banking regulation and risk management practices in banks were also delineated.

This led us to Part IV, which explained practical issues related to general banking management, including strategic decisions and day-to-day business operations as regards lending, investment, deposit mobilisation, borrowing, and so on. As compared to a broad macro approach in the first three parts of the book covering issues pertaining to the entire economy and the overall banking system, Part IV focused mainly on banking institutions as micro units.

In this part, the preceding chapter presented an assessment of banking performance in India using a variety of profitability, productivity and efficiency indicators. It reflected improvement in various indicators of profitability and operational efficiency during the post-reform period. Now, in this concluding chapter, we undertake a review of some contemporary issues pertaining to banks in India and also lay out a roadmap for the future.

The remainder of the chapter is organised as follows. Loan delinquencies during the 2010s in India, particularly in PSBs, were a considerable policy concern. They strangulated bank credit growth during the second half of the 2010s and undermined monetary policy effectiveness. The fiscal burden related to the recapitalisation of banks was also heavy. Incidence of high NPAs despite the banking sector reforms since the early 1990s added to the apprehensions. Section 12.2 in this chapter covers these issues.

India has adopted a process of bank consolidation since the early 2000s. Recently, in 2019 and 2020, amalgamation of 13 PSBs was undertaken, reducing the total number of PSBs to 12. Section 12.3 provides details of mergers and acquisitions (M&As) of banks in India and their relevance. During the post-reform period, there has been a debate on privatisation of PSBs. Section 12.4 provides a perspective on the issue.

In the last several decades, there has been rapid adoption of IT and ITES in banking. The payment and settlement system has witnessed growing digitalisation and entry of non-banking entities, facilitating growth of non-cash payments. Section 12.5 outlines related implications for banking in India.

Due to rapid industrialisation and urbanisation, there have been growing environmental concerns around the world. Particularly, global warming and related consequences of changing weather patterns are widely discussed. In this context, green banking, contributing towards an ecofriendly push, is highlighted in section 12.6. Inadequacy of the current banking regulatory framework and some innovative suggestions for the future are discussed in section 12.7. Finally, the broad conclusions of this chapter are presented in section 12.8.

12.2 Incidence of High Bank NPAs during the 2010s and Lessons Drawn

12.2.1 Recent Loan Delinquencies and Their Implications

Banks in India suffered high loan delinquencies in the post-GFC period. In the early part of this period, the problem was partly concealed by liberal loan restructuring strategies. Many problem loans which would have otherwise been classified as NPAs were negotiated and the terms of such loans, including the repayment period and interest charges, were modified.

Since inception of the asset classification regulation in 1992, the RBI had allowed for restructuring of NPAs if the borrower had commenced production and its performance for the previous two years had been satisfactory. This provision was diluted over the years; and by 2005, a liberal loan restructuring facility was available to large corporates as also small enterprises. It may be noted that loan restructuring favoured both banks and borrowers. Banks benefitted from the lower provisioning requirement of 2 per cent on restructured standard loans as compared to a provisioning requirement of 15 per cent on substandard assets until November 2012. Their financial position also looked better with underreporting of NPAs. Borrowers benefitted from continuing bank funding and protection from the stigma of being a defaulter.

In a nutshell, with such restructuring, even problem loans continued to be treated as standard assets. The following data highlights the gravity of the problem.

For PSBs, the ratio of gross NPAs (GNPAs) to advances was around 2 per cent during the period of 2007–08 to 2010–11. However, the *ratio of restructured standard assets to advances* had soared from 0.7 per cent in 2007–08 to 3.6 per cent in 2009–10. Assuming bulk of the restructured standard assets could have been problem loans, the ratio of stressed assets (RSAs) to advances accordingly rose from 2.9 to 5.8 per cent during the comparable period. Stressed assets include both assets classified as NPAs and restructured standard assets. This reflects the real problem of loan delinquencies which was understated as per the official figures on NPAs. By 2013–14, the GNPAs for PSBs were 4.4 per cent as compared to their RSAs of nearly 12 per cent.

The RBI was perhaps initially tolerant towards such rising restructuring of bank loans as it was helpful in guarding against negative fallouts of the GFC on the Indian economy. A stringent approach against restructuring and correct reflection of the loan delinquencies would have slowed down bank credit growth further on top of the deceleration experienced due to GFC-related negative sentiments. However, beyond a point the RBI had to ensure transparency in loan classification. It realised that banks and borrowers were taking undue advantage of the loan restructuring option. Since 2015, a realistic picture on bank loan delinquencies emerged with withdrawal of the scope for liberal loan restructuring. The GNPAs of PSBs increased from 5 per cent in 2014–15 to 9.3 per cent in 2015–16.

Initially, the bulk of such loan delinquencies were confined to PSBs. The GNPAs of PSBs reached a peak of 14.6 per cent in 2017–18 and thereafter gradually declined to 7.3 per cent in 2021–22. On the contrary, it was noticed that IPBs witnessed bulging NPAs in the second-half of the 2010s. Their GNPAs increased from around 2 per cent in the mid-2010s to 5.5 per cent in 2019–20. The GNPAs of foreign banks remained within a range of 2.3–4.2 per cent during the post-GFC period.

The GNPAs of PSBs dominated, shaping the overall trend of the GNPAs of SCBs, given their overwhelming dominance in bank credit. The GNPAs of SCBs gradually increased from about 2 per cent in the late 2000s to 11.2 per cent in 2017–18. Afterwards, there was a reversal of the trend due to a host of public policy initiatives undertaken to arrest loan delinquencies, details of which are discussed towards the end of this section. The GNPAs of SCBs stood at 3.9 per cent in 2022–23. According to the RBI's *Financial Stability Report* (June 2024), they declined to 2.8 per cent in the financial year 2023-24.

Why do we need to be concerned about loan delinquencies? As discussed in Chapter 6, NPAs are nothing but a manifestation of credit risk. Excessive NPAs cause a sudden drop in banking profitability. As scheduled principal repayments and interest charges are not received from NPAs, banking income is reduced. Moreover, higher provisioning requirements on NPAs put an additional burden on banks. Earnings from other assets are set aside as loan loss provisioning. Beyond a level, excessive NPAs can potentially cause bank collapse.

High incidence of bank NPAs makes monetary policy ineffective. In the backdrop of economic slowdown in India in the run up to the Covid-19 pandemic, the RBI had been pursuing an accommodative monetary policy to revive economic growth. It had reduced its policy rate—that is, the fixed repo rate under the LAF—from 8 per cent in late January 2014 to 5.15 per cent in October 2019. However, mainly because of high loan delinquencies, the credit growth of SCBs did not pick up; rather, it slowed down from an average of 16.7 per cent during 2009–14 to 9 per cent in 2014–15 and further decelerated to around 6 per cent both in 2019–20 and 2020–21. As indicated earlier, drying up of banking resources due to high NPAs constrains bank credit growth. Moreover, prevailing negative sentiments in an environment of high loan delinquencies affect assessment of the creditworthiness of loan seekers and exacerbate the problem of credit slowdown.

With reduction in the GNPAs of SCBs as indicated in the preceding paragraphs, there has been revival of growth in bank credit in the recent years. The growth in the bank credit of SCBs stood at 9.6 per cent in 2021–22 and accelerated to 15 per cent in 2022–23 (RBI, 2023b).

12.2.2 Incidence of High NPAs in the 1990s and Related Policy Response

Incidence of high NPAs in Indian banks is not a completely new experience. Adoption of prudential norms on asset classification and income recognition in 1992 had revealed the poor quality of bank assets (RBI, 1998). The GNPAs of PSBs were as high as 24.2 and 24.8 per cent in 1992–93 and 1993–94, respectively. Although this revelation raised serious concerns on banking health, it was not a matter of surprise. As discussed earlier, banks did not operate on commercial lines, pursuing socio-developmental goals prior to the 1990s. It is obvious that adoption of prudential norms on income recognition and asset classification from the early 1990s would reveal the true manifestation of weak asset quality.

To address the problem of high NPAs in the 1990s, several policy reforms were initiated to help banks recover debts. In terms of legal infrastructure, *Debt Recovery Tribunals* (DRTs) were set up with enactment of the Recovery of Debts due to Banks and Financial Institutions Act in August 1993. It envisaged expeditious adjudication and recovery of debts due to banks and financial institutions and provided for disposal of applications within six months. Enactment of the Securitisation and Reconstruction of Financial Assets and Enforcement of Security Interest (SARFAESI) Act, 2002, was a big boost for banks. It facilitated taking over the assets of loan defaulters and selling the same to *asset reconstruction companies* (ARCs). By 1997–98, the government provided INR 15.3 billion to some PSBs which suffered from high NPAs to write off their losses. By 1997–98, the government had infused nearly INR 200 billion for the recapitalisation of PSBs. Dilution of the government's stake in PSBs by selling a portion of its share helped in raising nearly INR 60 billion for nine PSBs. The management of banks also realised the importance of avoiding risky borrowers and became cautious about the quality of assets in their loan portfolio. Further details on such initiatives are provided in RBI (2008) and Panagariya (2020).

It is heartening to note that the policy-driven efforts to improve the asset quality of banks reduced the GNPAs of PSBs gradually to 17.8 per cent in 1996–97 and 9.4 per cent in 2002–03, reaching their lowest of 2 per cent in 2008–09. Commensurately, the GNPAs of SCBs gradually declined to 15.7 per cent in 1996–97, 8.8 per cent in 2002–03 and their lowest of 2.2 per cent in both 2007–08 and 2008–09.

12.2.3 Response to High Loan Delinquencies of the 2010s and the Road Ahead

Despite banking reforms to promote prudent banking in a market-oriented environment and considerable emphasis on asset quality, crystallisation of high NPAs during the 2010s was a significant policy concern. The existing legal provisions did not act as a deterrent for incidence of high NPAs at this time. Inadequacies of the risk management framework of banks as well as the weakness of the prevailing legal framework for resolution of bank NPAs thus stood exposed.

Several attempts were made to explore the causes of such high loan delinquencies. Excessive procyclicality of bank credit with adoption of the Basel norms on capital adequacy, rapid growth of bank credit in India during 2004–07 sowing the seeds of loan delinquencies, weak creditors' rights in the existing legal system, and political intervention in PSBs and related governance issues are cited as key factors (Samantaraya, 2016; Misra, Rajmal and Verma, 2016; Panagariya, 2020).

It is important to note that within the overall banking system, PSBs predominantly suffered from high NPAs during the 2010s. Drawing from Panagariya (2020), let us look into the reasons behind such a high concentration of loan delinquencies in PSBs:

- First, nudged by the government to promote infrastructure development, PSBs provided loans to borrowers engaged in building road infrastructure, steel, power projects, aviation, transportation, and so on. Several such projects could not be completed on time and commercial operations could not commence due to impediments including land acquisition, environmental clearances, and so on. Cancellation of allocated coal blocks and closure of iron ore mines, which were not anticipated earlier, added to the problem. Similarly, changes in government policy on energy prices made some projects commercially unviable. Global overcapacity and the consequent softening of steel prices affected some borrowers related to the steel industry. PSBs had limited experience in financing infrastructure projects which constrained their effective credit appraisal. The IPBs and foreign banks did not have much exposure to similar projects.

- Second, it is alleged that in several cases politically influential entities were able to manipulate the system and managed to obtain loans from PSBs. Many of them were believed to be wilful defaulters.
- Third, the government appoints all directors in the top executive body of PSBs—that is, the board of directors, except those elected by shareholders. Many such directors are political appointees lacking professional expertise in banking unlike their counterparts in private banks.
- Fourth, the term of appointment of the chairman and managing director (CMD) of PSBs used to be short which constrained long-term planning. Moreover, CMDs of PSBs are appointed by the government. It is perceived that their allegiance to the political leadership may not be conducive to banking soundness. For example, there were instances when the RBI adopted monetary tightening and required banks to slowdown credit growth in the backdrop of signs of overheating. On the contrary, the government viewed the RBI's concerns on overheating as imaginary. A CMD appointed by the government is more likely to align with the government and ignore the RBI's concerns on high credit growth.
- Fifth, business decisions of executives and officers of PSBs are subject to scrutiny by the Central Vigilance Commission (CVC) and investigative agencies like the Central Bureau of Investigation (CBI). While this can be useful for keeping corruption in check, at times it works against sensible business decisions. For example, when NPAs start mounting, it may be prudent to sell several problem loans to ARCs. However, the decision on the amount of haircut for such sales is tricky. The fear of scrutiny for such decisions in the future forced the top executives of PSBs to take the safe option and postpone the decision (leaving it to their successor). Long delays further depreciated the value of such assets.

There were concerted efforts to address the problem of loan delinquencies in the 2010s. Major initiatives included (*a*) ensuring realistic assessment of asset quality and allowing concessional treatment in cases with high chances of recovering the assets, (*b*) recapitalisation of banks, (*c*) improving governance in PSBs, (*d*) putting in place an effective resolution mechanism for NPAs and (*e*) amalgamation of selected PSBs. A broad outline of these measures is as follows.

12.2.3.1 Withdrawal of Liberal Policy on Loan Restructuring

As indicated in the preceding discussion, the RBI recognised misuse of restructuring norms for hiding real loan delinquencies. In April 2015, it prescribed that banks treat such restructured standard assets as substandard loans. However, to avoid a kneejerk reaction and sudden surge in NPAs, it provided several concessions. Under the *Strategic Debt Restructuring* (SDR) scheme introduced in June 2015, conversion of part of the problem loans into equity was allowed so that lending banks could become the majority shareholder and recover their dues by selling the company. Under this mechanism, problem loans were allowed to be classified as standard assets if the company (borrower) could be sold to a new promoter within 18 months.

The *Scheme for Sustainable Structuring of Stressed Assets* (S4A) was introduced in June 2016. It allowed lending banks to determine if more than half the dues in any NPA were sustainable and could be serviced under the original terms and conditions; if so, the banks were permitted to convert the sustainable part into equities or optionally convertible debentures. The lending banks could sell this stake to relieve themselves of the NPAs.

It may be noted that prior to withdrawal of the liberal policy on loan restructuring in April 2015, there were some initiatives in 2014 to relieve banks of their NPA burden. As loan delinquencies in sectors like infrastructure and energy were due to external factors beyond the control of banks as indicated in the previous discussion, they were given relaxations under the facility of *flexible structuring of long-term loans* for such sectors. Similarly, guidelines were issued for formation of a *Joint Lenders' Forum* (JLF) to facilitate timely recognition of problem assets and put in place a corrective action plan. Details of these policy measures are available in the relevant circulars issued by the RBI.

As noted by Panagariya (2020), all such initiatives were not effective in the resolution of NPAs; rather, they were misused to postpone the downgrading of problem assets.

12.2.3.2 Recapitalisation of Banks

Incidence of NPAs raises the capital requirement (numerator) of a bank to maintain the minimum regulatory CRAR as there is a rise in risk-weighted assets (denominator). This is because the risk weights on NPAs are higher with downgrading of asset quality. In view of capital constraints, banks fail to raise credit growth and suffer from potential income loss. It is an opportunity cost for banks as they must forego potentially profitable loan proposals. In view of these aspects, recapitalisation of banks is necessary to keep them afloat.

As PSBs had a significant proportion of NPAs in the 2010s, there was an imperative need for the government to recapitalise them. Initially, a recapitalisation plan of INR 700 billion for the four-year period of 2015–16 to 2018–19 was announced. Realising the inadequacy of the amount in view of the massive requirement, in October 2017 it was raised to INR 2.1 trillion.

While recapitalisation in itself is not a direct measure to mitigate the problem of loan delinquencies, it was a necessary policy initiative to address the financial health and income earning prospects of PSBs, particularly of those with high incidence of NPAs. Part of the recapitalisation of PSBs was also guided by the higher capital requirements under Basel III as detailed in Chapter 7.

12.2.3.3 Reforms in the Governance of PSBs under the Indradhanush Framework

As indicated earlier, there was a peculiarity in the loan delinquencies of the 2010s. The bulk of the problem loans were concentrated in PSBs. We also discussed that governance issues in PSBs partly contributed to the problem. In this context, the government brought about some cosmetic changes in the governance of PSBs. The *Indradhanush* initiative launched in 2015 aimed at reducing political interference in the business decisions of PSBs. Like the seven shades of the *indradhanush*, or rainbow, this scheme was composed of seven aspects, summarised as follows:

- *Appointment*: The position of CMD in PSBs (except in SBI) was bifurcated into two separate positions to reduce concentration of executive power. These were managing director and chief executive officer (MD–CEO) and non-executive chairman. Previously, CMDs were appointed from amongst the senior officers within PSBs. Now the position was opened up to professionals from private banks and other entities. The process of appointment of the non-official or independent directors was also revamped to make it more transparent.

- *Bank Boards Bureau (BBB)*: The BBB was established for professionalising appointments of the non-executive chairman and whole-time directors of the boards of PSBs. The BBB consists of a chairman and six members (out of which three are officials and three experts). It was envisaged that the BBB would guide the boards of PSBs towards formulating their strategy for the bank's growth and development.
- *Capitalisation*: We have already discussed recapitalisation of PSBs in the preceding section. It was a component of the Indradhanush plan.
- *De-Stressing PSBs*: As indicated earlier, several PSBs were burdened with high NPAs due to their exposures to various infrastructure-related projects. They undertook such lending induced by the government to meet developmental objectives, and it was realised that part of the problem was beyond their control. Various initiatives were undertaken to provide some relief to PSBs in this regard. These included coordination with different ministries and administrative authorities to promptly clear pending approvals for stalled projects, flexible restructuring of long-term project loans to infrastructure and core industries, tightening of the norms for ARCs, establishment of six new DRTs, and so on.
- *Empowerment*: To empower banks to take business decisions on commercial lines, a circular was issued doing away with any interference from the government. Banks were also provided greater flexibility in the recruitment process.
- *Framework of accountability*: Accountability in PSBs is considered to be a major concern. The remuneration in PSBs used to be independent of their performance. To overcome this issue, introduction of a *key performance indicator* (KPI) framework in PSBs was envisaged. The indicators in this regard included efficiency of capital use, diversification of business or processes, NPA management, financial inclusion and other strategic initiatives. To improve accountability at the top, it was proposed to link the performance bonus of the MD–CEO with the KPI framework. Several measures were also included to streamline the vigilance process within PSBs for controlling banking frauds and fixing accountability for bank staff.

- *Governance reforms*: Through Gyan Sangam, a platform was provided for interaction amongst all stakeholders relating to the governance and other policy decisions of PSBs. The prime minister, finance minister, RBI governor and CMDs of the banks participated in this platform, reflecting its importance. Several governance reforms including setting up of the BBB, the no-interference policy, and so on, germinated out of Gyan Sangam.

For further details about the Indradhanush initiative, one may refer to the report *Indradhanush: Plan for Revamp of Public Sector Banks*, published by the Department of Financial Services, Ministry of Finance (Press Information Bureau, 2018).

It may be noted that while the reform push under the Indradhanush framework was useful in several aspects, improving governance issues in PSBs, some of its provisions appear to be only cosmetic changes. One such measure is the no-interference policy. There are issues related to its implementation. Similarly, there are instances of persons without exemplary credentials and professional achievements being appointed as non-executive chairman in PSBs. This exposes the weakness of the BBB framework in infusing professionalism in PSB appointments at the top level.

12.2.3.4 Insolvency and Bankruptcy Code (IBC), 2016

The RBI acquired the legal mandate to issue directions to banks for initiating the insolvency resolution process against defaulters under the Insolvency and Bankruptcy Code (IBC), 2016. The IBC facilitated the NPA resolution process on several accounts. The RBI directive enabled banks to pursue proceedings against powerful defaulters including those that were politically connected. The hesitancy of the bank management to decide on the haircut in the resolution process with potential future vigilance scrutiny was mitigated as the RBI-appointed committee advised them in the matter. Immediately after its implementation, the IBC facilitated legal proceedings against 12 defaulters, each having outstanding dues of INR 5,000 crore or more. Put together, these accounted for NPAS worth nearly INR 1.75 trillion (Panagariya, 2020).

The IBC facilitated faster proceedings and higher recovery rates as compared to previous legal provisions under DRTs and the SARFAESI

Act. By end-December 2018, there were four accounts involving INR 920 billion that were restructured with a recovery rate of almost 51 per cent. As reported by Panagariya (2020), during 2017–18, the recovery rate under the IBC at nearly 50 per cent was much higher as compared to the recovery rates of 24.8 per cent under the SARFAESI Act and 5.4 per cent under the DRTs. The RBI revised the guidelines for resolution of stressed assets in June 2019 by providing a pre-IBC window for banks. It incentivised banks for early recognition, reporting and time-bound resolution of stressed assets as delays in such actions attracted additional provisioning. Additional provisions of 20 per cent were required if the resolution plan against a defaulter is not implemented within 180 days, which increased by 15 per cent after 365 days. The filing of an insolvency application under the IBC allowed reversing half of the additional provisioning while the remaining additional provisioning could be reversed with admission of the borrower under the IBC resolution process.

Overall, the IBC is popularly viewed as an effective legal framework for resolution of problem assets of banks despite the usual delays involved in the appeal and grievance redressal process in the Indian legal system. As of end-March 2023, the IBC had rescued 678 corporate debtors (RBI, 2023b). In value terms, more than 72 per cent of the distressed assets of the corporate debtors were rescued. On average, it took 512 days for conclusion of the resolution process. As of end-March 2023, 520 corporate debtors were completely liquidated. However, a mere INR 46.4 billion was realised from their liquidation as against a total claim of INR 1.2 trillion.

12.2.3.5 Amalgamation of PSBs

As indicated previously, high NPAs in the 2010s constrained lending in many PSBs due to higher capital requirements, adversely affecting their income and profitability. The government undertook amalgamation of select PSBs during 2019 and 2020 to address several concerns in this regard. First, an objective of the amalgamation of PSBs was to compensate the low capital position of one bank with the higher capital position of another. For example, as seen in Table 12.1, United Bank of India had a very low CRAR of just 5.56 per cent in 2019–20 (before its merger with PNB), but in 2020–21 the CRAR of the consolidated PNB increased to 14.32 per cent. Second, it was also observed that the consolidation process ensured merging of banks with low or negative profit with those with high profit. For example, both Dena Bank and Vijaya Bank registered negative ROAs in 2018–19. After their merger with BOB, the consolidated entity had an ROA of 0.06 per cent in 2019–20 (Table 12.1). This was closer to the ROA figure of the standalone BOB in 2018–19. Similarly, PNB had registered positive ROA of 0.04 in 2019–20, while Oriental Bank of Commerce had a negative ROA of (–)0.83. After the merger of the two, the ROA of the consolidated entity was 0.15 in 2020-21. Third, there was consideration of expansion of geographical reach in the merger of Allahabad Bank and Indian Bank. Prior to the merger, Indian Bank had a large presence in southern India while Allahabad Bank had most of its branches in northern India. After the merger, the consolidated entity could scale up its pan-India presence. As can be observed from Table 12.1, after the respective mergers, the capital position, quality of assets and profitability improved in all the consolidated entities.

As a consequence of the various policy measures discussed in the preceding paragraphs, there has been a turnaround in the loan delinquencies of banks in India. The GNPAs of SCBs had declined to 3.9 per cent in 2022–23, which dropped to 2.8 per cent in 2023–24.

As discussed, high incidence of NPAs mainly adversely affected the profitability of PSBs in the 2010s. Bank credit growth also decelerated, despite monetary policy accommodation. To avoid recurrence, lessons drawn from this experience should guide future business decisions of banks. Ultimately, correct credit appraisal and sound risk management techniques are fundamental for arresting loan delinquencies. PSBs need to ensure greater professionalism in their business decisions and insulate themselves from political intervention.

12.3 Bank Mergers and Consolidation

12.3.1 The Context and History

In Chapter 2, we had observed that in 2020–21 several PSBs were merged in a massive banking consolidation exercise in India. As part of this process, Allahabad Bank was merged with Indian Bank, Syndicate Bank was merged with Canara Bank, both Oriental Bank of Commerce and United Bank of India were merged with PNB, and both Andhra Bank and Corporation Bank were merged with Union Bank of India.

Table 12.1 Banking indicators before and after the recent mergers of PSBs

Bank	2017–18	2018–19	2019–20	Bank	2020–21	2021–22	2022–23
CRAR: capital adequacy ratio (per cent)							
Bank of Baroda	12.13	13.42	13.30				
Dena Bank	11.09	2.00		Bank of Baroda	14.99	15.68	16.24
Vijaya Bank	13.90	10.14					
Canara Bank	13.22	11.90	13.65	Canara Bank	13.18	14.90	16.68
Syndicate Bank	12.24	14.23	11.51				
Allahabad Bank	8.69	12.51	12.01	Indian Bank	15.71	16.53	16.49
Indian Bank	12.55	13.21	14.12				
Punjab National Bank	9.20	10.93	14.15				
Oriental Bank of Commerce	10.50	12.73	11.55	Punjab National Bank	14.32	14.50	15.50
United Bank of India	12.62	13.00	5.56				
Andhra Bank	11.00	13.68	11.12				
Corporation Bank	9.23	12.30	11.53	Union Bank of India	12.56	14.52	16.04
Union Bank of India	11.46	11.78	12.81				
Ratio of net NPAs to net advances (per cent)							
Bank of Baroda	5.49	3.33	3.13				
Dena Bank	11.95	8.02		Bank of Baroda	3.09	1.72	0.89
Vijaya Bank	4.32	3.08					

(Contd)

Table 12.1 *(Contd)*

Bank	2017–18	2018–19	2019–20	Bank	2020–21	2021–22	2022–23
Canara Bank	7.48	5.37	4.22	Canara Bank	3.82	2.65	1.73
Syndicate Bank	6.28	7.37	4.61				
Allahabad Bank	8.04	5.22	5.66	Indian Bank	3.37	2.27	0.90
Indian Bank	3.81	3.75	3.13				
Punjab National Bank	11.24	7.22	5.78				
Oriental Bank of Commerce	10.48	5.93	5.01	Punjab National Bank	5.73	4.80	2.72
United Bank of India	16.49	8.67	4.73				
Andhra Bank	8.48	5.73	4.92				
Corporation Bank	11.74	5.71	4.91	Union Bank of India	4.62	3.68	1.70
Union Bank of India	8.42	8.67	5.49				
ROA (per cent)							
Bank of Baroda	–0.34	0.06	0.06				
Dena Bank	–1.59	–5.49		Bank of Baroda	0.07	0.60	1.03
Vijaya Bank	0.44	–1.26					
Canara Bank	–0.75	0.06	–0.32	Canara Bank	0.23	0.48	0.81
Syndicate Bank	–1.05	–0.87	–1.20				

Allahabad Bank	−1.96	−3.48	−2.22	Indian Bank	0.50	0.63	0.77
Indian Bank	0.53	0.12	0.26				
Punjab National Bank	−1.60	−1.25	0.04	Punjab National Bank	0.15	0.26	0.18
Oriental Bank of Commerce	−2.31	0.02	−0.83				
United Bank of India	−1.04	−1.60	−4.17				
Andhra Bank	−1.46	−1.09	−0.50	Union Bank of India	0.27	0.47	0.69
Corporation Bank	−1.67	−3.14	−1.13				
Union Bank of India	−1.07	−0.59	−0.53				

Source: *Statistical Tables Relating to Banks in India*, various issues, downloaded from RBI website, www.rbi.org.in; official websites of the respective banks.

It may be noted that consolidation of banks through M&As is not new in India. The Indian banking system has witnessed several spells of bank consolidation and policy reversals, summarised as follows:

- Through closure and amalgamation of weak banks, the number of banks in India reduced from 561 in 1951 to 89 in 1969. Notably, in 1959, SBI had acquired the state-owned banks of eight former princely states. These were popularly referred to as SBI associate banks.
- After the bank nationalisation of 1969, the RBI did not permit entry of any NPB. However, during 1969–90, 12 private banks were merged with PSBs out of which 3 were acquired by SBI (RBI, 2008).
- In the early part of the post-reform period, there was a reversal of this policy to allow more new banks so that customers and the economy benefit from the highly competitive environment. Since 1993, entry of new IPBs and foreign banks was liberalised. The number of banks operating in India rapidly increased from 74 in 1990–91 to 92 in 1995–96 and peaked at 105 in 1998–99.
- Since the early 2000s, there has again been a turnaround in favour of consolidation. The RBI raised the capital requirement of old private banks to be at par with the NPBs in January 2001. The capital requirement was raised from INR 200 crore to INR 300 crore. It is observed that M&As undertaken amongst banks during the 2000s were mainly triggered by this requirement. Consequently, the number of banks reduced to 82 in 2006–07. It is to be noted that during this period, there were also a few instances in which M&As were undertaken because of the weak financial position of one of the concerned banks. For example, the merger of Global Trust Bank with Oriental Bank of Commerce in August 2004, that of Ganesh Bank of Kurundwad with Federal Bank in September 2006 and United Western Bank with IDBI Bank in October 2006 fall under this category.
- Subsequently, all seven SBI associate banks were merged with SBI in a phased manner over the period 2008–17. In 2019–20, Dena Bank and Vijaya Bank were merged with BOB. As indicated earlier, during 2020–21, 10 PSBs underwent an amalgamation process, being merged to form 4 PSBs.
- The recent process of M&As is not confined to PSBs alone. In 2020–21, Lakshmi Vilas Bank was acquired by DBS Bank.

12.3.2 Economic Rationale for Bank Mergers

Why do banks undertake M&As? What are the benefits of bank consolidation and what are the concerns? It is important to find answers to such questions to assess the relevance of bank consolidation.

M&As in the banking industry are undertaken mainly due to two reasons. The first is concerned with bank failures and the related public policy interventions to avoid the contagion effect in the entire banking system. As discussed earlier, if there is deterioration in the financial position of a bank, it may lead to a bank run which has potentially disastrous consequences for other banks too. Such costs were discussed at length in Chapter 6 and the same are summarised as follows:

- Depositors suffer heavily due to bank failures as they are unable to withdraw their savings from the concerned banks.
- Disruptions in banking lead to drops in savings and investments, constraining economic growth and causing losses to the entire economy.
- Monetary policy effectiveness is undermined.
- Resolution costs related to banking crises impose a heavy burden on taxpayers.

To avoid such costs, banking regulators proactively arrange for acquisition of the problem bank by a healthy bank. For example, Lakshmi Vilas Bank, a leading old private bank, had witnessed steady deterioration of its financial position since 2018. It failed to put in place any viable strategic plan for improving the state of affairs. Its NPAs kept mounting, capital position and net worth got eroded, and advances and liquidity position suffered. To prevent the situation from worsening further, the Government of India sanctioned amalgamation of Lakshmi Vilas Bank with DBS Bank (India) in November 2020.

The second reason is more voluntary in nature. Banks are found to undertake expansion of their business through M&As to survive and excel in a more competitive environment. In a liberalised environment in the post-reform period, the dominant PSBs are not only competing amongst themselves, but private banks are also challenging the status quo. As observed in Chapter 2, two NPBs found place amongst the top five banks in India in 2021–22. With increasing competition, the NII and the NIM of banks have been shrinking. With falling NII and NIM figures, banks can maximise their profit only through raising the volume of lending and mobilising cheaper sources of funds. This drives banks to opt for M&As as a way of acquiring more business.

Overall, the benefits of M&As amongst banks can be summarised as follows:

- Banking consolidation helps banks benefit from economies of scale and economies of scope. In microeconomics, economies of scale refer to raising the output of a firm with the same or lesser quantity of input by changing input combinations. The costs increase less than proportionately when there are economies of scale. Economies of scope refer to higher output of two different goods produced by a single firm (because of advantages of joint production) as compared to production of the same two goods separately by two individual firms. In other words, economies of scope imply that joint output (say, car and truck) of a single firm is greater than the sum of the output of both goods when each product (say, car or truck) is produced by two different firms, separately.
- A bank can raise its income due to M&As because of various reasons. It can increase its geographical spread. For example, Indian Bank used to have a large presence in the southern part of India while Allahabad Bank used to have a high proportion of its branches in the northern part of the country. After the merger, the consolidated Indian Bank could improve its presence covering both the southern and northern parts of the country.
- With consolidation and a larger size, the scope for accessing funds through the capital market improves.
- Greater diversification of assets across different geographical regions, a wide spectrum of economic activities and various categories of borrowers reduce banking risks. We have discussed in detail in Chapter 3 how diversification reduces banking risks.

However, the banking consolidation process has several drawbacks too. First, a major problem is related to increasing concentration in the banking industry. If bigger banks in the industry undergo M&As, their market power rises. This may lead to associated problems pertaining to monopoly or duopoly markets. Second, operational risks in a bank are related to its business size. So a bigger bank size after M&A may accentuate a bank's operational risks. Third, if a big bank which is systemically important fails, it is challenging to arrange for its induced amalgamation. The healthy bank which needs to take over the business of the troubled bank has to be very big itself.

12.3.3 Legal Framework for M&As of Banks

The BR Act, 1949, provides for amalgamations of banks in India, both for those undertaken voluntarily and those undertaken compulsorily through government intervention. Section 44A of the BR Act requires approval of the board of directors and subsequently that of the shareholders of both banking entities for voluntary amalgamation. The RBI's approval is also mandatory. Most voluntary amalgamations in India have been undertaken between healthy banks. This was part of restructuring in the banking system largely driven by business expansion and profitability considerations.

Section 45 of the BR Act provides for compulsory amalgamations of banks in India induced or obligated by the RBI in public interest. These are often undertaken where the financial health of a bank deteriorates severely, potentially threatening its very existence. By arranging its merger with a healthy bank, it is ensured that there is a change in the management of the distressed bank. This helps in protecting the interest of depositors and saving the entire banking system. The SOPs for induced amalgamation of a troubled bank are as follows:

- Based on its judgement on the failure of a bank to improve its financial position, the RBI recommends that the Government of India order a moratorium for the concerned bank in distress under section 45(2) of the BR Act.
- During the moratorium period, the RBI identifies a healthy bank which can take over the business of the troubled bank. After due analysis, the RBI prepares a scheme of amalgamation and sends the same to both the banking companies[1] for their suggestions and objections.
- After considering the feedback received, the RBI prepares the final scheme of amalgamation and sends the same to the Government of India for its sanction.
- The Government of India notifies the amalgamation and places the same for approval of the Parliament.

---

[1] This is referring to both the troubled bank and the healthy bank.

These statutory provisions on mergers are not applicable to PSBs. PSBs are established under special legislation of the Parliament and majority of their equity shares are held by the Government of India. For mergers of PSBs, the Government of India prepares a scheme of transfer of undertaking in consultation with the RBI. Transfers so far have taken place from one set of PSBs to another PSB. Under section 9(6) of the Banking Companies (Acquisitions and Transfer of Undertakings) Act, 1970 and 1980, the scheme of transfer is placed before the Parliament.

12.3.4 An Assessment

The process of banking consolidation in India during the post-reform period has been mainly guided by the recommendations of the Narasimham Committee on the Financial System (RBI, 1991). The committee recommended merger of banks and restructuring of the composition of the Indian banking system with regard to economic and commercial considerations. It was suggested that ultimately the Indian banking system should have 3 to 4 large banks with international presence along with 8 to 10 national banks with a pan-India geographical spread. The committee also envisaged the relevance of small banks catering to the banking needs of different regions and RRBs operating in rural areas.

It is difficult to determine the optimal size of a bank in a country. It depends on the size of the economy, composition of the financial sector, extent of diversification in the banking industry from traditional banking to universal banking, and so on. The progress in consolidation of the banking system in India during the post-reform period until now has been largely as per the blueprint provided by the Narasimham Committee as mentioned. The first PSB merger was undertaken in September 1993. With concerns about its weak financial position, New Bank of India was merged with PNB (RBI, 1994). In the subsequent consolidation process, as discussed earlier, the total number of PSBs has been reduced to 12 in 2020–21, as compared to 29 in the 1990s. Amongst them, SBI has an overwhelming dominance, accounting for nearly one-fifth share of the entire banking industry. There were four PSBs with a share of 5–7 per cent in the total advances of all SCBs in 2021–22. These were BOB, Canara Bank, PNB and Union Bank of India. There are several PSBs with bulk of their business activities confined to specific regions such as Bank of Maharashtra, IOB, Punjab and Sindh Bank and UCO Bank. Their individual share in the total advances of all SCBs in 2021–22 was about 1 per cent.

In 2021–22, the size of three IPBs was reasonably big. The biggest IPB and second biggest bank in India was HDFC Bank with a share of 11.1 per cent in the total advances of SCBs. ICICI Bank and Axis Bank had shares of 7 and 5.8 per cent, respectively. Kotak Mahindra Bank and IndusInd Bank each had a share of nearly 2 per cent, and Yes bank, IDBI Bank, Federal Bank, IDFC First Bank and Bandhan Bank had a share of 1 per cent each. Each of the remaining 11 IPBs had a share of less than 0.5 per cent. Perhaps there is some further scope for consolidation among such small private banks.

Thus, with the banking consolidation process undertaken so far, the number of PSBs was reduced to 12 and that of IPBs to 21 as of 2021–22. This is compared to the Indian banking system having 28 PSBs and 29 IPBs in 2004–05. A quick assessment of the performance of PSBs after the amalgamations in 2019–20 points to encouraging results (Table 12.1). It is observed that for the consolidated entities, CRAR and ROA consistently improved after amalgamation while the ratio of net NPAs to net advances declined.

Thus, going forward, there is need to further reduce the total number of Indian banks to around 20. There can be further consolidation of PSBs and IPBs so that the Indian banking system will have 10 PSBs and 10 IPBs. There is no need to reduce the number of foreign banks given their critical role in promoting foreign trade and investment with their respective home countries. With increasing competition amongst banks and consequent improvement in their efficiency, there could be further shrinking of NIM. In this backdrop, banks can improve their income and profitability by expanding their business volume. The proposed consolidation of banks is relevant in this context.

12.4. Debate on Government versus Private Ownership of Banks

12.4.1 Rationale for Privatisation of PSBs

A concern has resurfaced in the recent years on the government ownership of banks after PSBs suffered high incidence of NPAs during the 2010s. We have discussed in section 12.2 induced funding of infrastructure and power projects guided by the government's developmental objectives, political intervention, governance issues, and so on, which are popularly cited as the causes of such high loan delinquencies in PSBs.

The debate on private versus public ownership of banks is not new. The RBI (2008) has undertaken a survey of studies both in a cross-country perspective and in the Indian context highlighting the pros and cons of government ownership of banks.

Drawing from the literature (Joshi and Little, 1996; RBI, 2008; Panagariya, 2020), the main arguments against government ownership of banks are summarised as follows:

- PSBs suffer from management inefficiency due to political and administrative interference, particularly in allocation of bank credit.
- State ownership of banks gives an advantage to PSBs of mobilising deposits at a cheaper cost due to an implicit guarantee on deposits (as the government is highly unlikely to default). This puts private banks at a disadvantage and distorts competitiveness. Private banks are compelled to pay higher interest rates on their deposits to compensate for the implicit guarantee in the public perception.
- PSBs enjoy government backing with an implicit assurance of necessary recapitalisation as and when needed. This makes the bank management complacent and dilutes the professional approach that otherwise should have been adopted in a competitive environment.
- There is an unnecessary fiscal cost for recapitalisation when the financial position of PSBs becomes weak.
- PSBs fail to exploit the capital market for raising funds due to their financial weakness and inefficiency.

Overall, the banking system suffers due to the inefficiency of PSBs and strangulation of growth of private banks without a level playing field. Its service to the economy becomes suboptimal. Moreover, in extreme cases, even government ownership cannot prevent the occurrence of banking crises.

These aspects implicitly justify privatisation of PSBs.

12.4.2 Benefits of Public Ownership of Banks

Contrary to the general perception, empirical evidence does not support the proposition that bank privatisation produces superior performance as compared to government ownership. As highlighted in Chapter 11, PSBs have improved their performance in terms of profitability, productivity and operational efficiency during the post-reform period. In labour productivity and operational efficiency, PSBs have even performed better than IPBs. Ram Mohan and Ray (2004) observed that in terms of banking productivity and efficiency, PSBs do not lag behind private banks in India. In view of this, it is difficult to support privatisation of PSBs based on business performance. As long as a level playing field is provided without any preference for public versus privately owned banks and permitting maximum operational autonomy to PSBs, no issue arises.

PSBs have the advantage of implicit government backing with assurance of recapitalisation. This strengthens the confidence of depositors in PSBs and practically rules out bank run–like situations in these banks.

When any private bank is in trouble and if the size of the concerned bank is big, banking regulators can use PSBs for taking over the business of the troubled bank. Given the big size of a majority of PSBs, they can accommodate big private banks in the amalgamation process as and when required. Thus, the presence of PSBs is also helpful from the financial stability point of view.

12.4.3 Future Roadmap

Broadly, the observation of the Narasimham Committee (RBI, 1991) as regards bank ownership appears reasonable. The committee suggested that as far as the banking business is concerned, integrity and autonomy of the bank's management are more relevant. The profitability and efficiency of banks do not depend much on the ownership status, government *or* private.

Nevertheless, it was also observed in Chapter 11 that the incidence of high loan delinquencies in PSBs during the 2010s led to deterioration in their profitability. PSBs, particularly those that suffered from high loan delinquencies in the 2010s, need to learn from the mistakes, misjudgements, malfeasances and external factors responsible for their NPAs. Necessary corrective action will be helpful in avoidance of any recurrences. As far as governance issues are concerned, the government and the top management of PSBs need to realise that any compromise on commercial considerations in the banking business to promote political favouritism or crony capitalism can be costly in the long run. It is also not in the long-term interest of the bank or the general public. Any adverse consequence of politically driven banking decisions ends in fiscal burden in terms of recapitalisation of troubled banks.

It is also important to note that private banks are not immune to malfeasance or crony capitalism, which can be detrimental to a bank's commercial interest. The alleged loan fraud case involving Chanda Kochhar, former CEO and MD of ICICI Bank; her husband, Deepak Kochhar; and Videocon Group's V. N. Dhoot is a burning example. Therefore, the key is to improve governance standards in all banks with proper checks and balances, irrespective of ownership status.

Privatisation of PSBs will not necessarily do away with the fiscal burden of resolution costs when such banks are in crisis. If a private bank is systemically important, the public authority cannot allow it to fail given the potential disruption this can cause. During the GFC of 2007–08, some private banks were rescued with consequent cost on the exchequer. So the balance is in favour of retaining public ownership of existing PSBs given their importance from the financial stability point of view.

However, it is important to remove any differential treatment in policies and regulations pertaining to the banking business for public versus private banks. As recommended by the Committee on Fuller Capital Account Convertibility, chaired by former RBI deputy governor S. S. Tarapore, all commercial banks in India need to be subject to uniform banking legislation (RBI, 2006b).

12.5 Progress on ITES, Fintech and Implications for Banking

In Chapter 2, we had discussed rapid adoption of IT and ITES by banks in India from the 1980s. Particularly, computerisation and adoption of core banking solutions (CBSs) have radically transformed the way in which banking services are provided since the last two and half decades. Improvement in the communications network across bank branches and amongst banks and other financial institutions, both within India and abroad, has enabled faster transfer of data. This has helped in promoting online transfer of funds remotely and instantly using RTGS, NEFT, IMPS, and so on. CBSs in the form of ATMs, internet banking and mobile banking have tremendously expanded the mode and reach of banking services.

This technological revolution in banking through adoption of the latest communication and information technology has helped both customers and banks. Customers need not visit bank premises to avail regular banking services. They can avail such services instantly from anywhere and at any time. Banks benefit in terms of efficient data storage and faster computing facilities. They also save on operational costs. This, in turn, helps them to provide efficient customer friendly services at competitive prices.

However, as mentioned earlier, adoption of CBSs and provision of online banking services have significantly raised the operational risks for banks due to banking frauds. There are numerous instances where bank customers have suffered due to phishing and cybercrime. The RBI and banks have been very active in promoting awareness amongst customers about such scams. Despite this, banking frauds do occur.

In recent times, the term *fintech* has become very popular. It refers to application of advanced IT-based software and hardware to financial services and processes. Use of fintech makes banking transactions faster, more convenient and more secure, benefitting both banks and customers. Adoption of CBSs is nothing but an initial application of fintech.

Fintech has expanded the scope of providing financial services tremendously by integrating banking services with non-financial services and products. Use of blockchain technology, big data and distributed ledgers has brought lenders and borrowers on a common platform. Such platforms facilitate peer-to-peer (P2P), business-to-business (B2B) and business-to-consumer (B2C) interfaces. For example, fintech has facilitated banking services with e-commerce platforms. In the payments system, mobile applications like Google Pay, Paytm, and so on, are widely used for retail payments through the UPI. Such innovation has helped not only ordinary households, but small businesses have also benefitted in several ways. Use of UPI has been useful for MSMEs and 'buy now, pay later' (BNPL) players, helping in expanding their access to credit and credit-based transactions. Access to credit has thus become hassle-free.

The proposal mooted by the RBI to permit UPI transactions via pre-sanctioned credit lines is believed to be helpful for banks in providing seamless lending services to borrowers without any pressure on the existing physical infrastructure. This is particularly so for the numerous personal loans and working capital loans for which already pre-approved credit lines are prevailing. It will also benefit those borrowers who do not possess a credit card at the moment.

It is expected that UPI can provide a common platform integrating lenders, borrowers and payees of borrowers. Obviously, the move will hurt the credit card business, increasing competition from UPI-based transactions as also emerging innovations introducing new generations of revolving-credit products. Banks need to take cognisance of these developments and prepare a suitable response by reorienting their long-term business strategy.

The RBI has recently introduced its digital currency on a pilot basis. Central bank digital currency (CBDC)–wholesale was introduced from 1 November 2022 while CBDC-retail commenced from 1 December 2022.

Unlike cryptocurrencies, the CBDC is issued by the central bank. In future, the e-Rupee will develop as a common medium of exchange. Currency in electronic form is stored in a digital wallet unlike the physical form of paper currencies. Fuller implementation of CBDC in the future and widespread use of fintech for retail payments may substantially relive banks of the burden of day-to-day currency management. However, banks need to be mindful about the adverse impact of digital currency on the stickiness of their deposits. There is empirical evidence which suggests significantly high sensitivity of deposits of digital banks as compared to those of non-digital banks (RBI, 2023b). Moreover, with increasing digital banking, there is greater demand for enhancing protection against cybersecurity threats, data privacy, skill upgradation commensurate with the pace of technological change, and so on.

Rapid developments in fintech, while providing substantial scope for promoting financial inclusion, also pose proportionate challenges for financial regulation. Fintech involves non-financial firms. Regulation of such entities and their businesses needs to be integrated comprehensively. Lack of adequate skill and understanding regarding the technology used in fintech may be a handicap. Operational risks associated with any disruptions in the payment and settlement system caused by technological hazards, both accidental and manmade, are emerging concerns for financial stability.

12.6 Environmental Concerns and Green Banking

Concerns regarding climate change are ubiquitous. Abrupt shifts in weather patterns and global warming are part of such climate change. These are reflected in increase in the frequency of cyclones, droughts, heavy downpours and floods, intense heat waves, and so on. Part of the shifts in the weather pattern is quite natural. However, it is believed that growing industrialisation since the previous century, deforestation and rapid use of fossil fuels have aggravated environmental degradation and largely contributed to the observed climate change. Recognising its severe adverse consequences, there have been internationally coordinated efforts to contain ecological degradation worldwide.

The Kyoto Protocol is one such widely cited legally binding international treaty for mitigating greenhouse gas effects. It came into effect in 2005. In 2015, at the United Nations Climate Change Conference (COP21) held in Paris, a key international treaty on climate change was adopted. It is popularly referred to as the Paris Agreement and came into effect in November 2016. According to this agreement, greenhouse gas emissions must peak before the year 2025 and decline by 43 per cent by 2030. This may contain rise in global warming up to 1.5 degree Celsius (vis-à-vis pre-industrial levels) by the end of this century.

India is committed to the Paris Agreement and actively working to achieve the goal of net zero emissions by 2070. Several initiatives are being undertaken by the government including exploration and use of renewable energy such as solar power and strategies for energy conservation. The banking industry has also taken steps in this regard, promoting eco-friendly approaches in the banking business. This has been done in several ways.

As discussed in the preceding section, in the last several decades there has been rapid adoption of IT and ITES in banking services. Facilities like electronic fund transfers, online processing, record keeping, digital payments, and so on, have substantially reduced the use of paper in banking transactions. This has consequently helped in decreasing cutting of trees and deforestation. Thus, with large-scale automation, banks have adopted environment-friendly banking practices, facilitating reduction in the carbon footprint in banking.

12.6.1 Green Deposits in India

Very recently, India undertook a positive initiative towards enhancing the ecosystem and contributing to the achievement of the country's net zero policy. This is in terms of launching the scheme of green deposits on 1 June 2023.

As per RBI guidelines, banks can mobilise a special type of fixed deposits termed as *green deposits*. The returns on such deposits are comparable to ordinary fixed deposits. What separates them from ordinary fixed deposits is the end-use of the funds. The funds mobilised through green deposits need to be utilised for financing such activities and projects which the RBI has identified as contributing to reducing carbon emissions and greenhouse gases, protecting and promoting biodiversity and the natural ecosystem, enhancing energy efficiency, and so on. To encourage mobilisation of green deposits, banks can issue a certificate to depositors to the effect that they have contributed towards arresting global warming and ecological degradation.

The scheme of green deposits can be appreciated as a significant stride towards promoting environment-friendly activities through banking. While there is some moral satisfaction to responsible citizens of contributing towards eco-friendly initiatives, making green deposits financially more rewarding through tax incentives will certainly be helpful for adequate fund mobilisation. Further, treatment of green lending as a priority sector category will help banks to meet the shortfall in priority sector lending obligations.

However, as in any new initiative, there could be some teething problems in implementation of the scheme of green deposits. One such issue is related to matching the funds generated through green deposits with green lending. If adequate projects for green lending are not available, how would the funds mobilised for this purpose be deployed? One option could be investing such surplus funds in green bonds.

However, drawing from the experience of financing infrastructure and energy projects and consequent loan delinquencies in the 2010s, banks need to be careful in assessment of the financial viability of green projects. Overenthusiasm in this regard may be costly in the future.

12.6.2 Climate Change and Its Adverse Consequences for the Banking Business

Banks need to be aware of the adverse impact of climate change on society at large as indicated earlier. More importantly, they also need to be concerned about its damaging consequences for the banking sector itself. Climate change enhances banking risk on several accounts, such as raising physical risk and transition risk.

Severe weather events such as cloud bursts, frequent cyclones, catastrophic floods and extreme heatwaves can cause substantial losses to the banking business by raising the credit risk, operational risk and liquidity risk of banks. Damage to the production facility of a borrower, bank-financed residential property or automobiles due to severe weather events raising the default risk of borrowers is obvious. Moreover, disruptions in transport and communication networks exacerbate the problem. Damage to the buildings and premises of banks along with documents and its communication and data storage facilities raises the operational risks of a bank. These can be counted as physical risks to banks due to climate change. Tentative estimates are available to gauge the impact of severe natural disaster incidences on bank NPAs. For example, systemwide GNPAs are estimated to increase by 0.37 per cent in the year after a severe natural disaster event (RBI, 2023b). GNPAs in the second and third years after the event can rise by nearly 0.6 per cent each. Thus, the adverse impact on bank NPAs due to extreme natural disaster events appears to be enduring.

Similarly, we can consider the transition risks to banks due to climate change. With commitment to the target of net zero greenhouse gas set by India and other countries, there will be a shift towards products and production processes with a low carbon footprint. Accordingly, there will be changes in product preferences from the consumer side too. This may allow for exploiting lending opportunities to new eco-friendly business activities but may affect the businesses of existing borrowers. In the automobile industry, shifting from vehicles fuelled by fossil fuel (petrol and diesel) to those by electricity is a burning example. If such transitions are sudden and disruptive, they may raise banking risks.

In view of these aspects, as noted by the RBI (2023b), banks need to be aware of the challenges posed by climate change-related disruptive processes which raise banking risks. They need to calibrate their operations and business strategies so as to effectively address the economic disruptions related to net zero targets. The channels through which extreme weather events and green transition affect the banking business need to be traced. The quantum of associated risks needs to be counted. Consequently, necessary regulatory requirements and banking management practices have to be upgraded so that banks continue to be strong and resilient.

12.7 Banking Regulations for the Future

Since the late 2010s, the Basel III norms on capital adequacy and liquidity standards are the mainstay of the regulatory apparatus for promoting the safety and soundness of the banking system across the world. Notwithstanding the improvements as compared to its earlier versions, there is cynicism about the Basel III framework. It is alleged that the banking system remains as fragile and vulnerable as it was just before the GFC. The major deficiencies of Basel III are enumerated as follows:

- It is estimated that despite all claims about the revised Basel III framework, the actual ratio of equity to total assets of banks in many countries is less than 5 per cent (King, 2016). As asserted by Admati and Hellwig (2013), a low level of equity makes a bank vulnerable to insolvency and crisis. The minimum *leverage ratio* of 3 per cent under Basel III is considered to be very low.

- There has been criticism on the ground that Basel III is susceptible to application of dubious methods for calculation of risks and financial engineering, like the previous versions. This may undermine the genuine requirement of capital to be maintained by banks.
- At a more fundamental level, there have been concerns as regards the 'alchemy' involved in banking in transformation of risky assets into riskless liabilities. As noted by M. King (2016), this alchemy of apparent transformation of risk into safety seemed to be working satisfactorily in normal circumstances. But when confidence in banks was eroded, banking crises occurred and the alchemy was exposed. The liquidity requirements under the *liquidity coverage ratio* (LCR) and *net stable funding ratio* (NSFR) are yet to see testing times.

In this backdrop, a few useful regulatory prescriptions are proposed as the future roadmap to make the banking system sound and resilient. These are worth pondering over.

12.7.1 Raising Common Equity Capital to a Reasonably High Level

As is popularly asserted, banking involves socialising costs and privatising profits. A large part of the upside potential in the form of profits accrues to the shareholders and managers of banks despite their low stake in the banking business due to leveraging. On the contrary, a large part of the losses due to bank failures are borne by bank depositors and tax payers. As detailed in Chapter 7, low equity provides greater incentive to banks to take excessive risks due to this unique feature in banking. The best way to make banks both safe and sound is to substantially raise the requirement of minimum equity to be contributed by bank owners and shareholders. A higher equity capital requirement can certainly contain any reckless behaviour of the bank management as they would have to bear the costs of any excessively risky decisions.

Further, a higher level of equity capital provides a bigger cushion to banks to fall back on if there are asset delinquencies and/or losses. This not only protects the interest of depositors but also strengthens their confidence in the bank. On the contrary, banks with low equity have weak loss absorption power. Low equity capital in a bank impairs the confidence of the depositors and they desert the bank in a flash with the surfacing of any adverse news. Thus, both solvency and liquidity concerns can be addressed by raising equity stakes.

According to Admati and Hellwig (2013, p. 179), 'Requiring that banks' equity be at least in the order of 20–30 percent of their total assets would make the financial system substantially safer and healthier.' To raise the capital position in an orderly manner, they have suggested a three-pronged approach for banks with different financial conditions:

1. withholding of dividends and share purchase payouts of all shareholders until the banks have reached desired higher equity levels;
2. requiring banks to raise more equity from the stock market; and
3. winding-up of banks which are insolvent.

The first option is prescribed for all banks. The second option is thought to be suitable for healthy banks which can raise new capital from the market without much difficulty. The third option is found to be unavoidable for weaker banks in the larger long-term interest of the overall banking system despite its short-term costs. Admati and Hellwig (2013) have cited the experience of Japan to explain the harmful and costly consequences of keeping insolvent or 'zombie' banks. Carrying on with weak and vulnerable banks with budgetary support is tantamount to postponing the problem of insolvency rather than being a credible cure.

To infuse the countercyclical requirement of regulatory capital, Admati and Hellwig (2013) suggest that banks should have at least 30 per cent equity as a proportion of total assets during good times or economic booms. During economic recessions or downswings, if a bank incurs losses, the equity can be drawn on to compensate for the losses up to a threshold minimum level. This can be done without recourse to the public exchequer. As the equity–assets ratio of a bank approaches the minimum threshold—say, 20 per cent—it can be recouped by retained earnings and withholding payouts to shareholders. If it falls below 20 per cent, the bank will be required to rebuild its equity by issuing new shares in the market.

M. King (2016) has also observed that banks in the US and Europe held too little equity and too few liquid assets before unfolding of the GFC during 2007–08. Similar to Admati and Hellwig (2013), he prescribes raising the equity share of banks to maintain the safety and soundness of the banking system. To start the process, M. King (2016) recommends a minimum ratio of equity to total assets of 10 per cent.

12.7.2 Upgrading LOLR to a Robust Liquidity Provision Facility

King (2016) makes a novel recommendation that central banks act as a 'pawnbroker for all seasons' (PFAS). This is an ingenious and credible approach to arrest the vulnerability of banks. It overcomes the deficiencies of the prevailing LOLR facility used for addressing liquidity problems in banks. In addition to encompassing the features of the traditional LOLR facility, PFAS is envisaged to contain the liquidity risk of banks on a durable and sustained basis. This can replace many complex banking regulations once implemented fully.

The proposed PFAS system envisages liquidity support based on the composition and size of assets and liabilities of a bank. It is a two-pronged approach. First, it determines the amount of effective liquidity in the asset portfolio of a bank with a suitable haircut for each category, considering its illiquidity. Assets with high liquidity are assigned a lower weight for haircuts, while assets like term loans with low liquidity are assigned a higher haircut. This is akin to LCR and NSFR liquidity requirements adopted under Basel III in several ways. But unlike LCR and NSFR, PFAS is conceived as a mechanism to avail central bank liquidity support through a well-defined procedure. Let us understand this with a numerical example.

Let us assume that Bank A has total assets worth INR 1,91,000 crore. These are composed of INR 1,000 crore in cash, INR 40,000 crore in government securities and INR 1,50,000 crore in retail loans (Table 12.2). Let us assume the central bank applies a haircut of nil on cash, 10 per cent on government securities and 50 per cent on retail loans.

Table 12.2 Calculation of effective liquid assets under PFAS

Asset type	Amount (INR crore)	Haircut (per cent)	Effective liquid assets (INR crore)
Cash	1,000	0.0	1,000 × (1 – 0.0) = 1,000
Government securities	40,000	10.0	40,000 × (1 – 0.1) = 36,000
Retail bank loans	1,50,000	50.0	1,50,000 × (1 – 0.5) = 75,000
Total effective liquid assets			1,12,000 –

Source: Hypothetical example by the author.

The effective liquidity of each asset type is calculated by discounting the weightage for haircuts. In our example (Table 12.2), the discount or haircut for government securities is 10 per cent. Its effective liquidity then is 90 per cent, which is 100 – 10. Accordingly, the amount of government securities in the portfolio—that is, INR 40,000 crore—is multiplied by 90 per cent or 0.9 to arrive at a corresponding effective liquid asset worth INR 36,000 crore. Similarly, we have calculated the effective liquidity for cash and retail loans.

By adding the effective liquidity of all three forms of assets in the portfolio, the total *effective liquid assets* are calculated to be INR 1,12,000 crore. This sets the limit for what the bank is entitled to borrow from the central bank.

The second aspect of PFAS is related to the liabilities side. Bank deposits and unsecured short-term debts up to one year are to be treated as the effective liquid liabilities of a bank. M. King (2016) recommends that the total amount of *effective liquid assets* of a bank, as indicated, should be more than its *effective liquid liabilities*. If so, each bank can avoid liquidity problems within a one-year horizon. This is because a bank can avail central bank funds as long as its total effective liquid liabilities are less than its total effective liquid assets. The quantum of liquidity support from the central bank can be linked to the total effective liquid assets of a bank. Thus, the proposed PFAS can address the liquidity problems of banks most effectively. In our example, Bank A's total effective liquid liabilities cannot exceed INR 1,12,000 crore.

The central bank's liquidity support is the most reliable and assured and works as a formidable backup during a crisis. Not only can PFAS be very useful for addressing liquidity problems of banks, it can also do away with any penal rate for availing central bank liquidity support during times of distress.

Under PFAS, banks would be given the freedom to choose various types of assets with different risk characteristics as per their own business model. However, the application of the relevant haircut by the central bank for different types of assets will determine the amount of eligible liquidity support.

Needless to say, PFAS cannot be implemented overnight. It is suggested that the transition period can be extended over 10–20 years. Until full implementation of PFAS, it can run along with the present capital adequacy and liquidity related regulations parallelly. The adjustment can be gradual.

For example, assume in the case of Bank A, the total effective liquid liabilities at present are INR 1,27,000 crore and total effective liquid assets are INR 1,12,000 crore. Thus, there is a gap of INR 15,000 crore. If the transition period for full implementation of PFAS is 10 years, then there could be equal proportionate adjustments. Bank A would need to reduce its effective liquid liabilities by INR 1,500 crore every year. At the end of 10 years, Bank A can bridge the gap. Alternatively, depending on the prevailing economic and financial conditions, the adjustment process can be front-loaded or back-loaded, using appropriate judgement and priority.

It is important to note that the central bank must keep its discount or haircut rate constant for a durable period like 3–5 years. Such rates as are set during normal times should not be altered during a crisis. The discount or haircut rates for different assets should be set by the central bank mainly based on the time required by it to offload the acquired assets in the market without much loss of value.

However, there is one challenge for implementation of PFAS. The issue is related to determination of the haircut for different types of assets. The existing approach of capital adequacy norms under Basel III has even more serious challenges as to the determination of risk weights of various assets. So the issue of fixing the haircuts can be relatively easily handled by banking regulators. A similar procedure is already followed for LCR and NSFR requirements.

As suggested by King (2016), the combination of leverage ratio regulations and PFAS will eliminate alchemy in the banking business and will be helpful in building strong and resilient banks. They can address both solvency and liquidity concerns in banking and can replace all complicated banking regulations related to capital adequacy norms.

12.7.3 Status Quo under Collective Bargaining

The Basel III norms improve upon previous versions in several ways as detailed in Chapter 7. Nevertheless, the revised capital adequacy requirements under Basel III fall short of the capital or equity requirements proposed by Admati and Hellwig (2013) and King (2016) as discussed in the previous sections. There is no doubt that the proposed higher equity requirements combined with the system of PFAS will surely and substantially protect the safety and resilience of the banking system. As indicated earlier, a higher equity–assets ratio of 20–30 per cent will contain irrational risk-taking by banks and also provide an adequate cushion for risk absorption. Correspondingly, the exposure of bank depositors and tax payers in the event of bank losses or insolvency will remarkably diminish. Confidence of depositors in banks would be maintained even without deposit insurance. On the other hand, the system of PFAS would definitely improve upon the present-day LOLR system and would be very effective in addressing liquidity problems of banks.

The pertinent question, however, is whether these proposals can be implemented. Despite unfolding of the serious shortcomings of the prevailing risk-based capital adequacy norms for banking regulation during the GFC and availability of reliable and sound alternatives in the form of the combination of a higher leverage ratio and system of PFAS, will the proposed alternatives replace the former? The answer is perhaps no.

The political economy literature suggests that given the conflicts in collective decision-making in a society, the relative dominance and bargaining power of different interest groups may lead to a suboptimal equilibrium. A higher leverage ratio and PFAS system may be optimal to maintain solvency and liquidity in the banking system, protect depositors and promote the interest of tax payers. But such optimal option may not be implemented if it does not find adequate support in the collective bargaining process.

On the contrary, the present risk-based capital adequacy norms benefit bank owners and shareholders. Using the implicit government guarantee in terms of both deposit insurance and bailout packages, banks effectively raise funds at cheaper costs from depositors. They benefit from this implicit subsidy and substantial leveraging with their equity–assets ratio at the sub-5 per cent level in many countries. They make gains from the privatisation of profits and socialising of costs. If the leverage ratio were raised to 20–30 per cent, the shareholders would have to contribute more equity and consequently the rate of return on equity would fall. To protect their self-interest, the owners and shareholders of banks or their lobbyists misleadingly argue that by raising capital, banks will have less resources to lend, which will hurt the economy. It is also argued that raising higher equity capital will augment the cost of borrowings of banks and consequent higher lending rates will be inimical to borrowers.

In reality, addition of equity to the existing bank deposits will actually raise banking resources which can augment lending and investment. There could be a marginal hike in the overall cost of funding as equity owners expect a higher rate of return on their funds as compared to depositors. However, this need not lead to a rise in lending rates. A higher volume of banking resources (relatively higher supply) with equity infusion may, in fact, reduce lending rates despite a marginal hike in the overall cost of borrowing.

Therefore, borrowers and the economy can benefit from both a higher volume of bank lending as well as lower lending rates.

The bankers' lobby has been able to drive collective decision-making in their favour. Despite being suboptimal, the risk-based capital adequacy Basel norms are in vogue under the banner of international best practices. Time will tell if depositors and tax payers will gain bargaining power and win the collective bargaining in their favour. That will perhaps lead to a superior framework of banking regulation which is in the larger interest of society.

Another related issue is whether raising the leverage ratio to 20–30 per cent and/or adoption of PFAS can guarantee the safety and resilience of banks and the banking system. The answer is again no if the internal risk management system of banks is not adequate.

There is no doubt that banking entails inherent risks, as detailed earlier. Raising equity capital can compel bank owners and managers to be more involved and careful not to take excessive risks. Nevertheless, their intention alone is not sufficient to control the risks in banking. It has to be necessarily supported by a system of competent people and appropriate procedures for risk assessment and mitigation within each bank. This underscores strengthening risk management within banks as a complementary necessity along with higher equity requirements and the PFAS procedure.

12.8 Conclusion

The chapter flagged key contemporary issues related to the banking sector in India. These included the high loan delinquencies of the 2010s, the process of bank consolidation, the debate on public versus private ownership of banks, the use of the latest technological innovations and their implications for banking, adverse impact of climate change and the commencement of green banking, and a future roadmap for banking regulation through an augmented coverage ratio and innovative liquidity support facility.

It is widely recognised that in a global perspective India's banking sector has lagged behind as against its economic size. In terms of GDP, India has become the fifth largest economy. But only one Indian bank, namely SBI, appeared in the list of top 100 banks in the world in 2019, and that too at the 55th position. Comparatively, 18 banks from China, 12 banks from the US, 8 banks from Japan, and 6 banks each from France, South Korea and the UK appeared in the list of top 100 global banks.

Notwithstanding their declining share in the recent years, PSBs still account for bulk of the commercial banking business in India. Their share in the total advances of SCBs stood at around 60 per cent in 2019–20. To improve the relative performance of the Indian banking sector in a global perspective, it is necessary to improve the efficiency and profitability of PSBs.

As reported in *Economic Survey, 2019–20*, published by the Government of India, every INR 100 invested in PSBs returned a negative profit (loss) of INR 23 in 2019. On the contrary, every INR 100 invested in an NPB led to a positive profit of INR 9.60. This is in the backdrop of the high loan delinquencies suffered by PSBs during the 2010s. As both sets of banks are operating in the same domestic market, there is an imperative need to look into the issues faced by PSBs and initiate necessary corrective measures so that many of them become competitive in the global market. Improvement in their productivity and profitability will enable several PSBs to figure in the list of top global banks.

Moreover, *Economic Survey, 2019–20* also noted that India has remained a gross underperformer in a global perspective when we compare the penetration of credit into the private sector in relation to per capita GDP. There is a requirement for manifold increase in bank lending to address this disproportionality vis-à-vis the size of the economy. This will enable optimal contribution of the banking sector to propel economic progress and prosperity in our country. Nevertheless, the drive to expand credit is to be undertaken without compromising on prudential parameters so that banks do not face the problem of high loan delinquencies.

Revision Questions and Problems

1. How does high incidence of bank NPAs constrain bank credit flow and adversely affect monetary policy effectiveness?
2. What are the major factors which contributed to raising loan delinquencies of PSBs during the 2010s?
3. Briefly assess the role of the IBC and the Indradhanush framework in addressing the problem of high NPAs in PSBs during the later part of the 2010s.
4. What are the major arguments in favour of privatisation of PSBs in India? You may provide your objective assessment on the issue of bank ownership in the Indian context.

5. How do you assess the rationale and impact of mergers of PSBs in India during the post-reform period, particularly during the mega merger of 2019–20?
6. What are the implications of recent advances in digitalisation and entry of fintech companies for banks in India?
7. Briefly discuss the rationale for green banking in India.
8. How do you assess the impact of environmental concerns related to global warming and extreme weather conditions on the banking business in India?
9. Provide your objective assessment on 'pawnbroker for all seasons' (PFAS) as the future framework to provide central bank liquidity support to banks.

References

Acemoglu, Daron (2009). *Introduction to Modern Economic Growth*. Princeton (NJ) and Oxford: Princeton University Press.

Admati, Anat, and Martin Hellwig (2013). *The Bankers' New Clothes: What's Wrong with Banking and What to Do About It*. Princeton, NJ: Princeton University Press.

Ahluwalia, Montek S. (2000). 'Economic Performance of States in Post-Reforms Period'. *Economic and Political Weekly* 35, no. 19 (6 May), pp. 1637–48.

Akerlof, George A. (1970). 'The Market for Lemons: Quality Uncertainty and the Market Mechanism'. *Quarterly Journal of Economics* 84, no. 3 (August), pp. 488–500.

Alworth, Julian S., and Sudipto Bhattacharya (1998). 'The Emerging Framework of Bank Regulation and Capital Control'. In *The Emerging Framework of Financial Regulation*, edited by C. A. E. Goodhart, pp. 43–91. London: Central Banking Publications Limited.

Bank for International Settlements (BIS) (2004). *International Convergence of Capital Measurement and Capital Standards: A Revised Framework*. June. Basel: Bank for International Settlements.

——— (2010). *Basel III: A Global Regulatory Framework for More Resilient Banks and Banking Systems*. December. Basel: Bank for International Settlements.

——— (2017). *High-Level Summary of Basel III Reforms*. December. Basel: Bank for International Settlements.

Baral, Riyanka, and Debasis Patnaik (2023). 'Bank Efficiency and Governance: Evidence From Indian Banking'. *Journal of Management and Governance* 27, pp. 957–85, https://doi.org/10.1007/s10997-021-09610-9.

Barro, Robert J. (1991). 'Economic Growth in a Cross Section of Countries'. *Quarterly Journal of Economics* 106, no. 2 (May), pp. 407–43.

——— (2008). *Macroeconomics: A Modern Approach*. Mason, OH: Thomson South-Western.

Barro, Robert J., and Xavier Sala-i-Martin (1992). 'Convergence'. *Journal of Political Economy* 100, no. 2 (April), pp. 223–51.

——— (2004). *Economic Growth*. New Delhi: Prentice-Hall of India Private Limited.

Bernanke, Ben S. (1981). 'Bankruptcy, Liquidity and Recession'. *American Economic Review* 71, no. 2 (May), pp. 155–59.

——— (1983). 'Nonmonetary Effects of the Financial Crisis in the Propagation of the Great Depression'. *American Economic Review* 73, no. 3 (June), pp. 257–76.

——— (1993). 'Credit in the Macroeconomy'. *Federal Reserve Bank of New York Quarterly Review* 18, no. 1 (Spring), pp. 50–70.

Bernanke, Ben S., and Allan S. Blinder (1992). 'The Federal Funds Rate and the Channels of Monetary Transmission'. *American Economic Review* 82, no. 4 (September), pp. 901–21.

Bernanke, Ben S., and Mark Gertler (1995). 'Inside the Black Box: The Credit Channel of Monetary Policy Transmission'. *Journal of Economic Perspective* 9, no. 4 (Fall), pp. 27–48.

Bhattacharya, B. B., and S. Sakthivel (2004). 'Regional Growth and Disparity in India: Comparison of Pre- and Post-Reform Decades'. *Economic and Political Weekly* 39, no. 10 (6 March), pp. 1071–77.

Bhattacharya, Hrishikes (2011). *Banking Strategy, Credit Appraisal, and Lending Decisions*. 2nd edition. New Delhi: Oxford University Press.

Blinder, Alan S. (1994). 'On Sticky Prices: Academic Theories Meet the Real World'. In *Monetary Policy*, edited by N. G. Mankiw, pp. 117–154. Chicago, IL: University of Chicago Press.

Canara Bank (n.d.). 'Credit Sanctioning Powers'. www.canarabank.com/media/7671/credit-snactioning-powers.pdf. Accessed 11 May 2023.

Chakrabarty, K. C. (2013). 'Productivity Trends in Indian Banking in the Post-Reform Period: Experience, Issues and Future Challenges'. Speech delivered at FIBAC 2013, organised by the Federation of Indian Chambers of Commerce and Industry (FICCI) and Indian Bankers' Association (IBA), August 2013. https://www.rbi.org.in/Scripts/BS_SpeechesView.aspx?Id=829. Accessed on 24 March 2021.

Dandekar, V. M. (1993). 'Forty Years after Independence'. In *Indian Economy: Problems and Prospects*, edited by Bimal Jalan, pp. 33–44. New Delhi: Penguin Books.

Das, Abhiman, Ashok Nag and Subhash C. Ray (2005). 'Liberalisation, Ownership and Efficiency in Indian Banking'. *Economic and Political Weekly* 40, no. 12 (19 March), pp. 1190–97.

Diamond, Douglas W. (1984). 'Financial Intermediation and Delegated Monitoring'. *Review of Economic Studies* 51, no. 3 (July), pp. 393–414.

Diamond, Douglas W., and Philip H. Dybvig (1983). 'Bank Runs, Deposit Insurance and Liquidity'. *Journal of Political Economy* 91, no. 3 (June), pp. 401–19.

Dowd, K (1993). 'Deposit Insurance: A Skeptical View'. *Federal Reserve Bank of St. Louis Review* 75, no. 1 (January–February), pp. 14–17.

Federal Reserve System (2016). *The Federal Reserve System: Purposes & Functions*, 10th edition, October. Washington, DC: Federal Reserve System.

Friedman, Milton (1968). 'The Role of Monetary Policy'. *American Economic Review* 5, no. 1 (March), pp. 1–17.

Friedman, Milton, and A. J. Schwartz (1963). *A Monetary History of the United States, 1867–1960*. Princeton, NJ: Princeton University Press.

Gertler, Mark, and Simon Gilchrist (1993). 'The Role of Credit Market Imperfections in the Monetary Transmission Mechanism: Arguments and Evidences'. *Scandinavian Journal of Economics* 95, no. 1 (March), pp. 43–64.

——— (1994). 'Monetary Policy, Business Cycles, and the Behaviour of Small Manufacturing Firms'. *Quarterly Journal of Economics* 109, no. 2 (May), pp. 309–40.

Ghosh, Madhusudan (2008). 'Economic Reforms, Growth and Regional Divergence in India'. *Margin: The Journal of Applied Economic Research* 2, no. 3 (August), pp. 265–85.

Ghosh, Saurabh, Abhinav Narayanan and Pranav Garg (2021). 'Monetary Policy Transmission in India: New Evidence from Firm–Bank Matched Data'. RBI Working Paper Series No. WPS(DEPR): 01/2021, Reserve Bank of India, Mumbai.

Goodhart, Charles (1998). 'Some Regulatory Concerns'. In *The Emerging Framework of Financial Regulation*, edited by C. A. E. Goodhart, pp. 213–54. London: Central Banking Publications.

Government of India (2000). *Economic Survey 2019–20*. New Delhi: Ministry of Finance, Government of India.

Gurley, John G., and Edward S. Shaw (1955). 'Financial Aspects of Economic Development'. *American Economic Review* 45, no. 4 (September), pp. 515–38.

——— (1956). 'Financial Intermediaries and the Saving-Investment Process'. *Journal of Finance* 11, no. 2 (May), pp. 257–76.

Hull, John C. and Sankarshan Basu (2018). *Options, Futures, and Other Derivatives*. Noida: Pearson.

Insurance Regulatory and Development Authority of India (IRDAI) (2023). *Handbook on Indian Insurance Statistics 2022–23*. https://irdai.gov.in/handbook-of-indian-insurance. Accessed in February 2023.

Joshi, Vijay, and I. M. D Little (1996). *India's Economic Reforms: 1991–2001*. New Delhi: Oxford University Press.

Karlan, Dean, and Jonathan Morduch (2020). *Macroeconomics*. 3rd edition. New York: McGraw Hill Education.

Kashyap, A. K., and J. C. Stein (1994). 'The Impact of Monetary Policy on the Bank Balance Sheets'. NBER Working Paper, no. 4821, National Bureau of Economic Research, Cambridge, MA.

Kashyap, A. K., J. C. Stein and D. W. Wilcox (1993). 'Monetary Policy and Credit Conditions: Evidence from the Composition of External Finance'. *American Economic Review* 83, no. 1 (March), pp. 78–98.

Kim, Hyun E. (1999). 'Was Credit Channel a Key Monetary Transmission Mechanism Following the Recent Financial Crisis in the Republic of Korea?' World Bank Policy Research Working Paper, no. 3003, World Bank, Washington, DC.

King, Mervyn (2016). *End of Alchemy: Money, Banking and the Future of the Global Economy*. London: Little Brown.

King, Stephen R. (1986). 'Monetary Transmission: Through Bank Loans or Bank Liabilities?' *Journal of Money, Credit and Banking* 18, no. 3 (August), pp. 290–303.

Kreps, David M. (1990). *A Course in Microeconomic Theory*. Princeton, NJ: Princeton University Press.

Krishnan, Janaki (2023). 'Big Boost: SBI-Led Consortium to Fund Adani Group's ₹34,000-crore PVC Project in Mundra'. 20 July 2023. https://www.thehindubusinessline.com/companies/sbi-led-consortium-to-fund-adani-groups-34000-crore-pvc-project-in-mundra/article67097877.ece. Accessed 8 July 2024.

Kryshko, Maxym (2001). 'Bank Lending Channel and Monetary Transmission Mechanism in Ukraine'. Master's thesis, Economic Education and Research Consortium, National University of Kyiv-Mohyla Academy, Kyiv.

Kumar, Utsav, and Arvind Subramanian (2012). 'Growth in India's States in the First Decade of the 21st Century: Four Facts'. *Economic and Political Weekly* 47, no. 3 (21 January), pp. 48–57.

Kumbhakar, Subal C., and Subrata Sarkar (2003). 'Deregulation, Ownership, and Productivity Growth in the Banking Industry: Evidence from India'. *Journal of Money, Credit and Banking* 35, no. 3 (June), pp. 403–24.

Kydland, Finn E., and Edward C. Prescott (1982). 'Time to Build and Aggregate Fluctuations'. *Econometrica* 50, no. 6 (November), pp. 1345–70.

Lucas, Robert E. Jr. (1981). *Studies in Business Cycle Theory*. Cambridge, MA: MIT Press.

Mankiw, Gregory N. (2010). *Macroeconomics*. 7th edition. New York: Worth Publishers.

——— (2016). *Principles of Microeconomics*. 8th edition. Boston, MA: Cengage.

Mankiw, Gregory N., David Romer and David N. Weil (1992). 'A Contribution to the Empirics of Economic Growth'. *Quarterly Journal of Economics* 107, no. 2 (May), pp. 407–37.

Mishkin, Frederic S. (1996). 'The Channels of Monetary Transmission Mechanism: Lessons for Monetary Policy'. NBER Working Paper No. 5464, National Bureau of Economic Research, Cambridge, MA.

——— (2004). *The Economics of Money, Banking and Financial Markets*. Boston, MA: Pearson Addison-Wesley.

Misra, Rekha, Rajmal and Radheshyam Verma (2016). 'Determinants of Recovery of Stressed Assets in India: An Empirical Study'. *Economic and Political Weekly* 51, no. 43 (22 October), pp. 62–71.

Mohan, Rakesh (2005). 'Reforms, Productivity and Efficiency in Banking: The Indian Experience'. Speech delivered at the 21st Annual General Meeting and Conference of the Pakistan Society of Development Economists at Islamabad, December 2005. https://rbi.org.in/scripts/BS_SpeechesView.aspx?Id=269. Accessed 24 March 2021.

——— (2008). 'The Growth Record of the Indian Economy, 1950–2008: A Story of Sustained Savings and Investment'. *BIS Review* 18, pp. 1–21.

Morris, C. S., and G. H. Sellon Jr (1995). 'Bank Lending and Monetary Policy: Evidence of a Credit Channel'. *Federal Reserve Bank of Kansas City Economic Review* 80 (April), pp. 59–75.

Morsink, James, and Tamim Bayoumi (2001). 'A Peep Inside the Black Box: The Monetary Transmission Mechanism in Japan'. *IMF Staff Papers* 48, no. 1, pp. 22–57.

Mukhopadhyay, Hiranya (1999). 'Monetary Transmission Mechanism: The Credit Channel Hypothesis Revisited'. *International Journal of Development Banking* 17, no. 2, pp. 47–58.

Nachane, D. M., Saibal Ghosh and Partha Ray (2006). 'Basel II and Bank Lending Behaviour: Some Likely Implications for Monetary Policy'. *Economic and Political Weekly* 41, no. 11 (18 March), pp. 1053–58.

Nataraj, Geethanjali (2017). 'Demonetisation and Its Impact'. New Delhi: Indian Institute of Public Administration. https://www.iipa.org.in/new/upload/theme2017.pdf. Accessed 31 August 2024.

Panagariya, Arvind (2020). *India Unlimited: Reclaiming the Lost Glory.* Noida: HarperCollins Publishers India.

Pandit, B. L., Ajit Mittal, Mohua Roy and Saibal Ghosh (2006). *Transmission of Monetary Policy and the Bank Lending Channel: Analysis and Evidence for India.* Development Research Group (DRG) Study No. 25. Mumbai: Reserve Bank of India.

Pension Fund Regulatory and Development Authority (PFRDA) (2024). *Handbook of National Pension System Statistics, 2024.* https://www.pfrda.org.in/index1.cshtml?lsid=2026. Accessed on 30 August 2024.

PHD Chamber of Commerce and Industry (2017). *Impact of Demonetisation on Business, Economy and People: Suggestive Measures for Remonetisation.* New Delhi: PHD Chamber of Commerce and Industry. https://www.phdcci.in/wp-content/uploads/2021/08/Study-on-Impact.pdf. Accessed 31 August 2024.

Phelps, Edmund S. (1969). 'The New in Inflation and Employment Theory'. *American Economic Review* 59, no. 2 (May), pp. 147–60.

Pierce, David G., and Peter J. Tysome (1985). *Monetary Economics: Theories, Evidence and Policy.* London: Butterworths.

Pindyck, Robert S., and Daniel L. Rubinfeld (2013). *Microeconomics.* 8th edition. Delhi: Pearson.

Planning Commission (2009). *Report of the Expert Group to Review the Methodology for Estimation of Poverty (Chairman: Suresh D. Tendulkar).* December. New Delhi: Planning Commission, Government of India.

——— (2014). *Report of the Expert Group to Review the Methodology for Measurement of Poverty (Chairman: C. Rangarajan).* June. New Delhi: Planning Commission, Government of India.

Press Information Bureau (2018). 'Recapitalisation of Public Sector Banks'. https://pib.gov.in/newsite/PrintRelease.aspx?relid=175368. Accessed 2 September 2024.

Ram Mohan, T. T, and S. Ray (2004). 'Comparing Performance of Public and Private Sector Banks: A Revenue Maximisation Efficiency Approach'. *Economic and Political Weekly* 39, no. 12 (20 March), pp. 1271–75.

Rangarajan, C. (1998). *Indian Economy: Essays on Money and Finance.* New Delhi: UBSPD.

——— (2009). 'The Financial Crisis and Its Fallout'. In *India: Monetary Policy, Financial Stability and Other Essays*, pp. 405–09. New Delhi: Academic Foundation.

Reserve Bank of India (RBI) (1968). *Report of the Working Group on Industrial Financing through Co-operative Banks.* Mumbai: Reserve Bank of India. https://www.rbi.org.in/Scripts/PublicationReportDetails.aspx?UrlPage=&ID=1008. Accessed 6 October 2022.

——— (1987). *Report of the Working Group on Money Market.* Mumbai: Reserve Bank of India.

——— (1991). *Report of the Committee on the Financial System.* Mumbai: Reserve Bank of India.

——— (1994). *Report on Trend and Progress of Banking in India, 1992–93.* Mumbai: Reserve Bank of India.

——— (1996). *Report on Trend and Progress of Banking in India, 1995–96.* Mumbai: Reserve Bank of India.

——— (1998). *Report on Trend and Progress of Banking in India, 1997–98.* Mumbai: Reserve Bank of India.

——— (1999a). 'Asset–Liability Management System in Banks: Guidelines'. Issued by the RBI vide circular DBOD No. BP.BC.8/21.04.098/99, dated 10 February 1999. https://www.rbi.org.in/circulars/circject/download98b%5CDBOD.No.%20BP.BC.94_21.04.098_98.htm. Accessed 8 December 2021.

——— (1999b). *Report on Currency and Finance, 1998–99.* Mumbai: Reserve Bank of India.

——— (2005a). *Report on Currency and Finance, 2004–05.* Mumbai: Reserve Bank of India.

——— (2005b). *Report on Trend and Progress of Banking in India, 2004–05.* Mumbai: Reserve Bank of India.

——— (2005c). *Mid-Term Review of Annual Policy Statement, 2005–06.* Mumbai: Reserve Bank of India.

——— (2006a). *Report on Currency and Finance, 2005–06.* Mumbai: Reserve Bank of India.

——— (2006b). *Report of the Committee of Fuller Capital Account Convertibility.* Mumbai: Reserve Bank of India.

——— (2007). *Guidelines on Asset–Liability Management (ALM) System – Amendments.* Issued by the RBI vide their circular DBOD No. BP.BC.38/

21.04.098/2007-08 dated 24 October 2007. https://www.rbi.org.in/Scripts/NotificationUser.aspx?Id=3896&Mode=0. Accessed 17 July 2022.

——— (2008). *Report on Currency and Finance, 2006–08*. Mumbai: Reserve Bank of India.

——— (2009). *Report of the Committee on Financial Sector Assessment*. Issued as supplement to *RBI Bulletin*, May 2009 issue. Mumbai: Reserve Bank of India.

——— (2011). *Report on Trend and Progress of Banking in India, 2010–11*. Mumbai: Reserve Bank of India.

——— (2012). *Report on Trend and Progress of Banking in India, 2011–12*. Mumbai: Reserve Bank of India.

——— (2014). 'Basel III Framework on Liquidity Standards: Liquidity Coverage Ratio (LCR), Liquidity Risk Monitoring Tools and LCR Disclosure Standards'. Issued by the RBI vide circular DBOD No. BP.BC. No. 120/21.04.098/2013-14, dated 9 June 2014. https://www.rbi.org.in/Scripts/NotificationUser.aspx?Id=8934&Mode=0. Accessed 12 February 2023.

——— (2018). 'Basel III Framework on Liquidity Standards: Net Stable Funding Ratio (NSFR): Final Guidelines'. Issued by the RBI vide circular DBOD No. BP.BC. No. 106/21.04.098/2017-18, dated 17 May 2018. https://www.rbi.org.in/Scripts/NotificationUser.aspx?Id=11278&Mode=0. Accessed 12 February 2023.

——— (2019a). *RBI Annual Report, 2018–19*. Mumbai: Reserve Bank of India.

——— (2019b). *Report on Trend and Progress of Banking in India, 2018–19*. Mumbai: Reserve Bank of India.

——— (2019c). 'Large Exposures Framework'. https://www.rbi.org.in/Scripts/NotificationUser.aspx?Id=11573&Mode=0. Accessed 28 August 2024.

——— (2021a). 'Master Direction: Reserve Bank of India (Interest Rate on Advances) Directions, 2016'. Issued by the RBI on 3 March 2016 and updated as on 10 June 2021. https://www.rbi.org.in/Scripts/BS_ViewMasDirections.aspx?id=10295. Accessed 20 April 2023.

——— (2021b). 'Master Direction: Reserve Bank of India (Interest Rate on Deposits) Directions, 2016'. Issued vide Master Direction DBR. Dir. No. 84/13.03.00/2015-16, dated 3 March 2016 and updated as on 11 November 2016. https://www.rbi.org.in/Scripts/BS_ViewMasDirections.aspx?id=10296. Accessed 20 April 2023.

——— (2021c). *RBI Annual Report, 2020–21*. Mumbai: Reserve Bank of India.

——— (2022a). 'Master Direction: Classification, Valuation and Operation of Investment Portfolio of Commercial Banks (Directions), 2021', updated as on 31 March 2022. https://www.rbi.org.in/Scripts/NotificationUser.aspx?Id=12264&Mode=0. Accessed 26 April 2022.

——— (2022b). *Report on Trend and Progress of Banking in India, 2021–22.* Mumbai: Reserve Bank of India.

——— (2023a). *Annual Report 2022–23.* Mumbai: Reserve Bank of India.

——— (2023b). *Financial Stability Report, June 2023.* Mumbai: Reserve Bank of India.

——— (2023c). 'Master Circular: Prudential Norms on Income Recognition, Asset Classification and Provisioning Pertaining to Advances'. https://rbi.org.in/Scripts/BS_ViewMasCirculardetails.aspx?id=12472#. Accessed 20 April 2023.

——— (n.d.1). *Statistical Tables Relating to Banks in India.* https://data.rbi.org.in/DBIE/#/dbie/reports/Publication/Time-Series%20Publications/Statistical%20Tables%20Relating%20to%20Banks%20in%20India. Accessed 20 April 2023.

——— (n.d.2). *Handbook of Statistics on the Indian Economy.* https://data.rbi.org.in/#/dbie/reports/Publication/Time-Series%20Publications/Handbook%20of%20Statistics%20on%20the%20Indian%20Economy. Accessed 20 April 2023.

Reserve Bank Staff College (2017). *Reserve Bank of India: Functions and Working.* Chennai: Reserve Bank Staff College.

Romer, Christina D., and David H. Romer (1990). 'New Evidence on the Monetary Transmission Mechanism'. *Brookings Papers on Economic Activity* no. 1, pp. 149–213.

Romer, David (2011). *Advanced Macroeconomics.* 4th edition. New York: McGraw Hill.

Royal Swedish Academy of Sciences (2022). 'The Laureates Explained the Central Role of Banks in Financial Crises'. https://www.nobelprize.org/uploads/2022/10/popular-economicsciencesprize2022.pdf. Accessed 2 January 2023.

Samantaraya, Amaresh (2015). 'Role of Monetary Policy in Sustaining High Growth in India: Lessons from the Recent Dynamics in Determination of Bank Credit'. In *Reviving Growth in India*, edited by Pradeep Agrawal, pp. 170–93. New Delhi: Cambridge University Press.

——— (2016). 'Procyclical Credit Growth and Bank NPAs in India'. *Economic and Political Weekly* 51, no. 12 (19 March), pp. 112–19.

——— (2023). 'Conduct of Monetary Policy in India: The Journey So Far and Contemporary Challenges'. In *India's Contemporary Macroeconomic Themes,* edited by D. K. Srivastava and K. R. Shanmugam, pp. 315–41. Singapore: Springer Nature.

Samantaraya, Amaresh, A. K. Sahoo, Arundhati Mallick and B. Bhuyna (2014). 'Has Odisha Become Less Poor in the Last Decade?' *Economic and Political Weekly* 49, no. 46 (15 November), pp. 62–67.

Samantaraya, Amaresh, and B. Kamaiah (2011). 'An Empirical Analysis of Monetary Transmission in India in the Post-Reform Period: Relevance of the Banking Channel'. *IUP Journal of Applied Economics* 10, no. 4 (October), pp. 5–22.

Sayers, R. S. (1947). *Modern Banking.* 2nd edition. London: Oxford University Press.

Securities and Exchange Board of India (SEBI) (2005). *Report of the High Level Expert Committee on Corporate Bonds and Securitisation.* Mumbai: Securities and Exchange Board of India.

——— (2023). *Handbook of Statistics 2022.* https://www.sebi.gov.in/reports-and-statistics/publications/may-2023/handbook-of-statistics-2022_74606.html. Accessed on 16 October 2022.

Sengupta, Nandini (2014). 'Changes in Transmission Channels of Monetary Policy in India'. *Economic and Political Weekly* 49, no. 49 (6 December), pp. 62–71.

Sensarma, Rudra (2005). 'Cost and Profit Efficiency of Indian Banks during 1986–2003: A Stochastic Frontier Analysis'. *Economic and Political Weekly* 40, no. 12 (19 March), pp. 1198–1209.

Singh, Kanhaiya, and Vinay Dutta (2013). *The Commercial Bank Management.* Chennai: McGraw Hill Education.

Solow, Robert M. (1956). 'A Contribution to the Theory of Economic Growth'. *Quarterly Journal of Economics* 70, no. 1 (February), pp. 65–94.

Index

For EU product safety concerns, contact us at Calle de José Abascal, 56–1°, 28003 Madrid, Spain or eugpsr@cambridge.org.

www.ingramcontent.com/pod-product-compliance
Lightning Source LLC
LaVergne TN
LVHW100246210926
848480LV00003B/842

* 9 7 8 1 0 0 9 5 5 6 4 4 6 *